CHANGZHOU STATISTICAL YEARBOOK

常州统计年鉴 2012

（总第22期 No.22）

常州市统计局
国家统计局常州调查队 编

Compiled by Changzhou Municipal Statistics Bureau and
Changzhou Investigation Team of the national Bureau of Statistics

中国统计出版社
China Statistics Press

地区生产总值

Gross Domestic Product

单位：亿元(100 million yuan)

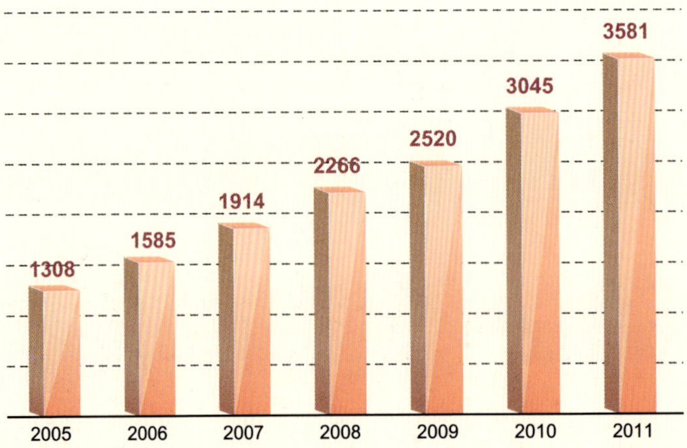

国民经济三次产业结构

Proportions in Gross Domestic Product

单位：%

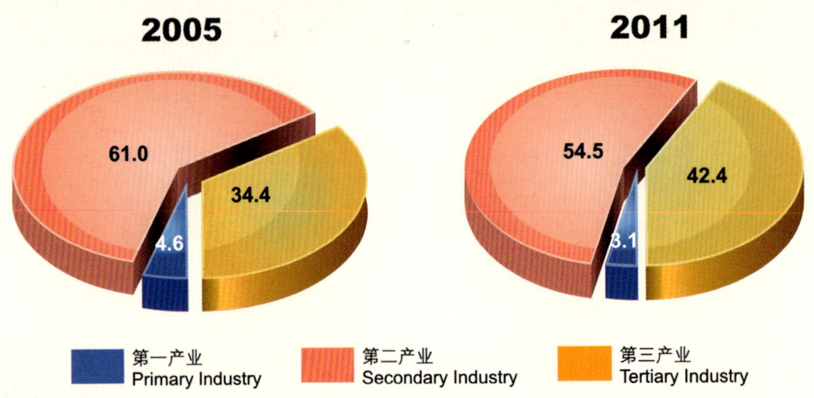

人均地区生产总值

Per Capita of Gross Domestic Product

单位：元(yuan)

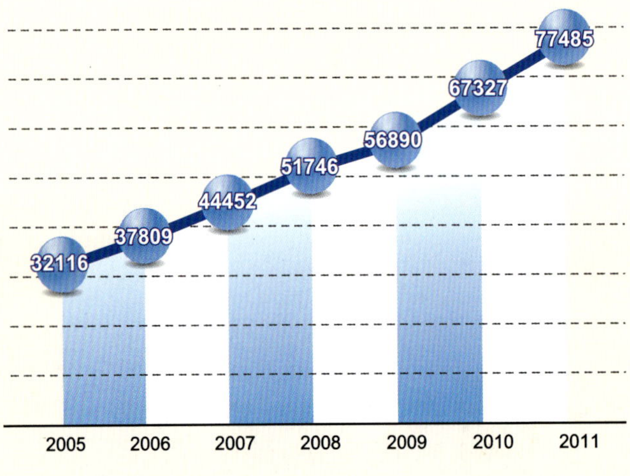

全社会固定资产投资完成额

Total Completed Investment in Fixed Assets

单位：亿元(100 million yuan)

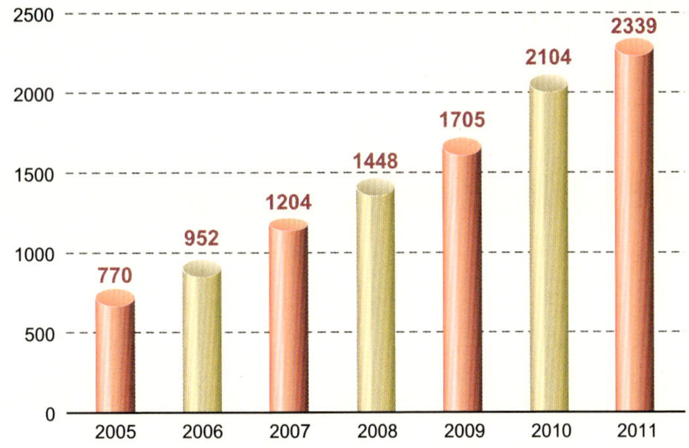

全社会固定资产投资构成

Total Investment in Fixed Assets

单位：%

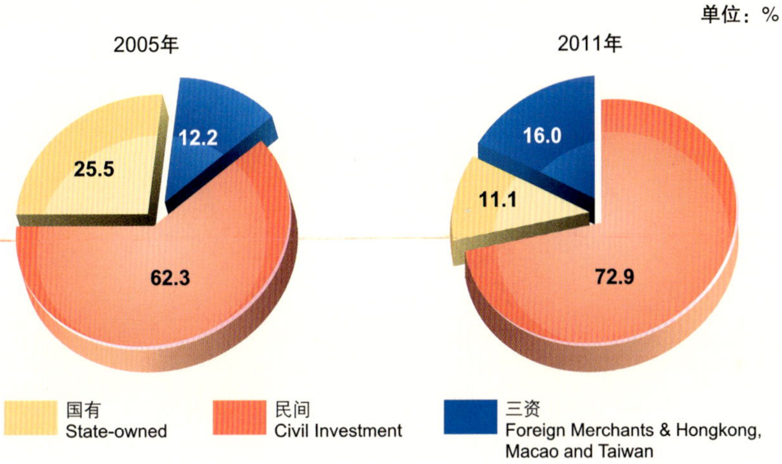

社会消费品零售总额

Total Retail Sales of Consumer Goods

单位：亿元(100 million yuan)

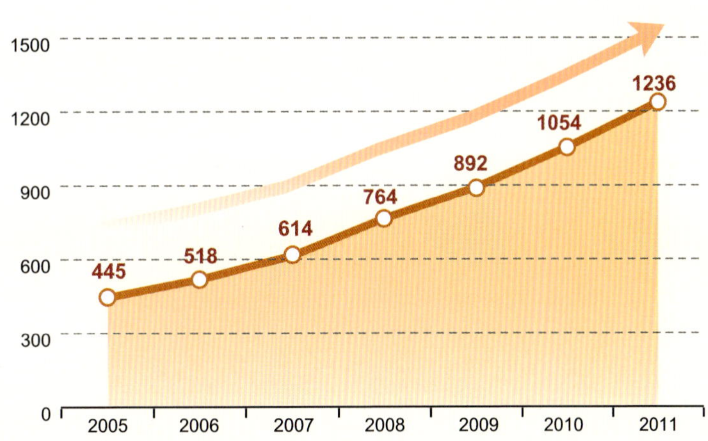

农林牧渔业总产值(现价)

Gross Output Value of Farming, Forestry,Animal Husbandry and Fishery (Current)

单位：亿元(100 million yuan)

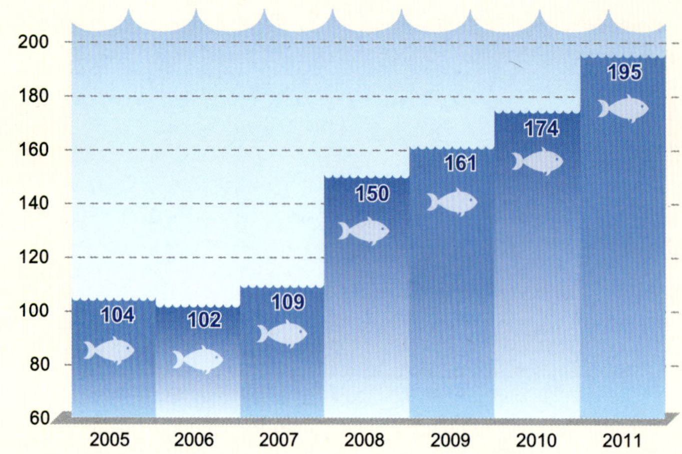

农村三次产业从业人员比重

Proportion of Employment in Tertiary Industry in Rural Area

单位：%

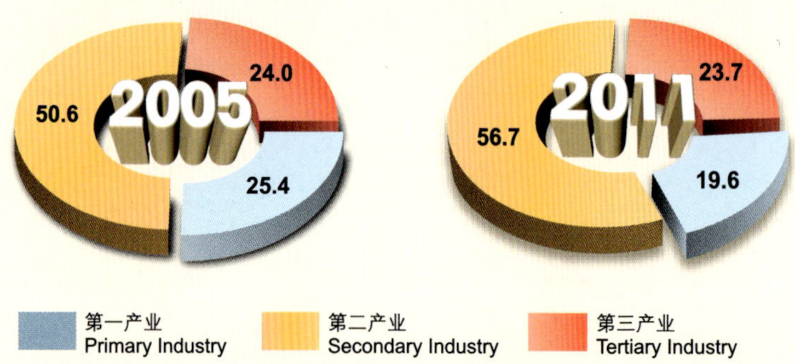

水稻单产

Per Hectare of Paddy Rice

单位：公斤/公顷(kg/hectare)

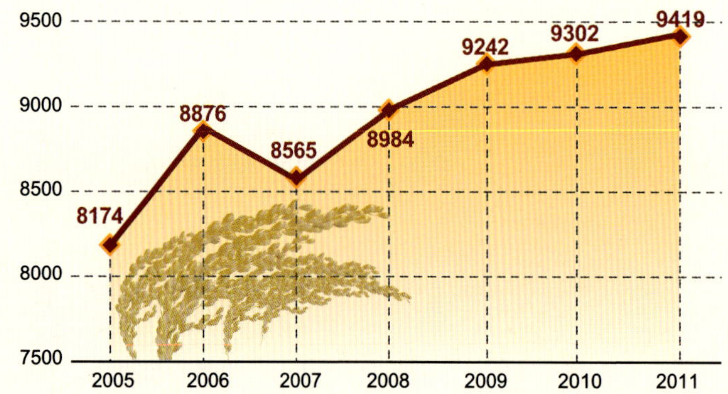

工业生产发展指数（以2000年为100）

Indices of Gross Industrial Output

(Calculated by Comparable Price:2000=100)

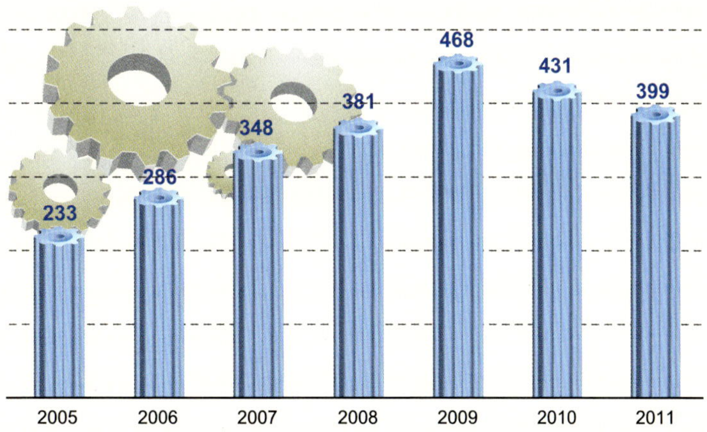

规模以上工业实现利润

Profit of Industries above Dseignated Size

单位：亿元(100 million yuan)

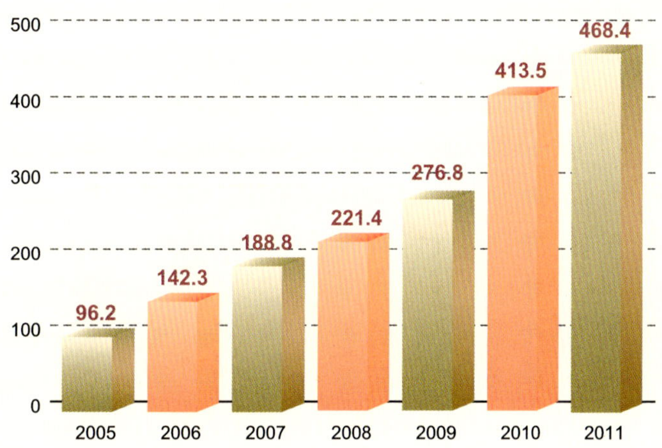

工业主要行业构成

Main Industry Structure

单位：%

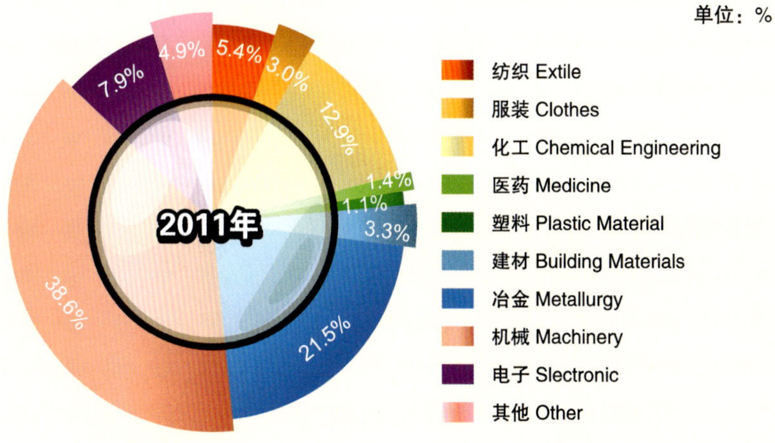

私营企业注册资本

Registered Capital of Private Enterprises

单位：亿元(100 million yuan)

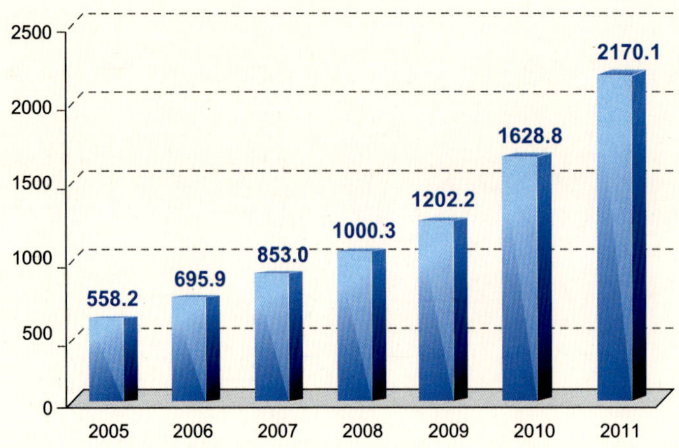

个私企业从业人数

Number of Employees in Individual and Private Enterprises at Year-end

单位：万人(10000 persons)

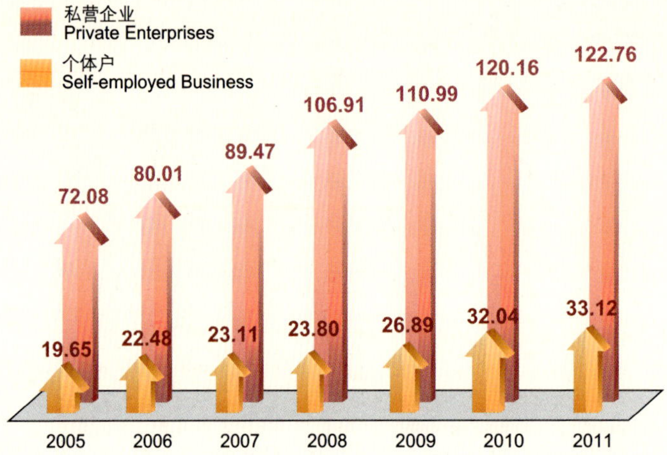

个私企业户数

Number of Individual and Private Economy at Year-end

单位：户(unit)

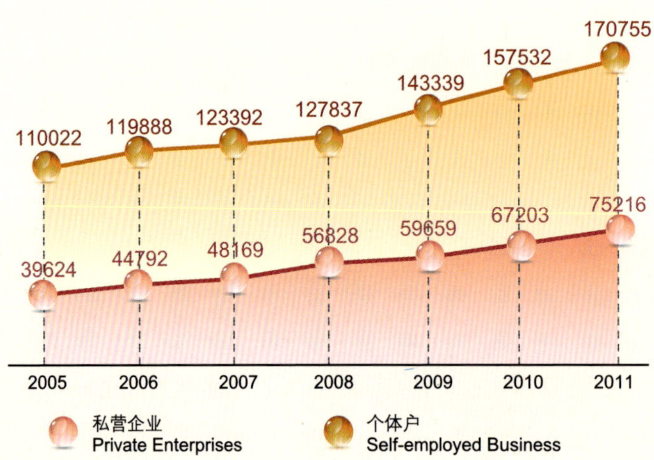

全社会固定资产投资完成额
Total Completed Investment in Fixed Assets

单位：亿元(100 million yuan)

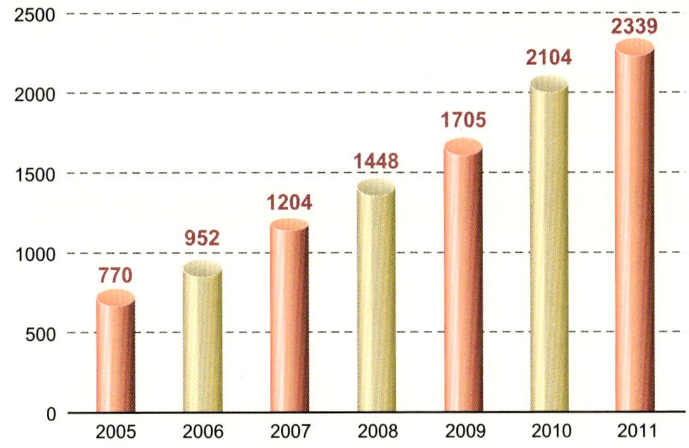

全社会固定资产投资构成
Total Investment in Fixed Assets

单位：%

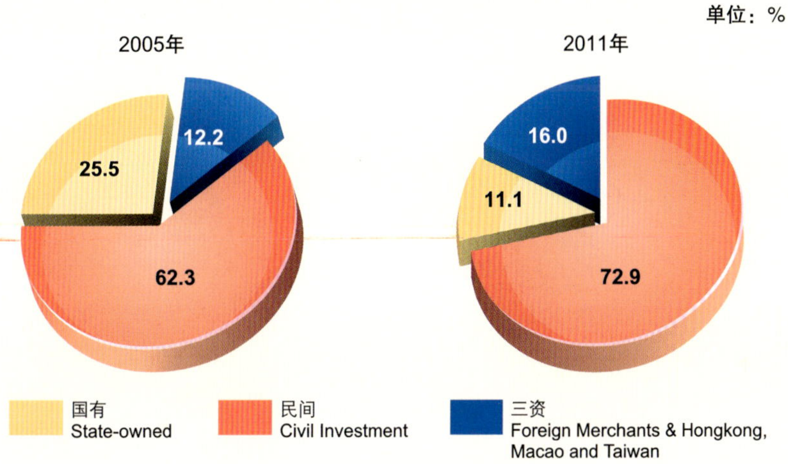

社会消费品零售总额
Total Retail Sales of Consumer Goods

单位：亿元(100 million yuan)

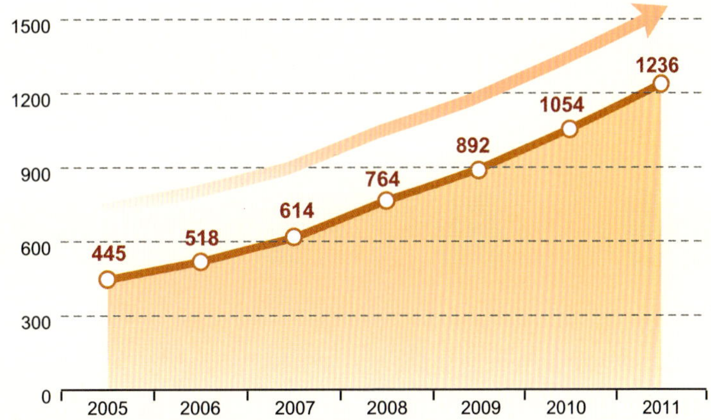

农林牧渔业总产值(现价)

Gross Output Value of Farming, Forestry, Animal Husbandry and Fishery (Current)

单位：亿元(100 million yuan)

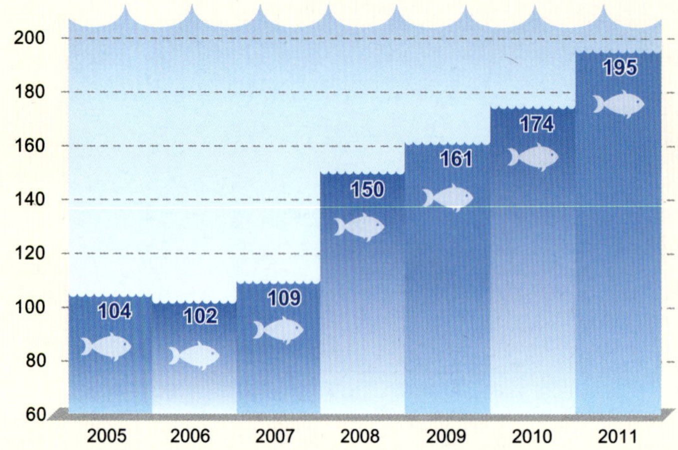

农村三次产业从业人员比重

Proportion of Employment in Tertiary Industry in Rural Area

单位：%

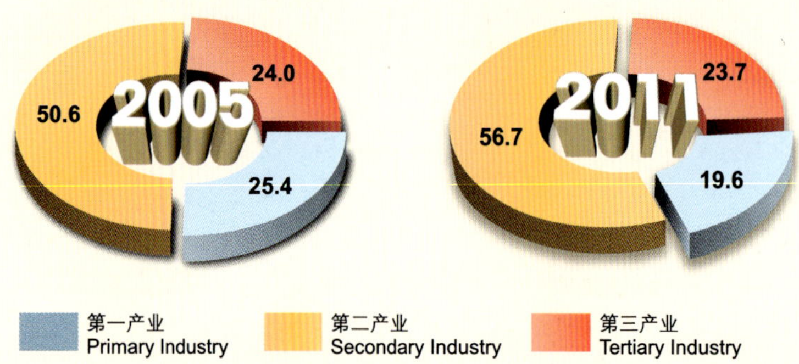

水稻单产

Per Hectare of Paddy Rice

单位：公斤/公顷(kg/hectare)

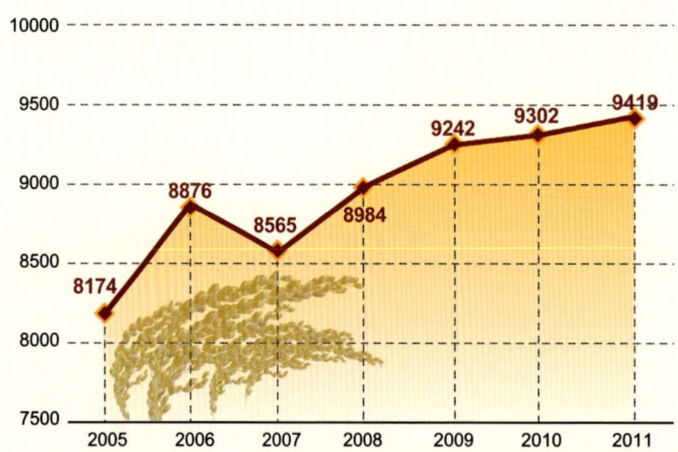

工业生产发展指数（以2000年为100）

Indices of Gross Industrial Output

(Calculated by Comparable Price:2000=100)

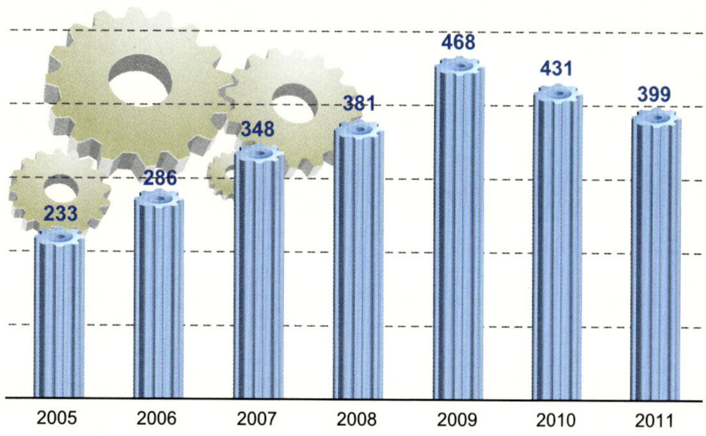

规模以上工业实现利润

Profit of Industries above Dseignated Size

单位：亿元(100 million yuan)

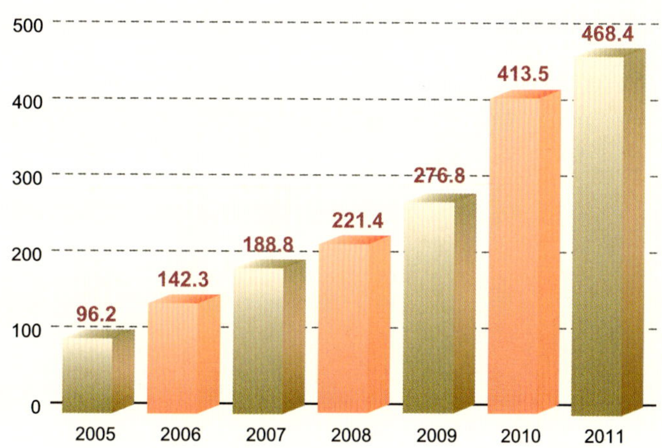

工业主要行业构成

Main Industry Structure

单位：%

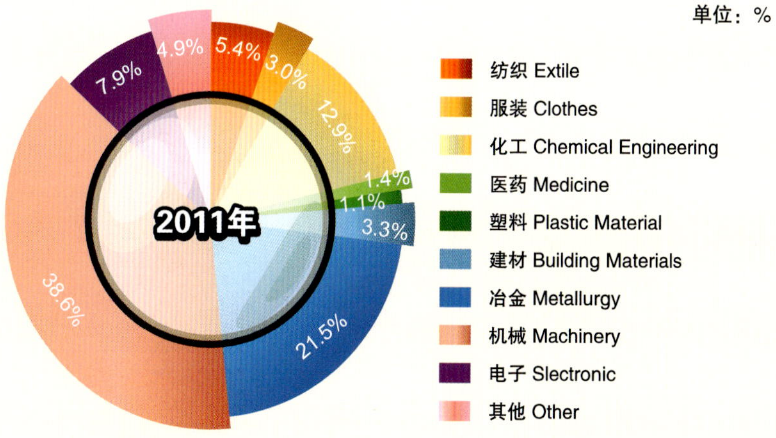

私营企业注册资本

Registered Capital of Private Enterprises

单位：亿元(100 million yuan)

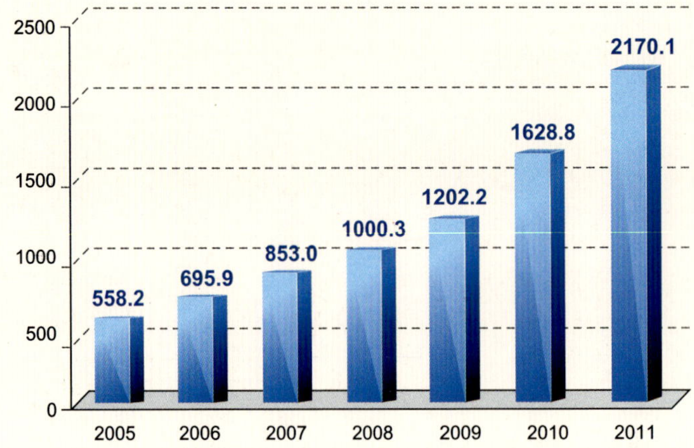

个私企业从业人数

Number of Employees in Individual and Private Enterprises at Year-end

单位：万人(10000 persons)

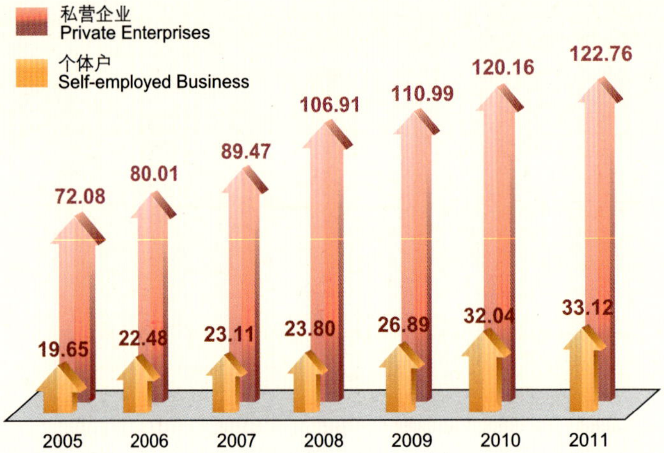

个私企业户数

Number of Individual and Private Economy at Year-end

单位：户(unit)

个私经济

进出口总额

Total Imports and Exports

单位：亿美元(USD 100 million)

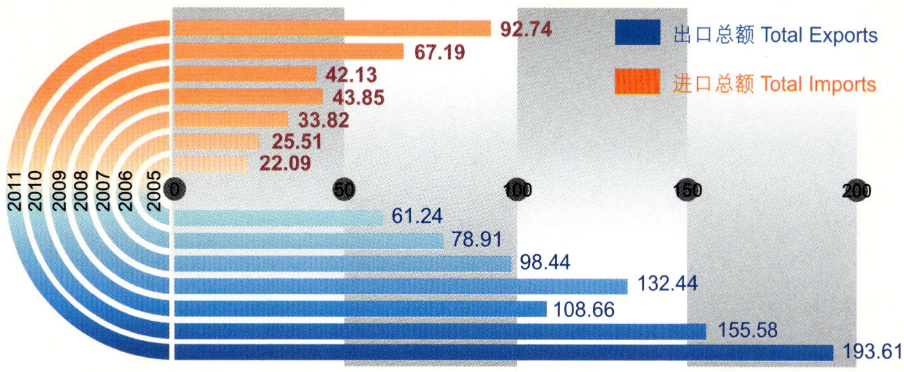

实际利用外资金额

Total Amount of Foreign Investment Actually Utilized

单位：亿美元(USD 100 million)

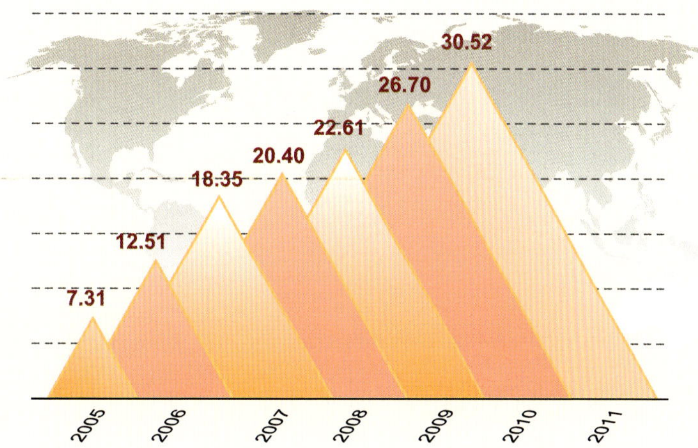

规模以上三资企业工业总产值

Total Output Value of Foreign-funded Industrial Enterprises Above Designated Size

单位：亿元(100 million yuan)

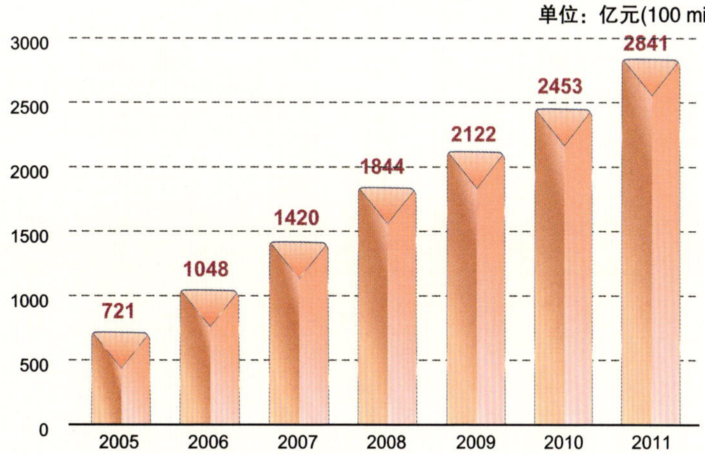

外向经济

财政总收入和支出

Total Financial Revenue & Finacial Expenditure

单位：亿元（100 million yuan）

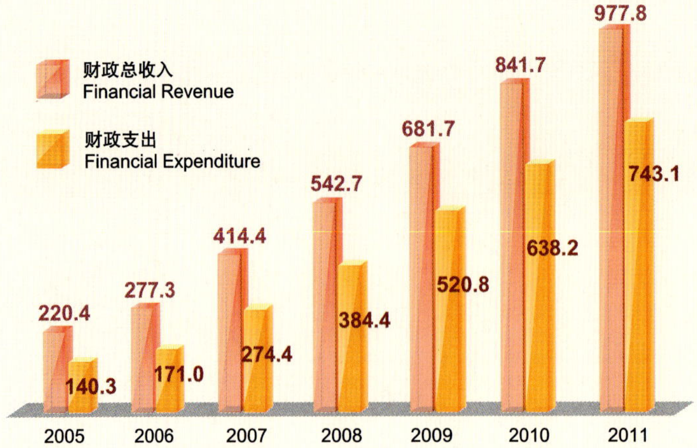

财政收入占GDP比重

Proportion of Revenue in GDP

单位：%

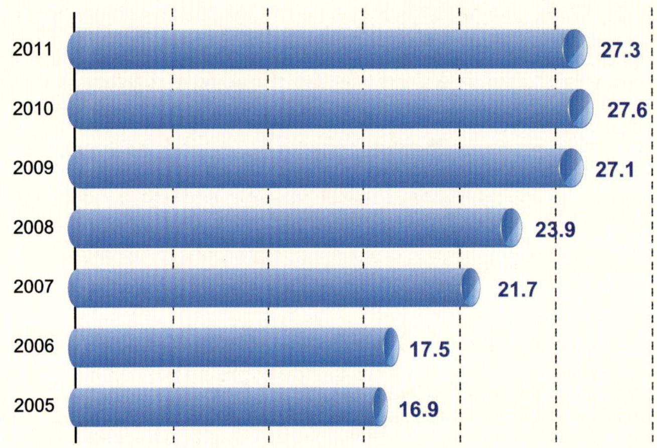

金融机构存贷款余额

Deposit and Loan Balance of National Banking Institutions

单位：亿元（100 million yuan）

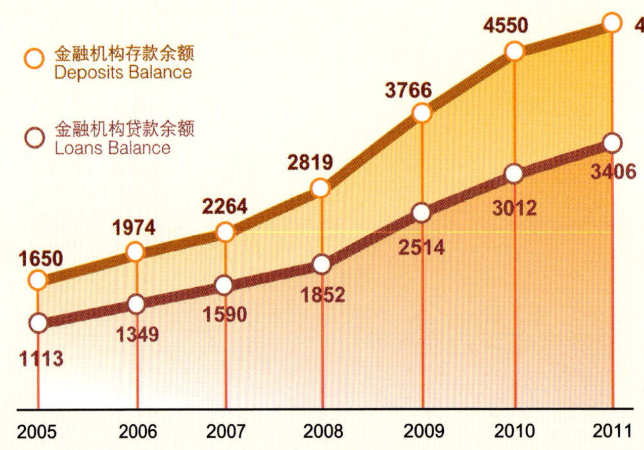

财政金融

市区居民人均可支配收入、农民人均纯收入

Per Capita Disposable Income and Net Income of Rural Residents

单位：元（yuan）

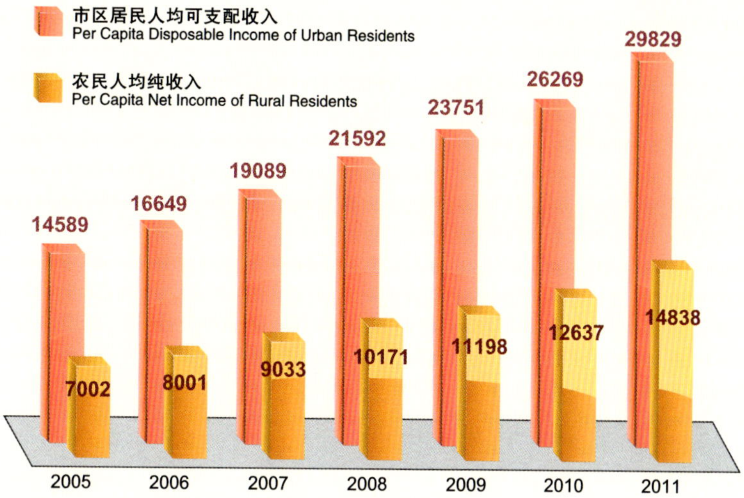

城镇、农村居民恩格尔系数

Engel Coefficient of Urban and Rual Residents

单位：%

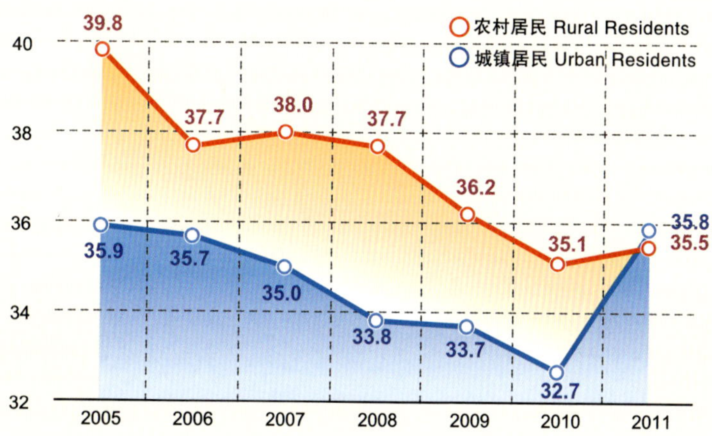

城乡居民人均储蓄存款余额

Per Capita Deposits of Urban and Rural Residents

单位：元(yuan)

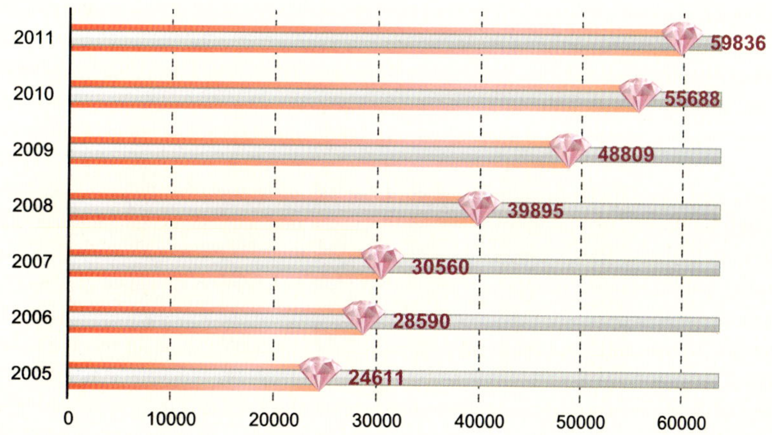

普通高等院校在校学生数

Students Enrollmed of Institutions of Higher Education

单位：人（person）

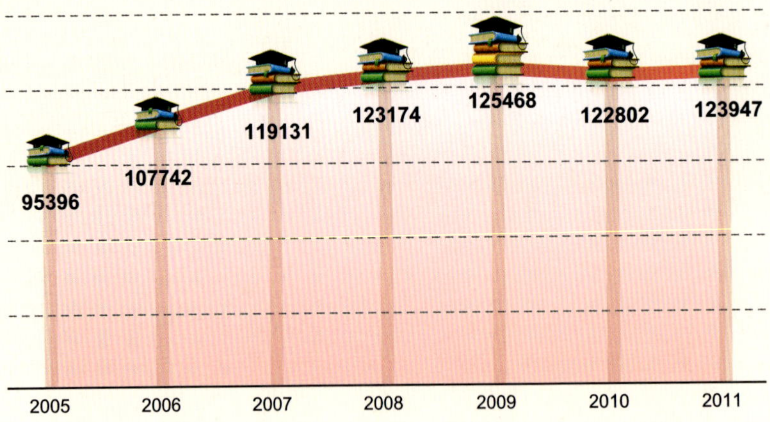

专利申请量、专利授权量

Number of Patent Authorizaions Examined and Granted

单位：项（unit）

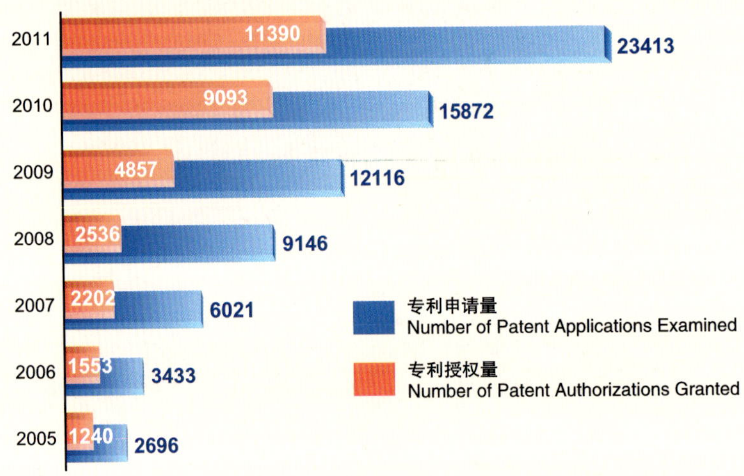

全社会卫生机构床位数

Beds of Health Care Institutions

单位：张（bed）

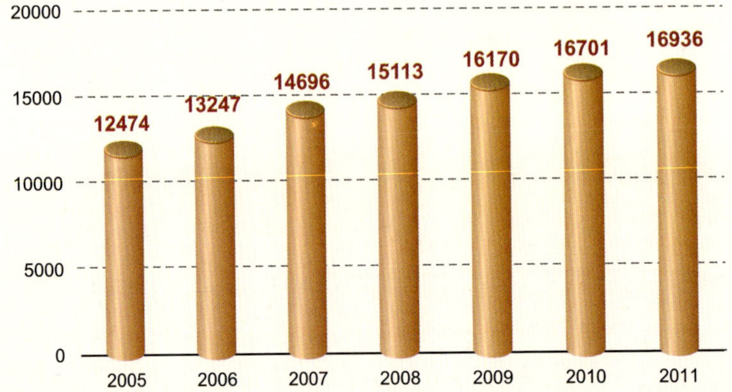

人均拥有道路面积

Per Capita Area of Roads

单位：平方米（sq.m）

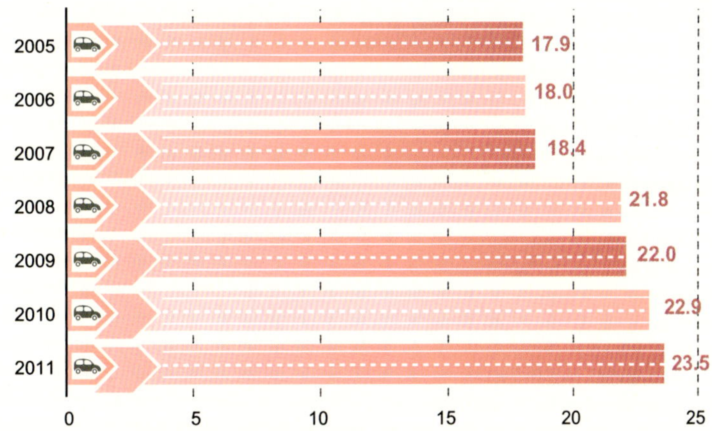

人均公园绿地面积

Per Capita Green Area of Parks

单位：平方米（sq.m）

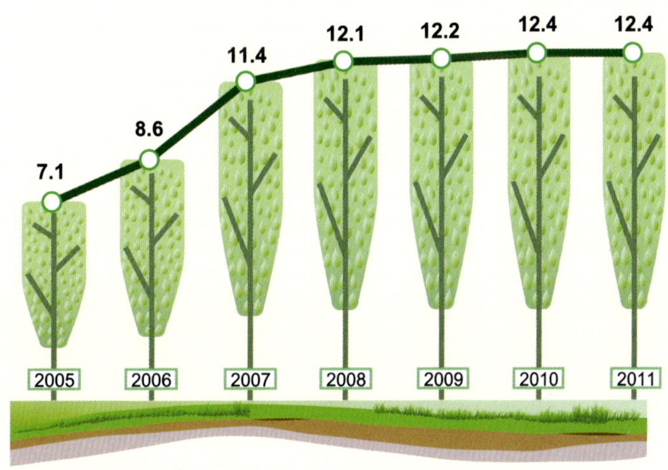

建成区面积

Area of Constructed Regions

单位：平方公里（sq.km）

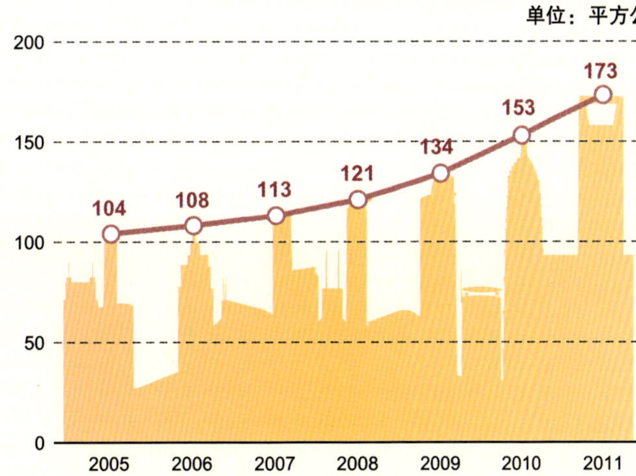

常州统计年鉴

2012 STATISTICAL YEARBOOK

编 者 说 明

一、《常州统计年鉴—2012》是一本信息高度密集的资料和工具书。它以翔实的统计数据反映了2011年常州经济、科技、社会各方面的发展变革情况，以及历史年份和改革开放以来大量的统计数据。

二、全书内容分为23部分，即：1. 概述；2. 排名榜；3. 行政区划、自然概况；4. 综合；5. 人口；6. 从业人员、工资总额；7. 物价指数；8. 人民生活；9. 固定资产投资；10. 农业；11. 工业；12. 建筑业；13. 交通运输、邮电通信；14. 贸易、住宿餐饮业；15. 个体、私营经济；16. 对外经济、旅游；17. 能源消费；18. 财政、金融、保险；19. 企业调查；20. 城市建设、环境保护；21. 科技、教育、文化；22. 卫生、体育；23. 民政、司法、其他。书末附有主要统计指标解释等附录资料。

三、本书中所使用的度量衡单位采用国际统一标准计量单位，价值量指标凡未标明何种价格的，均为以现行价格计算。

四、本书中的简称和符号使用说明：年主营业务收入2000万元以上的法人工业企业，简称“规模以上”工业企业；“…”表示数据不足本表最小单位数；“空格”表示数据不详或无该项数据；“＃”表示其中数。

《常州统计年鉴》公开出版以来，受到社会各界关心和支持，并提出了许多宝贵意见，对此，我们深表谢意。热忱欢迎读者继续对年鉴的不足之处批评指正，帮助我们进一步提高编辑水平。

Preface

I. *Changzhou Statistical Yearbook-2011* is a reference book, which reflects the economic, scientific and technological, social development in Changzhou city in 2011 by means of full and accurate statistical data. It also provides abundant statistical data about past years and the years since reform and opening-up.

II. This book contains the following twenty-three parts: 1.General Description; 2.List of Top Strengths; 3. Division of Administration Areas and Natural Resources; 4.General Survey; 5.Population; 6.Employment and Total Wages; 7.Price Indices; 8.People's Livelihood; 9.Investment in Fixed Assets; 10.Agriculture; 11.Industry; 12.Construction; 13.Transportation, Post and Telecommunications; 14.Trade, Accommodation and Catering Trade; 15.Individual and Private Economy; 16.Foreign Economy and Tourism; 17.Energy Consumption; 18.Public Finance, Banking and Insurance; 19.Enterprises Survey; 20.Urban Construction and Environmental Protection; 21.Science Technology, Education and Culture; 22.Health and Sports; 23.Civil Administration, Judicature and Others. In addition, Explanatory Notes on Main Statistical Indicators are provided at the end of each part.

III. The units of measurement used in this book are internationally standard measurement units. Those undefined price indices should be calculated in accordance with current prices.

IV. Abbreviations and Notations used in this book:

Corporate industrial enterprises with main business income of 20 million yuan and above are referred to the statistical coverage of industrial enterprises "above designated size" for short."…" indicates that the figure is not big enough to be measured with the smallest unit in the table, "(blank)" indicates that the data are not available, "#" indicates the items of the total.

Here we'd like to express our sincere thanks to the readers who have offered us so many invaluable suggestions on content selection and compilation of the yearbook. Our thanks also go to those friends in all circles of society who have shown their support and care to the publication of the yearbook. We welcome any suggestions and comments from readers so as to help us to further improve our work of compilation.

目 录

CONTENTS

第一篇 概 述

CHAPTER 1 GENERAL DESCRIPTION

第二篇 排名榜

CHAPTER 2 LIST OF TOP STRENGTHS

第三篇 行政区划 自然概况

CHAPTER 3 ADMINISTRATIVE DIVISION AND NATURAL RESOURCES

第四编 综 合

CHAPTER 4 GENERAL SURVEY

第五篇 人 口

CHAPTER 5 POPULATION

第六篇 从业人员 工资总额

CHAPTER 6 EMPLOYMENT AND TOTAL WAGES

第七篇 物价指数

CHAPTER 7 PRICE INDEX

第八篇 人民生活

CHAPTER 8 PEOPLE'S LIVELIHOOD

第九篇 固定资产投资

CHAPTER 9 INVESTMENT IN FIXED ASSETS

第十篇 农 业

CHAPTER 10 AGRICULTURE

第十一篇 工 业

CHAPTER 11 INDUSTRY

第十二篇 建筑业

CHAPTER 12 CONSTRUCTION

第十三篇 交通运输 邮电通信

CHAPTER 13 TRANSPORTATION, POST AND TELECOMMUNICATIONS

第十四篇 贸易 住宿餐饮业

CHAPTER 14 TRADE, ACCOMMODATION AND CATERING TRADE

第十五篇 个体 私营经济

CHAPTER 15 INDIVIDUAL AND PRIVATE ECONOMY

第十六篇 对外经济 旅游

CHAPTER 16 FOREIGN ECONOMY AND TOUEISM

第十七篇 能源消费

CHAPTER 17 CONSUMPTION OF ENERGY

第十八篇 财政 金融 保险

CHAPTER 18 PUBLIC FINANCE, BANKING AND INSURANCE

第十九篇 企业调查

CHAPTER 19 ENTERPRISES SURVEY

第二十篇 城市建设 环境保护

CHAPTER 20 URBAN CONSTRUCTION AND ENVIRONMENTAL PROTECTION

第二十一篇 科技 教育 文化

CHAPTER 21 SCIENCE, TECHNOLOGY, EDUCATION AND CULTURE

第二十二篇 卫生 体育

CHAPTER 22 HEALTH AND SPORTS

第二十三篇 民政 司法 其他

CHAPTER 23 CIVIL ADMINISTRATION, JUDICATURE AND OTHERS

附 录

APPENDIX

1

CHAPTER 1

概 述

GENERAL DESCRIPTION

常州市
2011年国民经济和社会发展统计公报

2011年，面对国际金融危机再掀波澜、国内经济运行遭遇多重挑战的复杂局面，全市人民在市委、市政府的正确领导下，坚持以“加快转型升级年”活动为主线，以改革开放和创新驱动为动力，努力在保增长中调结构、促转型，在快发展中惠民生、促和谐，全市国民经济呈现运行态势总体平稳、发展质量稳步提高、民生民计持续改善的良好局面，圆满完成了人代会确定的各项目标任务，实现了“十二五”规划的良好开局。

一、经济运行

【综合】产业结构持续改善。全年实现地区生产总值（GDP）3581.0亿元，按可比价计算增长12.2%，其中一、二、三次产业分别实现增加值111.8亿元、1950.8亿元和1518.4亿元，分别比上年增长4.0%、12.2%和12.8%。全市产业结构继续得到优化，三次产业比重由上年的3.3：55.3：41.4调整为3.1：54.5：42.4，服务业增加值在全市经济总量中所占比重较上年提高1.0个百分点，对经济增长的贡献率达47.9%。按常住人口计算，全市人均生产总值达77485元，依据当年平均汇率折算达11997美元。

财政收支稳步增长。全年实现地方一般预算收入350.9亿元，比上年增长22.6%。主要税种保持较快增长态势，其中增值税、营业税、个人所得税分别入库48.6亿元、74.1亿元和19.2亿元，增长21.5%、14.1%和32%。民生投入力度进一步加大，全年一般预算财政支出361.8亿元，比上年增长28.6%，其中教育支出54.9亿元，社会保障和就业支出36.4亿元，医疗卫生支出19.7亿元，城乡社区事务支出68.0亿元，交通运输支出12.1亿元，分别比上年增长35.2%、46.1%、34.0%、67.6%和44.0%。

【农业与农村经济】农业生产成果丰硕。全市实现农林牧渔业总产值194.7亿元，比上年增长11.8%。粮食生产稳中略升，全市粮食播种面积159.5千公顷，比上年略有下降；粮食总产量115.2万吨，较上年基本持平。粮食亩产481.4公斤，其中水稻亩产再创新高，达到627.9公斤，比上年增产7.8公斤，实现全省“九连冠”。高效设施农业继续推进，“双百万亩”工程建设任务全面完成，全市新建高标准农田14万亩，新增高效农业面积达13.9万亩（其中设施农业7.6万亩），高效渔业面积10.3万亩；累计建成高标准农田113.3万亩，高效农业113万亩（其中设施农业30.4万亩），高效渔业45.7万亩。截至年末，全市共有无公害农产品生产基地414个，省级以上认证的无公害农产品624只，省级名优农产品42个，获得绿色标志的农产品343只，有机食品140个。

新农村建设成效显著。全年新建、改建农村公路58公里，改造农危桥185座。农村水利工作稳步推进，全年实现农村水利建设投资3亿元，完成各类水利建设土方1599万立方米，疏浚县级河道5条，疏浚乡级河道104条，整治178个村庄的865个河塘，完成圩堤加固61.7公里，建设小沟以上建筑物3526座，新建防渗渠道267公里，新建改造塘坝187座，新建改造机电泵站256座，新建改造圩口闸48座，治理水土流失面积16平方公里，新增节水灌溉面积7.6万亩，增加有效灌溉面积1.2万亩，恢复改善灌溉面积10.5万亩，改造中低产田2.8万亩。

产业化发展成效显著。当年新增农民专业合作经济组织447家，累计2350家；新增省级以上农业龙头企业6家，其中国家级1家。48家市级以上农业龙头企业带动基地种植面积超100万亩，全年实现销售收入388亿元，比上年增长21.5%。休闲观光农业快速发展，全年建成各类休闲观光农业景点300余个，创成全国农业旅游示范点17家，评出市级三星级以上景点41家，年内接待游客550多万人次，实现旅游收入10亿元。

【工业】经济总量稳步提升。全年完成规模以上工业产值8270.8亿元，比上年增长18.5%，其中轻工业完成产值1547.8亿元，增长5.6%；重工业完成产值6722.9亿元，增长21.9%。规模以上工业中，民营企业完成产值5139.6亿元，增长20.0%，其中私营企业完成产值4616.7亿元，增长24.6%；外商及港澳台商投资企业完成产值2841.2亿元，增长17.4%。全市完成主营业务收入8212.5亿元，实现利税713.3亿元，利润总额468.4亿元，分别比上年增长19.5%、18.6%、15.7%。

产业结构持续优化。全市五大产业规模以上企业完成工业产值5620.9亿元，较上年增长33.7%，占规模以上工业总产值的比重达67.7%，对规模以上工业增长的贡献份额达80.7%。高新技术产业蓬勃发展，贡献份额显著增强，全市规模以上高新技术企业完成产值3100.6亿元，比上年增长38.6%，占规模以上工业产值的比重由上年的32.1%上升到37.3%，拉动全市工业增长12.8个百分点，对全市工业增长的贡献份额由上年的30.7%提高到47.7%。

【建筑业】建筑行业稳步发展。全年实现建筑业增加值181.5

亿元，按可比价计算增长7.8%；建筑企业完成施工产值899.6亿元，比上年增长20.6%；施工面积7657.2万平方米，增长23.7%；竣工面积2831.5万平方米，增长6.5%。建筑业劳动效率不断提高，按施工产值计算的全员劳动生产率达24.5万元/人，比上年提高6.5%。常州高架道路一期工程荣获中国工程质量最高奖“鲁班奖”。

【国内贸易】国内贸易平稳增长。全年完成社会消费品零售总额1236.1亿元，比上年增长17.3%，其中批发零售业共实现消费品零售额1133.8亿元，增长16.6%；住宿餐饮业实现零售额102.3亿元，增长24.8%。城乡市场消费基本保持同步增长，其中城镇地区实现社会消费品零售额1154.3亿元，比上年增长17.3%；乡村地区实现社会消费品零售额81.8亿元，增长16.4%。

商品市场繁荣兴旺。截至年末，全市拥有亿元以上商品交易市场59家，营业面积428.7万平方米，比上年增长5.3%；成交额1623.1亿元，比上年增长21.4%。全市有5家市场年成交额突破百亿元，分别是江苏凌家塘市场、江苏长江塑料化工交易市场、江苏湖塘纺织城、常州钢材现货交易市场、常州龙成钢材城，成交额分别达到206.1亿元、202亿元、184亿元、120.8亿元、116.7亿元。

【交通运输和邮电通讯】交通运能不断提升。全年完成货物运输量15644万吨，货物周转量109.8亿吨公里，分别比上年增长19.3%、22.2%；完成旅客运输量15845万人次，旅客周转量89.8亿人公里，分别比上年增长19.4%、22.9%。港口货物吞吐量9521万吨，其中长江常州港货物吞吐量2768.7万吨。全年外贸货物吞吐量390.6万吨，比上年增长14.3%；集装箱吞吐量13.4万标准箱，比上年增长26.4%。民航常州机场全年进出港旅客93.4万人次，航空运输货物8362.7吨，分别比上年增长41.9% 、24.5%。全市机动车拥有量继续增长，年末全市民用汽车拥有量56万辆，比上年末增长23.5%，其中私人汽车43.4万辆，增长28%。

通信行业加速发展。全年邮政业务总收入6亿元，比上年增长14.8%；发送特快专递425.1万件，增长28.6%。通信业务收入54亿元，比上年增长6.9%。年末本地电话用户数158.7万户，移动电话用户560.5万户，其中3G用户达到84.3万户，全年短信业务量44.3亿条。年末全市互联网用户数达107.8万户，比上年末增长21.3%，其中宽带网用户104.51万户，增长33.6%。

【金融保险业】金融信贷有序运行。年末全市金融机构人民币存款余额4902.2亿元，比年初增长7.7%；贷款余额3406.4亿元，比年初增长12.8%，其中各项短期贷款1840亿元，比年初增长21.1%。个人中长期消费贷款余额483.6亿元，比年初增长14.2%，其中个人住房贷款462.3亿元，比年初增长13.5%。

保险业务发展较快。截至年末，全市纳入统计范围的保险公司共57家，比上年增加9家，全年实现保费收入99.3亿元，比上年增长14.7%，其中财产险保费收入29.7亿元，增长21.3%；寿险保费收入69.6亿元，增长12.1%。全年保险赔款、其它各类给付支出25.2亿元，比上年增长34.2%，其中财产险赔付支出14.6亿元，比上年增长38.2%；寿险赔付支出2.0亿元，增长27.9%，其它各类给付支出8.6亿元，增长29.2%。

证券市场交易趋冷。年内新增5家证券营业部。23个证券营业部全年证券交易总额4839.1亿元，比上年下降27.3%，其中股票、基金、债券分别成交4779.2亿元、53亿元、6.8亿元，分别下降27.3%、28.9%、17.3%。年底资金账户53.5万户，下降4.7%，持有A股股票市值293亿元，下降14.1%。

【旅游业】旅游产业快速发展。全年实现旅游总收入425.9亿元，比上年增长21.8%；接待国内游客3360.9万人次，增长19.9%；国内旅游收入398.5亿元，增长22.2%。全年接待入境游客41.3万人次，旅游外汇收入4.2亿美元，分别比上年增长15.1%和21.4%。环球动漫嬉戏谷、环球恐龙城5D互动电影、超级大海啸、南山竹海二期历史文化区、春秋淹城旅游区百灵水世界、春秋王宫等一大批旅游新项目先后建成开放。至年末，全市共有国家5A级景区1家，国家4A级景区11家，全国工农业旅游示范点17家。旅行社发展到111家，1家旅行社进入全省旅行社20强，1家旅行社进入全国旅行社100强；星级酒店发展到65家，其中五星级酒店6家，四星级酒店26家。

【固定资产投资】有效投入不断加大。全年完成全社会固定资产投资2338.9亿元，比上年增长20%，其中一、二、三次产业分别完成投资10亿元、1295.8亿元和1033.1亿元，分别比上年增长42.2%、19.3%和20.7%。工业投资稳定增长，投入结构持续优化，全年完成工业投资1293.4亿元，比上年增长19.7%，其中五大产业完成投资961亿元，比上年增长27.9%，占工业投资的比重达74.3%，比上年提高4.8个百分点。高新技术产业投资增势明显，全年完成投资576.7亿元，比上年增长95.2%，占工业投资的比重达44.6%，比上年提高17.2个百分点。

房产投资较快增长。列统房地产开发企业全年完成投资565.9亿元，比上年增长33.2%，其中住宅完成投资402.9亿元，比上年增长39%；商业营业用房、办公楼分别完成投资82.5亿元、28.3亿元，增长21.3%、51.5%。全年商品房屋施工面积达3926.8万平方米，比上年增长22.4%，其中新开工面积1451.1万平方米，增长9.7%；商品房竣工面积682.2万平方米，比上年下降6.9%。年末商品房待售面积191.5万平方米，下降0.9%，其中住宅待售面积71.2万平方米，下降17.7%。

二、改革开放

【民营经济】民营经济快速发展。年内新增私营企业1.2万户，私营企业累计达7.5万户，比上年末增长11.9%；新增个体工商户3.8万户，个体工商户累计达17.1万户，比上年末增长8.4%。全市私营企业注册资本2170.1亿元，个体工商户注册资本70.6亿元，分别比上年增长33.2%、18.9%。民营经济全年完成增加值2393亿元，按可比价计算增长12.9%，在全市经济总量中所占比重由上年的66.2%提高到66.8%；上缴税收362.5亿元，比上年增长23.4%，在全市税收总收入中所占比重由上年的63.4%提高到63.8%。

【开放型经济】外贸实力不断增强。全年完成进出口总额286.3亿美元，比上年增长28.5%，其中出口193.6亿美元，增长24.4%；进口92.7亿美元，增长38.1%。机电产品出口103.4亿美元，占全市出口份额的53.4%；高新技术产品出口41.1亿美元（按商务部高新技术类统计口径），占全市出口份额的21.2%。全年出口额超1000万美元的企业共360家，比上年增长25.4%。全市新增国家级出口基地1家，新获认定省级出口品牌32家，市级出口品牌53家。传统市场出口规模继续扩大，全年对欧盟、美国、东盟和日本市场的出口分别为51.5亿美元、35.4亿美元、17.4亿美元、18.4亿美元，分别比上年增长12%、24.4%、22.1%和32.3%。新兴市场开拓力度进一步加大，全年对东欧、拉美、大洋洲和中东等市场的出口增幅分别达68.9%、46.6%、29%和42.3%。

招商引资结构优化。全年完成实际到帐外资上报数32.2亿美元，比上年增长20.6%；实际到帐外资确认数30.5亿美元，增长14.3%。其中制造业实际到帐外资19.8亿美元，生产性服务业实际到帐外资2.5亿美元。项目引进成效显著，全年新增工商登记注册外资3000万美元以上项目43个，其中制造业项目29个；实际到帐外资超1000万美元项目81个。外商投资企业设备进口7.6亿美元，增长126.7%。新增世界500强投资项目9个，已有56家世界500强企业在我市投资85个项目。

外经合作稳步推进。全年新签外经合同额5.8亿美元，与上年持平，完成外经营业额5亿美元，比上年增长5.5%。走出去步伐有所加快，全市新核准境外投资项目49个，比上年增加9个；中方协议投资额4.5亿美元，增长30.1%。金昇公司斥资1亿欧元收购德国埃马克集团股权，常发集团投资5000万美元开发赞比亚铜矿。

【开发区建设】开发区竞争力不断增强。载体建设不断加快，省级以上开发区累计完成开发面积149.9平方公里，全年基础设施和功能性平台建设投入127亿元，工业投入798亿元。常州高新区、武进高新区和钟楼开发区获得江苏省知识产权保护试点园区，常州高新区通过国家生态园区评审。外资集聚效应凸显，省级以上开发区全年实际到帐注册外资26.5亿美元，占全市82.2%。其中制造业实际到帐17.5亿美元，占全市88.6%。新批协议外资1000万美元以上项目105个，占全市的86.8%。新增工商登记超3000万美元项目35个，其中制造业项目27个，分别占全市的81.4%和93.1%。

【外事】对外交往活跃频繁。全年接待外宾117批、1019人次，其中副部长以上团组5批、82人次；接待来常考察访问的外国驻华使、领馆官员29批、145人次，接待来访外国记者17批、62人次。年内有3个外国城市与我市结为友好城市，至年底，累计15个外国城市与我市结为友好城市，友好城市年内来访团组44批、302人次，组织25个团组、170人次出访友好城市。

三、社会事业

【科技事业】科技创新成绩斐然。全年政府科技经费投入15.7亿元，比上年增长41.8%；全社会研发投入占地区生产总值的比重达2.3%。全市新增高新技术企业165家，累计618家；新增省创新型企业59家，累计164家；新增省民营科技型企业961家，累计3306家；新增科技上市企业11家。全年共争取国家、省科技计划项目444项，争取资金4.2亿元，比上年增长26%，其中国家科技计划项目141项，争取资金1.9亿元。全年专利申请量达到23413件，比上年增长47.5%，其中发明专利6125件，增长84.8%；专利授权11390件，增长25.3%，其中发明专利授权744件，增长33 %。

创新平台建设加快。“一核八园”建设稳步推进，科教城入驻机构达520家，研发人才超万人；科技金融中心引入创投、担保、科技小额贷款、金融租赁等机构50家，资金规模20亿元。实施产学研合作项目556项，科研总收入4.4亿元。全市新建“两站三中心”149家，累计625家；新增国家级孵化器1家、省级孵化器5家、市级孵化器10家，新增孵化面积60.6万平方米，累计达364.6万平方米，在孵企业3610家。新增省级工程技术研究中心15家、企业技术中心12家、博士后科研工作站4家。

产学研合作不断深化。成功举办2011中国常州先进制造技术成果展示洽谈会，吸引140多家高校和科研院所、1400多位专家、1800多位企业家参加，达成合作项目160多项，其中108个项目现场签约，协议金额4.3亿元。充分发挥国际技术转移服务平台作用，重点开展与俄罗斯、以色列、英国、澳大利亚等国的交流合作；以“医疗器械和转化医学”为主题，举办第二届中英科技桥开放创新研讨会，“干细胞/微载体创面敷料”等7个项目达成实质性合作协议。年内共组织国际科技合作与交流27次，开展重大产学研合作活动13场，正式签订产学研合作项目310项。

人才高地加快构筑。启动实施“龙城英才计划”，全年引进250个领军人才创新创业团队，30多名国家“千人计划”签约来常创新创业。实施企业高层次科技人才培育计划236个，入选省优秀科技创新团队1个、省“双创人才”25名，获得国家和省级科技人才项目的支持经费5000万元，领军型创业人才创办的企业累计获得2.6亿元科技和人才专项资金。年末全市拥有各类专业技术人员41.4万人，比上年增长11.3%。全年接收大中专毕业生、引进各类技术人员37185人，其中博士157人，硕士1842人。

【教育事业】教育事业稳步推进。年末全市共有各类学校600所，在校学生74.5万人，教职工5.2万人，其中专任教师4万人。继续推进校舍安全工程，累计建设、改造校舍30万平方米。成立教育服务中心，举办“常州公开课”3讲、“龙城心理讲堂”大型公益讲座4场、龙城网校公益讲座155场，受众超过12万人次。教育信息化水平不断提升，全市100%学校建成一级校园网，8所学校获省中小学优秀校园网站评比活动一等奖，57所学校被确认为全国动漫实验学校。积极推进合作办学、境外培训和双向交流，新增聘外资格学校2所，年内有3所学校与国外4所学校缔结友好学校，165名教师赴境外教学、培训、考察，近千名学生赴境外修学、访问，11名学生获新加坡政府奖学金项目，300多名国外中小学生来常州留学、交流，美国总统奖学生首次来常州访问。落实各类学生资助3329万元。

基础教育不断强化。全市基础教育阶段省级优质学校达407所，占比率和就读率分别达到72.9%、83.6%。义务教育阶段起始年级小班化教学试点逐步推开，流动就业人员随迁子女公办学校吸纳比例达87%以上，市直属小学、幼儿园移交辖区管理，热点高中55%的统招名额分配到各初中学校，新组建25个优质名校教育集团。高考二本以上进线率位列全省前茅。省常中生物学科、前黄高中环境•生命学科被评为江苏省普通高中课程基地建设项目，省常中被评为全省14所普通高中创新人才培养试点学校之一。

职业教育创新发展。推进省职业教育创新发展实验区建设工程，形成殷村职教园建设思路和总体方案并启动建设，100%职业学校成为省优质职业学校，探索地方本科院校培养本科高职（技师）工作，省职校单招考试蝉联全省十二连冠，1名学生获全国光华创业精神大奖。

终身教育优化发展。推行社会办学规范管理、属地管理，编印《常州市社会办学服务指南》。年内新增省级乡镇（街道）社区教育中心3个，确定社区教育实验项目10个、市标准化乡镇（街道）成人教育中心6个、居民（村民）学校32家，开发社区教育课程200讲并每周在市电视台科教频道播出，引进、嫁接社区教育课程总量达15万讲，举办“2011年全国终身学习常州论坛”和第六届“全民终身学习推进周”活动。

【文化事业】文化工作成效显著。全年公共图书馆图书总流通132.2万人次，书刊文献外借125.3万册次，博物馆全年接待参观者94万人次。常州市图书馆戚区分馆、上书房分馆分别挂牌，在江苏省内率先探索开通了电视图书馆，推进城区街道社区信息共享工程按新标准建设。启动并推进“我为城市文明添光彩”主题活动和“幸福广场周周演”系列活动。通过全国第三次文化馆站评估定级省级验收。文化惠民工作深入开展，完成各类公益性演出1900场，低票价经营性演出3200场。公益文化场所免费开放服务水准不断提升，接待观众400万人次，举办各类文化艺术展览110个。农村文化工作有序推进，央视于2011年11月初进行了专题报道。

文艺精品异彩纷呈。常州历史上投资最大、阵容最强的大型交响锡剧《天涯歌女》社会反响强烈，成为江苏省戏剧节开幕式剧目并晋京演出。原创滑稽戏《逼煞钱师爷》成功上演。地方文献《常州词派研究丛书》（6册）、清代地方文史大成《常州赋》、《常州锡剧论文荟萃1950—2010》正式出版发行。广播电影电视节目48件作品获省政府奖，其中一等奖11件，二等奖19件，三等奖18件，为历年最好成绩。《长湖荡歌》获全省“市县代表性歌曲大赛”优秀作品奖。《常州白泰官》获第四届江苏曲艺“芦花奖”文学奖，《七彩人生》获节目奖、表演奖。建党90周年献礼片《秋之白华》获得较好反响。全市13个项目入选江苏省文化产业引导资金，共获得总额为1680万元的资金扶持。

广电事业稳步发展。全市拥有自办广播节目套数7套，全年播出时间44330小时，自办电视节目8套，全年播出时间56154小时，广播、电视节目综合覆盖率均为100%。网络改造力度加大，全年完成有线电视网络双向传输改造33.3万户，有线电视用户达112.7万户，比上年增加5.1万户，其中数字电视用户106.8万户，比上年增加15.7万户。获得广播电视科技创新奖、金鹿奖、金帆奖等45个省级奖项，为全省第一。江苏省5个国家级广播电视先进台站常州占2席。全年《常州广播电视报》发行量327.6万份。

文化遗产保护加强。全面完成常州市第三次全国文物普查工作，全市共普查文物点1677处，其中新发现文物点1270处。新增省级文保单位23个，累计达50个。完成清凉寺修缮与环境整治工程（一期）、大成一厂老厂房刘国钧办公楼修缮工程、孟河古城墙修复工程等项目；完成武进胥城遗址建设控制地带内的考古调查勘探、戚机厂燃机二期工程考古调查勘探、溧阳弘博热电二期工程考古调查勘探等多项工作；8个项目入选第三批江苏省非遗名录，3个项目入选国家级非遗名录。出版发行《常州市非物质文化遗产集萃》。组织参加2011中国（深圳）文化产业博览交易会，获得一金三银。在“2011江苏省工艺美术精品博览会”上摘得12金、13银、11铜和2个优秀奖。

【卫生事业】医疗体系不断完善。年末全市共有各类医疗卫生机构1101个，其中各级各类医院、卫生院92家，疾病预防控制机构8个，妇幼保健机构8个；卫生技术人员2.3万人，其中医生10376人、注册护士8550人。全市平均每千常住人口拥有卫生技术人员4.9人、医生2.2人、床位3.6张。累计建立居民健康档案344.2万份，建档率为75%，其中65岁以上老人建档率达到95%；高血压、Ⅱ型糖尿病、重性精神病规范化管理率分别达到98.1%、98.1%和97.5%。全面推行基本药物制度，所有基层医疗卫生机构全部配备使用规定目录范围内的基本药品，统一网上采购并实行零差率销售。截至年底，网上采购基本药物4.4亿元，销售4.2亿元，让利幅度35%以上。科研教学实现突破，创建省级重点学科2个、省级医学领军人才与创新团队2个，7人入选省医学重点人才。

农村医疗稳步推进。新型农村合作医疗参保人口达187万人，参保率继续保持100%。人均筹资305元，比上年提高60元。县乡两级政策范围内住院补偿比为73.5%，实际住院补偿比52.5%。全面开展农村儿童重大疾病医疗保障工作，2例白血病、17例先心病患儿得到新农合基金补偿。截至年末，全市拥有省级卫生镇27个、省级卫生村542个。

【体育事业】体育事业蓬勃发展。成功举办2011李宁杯中国羽毛球大师赛、环太湖国际公路自行车赛（常州站）、2011亚洲女子手球锦标赛暨2012伦敦奥运会资格赛、中美篮球对抗赛等4项国际级比赛、14项国家级比赛、15项省级赛事，央视直播、转播29小时。常州籍运动员全年在重大比赛中获得25项冠军，其中世界冠军2项，亚洲冠军1项，全国冠军22项。

全民健身扎实推进。全面实施城市社区和农村公共体育基础设施“提档工程”，全市新增社区健身活动场所63个，完成了对城区2004年以前建设的190个健身工程（点）的器材整新工作，对城区2004年以后建设的630个健身工程（点）下拨器材维修管理经费，对老小区改造过程中的7处场所配套建设了公共体育设施，清潭全民健身中心开工建设。青枫公园、武进健身广场被评为江苏省仅有的两家“国家级健身广场”。广泛开展全民健身活动，全市组织开展区级以上全民健身活动150多场，乡镇、街道以上活动200多项次，参与活动人数超过35万人。新建市级社区体育健身俱乐部10所，发展俱乐部会员2500人。整合社区晨晚练点的项目布局，新建社区晨晚练点80个。全市经常性参加体育锻炼的人数比重达52.6%。连续第15年获全民健身活动优秀组织奖和先进单位荣誉称号。全年发行体育彩票10.8亿元，比上年增长48%。

四、人口、民生与社会保障

【人口与就业】人口规模保持稳定。年末全市户籍人口达362.9万人，比上年末增长0.6%；暂住人口达133.1万人，比上年末增长0.2%。全市计划生育率达98.7%，节育率达88 %，独生子女率为79.7%；当年全市出生人口29007人，死亡人口22144人，人口自然增长率为1.9‰。

创业就业工作不断推进。全市新增就业岗位18万个，比上年增长3.3%，新增就业10.6万人，增长17.1%；扶持创业3595人，创业带动就业1.8万人，失业人员实现再就业5.9万人，其中就业困难对象再就业1.1万人；城镇登记失业率2.6%。继续强化技能培训工作，全年完成城乡劳动者职业技能培训6.2万人，城乡新成长劳动力技能培训1.1万人，高技能人才培养2.3万人。

【人民生活】居民收支稳步增长。抽样调查结果显示，全年城镇居民人均可支配收入29829元，人均消费性支出18893元，分别比上年增长13.6%、10.3%，居民恩格尔系数为35.8%，比上年上升3.1个百分点；农民人均纯收入14838元，人均生活消费支出11208元，分别比上年增长17.4%、13.1%，居民恩格尔系数35.5%，比上年上升0.5个百分点。居民储蓄继续增加，年末居民储蓄存款余额2171.2亿元，当年新增150.3亿元。

安居工程继续推进。截至年末，城镇居民人均住房建筑面积34.8平方米，比上年末增加1.6平方米；农村居民人均住房面积61.5平方米，比上年末增加3平方米。保障性安居工程建设继续推进，全年新开工建设廉租住房1022套、新开工公共租赁住房14013套、新增经济适用住房1376套、新建限价商品房3389套、城市棚户区危旧房改造56.5万平方米，发放廉租住房租赁补贴5016户。住房保障覆盖面进一步扩大，中心城区（天宁区、钟楼区、戚墅堰区）新增经济适用房购房签约461户，新增廉租住房保障家庭718户，新增经济适用房货币补贴保障家庭461户，新增公共租赁住房保障家庭1131户，新增廉租住房和公共租赁住房实物配租1567户。全市住房公积金扩面人数11.4万人，全年发放公积金贷款1.1万户，金额28.6亿元。全市老小区综合整治80万平方米。

【市场物价】物价指数高位运行。全年居民消费价格指数（CPI）为105。八大类商品和服务项目价格呈现“七涨一平”的格局，其中食品类价格上涨11.7%，家庭设备用品及维修服务类、居住类、烟酒类价格分别上涨6.3%、4.4%、3.7%，医疗保健和个人用品类、娱乐教育文化用品类、衣着类价格分别上涨2.4%、1.5%、1.6%、交通和通讯类价格与上年持平。

【社会保障】社保体系不断完善。截至年末，共有113.8万人参加企业养老保险，比上年末增长6%；88.9万人参加失业保险，增长11.9%；149.1万人参加城镇职工医疗保险，增长11.9%。养老、医疗、失业保险综合覆盖率在98%以上。五大保险基金征收达118.6亿元，比上年增长22.6%；支出94.2亿元，增长23.2%。全市医保定点住院医疗机构152家，门诊医疗机构206家，定点零售药店627家。市区企业退休人员月养老金提高至1661元，城乡居民社会养老保险月基础养老金提高至80元，城镇老年居民月养老补贴提高至220元，职工医保、城镇居民医保参保人员住院制度规定范围内医药费用报销比例分别达到80%和60%。全市参加城乡居民社会养老保险人数为90.7万人，享受基础养老金41.1万人。

【社会福利与救济】慈善救助有序开展。年末全市拥有各类养老机构92个，床位总数达14453张，收养人数达9704人；福利企业总数达到282个。全市30283户、56712人纳入低保范围，其中城镇低保对象10891户、20439人，农村低保对象19392户，36273人，累计发放保障金1.4亿元，15582人次得到医疗救助，比上年增加3088人次；救助金额达2383万元，增长56.3%。全年发行福利彩票9.3亿元，增长59.5%。慈善事业保持快速发展态势，截至年末，全市各级慈善会累计募集和认捐慈善总额达18.79亿元，累计发放救助金3.95亿元，救助惠及各类困难群众40.56万人次。年内全市各级慈善会共发放救助金8348万元，救助各类困难群众5.56万人次，市慈善总会共发放各类救助金2490.58万元，救助困难群众1.9万余人次。

五、城乡建设

【基础设施建设】基础设施日益完善。常州机场新航站楼、京沪高铁常州北站建成运营，西绕城高速公路、龙江路高架南延等工程建成通车，常溧高速公路建设积极推进，苏南运河、丹金溧漕河等三级航道整治工程进展顺利，串新河枢纽、南运河枢纽、大运河东枢纽等城市防洪节点工程全力推进。城市功能不断完善，中心城区完成永宁北路、中吴大道东延等道路建设，南部新城扎实推进武宜路片区综合改造工程，滨湖新城商业综合体项目启动实施。

【公用事业】公交优先成效显著。全年新辟公交线路11条，优化调整公交线路19条，年末拥有公交线路167条，公交线路长度3138公里，运营车辆2600辆，分别较上年末增长3.7%、5.3%、3.3%。车辆安全舒适以及智能化水平不断提高，全年新增空调公交车辆689辆，市区公交车实现100%空调化，GPS安装率达100%。公交总行驶里程1.5亿公里，比上年增长2.1%；总客运量4.1亿人次，增长4.5%，日均客运量111.6万人次。快速公交日均客运量29万人次，达到公交日均总客运量的26%，最高峰客运量达到46.3万人次。快速公交系统成功入选全国“百年百项杰出土木工程”。

公共服务不断完善。数字化城市长效综合管理机制不断完善，生活垃圾无害化处理率达100%。居民住宅区治安防范进一步加强。156个老小区门岗设施已基本投入使用；80万平方米老小区提升工程防范设施补建到位，实现老小区保洁、保绿与保安一体化管理。城区供水总量2.9亿立方米，其中居民生活用水1.2亿立方米，供水普及率达100%。全社会用电量331.7亿千瓦时，比上年增长13.9%，其中城乡居民生活用电28亿千瓦时，增长1.9%。年末市区管道燃气用户达49.7万户，比上年末增长13.9%；城市供气气化率达99.1%。全市生活污水日处理能力53.5万吨，城区生活污水处理率达93.2%。年底城市路灯总数16.3万盏，比上年末增长7.2%。

六、环境保护与资源节约

【环境保护与治理】生态环境不断改善。巩固提升市区60条河道整治成果，完成市区外围黑臭河道整治40条，3条入太湖河道和主要湖泊水质总体有所改善。全市空气质量优良天数达343天，占总天数的94%。生态市建设通过国家级考核验收，成为全国第二个通过生态市建设国家考核的地级市。区域环境噪声平均值为54.7分贝，交通干线噪声平均值为67.3分贝，集中式饮用水水源地水质达标率为100%。15个全国环境优美镇提升创建为国家级生态镇，建成国家级生态街道2个、国家级生态村5个，新增省、市级生态村85个、绿色社区34家、绿色学校54所和环境教育基地3个。

【城市绿化】城市绿化品质提升。实施深化五大特色绿化工程，完成投资 8.3亿元，新增绿地578.1公顷。高铁生态公园总投资1.8亿元，已新增绿化面积32公顷；太湖湾嬉戏谷绿化工程已完工，新增绿地面积44公顷；高铁南北广场绿化、玲珑花园北侧绿地、太湖路北侧绿地、龙江路—黄河路交叉口绿地已完工，新增面积9.9公顷；紫荆公园东经120° 标志塔框架完成吊装。组织实施西绕城高速公路和泰州长江公路大桥连接线常州段绿化、锡溧漕河航道整治绿化、花海大道南段绿化以及新北区多条道路绿化工程，完成高架桥二期桥柱、城际铁路地道垂直绿化。年末建成区绿地面积达6648.7公顷，其中公园绿地面积1703公顷，分别比上年末增长13.4%和4.4%；城区人均公园绿地达到12.4平方米；建成区绿化覆盖率达42.2%，比上年提高0.02个百分点，建成区绿地率38.4%，比上年提高0.1个百分点。

注：公报中各项统计数据除注明按可比价格计算外，均按现行价格计算。

STATISTICAL COMMUNIQUE OF CHANGZHOU MUNICIPALITY ON THE 2011 NATIONAL ECONOMIC AND SOCIAL DEVELOPMENT

In 2011, facing the international financial crisis once again, under the complicated situation with multiple challenges suffered by the national economy, under the leadership of Changzhou Municipal Committee of the CPC and Changzhou Municipal People's Government, the whole city insisted on taking "Year of Accelerating Transformation & Upgrade" campaign as the mainstream, with the motivation of reform, opening and innovation. By ensuring the increase, all social sectors have tried their best to adjust the structure and accelerate the transition, as well as benefiting people and to be in harmony with the high-speed development. The national economy of the whole city turned out to be generally steady, the development quality increased stably, and people's living conditions improved continuously. So far, Changzhou has fulfilled the targets confirmed by the People's Congress and realized the good start of the "Twelfth Five-year Plan".

I. Economic Development

Economic Aggregate

The industrial structure was improving continuously. The gross domestic product (GDP) of the whole city reached RMB 358.10 billion, increased by 12.2% over the previous year calculated on comparable prices. The value added of three industries, namely, primary industry, secondary industry and tertiary industry reached RMB 11.18 billion, 195.08 billion and 151.84 billion respectively, was up 4.0%, 12.2% and 12.8% respectively over the previous year. The industrial structure of the whole city was optimized continuously. The proportion of the outputs of three industries was adjusted to 3.1:54.5:42.4 from 3.3:55.3:41.4 of last year, the proportion of the value added of the tertiary industry to the city's total economic output increased one percentage point over last year, with the rate of economic development reaching 47.9%. The per capita GDP based on resident population reached RMB 77,485, approximately USD 11997 based on the current exchange rate.

Financial income and expenses increased stably. The revenue of local general budget of the whole year reached RMB 35.09 billion, increased by 22.6% over last year. Major taxes maintained relatively rapid growth. Among them, the value-added tax, the sales tax, and individual income tax achieved RMB 4.86 billion, RMB 7.41 billion and RMB 1.92 billion respectively, up 21.5%, 14.1% and 32% respectively. The investment of people's livelihood kept increasing. All the year through, the fiscal expenditure of general budget of the whole year hit RMB 36.18 billion, up 28.6%, of which RMB 5.49 billion was paid for education, RMB 3.64 billion was paid for social security and other programs in fields of employment, RMB 1.97 billion was paid for health and medical services, RMB 6.80 billion was paid for urban and rural community affairs and RMB 1.21 billion was paid for traffic and transportations, increased by 35.2%, 46.1%, 34.0%, 67.6% and 44.0% respectively.

Agriculture and Rural Economy

The agricultural production got tremendous achievements. The total output value of agriculture, forestry, animal husbandry and fishery achieved RMB 19.47 billion, up 11.8% over the previous year. Grain production increased little in steady. Total sown areas of the whole city reached 159.5 thousand hectares, down a little over the previous year; and the capacity of grain production hit 1.152 million tons, nearly equivalent to the previous year. The output of grains achieved 481.4 kilograms per mu, of which the output of grains achieved new high, 627.9 kilograms per mu, increased by 7.8 kilograms over the previous year, ranking at the first place in Jiangsu province for nine straight years. The construction of high-efficiency industrialized agriculture continued promoting, the project called "Double Million mu" has been fully completed. The area of high-standard farmland was enlarged by another 140,000 mu, the area of high-efficiency farmland was enlarged by another 139,000 mu, including 76,000 mu for industrialized agriculture, the area of high-efficiency fishery was 103,000 mu. The area of high-standard farmland increased to 1,133,000 mu, the area of high-efficiency agriculture was 1,130,000 mu, including 304,000 mu for industrialized agriculture, the area of high-efficiency fishery was 457,000 mu. By the end of 2011, the number of pollution-free agricultural products manufacturing bases amounted to 414; the numbers of certified pollution-free agricultural products at or above provincial level, provincial famous agricultural products, agricultural products with green label and organic food products reached 624, 42, 343 and140 respectively.

The construction of "New Countryside" achieved marked results. During the whole year, 58 kilometers of rural road were newly built or reconstructed, and 185 dangerous bridges in countryside were reinforced. The infrastructure of water conservancy projects was carried out in stable progress. By the end of year, investment on water conservancy projects reached RMB 300 million in total; all kinds of water conservancy construction earthworks completed 15.99 million cubic meters; 5 rivers running in the countryside and 104 rivers running in the town, 865 ponds in 178 villages were dredged; 61.7 kilometers dike construction was completed, 3526 buildings above canaliculus level were built, 267 kilometers of anti-seepage channels were newly built; 187 reformed embankments were newly built; 256 reformed pump stations were newly built; 48 watergates were reconstructed; 16 square kilometers of soil erosion area were restored, adding water-saving irrigation area by 76,000 mu, adding efficient irrigation area by 12,000 mu, 105,000 mu irrigation area was improved, 28,000 mu low and medium-yield farmland was rebuilt.

The industrialization development achieved marked results. During the whole year, the farmers' specialized cooperative economic organizations were increased by 447, added up to 2350. The leading enterprises at provincial level or above increased by 6, including one with national level. 48 leading enterprises at municipal level or above drove the increase of more than 1 million mu of planting area. The sales income reached RMB 38.8 billion all the year around, increased by 21.5% over the last year. Leisure sight-seeing agriculture developed rapidly; more than 300 various kinds of leisure sight-seeing agriculture spot were built; 17 national agricultural tours demonstrations were created, as well as 41 sight spot with 3 stars or above at city level were born. The number of the tourists reached to more than 5.5 million in the whole year, which made tourism income reaching to RMB 1 billion.

Industry

The economic aggregate was increased steadily. The above-scale industrial output value achieved RMB 827.08 billion all the year around, an increase of 18.5% over the previous year, of which the light industry contributed RMB 154.78 billion, up 5.6%; and the heavy industry produced RMB 672.29 billion, up 21.9%. Among the above-scale industries, non-government companies achieved the output value of RMB 513.96 billion, increased by 20.0%, of which private enterprises made RMB 461.67 billion, up 24.6%; while the foreign invested and Hong Kong-, Macao- or Taiwan- funded industrial enterprises achieved the output value of RMB 284.12 billion, an increase of 17.4%. The main industrial income reached RMB 821.25 billion of the whole city, the profit and tax amount reached RMB 71.33 billion, and the contribution margin achieved RMB 46.84billion, increased by 19.5%, 18.6%, 15.7% respectively over the previous year.

The industrial structure continued optimizing. The output value of five major above-scale industrial enterprises achieved RMB 562.09 billion, up 33.7%, taking 67.7% of the overall industrial output value, contributing the rate of 80.7% to the above-scale industrial growth. High-tech industry developed rapidly, bringing much more contribution rate. High-tech above-scale industrial enterprises achieved the output value of RMB 310.06 billion, up 38.6%, taking 37.4% of the overall industrial output value, while the proportion was 32.1% last year, bringing the rate of 12.8 percentage points of industrial economic growth, the contributed rate of industrial growth reached to 47.7%. while it was 30.7% last year.

Architecture Industry

The architecture industry was in a stage of steady development. The value added of architecture industry reached RMB 18.15 billion, up 7.8% calculated at comparable prices; the construction output of architecture companies achieved RMB 89.96 billion, up 20.6%; the construction area reached 76.572 million square meters, increased by 23.7%; the completed construction area reached 28.315 million square meters, an increase of 6.5%. The efficiency of architecture industry kept improving. All-personnel labor productivity hit RMB 245,000/person calculated on its output value, up 6.5% over the previous year. The first-term project of

Changzhou Elevated Road won the "Luban Award," which is China's highest honor for architecture quality.

Domestic Trade

The domestic trade had stable growth. The total retail sales of consumer goods achieved RMB123.61 billion, increased by 17.3% over the previous year, of which wholesale and retail industry contributed RMB 113.38 billion, up 16.6%, the sales of the catering industry contributed RMB 10.23 billion, up 24.8%. Meanwhile the consumption of urban and rural market maintained the equal growth, of which the retail sales of consumer goods in urban area achieved RMB 115.43 billion, up 17.3%, while in the rural area achieved RMB 8.18 billion, up 16.4%.

The commodity market was prosperous. By the end of year, there were 59 products trading markets of which sales achieved over RMB 100 million, and the area of business achieved 4.287 million square meters, up 5.3% over last year. The volume of business achieved RMB 162.31 billion, up 21.4% over last year. 5 markets achieved RMB 10 billion in turnover, namely Jiangsu Lingjiatang Market, Jiangsu Yangzi River Plastic and Chemistry Trade Market, Jiangsu Hutang Textile City, Changzhou Steel Spot Market, and Changzhou Dragon City Steel City, making turnover of RMB 20.61 billion, RMB 20.2 billion, RMB 18.4 billion, RMB 12.08 billion, RMB 11.67 billion respectively.

Transportation and Post and Telecommunication

Transportation capacity continued growing. The total volume of cargo transportation amounted to 156.44 million tons, and the cargo circulation volume reached 10.98 billion tons/km all the year around, up 19.3% and 22.2% respectively. The passenger volume hit 158.45million person-times and the total volume of passenger circulation reached 8.98 billion persons / km, up 19.4% and 22.9% respectively. The volume of freight handled at ports achieved 95.21 million tons, of which Yangtze River Changzhou Port contributed 27.687 million tons. Throughput of foreign trade reached 3.906 million tons, an increase of 14.3%; the container throughput reached 134,000 TEUs, up 26.4%; the number of incoming and outgoing passengers at Changzhou Civil Airport achieved 934,000 person-times; the volume of air transportation reached 8362.7tons, increased by 41.9% and 24.5% respectively. The amount of vehicle kept the trend of a rapid growth. By the end of year, the amount of private vehicles reached 560,000 sets, a rise of 23.5%, including 434,000 sets of private cars, up 28%.

Telecommunication services made a rapid development. The income of post business reached RMB 6 billion all the year around, up 14.8% over the previous year. The number of express mail service was 4.251 million, up 28.6%. The income of communication business reached RMB 5.4 billion, up 6.9% over the previous year. The number of local telephone subscribers was 1.587 million. The number of mobile phone subscribers was 5.605 million. The number of 3G phone subscribers was 843,000. The number of SMS business was 4.43 billion. By the end of 2011, the number of Internet subscribers of the whole city reached 1.078 million, an increase of 21.3% over the previous year. The number of broadband networks subscribers was 1045,100, up 33.6%.

Finance and Insurance

Credit financing was in an orderly procedure. By the end of 2011, the balance of deposits among financial institutions reached RMB 490.22 billion, 7.7% higher than that at the beginning of 2011; while the balance of loans achieved RMB 340.64 billion, up 12.8% over the beginning of year, of which various kinds of short-term loans reached RMB 184 billion, 21.1% higher than that at the beginning of 2011. Personal medium and long-term loans made RMB 48.36 billion, increased by 14.2%, of which personal housing loans contributed RMB 46.23 billion, increased by 13.5%.

Insurance business develops comparatively fast. By the end of 2011, 57 insurance institutions were included into the statistical range, an increase of 9 institutions over last year. In 2011, the gross income of insurance amounted to RMB 9.93 billion, up 14.7%, including RMB 2.97 billion of property insurance and RMB 6.96 billion of life insurance, increased by 21.3% and 12.1% respectively. The expenditure of insurance indemnity reached RMB 2.52 billion, increased by 34.2% , of which RMB 1.46 billion was spent on property insurance, an increase of 38.2%, and RMB 200 million was paid for life insurance, an increase of 27.9%, and

RMB 860 million was spent on other insurance indemnity, a increase of 29.2%.

Security market was depressed. Five more security exchange offices were built during the year of 2011.The turnover of various securities in 23 security exchange offices reached RMB 483.91 billion, decrease 27.3%, of which the turnover of stock exchange, fund exchange and bond exchange contributed RMB 477.92 billion, RMB 5.3 billion and RMB 680 million respectively, decreased by 27.3%, 28.9% and 17.3% respectively. The number of cash accounts was 535,000, a decrease of 4.7%, including a stock exchange amount reached RMB 29.3 billion, decreased by 14.1%.

Tourism

Tourism industry develops fast. The total tourism income of the city achieved RMB 42.59 billion all the year around, up 21.8% over the previous year. The city received 33.609 million person-times of domestic tourists, contributing RMB 39.85 billion to the tourism income, up 19.9% and 22.2% respectively; and received 413,000 person-times of oversea tourists, producing foreign exchange earnings from tourism of USD 420 million, up 15.1% and 21.4% respectively. A group of new programs were completed and open, such as the Universal Dinosaur Town, Kuka Suka Grand Valley, the Grand Theatre of Dinosaur Town, the scenic spots of Three Rivers and Three Parks, the Amusement Park of Yancheng Remains of Spring & Autumn Period, the 4th floor of Tianning Pagoda and the creative business quarter called Canal No.5. By the end of 2011, Changzhou had one Class 5A tourist attractions, eleven Class 4A scenic spots, 17 domestic industry and agricultural scenic spots, 111 travel agencies, one of which were ranked among the Top 20 Travel Agencies of Outstanding Contribution in Jiangsu Province; one of which were ranked among the Top 100 Travel Agencies for Outstanding Contribution in China; and 65 hotels with stars, including six five-star hotels and 26 four-star hotels.

Investment in Fixed Assets

The scale of investment continued expanding. The amount of overall social investment in fixed assets hit RMB 233.89 billion, up 20% over the previous year, of which the investment in first industry reached RMB 1 billion, an increase of 42.2%; the investment in second industry made RMB 129.58 billion, increased by 19.3%; the investment in third industry made RMB 103.31 billion, up 20.7%. The industrial investment structure was optimized, making RMB 129.34 billion, up 19.7%. The investment proportion in five pillar industries and hi-tech industries was significantly increased. The total investment in major five pillar industries reached RMB 96.1 billion, increased by 27.9%, and the investment in hi-tech industries made RMB 57.67 billion, increased by 95.2%, and the proportion in total investment climbed to 74.3% and 44.6% respectively, the growth rates of which were 4.8 and 17.2 percentage points higher than the overall industrial investments respectively.

Real estate develops fast. Real estate companies completed investment of RMB 56.59 billion all the year around, up 33.2% over the previous year, among which the residential investment contributed RMB 40.29 billion, up 39%; the investment of commercial business and offices contributed RMB 8.25 billion and RMB 2.83 billion respectively, a rise of 21.3% and 51.5% respectively. The area of commercial residential building under construction reached 39.268 million square meters, an increase of 22.4%, of which the newly commenced construction took an area of 14.511 million square meters, increased by 9.7%; completed construction covered the area of 6.822million square meters, down 6.9%. By the end of year, area of commercial buildings held for sale reached 1.915 million square meters, down 0.9%, of which the residential area for sale was 712,000 square meters, 17.7% lower than last year.

II. Reform and Opening-up

Private Economy

Private economy maintained rapid development. By the end of 2011, Changzhou had newly increased 12,000 private enterprises, amounting to 75,000 private enterprises, up 11.9%; and newly increased 38,000 individually-owned businesses, amounting to 171,000 individually-owned businesses, up 8.4%. The total registered capital of private enterprises hit RMB 217.01

billion and the total registered capital of individually-owned businesses reached RMB 7.06 billion, increased by 33.2% and 18.9% respectively. The total added value of private economy in the city achieved RMB 239.3 billion, 12.9% higher than that of the previous year calculated on comparable prices, the proportion of that to the city's total economic output increased from 66.2% to 66.8%; while the tax revenue of private economy reached RMB 36.25 billion, the proportion of that to the city's total tax revenue increased from 63.4% to 63.8%.

Open Economy

Foreign trade obtained great progress. During the whole year, the total volume of imports and exports reached USD 28.63 billion, up 28.5%. The total export volume achieved USD 19.36 billion, up 24.4%; while the total import volume made USD 9.27 billion, up 38.1%. The annual export volume of electromechanical products reached USD 10.34 billion, which accounted for 53.4% of total exports volume; the annual export volume of hi-tech products reached USD 4.11 billion, which accounted for 21.2% of total exports volume. The number of enterprises with annual export volume of more than USD 10 million reached 360, an increase of 25.4% over the previous year. In addition, the city newly added one state export base, 32 approved provincial export brands and 53 municipal export brands. The traditional market export was expanded. The export volume to regions of EU, USA, ASEAN and Japan achieved USD 5.15 billion, USD 3.54 billion, USD 1.74 billion and USD 1.84 billion, increased by 12%, 24.4%, 22.1% and 32.3% respectively. Emerging markets achieved further development. The export growth to Eastern Europe, Latin America, Oceania and Middle East markets reached 68.9%, 46.6%, 29% and 42.3%.

Investment promotion structure was optimized. In the year of 2011, the reported paid-in foreign capital was USD 3.22 billion, an increase of 20.6% over the previous year; the confirmed paid-in foreign capital was USD 3.05 billion, an increase of 14.3%. The actual paid-in foreign capital in manufacturing was USD 1.98 billion while that in producer service was USD 250 million. The introduction of projects achieved marked results. The city added 43 projects each with industrial and commercial registered foreign capital above USD 30 million, including 29 manufacturing projects, and 81 projects each with actual paid-in foreign capital above USD 10 million. The equipment importing expense by foreign-invested enterprises reached USD 760 million, an increase of 126.7%. So far, there have been 85 projects invested by 56 Fortune 500 Companies in Changzhou, including 9 newly invested projects.

Foreign economic cooperation moved forward steadily. All the year around, the amount of newly contracted foreign investment was USD 580 million, maintaining the same level as that in the previous year. And the foreign trade turnover was USD 500 million, increased by 5.5%. The pace of "going out" was accelerated. Within the year, Changzhou newly authorized 49 foreign investment projects, 9 more than that of last year. The amount of Chinese agreed investment reached USD 450 million, an increase of 30.1%. Jiangsu Jinsheng Industry Co., Ltd. took over Germany EMAG Group with EUR 100 million. Changfa Group invested USD 50 million in developing Zambia copper mine.

Construction of Development Zones

Competitiveness of development zones was continuously enhanced. The carrier construction was accelerating. In 2011, the construction area of development zones above the provincial level totaled 149.9 square kilometers. The investment in infrastructure and functional platforms construction reached RMB 12.7 billion, and the investment in industry reached RMB 79.8 billion. Changzhou National Development Zone, Wujin Hi-tech Development Zone and Zhonglou Development Zone were recognized as Jiangsu Provincial Intellectual Property Right Protection Pilot Parks. And Changzhou National Development Zone passed the assessment of National Ecological Garden. Foreign capital agglomeration effects were significant. The actual paid-in foreign investment of development zones above provincial level reached USD 2.65 billion, accounting for 82.2% of the city's total amount. And the actual paid-in foreign investment in manufacturing reached USSD 1.75 billion, accounting for 88.6% of the city's total amount. The new approved projects with agreed foreign-capital of more than USD 10 million achieved 105, accounting for 86.8%. The new projects with the industrial and commercial registered capital of more than USD 30 million achieved 35, including 27 manufacturing projects, accounting for 81.4% and 93.1 % respectively.

Foreign Affairs

Foreign exchange became more frequent. In 2011, the city received 117 foreign delegations with total 1,019 visitors, including 5 delegations with total 82 members at vice-minister level and above; 29 investigation missions with total 145 officials from foreign embassies and consulates; and 17 journalist delegations with total 62 members. Changzhou has established sister-city relationship with 15 foreign cities, including 3 new sister cities established within this year. By the end of the year, the city has received 44 delegations with total 302 visitors from these cities and sent 25 delegations with total 170 members to visit them.

III. Social Undertaking

Science and Technology

Science and technology innovation achieved remarkable success. In 2011, the government invested RMB 1.57 billion in science and technology research, increased by 41.8%; the total R&D input occupied 2.3% of the GDP. The city has owned 618 hi-tech enterprises, including 165 newly added ones; 164 provincial innovative enterprises, including 59 newly added ones; 3,306 provincial private technological enterprises, including 961 newly added ones. In addition, the city newly added 11 listed hi-tech enterprises. In the past year, the city has obtained 444 state and provincial science and technology projects, involving the fund of RMB 420 million, increased by 26%, among which, there were 141 state science and technology plan projects, involving the fund of RMB 190 million. The patent applications amounted to 23,413, increased by 47.5% over the previous year, among which 6,125were patent of invention applications, accounting for 84.8% of the total amount. Besides, the number of patent authorizations was 11,390, grew by 25.3%, among which 774 were patent of invention authorizations, grew by 33%. .

The pace of platform building was accelerated. The construction of "One scientific center and eight industrial parks" moved forward steadily. Changzhou Science and Education Town has attracted 520 institutes to settle in and employed more than 10,000 R&D personnel. Changzhou Technology Financial Center introduced over 50 agencies for venture capital, guarantees, micro-loans and financial leasing, which covers the fund of RMB 2 billion. It has implemented 556 production-teaching-research projects, realizing the revenue in scientific research of RMB 440 million. The city newly built 149 "two stations and three centers", and the total number reached 625. Besides, the city has newly added 1 state incubator, 5 provincial incubators and 10 municipal incubators, which added the incubator area of 606,000 square meters. So far, the total area of all incubators reached 3,646,000 square meters, and the enterprises being incubated reached 3,610. Moreover, the city newly built 15 engineering technology research centers at provincial level, 12 enterprise technology centers and 4 post-doctoral research stations.

The cooperation of enterprises, universities and research institutes was further deepened. 2011 China (Changzhou) Advanced Manufacturing Technology Exhibition was successfully held and attracted more than 140 universities and research institutes, over 1,400 experts and 1,800 entrepreneurs to participate in. As a result, more than 160 cooperation projects were reached in the exhibition and 108 projects were signed on the spot involving the agreed capital of RMB 430 million. By fully playing the function of service platform for transferring international technology, the city focused on the exchange and cooperation with Russia, Israel, Britain, Australia and other countries. Besides, the city held the 2nd Sino-British Bridge Opening and Innovation Seminar based on the theme of "medical devices and translational medicine". The seven projects achieved substantive cooperation agreements, including the project of "stem cells / micro carrier wound dressing". In the whole year, the city has organized 27 international scientific and technological cooperation and exchanges, carried out 13 significant production-teaching-research cooperation activities and officially signed 310 production-teaching-research cooperation projects.

The construction of talents cluster was speeded up. With the implementation of "Talents Gathering Plan", Changzhou has introduced 250 innovative and entrepreneurial talents teams and signed more than 30 talents selected from "National Thousand Talents Introduction Plan" to start the business in Changzhou. In 2011, the city carried out 236 training programs for high-level scientific and technological personnel. One team was selected as provincial outstanding scientific and technological innovation team and 25 personnel were recognized as provincial "Innovation and Entrepreneurship talents". The support fund for national and provincial technological talents projects of Changzhou reached RMB 50 million. And the technology & talents special funds for enterprises set up by leading innovation and entrepreneurship talents reached RMB 260 million. By the end of 2011, the number of various types of professional and technical personnel reached 414,000, increasing 11.3% over the previous year and 37,185 college graduates and professional and technical personnel were brought in, including 157 doctors and 1,842 masters.

Education

The educational undertaking was steadily advanced. By the end of the year, the city owned a total of 600 various kinds of full-time schools, 745,000 enrolled full-time students and 52,000 faculty members, among which 40,000 were full-time teachers. The construction project of school buildings was advanced, covering a total area of 300,000 square meters. The city also set up an educational service center to organize 3 "Changzhou open classes", 4 large public lectures of "psychology" and 155 public lectures through network schools, which covered over 120,000 audiences. The informationization of education was improved. The First-level campus network accounted for 100% of the schools. 8 schools won the first prizes in Jiangsu provincial excellent primary and secondary campus networks assessment activities, and 57 schools were recognized as national animation experimental schools. Cooperative education, overseas training and two-way exchange were actively moved forward. In 2011, 2 more schools were authorized the qualification of recruiting foreign faculty; 3 schools established sister-school relationship with 4 foreign schools; 165 teachers went abroad for teaching, training and investigation and about 10,000 students went abroad for further education and visit; 11 students were granted the scholarship by the Singapore Government; more than 300 foreign primary and secondary school students came to Changzhou for education and exchange; the student granted United States Presidential Scholars Program visited Changzhou for the first time. A total of RMB 33.29 million was used for aiding all kinds of students.

Basic education was continuously strengthened. The city has 407 provincial quality schools at the basic education stage, the number proportion and enrollment rate reaching 72.9% and 83.6%. Small-class education mode at compulsory education stage was gradually spread. 87% children of migrant employees were enrolled into public schools. The primary schools and kindergartens under city-direct administration were handed over to the prefecture districts. 55% entrance quota of hot high schools was allocated to all junior high schools. 25 new famed school education groups were set up. The admission scores (the second batch) of college entrance examination of Changzhou ranked in the forefront in Jiangsu province. Biological science course of Changzhou Senior High School of Jiangsu Province, and environment • life science course of Qianhuang Senior High School were recognized as Jiangsu High School Curriculum Base Construction Project. And Changzhou Senior High School of Jiangsu Province was selected as one of 14 experimental site senior schools for training innovative personnel in Jiangsu province.

Vocational education achieved development in innovation. The construction project of the provincial innovation and development experimental zone of vocational education was improved. The overall program of Yincun Vocational Education Park was formed and the construction was launched. 100% of the vocational schools became provincial high-quality vocational schools. The training of vocational undergraduates (technicians) by local universities and colleges was exploring. The examination of enrollment with the specialty in vocational schools ranked the first place for 12 consecutive years. One student won the Spirit Award of National Guanghua Entrepreneurial Competition.

Lifelong education was optimized. The city actively implemented standardized management and territorial management of social sponsoring education, complied and printed "Changzhou Social Sponsoring School Service Guide". In the year of 2011, the city newly built 3 provincial-level towns (sub districts) and community education centers, 10 community education experimental projects, 6 city standardized towns (streets) adult education centers, 32 residents (villagers) schools, and offered 200 lecture courses of community education, which were broadcast weekly in Changzhou TV Science Channel. Moreover, the city published a total of 150,000 lectures of community educational courses by introduction and cooperation, and held "2011 National Lifelong Education Changzhou Forum" and "Sixth Promotion Week of Lifelong Education".

Culture

The cultural undertaking achieved marked results. In 2011, all public libraries received 1.322 million people and lent 1.253 million books and literatures. The museum received 940,000 visitors. Qishuyan District Sub-library and Shangshufang Sub-library of Changzhou Library were opened. TV Library was first opened in Jiangsu province, which greatly promoted the construction of information sharing project in urban and sub-district communities. Besides, the city carried out the activities of "Brightening the Culture of City" and "Weekly Performance in Happiness Plaza", and successfully passed the provincial inspection of Third National Culture Centers/Station Assessment and Grading. The projects of "Benefiting People" were deeply implemented, including 1,900 charity performances and 3,200 low-fare performances. The public culture centers continuously improved the service level, and totally received 4 million audiences and held 110 various cultural and art exhibitions. Cultural work in rural areas was advanced in an orderly way. In November 2011, CCTV had a special report for Changzhou's rural cultural work.

Literary and artistic creation produced many excellent works. In possession of largest investment and strongest cast team in Changzhou's history, the symphony Wuxi opera "The Wandering Songstress" achieved great success and was performed as the opening drama in Jiangsu Drama Festival, even obtained the opportunity of performing in Beijing. The original antimask "The story of Jurisprudence Secretary Qian Foduo" was successfully staged. Local literature "Research on Changzhou Poems" (6 volumes), the book about Changzhou local history in Qing dynasty "The Ode of Changzhou", and "Changzhou Wuxi Opera Papers Collection 1950-2010" were officially published. 48 broadcast, movies and TV programs won the provincial government awards, including 11 first prizes, 19 second prizes and18 third prizes, which was the best result over the years. "The Song of Changdang Lake" won the Outstanding Work Award of Cities and Counties Representative Songs Contest in Jiangsu province. "Changzhou Bai Tai Guan" won the prize for literature in 4th Jiangsu Folk Art Luhua Award. "Colorful Life" won the Best Program and Performance Awards. The tribute film for 90th anniversary of CPC "The Seal of Love" received warm social repercussions. The city's 13 projects received the supporting funds for cultural industries of Jiangsu province, involving the total capital of RMB 16.8 million.

Broadcasting and television undertakings maintained steady development. Changzhou owned 7 self-running radio broadcasting programs with the annual telecast time reaching 44,330 hours; and 8 self-running TV programs with the annual telecast time reaching 56,154 hours, and the comprehensive coverage rate of radio and TV programs reaching 100%. The city also accelerated the network rebuilding and completed the transformation of the two-way transmission of cable TV network in 333,000 households. The number of cable TV subscribers reached 1.127 million, increasing 51,000 subscribers over the previous year. And the number of digital TV subscribers reached 1.068 million, increasing 157,000 subscribers over the previous year. Furthermore, the city was honored with 45 provincial-level awards, including Broadcast and TV Technology Innovation Award, Golden Deer Award, Golden Sail Award and so on. Among the five advanced State Broadcast and TV Stations in Jiangsu, Changzhou occupied two seats. A total of 3.276 million copies of the Changzhou Radio and Television Newspaper were published during 2011.

The protection of cultural relics was strengthened. The city completed the third National Cultural Relics Census and totally checked 1,677 cultural relic sites, including 1,270 new discovered sites. The total number of provincial cultural relic protection units reached 50, including 23 newly added units. Some projects about cultural relics have been successfully completed, including the repair and environmental restoration project for Qingliang Temple (first phase), renovation project of Liu Guojun's office building in Dacheng Factory, restoration project for ancient wall of Menghe Town, archaeological survey and exploration of Xucheng Ruins within the construction control areas, archaeological survey and exploration of the second-phase combustion engine project of CSR Qishuyan Locomotive Co., Ltd., archaeological survey and exploration of the second-phase thermoelectricity project of Liyang Hongbo Co., Ltd. Eight projects were selected in the third batch of Jiangsu Province Intangible Cultural Heritage List, and three projects were selected in National Intangible Cultural Heritage List. In the year, Changzhou published "Changzhou Intangible Cultural Heritage Collection", participated in 2011 China (Shenzhen) Cultural Industry Fair and won one gold award and three silver awards. Moreover, Changzhou won 12 gold awards, 13 silver awards, 11 bronze awards and 2 recognition awards in 2011 Jiangsu Arts and Crafts Expo.

Health Care

Medical system was constantly improved. By the end of the year, the city has owned 1,101 medical institutions of various kinds, including 92 hospitals and clinics, 8 disease prevention and control institutions and 8 women and children's health care centers. Besides, there were 23,000 health technical personnel including 10,376 doctors and 8,550 registered nurses. For per 1,000 permanent residents, there were 4.9 health technical personnel, 2.2 doctors and 3.6 hospital beds available. And the city set up 3.442 million record files of residents' health with the average coverage rate reaching 75% and coverage rate for the aged over 65 years old reaching 95%. The standardized management rate of hypertension, type II diabetes and severe psychosis reached 98.1%, 98.1% and 97.5 % respectively. The essential drug system was fully implemented. All primary health care institutions should use essential drugs in prescribed list and carried out unified online purchasing and zero profit sales. At the end of the year, the cost of essential drugs purchased online reached RMB 440 million and the sales revenue reached RMB 420 million. The profit reducing rate reached over 35%. Research and teaching achieved a breakthrough, establishing 2 provincial key disciplines, organizing 2 provincial leading medical and innovative talent teams and training 7 provincial key medical personnel.

Medical care in rural areas was steadily improved. The population covered by the new-type rural cooperative medical care system reached 1.87 million, with 100% coverage rate and per capital funding of 305 yuan, increasing 60 yuan over the previous year. The hospitalization subsidy ratio on the range of county and township policy was 73.5%, and the actual hospitalization subsidy ratio was 52.5%. Medical security for rural children with major diseases was comprehensively progressed. Two children patients with leukemia and 17 children patients with congenital heart disease got the new rural cooperative fund compensation. By the end of the year, Changzhou had 27 provincial hygiene towns and 542 provincial hygiene villages.

Sports

Sports undertaking was vigorously developed. In 2011, Changzhou successfully held four world-class competitions, namely, 2011 Lining China Badminton Masters, 2011 Taihu Lake International Road Cycling Race (Changzhou Station), 2011 Asia Women's Handball Championship & Qualifying Trial for London 2012 Olympic Games and Sino-US Basketball Championship, as well as 14 national competitions and 15 provincial competitions. The CCTV broadcasting and rebroadcasting time reached 29 hours. Throughout the year, Changzhou athletes won 25 champions in major competitions, including 2 world champions, 1 Asian champion and 22 national champions.

The nationwide fitness campaign was effectively promoted. With the implementation of public sports infrastructure improvement projects in urban communities and rural areas, Changzhou newly built 63 community fitness centers, renewed the sports facilities for 190 urban fitness centers (sites) built before 2004, allocated the sports facility maintenance fund for 630 fitness centers (sites) built after 2004, installed public sports facilities in 7 sites of old residential communities, and started the construction of Qingtan Nationwide Fitness Center. Qingfeng Park and Wujin Fitness Square were named "National Fitness Square", which were only two units receiving the honors in Jiangsu province. The nationwide fitness campaign was extensively developed. The City organized more than 150 fitness activities over the district level and more than 200 fitness activities over the township and sub-district level, involving more than 350,000 participants. Besides, the city newly built 10 city-level community fitness clubs and developed 2,500 club members, and newly built 80 community exercise centers in the year based on the layout of existing community morning and evening exercise centers. The proportion of population who participate in physical exercise regularly in the city reached 52.6%, winning the honors of National Outstanding Organization Award and Advanced Units for Nationwide Fitness for 15 consecutive years. The sales volume of sports lottery in the whole year reached RMB 1.08 billion, increased 48% year-on-year.

IV. Population, Livelihood and Social Security

Population & Employment

The population size remained stable. By the end of the year, the registered household population of Changzhou totaled 3.629

million, 0.6% higher than the same period of last year. The population of temporary residents reached 1.331 million, up 0.2% over the previous year. The planned birth rate was 98.7%, and the controlled birth rate and one-child per family rate reached 88% and 79.7% respectively. In 2011, the newly-born population was 29,007, while the death population was 22,144. The natural population growth was 1.9%.

The process of entrepreneurship and employment kept advancing. 180,000 new jobs were offered, 3.3% higher than the number of last year. 106,000 workers were employed, up 17.1% over the previous year. 3,595 people who started their own business got government support, which in turn created 18,000 jobs. 59,000 laid-off workers were reemployed, among which 11,000 used to have difficulties in getting jobs. The unemployment rate registered in urban areas was within 2.6%. The skill training program was continuously strengthened. During the whole year, 62,000 urban and rural labors received vocational skill training, 11,000 new labors received working skill training and 23,000 highly skilled personnel were cultivated.

People's Lives

The residents' income and expenditure maintained steady growth. The result of sampling survey showed urban residents' annual per capita disposable income reached 29,829 yuan, increased by 13.6% year-on-year; while the per capita expenditure on consumption amounted to 18,893 yuan, grew by 10.3%. The urban residents' Engel coefficient reached 35.8%, 3.1% higher than that of last year. The per capita net income of rural residents made 14,838 yuan, an increase of 17.4% year-on-year. The per capita living expenditure achieved 11,208 yuan, rose by 13.1% over last year. The Engel coefficient (the proportion of food expenditure in consumer expenditure) of rural residents was 35.5%, 0.5 percentage points higher than that of the previous year. Bank savings deposits of urban and rural residents increased continuously. By the end of 2011, the balance of savings deposits of residents had surged to 217.12 billion yuan, and 15.03 billion yuan was newly added this year.

The housing project for low-income urban residents was continuously boosted. The per capital living space of urban residents was 34.8 square meters by the end of 2011, an increase of 1.6 square meters over last year, while that of rural residents was 61.5 square meters, increased by 3 square meters compared with the previous year. The housing security program was continuously moving ahead. The newly-built 1,022 sets of low-rent apartments, 14,013 sets of public-rent apartments, 1,376 sets of economically affordable apartments and 3,389 sets of commodity apartments with limited prices were under construction; while the dilapidated and old buildings covering 565,000 square meters in shantytown were transformed. 5,016 families received subsidy for low-rent apartment from government. The area of housing security program expanded more in the center of downtown (Tianning District, Zhonglou District and Qishuyan District). 461 families signed the contract of buying economically affordable housing; 718 new households were qualified for the low-rent houses; 461 families enjoyed the currency subsidy for economically affordable housing; 1,131 families were eligible for the public-rent apartments; and 1,567 households moved in to the low-rent or public-rent houses provided by the government and paid relevant rents. 114,000 people were included in the public housing accumulation fund expansion program. 2.86 billon of the housing accumulation loan was provided to 11,000 families. 800,000 square meters of the old residential areas completed their improvement programs.

Market Prices

The consumer price index (CPI) kept running high. The CPI of the whole year was 105. Among the prices of eight major categories of commodities and services, seven of them rose and only one remained the same: the food prices increased by 11.7%, the household appliances and maintenance, housing and wine and tobacco respectively grew by 6.3%, 4.4% and 3.7%. The prices of medical care and personal items, entertainment, education, cultural products and services and clothing climbed by 2.4%, 1.5% and 1.6% respectively. The prices of transportation and telecommunications remained the same as last year.

Social Security

Social security system was continuously optimized. By the end of the year, 1,138,000 people joined the enterprise insurance for aged, up 6% over the same period of last year. 889,000 people joined the unemployment insurance, 11.9% higher than previous year. 1,491,000 people joined the medical insurance for workers in town, 11.9% higher than last year. The comprehensive coverage rate of endowment insurance, medical insurance and unemployment insurance was over 98%. The five major social security fund of Changzhou all together collected 11.86 billion yuan, 22.6% higher than last year and spent 9.42 billion yuan, 23.2% higher than last year. There were totally 152 specified medical establishments for medical insurance, 206 medical establishments of outpatient service and 627 specified medicine retail shops. The average monthly pension of urban enterprise employees reached 1,661 yuan. The basic monthly pension of social endowment insurance of urban and rural residents increased to 80 yuan, and the monthly pension allowance of aged urban residents rose to 220 yuan. The ratio of people applying for reimbursement within the prescribed limit hospitalization reached 80% and 60% respectively for labors and urban residents who joined medical care. By the end of 2011,there were 907,000 people joined the urban and rural social endowment insurance.411,000 rural residents received their basic pension payments directly.

Social Welfare & Relief

The social charitable aid was well promoted. By the end of 2011, the number of various nursing homes reached 92, with a total of 14,453 beds and 9,704 old people adopted. The number of welfare enterprises reached 282. 56,712 residents from 30,283 households were included in the subsistence allowance system among which there were 20,439 residents from 10,891 urban households and 36,273 residents from 19,392 rural households. RMB 140 million yuan of subsistence allowance was issued and 15,582 person-times got medical aid, 3,088 more than last year. The sum of salvation reached 23.83 million yuan, up 56.3%. Welfare lottery tickets worth RMB 930 million yuan were released throughout the year, up 59.5% over the previous year. The charities kept advancing rapidly. By the end of the year, all levels of charity federation raised and subscribed 1.879 billon yuan totally, and 395 million yuan of salvage money was issued. 405,600 person-times got the aid. During the whole year, all levels of charity federations issued 83.48 million yuan salvage money, and among people in straitened situation 55,600 person-times received aid; Changzhou charity federation issued various kinds of salvage money by 24.9058 million yuan and 19,000 people got benefit from it.

V. Urban and Rural Construction

Infrastructure Construction

The city construction was comprehensively improved. The new terminal building of the airport and the new line of the high speed railway both were finished and put into operation. The West City Loop Highway and the Longjiang Viaduct south extension program were both finished and opened to traffic. The Changzhou-Liyang highway was actively promoted. The improvement programs of Suzhou-Nanjing Canal and Danyang-Jintan-Liyang Canal went well. Great efforts were made to the programs of Chuanxin River pivot, South Canal pivot & the east pivot of the Grand Canal for preventing flood. The city's infrastructures and functions were constantly improved day by day. In the center of the city, the Yongning North Road Zhongwu Blvd. east extension project and other road programs were completed. The comprehensive reform of the Wuyi Road area and the Binghu Commercial Complex in the south of the city were under construction.

Public Utility

The Strategy of "Putting Public Transportation First" had in-depth development. In 2011, the city added 11 new bus lines and adjusted 19 lines for optimization. At the end of the year, there were 167 lines with total 3,138 km, and 2,600 buses were in service, up 3.7%, 5.3% and 3.3% respectively over the previous year. 689 air conditioning buses were newly added, making 100% air conditioning buses in downtown, and the GPS assembling rate reached 100%. The total mileage was 150 million km, up 2.1% over the previous year; the total transport capacity made 410 million passengers, up 4.5%, with daily transport capacity of 1.116 million passengers. The daily transport capacity of BRT was 290,000 passengers, the ratio of which achieved 26% of daily transport capacity, and there were around

463,000 passengers at the peak. The BRT had been selected into the "100 Remarkable Civil Engineering Projects in 100 Years."

The public services system kept improving. The system of digital city kept improving and the non-hazardous treatment ratio of household garbage reached 100%. The security of Residential areas was improved a lot. Gate entries have been used in those 156 old residential areas. The supplemental construction of containment facilities in old neighborhood covering 800,000 square meters was completed. Integration management of cleanliness, virescence and security of old neighborhood was realized. The total urban water supply amount reached 290 million cubic meters, including domestic water use of 120 million cubic meters, with the coverage rate of running water reaching 100%. The total consumption of electricity in the city reached 33.17 billion kwh, up 13.9% over the previous year, among which the household electricity consumption of urban and rural residents amounted to 2.8 billion kwh, increased by 1.9%. By the end of 2011,497,000 families became users of pipeline gas, up 13.9% than 2010. The rate of liquefied gas supply of whole city reached 99.1%. The daily treatment capacity of domestic sewage reached 535,000 tons, and sewage water treatment rate in the urban area reached 93.2%. By the end of the year, the number of street lamps was 163,000, increased by 7.2% compared to the end of last year.

VI. Environmental Protection and Resource Conservation

Environmental Protection and Treatment

The Environmental quality continuously improved. The achievements of the renovation of 60 water channels in urban area were enhanced. The renovations for 40 black and odorous water channels in suburban area were finished. The quality of the three water channels flowing into Taihu Lake, as well as the other lakes was improved generally. In 2011, there were 343 days with air quality above the good level, accounting for 94% of the whole year. The construction of National Ecological City successfully passed the national technology assessment, which made the city the second Prefecture-level City that passed the national assessment. The city produced average environmental noise of 54.7 decibels and average traffic noise of 67.3 decibels. The compliance rate of water quality of centralized drinking water sources achieved 100%. 15 towns which were awarded as "National Towns with Good Environment" were upgraded to "National Ecological Towns." Four "National Eco-Street" and five "National Eco-Village" were constructed. 85 Provincial Eco-Villages and Municipal Eco-Villages, 34 Green Residential Areas, 54 Green Schools and three bases for environmental education were newly constructed.

Urban Greening

The quality of urban greening was improved. The five featured greening projects were implemented with big efforts. The total investment made RMB 830 million with 578.1 hectares of newly built green areas. With an investment of RMB 180 million, there was a newly built green area of 32 hectares in the High-speed Railway Eco-Park. 44 hectares of green areas were added along with the completion of Joyland near Taihu Lake. A number of greening projects were completed, such as both south and north squares of railway station, the northern part of Linglong Garden, the north side of Taihu Road and the crossroads of Longjiang Road and Huanghe Road, adding 9.9 hectares of green land. The framework of symbolic tower in Zijing Park located in longitude 120° had finished hoisting. Projects including the interconnecting road of the Changzhou West Loop Highway with Taizhou Changjiang Highroad, the waterway regulation of Wuxi-Liyang River, the greening work of south Huahai Road and an amount of roads in Xinbei district were under construction. The secondary phase construction of posts of viaduct and the vertical greening of tunnel of the Intercity Railway stations were completed. By the end of year, the green areas of built-up regions covered 6,648.7 hectares, including the park green lands of 1,703 hectares, up 13.4% and 4.4% respectively; and the per capita park green area in urban Changzhou achieved 12.4 square meters. The rate of greenery coverage of built up area was 42.2%, an increase of 0.02%; meanwhile, the rate of green land coverage of built up area was 38.4%, up 0.1% over the previous yeas.

Note:The statistical data in the communique are calculated on current price except those calculated on comparable price as specially defined.

2

CHAPTER 2

排 名 榜

LIST OF TOP STRENGTHS

2-1 工业企业主营业务收入前 100 名单位（2011 年）
TOP 100 INDUSTRIAL ENTERPRISES BY MAIN BUSINESS LNCOME（2011）

序号 No.	企业名称 Name of Enterprises	序号 No.	企业名称 Name of Enterprises
1	中天钢铁集团有限公司	26	常州现代通讯光缆有限公司
2	江苏申特钢铁有限公司	27	常柴股份有限公司
3	常州金源铜业有限公司	28	百兴集团有限公司
4	亚邦投资控股集团有限公司	29	江苏新科数字技术股份有限公司
5	常州天合光能有限公司	30	常州龙祥钢铁有限公司
6	江苏新时代铜业有限公司	31	常州常发动力机械有限公司
7	江苏上上电缆集团有限公司	32	常州协鑫光伏科技有限公司
8	常州东方特钢有限公司	33	常州安凯特电缆有限公司
9	常州市盛洲铜业有限公司	34	江苏华电戚墅堰发电有限公司
10	现代（江苏）工程机械有限公司	35	常州市丽岛金属材料制造有限公司
11	小松（常州）工程机械有限公司	36	国电常州发电有限公司
12	华润包装材料有限公司	37	国茂减速机集团有限公司
13	江苏江南实业集团有限公司	38	溧阳罗地亚稀土新材料有限公司
14	江苏国强镀锌实业有限公司	39	盘固水泥集团有限公司
15	南车戚墅堰机车有限公司	40	溧阳市宏峰水泥有限公司
16	新誉集团有限公司	41	江苏常宝钢管股份有限公司
17	今创集团有限公司	42	常州岩松金属制品有限公司
18	江苏华朋变压器有限公司	43	常州新日化学有限公司
19	常州亿晶光电科技有限公司	44	常州龙源港机重工集团有限公司
20	新华昌集团有限公司	45	常州老三集团有限公司
21	常州亚邦化学有限公司	46	常林股份有限公司
22	江苏蓝色星球环保科技股份有限公司	47	江苏诚达石化工业有限公司
23	江苏常发农业装备股份有限公司	48	常州东风农机集团有限公司
24	光宝科技（常州）有限公司	49	江苏旷达汽车织物集团股份有限公司
25	瑞声声学科技（常州）有限公司	50	常州宝马机电有限公司

2-1　续表　continued

序号 No.	企业名称 Name of Enterprises	序号 No.	企业名称 Name of Enterprises
51	常州华利达服装集团有限公司	76	江苏金牛线缆集团有限公司
52	南车戚墅堰机车车辆工艺研究所有限公司	77	莱尼电气线缆（常州）有限公司
53	江苏顺风光电科技有限公司	78	江苏中再生投资开发有限公司
54	江苏金峰水泥集团有限公司	79	江苏新鸿联集团有限公司
55	江苏常隆化工有限公司	80	江苏正信新能源科技集团有限公司
56	江苏金昇实业股份有限公司	81	常州盘石水泥有限公司
57	常州东昊化工有限公司	82	常州市正和电磁线有限公司
58	常州兆阳光能科技有限公司	83	黑牡丹集团股份有限公司
59	常州常松金属复合材料有限公司	84	常州市亚达铜业有限公司
60	江苏武进不锈钢管厂集团有限公司	85	常州市神力电机有限公司
61	江苏正昌集团有限公司	86	常州明谛树脂有限公司
62	常州海杰冶金机械制造有限公司	87	江苏丰润电器有限公司
63	常州市英中电气有限公司	88	溧阳市三元钢铁有限公司
64	常州西电变压器有限责任公司	89	常州格力博工具有限公司
65	常州市长润石油有限公司	90	常州华盛恒能光电有限公司
66	江苏常发制冷股份有限公司	91	天合光能（常州）科技有限公司
67	江苏沙钢集团鑫瑞特钢有限公司	92	溧阳市新金峰水泥有限公司
68	卡尔迈耶（中国）有限公司	93	常州旭荣针织印染有限公司
69	永祺（常州）车业有限公司	94	金坛正信光伏电子有限公司
70	江苏兴荣美乐铜业有限公司	95	常州阻燃材料工程技术研究中心有限公司
71	江苏中东化肥股份有限公司	96	江苏华威世纪电子集团有限公司
72	常州宝菱重工机械有限公司	97	常州华日升反光材料有限公司
73	梅特勒-托利多（常州）测量技术有限公司	98	常州中弘光伏有限公司
74	中电装备东芝（常州）变压器有限公司	99	中盐常州化工股份有限公司
75	东华纺织集团有限公司	100	常州常宝精特钢管有限公司

2-2 工业企业实现利税前 100 名单位（2011 年）
TOP 100 INDUSTRIAL ENTERPRISES BY PROFITS AND TAXES（2011）

序号 No.	企业名称 Name of Enterprises	序号 No.	企业名称 Name of Enterprises
1	中天钢铁集团有限公司	26	华润包装材料有限公司
2	江苏申特钢铁有限公司	27	江苏上上电缆集团有限公司
3	常州天合光能有限公司	28	江苏恒立高压油缸股份有限公司
4	现代（江苏）工程机械有限公司	29	南车戚墅堰机车有限公司
5	新誉集团有限公司	30	溧阳市宏峰水泥有限公司
6	亚邦投资控股集团有限公司	31	盘固水泥集团有限公司
7	今创集团有限公司	32	江苏旷达汽车织物集团股份有限公司
8	小松（常州）工程机械有限公司	33	常州康美化工有限公司
9	江苏国强镀锌实业有限公司	34	安费诺（常州）连接系统有限公司
10	江苏金峰水泥集团有限公司	35	江苏新时代铜业有限公司
11	溧阳罗地亚稀土新材料有限公司	36	常州亚玛顿股份有限公司
12	瑞声声学科技（常州）有限公司	37	常州首创服饰有限公司
13	江苏江南实业集团有限公司	38	江苏正信新能源科技集团有限公司
14	常州亿晶光电科技有限公司	39	百兴集团有限公司
15	江苏蓝色星球环保科技股份有限公司	40	常州金源铜业有限公司
16	江苏华朋变压器有限公司	41	常州市丽岛金属材料制造有限公司
17	江苏华电戚墅堰发电有限公司	42	常州四药制药有限公司
18	常州市盛洲铜业有限公司	43	常州港华燃气有限公司
19	常州现代通讯光缆有限公司	44	常州龙祥钢铁有限公司
20	江苏常发农业装备股份有限公司	45	常州龙源港机重工集团有限公司
21	常州安凯特电缆有限公司	46	国电常州发电有限公司
22	新华昌集团有限公司	47	常州常发动力机械有限公司
23	卡尔迈耶（中国）有限公司	48	常州协鑫光伏科技有限公司
24	黑牡丹集团股份有限公司	49	国茂减速机集团有限公司
25	常州东方特钢有限公司	50	森萨塔科技（常州）有限公司

2-2 续表 continued

序号 No.	企业名称 Name of Enterprises	序号 No.	企业名称 Name of Enterprises
51	梅特勒–托利多（常州）测量技术有限公司	76	光宝科技（常州）有限公司
52	江苏艾贝时尚服饰有限公司	77	中盐金坛盐化有限责任公司
53	江苏顺风光电科技有限公司	78	常州华盛恒能光电有限公司
54	常州制药厂有限公司	79	常州市神力电机有限公司
55	常州海杰冶金机械制造有限公司	80	普利司通（常州）汽车配件有限公司
56	常州星宇车灯股份有限公司	81	江苏天常复合材料股份有限公司
57	金坛正信光伏电子有限公司	82	常林股份有限公司
58	江苏华盛天龙光电设备股份有限公司	83	江苏裕兴薄膜科技股份有限公司
59	常州市英中电气有限公司	84	江苏国光信息产业股份有限公司
60	常州常宝精特钢管有限公司	85	江苏溧阳南方水泥有限公司
61	江苏兴荣美乐铜业有限公司	86	常州赛迪电气制造有限公司
62	凡登（常州）新型金属材料技术有限公司	87	常州市名杰建材设备制造有限公司
63	常州千红生化制药股份有限公司	88	重庆啤酒集团公司常州天目湖啤酒有限公司
64	常州盘石水泥有限公司	89	常州市康辉医疗器械有限公司
65	江苏武进不锈钢管厂集团有限公司	90	溧阳市万兴特种建材有限公司
66	创生医疗器械（江苏）有限公司	91	江苏常发制冷股份有限公司
67	常州华利达服装集团有限公司	92	常州博瑞电力自动化设备有限公司
68	江苏正昌集团有限公司	93	溧阳市中材重型机器有限公司
69	江苏常宝钢管股份有限公司	94	江苏智思机械集团有限公司
70	常州科研试制中心有限公司	95	常州市新东方电缆有限公司
71	安费诺–泰姆斯（常州）通讯设备有限公司	96	江苏常宝普莱森钢管有限公司
72	南车戚墅堰机车车辆工艺研究所有限公司	97	常州润源电力建设有限公司
73	梅特勒–托利多（常州）精密仪器有限公司	98	金坛市第二铸钢厂
74	江苏海翔新能源科技有限公司	99	常州小糸今创交通设备有限公司
75	江苏金昇实业股份有限公司	100	中电装备东芝（常州）变压器有限公司

2-3 工业企业实现利润前 100 名单位（2011 年）
TOP 100 INDUSTRIAL ENTERPRISES BY PROFITS（2011）

序号 No.	企业名称 Name of Enterprises	序号 No.	企业名称 Name of Enterprises
1	中天钢铁集团有限公司	26	江苏江南实业集团有限公司
2	现代（江苏）工程机械有限公司	27	常州康美化工有限公司
3	江苏申特钢铁有限公司	28	常州首创服饰有限公司
4	新誉集团有限公司	29	江苏旷达汽车织物集团股份有限公司
5	亚邦投资控股集团有限公司	30	盘固水泥集团有限公司
6	今创集团有限公司	31	江苏正信新能源科技集团有限公司
7	常州亿晶光电科技有限公司	32	江苏新时代铜业有限公司
8	小松（常州）工程机械有限公司	33	常州亚玛顿股份有限公司
9	江苏金峰水泥集团有限公司	34	常州东方特钢有限公司
10	江苏国强镀锌实业有限公司	35	常州常发动力机械有限公司
11	江苏常发农业装备股份有限公司	36	常州港华燃气有限公司
12	江苏华电戚墅堰发电有限公司	37	森萨塔科技（常州）有限公司
13	瑞声声学科技（常州）有限公司	38	常州协鑫光伏科技有限公司
14	常州安凯特电缆有限公司	39	常州天合光能有限公司
15	常州市盛洲铜业有限公司	40	常州龙源港机重工集团有限公司
16	黑牡丹集团股份有限公司	41	华润包装材料有限公司
17	卡尔迈耶（中国）有限公司	42	溧阳市宏峰水泥有限公司
18	江苏华朋变压器有限公司	43	梅特勒-托利多（常州）测量技术有限公司
19	江苏蓝色星球环保科技股份有限公司	44	南车戚墅堰机车有限公司
20	江苏上上电缆集团有限公司	45	江苏顺风光电科技有限公司
21	溧阳罗地亚稀土新材料有限公司	46	金坛正信光伏电子有限公司
22	新华昌集团有限公司	47	江苏华盛天龙光电设备股份有限公司
23	江苏恒立高压油缸股份有限公司	48	江苏艾贝时尚服饰有限公司
24	常州现代通讯光缆有限公司	49	常州星宇车灯股份有限公司
25	安费诺（常州）连接系统有限公司	50	常州华利达服装集团有限公司

2-3 续表 continued

序号 No.	企业名称 Name of Enterprises	序号 No.	企业名称 Name of Enterprises
51	凡登（常州）新型金属材料技术有限公司	76	立达（常州）纺织仪器有限公司
52	常州千红生化制药股份有限公司	77	常州市神力电机有限公司
53	江苏常宝钢管股份有限公司	78	江苏国光信息产业股份有限公司
54	常州常宝精特钢管有限公司	79	常州博瑞电力自动化设备有限公司
55	江苏兴荣美乐铜业有限公司	80	常州盘石水泥有限公司
56	常州制药厂有限公司	81	常州市康辉医疗器械有限公司
57	常州市丽岛金属材料制造有限公司	82	金坛市第二铸钢厂
58	南车戚墅堰机车车辆工艺研究所有限公司	83	国电常州发电有限公司
59	创生医疗器械（江苏）有限公司	84	常林股份有限公司
60	百兴集团有限公司	85	江苏武进不锈钢管厂集团有限公司
61	常州海杰冶金机械制造有限公司	86	常州华盛恒能光电有限公司
62	常州金源铜业有限公司	87	常州小糸今创交通设备有限公司
63	梅特勒–托利多（常州）精密仪器有限公司	88	江苏常宝普莱森钢管有限公司
64	国茂减速机集团有限公司	89	江苏天常复合材料股份有限公司
65	光宝科技（常州）有限公司	90	江苏省激素研究所股份有限公司
66	常州市英中电气有限公司	91	常州润源电力建设有限公司
67	常州四药制药有限公司	92	常州三菱电机士林电装品有限公司
68	安费诺–泰姆斯（常州）通讯设备有限公司	93	江苏金源锻造股份有限公司
69	江苏常发制冷股份有限公司	94	江苏溧阳南方水泥有限公司
70	常州龙祥钢铁有限公司	95	江苏省健尔康医用敷料有限公司
71	常州科研试制中心有限公司	96	常州旭荣针织印染有限公司
72	常州市新东方电缆有限公司	97	常州市武进凤市电子集团有限公司
73	江苏裕兴薄膜科技股份有限公司	98	常州依索沃尔塔合成材料有限公司
74	江苏海翔新能源科技有限公司	99	普利司通（常州）汽车配件有限公司
75	江苏正昌集团有限公司	100	常州新日化学有限公司

2-4 批发贸易业企业商品销售总额前 10 名单位（2011 年）
TOP TEN WHOLESALE TRADE ENTERPRISES BY COMMODITIES SALES VOLUME（2011）

序号 No.	单位名称 Name of Units	序号 No.	单位名称 Name of Units
1	江苏省烟草公司常州市公司	6	常州市中油石油销售有限公司
2	常州市化工轻工材料总公司	7	常州市联众商贸有限公司
3	常州市大江铜业有限公司	8	江苏沙兴钢材销售有限公司
4	江苏和瑞升金属资源有限公司	9	梅特勒–托利多（常州）称重系统设备有限公司
5	常州大华进出口（集团）有限公司	10	常州对外贸易有限公司

2-5 批发贸易业企业利税总额前 10 名单位（2011 年）
TOP TEN WHOLESALE TRADE ENTERPRISES BY PROFITS AND TAXES（2011）

序号 No.	单位名称 Name of Units	序号 No.	单位名称 Name of Units
1	江苏省烟草公司常州市公司	6	江苏中再物资回收有限公司
2	梅特勒–托利多（常州）称重系统设备有限公司	7	常州苏南物资再生利用有限公司
3	常州市顺统物资再生有限公司	8	常州国电常发能源有限公司
4	常州正华物资回收有限公司	9	常州市丽华金属材料有限公司
5	常州老三集团进出口有限公司	10	常州市中油石油销售有限公司

2-6 零售贸易业企业商品销售总额前 10 名单位（2011 年）
TOP TEN RETAIL TRADE ENTERPRISES BY COMMODITIES SALES VOLUME（2011）

序号 No.	单位名称 Name of Unitss	序号 No.	单位名称 Name of Units
1	江苏明都汽车集团有限公司	6	常州市凯歌汽车销售有限公司
2	常州药业股份有限公司	7	常州宝尊汽车销售服务有限公司
3	国药控股常州有限公司	8	常州市五星电器有限公司
4	常州百货大楼股份有限公司	9	常州金太阳至尊家电有限公司
5	江苏万帮明都汽车有限公司	10	常州泰富百货集团有限责任公司

2-7　零售贸易业企业利税总额前 10 名单位（2011 年）
TOP TEN RETAIL TRADE ENTERPRISES BY PROFITS AND TAXES（2011）

序号 No.	单位名称 Name of Units	序号 No.	单位名称 Name of Units
1	常州百货大楼股份有限公司	6	常州药业股份有限公司
2	常州新世纪商城有限公司	7	溧阳市华地百货有限公司
3	江苏常金首饰集团有限公司	8	常州金太阳至尊家电有限公司
4	常州市五星电器有限公司	9	江苏明都汽车集团有限公司
5	常州金店有限公司	10	常州关河大润发商业有限公司

2-8　批发零售贸易业企业利润总额前 10 名单位（2011 年）
TOP TEN WHOLESALE AND RETAIL TRADE ENTERPRISES BY PROFITS （2011）

序号 No.	单位名称 Name of Units	序号 No.	单位名称 Name of Units
1	江苏省烟草公司常州市公司	6	常州市五星电器有限公司
2	常州百货大楼股份有限公司	7	常州金店有限公司
3	梅特勒–托利多（常州）称重系统设备有限公司	8	常州药业股份有限公司
4	江苏常金首饰集团有限公司	9	溧阳市华地百货有限公司
5	常州新世纪商城有限公司	10	常州金太阳至尊家电有限公司

2-9　餐饮业企业营业收入前 10 名单位（2011 年）
TOP TEN CATERING TRADE ENTERPRISES BY BUSINESS INCOME（2011）

序号 No.	单位名称 Name of Unitss	序号 No.	单位名称 Name of Units
1	大娘水饺餐饮集团股份有限公司	6	常州市长兴楼饭店有限公司
2	常州丽华快餐集团有限公司	7	常州锦湖酒店管理有限公司
3	常州福记餐饮投资管理有限公司	8	常州亿家乐早餐工程有限公司
4	莱蒙水榭花都房地产开发有限公司武进假日酒店	9	常州紫缘大酒店有限公司
5	常州听松楼花园酒店有限公司	10	溧阳泰丰餐饮有限公司

2-10 餐饮业企业利税总额前 10 名单位（2011 年）
TOP TEN CATERING TRADE ENTERPRISES BY PROFITS AND TAXES（2011）

序号 No.	单位名称 Name of Units	序号 No.	单位名称 Name of Units
1	大娘水饺餐饮集团股份有限公司	6	常州锦湖酒店管理有限公司
2	莱蒙水榭花都房地产开发有限公司武进假日酒店	7	常州听松楼花园酒店有限公司
3	常州丽华快餐集团有限公司	8	常州奥体明都国际饭店有限公司
4	溧阳泰丰餐饮有限公司	9	常州国安大酒店有限公司
5	常州福记餐饮投资管理有限公司	10	常州紫缘大酒店有限公司

2-11 住宿业企业营业收入前 10 名单位（2011 年）
TOP TEN HOTELS BY BUSINESS INCOME（2011）

序号 No.	单位名称 Name of Units	序号 No.	单位名称 Name of Units
1	常州富都大酒店有限公司	6	常州阳光国际大酒店有限公司
2	江苏天目湖宾馆有限公司	7	常州大酒店有限公司
3	溧阳宾馆有限公司	8	常州锦江国际大酒店有限公司
4	常州涵田渡假村酒店管理有限公司	9	常州香树湾花园酒店有限公司
5	常州金陵江南大饭店有限公司	10	常州市明都大饭店管理有限公司

2-12 住宿业企业利税总额前 10 名单位（2011 年）
TOP TEN HOTELS BY PROFITS AND TAXES（2011）

序号 No.	单位名称 Name of Unitss	序号 No.	单位名称 Name of Units
1	常州富都大酒店有限公司	6	溧阳市天目湖大酒店
2	溧阳宾馆有限公司	7	常州市明都大饭店管理有限公司
3	常州涵田渡假村酒店管理有限公司	8	常州锦江国际大酒店有限公司
4	常州金陵江南大饭店有限公司	9	溧阳市扬子国际大酒店有限公司
5	江苏天目湖宾馆有限公司	10	溧阳假日酒店有限公司

2-13　住宿餐饮企业利润总额前 10 名单位（2011 年）
TOP TEN ACCOMMODATION AND CATERING TRADE ENTERPRISES BY PROFITS（2011）

序号 No.	单位名称 Name of Units	序号 No.	单位名称 Name of Units
1	大娘水饺餐饮集团股份有限公司	6	常州涵田渡假村酒店管理有限公司
2	常州富都大酒店有限公司	7	溧阳市天目湖大酒店
3	莱蒙水榭花都房地产开发有限公司武进假日酒店	8	常州金陵江南大饭店有限公司
4	溧阳宾馆有限公司	9	常州国安大酒店有限公司
5	溧阳泰丰餐饮有限公司	10	常州锦湖酒店管理有限公司

2-14　成交额超亿元市场前 10 名单位（2011 年）
TOP TEN MARKETS BY TANSACTION VOLUME ABOVE RMB100 MILLION （2011）

序号 No.	单位名称 Name of Units	序号 No.	单位名称 Name of Units
1	江苏凌家塘市场发展有限公司	6	常州市武进夏溪花木市场发展有限公司
2	江苏长江塑料化工交易市场有限公司	7	江苏苏浙皖边界市场发展有限公司
3	江苏湖塘纺织城投资发展有限公司	8	江苏万商商贸城有限责任公司
4	常州钢材现货交易市场有限公司	9	江苏亚邦医药物流中心有限公司
5	常州龙成钢材城有限公司	10	常州长贸中心市场发展有限公司

2-15　出口额前 10 名单位（2011 年）
TOP TEN ENTERPRISES BY EXPORT VALUE（2011）

序号 No.	单位名称 Name of Unitss	序号 No.	单位名称 Name of Units
1	常州天合光能有限公司	6	常州对外贸易有限公司
2	常州亿晶光电科技有限公司	7	常州机械设备进出口有限公司
3	溧阳罗地亚方正稀土新材料有限公司	8	常州兆阳光能科技有限公司
4	常州大华进出口(集团)有限公司	9	常州华利达服装集团有限公司
5	华润包装材料有限公司	10	常州新华昌国际集装箱有限公司

2-16 驰名商标和著名商标一览
RENOWNED AND DISTINGUISHED BRANDS

企业名称 Name of Enterprises	商标名称 Brand Name	主要产品 Mostly Product	颁布时间 Time of Release	所在地区 Region
驰名商标 Renowned Brand				
常柴股份有限公司	CHANGCHAI及图; 常柴CC及图	柴油机	1995年	钟楼
常州东风农机集团有限公司	东风及图；DF及图	拖拉机	1999年	钟楼
新科电子集团有限公司	新科Shinco	影碟机	1999年	武进
江苏正昌集团有限公司	正　昌	饲料机械	2000年	溧阳
常州常发动力机械有限公司	常　发	柴油机	2002年	武进
黑牡丹（集团）股份有限公司	黑牡丹HEIMUDAN及图	牛仔布、色织布	2005年	天宁
江苏华鹏变压器有限公司	华鹏HUA PENG	变压器	2005年	溧阳
江苏庄臣同大有限公司	全无敌	杀虫剂、蚊香	2006年	新北
江苏上上电缆集团有限公司	上上及图	电线、电缆	2006年	溧阳
江苏新鸿联集团有限公司	红联及图	灯　具	2006年	武进
亚邦投资控股集团有限公司	亚邦及图	染料、涂料	2007年	武进
江苏兰陵化工集团有限公司	兰陵及图	防腐涂料、防火涂料	2008年	武进
顶呱呱彩棉服饰有限公司	顶呱呱	内衣等	2008年	武进
江苏天容集团股份有限公司	溧化LIHUA及图	农　药	2008年	溧阳
亚邦投资控股集团有限公司	光辉GUANGHUI及图	油漆、耐酸漆	2009年	武进
江苏庄臣同大有限公司	爱家及图	空气清新剂、杀害虫剂等	2009年	新北
常州市武进五洋纺织机械有限公司	五洋WYFJ及图	针织机械、编织机	2010年	武进
江苏迪邦三星轴承有限公司	三鑫SANXIN及图	圆柱滚子轴承、四列圆锥滚子轴承	2010年	武进
江苏旷达汽车织物集团股份有限公司	旷　达	装饰布	2010年	武进
江海环保股份有限公司	江海及图	水质稳定剂	2010年	武进
国茂减速机集团有限公司	国茂GUOMAO及图	减速机	2010年	武进
江苏洛基木业有限公司	洛基LODGI及图	地板、铺地木材、非金属地板等	2010年	武进
江苏开利地毯股份有限公司	天目湖及图	地　毯	2010年	溧阳
江苏天容集团股份有限公司	天容及图	杀害虫剂、除草剂、消灭有害植物剂	2010年	溧阳
常州光洋轴承股份有限公司	NRB	轴承（机器零件）、传动轴承	2011年	新北
常州银河电器有限公司	BILIN	晶体管（电子）、半导体器件、晶片（锗片）	2011年	新北
常州市常欣电子衡器有限公司	常欣CHANGXIN及图	超载限制器	2011年	新北
灵通投资集团有限公司	LING TONG及图	金属陈列架	2011年	武进
常州迪邦纺织有限公司	迪邦DiBang	纱、线、棉线和棉纱	2011年	武进
江苏太阳宝新能源有限公司	太阳宝	太阳能热水器	2011年	武进

2-16 续表 1　continued 1

企业名称 Name of Enterprises	商标名称 Brand Name	主要产品 Mostly Product	颁布时间 Time of Release	所在地区 Region
江苏亚示照明集团有限公司	YASHIPS	灯、照明器	2011年	武进
江苏裕成电子有限公司	裕成YUCHENG及图	自行车发动机	2011年	武进
常州玉宇电光器件有限公司	玉　宇	灯泡、电灯	2011年	武进
常州市武进五洋纺织机械有限公司	柳绿LLPJ及图	纺织织物、布、编织织物	2011年	武进
今创集团股份有限公司	KTK及图	车辆行李架、车辆座位、车辆内装饰品	2011年	武进
新城控股集团有限公司	新城及图	建筑、砖石建筑、商业摊位及商店的建筑	2011年	武进
著名商标 Distinguished Brand				
金坛市峨嵋农机动力机械厂	金田及图形	柴油机、内燃机、发电机（组）等	2009年	金坛
金坛市金动柴油机厂	金动及图形	柴油机、汽油机	2009年	金坛
江苏凯灵汽车电器有限公司	凯灵及图形	汽车综合开关、汽车地板	2009年	金坛
江苏飞洋鱼制衣有限公司	飛洋魚	衣物、衬衫、裤子等	2009年	金坛
金坛市江南制粉有限公司	沁雪及图形	谷类制品、面粉、生糯粉等	2009年	金坛
金坛市江南春米业有限公司	苏及图形	米、谷类制品、锅巴等	2009年	金坛
江苏冶建防腐材料有限公司	天虎及图形	涂　料	2009年	溧阳
江苏天容集团股份有限公司	天容及图形	杀害虫剂、除草剂、消灭有害植物制剂等	2009年	溧阳
溧阳市四方不锈钢制品有限公司	利洋四方及图形	金属管道弯头、金属管道接头	2009年	溧阳
江苏山湖电缆有限公司	山湖及图形	电缆、电线、接线盒	2009年	溧阳
江苏开利地毯股份有限公司	天目湖及图形	地　毯	2009年	溧阳
江苏常隆化工有限公司	天宁及图形	农　药	2009年	市属
常州机械设备进出口有限公司	亚美柯及图形	柴油机、发电机、泵（机器）等	2009年	市属
常州伊顿森源开关有限公司	常森及图形	断路器、低压电器元件、高低压开关柜等	2009年	天宁
常州特种变压器有限公司	稳福及图形	变压器（电）、配电箱（电）	2009年	天宁
江苏上能变压器有限公司	sunel	变压器、整流用电力装置等	2009年	天宁
常州武帆合金有限公司	武帆及图形	铝锰铁复合脱氧剂	2009年	武进
江苏中东集团有限公司	中东及图形	肥料、混合肥料、化学肥料等	2009年	武进
江苏安格特新材料科技有限公司	安格特及图形	未加工塑料、聚丙烯、聚氯乙烯树脂等	2009年	武进
江苏华光粉末有限公司	剑亮及图形	粉末涂料	2009年	武进
江苏晨光涂料有限公司	晨光及图形	油漆、底漆、刷墙用白浆（白垩灰浆）等	2009年	武进
常州市长润石油有限公司	江	各种机油、工业脂、高温脂	2009年	武进
常州华联保健敷料有限公司	华联及图形	卫生绷带、医用胶布、医用敷料等	2009年	武进
常州丰顺建筑装饰材料有限公司	FENGSHUN及图形	金属建筑材料、金属天花板等	2009年	武进
常州凯达轧辊集团有限公司	凯达及图形	铸铁轧辊	2009年	武进

2-16 续表 2 continued 2

企业名称 Name of Enterprises	商标名称 Brand Name	主要产品 Mostly Product	颁布时间 Time of Release	所在地区 Region
常州市武进协昌机械有限公司	协昌及图形	橡胶塑料工业设备	2009年	武进
常州一步干燥设备有限公司	一步及图形	食品、制药工业用机械及部件、化肥设备等	2009年	武进
常州市薛巷电讯元件有限公司	桑乐及图形	电线、电器接插件、电器插头（触点）等	2009年	武进
常州日盈电器有限公司	图　形	电器接插件、电线、插头等	2009年	武进
常州晶雪冷冻设备有限公司	晶雪及图形	冷藏室、空气调节器	2009年	武进
常州市太阳宝热水器有限公司	太阳宝	太阳能热水器	2009年	武进
江苏常武起动电机有限公司	常威及图形	汽车发电机、汽车起动机	2009年	武进
江苏龙城精锻有限公司	图　形	陆地车辆传动齿轮、陆地车辆传动马达等	2009年	武进
常州市河马塑胶有限公司	河马及图形	塑料管、管子接头、非金属软管	2009年	武进
江苏红日防静电地板有限公司	红日及图形	建筑用木材、铺地木材、地板	2009年	武进
江苏南洋木业有限公司	图　形	铺地木材、成品木材、拼花地板材料等	2009年	武进
常州市赛力木业有限公司	圣力及图形	建筑用木材、胶合板、地板等	2009年	武进
江苏科利达装饰材料有限公司	科利达	地板、非金属建筑材料、木材等	2009年	武进
灵通投资集团有限公司	灵通及图形	陈列柜、金属陈列衣架、茶几等	2009年	武进
常州鸿联家私有限公司	鸿联及图形	家具、金属家具、办公用家具等	2009年	武进
江苏阳湖纺织集团股份有限公司	阳湖及图形	棉纱和棉线、精纺棉、弹力丝（纺织用）等	2009年	武进
江苏华达化工集团有限公司	常恒及图形	胶粘剂、染料中间体	2009年	新北
常州市卓云精细化工有限公司	康力及图形	表面活性化学剂人造增甜剂（化学制剂）等	2009年	新北
常州光洋轴承有限公司	NRB	轴承（机器零件）、传动轴承、滚珠轴承等	2009年	新北
常州联力自动化科技有限公司	联力及图形	用于计算机操作仪器的机械装置等	2009年	新北
常州星宇车灯股份有限公司	星　怡	灯　具	2009年	新北
常州九鼎车业有限公司	JUDNG	车辆灯、汽车照明设备等	2009年	新北
常州市飞拓模塑有限公司	飞拓及图形	后视镜、车辆保险杠、汽车配件等	2009年	新北
常州市盛扬电动自行车有限公司	盛扬及图形	电动车辆、陆地车辆传动马达、机动自行车等	2009年	新北
常州工业技术玻璃有限公司	长江及图形	车窗玻璃、钢化玻璃	2009年	新北
江苏常松机械集团有限公司	常松及图形	推土机、运土机、挖掘机（机械）等	2009年	钟楼
常州金店有限公司	皆是缘及图形	宝石（珠宝）、翡翠、黄金首饰等	2009年	钟楼
南京化工学院常州市武进水质稳定剂厂	颂歌及图形	水质稳定剂	2010年	武进
常州市国宇环保科技有限公司	玉宇及图形	硝酸银、催化剂、工业用纤维素醚等	2010年	武进
江苏猴王涂料有限公司	猴王牌及图形	涂 料	2010年	武进
金隆化工集团有限公司	华隆及图形	染　料	2010年	武进

2-16 续表 3　continued 3

企业名称 Name of Enterprises	商标名称 Brand Name	主要产品 Mostly Product	颁布时间 Time of Release	所在地区 Region
江苏玉兰木业有限公司	图　形	金属地板、建筑用金属框架	2010年	武进
江苏双菱链传动有限公司	双菱及图形	滚子链条	2010年	武进
常州市武进五菱柴油机有限公司	五菱牌及图形	柴油机	2010年	武进
常州钢筘有限公司	蓝箭及图形	梳理机用齿条、钢筘	2010年	武进
常州远东连杆集团有限公司	滆湖及图形	泵油扳手总成、连杆总成	2010年	武进
江苏常嘉电器有限公司	吉诺尔及图形	洗衣机	2010年	武进
常州市永安电机有限公司	图　形	电　机	2010年	武进
江苏省范群干燥设备厂	范群及图形	电动食品加工机、制药加工工业用机器等	2010年	武进
常州常发农业装备有限公司	常发及图形	泵（机器）、液压泵、发电机（组）等	2010年	武进
江苏智思机械集团有限公司	ZS及图形	工业用卷烟机、烟草加工机	2010年	武进
常州东吴链传动制造有限公司	東傳及图形	非陆地车辆传动链、机器传动、转动装置等	2010年	武进
常州欧凯电器有限公司	OUCK	马达和引擎起动器、发电机、冰箱电机等	2010年	武进
常州联发机械有限公司	常联发及图形	柴油机、农业机械、汽油机等	2010年	武进
常州市润源经编机械有限公司	润源及图形	纺织机、编织机、缝编机等	2010年	武进
江苏金牛线缆集团有限公司	金牛及图形	电缆、电线、绝缘铜线等	2010年	武进
创生医疗器械（江苏）有限公司	创生及图形	骨科手术器械	2010年	武进
江苏康进医疗器材有限公司	康进及图形	医用导管、医用注射器、医疗器械和仪器等	2010年	武进
常州西武暖通设备有限公司	真乐及图形	散热器、空气调节设备	2010年	武进
常州市凯凯照明电器有限公司	图　形	照明灯（照明灯笼）、照明防护装置、弧光灯等	2010年	武进
普罗斯电器（江苏）有限公司	Plusrite	灯、照明防护装置、照明器械及装置等	2010年	武进
常州常发农业装备有限公司	常发及图形	拖车（车辆）、拖拉机、陆地车辆动力装置	2010年	武进
今创集团有限公司	KTK	车辆卧铺、车辆行李架、车辆内装饰品等	2010年	武进
常州华日升反光材料有限公司	通明及图形	反光膜	2010年	武进
江苏润德医用材料有限公司	润德及图形	密封橡皮圈、橡皮塞子、垫片（密封垫）等	2010年	武进
常州市欧太装饰材料有限公司	欧运及图形	非金属地板、非金属建筑材料、非金属门等	2010年	武进
江苏尼高科技有限公司	尼高科技及图形	建筑灰浆、非金属建筑、涂面材料等	2010年	武进
常州市佳安装饰材料有限公司	好佳好HAOJIAHAO	地板、贴面板、半成品木材等	2010年	武进
常州迪邦纺织有限公司	迪邦DiBang	纱、线、棉线和绵纱等	2010年	武进
常州市武进五洋纺织机械有限公司	柳绿及图形	纺织织物、布、编织织物等	2010年	武进
江苏长海复合材料股份有限公司	常海及图形	热敷胶粘纤维布、纺织用玻璃纤维织物、毡等	2010年	武进
江苏天香集团有限公司	香雪及图形	酱油、味精	2010年	武进

2-16 续表 4 continued 4

企业名称 Name of Enterprises	商标名称 Brand Name	主要产品 Mostly Product	颁布时间 Time of Release	所在地区 Region
常州市立华畜禽有限公司	雪山及图形	活动物、活家禽、种家禽等	2010年	武进
常州市翟家果品专业合作社	常溪及图形	鲜水果、鲜葡萄、杏仁（水果）等	2010年	武进
常州市武进夏溪花木市场发展有限公司	夏溪花木市场及图形	树木评估、组织商业或广告交易会等	2010年	武进
新城控股集团有限公司	新城及图形	建筑、砖石建筑、商业摊位及商店的建筑等	2010年	武进
常州华钛化学股份有限公司	图形	工业用化学品、紫外线吸收剂、光引发剂	2010年	金坛
江苏省激素研究所股份有限公司	金珠及图形	农　药	2010年	金坛
金坛柴油机有限公司	天鹅及图形	柴油机、发电机组	2010年	金坛
金坛市旺达喷灌机有限公司	大网及图形	排水机、农业用排灌机、泵等	2010年	金坛
常州而今太阳能设备制造有限公司	而今ERJIN	太阳能收集器、太阳能热水器、太阳能淋浴器	2010年	金坛
江苏省金坛密封件厂	JMP及图形	橡皮圈、密封用橡皮圈、橡皮减震器等	2010年	金坛
盘固水泥集团有限公司	盘固及图形	水　泥	2010年	金坛
金坛市博天鞋业有限公司	博天BOTIAN	鞋（脚上的穿着物）	2010年	金坛
江苏茅山青锋茶叶有限公司	金鹿及图形	茶　叶	2010年	金坛
金坛市方麓茶场有限公司	百园春及图形	茶　叶	2010年	金坛
江苏鑫品茶业有限公司	鑫品及图形	茶、茶叶代用品	2010年	金坛
金坛市御庭春茶业有限公司	天壶及图形	茶、茶叶代用品	2010年	金坛
江苏瑞阳化工股份有限公司	瑞阳及图形	季戊四醇、甲酸等	2010年	溧阳
江苏江南农化有限公司	巨能及图形	农药、杀虫剂、灭杂草剂等	2010年	溧阳
江苏竹箦阀业有限公司	竹机ZJ	闸　阀	2010年	溧阳
江苏省社渚轴承有限公司	球星牌及图形	轴　承	2010年	溧阳
溧阳市重型机械厂有限公司	麦重及图形	破碎机、喂料机等	2010年	溧阳
江苏保龙机电制造有限公司	保龙及图形	刨削机、刨花机、风力机和其配件等	2010年	溧阳
江苏省溧阳市汽车座椅调角器总厂	力乐及图形	汽车配件（汽车座椅调角器）	2010年	溧阳
江苏金峰水泥集团有限公司	金峰 JINFENGPAI	水　泥	2010年	溧阳
江苏天目湖宾馆有限公司	天目湖及图形	鱼制食品等	2010年	溧阳
江苏省前峰茶厂	前峰及图形	茶　叶	2010年	溧阳
溧阳市天目湖玉莲珍稀茶果场	玉莲及图形	茶、茶叶代用品	2010年	溧阳
重庆啤酒集团常州天目湖啤酒有限公司	天目湖及图形	啤酒、汽水	2010年	溧阳
江苏华能建设工程集团有限公司	苏华及图形	锅炉清垢与修理、供暖设备的安装和修理等	2010年	溧阳
常州亚玛顿光伏玻璃有限公司	亚玛顿	光学玻璃、太阳能电池、表面带电导体的玻璃等	2010年	天宁

2-16 续表 5　continued 5

企业名称 Name of Enterprises	商标名称 Brand Name	主要产品 Mostly Product	颁布时间 Time of Release	所在地区 Region
常州新华陵汽车电器有限公司	超灵及图形	汽车配件	2010年	天宁
江苏恒利集团有限公司	恒利及图形	棉布、色织布、牛仔布等	2010年	天宁
常州丽华快餐集团有限公司	丽华快餐	餐厅、快餐馆、流动饮食供应等	2010年	天宁
常州红梅乳业有限公司	红梅及图形	牛奶、牛奶饮料（以牛奶为主的）、牛奶制品等	2010年	钟楼
常州千红生化制药股份有限公司	怡　开	人用药、原料药、生化药品等	2010年	新北
常州市常欣电子衡器有限公司	常欣及图形	超载限制器	2010年	新北
常州银河电器有限公司	BILIN	晶体管（电子）、半导体器件、晶片（锗片）等	2010年	新北
江苏三恒科技集团有限公司	三　恒	报警器、监视器（计算机硬件）等	2010年	新北
常州市康辉医疗器械有限公司	康辉及图形	外科器械、止血缝合器械	2010年	新北
常州市常蒸蒸发器有限公司	常蒸及图形	蒸发器	2010年	新北
常州亨达车业部件有限公司	一帆顺YIFANSHUN	汽车照明设备、车灯、车辆反光镜等	2010年	新北
江苏贝德莱特太阳能科技有限公司	BadeLite	太阳能热水器、太阳能集热器、空气调节设备等	2010年	新北
常州市曙光车业有限公司	知音及图形	车辆油箱盖（气）、车辆内装饰品等	2010年	新北
江苏华生塑业有限公司	华生及图形	塑料管、管子接头、非金属软管	2010年	新北
常州丰盛光电科技股份有限公司	Julite	半加工塑料物质、有机玻璃、塑料板等	2010年	新北
常州市宏发纵横新材料科技有限公司	PGTEX	纺织织物、航空气球用不透气织物等	2010年	新北
常州市祥兴电机有限公司	图　形	马达及其部件	2010年	戚墅堰
常州市同和纺织机械制造有限公司	TONGHE	纺织工业用机器、纺织机、精纺机等	2010年	戚墅堰
江苏凯隆电器有限公司	KRAO及图形	断路器、高低压开关板、工业操作遥控电器设备等	2010年	戚墅堰
常州亚联灯具有限公司	FANOYA	路灯、探照灯、安全灯等	2010年	戚墅堰
常州制药厂有限公司	常药及图形	西药、原料药	2010年	市属
常州金源铜业有限公司	金线及图形	金属杆、金属板条	2010年	市属
常林股份有限公司	常林及图形	装载机	2010年	市属
常林股份有限公司	CHANGLIN	装载机、压路机、平地机等	2010年	市属
常州能源设备总厂有限公司	CEEF及图形	载热体加热炉	2010年	市属
月星集团有限公司	图　形	家具、非纺织品壁饰（家具）、陈列架等	2010年	市属
常州月兔调味食品有限公司	月兔牌及图形	味　精	2010年	市属
常州神龙饲料有限公司	水神及图形	饲料（包括非医用饲料添加剂及催化剂）	2010年	市属
中盐金坛盐化有限责任公司	金赛盐业及图形	岩盐、原盐、工业用盐	2011年	金坛
江苏丰登农药有限公司	丰登及图形	农　药	2011年	金坛

2-16 续表 6 continued 6

企业名称 Name of Enterprises	商标名称 Brand Name	主要产品 Mostly Product	颁布时间 Time of Release	所在地区 Region
常州金土木工程仪器有限公司	金土木	信号遥控电子启动设备、声波定位仪器等	2011年	金坛
江苏华兴电子有限公司	FY及图形	磁铁、扼流圈（阻抗）、半导体器件等	2011年	金坛
常州亿晶光电科技有限公司	EGNG及图形	单晶硅、多晶硅、碳电极等	2011年	金坛
常州市龙泉太阳能设备厂	龍全及图形	太阳能热水器、浴用加热器、太阳能集热器等	2011年	金坛
金坛市明日春花盆有限公司	树春及图形	花和植物用盆（花展用）、花盆、非纸制花盆套	2011年	金坛
江苏鸿瑞昌泰纺织有限公司	HRCT及图形	织物、纺织织物、毛织品等	2011年	金坛
常州金松时装有限公司	G&P	服装、女紧身衣裤、连裤内衣等	2011年	金坛
江苏波仕曼制衣有限公司	波仕曼及图形	服装、袜、游泳衣等	2011年	金坛
溧阳市幽香苏茶有限公司	幽香苏及图形	茶，茶叶代用品	2011年	金坛
金坛丰登酒业有限公司	丰登及图形	酒	2011年	金坛
江苏竹溪活性炭有限公司	竹溪及图形	活性炭	2011年	溧阳
江苏天容集团股份有限公司	瑞禾及图形	杀害虫剂、除草剂、除莠剂等	2011年	溧阳
江苏溧阳南方水泥有限公司	苏特SUTE	水泥	2011年	溧阳
溧阳市天目湖玉枝特种茶果园艺场	玉枝及图形	茶、茶叶代用品	2011年	溧阳
江苏天目湖生态农业有限公司	富子fz	茶	2011年	溧阳
江苏天目湖集团公司	天目湖及图形	观光旅游、安排游览、旅行预订等	2011年	溧阳
江苏金源锻造股份有限公司	金石Jinshi	研磨加工、金属锻造、金属冶炼等	2011年	溧阳
常州市宏达机床数控设备有限公司	宏瑞达	机械台架、切削工具（包括机械刀片）、刀座	2011年	戚墅堰
常州市新东方电缆有限公司	神鸡及图形	电线、电缆	2011年	戚墅堰
常州普灵仕制衣有限公司	蓝豹及图形	服装、女衣裤、内衣等	2011年	戚墅堰
常州东风农机集团有限公司	常拖及图形	内燃机（不包括汽车、拖拉机、谷物联合收割机）	2011年	市属
常州天马集团有限公司	天马及图形	纺织用玻纤织物、纺织品用玻纤织物	2011年	市属
江苏常宝钢管股份有限公司	环球及图形	钢管、钢带、钢坯	2011年	市属
常州耀春格瑞纺织品有限公司	春格儿及图形	床罩、被子、床单等	2011年	市属
常州四药制药有限公司	奥　克	西　药	2011年	天宁
常州航月纺织机件有限公司	航月及图形	纺织机、纺纱车、纺织工业用机器等	2011年	天宁
常州亚泰纺织染整有限公司	SYT及图形	织物、布、棉织品等	2011年	天宁
大娘水饺餐饮集团股份有限公司	WUDANIANG及图形	馅饼、饺子、八宝饭等	2011年	天宁
常州市牛塘化工厂有限公司	牛塘及图形	氰尿酸聚丁脂、癸二酸二酰肼、三羟二基尿酸脂等	2011年	武进
江苏江海化工集团有限公司	江海及图形	水质稳定剂	2011年	武进

2-16 续表 7　continued 7

企业名称 Name of Enterprises	商标名称 Brand Name	主要产品 Mostly Product	颁布时间 Time of Release	所在地区 Region
常州市源恩合成材料有限公司	源恩及图形	工业用粘合剂、鞋粘合剂、皮革粘合剂等	2011年	武进
常州市方鑫化工物资有限公司	方鑫FANGXIN及图形	未加工环氧树脂、未加工合成、人造树脂等	2011年	武进
常州市南方卫生器材厂有限公司	妙手及图形	外科敷料，医用橡皮膏，医用胶布等	2011年	武进
江苏聚荣制药集团有限公司	聚荣及图形	人用药	2011年	武进
常州市运河焊材有限公司	大运河及图形	焊　丝	2011年	武进
江苏武进液压启闭机有限公司	五叶WY及图形	液压启闭机	2011年	武进
常州市武起汽车电机有限公司	常乐及图形	起动机电机	2011年	武进
江苏恒力电机集团股份有限公司	WUDIAN及图形	直流起动机、发电机、发动机等	2011年	武进
常州市华立液压润滑设备有限公司	华润HUARUN及图形	液压润滑设备、液压元件、油箱等	2011年	武进
江苏金鼎电动工具集团有限公司	金鼎及图形	机械操纵的手持工具、电动手工操作钻孔器等	2011年	武进
常州市永明机械制造有限公司	常明及图形	纺织工业用机器、压平机、马达和引擎起动器等	2011年	武进
江苏洛凯机电制造集团有限公司	洛凯及图形	非陆地车辆传动马达、定子、马达和引擎用风扇等	2011年	武进
江苏武东机械有限公司	武东及图形	机器、马达和引擎调速器、联轴器等	2011年	武进
常州市传动输送机械有限公司	霸宇及图形	传动装置（机器）、机器、马达和引擎调速器等	2011年	武进
江苏容天乐机械股份有限公司	WJT	自动加油轴承、滚珠轴承、机器轴承托架等	2011年	武进
江苏昌盛电缆集团有限公司	昌盛及图形	防火线缆、电线、电缆	2011年	武进
江苏华鑫合金有限公司	热工及图形	热电耦丝、补偿导线	2011年	武进
江苏宏事达电气制造有限公司	宏事达	电子计算机及其外部设备、计时装置等	2011年	武进
江苏南方通信科技有限公司	精科及图形	电缆、电线、电源材料等	2011年	武进
江苏英特曼电器有限公司	ETMAN及图形	插头、插座及其他接触器（电）、电开关等	2011年	武进
常州市钱璟康复器材有限公司	钱璟及图形	按摩器械、振动按摩器、医用体育活动器械等	2011年	武进
常州市云涛洁具有限公司	云涛及图形	玛瑙浴缸、脸盆、澡盆等	2011年	武进
新科电子集团有限公司	Shinco	空调、电热水器、冷藏箱（集装箱）等	2011年	武进
江苏常嘉电器有限公司	首都CAPITAL	照明灯、卫生器械及设备、水净化装置等	2011年	武进
江苏环球龙圣环境科技发展有限公司	宇球及图形	水冷却装置、冷却设备和装置	2011年	武进
江苏亚示照明集团有限公司	YASHIPS	灯、照明器、灯泡等	2011年	武进
江苏海鸥冷却塔股份有限公司	图形	水冷却装置、冷却设备和装置	2011年	武进
江苏友奥电器有限公司	YOAU	制冰机和设备、空气调节设备、干燥设备等	2011年	武进
常州玉宇电光器件有限公司	Yuyu	照明器、灯泡、灯等	2011年	武进
江苏裕成电子有限公司	裕成及图形	陆地车辆传送马达、联动机件、动力装置等	2011年	武进

2-16 续表 8 continued 8

企业名称 Name of Enterprises	商标名称 Brand Name	主要产品 Mostly Product	颁布时间 Time of Release	所在地区 Region
江苏逸盛投资集团有限公司	逸盛CES	车辆轮胎、汽车轮胎、飞机轮胎等	2011年	武进
常州市宇锋车辆厂	宇锋及图形	机动自行车、电动车辆、小型机动车等	2011年	武进
常州市铭锦弹簧有限公司	铭锦及图形	车辆减震器、机动车减震器、车辆减震弹簧等	2011年	武进
常州精科实业有限公司	CONTIN	钟表及其零部件、计时器（时钟）、记时计等	2011年	武进
江苏恒耐炉料集团有限公司	恒耐及图形	耐火材料	2011年	武进
常州市洁丽木业有限公司	洁丽及图形	地板、护墙板、已加工木材等	2011年	武进
江苏博大木业有限公司	博瑞得及图形	地板、胶合板、耐火材料等	2011年	武进
江苏贝尔装饰材料有限公司	贝尔BeiEr	木材、铺地木材、制家用器具用木材等	2011年	武进
江苏玉兰木业有限公司	帕伦克及图形	地板、拼花地板条、贴面板等	2011年	武进
江苏中鑫德赛木业有限公司	荣登及图形	木地板、铺地木材、地板等	2011年	武进
江苏欧龙地板有限公司	伊恩YIEN	半成品木材、地板、耐火材料等	2011年	武进
常州市锦纶厂有限公司	威美WEIMEI及图形	丙纶丝、锦纶丝	2011年	武进
常州市棱光化工材料有限公司	棱光及图形	铝鞋眼	2011年	武进
江苏吉祥贺盛食品有限公司	贺盛及图形	味精、调味品等	2011年	武进
江苏中江焊丝有限公司	鲀鱼及图形	金属焊丝；金焊锡；锡焊锡等	2011年	新北
常州市第八纺织机械有限公司	华发及图形	纺织机械及零件、针织机械及零件等	2011年	新北
常州市西夏墅工具研究所有限公司	合力HL	刀具（机器零件）、切削工具（包括机械刀片）	2011年	新北
常州宝隆冶金设备制造有限公司	常　冶	输送机、包装机、轧钢机滚筒等	2011年	新北
常州市南港港口机械有限公司	NGPMC及图形	起重机、装卸设备	2011年	新北
常州天山重工机械有限公司	TS·HI及图形	机器传动装置、非陆地车辆变速箱等	2011年	新北
常州太平洋电力设备（集团）有限公司	常太及图形	配电箱（电）、配电盘、配电控制台（电）等	2011年	新北
常州太平电器有限公司	太平通信TAIPING	光通信设备、电源材料（电线、电缆）等	2011年	新北
常州市永光车业有限公司	永兆及图形	汽车灯、车辆灯	2011年	新北
常州星宇车灯股份有限公司	星宇及图形	荧光灯、照明防护装置等	2011年	新北
常州市瑞悦车业有限公司	富满及图形	车门、车辆轮辐、后视镜等	2011年	新北
吟飞科技（江苏）有限公司	吟飞及图形	手风琴、钢琴、乐器等	2011年	新北
常州市墅乐厨具有限公司	墅乐及图形	家用压面机	2011年	新北
常州中华恐龙园有限公司	恐龙及图形	帘子布、无纺布、纺织品壁挂等	2011年	新北
常州市丽岛金属材料制造有限公司	丽岛LIDAO	建筑用金属包层、金属地板、金属建筑材料等	2011年	钟楼
江苏洛克电气有限公司	洛克及图形	电　机	2011年	钟楼

2-17　名牌产品一览
GENERAL VIEW OF FAMOUS BRAND PRODUCTS

企业名称 Name of Enterprises	产品名称 Product Name	颁布时间 Time of Release
中国名牌产品　China Top Brand Products		
江苏上上电缆集团	上上牌交联聚乙烯电力电缆	2004年
黑牡丹（集团）股份有限公司	黑牡丹牌牛仔布	2005年
常州月夜灯芯绒有限公司	月夜牌灯芯绒	2005年
常柴股份有限公司	常柴牌单缸柴油机	2005年
江苏常发集团常州常发动力机械有限公司	常发牌单缸柴油机	2005年
江苏华鹏变压器有限公司	华鹏牌干式电力变压器	2005年
江苏华鹏变压器有限公司	华鹏牌110KV及以下油浸式电力变压器	2005年
常州华电变压器集团公司常州变压器厂	常州牌110KV及以下油浸式电力变压器	2005年
常州天马集团有限公司	天马牌无碱玻璃纤维短切原丝毡	2005年
江苏多棱数控机床股份有限公司	SDL牌重型数控镗铣床	2006年
常州东风农机集团有限公司	东风牌手扶拖拉机	2006年
江苏常发集团常州常发动力机械有限公司	常发牌手扶拖拉机	2006年
新科电子集团有限公司	新科、Shinco牌激光视盘机	2006年
江苏康泰氟化工有限公司	蓝色星球牌HFC-134A制冷剂	2006年
江苏常隆化工有限公司	天宁牌吡虫啉杀虫剂	2006年
江苏同大股份有限公司	全无敌牌气雾杀虫剂	2006年
月星集团有限公司	月星牌实木家具	2006年
江苏鸿联集团有限公司	红联牌室内灯具	2006年
常州天马集团有限公司	天马牌玻璃纤维土工格栅	2006年
江苏金鼎电动工具集团有限公司	金鼎牌电动工具	2007年
常州市永明机械制造有限公司	常明牌PP编织物机	2007年
常州市武进不锈钢管厂有限公司	阳湖牌锅炉用不锈钢无缝钢管	2007年
江苏常隆化工有限公司	天宁牌乙草胺	2007年
常林股份有限公司	常林牌装载机	2007年
新科电子集团有限公司	新科、Shinco牌家用分体空调	2007年

2-17 续表 1 continued 1

企业名称 Name of Enterprises	产品名称 Product Name	颁布时间 Time of Release
江苏名牌产品 Jiangsu Famous Brand Products		
常州华威电子有限公司	Chang牌铝电解电容器	2009年
新科电子集团有限公司	新科Shinco牌DVD视盘机、房间空气调节器	2009年
溧阳开利地毯材料有限公司	天目湖牌地毯	2009年
江苏鸿瑞昌泰纺织有限公司	HRCT牌化纤仿毛毛毯	2009年
溧阳新元窗帘制品有限公司	新元牌窗帘	2009年
黑牡丹（集团）股份有限公司	黑牡丹牌牛仔布	2009年
华润包装材料有限公司	安德利、华蕾牌瓶用聚对苯二甲酸乙二醇酯（PET）树脂	2009年
江苏瑞阳化工股份有限公司	瑞阳牌工业用季戊四醇	2009年
中盐金坛盐化有限责任公司	金赛盐业牌盐	2009年
江苏天容集团股份有限公司	溧化牌苄嘧磺隆除草剂	2009年
江苏常隆化工有限公司	天宁牌乙草胺等酰胺类除草剂、拟除虫菊酯类杀虫剂、氨基甲酸酯类农药、吡虫啉、磺酰脲类除草剂	2009年
常州光辉化工有限公司	光辉牌油漆涂料	2009年
江苏兰陵化工集团有限公司	兰陵牌涂料	2009年
江苏晨光涂料有限公司	晨光牌内外墙涂料	2009年
亚邦牌化工集团有限公司	亚邦牌分散染料	2009年
常茂生物化学工程股份有限公司	常茂（图形）牌酒石酸	2009年
常州华钛化学股份有限公司	RUNTECURE牌光引发剂	2009年
南京化工学院常州市武进水质稳定剂厂	颂歌牌水处理剂	2009年
常州市宏发纵横新材料科技有限公司	PGTEX牌连续树脂基预浸料用多轴向经编增强复合材料	2009年
江苏省竹箦阀业有限公司	ZJ牌阀门	2009年
常州市裕成电子有限公司	裕成牌电动自行车用轮毂电机	2009年
江苏上上电缆集团有限公司	上上牌电线电缆	2009年
江苏金牛线缆集团有限公司	金牛牌电线电缆	2009年
梅特勒-托利多（常州）测量技术有限公司	METTLER TOLEDO牌电子衡器	2009年
江苏常发制冷股份有限公司	常发牌冰箱、空调用蒸发器、冷凝器	2009年
金坛市金动柴油机厂	金动牌柴油机	2009年

2-17 续表 2　continued 2

企业名称 Name of Enterprises	产品名称 Product Name	颁布时间 Time of Release
常州市华立液压润滑设备有限公司	华润牌稀油润滑装置	2009年
溧阳市重型机械厂	麦重牌破碎机	2009年
常州常发农业装备有限公司	常发牌轮式拖拉机	2009年
常州星宇车灯有限公司	星怡牌汽车车灯	2009年
江苏上齿集团有限公司	上溧牌汽车及工程车螺旋锥齿轮	2009年
常州光洋轴承有限公司	NRB牌滚动轴承	2009年
江苏正昌集团有限公司	正昌牌成套工程设备、饲料压制机、粉碎机	2009年
江苏华鹏变压器有限公司	华鹏牌电力变压器	2009年
金坛市金榆互感器有限公司	金低牌电流互感器	2009年
江苏省金坛密封件厂	JMP牌汽车空调（HFC-134a）密封件	2009年
常州联力自动化科技有限公司	联力LIANLI及图牌矿用隔爆兼本质安全型真空组合开关	2009年
常州天马集团有限公司	天马牌不饱和聚酯树脂、玻璃纤维制品	2009年
江苏金峰水泥集团有限公司	金峰牌水泥	2009年
常州市龙泉太阳能设备厂	全牌太阳能热水器	2009年
月星集团有限公司	月星（图形）牌实木家具	2009年
常州市洁丽木业有限公司	洁丽牌实木地板	2009年
江苏玉兰木业有限公司	东方玉兰牌浸渍纸层压木质地板	2009年
常州市德威木业有限公司	德威牌强化木地板	2009年
江苏博大木业有限公司	博瑞得牌热固性树脂浸渍纸高压装饰层积板	2009年
江苏凯莱木业有限公司	凯莱牌浸渍纸层压木质地板	2009年
江苏好佳好木业有限公司	斯诺比牌浸渍纸层压木质地板	2009年
江苏双奇木业有限公司	双奇牌浸渍纸层压木质地板	2009年
常州市墅乐厨具有限公司	墅乐牌家用制面机	2009年
金坛市鑫隆防水塑胶制品有限公司	隆坛牌高分子防水材料	2009年
江苏鸿联集团有限公司	红联牌照明灯具	2009年
江苏亚示照明灯具有限公司	YASHIPS牌室外灯具	2009年
常州市第二石英钟表厂	CONTIN牌指针式石英钟	2009年

2-17 续表 3　continued 3

企业名称 Name of Enterprises	产品名称 Product Name	颁布时间 Time of Release
江西洪都航空工业集团常州洪都电动车有限公司	洪都牌电动自行车	2009年
常州鸿尔达车业有限公司	鸿尔靓达牌电动自行车	2009年
溧阳市四方不锈钢制品有限公司	利洋四方牌不锈钢卫生级管阀件	2009年
江苏常宝钢管股份有限公司	环球牌无缝钢管	2009年
中天钢铁集团有限公司	ZENITH牌热轧光圆钢筋、热轧带肋钢筋	2009年
常州金源铜业有限公司	金线牌电工用铜线坯（Φ8.0mm光亮铜杆）	2009年
常州方圆制药有限公司	创成牌硫酸依替米星制剂	2009年
常州千红生化制药股份有限公司	常生千红牌肝素系列产品及其制剂	2009年
江苏省健尔康医用敷料有限公司	健尔康牌脱脂纱布	2009年
常州市南方卫生器材厂有限公司	妙手牌创可贴	2010年
常州环球地毯制造有限公司	环球牌阿克敏斯特地毯（手工剪花）	2009年
金坛市鑫品茶业有限公司	鑫品牌金坛雀舌茶	2009年
金坛市茅麓茶厂	巨鹿牌绿茶	2009年
金坛市茅山青锋茶叶有限公司	金鹿牌茅山青锋	2009年
常州阳湖新月茶业有限公司	阳湖新月牌绿茶	2009年
江苏天香集团有限公司	香雪牌味精	2009年
常州市立华畜禽有限公司	雪山牌雪山鸡	2009年
金坛丰登酒业有限公司	丰登牌黄酒（封缸酒）	2009年
重庆啤酒集团常州天目湖啤酒有限公司	天目湖啤酒	2009年
溧阳市天目湖宾馆有限公司	天目湖牌砂锅鱼头及真空包装鱼头	2009年
常州市艺林园花木有限公司	厚余牌樟树苗木	2009年
常州神龙饲料有限公司	水神牌水产饲料	2009年
江苏大娘水饺餐饮有限公司	江苏服务业名牌	2009年
常州国旅旅行社有限公司	江苏服务业名牌	2009年
常州亿晶光电科技有限公司	EGNG（图形）牌晶体硅光伏组件	2009年
江苏裕成电子有限公司	（YC字样图案）牌微型动圈式受话器/扬声器	2010年
常州星海电子有限公司	灵杰牌硅半导体二极管	2010年
常州天合光能有限公司	天合光能牌太阳能电池组件	2010年

2-17 续表 4　continued 4

企业名称 Name of Enterprises	产品名称 Product Name	颁布时间 Time of Release
常州成业服饰有限公司	CY牌短裤	2010年
江苏波仕曼制衣有限公司	波仕曼牌羽绒服装	2010年
顶呱呱彩棉服饰有限公司	顶瓜瓜牌天然彩棉内衣	2010年
江苏旷达汽车织物集团股份有限公司	旷达牌汽车内饰面料	2010年
江苏中东集团有限公司	中东牌复混肥料	2010年
常州亚邦化学有限公司	亚邦牌顺丁烯二酸酐	2010年
江苏省激素研究所股份有限公司	金珠牌除草剂、杀虫剂、植物生长调节剂	2010年
江苏丰登农药有限公司	丰登牌三唑类杀菌剂	2010年
江苏瑞邦农药厂有限公司	瑞邦牌75%苯磺隆水分散粒剂	2010年
常州市国宇环保科技有限公司	玉宇牌硝酸银	2010年
江苏天容集团股份有限公司	溧化牌苄嘧磺隆除草剂；天容牌杀虫双（单）、杀螟丹、精噁唑禾草灵	2010年
江苏恒立高压油缸有限公司	恒立牌液压油缸	2010年
金坛市农用水泵厂	国农牌自吸泵	2010年
常州市永安电机有限公司	M牌房间空调器用电动机	2010年
常州市武起汽车电机有限公司	常乐牌汽车用起动机	2010年
常州市武进五洋纺织机械有限公司	五洋牌GE-288A型中绒双针床经编机	2010年
江苏金鼎电动工具集团有限公司	金鼎牌电动工具	2010年
江苏鑫和泰机械集团有限公司	常动牌单缸柴油机铸铁机体	2010年
常柴股份有限公司	常柴牌柴油机	2010年
常州常发动力机械有限公司	常发牌柴油机、常发系列旋耕机	2010年
常州亚美柯机械设备有限公司	亚美柯牌柴油机	2010年
江苏保龙机电制造有限公司	保龙牌木材加工机械	2010年
常州联发凯迪机械有限公司	联发凯迪牌轮式拖拉机	2010年
常州太平洋电力设备（集团）有限公司	常太牌常太牌高低压开关柜	2010年
江苏安靠超高压电缆附件有限公司	安靠牌高压及超高压交联聚乙稀绝缘电力电缆附件系列产品	2010年
常州市拓源电气制造有限公司	常州拓源（图形）牌低压成套开关设备和控制设备	2010年
国茂减速机集团有限公司	国茂牌减速机	2010年
常州市永明机械制造有限公司	常明牌PP编织物机	2010年

2-17 续表 5 continued 5

企业名称 Name of Enterprises	产品名称 Product Name	颁布时间 Time of Release
常州市润源经编机械有限公司	润源牌经编机	2010年
江苏南方轴承股份有限公司	南方牌滚针轴承	2010年
盘固水泥集团有限公司	盘固牌通用硅酸盐水泥	2010年
江苏扬子水泥有限公司	长荡湖牌PO42.5水泥	2010年
江苏长海复合材料股份有限公司	常海牌薄型玻璃纤维短切毡	2010年
常州而今太阳能设备制造有限公司	而今牌家用太阳热水系统	2010年
江苏太阳宝新能源有限公司	太阳宝牌太阳能热水器	2010年
溧阳军荣旅游用品有限公司	JUNRONG牌旅行箱包	2010年
江苏力强化工有限公司	力洋牌酚醛模塑料	2010年
江苏凯灵汽车电器有限公司	凯灵牌汽车组合开关	2010年
江苏洛基木业有限公司	洛基牌浸渍纸层压木质地板	2010年
常州市佳安装饰材料有限公司	好佳好牌浸渍纸层压木质地板	2010年
常州市赛力木业有限公司	圣力牌浸渍纸层压木质地板	2010年
江苏科利达装饰材料有限公司	科利达牌浸渍纸层压木质地板	2010年
常州市赛欧地板有限公司	大欧牌浸渍纸层压木质地板	2010年
常州市森尼装饰材料有限公司	森尼牌浸渍纸层压木质地板	2010年
常州市欧太装饰材料有限公司	欧运牌浸渍纸层压木质地板	2010年
江苏太平洋印刷有限公司	小白豚牌相册	2010年
常州速派奇车业有限公司	速派奇牌电动自行车	2010年
江苏武进不锈钢管厂集团有限公司	阳湖牌锅炉用不锈钢无缝钢管	2010年
常州灵通展览用品有限公司	灵通LINGTONG牌展览展示器材	2010年
江苏国强镀锌实业有限公司	国强牌镀锌焊接钢管、高速公路波形梁护栏	2010年
常州制药厂有限公司	常药牌卡托普利系列、盐酸多西环素、复方利血平片	2010年
常州四药制药有限公司	奥克牌奥美拉唑系列、兰苏牌盐酸氨溴索系列、缬克牌缬沙坦胶囊	2010年
江苏康友医用器械有限公司	康友牌一次性使用无菌注射器	2010年
江苏康进医疗器材有限公司	康进牌一次性使用无菌注射器、输液器（带针）	2010年
常州医疗器材总厂有限公司	乐伦牌一次性使用无菌注射器输液器	2010年
常州千红生化制药股份有限公司	常生千红牌肝素系列产品及其制剂；怡开牌胰激肽原酶及其制剂系列产品	2010年

2-17 续表 6　continued 6

企业名称 Name of Enterprises	产品名称 Product Name	颁布时间 Time of Release
江苏省前峰茶厂	前峰牌绿茶	2010年
金坛市方麓茶场有限公司	百园春牌金坛雀舌茶	2010年
江苏德盛食品有限公司	德盛牌米果	2010年
江苏常州城北国家粮食储备库	诚百牌大米	2010年
江苏南顺食品有限公司	满天星牌小麦粉、挂面	2010年
金坛市江南制粉有限公司	沁雪牌水磨糯米粉	2010年
常州长江水产有限公司冷冻加工厂	江南牌太湖冻银鱼	2010年
金坛市绿野农业服务中心	碧润牌无节水芹	2010年
江苏吉祥贺盛食品有限公司	贺盛牌鸡精调味料	2010年
常州市康乐农牧有限公司	中东牌商品猪	2010年
江苏正平技术服务事务所有限公司	江苏服务业名牌	2010年
常州市维益专利事务所	江苏服务业名牌	2010年
常州大华进出口（集团）有限公司	江苏服务业名牌	2010年
常州中华恐龙园有限公司	江苏服务业名牌	2010年
江苏南方通信科技有限公司	精科牌铜芯聚烯烃绝缘铝塑综合护套市内通信电缆	2011年
常州金松时装有限公司	G&P牌衬衫	2011年
江苏华达化工集团有限公司	常恒牌1-萘胺、1-萘酚系列产品	2011年
冶建新材料股份有限公司	天虎牌TH-2型硅酸锌车间底漆	2011年
常州华日升反光材料有限公司	通明牌反光膜	2011年
常州市源恩合成材料有限公司	源恩牌聚氨酯胶粘剂	2011年
江苏华盛天龙光电设备股份有限公司	华盛天龙牌DRF系列直拉式单晶炉	2011年
金坛天鹅喷灌机械有限公司	天鹅牌轻小型喷灌机	2011年
常州联凯动力机械有限公司	常联发牌单缸柴油机	2011年
金坛柴油机有限公司	天鹅牌单缸柴油机	2011年
江苏海鸥冷却塔股份有限公司	海鸥牌冷却塔	2011年
金坛市旺达喷灌机有限公司	大网牌轻小型喷灌机	2011年
常州市第八纺织机械有限公司	华发牌整经机	2011年
江苏峨嵋动力机械有限公司	金田牌单缸柴油机	2011年

2-17 续表 7 continued 7

企业名称 Name of Enterprises	产品名称 Product Name	颁布时间 Time of Release
江苏天元工程机械有限公司	teeyer牌蒸压加气混凝土切割机	2011年
常州常瑞天力动力机械有限公司	常瑞牌单缸燃气机	2011年
江苏省社渚轴承有限公司	球星牌圆锥滚子轴承	2011年
江苏华阳电器有限公司	华阳huayang牌BYJ系列减速永磁步进电动机	2011年
常州亚玛顿股份有限公司	亞瑪頓牌太阳能电池用光伏镀膜玻璃	2011年
江苏丰顺新材料科技有限公司	丰顺牌建筑幕墙用铝塑复合板	2011年
江苏红日防静电地板有限公司	红日牌防静电活动地板	2011年
江苏欧龙地板有限公司	欧塞牌浸渍纸层压木质地板	2011年
江苏中鑫德赛木业有限公司	荣登牌浸渍纸层压木质地板	2011年
江苏亿家美木业有限公司	申嘉牌浸渍纸层压木质地板	2011年
常州市零点木业有限公司	零点牌浸渍纸层压木质地板	2011年
常州市东家装饰材料有限公司	东家牌浸渍纸层压木质地板	2011年
百兴集团有限公司	百兴牌聚氯乙烯硬片、膜	2011年
江苏南洋木业有限公司	南洋牌实木地板	2011年
江苏友奥电器有限公司	友奥牌移动式空调器	2011年
江苏德莱仕电器有限公司	中韩牌冷藏冷冻箱	2011年
常州市常蒸蒸发器有限公司	常蒸牌蒸发器、冷凝器（高效节能换热器）	2011年
常州华通焊丝有限公司	华通牌碳钢焊丝	2011年
江苏吉景金属科技有限公司	吉景牌连续热镀锌钢带	2011年
江苏康华医疗器材有限公司	常宝牌一次性使用无菌注射器、输液器	2011年
江苏润德医用材料有限公司	润德（+图形）牌注射液用卤化丁基橡胶塞	2011年
金坛市江南春米业有限公司	蘇牌大米	2011年
金坛市碧润水芹专业合作社	碧润牌无节水芹	2011年
常州市常洛果品专业合作社	苏常鲜牌绿色食品（葡萄）	2011年
金坛市后渎特种水产养殖场有限公司	苏标牌长荡湖中华绒螯蟹	2011年
江苏新城房产股份有限公司	江苏服务业名牌	2011年
常州市春秋乐园旅游发展有限公司	江苏服务业名牌	2011年
江苏凌家塘市场发展有限公司	江苏服务业名牌	2011年

2-17 续表 8　continued 8

企业名称 Name of Enterprises	产品名称 Product Name	颁布时间 Time of Release
常州名牌产品　Changzhou Famous Brand Products		
常州市杨程禹渔业专业合作社	青　鱼	2011年
常州市雅浦酿酒有限公司	黄　酒	2011年
常州市常丰食品有限公司	肉制品	2011年
金坛市荣华制粉厂	水磨糯米粉	2011年
溧阳维多生物工程有限公司	阿斯巴甜	2011年
溧阳市天目湖玉枝特种茶果园艺场	白　茶	2011年
溧阳市天目湖茶叶研究所	绿　茶	2011年
溧阳市天目湖燕山茶园有限公司	绿　茶	2011年
溧阳市天目佳农业生态园	绿　茶	2011年
溧阳市天目香茶厂	绿　茶	2011年
溧阳市周城汤山茶厂	绿　茶	2011年
溧阳市留云茶厂	绿　茶	2011年
溧阳市江南一叶茶场	绿　茶	2011年
金坛市万方光头牛肉有限公司	真空包装牛肉	2011年
金坛市马达山园艺有限公司	砂　梨	2011年
常州市武进区寨桥西湖山庄垂钓中心	中华绒螯蟹	2011年
常州市国宇环保科技有限公司	羧甲基纤维素钠（食品级）	2011年
常州亚美柯机械设备有限公司	单缸柴油机	2011年
江苏山湖电缆有限公司	物理发泡同轴射频电缆	2011年
江苏竹溪活性炭有限公司	活性炭	2011年
冶建新材料股份有限公司	硅酸锌车间底漆	2011年
溧阳市四方不锈钢制品有限公司	不锈钢卫生流体设备	2011年
溧阳市万兴特种建材有限公司	预应力混凝土用钢绞线	2011年
常州市丰宇五金工艺有限公司	网　篮	2011年
常州市飞拓模塑有限公司	汽车车灯	2011年
江苏贝德莱特太阳能科技有限公司	太阳能热水器	2011年
江苏德春电力科技有限公司	交流高压六氟化硫负荷开关	2011年
常州市黄河车灯有限公司	汽车燃油箱	2011年
常州市长力冲压机床有限公司	开式压力机	2011年

2-17 续表 9 continued 9

企业名称 Name of Enterprises	产品名称 Product Name	颁布时间 Time of Release
常州市曙光车业有限公司	汽车内饰件	2011年
常州市康辉医疗器械有限公司	骨科植入物（接骨钢板等）	2011年
常州市明宇交通器材有限公司	汽车灯具	2011年
江苏中江焊丝有限公司	CO2气体保护焊丝	2011年
常州市宏发纵横新材料科技有限公司	连续树脂基预浸料用多轴向经编增强复合材料	2011年
常州五王电机有限公司	罩极异步电动机	2011年
江苏亚示照明集团有限公司	照明灯具	2011年
普罗斯电器（中国）有限公司	节能高强度气体放电灯	2011年
常州顺风发电设备有限公司	柴油发电机组	2011年
常州市运河焊材有限公司	气体保护焊丝	2011年
江苏华光粉末有限公司	热固性粉末涂料	2011年
常州东吴链传动制造有限公司	链条、链轮	2011年
常州润达铁合金有限公司	硅铝铁合金复合脱氧剂、铸造孕育剂	2011年
江苏福昌环保科技集团有限公司	免燃料型有机化工废渣焚烧炉	2011年
江苏恒耐炉料集团有限公司	早强防爆浇注料	2011年
江苏联盟化学有限公司	PVC复合稳定剂	2011年
常州金马炉业设备有限公司	锅炉链条炉排	2011年
常州市科能电器有限公司	SF6气体泄漏监控报警系统	2011年
常州博万达汽车安全设备有限公司	BWD型汽车安全带	2011年
江苏恒益木业有限公司	浸渍纸层压木质地板	2011年
常州高力彩钢板有限公司	彩钢卷	2011年
常州市武进骏宇汽配涂料有限公司	制动气室系列	2011年
常州市华辉油泵油嘴厂	油泵、油嘴	2011年
江苏通洋船舶有限公司	船、艇	2011年
金坛市杰力农机精密铸造有限公司	微型耕作机	2011年
江苏恒亮离心机制造有限公司	卧式螺旋卸料沉降离心机	2011年
常州亨达车业部件有限公司	汽车后视镜（含广角后视镜）、汽车补盲外后视镜	2011年
常州曙光化工厂	工业用顺丁烯二酸酐	2011年
江苏吉景金属科技有限公司	连续热镀锌钢带	2011年
常州依丽雅斯遮阳技术有限公司	窗帘布	2011年

2-17 续表 10　continued 10

企业名称 Name of Enterprises	产品名称 Product Name	颁布时间 Time of Release
常州市天龙光电设备有限公司	铸造（锭）机	2011年
常州市武滚轴承有限公司	滚动轴承	2011年
常州市佳乐车辆配件制造有限公司	汽车空调系统壳体及金属支架	2011年
常州市南港港口机械有限公司	集装箱吊具	2011年
江苏天元工程机械有限公司	蒸压加气混凝土切割机	2011年
常州市常欣电子衡器有限公司	起重量限制器	2011年
常州雷利电机科技有限公司	排水泵用电动机	2011年
江苏三信环保设备有限公司	垃圾焚烧及烟气净化系统成套设备	2011年
常州市伟泰电子科技有限公司	轨道交通用空调机架、风道、车下箱体	2011年
江苏昌盛电缆集团有限公司	电线电缆	2011年
常州市武进洛阳新型保温材料厂	硬质聚氨酯泡沫	2011年
常州市飞扬粉末涂料有限公司	热固性粉末涂料	2011年
江苏德莱仕电器有限公司	家用冷藏冷冻箱	2011年
常州市金陵干燥设备有限公司	干燥设备	2011年
常州姚氏同德化工有限公司	水处理剂 有机膦酸盐	2011年
常州腾跃不锈钢管有限公司	无缝不锈钢管	2011年
常州市宇通干燥设备有限公司	干燥设备	2011年
江苏恒鑫富奥汽车零部件有限公司	制动气室	2011年
常州武帆合金有限公司	铝锰铁复合脱氧剂	2011年
江苏华阳电器有限公司	爪极式永磁同步电动机	2011年
常州欧凯电器有限公司	减速永磁式步进电动机	2011年
江苏龙城精锻有限公司	汽车发电机精锻爪极	2011年
常州市拓源电气制造有限公司	户内金属铠装抽出式开关设备	2011年
江苏新瑞重工科技有限公司	立式加工中心	2011年
常州市佳辰机房设备有限公司	防静电活动地板	2011年
常州牛顿力称重系统有限公司	电子天平	2011年
常州市合达油泵有限公司	高压喷油泵总成	2011年
常州信发汽车配件有限公司	电磁开关	2011年
常州市美意达木业有限公司	浸渍纸层压木质地板	2011年
常州乐士雷利电机有限公司	步进电机	2011年
常州乐士雷利电机有限公司	排水电机	2011年

2-17 续表 11 continued 11

企业名称 Name of Enterprises	产品名称 Product Name	颁布时间 Time of Release
常州腾龙汽车零部件股份有限公司	汽车空调用软管及软管组合件	2011年
常州市武进电力管件有限公司	压力管件元件	2011年
常州市河马塑胶有限公司	建筑小区排水用塑料检查井	2011年
常州康普药业有限公司	盐酸氯丙嗪系列产品	2011年
常州市武进红光无线电有限公司	机顶盒电源系列	2011年
常州森鸿装饰材料有限公司	浸渍纸层压木质地板	2011年
常州市鼎鸿木业有限公司	浸渍纸层压木质地板	2011年
江苏丰顺新材料科技有限公司	铝塑板、铝单板、铝蜂窝板	2011年
常州液压成套设备厂有限公司	液压启闭机及接力器	2011年
江苏源力汽车内饰件有限公司	汽车内饰件	2011年
江苏省巨变变压器有限公司	35KV及以下电力变压器	2011年
金坛市明日春花盆有限公司	实木复合花盆	2011年
江苏易成电力器材有限公司	玻璃纤维增强塑料电缆导管	2011年
常州市赛尔交通器材有限公司	轨道交通用前组合灯系列	2011年
江苏苏阳电工机械有限公司	笼式成缆机	2011年
常州亚泰焊材有限公司	气体保护电弧焊用碳钢焊丝	2011年
冶建新材料股份有限公司	通用耐磨环氧涂料	2011年
常州华迪特种变压器有限公司	20KV低损耗干式变压器	2011年
常州华迪特种变压器有限公司	非晶合金变压器	2011年
常州亚玛顿股份有限公司	光伏镀膜玻璃	2011年
常州市范群干燥设备有限公司	高效颜料烘干机	2011年
常州旭荣针织印染有限公司	针织面料	2011年
常州市默顿电气有限公司	电容补偿投切开关	2011年
常州中房物业有限公司	物业服务	2011年
常州丽华快餐集团有限公司	中式快餐（套餐）销售和服务	2011年
常州港华燃气有限公司	天然气供应与服务	2011年
常州产权交易所	产权交易、招投标服务	2011年
常州航天信息有限公司	防伪税控系统及增值产品的销售和服务	2011年
常州三晶世界科技产业发展有限公司	科技创业孵化服务	2011年
常州湟里金鼎国际大酒店有限公司	酒店服务	2011年
江苏天目湖宾馆有限公司	酒店服务	2011年

3

CHAPTER 3

行政区划　自然概况

ADMINISTRATIVE DIVISION AND NATURAL RESOURCES

3 行政区划　自然概况
ADMINISTRATIVE DIVISION AND NATURAL RESOURCES

行政区划　自然概况

行政区划

常州市下辖溧阳、金坛两市及武进、新北、天宁、钟楼、戚墅堰五区。溧阳、金坛二市下辖17个镇、83个居民委员会（社区居委会）和332个村民委员会；武进、新北、天宁、钟楼、戚墅堰区下辖 21个街道办事处、 20个镇，276个居民委员会（社区居委会）和 450个村民委员会。

位　置

常州地处江苏省南部，沪宁线中段，属长江三角洲沿海经济开放区。位于北纬31° 09'至32° 04'，东经119° 08'至120° 12'之间，北倚长江天堑，南与安徽省交界，东濒太湖与无锡市相连，西与南京、镇江两市接壤。

常州水陆空交通便利。沪宁铁路、沪宁与宁杭高速公路、312国道、京杭大运河穿境而过。全市水网纵横交织，连江通海。长江常州港为一类口岸，常州民航站已开通至北京、广州、大连、厦门、深圳、海口、西安等国内近20个大中城市的航线。

地　势

常州地貌类型属高沙平原，山丘平圩兼有。南为天目山余脉，西为茅山山脉，北为宁镇山脉尾部，中部和东部为宽广的平原、圩区。境内地势西南略高，东北略低，高低相差1.5 ~ 2米左右。

面　积

常州市总面积4372平方公里，市区面积为1862平方公里。

河　流

常州境内河道纵横交织，湖塘星罗棋布。著名的有泊洮湖（长荡湖）、滆湖、太湖3大天然湖泊，并有沙河（天目湖）、大溪两大人工水库，贯通全境的京杭大运河更是支流密布，脉脉相连，形成江河相通，3湖相连的水系网络。

Administrative Division and Natural Resources

Administrative Division

Changzhou has jurisdiction over two county-level cities and five districts. There are 17 towns, 83 neighborhood committees (community committees), and 332 villagers' committees under the jurisdiction of Jintan city and Liyang city; and Wujin district, Xinbei district, Tianning district, Zhonglou district, Qishuyan district totally administer 21 subdistrict offices, 20 towns, 276 neighborhood committees (community committees) and 450 villagers' committees.

Location

Changzhou, located in the southeast of Jiangsu province and the central section of Shanghai-Nanjing railway, belongs to the coastal economic open zone. Between north latitude 31°09' to 32°04' and east longitude 119°08' to 120°12', bordering the great Yangtze River in the north, Anhui province in the south and facing Taihu Lake and Wuxi city in the east and neighboring Nanjing city, Zhenjiang city in the west.

Changzhou is easily accessed by water, land and air since it is traversed by railways and expressways, including Shanghai-Nanjing Railway, Shanghai-Nanjing expressway, Nanjing-Hangzhou Expressway, Yangtze Riverside Expressway, Wuxi-Yixing Expressway,Yangzhou-Liyang Expressway, National Highway 312 and Beijing-Hangzhou Grand Canal; Besides, it owns the crisscross network of waters, connecting Yangtze River and leading to the sea. Changzhou Port of the Yangtze River is listed as the state category-1 port; and Changzhou civil airport has scheduled flights to nearly 20 large and medium size domestic cities, such as Beijing, Guangzhou, Dalian, Xiamen, Shenzhen, Haikou and Xi'an, etc.

Topography

The relief type of Changzhou is combined with plain and hills and polders. It has Tianmu Mountain ranges in the south, Maoshan Mountain ranges in the west, Tailing edge of Ningzhen Mountain in the north, vast plain and polder in the central section and east. The terrain is relatively higher in southwest and relatively lower in the northeast with a difference of 1.5～2 meters.

Area

The total area of Changzhou is 4372sq.km,The urban area covers1862sq.km.

Rivers

The rivers cross the city in a crisscross pattern, and lakes spread all over the city like the stars in the sky and scattered like the pieces on a chessboard.There are three famous natural lakes, such as Taohu Lake (Changdang Lake), Gehu Lake, Taihu Lake and two artificial reservoirs, namely, Shahe (Tianmu), Daxi reservoirs. The Beijing-Hangzhou Grand Canal goes through the city properly with many branches interlinked with rivers, which forms the water system network of canal, rivers interlinked and three lakes connected.

3-1 行政区划和土地面积（2011 年底）
ADMINISTRATIVE DIVISION AND LAND AREA（END OF 2011）

单位：个（unit）

地 区	Region	镇 Town	村民委员会 Villagers Committee	街 道 Subdistrict	居民委员会（社区居委会）Neighborhood Committee (Community Committee)	土地面积（平方公里）Area of Land(sq.km)
全 市	**Whole Municipality**	**37**	**782**	**21**	**359**	**4372.15**
市 区	**Urban Area**	**20**	**450**	**21**	**276**	**1861.96**
武进区	Wujin District	14	246	2	120	1245.84
新北区	Xinbei District	6	120	3	35	452.60
天宁区	Tianning District		34	6	61	65.03
钟楼区	Zhonglou District		41	7	53	66.81
戚墅堰区	Qishuyan District		9	3	7	31.68
县级市	**Cities at Country Level**	**17**	**332**		**83**	**2510.20**
溧阳市	Liyang City	10	175		67	1534.52
金坛市	Jintan City	7	157		16	975.68

3-2　行政区划（1983-2011 年）
ADMINISTRATIVE DIVISION（1983-2011）

单位：个（unit）

年　份 Year	街道办事处 Urban Subdistrict Office	居民委员会（社区居委会） Neighborhood Committee (Community Committee)	镇人民政府 Town Governments	乡人民政府 Township Governments	村民委员会 Villagers Committee
1983	18	236	7	136	1868
1984	18	265	7	136	1886
1985	19	288	16	125	1914
1986	18	303	16	125	1922
1987	18	329	22	119	1918
1988	19	336	35	106	1922
1989	18	339	39	102	1969
1990	18	363	39	102	1920
1991	18	375	48	93	1919
1992	18	388	49	88	1913
1993	20	414	65	72	1913
1994	19	429	71	66	1915
1995	18	450	74	63	1908
1996	18	460	81	56	1907
1997	19	471	81	56	1903
1998	19	482	81	55	1902
1999	20	505	70	9	1900
2000	23	344	70	9	1888
2001	25	336	70	9	1104
2002	22	339	70	9	1103
2003	27	273	65		1085
2004	27	273	65		1092
2005	24	293	64		1092
2006	16	289	64		1092
2007	20	291	37		1078
2008	20	304	37		1073
2009	21	292	37		940
2010	21	323	37		807
2011	21	359	37		782

3-3 分地区镇、街道数及名称（2011 年底）
NUMBER AND NAME OF SUBDISTRICT AND TOWN BY REGION（END OF 2011）

单位：个（unit）

指　标	Item	镇、街道数 Number of Subdistricts and Towns	镇、街道名称 Names of Subdistricts and Towns
总　计	**Total**	**58**	
街　道	**Subdistrict**	**21**	
按地区分	By Region		
武进区	Wujin District	2	南夏墅、西湖
新北区	Xinbei District	3	河海、三井、龙虎塘
天宁区	Tianning District	6	天宁、兰陵、茶山、雕庄、红梅、青龙
钟楼区	Zhonglou District	7	南大街、荷花池、新闸、五星、永红、北港、西林
戚墅堰区	Qishuyan District	3	戚墅堰、丁堰、潞城
镇	**Town**	**37**	
按地区分	By Region		
市　区	Urban Area	20	
武进区	WujinDistrict	14	湖塘、前黄、洛阳、遥观、横林、横山桥、郑陆、牛塘、奔牛、嘉泽、湟里、雪堰、邹区、礼嘉
新北区	Xinbei District	6	春江、新桥、孟河、西夏墅、薛家、罗溪
溧阳市	Liyang City	10	溧城、社渚 、南渡、上兴、别桥、上黄、竹箦、戴埠、埭头、天目湖
金坛市	Jintan City	7	金城、薛埠、尧塘、直溪、儒林、朱林、指前

NUMBER AND NAME OF SUBDISTRICT AND TOWNS BY REGIONS (END OF 2011)

4

CHAPTER 4

常州统计年鉴

综　合

GENERAL SURVEY

4 综　合
GENERAL SURVEY

从统计数字看 2011 年的常州
CHANGZHOU IN STATISTICS OF 2011

一、常州的人口
POPULATION OF CHANGZHOU

年末常住人口	Permanent Population at Year-end	464.97 万人	(10000 persons)
# 城镇人口	Urban Population	303.16 万人	(10000 persons)
人口密度	Density of population	1063 人 / 平方公里	(person/sq.km)

二、常州在全省的地位
POSITION OF CHANGZHOU IN JIANGSU PROVINCE

地区生产总值	Gross Domestic Product	居全省第 5 位	No.5 in Jiangsu
人均地区生产总值	Per Capita GDP	居全省第 3 位	No.3 in Jiangsu
地方一般预算收入	Local Government Budgetary	居全省第 5 位	No.5 in Jiangsu
进出口总额（海关数）	Total Imports and Exports	居全省第 4 位	No.4 in Jiangsu
# 出　口	Exports	居全省第 4 位	No.4 in Jiangsu
城镇居民人均可支配收入	Per Capita Disposable Income of Urban and Town Residents	居全省第 4 位	No.4 in Jiangsu
农民人均纯收入	Average Net Income Per Farmer	居全省第 3 位	No.3 in Jiangsu

三、常州市区的市政建设和公用事业
URBAN CONSTRUCTION AND PUBLIC UTILITIES OF CHANGZHOU

年末建成区面积	Total Area of the Constructed Regions at Year-end	173.15 平方公里	(sq.km)
年末城市道路长度	Length of Roads at Year-end	1810.74 公里	(km)
年末城市道路面积	Area of Roads at Year-end	3230 万平方米	(10000 sq.m)
年末城市桥梁数	Number of Bridges in Urban Area at Year-end	1000 座	(unit)
公共汽车客运总数	Total Volume of Passengers Traffic by Public Buses	40717 万人次	(10000 person-times)
年末供水综合生产能力	Production Capacity of Water Supply at Year-end	157.5 万吨 / 日	(10000 tons/day)
居民家庭用水	Family Water Consumption	8506.6 万立方米	(10000 m^3)
年末家庭燃气用户数	Number of Consumer of Gas and LPG at Year-end	49.52 万户	(10000 household)
燃气普及率	Percentage of Population with Access to Gas and LGP	99.1%	
年末城市园林绿地面积	Total Area of Parks,Gardens and Green Area in City at Year-end	7535 公顷	(hectare)
建城区绿化覆盖率	Coverage Rate of Green Area in the Constructed Area	42.2%	

四、常州的经济

ECONOMIC OF CHANGZHOU

	2011年实绩 Achievements in 2011	人均水平 Per Capita	日均水平 Per Dialy
地区生产总值 Gross Domestic Produc	3580.99亿元 (100 million yuan)	77485元 (yuan)	98109万元 (10000 yuan)
# 第三产业 Tertiary Industry	1518.37亿元 (100 million yuan)	32854元 (yuan)	41599万元 (10000 yuan)
农林牧渔业总产值 Total Output Value of Farming,forestry,Animal Husbandry and Fishing	194.68亿元 (100 million yuan)	5380元 (yuan)	5334万元 (10000 yuan)
# 农　业 Agriculture	107.78亿元 (100 million yuan)	2979元 (yuan)	2953万元 (10000 yuan)
规模以上工业总产值 Gross Output Value of Industrial Enterprises above Designated Size	8270.77亿元 (100 million yuan)	228582元 (yuan)	22660万元 (10000 yuan)
社会消费品零售总额 Total Retail Sales of Consumer Goods	1236.10亿元 (100 million yuan)	34162元 (yuan)	33866万元 (10000 yuan)
进出口总额 Total Imports and Exports	286.35亿美元 (USD 100 million)	7914美元 (USD)	7845万美元 (USD 10000)
# 出　口 Exports	193.61亿美元 (USD 100 million)	5351美元 (USD)	5304万美元 (USD 10000)
实际利用外资金额 Foreign Capital Actually Used	30.52亿美元 (USD 100 million)	843美元 (USD)	836万美元 (USD 10000)
全社会固定资产投资额 Total Investment in Fixed Assets	2338.94亿元 (100 million yuan)	64641元 (yuan)	64079万元 (10000 yuan)
房地产开发企业竣工住宅建筑面积 Completed Housing Area by Real Estate Development Enterrpises	472.38万平方米 (10000 sq.m)	1.31平方米 (sq.m)	12942平方米 (sq.m)
财政总收入 Financial Revenue	977.79亿元 (100 million yuan)	27023元 (yuan)	26789万元 (10000 yuan)
# 地方一般预算收入 Budgetary Revenue of Local Government	350.88亿元 (100 million yuan)	9697元 (yuan)	9613万元 (10000 yuan)
邮电业务收入 Revenue from Post & Telecommunication Services	59.95亿元 (100 million yuan)	1657元 (yuan)	1642万元 (10000 yuan)
全社会用电量 Total Electricity Consumed	331.66亿千瓦时 (100 million kw.h)	9166千瓦时 (kw.h)	9087万千瓦时 (10000 kw.h)

注：人均地区生产总值、人均第三产业增加值按常住人口计算。
Note: Per capita of gross regional product and per capita value added of tertiary industry are calculated as per permanent population.

4-1 历年地区生产总值
GROSS DOMESTIC PRODUCT OVER THE YEARS

单位：万元（10000 yuan）

年 份 Year	地区生产总值 Gross Domestic Product	其中 of which 第一产业 Primary Industry	第二产业 Secondary Industry	其中 of which 工 业 Industry	建筑业 Construction	第三产业 Tertiary Industry
1949	24979	17434	3193	3129	64	4352
1950	28470	18951	4463	4339	124	5056
1951	31080	19497	5310	5114	196	6273
1952	34493	21086	6620	5980	640	6787
1953	38228	21944	8331	7865	466	7953
1954	37536	20704	8482	7978	504	8350
1955	37985	21262	7539	6959	580	9184
1956	42016	21606	9713	8849	864	10697
1957	41120	20269	11410	10565	845	9441
1958	50377	20110	19284	17632	1652	10983
1959	53880	16766	24578	22848	1730	12536
1960	62495	18720	27681	26005	1676	16094
1961	45580	16215	16742	16001	741	12623
1962	46409	19128	15090	14311	779	12191
1963	49362	22345	15418	14513	905	11599
1964	53181	24631	17678	16711	967	10872
1965	62909	29268	21549	20524	1025	12092
1966	68993	31178	25295	24176	1119	12520
1967	63602	30983	20405	19306	1099	12214
1968	62681	27946	22896	21798	1098	11839
1969	71965	29154	29640	28420	1220	13171
1970	81090	27892	39166	37189	1977	14032
1971	96559	33300	48162	45761	2401	15097
1972	108835	33843	56735	53487	3248	18257
1973	122521	35367	67591	63108	4483	19563
1974	125285	35160	70303	66170	4133	19822
1975	131084	30945	78314	74137	4177	21825
1976	144282	35323	86637	81957	4680	22322
1977	154405	30472	99584	94311	5273	24349
1978	175707	38525	112468	105407	7061	24714
1979	201753	49760	122481	112412	10069	29512

4-1 续表 continued　　　　单位：万元（10000 yuan）

年 份 Year	地区生产总值 Gross Domestic Product	其中 of which 第一产业 Primary Industry	第二产业 Secondary Industry	其中 of which 工 业 Industry	建筑业 Construction	第三产业 Tertiary Industry
1980	227642	48897	142729	133235	9494	36016
1981	247378	51946	158129	147001	11128	37303
1982	260487	62795	160469	147281	13188	37223
1983	298476	70682	180162	166110	14052	47632
1984	387700	97530	218908	203098	15810	71262
1985	495896	105195	304811	280504	24307	85890
1986	547374	117724	328039	297125	30914	101611
1987	664549	125279	412259	376766	35493	127011
1988	821138	153477	505986	461754	44232	161675
1989	872397	165070	521667	483264	38403	185660
1990	948687	176805	579610	540600	39010	192272
1991	1021751	160573	656120	610693	45427	205058
1992	1443961	190338	929968	859302	70666	323655
1993	2238962	250531	1481661	1366806	114855	506770
1994	3149332	338176	2009160	1861541	147619	801996
1995	3697000	398160	2206420	2028562	177858	1092420
1996	4311541	455496	2465057	2236314	228743	1390988
1997	4701069	443684	2658167	2400789	257378	1599218
1998	5045974	444352	2810279	2526923	283356	1791343
1999	5387217	440113	2995019	2689386	305633	1952085
2000	6006573	451378	3366847	3019891	346956	2188348
2001	6729008	471137	3807601	3416841	390760	2450270
2002	7606035	488378	4315041	3877933	437108	2802616
2003	9014200	471800	5202500	4689100	513400	3339900
2004	11021900	541900	6618600	5929600	689000	3861400
2005	13081800	596200	7990500	7199500	791000	4495100
2006	15851100	660700	9544500	8750400	794100	5645900
2007	19135000	743200	11351300	10476100	875200	7040500
2008	22663200	845000	13170500	12094000	1076500	8647700
2009	25199300	917500	14297300	13016300	1281000	9984500
2010	30448900	997800	16836800	15308600	1528200	12614300
2011	35809900	1117800	19508400	17689100	1819300	15183700

注：2000-2003年数据根据第一次经济普查结果进行了调整，2005-2007年数据根据第二次经济普查结果进行了调整。

Note: The data collected during 2000-2003 were adjusted according to the record of the first Economic Census; and the data collected during 2005-2007 were adjusted according to the record of the second Economic Census.

4-2 地区生产总值指数（1978-2011 年，上年 =100）
GROSS DOMESTIC PRODUCT INDEX NUMBER （1978-2011， PRECEDING YEAR=100）

按可比价格计算 Calculated by comparable price

年份 Year	地区生产总值 Gross Domestic Product	其中 of which 第一产业 Primary Industry	第二产业 Secondary Industry	其中 of which 工业 Industry	第三产业 Tertiary Industry	人均地区生产总值 Per Capita Gross Domestic Product
1978	100.0	100.0	100.0	100.0	100.0	100.0
1979	108.6	104.4	108.0	106.2	117.9	107.8
1980	112.2	97.4	116.4	118.1	115.2	111.3
1981	108.5	103.2	111.3	110.9	102.2	107.6
1982	104.1	113.5	102.9	101.8	98.9	103.1
1983	114.8	108.4	113.9	114.4	127.8	113.8
1984	126.6	131.0	120.7	121.4	146.0	125.7
1985	122.8	97.9	133.7	132.4	110.1	122.2
1986	105.9	103.2	105.4	103.8	110.5	105.2
1987	116.3	96.0	121.1	122.1	114.3	115.1
1988	110.6	99.7	113.9	113.6	104.1	109.3
1989	94.7	102.9	92.8	94.0	98.3	93.5
1990	107.9	98.8	110.8	111.6	101.3	106.5
1991	107.3	88.8	114.6	114.9	102.2	106.4
1992	134.8	107.9	136.5	136.4	150.6	134.0
1993	133.9	110.1	137.8	139.5	135.6	133.4
1994	116.6	114.2	112.3	112.7	130.2	116.1
1995	113.6	109.6	113.1	113.1	116.5	112.8
1996	110.8	105.6	109.6	108.8	116.0	109.8
1997	109.1	101.3	108.5	108.3	113.1	108.2
1998	110.8	100.0	111.3	111.4	112.8	110.3
1999	110.2	104.6	110.6	110.7	110.6	110.1
2000	111.0	104.3	111.3	111.3	112.1	110.9
2001	112.0	105.7	112.9	113.1	112.0	111.7
2002	112.4	105.2	113.4	113.5	112.3	112.1
2003	114.5	102.4	116.5	117.3	113.3	113.7
2004	115.5	102.7	117.6	118.1	114.1	114.6
2005	115.1	105.0	116.3	116.5	114.8	113.6
2006	115.2	105.0	115.8	117.6	115.5	112.0
2007	115.6	103.5	116.2	117.3	116.0	112.6
2008	112.4	103.8	112.1	112.6	113.7	110.4
2009	111.7	104.7	110.8	110.4	114.1	110.5
2010	113.1	104.3	113.2	113.3	113.6	110.7
2011	112.2	103.9	112.2	112.6	112.8	109.8

4-3　地区生产总值指数（1978-2011年，1978=100）
GROSS DOMESTIC PRODUCT INDEX NUMBER（1978-2011，1978=100）

按可比价格计算　　Calculated by comparable price

年份 Year	地区生产总值 Gross Domestic Product	其中 of which 第一产业 Primary Industry	第二产业 Secondary Industry	其中 of which 工业 Industry	第三产业 Tertiary Industry	人均地区生产总值 Per Capita Gross Domestic Product
1978	100.0	100.0	100.0	100.0	100.0	100.0
1979	108.6	104.4	108.0	106.2	117.9	107.8
1980	121.8	101.7	125.7	125.4	135.8	120.0
1981	132.1	105.0	139.9	139.1	138.8	129.1
1982	137.5	119.2	144.0	141.6	137.3	133.1
1983	157.8	129.2	164.0	162.0	175.5	151.5
1984	199.7	169.2	197.9	196.7	256.2	190.4
1985	245.2	165.6	264.6	260.4	282.1	232.7
1986	259.7	170.9	278.9	270.3	311.7	244.8
1987	302.0	164.1	337.8	330.0	356.2	281.7
1988	334.0	163.6	384.7	374.9	370.9	307.9
1989	316.3	168.3	357.0	352.4	364.5	287.9
1990	341.3	166.3	395.6	393.3	369.3	306.6
1991	366.2	147.7	453.4	451.9	377.4	326.2
1992	493.7	159.4	618.8	616.4	568.4	437.2
1993	661.0	175.5	852.8	859.9	770.8	583.2
1994	770.7	200.4	957.6	969.1	1003.5	677.1
1995	875.6	219.6	1083.1	1096.0	1169.1	763.7
1996	970.1	231.9	1187.1	1192.5	1356.2	838.6
1997	1058.4	234.9	1288.0	1291.5	1533.9	907.4
1998	1172.7	234.9	1433.5	1438.7	1730.2	1000.8
1999	1292.3	245.7	1585.5	1592.6	1913.6	1101.9
2000	1434.5	256.3	1764.7	1772.6	2145.1	1222.0
2001	1606.6	270.9	1992.3	2004.8	2402.5	1365.0
2002	1805.8	285.0	2259.3	2275.4	2698.0	1530.2
2003	2067.6	291.8	2632.1	2669.0	3056.8	1739.8
2004	2388.1	299.7	3095.3	3152.1	3487.8	1993.8
2005	2748.7	314.7	3599.8	3672.2	4000.5	2265.0
2006	3166.5	330.4	4168.6	4267.1	4620.6	2536.8
2007	3660.5	342.0	4843.9	5005.3	5359.8	2856.4
2008	4114.4	356.4	5430.0	5636.0	6094.2	3153.5
2009	4595.8	373.1	6016.4	6227.8	6953.3	3484.6
2010	5197.8	389.1	6810.6	7056.1	7898.9	3857.5
2011	5832.0	404.3	7641.5	7945.2	8910.0	4235.5

4-4 历年地区生产总值构成
PROPORTIONS IN GROSS DOMESTIC PRODUCT OVER THE YEARS

单位：%

年 份 Year	地区生产总值 Gross Domestic Product	其中 of which 第一产业 Primary Industry	第二产业 Secondary Industry	其中 of which 工 业 Industry	建筑业 Construction	第三产业 Tertiary Industry
1949	100	69.8	12.8	12.5	0.3	17.4
1950	100	66.6	15.7	15.2	0.4	17.8
1951	100	62.7	17.1	16.5	0.6	20.2
1952	100	61.1	19.2	17.3	1.9	19.7
1953	100	57.4	21.8	20.6	1.2	20.8
1954	100	55.2	22.6	21.3	1.3	22.2
1955	100	56.0	19.8	18.3	1.5	24.2
1956	100	51.4	23.1	21.1	2.1	25.5
1957	100	49.3	27.7	25.7	2.1	23.0
1958	100	39.9	38.3	35.0	3.3	21.8
1959	100	31.1	45.6	42.4	3.2	23.3
1960	100	30.0	44.3	41.6	2.7	25.8
1961	100	35.6	36.7	35.1	1.6	27.7
1962	100	41.2	32.5	30.8	1.7	26.3
1963	100	45.3	31.2	29.4	1.8	23.5
1964	100	46.3	33.2	31.4	1.8	20.4
1965	100	46.5	34.3	32.6	1.6	19.2
1966	100	45.2	36.7	35.0	1.6	18.1
1967	100	48.7	32.1	30.4	1.7	19.2
1968	100	44.6	36.5	34.8	1.8	18.9
1969	100	40.5	41.2	39.5	1.7	18.3
1970	100	34.4	48.3	45.9	2.4	17.3
1971	100	34.5	49.9	47.4	2.5	15.6
1972	100	31.1	52.1	49.1	3.0	16.8
1973	100	28.9	55.2	51.5	3.7	16.0
1974	100	28.1	56.1	52.8	3.3	15.8
1975	100	23.6	59.7	56.6	3.2	16.6
1976	100	24.5	60.0	56.8	3.2	15.5
1977	100	19.7	64.5	61.1	3.4	15.8
1978	100	21.9	64.0	60.0	4.0	14.1
1979	100	24.7	60.7	55.7	5.0	14.6

4-4 续表 continued　　单位：%

年 份 Year	地区生产总值 Gross Domestic Product	其中 of which 第一产业 Primary Industry	第二产业 Secondary Industry	其中 of which 工业 Industry	建筑业 Construction	第三产业 Tertiary Industry
1980	100	21.5	62.7	58.5	4.2	15.8
1981	100	21.0	63.9	59.4	4.5	15.1
1982	100	24.1	61.6	56.5	5.1	14.3
1983	100	23.7	60.4	55.7	4.7	16.0
1984	100	25.2	56.5	52.4	4.1	18.4
1985	100	21.2	61.5	56.6	4.9	17.3
1986	100	21.5	59.9	54.3	5.6	18.6
1987	100	18.9	62.0	56.7	5.3	19.1
1988	100	18.7	61.6	56.2	5.4	19.7
1989	100	18.9	59.8	55.4	4.4	21.3
1990	100	18.6	61.1	57.0	4.1	20.3
1991	100	15.7	64.2	59.8	4.4	20.1
1992	100	13.2	64.4	59.5	4.9	22.4
1993	100	11.2	66.2	61.0	5.1	22.6
1994	100	10.7	63.8	59.1	4.7	25.5
1995	100	10.8	59.7	54.9	4.8	29.5
1996	100	10.6	57.2	51.9	5.3	32.3
1997	100	9.4	56.5	51.1	5.5	34.0
1998	100	8.8	55.7	50.1	5.6	35.5
1999	100	8.2	55.6	49.9	5.7	36.2
2000	100	7.5	56.1	50.3	5.8	36.4
2001	100	7.0	56.6	50.8	5.8	36.4
2002	100	6.4	56.8	51.0	5.8	36.8
2003	100	5.2	57.7	52.0	5.7	37.1
2004	100	4.7	58.8	53.1	5.7	36.5
2005	100	4.6	61.0	55.0	6.0	34.4
2006	100	4.2	60.2	55.2	5.0	35.6
2007	100	3.9	59.3	54.7	4.6	36.8
2008	100	3.7	58.1	53.4	4.7	38.2
2009	100	3.6	56.8	51.7	5.1	39.6
2010	100	3.3	55.3	50.3	5.0	41.4
2011	100	3.1	54.5	49.4	5.1	42.4

注：2000-2003年数据根据第一次经济普查结果进行了调整，2005-2007年数据根据第二次经济普查结果进行了调整。
Note: The data collected during 2000-2003 were adjusted according to the record of the first Economic Census; and the data collected during 2005-2007 were adjusted according to the record of the second Economic Census.

4-5 历年分地区人均生产总值
PER CAPITA OF GROSS DOMESTIC PRODUCT BY REGION OVER THE YEARS

单位：元（yuan）

年 份 Year	全 市 Whole Municipality	市 区 Urban Area	溧阳市 Liyang City	金坛市 Jintan City	年 份 Year	全 市 Whole Municipality	市 区 Urban Area	溧阳市 Liyang City	金坛市 Jintan City
1949	144	183	73	83	1981	832	1088	432	482
1950	163	208	89	84	1982	867	1120	454	545
1951	174	223	98	88	1983	985	1276	518	599
1952	190	238	117	105	1984	1272	1615	748	781
1953	206	262	114	116	1985	1620	2101	901	905
1954	198	252	112	110	1986	1775	2271	1007	1071
1955	196	249	115	109	1987	2134	2722	1231	1273
1956	213	279	118	98	1988	2606	3225	1597	1778
1957	205	264	119	106	1989	2732	3404	1618	1859
1958	243	321	135	103	1990	2935	3709	1662	1917
1959	253	342	128	87	1991	3136	4000	1740	1959
1960	291	400	123	96	1992	4404	5568	2499	2853
1961	211	289	80	92	1993	6806	8569	4075	4208
1962	212	285	90	106	1994	9532	11714	6121	6313
1963	219	283	120	116	1995	11117	13870	7912	7612
1964	229	290	126	147	1996	12847	15369	9294	9486
1965	264	343	139	151	1997	13892	16204	8174	8420
1966	283	373	140	155	1998	14842	16962	8869	9472
1967	256	323	143	173	1999	15834	18323	9431	10399
1968	247	327	124	138	2000	17635	20744	10344	11648
1969	279	375	133	147	2001	19704	23370	11563	13392
1970	308	429	126	147	2002	22215	26744	13005	15662
1971	358	485	198	153	2003	26149	31920	15415	18648
1972	397	529	245	165	2004	31665	38601	18968	22594
1973	441	583	264	205	2005	32116	34874	24456	27986
1974	445	604	239	188	2006	37809	40574	29658	33008
1975	462	645	221	166	2007	44452	46994	36039	38771
1976	504	696	261	181	2008	51746	53788	43186	43486
1977	535	739	273	189	2009	56890	60756	48488	47863
1978	605	810	309	305	2010	67327	71812	56784	56127
1979	689	914	334	395	2011	77485	81897	66934	65946
1980	771	1000	405	470					

注：1.2005年起人均地区生产总值按常住人口计算。
2.2000-2003年数据根据第一次经济普查结果进行了调整，2005-2007年数据根据第二次经济普查结果进行了调整。

Note: 1.Per capita regional GDP is calculated as per permanent population since 2005.
2.The data collected during 2000-2003 were adjusted according to the record of the first Economic Census; and the data collected during2005-2007 were adjusted according to the record of the second Economic Census.

4-6　分地区生产总值（2011 年）
GROSS DOMESTIC PRODUCT BY REGION（2011）

单位：亿元（100 million yuan）

指　标	Item	全　市 Whole Municipality	其中 of which 市　区 Urban Area	溧阳市 Liyang City	金坛市 Jintan City
地区生产总值	**Gross Domestic Product**	**3580.99**	**2715.04**	**503.78**	**365.10**
第一产业	Primary Industry	111.78	52.75	34.49	24.08
第二产业	Secondary Industry	1950.84	1517.84	283.92	203.94
工　业	Industry	1768.91	1418.92	257.58	180.56
建筑业	Construction	181.93	98.92	26.34	23.38
第三产业	Tertiary Industry	1518.37	1144.45	185.37	137.08
交通运输、仓储和邮政业	Transport ation、Storage and Post	126.66	97.76	36.85	24.79
信息传输、计算机服务和软件业	Information Transmission, Computer Servcie and Software Industries	46.42	32.61	3.75	4.60
批发和零售业	Retail and Wholesale Industries	389.04	323.87	40.77	21.73
住宿和餐饮业	Hoteling and Cateries	94.18	75.11	10.09	5.25
金融业	Financial	199.36	155.41	21.91	10.93
银行及其他金融活动	Banking and Other Financing Activities	191.58	148.83	21.56	9.67
保险业	Insurance	7.78	6.58	0.35	1.26
房地产业	Real Estate	197.23	146.95	23.60	10.22
房地产开发经营业	Real Estate Development Industry	107.72	96.20	12.87	3.42
物业管理、中介服务业和其他房地产	Property Management, Agency Service Industry and Other Real Estate	16.90	13.67	0.99	1.72
居民自有住房服务业	Resident Private House Service Industry	72.61	37.09	9.74	5.08
租赁和商务服务业	Leasehold and Business in Services	150.21	111.84	10.40	10.23
科学研究、技术服务和地质勘查业	Scientific Research, Technology Service and Geological Prospecting	20.82	16.49	1.02	2.76
水利、环境和公共设施管理业	Water Conservancy, Environment and Public Facility Management	32.99	12.34	1.87	16.33
居民服务和其他服务业	Community Service and Other Service	45.79	22.45	3.86	2.83
教　育	Education	73.62	51.21	8.79	8.57
卫生、社会保障和社会福利业	Health, Social Security and Welfare	31.69	24.85	3.08	4.01
文化、体育和娱乐业	Culture, Sports and Entertainment	25.56	15.87	4.89	4.44
公共管理和社会组织	Public Administration and Social Organizations	84.82	57.70	14.49	10.39

4-7 主要年份社会经济主要指标
MAJOR SOCIAL AND ECONOMIC INDICATORS IN MAIN YEARS

指 标	Item	1990	1995	2000	2005	2011
人口与就业	Population and Employment					
人 口	Population					
年末总人口（万人）	Year-end Population (10000 persons)	324.85	333.65	341.48	351.63	362.86
#非农业人口	Non-agricultural Population	81.40	120.48	147.81	160.56	186.02
就 业	Employment					
从业人员（万人）	Employment (10000 persons)	186.06	188.78	179.36	222.31	277.72
在岗职工人数（万人）	Number of Fully Employed Staff and Workers (10000 persons)	56.17	54.42	40.39	35.11	38.07
宏观经济	Macroeconomy					
国民经济核算	National Accounting					
地区生产总值（亿元）	Gross Domestic Products (100 million yuan)	94.87	369.70	600.66	1308.18	3580.99
第一产业	Primary Industry	17.68	39.82	45.14	59.62	111.78
第二产业	Secondary Industry	57.96	220.64	336.68	799.05	1950.84
#工　业	Industy	54.06	202.86	301.99	719.95	1768.91
第三产业	Tertiary Industry	19.23	109.24	218.83	449.51	1518.37
固定资产投资	Investment in Fixed Assets					
全社会固定资产投资完成额（亿元）	Total Investment in Fixed Assets (100 million yuan)	22.71	115.06	163.43	769.80	2338.94
城镇投资	Urban Investment		47.80	103.76	534.70	1723.36
#房地产开发	Real Estate Investment		18.47	29.98	114.27	565.91
农村投资	Rural Investment		39.61	34.23	235.10	615.58
财 政	Government Finance					
财政总收入（亿元）	Financial Revenue (100 million yuan)	13.10	28.50	60.23	220.45	977.79
#地方财政收入	Local Revenue		13.49	32.92	138.26	733.59
地方财政支出（亿元）	Local Expenditure (100 million yuan)	5.11	13.33	32.50	140.28	743.08
吸收外资	Forign Capital Inducement					
协议外商直接投资项目（个）	Number of Newly Signed Foreign Capital Agreement Contract (piece)	40	292	167	509	308
协议外商直接投资（亿美元）	Amount of Newly Signed Foreign Capital Agreement Contract (USD 100 million)	0.18	8.87	10.03	28.51	46.32
实际外商直接投资（亿美元）	Amount of Foreign Capital Actually Utilized（USD 100 million）	0.07	3.29	7.00	7.31	30.52

4-7 续表1 continued 1

指 标	Item	1990	1995	2000	2005	2011
产 业	**Industries**					
农 业	**Agriculture**					
耕地面积（千公顷）	Cultivated Areas (1000 hectares)	204.54	200.88	204.25	176.32	150.00
从业人员（万人）	Employment (10000 persons)	135.80	136.31	128.67	126.86	132.81
农林牧渔业总产值（亿元）	Gross Output Value of Agriculture (100 million yuan)	29.06	74.74	85.88	104.10	194.68
主要农副产品产量	Output of Major Farm and Sideline Products					
粮　食（万吨）	Grain (10000 tons)	164.50	159.57	136.22	98.06	115.19
油　料（吨）	Oil-Bearing Crop (ton)	63899	72786	91629	85960	32048
水产品（吨）	Aquatic Products (ton)	53149	90571	111188	130198	164421
蚕　茧（吨）	Silkworm Cocoons (ton)	8726	10055	4815	2843	544
水　果（吨）	Fruits (ton)	9670	22716	29639	67275	92918
茶　叶（吨）	Tea (ton)	3730	2550	2680	2762	3449
工 业	**Industry**					
规模以上工业企业主要经济指标	Major Economy Indictors of Industrial Enterprises above Designated Size					
工业总产值（亿元）	Gross Output Value of Industry (100 million yuan)	196.20	579.62	874.63	2504.19	8270.77
固定资产原价（亿元）	Original Value of Fixed Assets (100 million yuan)	80.42	252.19	395.90	796.70	2485.28
主营业务收入（亿元）	Main Business Income (100 million yuan)	160.85	542.82	836.10	2459.56	8212.53
实现利税（亿元）	Total Pre-tax Profits(100 million yuan)	13.21	34.65	59.64	161.84	713.30
建筑业	**Construction**					
建筑业企业施工产值（亿元）	Output Value of Construction Enterprises (100 million yuan)	8.64	30.93	123.18	283.48	883.87
房屋竣工建筑面积（万平方米）	Floor Space of Buildings Completed (10000 sq.m)	193.97	194.70	630.28	1588.83	2831.52
交通运输、邮电通信	**Transportation,Post and Telecommunications**					
货物运输量（万吨）	Freight Traffic (10000 tons)	4375	5804	4696	6032	15644
旅客发送量（万人次）	Number of Passenger Despatched (10000 person-times)	5048	7270	10196	15235	15845
邮电业务收入（亿元）	Total Busines Volume of Post and Telecommunications (100 million yuan)	0.65	5.46	16.84	34.36	59.95
年末固定电话用户（万户）	Number of Fixed Telephone Subscribers at Year-end (10000 Subscribers)	15.57	19.79	75.88	202.08	158.75

4-7 续表 2 continued 2

指 标	Item	1990	1995	2000	2005	2011
年末移动电话用户（万户）	Number of Mobile Telephone Subscribers at Year-end (10000 Subscribers)		1.80	56.68	207.46	560.46
电话交换机容量（万门）	Capacity of Telephone Exchanges (10000 line)	5.16	29.79	118.30	160.33	309.96
国内商业	**Domestic Trade**					
社会消费品零售总额（亿元）	Total Retail Sales of Consumer Goods (100 million yuan)	38.19	131.78	202.31	444.94	1236.10
对外经济贸易	**Foreign Trade**					
进出口总额（亿美元）	Total Exports and Imports (USD 100 million)	0.62	9.93	28.22	83.34	286.35
进 口	Imports	0.12	2.24	9.62	22.09	92.74
出 口	Exports	0.50	7.69	18.60	61.24	193.61
国际旅游	**International Tourism**					
来常旅游人数（万人次）	Number of Tourists from Abroad (10000 person-times)	0.70	1.95	3.31	18.20	41.31
旅游外汇收入（亿美元）	Foreign Exchange Earnings from Tourism (USD 100 million)		0.10	0.24	1.44	4.21
金融保险	**Banking & Insurance**					
金融机构存款余额（亿元）	Deposit Balance of Financial Institutions (100 million yuan)	59.37	257.61	629.36	1649.61	4902.15
金融机构贷款余额（亿元）	Loans Balance of Financial Institutions (100 million. yuan)	74.24	211.88	389.26	1113.25	3406.35
保险费收入（亿元）	Income From Insurances (100 million yuan)	1.00	4.44	12.10	37.88	99.28
保险赔（结）款支出（亿元）	Expenditure for Insurance Claims (100 million yuan)	0.25	1.28	3.59	10.42	16.57
教育、科技	**Education,Science and Technology**					
教 育	**Education**					
专任教师数（万人）	Full-time Teachers (10000 persons)	2.52	2.74	2.82	3.16	3.43
#普通高等学校	Institutions of Higher Education	0.07	0.10	0.12	0.45	0.53
普通中学	Regular Secondary Schools	0.91	0.96	1.04	1.29	1.38
小 学	Primary Schools	1.31	1.36	1.30	1.14	1.19
在校学生数（万人）	Students Enrollment (10000 persons)	46.10	50.19	57.10	64.88	60.04
#普通高等学校	Institutions of Higher Education	0.51	1.16	2.00	9.54	12.39
普通中学	Regular Secondary Schools	14.90	15.86	18.23	22.07	17.76
小 学	Primary Schools	27.70	27.16	30.01	24.46	22.90

4-7 续表3 continued 3

指 标	Item	1990	1995	2000	2005	2011
科 技	**Science and Technology**					
专利申请量（项）	Number of Patent Applications Examined (unit)		547	837	2696	23413
专利授权量（项）	Number of Patent Authorizations Granted (unit)		255	731	1240	11390
家庭、生活、环境	**Family, Livelihood and Environment**					
家 庭	**Family**					
家庭总户数（万户）	Total Number of Household (10000 households)	106.91	114.00	117.89	121.97	128.10
平均每户家庭人口（人）	Average Number of Household Size (person)	3.04	2.93	2.90	2.88	2.83
婚 姻	**Marriages and Divorces**					
准予登记结婚（对）	Marriage Leagally Registered (couple)	24093	31889	23916	26536	38945
准予登记离婚数（对）	Divorce Leagally Registered (couple)	604	1399	2203	5001	8186
住 宅	**Housing**					
农村居民人均住房面积（平方米）	Per Capita Living Space Of Rural Residents (sq.m)	31.66	35.90	49.27	56.20	61.52
生 活	**People's Livelihood**					
农村居民人均纯收入（元）	Per Capita Net Income Of Rural Residents (yuan)	1401	3397	4430	7002	14838
农村居民人均生活消费支出（元）	Per Capita Living Expenditure of Rural Residents (yuan)	1231	2952	3243	5712	11208
城乡居民储蓄存款余额（亿元）	Balance of Saving Deposits in Urban and Rural Residents (100 million yuan)	34.29	128.65	355.57	865.39	2157.39
工 资	**Wages**					
在岗职工工资总额（亿元）	Total Wages of Fully Employde Staff and Workers (100 million yuan)	12.90	38.68	48.97	78.57	227.13
卫 生	**Health Care**					
医 院（包括卫生院，个）	Hospitals (include Township Hospitals,unit)	163	161	117	113	92
医 生（人）	Doctors (person)	6144	7073	7779	8356	10376
医院床位数（包括卫生院，张）	Number of Hospital Beds (include Township Hospitals,unit)	9495	10339	10730	11734	15039
火灾、交通事故	**Fire Loss and Road Accidents**					
火灾发生数（起）	Number of Fire Disasters (time)	262	229	1371	2209	396
火灾损失额（万元）	Fire Loss (10000 yuan)	140	430	507	460	658
道路交通事故发生数（起）	Number of Road Accidents (time)	1163	1425	3405	2993	1348
道路交通事故损失额（万元）	Loss of Road Accidents (10000 yuan)	144	765	1301	770	303

4-8 主要年份市区社会经济主要指标
MAJOR SOCIAL AND ECONOMIC INDICATORS OF URBAN DISTRICTS IN MAIN YEARS

指 标	Item	1990	1995	2000	2005	2011
人口与就业	**Population and Employment**					
人 口	**Population**					
年末总人口（万人）	Year-end Population (10000 persons)	195.24	202.20	208.18	220.76	228.98
#非农业人口	Non-agricultural Population	64.74	84.50	104.39	110.38	124.74
就 业	**Employment**					
从业人员（万人）	Employment (10000 persons)	117.84	118.01	111.55	148.55	193.55
在岗职工人（万人）	Number of Fully Employed Staff and Workers (10000 persons)	45.19	42.44	29.90	25.36	27.50
宏观经济	**Macroeconomy**					
国民经济核算	**National Accounting**					
地区生产总值（亿元）	Gross Domestic Products (100 million yuan)	72.06	279.19	430.89	981.45	2715.04
第一产业	Primary Industry	9.07	20.95	22.75	27.03	52.75
第二产业	Secondary Industry	48.54	179.22	256.10	620.51	1517.84
#工 业	Industy	45.91	170.20	239.46	571.46	1418.92
第三产业	Tertiary Industry	14.44	79.02	152.04	333.91	1144.45
固定资产投资	**Investment in Fixed Assets**					
全社会固定资产投资完成额（亿元）	Total Investment in Fixed Assets (100 million yuan)	17.09	85.23	126.90	609.75	1821.18
城镇投资	Urban Investment		38.81	67.81	450.31	1385.72
#房地产开发	Real Estate Investment	0.78	14.62	25.46	97.76	506.69
农村投资	Rural Investment		8.12	9.97	159.44	435.46
财 政	**Government Finance**					
财政总收入（亿元）	Financial Revenue (100 million yuan)	11.66	23.99	50.77	182.12	810.28
#地方财政收入	Local Revenue		11.19	27.60	113.29	610.98
地方财政支出	Local Expenditure	3.87	10.16	25.98	112.69	605.04
#用于教育	Education Expenditure	0.66	2.00	4.05	9.55	39.95
价 格	**Price**					
居民消费价格指数（上年=100）	Consumer Price Index (preceding year=100)	104.2	114.9	99.5	102.8	105.0
商品零售价格指数（上年=100）	Retail Price Index (preceding year=100)	103.4	112.8	98.0	101.3	104.4

注：本表资料1990、1995、2000年数据除城市建设外均按新行政区划作了调整，2005年起均为新行政区划数据。
Note: The data of 1990, 1995 and 2000 in this table had been adjusted according to the new administrative division, except those of urban construction. The data are all under new administrative division since 2005.

4-8 续表 1 continued 1

指　标	Item	1990	1995	2000	2005	2011
吸收外资	**Forign Capital Inducement**					
协议外商直接投资项目（个）	Number of Newly Signed ForeignCapital Agreement Contract (piece)	39	243	132	355	219
协议外商直接投资（亿美元）	Amount of Newly Signed Foreign Capital Agreement Contract (USD 100 million)	0.15	7.05	4.78	20.33	33.20
产　业	**Industries**					
农　业	**Agriculture**					
耕地面积（千公顷）	Cultivated Areas (1000 hectares)	97.01	94.80	88.75	64.27	58.60
从业人员（万人）	Employment (10000 persons)	76.65	75.96	71.22	75.19	80.38
农林牧渔业总产值（亿元）	Gross Output Value of Agriculture (100 million yuan)	15.48	39.34	43.81	47.90	86.69
主要农副产品产量	Output of Major Farm and Sideline Products					
粮　食（万吨）	Grain (10000 tons)	89.07	81.30	66.11	39.28	32.34
油　料（吨）	Oil-Bearing Crop (ton)	11710	12068	17412	8489	3138
水产品（吨）	Aquatic Products (ton)	16049	45321	35588	57173	63420
水　果（吨）	Fruits (ton)	6038	18527	21811	49747	53783
工　业	**Industry**					
规模以上工业企业主要经济指标	Major Economy Indictors of Industrial Enterprises above Designated Size					
工业总产值（亿元）	Gross Output Value of Industry (100 million yuan)	163.78	474.76	730.74	2032.39	6446.64
固定资产原价（亿元）	Original Value of Fixed Assets (100 million yuan)	69.40	215.79	339.76	660.42	2036.72
主营业务收入（亿元）	Main Business Income (100 million yuan)	136.76	446.40	704.23	2016.20	6400.71
实现利税（亿元）	Total Pre-tax Profits (100 million yuan)	11.67	28.13	50.94	119.96	519.38
建筑业	**Construction**					
建筑业企业施工产值（亿元）	Output Value of Construction Enterprises (100 million yuan)			46.65	154.51	400.79
房屋竣工建筑面积（万平方米）	Floor Space of Buildings Completed (10000 sq.m)		80.50	320.17	830.89	1216.01
交通运输、邮电通信	**Transportation,Post and Telecommunications**					
货物运输量（万吨）	Freight Traffic (10000 tons)	2349	4483	3100	3857	10668
旅客发送量（万人次）	Number of Passenger Despatched (10000 person-times)	2849	4383	6924	10308	11360
邮电业务收入（亿元）	Total Busines Volume of Post and Telecommunications (100 million yuan)	0.55	4.42	14.11	27.74	47.69
年末固定电话用户（万户）	Number of Fixed Telephone Subscribers at Year-end (10000 Subscribers)	2.46	11.68	53.43	145.97	114.24
年末移动电话用户（万户）	Number of Mobile Telephone Subscribers at Year-end (10000 Subscribers)		1.35	46.96	162.58	423.80
电话交换机容量（万门）	Capacity of Telephone Exchanges (10000 line)	4.23	21.53	82.45	114.35	225.34

4-8 续表 2 continued 2

	指 标 Item	1990	1995	2000	2005	2011
国内商业	**Domestic Trade**					
社会消费品零售总额（亿元）	Total Retail Sales of Consumer Goods (100 million yuan)	26.21	84.99	133.88	329.21	926.23
对外经济贸易	**Foreign Trade**					
进出口总额（亿美元）	Total Exports and Imports (USD 100 million)	0.61	9.43	25.15	76.03	255.72
进　口	Imports	0.11	2.22	8.81	21.11	87.17
出　口	Exports	0.50	7.21	16.34	54.92	168.55
国际旅游	**International Tourism**					
来常旅游人数（万人次）	Number of Tourists from Abroad (10000 person-times)	0.65	1.90	3.11	17.28	39.48
旅游外汇收入（亿美元）	Foreign Exchange Earnings from Tourism (USD 100 million)		0.09	0.23	1.38	4.02
金融保险	**Banking & Insurance**					
金融机构存款余额（亿元）	Deposit Balance of Financial Institutions (100 million yuan)	46.24	205.93	511.00	1375.25	4024.70
金融机构贷款余额（亿元）	Loans Balance of Financial Institutions (100 million yuan)	58.52	170.12	324.19	966.84	2817.27
保险费收入（亿元）	Income From Insurances (100 million yuan)	0.84	4.38	10.27	30.54	83.33
保险赔（结）款支出（亿元）	Expenditure for Insurance Claims (100 million yuan)	0.19	1.16	3.04	8.97	13.54
教育、科技	**Education,Science and Technology**					
教　育	**Education**					
专任教师数（万人）	Full-time Teachers (10000 persons)	1.59	1.76	1.82	2.15	2.42
# 普通高等学校	Institutions of Higher Education	0.07	0.10	0.12	0.45	0.53
普通中学	Regular Secondary Schools	0.56	0.60	0.64	0.79	0.86
小　学	Primary Schools	0.75	0.78	0.75	0.71	0.78
在校学生数（万人）	Students Enrollment (10000 persons)	28.82	15.94	37.33	46.45	46.47
# 普通高等学校	Institutions of Higher Education	0.51	1.16	2.00	9.54	12.33
普通中学	Regular Secondary Schools	9.17	9.84	11.11	13.52	11.92
小　学	Primary Schools	16.46	15.95	17.69	15.95	16.63
科　技	**Science and Technology**					
专利申请量（项）	Number of Patent Applications Examined (unit)				1976	17573
专利授权量（项）	Number of Patent Authorizations Granted (unit)				1021	8884
家庭、生活、环境	**Family, Livelihood and Environment**					
家　庭	**Family**					
家庭总户数（万户）	Total Number of Household (10000 households)	63.65	67.67	70.77	74.36	80.53
平均每户家庭人口（人）	Average Number of Household Size (person)	3.07	2.98	2.94	2.97	2.83

4-8 续表 3 continued 3

指 标	Item	1990	1995	2000	2005	2011
婚　姻	**Marriages and Divorces**					
准予登记结婚（对）	Marriage Leagally Registered (couple)	11058	19048	14848	17002	24003
准予登记离婚数（对）	Divorce Leagally Registered (couple)	496	1165	1280	3494	5266
住　宅	**Housing**					
城市居民人均使用面积（平方米）	Per Capita Usable Floor Space ofUrban Residents (sq.m)	13.22	15.04	15.19	21.04	26.11
生　活	**People's Livelihood**					
市区居民人均可支配收入（元）	Per Capita Disposable Income Of Urban Residents (yuan)	1769	5632	8540	14589	29829
市区居民人均生活消费支出（元）	Per Capita Living Expenditure of Urban Residents (yuan)	1498	4426	6759	10718	18893
城乡居民储蓄存款余额（亿元）	Balance of Saving Deposits in Urban and Rural Residents (100 million yuan)	25.45	96.92	268.11	671.82	1674.01
工　资	**Wages**					
在岗职工工资总额（亿元）	Total Wages of Fully Employed Staff (100 million yuan)	10.82	31.91	38.59	60.26	183.70
卫　生	**Health Care**					
医　院（包括卫生院，个）	Hospitals (include Township Hospitals,unit)	90	91	64	61	47
医　生（人）	Doctors (person)	4636	5146	5616	4751	7167
医院床位数（包括卫生院，张）	Number of Hospital Beds (include Township Hospitals,unit)	6506	7236	7774	8467	11136
城市建设	**Urban construction**					
自来水供水量（万吨）	Annual Consumption of Tap Water (100 million tons)	25994	11257	16631	32384	21664
城市排水管道长度（公里）	Length of Sewer Piplelines of Urban Districts (km)	231	698	929	2918	3807
用电量（万千瓦时）	Electric Power Consumption (10000 kw/h)	147215	224394	327410	1432121	2408214
城市煤气供应量（万立方米）	Goal Gas Supply of Urban Districts (10000 m3)	1601	1783	4256	8030	60537
年末出租车运营数（辆）	Number of Operating Taxi at Year-end (coach)	137	592	1443	1842	2542
年末运营公交车辆数（辆）	Number of Public Transit Vehicles at Year-end (coach)	232	307	1572	2105	2600
铺装道路长度（公里）	Length of Paved Roads(km)	336	483	697	3584	1811
公园绿地面积（公顷）	Green Space of Park(hectare)	121	283	458	1568	1704
火灾、交通事故	**Fire Loss and Road Accidents**					
火灾发生数（起）	Number of Fire Disasters (time)	162	139	1119	1605	299
火灾损失额（万元）	Fire Loss (10000 yuan)	93	317	370	383	458
道路交通事故发生数（起）	Number of Road Accidents (time)	702	925	2339	2074	990
道路交通事故损失额（万元）	Loss of Road Accidents (10000 yuan)	92	557	868	506	161

4-9 主要年份社会经济主要指标增长速度
GROWTH RATE OF MAJOR SOCIAL AND ECONOMIC INDICATORS IN MAIN YEARS

单位：%

指 标	Item	2011年比下列各年增长 Growth Rates of 2011 over Following Years			
		1978	1990	2000	2010
人口与就业	**Population and Employment**				
年末总人口	Total Population at year-end	24.7	11.7	6.3	0.6
从业人员	Number of Employed Persons	86.0	49.3	54.8	2.1
在岗职工人	Number of Fully Employed Staff and Workers	3.9	-32.2	-5.7	3.7
宏观经济	**Macroeconomy**				
地区生产总值	Gross Domestic Product	57.3倍	16.1倍	3.1倍	12.2
第一产业	Primary Industry	3.0倍	1.4倍	57.7	3.9
第二产业	Secondary Industry	75.4倍	18.3倍	3.3倍	12.2
#工 业	Industry	78.5倍	19.2倍	3.5倍	12.6
第三产业	Tertiary Industry	88.1倍	23.1倍	3.2倍	12.8
全社会固定资产投资完成额	Total Investment in Fixed Assets	2641.3倍	102.0倍	3.1倍	20.0
财政总收入	Total Financial Revenue	156.5倍	73.6倍	15.2倍	16.2
#地方一般预算收入	Local Government Budgetary Revenue			9.9倍	22.6
地方财政支出	Local Expenditure	798.0倍	144.4倍	21.9倍	16.4
协议外商直接投资项目	Number of Newly Signed Foreign Capital Agreement Contract		670.0	84.4	-5.8
协议外商直接投资	Amount of Newly Signed Foreign Capital Agreement Contract		256.3倍	3.6倍	-2.3
实际外商直接投资	Amount of Foreign Capital Actually Utilized		435.0倍	3.4倍	14.3
产 业	**Industries**				
农林牧渔业总产值	Gross Output Value of Agriculture	27.0倍	5.7倍	1.3倍	11.8
邮电业务收入	Total Busines Volume of Post and Tele- communications		91.4倍	2.6倍	7.6
社会消费品零售总额	Total Retail Sales of Consumer Goods	255.3倍	31.4倍	5.1倍	17.3
进出口总额	Total Exports and Imports		464.4倍	9.1倍	28.5
进 口	Imports		784.9倍	8.6倍	38.0
出 口	Exports		386.2倍	9.4倍	24.4

注：地区生产总值按可比价计算。
Note:GDP can be calculated by comparable price.

4-9 续表 continued　　　　单位：%

指　标	Item	2011年比下列各年增长 Growth Rates of 2011 over Following Years			
		1978	1990	2000	2010
来常旅游人数	Number of Tourists from Abroad			6.9倍	19.8
旅游外汇收入	Foreign Exchange Earnings from Tourism			16.5倍	21.4
金融机构存款余额	Deposit Balance of Financial Institutions	1436.6倍	81.6倍	6.8倍	7.7
# 储蓄存款	Savings Deposits	2995.4倍	61.9倍	5.1倍	7.4
金融机构贷款余额	Loans Balance of Financial Institutions	370.1倍	44.9倍	7.8倍	13.1
保费收入	Income From Insurances		98.3倍	7.2倍	14.7
赔款支出	Expenditure for Insurance Claims		65.3倍	3.6倍	-11.7
教育、科技	**Education,Science and Technology**				
在校学生数	Students Enrollment	0.3	30.2	5.2	-0.6
# 普通高等学校	Institutions of Higher Education	284.6倍	23.4倍	5.2倍	0.9
普通中学	Regular Secondary Schools	-17.6	19.2	-2.6	-5.7
小　学	Primary Schools	-39.6	-17.3	-23.7	3.4
专利申请量	Number of Patent Applications Examined			27.0倍	47.5
专利授权量	Number of Patent Authorizations Granted			14.6倍	25.3
家庭、生活、环境	**Family,Livelihood and Environment**				
市区居民人均可支配收入	Per Capita Net Income of Urban Residents		15.9倍	2.5倍	13.6
市区居民人均生活消费支出	Per Capita Living Expenditure of Urban Residents		11.6倍	1.8倍	10.3
医　生	Doctors	2.4倍	68.9	33.4	4.2
医院、卫生院床位数	Number of Hospital Beds	1.2倍	61.2	42.7	0.3
自来水供水量	Annual Volume of Tap Water Supply	5.3	-16.7	30.3	-1.4
城市排水管道长度	Length of Sewer Piplelines of Urban Districts		15.5倍	3.1倍	5.0
用电量	Electric Power Consumption		10.3倍	3.5倍	13.9
城市煤气供应量	Goal Gas Supply of Urban Districts		36.8倍	13.2倍	2.4

4-10 主要时期社会经济主要指标平均增长率
AVERAGE GROWTH RATE OF MAJOR SOCIAL AND ECONOMIC INDICATORS OF MAIN PERIOD

单位：%

指 标	Item	"九五" 时期 "Ninth Five-Year Plan" Period	"十五" 时期 "Tenth Five-Year Plan" Period	"十一五" 时期 "Eleventh Five-Year Plan" Period	1979～2011
年末总人口	Year-end Population	0.5	0.6	0.5	0.7
从业人员	Number of Employed Persons	-1.0	3.3	4.1	1.9
在岗职工人数	Number of Fully Employed Staff and Workers	-5.8	-2.8	0.9	0.1
地区生产总值	Gross Domestic Product	10.4	13.9	13.6	13.1
第一产业	Primary Industry	3.1	4.2	4.3	4.3
第二产业	Secondary Industry	10.3	15.3	13.6	14.0
第三产业	Tertiary Industry	12.9	13.3	14.6	14.6
全社会固定资产投资完成额	Financial in Fixed Assets	7.3	36.3	22.3	27.0
财政总收入	Total Government Revenue	16.1	29.6	30.7	16.6
地方财政支出	Local Expenditure	19.5	34.0	35.4	22.4
协议外商直接投资项目	Number of Newly Signed Foreign Capital Agreement Contract	-10.6	25.0	-8.5	
协议外商直接投资	Amount of Newly Signed Foreign Capital Agreement Contract	-13.0	36.9	10.7	
实际外商直接投资	Amount of Foreign Capital Actually Utilized	16.4	5.5	29.6	
农林牧渔业总产值	Total Output value of Farming,Forestry,Animal Husbandry and Fishing	2.8	3.9	10.8	10.6
规模以上工业总产值	Total Output Value of Industry above Designated Size	8.6	23.4	24.2	
货物运输量	Freight Traffic	-4.1	5.1	16.8	
旅客发送量	Number of Passenger Despatched	7.0	8.4	13.9	
邮电业务收入	Total Busines Volume of Post and Telecommunications	25.3	15.3	10.1	
社会消费品零售总额	Total Retail Sales of Consumer Goods	9.0	17.0	18.8	18.3
进出口总额	Total Exports and Imports	23.2	24.2	21.7	
进 口	Imports	33.8	18.1	24.9	
出 口	Exports	19.3	26.9	20.5	
市区居民人均可支配收入	Per Capita Dispoable Income of Urban Household	8.7	11.3	12.5	
市区居民人均消费性支出	Per Capita Living Expenditures of Urban Household	8.8	9.7	9.8	
农村居民人均纯收入	Per Capita Net Income of Rural Residents	5.5	9.6	12.5	
农村居民人均生活消费支出	Per Capita Living Expenditure of RuralResidents	1.9	12.0	11.7	
在岗职工年平均工资	Average Annual Wages of Fully Employed Staff and Workers	10.2	14.8	14.0	14.7
平均每人储蓄存款余额	Per Capita Balance of Savings Deposits	22.0	18.8	17.7	26.6
医 生	Doctors	1.9	1.4	3.6	3.8
在校学生数	Students Enrollment	2.6	2.6	-1.4	0.0
# 高等学校	Institutions of Higher Education	11.4	36.7	5.2	18.7

4-11 主要年份社会经济发展结构指标
STRUCTURAL INDICATORS ON ECONOMIC AND SOCIAL DEVELOPMENT IN MAIN YEARS

单位：%

指 标	Item	1990	1995	2000	2005	2011
人 口	**Population**					
农业非农业结构	Agricultural and Non-agricultural Structure	100.0	100.0	100.0	100.0	100.0
农 业	Agriculture	74.9	63.9	56.7	54.3	48.7
非农业	Non-agricultural	25.1	36.1	43.3	45.7	51.3
性别结构	Sexual Structure	100.0	100.0	100.0	100.0	100.0
男	Male	51.5	51.4	50.8	50.5	49.8
女	Female	48.5	48.6	49.2	49.5	50.2
就 业	**Employment**					
从业人员产业结构	Industrial Structure	100.0	100.0	100.0	100.0	100.0
第一产业	Primary Industry	35.9	29.4	28.9	13.5	8.0
第二产业	Secondary Industry	45.6	47.3	43.6	53.4	55.2
第三产业	Tertiary Industry	18.5	23.3	27.5	33.1	36.8
国民经济核算	**National Accounting**					
地区生产总值产业结构	Industrial Structure	100.0	100.0	100.0	100.0	100.0
第一产业	Primary Industry	18.6	10.8	7.5	4.3	3.1
第二产业	Secondary Industry	61.1	59.7	56.1	61.1	54.5
第三产业	Tertiary Industry	20.3	29.5	36.4	34.6	42.4
固定资产投资	**Investment in Fixed Assets**					
全社会固定资产投资结构	Investment Structure of Fixed Assets		100.0	100.0	100.0	100.0
# 城镇投资	Urban Investment		41.5	63.5	69.5	73.7
房地产开发	Real Estate Development		16.1	18.3	14.8	24.2
财 政	**Government Finance**					
地方一般预算收入结构	Structure of Local Government Budgetary Revenue			100.0	100.0	100.0
# 税收收入	Income from Taxes			92.1	84.1	80.0
吸收外资	**Utilization of Foreign Capital**					
实际吸收外资结构	Structure of Foreign Capital Actually Utilized		100.0	100.0	100.0	100.0
合资企业	Joint-ventures		86.4	51.5	22.1	25.2
合作企业	Cooperative Enterprises		4.2	9.1	4.0	0.2
独资企业	Foreign Funded Enterprises		9.4	39.4	73.9	74.6
农 业	**Agriculture**					
农林牧渔业总产值结构	Structure of Gross Agricultural Output Value	100.0	100.0	100.0	100.0	100.0
农 业	Planting	61.9	59.7	59.8	48.2	55.4
林 业	Forestry	0.6	0.7	1.0	1.2	0.7

4-11 续表 1 continued 1

单位：%

指 标	Item	1990	1995	2000	2005	2011
牧 业	Animal Husbandry	28.5	23.4	15.1	18.0	16.5
渔 业	Fishery	8.9	16.1	24.1	27.9	22.9
农林牧渔服务业	Service Industry for Planting, Forestry, Animal Husbandry and Fishery				4.7	4.5
工 业	**Industry**					
工业总产值结构	Structure of Gross Industrial Output Value	100.0	100.0	100.0	100.0	100.0
轻工业	Light Industry	49.5	40.0	41.4	34.9	18.7
重工业	Heavy Industry	50.5	60.0	58.6	65.1	81.3
建筑业	**Construction**					
建筑业企业总产值结构	Structure of Total Output Value of Construction Enterprises		100.0	100.0	100.0	100.0
# 房屋土木工程建筑业	Building and Civil Engineering Construction		78.6	75.1	79.7	80.8
建筑安装业	Installation		11.7	13.8	11.2	11.1
建筑装饰业	Decoration		9.6	11.1	5.2	6.8
运输业	**Transportation**					
货运量结构	Structure of Freight Traffic	100.0	100.0	100.0	100.0	100.0
铁 路	Railways	2.9	3.2	4.7	4.9	1.2
公 路	Highways	67.3	61.2	71.0	82.1	89.1
水 运	Waterway	29.9	35.6	24.2	13.0	9.7
民用航空	Civil Aviation	…	…	…	…	…
国内商业	**Domestic Trade**					
社会消费品零售总额结构	Total Retail Sale of Consumer Goods		100.0	100.0	100.0	100.0
市的零售额	Retail Prices of Urban Districts		62.2	67.6	89.7	93.4
县以下零售额	Retail Prices of County Level and Below		37.8	32.4	10.3	6.6
对外经济贸易	**Foreign Trade**					
进出口结构	Structure of Imports and Exports	100.0	100.0	100.0	100.0	100.0
出 口	Exports	80.8	77.5	65.9	73.5	67.6
进 口	Imports	19.2	22.5	34.1	26.5	32.4
国际旅游	**International Tourism**					
来常旅游人数结构	Structure of Foreign Tourists	100.0	100.0	100.0	100.0	100.0
外国人	Foreigners	47.1	61.9	66.8	73.4	87.1
港澳台同胞	Compartiots from Hongkong, Macao,Taiwan	52.9	38.1	33.2	26.6	12.9
金 融	**Banking**					
金融机构存款结构	Structure of Savings Deposits in Banking Institutions	100.0	100.0	100.0	100.0	100.0
# 企业存款	Deposits of Enterprises	23.5	33.7	33.4	28.7	53.2
储蓄存款	Savings Deposits	57.8	49.9	56.5	52.5	44.0

4-11 续表2 continued 2

单位：%

指 标	Item	1990	1995	2000	2005	2011
金融机构贷款结构	Structure Loans in Banking Institutions		100.0	100.0	100.0	100.0
#短期贷款	Short-term Loans		74.3	82.0	63.7	54.0
中长期贷款	Medium-term and Long-term Loans		11.8	8.5	26.0	43.5
教 育	**Education**					
在校学生结构	Structure of Student Enrollment	100.0	100.0	100.0	100.0	100.0
#大学生	College and University Students	1.1	2.3	3.5	14.7	20.6
中学生	Secondary School Students	32.3	31.6	31.9	34.0	29.6
小学生	Primary School Students	60.1	54.1	52.6	37.7	38.1
专任教师结构	Full-time Teachers by Type	100.0	100.0	100.0	100.0	100.0
#高等教育	Higher Education	2.8	3.5	4.4	14.3	15.3
普通中学	Regular Secondary Schools	35.9	35.2	36.7	40.8	40.3
小 学	Primary Schools	51.9	49.6	46.0	36.2	34.6
生 活	**Livelihood**					
市区居民消费结构	Consumption Structure of Urban Residents	100.0	100.0	100.0	100.0	100.0
食品类	Food	61.6	54.9	40.1	35.9	35.8
衣着类	Clothing	11.1	10.4	7.9	9.7	9.3
家庭设备、用品及服务	Household Appliances	5.0	5.7	10.5	6.5	6.9
医疗保健	Health Care	1.5	1.4	6.1	7.6	7.5
交通和通信	Transportation and Communication	3.0	4.7	5.9	12.2	15.7
娱乐、教育、文化服务	Recreational,Educational and Cultural Services	6.7	9.7	12.2	13.8	15.7
居 住	Housing	7.5	8.6	11.0	9.9	6.6
杂项商品和服务	Miscellaneous Commodities and Services	3.6	4.6	6.3	4.3	2.7
农村居民消费结构	Consumption Structure of Rural Residents		100.0	100.0	100.0	100.0
食品类	Food		49.9	43.1	39.8	35.5
衣着类	Clothing		7.1	5.5	6.5	7.1
居 住	Housing		15.8	17.8	14.0	12.0
家庭设备、用品及服务	Household Appliances		8.5	5.1	6.1	6.2
医疗保健	Health Care		2.0	5.5	6.6	8.0
交通和通信	Transportation and Communication		1.8	8.1	11.6	12.6
文教娱乐用品及服务	Recreational,Educational and Cultural Services		12.4	11.8	13.1	16.1
其他商品和服务	Other Commodities and Services		2.5	3.1	2.4	2.5
卫 生	**Public Health**					
卫生机构数结构	Number of Health Institutions	100.0	100.0	100.0	100.0	100.0
#医院（包括卫生院）	Hospitals（include Township Hospitals）	18.3	18.8	15.0	8.9	8.3
门诊部、所	Clinics	77.1	76.0	79.2	36.9	32.2
卫生技术人员结构	Structure of Medical Technical Personnel	100.0	100.0	100.0	100.0	100.0
#医 生	Doctors	47.5	47.3	46.5	46.8	45.4
护师、护士	Nurses	26.5	28.0	29.7	32.8	37.4

4-12 主要年份社会经济发展相对指标
RELATIVE INDICATORS ON ECONOMIC AND SOCIAL DEVELOPMENT IN MAIN YEARS

指 标	Item	1990	1995	2000	2005	2011
人 口	**Population**					
出生率 (‰)	Birth Rate (‰)	15.1	11.7	12.6	8.3	8.0
死亡率 (‰)	Death Rate (‰)	6.4	6.4	6.8	6.2	6.1
自然增长率 (‰)	Natural Growth Rate (‰)	8.7	5.3	5.8	2.1	1.9
国民经济核算	**National Accounting**					
经济增长贡献率(%)	Growth Rate of Economy (%)					
第一产业	Primary Industry	15.4	11.0	1.8	2.6	2.2
第二产业	Secondary Industry	76.0	36.0	60.0	66.6	49.8
#工 业	Industy	75.2	30.5	53.4	61.6	44.4
第三产业	Tertiary Industry	8.7	53.0	38.2	30.8	47.9
人均地区生产总值（元）	Per Capita Gross Domestic Product (yuan)	2935	11117	17635	32116	77485
固定资产投资	**Investment in Fixed Assets**					
全社会固定资产投资相当于地区生产总值比例 (%)	Proportion of Total Investment in Fixed Assets to GDP (%)	23.9	31.1	27.2	59.1	65.3
城镇集体以上房屋建筑面积竣工率 (%)	Rate of Floor Space of Buildings Completed (%)		49.7	48.8	42.1	53.4
城镇固定资产交付使用率 (%)	Rate of Fixed Assets Completed in Urban Investment and Put into Use (%)			72.0	70.0	77.3
城镇固定资产项目建成投产率 (%)	Rate of Projects Completed in Urban Investment and Put into Use (%)			69.1	58.0	69.8
财 政	**Government Finance**					
全市财政收入相当于地区生产总值比例 (%)	Proportion of Government Revenue to GDP (%)	13.8	7.7	10.0	16.9	27.3
地方一般预算收入相当于地区生产总值比例 (%)	Proportion of Local Financial Revenue to GDP (%)			5.4	7.3	9.8
吸收外资	**Utilization of Foreign Capital**					
实际利用外资额相当于签订利用外资比例 (%)	Proportion of Foreign Capital Actually Utilized (%)	29.1	33.3	94.5	25.6	65.9
农 业	**Agriculture**					
平均每个农村人口占有耕地（平方米）	Cultivated Land per Rural Population (sq.m)	846	839	859	749	636

4-12 续表1 continued 1

指 标	Item	1990	1995	2000	2005	2011
每公顷耕地农业机械总动力（千瓦）	Total Power of Agricultural Machinery per Hectare of Cultivated Land (kw)	5.71	6.80	8.20	9.19	10.35
农民人均农产品产量（公斤）	Output of Farm Products per Agricultural Laborer (kg)					
粮 食	Grain	506.40	478.25	398.90	278.88	317.45
油 料	Oil-bearing Crops	19.67	21.82	26.83	24.45	8.83
茶 叶	Tea	1.15	0.76	0.79	0.79	0.95
水 果	Fruits	2.98	6.81	8.68	19.13	25.61
猪 肉	Pork	21.55	26.97	18.83	18.46	16.74
水产品	Aquatic Products	16.36	27.15	32.51	37.03	45.31
每公顷播种面积农产品产量（公斤）	Output of Farm Crops per Hectare of Sown Area (kg)					
粮 食	Grain	5720	6666	6982	6772	7221
棉 花	Cotton	552	577	967	764	847
油 料	Oil-bearing Crops	1594	1644	1850	1952	1995
工 业	**Industry**					
资产负债率（%）	Asstes-Liability Ratio (%)		64.82	61.70	65.61	60.93
成本费用利润率（%）	Ratio of Pre-tax Profits to Gross Output Value (%)		2.23	3.13	4.06	6.09
工业产品销售率（%）	Ratio of Industrial Products Sales (%)		96.13	97.12	97.77	98.76
全员劳动生产率（元/人）	Overall Labor Productivity(yuan/person)		23586	44066	98345	232020
建筑业	**Construction**					
全员劳动生产率（元/人,按施工产值计算）	Overall Labor Productivity (yuan/person, In Terms of Construction Output Value)	11326	39838	77513	163100	244984
交通、通信业	**Transportation and Telecommunication Services**					
每万人拥有公共车辆（标台）	Number of Public Transit Vehicles Owned per 10000 Persons (set)	4.30	4.80	15.60	9.02	14.30
住宅电话普及率（部/百人）	Access to Home Telephone (set/100 persons)		11.88	18.81	32.30	21.43
移动电话普及率（部/百人）	Access to Mobile Telephone (set/100 persons)		0.54	16.64	45.50	154.46

4-12 续表 2 continued 2

指 标	Item	1990	1995	2000	2005	2011
国内商业	**Domestic Trade**					
人均消费品零售额（元）	Per Capita Consumption Retail Sale (yuan)	1181	3963	5940	12677	34162
对外经济贸易	**Foreign Trade and Economic Cooperation**					
进出口总额相当于地区生产总值比例 (%)	Ratio of Total Imports and Exports and Gross Domestic Product (%)	3.46	22.44	38.89	51.60	51.64
出口总额相当于地区生产总值比例 (%)	Ratio of Total Exports and Gross Domestic Product (%)	2.79	17.38	25.63	37.90	34.92
教 育	**Education**					
学龄儿童入学率 (%)	Rate of School-age Children Enrollment (%)	100.00	99.65	100.00	100.00	100.00
中学毕业生升学率 (%)	Rate of Secondary School Graduates Entering Higher Level Schools (%)	49.02	72.53	90.28	96.51	99.90
平均每个教师负担学生数（人）	Number of Students Burdened Per Teacher (person)	18.28	18.32	20.22	20.51	17.49
高等学校	Institutions of Higher Education	7.30	12.17	16.23	21.13	23.59
普通中学	Regular Secondary School	16.46	16.45	17.61	17.12	12.83
小 学	Primary School	21.17	19.97	23.08	21.37	19.28
婚 姻	**Marriage**					
离婚率 (‰)	Divorce Rate (‰)	0.19	0.42	0.65	1.43	2.26
生 活	**Livelihood**					
城市与农村居民收入比例	Proportion of Income of Urban Residents to Income of Rural Residents	1.26:1	1.66:1	1.93:1	2.08:1	2.01:1
卫 生	**Health Care**					
每万人拥有医院数（包括卫生院，个）	Number of Hospitals Per 10000 Persons (unit)	0.50	0.48	0.34	0.32	0.25
每万人拥有医生数（人）	Number of Doctors Per 10000 Persons (person)	19.01	21.27	22.80	23.80	28.60
每万人拥有医院床位数（包括卫生院，张）	Number of Hospital Beds Per 10000 Persons (bed)	29.37	31.10	31.50	33.37	41.44
城市建设	**Urban Construction**					
人均公园绿地面积（平方米）	Per Capita Green Area of Park (sq.m)	1.83	4.10	5.64	7.10	12.40
建成区绿化覆盖率（%）	Coverage Rate of Green Areas (%)	15.13	29.80	31.69	38.80	42.17
人均拥有道路面积（平方米）	Per Capita Area of Road (sq.m)	5.50	6.50	10.68	17.90	23.53

4-13　常州国民经济主要指标占全省的比重（2011 年）
PERCENTAGE OF CHANGZHOU'S MAJOR NATIONAL ECONOMIC INDICATORS IN THE PROVINCE（2011）

指　标	Item	常州市 Changzhou City	江苏省 Jiangsu Province	常州市占全省的比重（%） Percentage of Changzhou in Jiangsu
土地面积（平方公里）	Area of Land (sq.km)	4372.15	102600	4.3
常住人口（万人）	Permanent Populationn (10000 persons)	464.97	7898.80	5.9
社会从业人员（万人）	Social Employment (10000 persons)	277.72	4758.23	5.8
地区生产总值（亿元）	Gross Domestic Product (100 million yuan)	3580.99	49110.27	7.3
第一产业	Primary Industry	111.78	3064.78	3.6
第二产业	Secondary Industry	1950.84	25023.78	7.8
第三产业	Tertiary Industry	1518.37	20842.21	7.3
全社会固定资产投资完成额（亿元）	Total Investment in Fixed Assets(100 million yuan)	2338.94	26693.82	8.8
地方一般预算收入（亿元）	Local Government Budgetary Revenue (100 million yuan)	350.88	5147.89	6.8
一般预算支出（亿元）	Budgetary Expenditure(100 million yuan)	361.81	6221.72	5.8
城镇居民人均可支配收入（元）	Per Capita Disposable Income of Urban Residents (yuan)	29829	26341	高出全省3488元
农民人均纯收入（元）	Per Capita Net Income of Rural Residents (yuan)	14838	10805	高出全省4033元
城乡居民储蓄存款余额（亿元）	Balance Amount of Saving Deposits of Urban and Rural Residents (100 million yuan)	2157.39	25914.74	8.3
粮食产量（万吨）	Output of Grain (10000 tons)	115.19	3307.76	3.5
油料产量（万吨）	Output of Oil-bearing Crops (10000 tons)	3.20	144.05	2.2
社会消费品零售总额（亿元）	Total Retail Sales of Consumer Goods (100 million yuan)	1236.10	15988.38	7.7
进出口总额（亿美元）	Total Exports & Imports(USD 100 million)	286.35	5397.59	5.3
# 出　口	Exports	193.61	3126.23	6.2
实际利用外资（亿美元）	Amount of Foreign Capital Actually Utilized (USD 100 million)	30.52	321.32	9.5

4-14 五区社会经济主要指标（2011 年）
MAJOR SOCIAL AND ECONOMIC INDICATORS OF FIVE DISTRICTS（2011）

指 标	Item	武进区 wujin District	新北区 Xinbei District	天宁区 Tianning District	钟楼区 Zhonglou District	戚墅堰区 Qishuyan District
人口与就业	**Population and Employment**					
年末总户数（万户）	Total Number of Households at Year-end (1000 households)	36.34	14.75	13.72	12.88	2.83
年末户籍总人口（万人）	Total Population at Year-end (10000 persons)	102.37	46.05	37.31	35.37	7.88
年末常住人口（万人）	Permanent Population at Year-end (10000 persons)	159.30	60.58	52.06	51.27	10.65
#城镇人口	Non-agricultural Population	87.06	33.87	52.06	51.27	10.65
暂住人口（一个月及以上，万人）	Population of Temporary Residents (above one month，10000 persons)	61.65	19.23	13.33	12.83	3.26
年末在岗职工人数（万人）	Number of Staff & Workers Employed at Year-end (10000 persons)	7.77	5.33	8.00	4.68	1.72
年末私营企业从业人员（万人）	Employees of Urban Private Enterprises at Year-end (10000 persons)	47.59	20.06	8.50	7.18	2.59
年末个体从业人员（万人）	Urban Self-employed Individuals at Year-end (10000 persons)	11.24	4.10	5.33	3.80	0.72
城镇登记失业人员（人）	Urban Registered Unemployed Persons at Year-end (person)	9040	392	10276	5660	1445
综合经济	**Aggregative Economy**					
地区生产总值（亿元）	Gross Domestic Product (100 million yuan)	1376.96	623.15	350.63	326.51	81.85
第一产业	Primary Industry	40.65	11.22	0.10	0.15	0.02
第二产业	Secondary Industry	867.14	410.57	121.01	159.94	59.49
#工 业	Industry	823.24	388.71	108.36	145.00	56.53
第三产业	Tertiary Industry	469.17	201.36	229.52	166.42	22.34
固定资产投资	**Investment in Fixed Assets**					
全社会固定资产投资完成额（亿元）	Total Investment in Fixed Assets (100 million yuan)	715.73	477.19	236.05	227.86	58.52
城镇固定资产投资	Investment in Fixed Assets of Cities and Township	407.83	349.64	236.05	227.86	58.52
#房地产投资	Investment in Real Estate	131.38	116.77	145.14	89.79	23.60
农村投资	Investment in Rural Collective Units	307.90	127.56			
财 政	**Finance**					
财政总收入（亿元）	Total Financial Revenue (100 million yuan)	315.56	204.11	61.76	53.21	18.97
#地方一般预算收入	Budgetary Revenue	105.28	73.02	35.67	31.29	8.55
#各项税收	Taxes	84.95	63.63	32.30	25.92	7.93

4-14 续表 1 continued 1

指　标	Item	武进区 wujin District	新北区 Xinbei District	天宁区 Tianning District	钟楼区 Zhonglou District	戚墅堰区 Qishuyan District
财政支出（亿元）	Fiscal Expenditure (100 million yuan)	232.34	112.15	16.21	20.58	6.00
#一般预算支出	Budgetary Revenue	105.90	38.77	15.18	17.72	4.96
工　业	**Industry**					
规模以上工业企业主要经济指标	Main Indicators of Enterprises Above Designated Size					
企业单位数（个）	Number of Enterprises Above Designated Size (unit)	1613	769	236	248	89
内资企业	Domestic-funded Enterprises	1403	520	163	198	75
港、澳、台商投资企业	Enterprises with Investment from Hongkong,Macao and Taiwan	95	70	35	16	7
外商投资企业	Enterprises with Foreign Investment	115	179	38	34	7
工业总产值（亿元）	Gross Industrial Output Value (100 million yuan)	3223.30	1707.93	636.53	644.12	234.76
内资企业	Domestic-funded Enterprises	2625.78	740.26	294.66	442.12	169.06
港、澳、台商投资企业	Enterprises with Investment from Hongkong,Macao and Taiwan	323.61	222.86	87.24	108.60	32.69
外商投资企业	Enterprises with Foreign Investment	273.91	744.82	254.63	93.40	33.01
#制造业	Manufacturing	3206.17	1675.61	619.99	644.12	207.64
#重工业	Heavy Industry	2582.38	1454.72	322.63	583.37	220.91
总资产（亿元）	Total Assets (100 million yuan)	2609.90	1469.49	415.51	340.29	225.01
固定资产原值（亿元）	Original Value of Fixed Assets (100 million yuan)	845.90	771.72	152.61	166.44	100.05
所有者权益合计（亿元）	Total Owners Equity (100 million yuan)	1021.42	615.69	185.73	134.77	98.56
主营业务收入（亿元）	Main Business Income (100 million yuan)	3158.97	1672.46	644.05	669.66	255.57
利税总额（亿元）	Total Pre-tax Profits (100 million yuan)	244.32	141.23	45.27	54.51	34.04
利润总额（亿元）	Total Profits (100 million yuan)	155.99	91.18	31.96	34.87	27.60
贸易、外经	**Trade, Foreign Trade**					
社会消费品零售总额（亿元）	Total Retail Sales of Consumption Goods (100 million yuan)	316.12	161.65	256.55	178.64	13.27
进出口总额（亿美元）	Total Imports & Exports (USD 100 million)	79.50	113.24	30.48	25.42	5.48
#出　口	Exports	51.95	66.39	25.15	20.65	3.88

4-14 续表 2 continued 2

	指 标 Item	武进区 wujin District	新北区 Xinbei District	天宁区 Tianning District	钟楼区 Zhonglou District	戚墅堰区 Qishuyan District
新签协议合同（个）	Number of Newly Signed Agreement contracts (unit)	103	72	20	18	6
协议合同外资金额（亿美元）	Amount of Negotiated Investment from Abroad (USD 100 million)	11.11	12.79	3.70	4.00	1.61
教育、卫生	**Education and Public Health**					
普通中学学校数（个）	Number of Regular Secondary Schools (unit)	49	17	3	3	3
小学学校数（个）	Number of Primary Schools (unit)	46	21	23	22	4
普通中学在校学生数（人）	Number of Student Enrollment of Regular Secondary Schools (person)	57137	16691	2335	2024	3082
小学在校学生数（人）	Number of Student Enrollment of Primary Schools (person)	82499	27121	26370	25348	4912
普通中学专任教师数（人）	Number of Full-time Teachers of Regular Secondary Schools (person)	4067	1298	207	132	230
小学专任教师数（人）	Number of Full-time Teachers of Primary Schools (person)	3597	1310	1301	1249	293
幼儿园数（个）	Number of Kindergartens(unit)	54	27	25	24	4
入园儿童数（人）	Number of Newly Enrolled in Kindergartens (person)	33828	14493	9630	12884	2237
卫生机构数（个）	Number of Health Institutions (unit)	342	111	149	87	21
#医院、卫生院	Hospitals	30	9	6	1	1
卫生机构床位数（张）	Number of Beds in Health Institutions (unit)	4985	816	5966	684	279
#医院、卫生院	Hospitals	4615	581	5196	500	244
卫生技术人员（人）	Number of Medical Personnel (person)	5166	1222	8262	1642	498
#医 生	Doctors	2423	675	3161	695	213
#执业（助理）医师	Practicing (Assistant) Doctors	1884	476	2924	625	165
人民生活	**People's Livelihood**					
参加养老保险的人数（万人）	Number of Persons Covered by Endowment Insurance (10000 persons)	29.47	18.08	10.10	9.85	2.34
城镇居民可支配收入（元）	Per Capita Disposable Income of Urban Residents (yuan)	31003				
农民人均纯收入（元）	Per Capita Net Income of Rural Residents (yuan)	16373	14718			
社会治安	**Security of Society**					
刑事案件立案数（件）	Number of Criminal Cases Registered (case)	1352	526	632	562	101
犯罪人数（人）	Number of Criminals (person)	2132	853	831	793	172
民事案件发案数（人）	Number of Civil Cases Arised (person)	7967	4063	3757	3946	471

5

CHAPTER 5

人　口

POPULATION

5 人 口 POPULATION

2011 年主要统计指标 MAJOR STATISTICAL INDICATORS OF 2011

年底总户数	Total Households	128.10万户	(10000 households)
比上年增长	Over the Previous Year	0.8%	
年底总人口	Total Population	362.86万人	(10000 persons)
比上年增长	Over the Previous Year	0.6%	
年底市区人口	Urban Districts Population	228.98万人	(10000 persons)
比上年增长	Over the Previous Year	0.5%	
年底常住人口	Permanent population	464.97万人	(10000 persons)
比上年增长	Over the Previous Year	1.2%	
年底暂住人口	Temporary Resident Population At Year-end	133.09万人	(10000 persons)
比上年增长	Over the Previous Year	-0.3%	
暂住一个月以上人口	Temporary Resident Population Over One Month	123.11万人	(10000 persons)
比上年增长	Over the Previous Year	-1.7%	

5-1　历年年末户籍户数、人口数
YEAR-END HOUSEHOLDS AND POPULATION OVER THE YEARS

年　份 Year	总户数（万户） Total Number of Households (10000 households)	总人口（万人） Total Population (10000 persons)	城镇人口（万人） Urban Population (10000 persons)	年平均人口（万人） Average Population Per Year (10000 persons)	平均每户人口（人） Average Person Per Household (person)
1949	40.88	173.89	33.77	173.89	4.25
1950	42.37	176.45	31.86	175.17	4.16
1951	43.52	179.87	30.44	178.16	4.13
1952	44.23	183.34	31.31	181.61	4.15
1953	45.76	187.99	32.46	185.67	4.11
1954	45.86	191.54	34.38	189.77	4.18
1955	46.96	196.35	36.82	193.95	4.18
1956	47.03	198.34	37.45	197.35	4.22
1957	47.94	203.70	38.79	201.02	4.25
1958	48.60	211.66	48.22	207.68	4.36
1959	50.31	214.43	49.18	213.05	4.26
1960	50.87	215.49	50.04	214.96	4.24
1961	52.86	215.57	45.10	215.53	4.08
1962	53.18	222.13	39.49	218.85	4.18
1963	54.67	229.31	39.15	225.72	4.19
1964	55.26	235.39	38.84	232.35	4.26
1965	55.78	240.79	39.48	238.09	4.32
1966	56.20	246.69	40.12	243.74	4.39
1967	57.60	250.36	41.10	248.53	4.35
1968	59.10	256.51	43.01	253.44	4.34
1969	60.47	260.19	36.82	258.35	4.30
1970	61.93	266.82	37.58	263.51	4.31
1971	63.33	272.22	38.61	269.52	4.30
1972	64.16	275.67	39.00	273.95	4.30
1973	65.71	279.95	41.97	277.81	4.26
1974	66.81	282.61	40.86	281.28	4.23
1975	68.01	284.69	40.74	283.65	4.19
1976	69.98	287.32	42.25	286.01	4.11
1977	71.63	289.64	42.75	288.48	4.04
1978	73.23	291.00	45.22	290.32	3.97
1979	74.41	294.42	51.79	292.71	3.96

5-1 续表 continued

年 份 Year	总户数（万户） Total Number of Households (10000 households)	总人口（万人） Total Population (10000 persons)	城镇人口（万人） Urban Population (10000 persons)	年平均人口（万人） Average Population Per Year (10000 persons)	平均每户人口（人） Average Person Per Household (person)
1980	77.19	295.92	53.48	295.17	3.83
1981	79.93	298.75	55.17	297.34	3.74
1982	81.59	301.98	57.68	300.37	3.70
1983	83.73	304.26	59.47	303.12	3.63
1984	85.60	305.48	61.46	304.87	3.57
1985	88.21	306.87	64.20	306.18	3.48
1986	91.06	309.74	67.92	308.31	3.40
1987	93.67	313.22	69.21	311.48	3.34
1988	100.32	317.06	75.08	315.14	3.16
1989	104.80	321.65	79.32	319.36	3.07
1990	106.91	324.85	81.40	323.25	3.04
1991	108.61	326.87	82.80	325.86	3.01
1992	110.41	328.57	97.58	327.72	2.98
1993	111.63	329.33	115.11	328.95	2.95
1994	111.84	331.44	116.02	330.39	2.96
1995	114.00	333.65	120.48	332.55	2.93
1996	114.73	337.54	124.71	335.60	2.94
1997	115.69	339.23	128.47	338.39	2.93
1998	116.57	340.75	130.43	339.99	2.92
1999	117.44	339.71	139.43	340.23	2.89
2000	117.89	341.48	147.81	340.60	2.90
2001	118.65	341.52	152.40	341.50	2.88
2002	119.74	343.24	157.82	342.38	2.86
2003	121.04	346.22	201.01	344.73	2.86
2004	121.63	348.96	206.75	347.59	2.87
2005	121.97	351.63	212.56	350.30	2.88
2006	122.32	354.67	223.99	353.15	2.90
2007	122.21	357.38	264.84	356.03	2.92
2008	123.40	358.74	268.66	358.06	2.91
2009	125.47	359.82	272.27	359.28	2.87
2010	127.11	360.80	293.74	360.31	2.84
2011	128.10	362.86	303.16	361.83	2.83

注：2003年前城镇人口为非农业人口数据，2006年起城镇人口按常住人口计算。

Note: The data of urban population belong to the data of non-agricultural before the year of 2003, the urban population is calculated as permanent population since 2006.

5-2　历年人口自然变动情况
POPULATION NATURAL CHANGE OVER THE YEARS

年　份 Year	出生人数（人） Birth Population (person)	出生率（‰） Birth Rate (‰)	死亡人数（人） Death Population (person)	死亡率（‰） Death Rate (‰)	自然增长人数（人） Natural Growth Population (person)	自然增长率（‰） Natural Growth Rate (‰)
1949	68233	39.2	28572	16.4	39661	22.8
1950	69811	39.9	28921	16.5	40890	23.3
1951	73147	41.1	28458	16.0	44689	25.1
1952	76275	42.0	28956	15.9	47319	26.1
1953	79065	42.6	28832	15.2	50233	27.1
1954	74832	39.4	23251	12.3	51581	27.2
1955	70118	36.2	21094	10.9	49024	25.3
1956	70379	35.7	23938	12.1	46441	23.5
1957	73364	36.5	19413	9.7	53951	26.8
1958	64609	31.1	18203	8.8	46406	22.3
1959	44026	20.7	26971	12.7	17055	8.0
1960	44985	20.9	32791	15.3	12194	5.7
1961	46124	21.4	26508	12.3	19616	9.1
1962	80239	36.7	20515	9.4	59724	27.3
1963	89412	39.6	18889	8.4	70523	31.2
1964	83705	36.0	18644	8.0	65061	28.0
1965	77946	32.7	18188	7.6	59758	25.1
1966	73364	30.1	16995	7.0	56369	23.1
1967	73418	29.5	16405	6.6	57013	22.9
1968	75064	29.6	15607	6.2	59457	23.5
1969	71259	27.6	14611	5.7	56648	21.9
1970	70116	26.6	16094	6.1	54022	20.5
1971	66295	24.6	16815	6.2	49480	18.4
1972	56287	20.5	16850	6.2	39437	14.4
1973	46210	16.6	17319	6.2	28891	10.4
1974	43963	15.6	17964	6.3	25999	9.2
1975	42669	15.0	17906	6.3	24763	8.7
1976	40004	14.0	17748	6.2	22256	7.8
1977	42121	14.6	18985	6.6	23136	8.0
1978	41310	14.2	18293	6.3	23017	7.9
1979	37548	12.8	18392	6.3	19156	6.5

5-2 续表 continued

年 份 Year	出生人数（人） Birth Population (person)	出生率（‰） Birth Rate (‰)	死亡人数（人） Death Population (person)	死亡率（‰） Death Rate (‰)	自然增长人数（人） Natural Growth Population (person)	自然增长率（‰） Natural Growth Rate (‰)
1980	35260	11.9	19086	6.5	16174	5.5
1981	46288	15.6	18865	6.3	27423	9.2
1982	46030	15.3	18086	6.0	27944	9.3
1983	32485	10.7	19710	6.5	12775	4.2
1984	29331	9.6	19340	6.3	9991	3.3
1985	30971	10.1	19082	6.2	11889	3.9
1986	40329	13.1	19067	6.2	21262	6.9
1987	47636	15.3	19274	6.2	28362	9.1
1988	48901	15.5	20204	6.4	28697	9.1
1989	50730	15.9	19115	6.0	31615	9.9
1990	48772	15.1	20595	6.4	28177	8.7
1991	41384	12.7	20412	6.3	20972	6.4
1992	39676	12.1	20979	6.4	18697	5.7
1993	37130	11.3	20176	6.1	16954	5.2
1994	35638	10.8	20248	6.1	15390	4.7
1995	38830	11.7	21292	6.4	17538	5.3
1996	33464	10.0	22239	6.6	11225	3.3
1997	48469	14.3	20008	5.9	28461	8.4
1998	40230	11.8	22255	6.5	17975	5.3
1999	31975	9.4	20355	6.0	11620	3.4
2000	42845	12.6	22998	6.8	19847	5.8
2001	28713	8.4	18720	5.5	9993	2.9
2002	30949	9.0	19746	5.8	11203	3.2
2003	25490	7.4	19867	5.8	5623	1.6
2004	27992	8.1	24266	7.0	3726	1.1
2005	29049	8.3	21624	6.2	7425	2.1
2006	28166	8.0	21465	6.1	6701	1.9
2007	27236	7.7	23811	6.7	3425	1.0
2008	25273	7.1	24734	6.9	539	0.2
2009	26142	7.3	27577	7.7	-1435	-0.4
2010	27950	7.8	30510	8.5	-2560	-0.7
2011	29007	8.0	22144	6.1	6863	1.9

5-3　分地区户数和人口情况（2011年底）
NUMBER OF HOUSHOLD AND POPULATION BY REGION（END OF 2011）

地　区 Region		总户数（户）Total Number of Households (household)	户籍人口（人）Household register Population (person)	按性别分 By Sex 男 Male	女 Female	按年龄分 By Age #18岁以下 Age 18 and Under	#60岁以上 Age 60 and Over	常住人口（万人）permanent population (10000 persons)	其中 of which #城镇人口 Urban Population
总　计	**Total**	**1280965**	**3628615**	**1808623**	**1819992**	**482060**	**733361**	**464.97**	**303.16**
市　区	Urban Area	805282	2289831	1134471	1155360	309539	462161	333.86	234.91
武进区	Wujin District	363385	1023675	505514	518161	133059	217599	159.30	87.06
新北区	Xinbei District	147518	460515	228860	231655	67535	81198	60.58	33.87
天宁区	Tianning District	137241	373068	183570	189498	51644	74268	52.06	52.06
钟楼区	Zhonglou District	128791	353737	176363	177374	47971	70851	51.27	51.27
戚墅堰区	Qishuyan District	28347	78836	40164	38672	9330	18245	10.65	10.65
溧阳市	Liyang City	265333	787333	398769	388564	109868	156766	75.58	39.01
金坛市	Jintan City	210350	551451	275383	276068	62653	114434	55.53	29.24

5-4　分地区暂住人口情况（2011年底）
TEMPORARY RESIDENT POPULATION BY REGION（END OF 2011）

单位：人（person）

指　标	Item	全　市 Whole Municipality	其中 of which 市　区 Urban Area	溧阳市 Liyang City	金坛市 Jintan City
总　计	**Total**	**1330945**	**1183439**	**69200**	**78306**
按时间分	By Time				
#一个月以上	Over One Month	1231076	1102995	59035	69046
#一年以上	Over One Year	240517	200092	8058	32367
按活动类型分	By Active Type				
#务　工	Engaged into Industry or Project	934726	837314	34787	62625
务　农	Engaged into Agriculture	60298	49926	3954	6418
经　商	Business	137410	127786	7196	2428
服　务	Service	78494	68787	6828	2879

5-5 分地区人口自然增长和迁移情况（2011 年）
NATURAL GROWTH AND MIGRATION OF POPULATION BY REGION（2011）

地 区	Region	出生人数（人）Birth Population (person)	出生率（‰）Birth Rate (‰)	死亡人数（人）Death Population (person)	死亡率（‰）Death Rate (‰)
总 计	**Total**	**29007**	**8.0**	**22144**	**6.1**
市 区	Urban Area	18700	8.2	15316	6.7
武进区	Wujin District	7754	7.6	7288	7.1
新北区	Xinbei District	5040	11.1	3354	7.4
天宁区	Tianning District	2644	7.1	2151	5.8
钟楼区	Zhonglou District	2748	7.8	2002	5.7
戚墅堰区	Qishuyan District	514	6.5	521	6.6
溧阳市	Liyang City	6312	8.0	2885	3.7
金坛市	Jintan City	3995	7.3	3943	7.2

5-5 续表 continued

地 区	Region	自然增长人数（人）Natural Growth Population (person)	自然增长率（‰）Natural Growth Rate (‰)	迁入人数（人）Number of the Transferred From Outside (person)	迁出人数（人）Number of the Transferred to Outside (person)
总 计	**Total**	**6863**	**1.9**	**44674**	**27278**
市 区	Urban Area	3384	1.5	39176	23338
武进区	Wujin District	466	0.5	15078	12591
新北区	Xinbei District	1686	3.7	8752	2517
天宁区	Tianning District	493	1.3	5256	3058
钟楼区	Zhonglou District	746	2.1	5809	4543
戚墅堰区	Qishuyan District	-7	-0.1	1281	629
溧阳市	Liyang City	3427	4.4	4314	2353
金坛市	Jintan City	52	0.1	4184	1587

5-6 预期寿命
LIFE EXPECTANCY

单位：岁（age）

年 代	year	平均预期寿命 Average Life Expectancy	其 中 of which 男 性 Male	女 性 Female
全 市	**Whole Municipality**			
20世纪80年代（1982年）	1980s (year of 1982)	67.8	66.5	73.2
20世纪90年代（1990年）	1990s (year of 1990)	72.2	70.1	74.3
20世纪末（2000年）	End of 20th Century (year of 2000)	75.5	73.3	77.8
市 区	**Urban Area**			
20世纪50年代（1957年）	1950s (year of 1957)	63.3	62.9	66.6
20世纪60年代（1960年）	1960s (year of 1960)	57.1	54.3	60.7
20世纪80年代（1982年）	1980s (year of 1982)	71.6	69.1	74.4
20世纪90年代（1990年）	1990s (year of 1990)	74.7	72.7	76.6
20世纪末（2000年）	End of 20th Century (year of 2000)	77.8	75.8	79.8

5-7 分地区计划生育情况（2011年）
STATISTICS ON BIRTH CONTROL BY REGION（2011）

指 标	Item	全 市 Whole Municipality	其 中 of which 市 区 Urban Area	溧阳市 Liyang City	金坛市 Jintan City
计划生育率（%）	Family Planning Rate (%)	98.7	98.8	98.0	98.4
独生子女率（%）	Only-child Rate (%)	79.7	79.3	75.8	86.3
育龄妇女人数（万人）	Number of Woman of Child-bearing Age (10000 persons)	103.32	66.71	20.96	15.65
#已婚育龄妇女数	Number of Married Woman of Child-bearing Age	81.99	52.68	16.73	12.57
有效领独生子女证人数（万人）	Number of Only-child Certificare Obtained (10000 persons)	28.42	19.31	4.76	4.35
晚婚率（%）	Deferred Marriage Rate (%)	74.3	79.1	62.4	66.1
现家庭只有一个孩子的妇女人数（万人）	Number of Woman Owns One-child in Family (10000 persons)	65.31	41.79	12.68	10.85

6

CHAPTER 6

从业人员　工资总额

EMPLOYMENT AND TOTAL WAGES

6 从业人员　工资总额
EMPLOYMENT AND TOTAL WAGES

2011 年主要统计指标
MAJOR STATISTICAL INDICATORS OF 2011

年底社会从业人员数	Number of Employment	277.72万人	(10000 persons)
比上年增长	Over the Previous Year	2.1 %	
城镇非私营单位年底在岗职工人数	Number of Fully Employed Staff and Workers of Urban Non-Private Entities by the End of Year	38.07万人	(10000 persons)
比上年增长	Over the Previous Year	3.7%	
城镇非私营单位在岗职工平均工资	Average Wage of On-Post Employees of Urban Non-Private Entities	49755元	(yuan)
比上年增长	Over the Previous Year	12.5%	
私营单位从业人员平均工资	Average Wage of Employees of Private Entities	29306 元	(yuan)
比上年增长	Over the Previous Year	16.7%	

6-1　历年年末从业人员及构成
NUMBER AND COMPOSITION OF EMPLOYED PERSONS OVER THE YEARS

年　份 Year	年末从业人员（万人） Number of Employed persons (10000 persons)	其　中　of which 第一产业 Primary Industry	第二产业 Secondary Industry	第三产业 Tertiary Industry	构　成（%） Composition (%)	其　中　of which 第一产业 Primary Industry	第二产业 Secondary Industry	第三产业 Tertiary Industry
1949	67.24	56.96	4.08	6.20	100	84.7	6.1	9.2
1950	70.06	58.53	5.46	6.07	100	83.5	7.8	8.7
1951	72.82	61.64	5.49	5.69	100	84.6	7.5	7.8
1952	78.04	65.81	6.44	5.79	100	84.3	8.3	7.4
1953	80.06	66.77	7.46	5.83	100	83.4	9.3	7.3
1954	82.70	69.68	7.38	5.64	100	84.3	8.9	6.8
1955	84.64	72.22	6.85	5.57	100	85.3	8.1	6.6
1956	84.81	71.67	7.13	6.01	100	84.5	8.4	7.1
1957	84.80	71.31	7.41	6.07	100	84.1	8.7	7.2
1958	87.44	62.17	18.78	6.49	100	71.1	21.5	7.4
1959	87.82	63.36	17.30	7.16	100	72.1	19.7	8.2
1960	89.23	67.06	14.61	7.61	100	75.2	16.4	8.5
1961	91.28	69.54	13.28	8.47	100	76.2	14.5	9.3
1962	98.92	80.91	8.98	9.03	100	81.8	9.1	9.1
1963	101.81	84.14	8.93	8.74	100	82.6	8.8	8.6
1964	100.72	82.34	10.05	8.33	100	81.8	10.0	8.3
1965	106.33	85.77	11.36	9.21	100	80.7	10.7	8.7
1966	106.80	85.30	12.60	8.90	100	79.9	11.8	8.3
1967	110.36	88.85	12.78	8.73	100	80.5	11.6	7.9
1968	115.08	92.74	13.39	8.95	100	80.6	11.6	7.8
1969	118.59	95.82	14.13	8.64	100	80.8	11.9	7.3
1970	127.24	100.81	16.10	10.33	100	79.2	12.7	8.1
1971	131.32	101.71	18.83	10.78	100	77.5	14.3	8.2
1972	134.45	101.22	21.40	11.83	100	75.3	15.9	8.8
1973	136.12	100.92	22.72	12.48	100	74.1	16.7	9.2
1974	138.01	100.05	24.71	13.25	100	72.5	17.9	9.6
1975	138.69	97.10	27.79	13.80	100	70.0	20.0	10.0
1976	140.81	97.19	30.58	13.04	100	69.0	21.7	9.3
1977	144.43	93.53	36.11	14.79	100	64.8	25.0	10.2
1978	149.35	90.36	40.20	18.79	100	60.5	26.9	12.6
1979	151.59	92.75	43.17	15.67	100	61.2	28.5	10.3

6-1 续表 continued

年 份 Year	年末从业人员（万人） Number of Employed persons (10000 persons)	其 中 of which			构 成（%） Composition (%)	其 中 of which		
		第一产业 Primary Industry	第二产业 Secondary Industry	第三产业 Tertiary Industry		第一产业 Primary Industry	第二产业 Secondary Industry	第三产业 Tertiary Industry
1980	155.45	90.25	49.18	16.02	100	58.1	31.6	10.3
1981	157.23	87.90	51.84	17.49	100	55.9	33.0	11.1
1982	160.65	84.48	55.32	20.85	100	52.6	34.4	13.0
1983	168.92	87.09	59.26	22.57	100	51.6	35.1	13.4
1984	173.73	78.25	67.98	27.50	100	45.0	39.1	15.8
1985	178.64	70.19	77.50	30.96	100	39.3	43.4	17.3
1986	181.69	67.84	80.62	33.23	100	37.3	44.4	18.3
1987	187.00	65.96	84.95	36.09	100	35.3	45.4	19.3
1988	185.59	65.24	86.90	33.44	100	35.2	46.8	18.0
1989	184.55	66.88	84.09	33.58	100	36.2	45.6	18.2
1990	186.06	66.82	84.83	34.42	100	35.9	45.6	18.5
1991	187.39	67.33	84.15	35.90	100	35.9	44.9	19.2
1992	187.00	65.03	84.80	37.17	100	34.7	45.3	19.9
1993	188.65	63.70	86.56	38.39	100	33.8	45.9	20.3
1994	187.19	61.42	85.75	40.02	100	32.8	45.8	21.5
1995	188.78	55.51	89.23	44.04	100	29.4	47.3	23.3
1996	188.75	53.68	88.02	47.05	100	28.4	46.6	24.9
1997	185.23	54.69	84.05	46.49	100	29.5	45.4	25.1
1998	183.96	55.04	80.17	48.75	100	29.9	43.6	26.5
1999	185.60	54.38	79.64	51.57	100	29.3	42.9	27.8
2000	179.36	51.82	78.13	49.41	100	28.9	43.6	27.5
2001	189.11	49.81	85.26	54.04	100	26.3	45.1	28.6
2002	192.14	46.22	88.47	57.45	100	24.1	46.0	29.9
2003	199.74	38.77	98.92	62.05	100	19.4	49.5	31.1
2004	217.42	34.57	114.52	68.32	100	15.9	52.7	31.4
2005	222.31	30.01	118.71	73.58	100	13.5	53.4	33.1
2006	225.81	27.32	123.52	74.97	100	12.1	54.7	33.2
2007	233.18	25.88	129.65	77.65	100	11.1	55.6	33.3
2008	242.71	24.76	136.16	81.79	100	10.2	56.1	33.7
2009	251.56	24.40	140.87	86.29	100	9.7	56.0	34.3
2010	272.00	23.66	151.23	97.10	100	8.7	55.6	35.7
2011	277.72	22.26	153.21	102.25	100	8.0	55.2	36.8

6-2　历年年末市区从业人员及构成
NUMBER AND COMPOSITION OF URBAN EMPLOYED PERSONS OVER THE YEARS

年份 Year	年末从业人员（万人） Number of Employed persons (10000 persons)	其中 of which 第一产业 Primary Industry	第二产业 Secondary Industry	第三产业 Tertiary Industry	构成（%） Composition (%)	其中 of which 第一产业 Primary Industry	第二产业 Secondary Industry	第三产业 Tertiary Industry
1949	43.68	34.17	3.90	5.61	100	78.2	8.9	12.8
1950	45.54	34.97	5.23	5.34	100	76.8	11.5	11.7
1951	47.35	37.35	5.14	4.85	100	78.9	10.9	10.2
1952	51.91	41.19	6.02	4.70	100	79.3	11.6	9.1
1953	53.59	41.93	7.04	4.63	100	78.2	13.1	8.6
1954	53.81	42.60	6.87	4.34	100	79.2	12.8	8.1
1955	54.73	43.91	6.43	4.39	100	80.2	11.7	8.0
1956	53.90	42.58	6.70	4.63	100	79.0	12.4	8.6
1957	52.50	41.04	6.87	4.59	100	78.2	13.1	8.7
1958	53.07	34.97	14.01	4.09	100	65.9	26.4	7.7
1959	55.92	37.84	13.18	4.92	100	67.7	23.6	8.8
1960	56.96	39.81	11.64	5.51	100	69.9	20.4	9.7
1961	57.20	41.78	9.29	6.13	100	73.0	16.2	10.7
1962	62.26	48.25	8.02	5.99	100	77.5	12.9	9.6
1963	63.92	49.93	8.03	5.96	100	78.1	12.6	9.3
1964	60.98	45.89	9.22	5.87	100	75.3	15.1	9.6
1965	65.26	48.38	10.46	6.42	100	74.1	16.0	9.8
1966	65.42	47.52	11.65	6.25	100	72.6	17.8	9.6
1967	67.77	49.87	11.79	6.11	100	73.6	17.4	9.0
1968	71.56	53.15	12.30	6.11	100	74.3	17.2	8.5
1969	73.98	55.02	12.94	6.01	100	74.4	17.5	8.1
1970	81.33	59.44	14.62	7.27	100	73.1	18.0	8.9
1971	83.32	58.76	16.77	7.80	100	70.5	20.1	9.4
1972	84.70	58.52	18.14	8.04	100	69.1	21.4	9.5
1973	85.32	57.38	19.46	8.48	100	67.3	22.8	9.9
1974	86.40	56.37	21.05	8.98	100	65.2	24.4	10.4
1975	86.86	53.75	23.96	9.15	100	61.9	27.6	10.5
1976	88.70	53.48	26.57	8.65	100	60.3	30.0	9.8
1977	90.55	50.47	30.04	10.03	100	55.7	33.2	11.1
1978	94.91	48.72	32.99	13.19	100	51.3	34.8	13.9
1979	96.41	49.59	36.63	10.19	100	51.4	38.0	10.6

6-2 续表 continued

年 份 Year	年末从业人员（万人） Number of Employed persons (10000 persons)	其 中 of which 第一产业 Primary Industry	第二产业 Secondary Industry	第三产业 Tertiary Industry	构 成（%） Composition (%)	其 中 of which 第一产业 Primary Industry	第二产业 Secondary Industry	第三产业 Tertiary Industry
1980	98.05	46.67	40.30	11.08	100	47.6	41.1	11.3
1981	99.87	45.00	42.99	11.89	100	45.1	43.0	11.9
1982	101.92	43.42	43.84	14.66	100	42.6	43.0	14.4
1983	109.08	45.74	47.34	16.01	100	41.9	43.4	14.7
1984	112.35	40.25	52.73	19.39	100	35.8	46.9	17.3
1985	115.20	34.77	58.77	21.66	100	30.2	51.0	18.8
1986	116.71	33.34	59.93	23.45	100	28.6	51.3	20.1
1987	116.23	32.10	62.60	21.55	100	27.6	53.9	18.5
1988	118.03	31.43	63.55	23.06	100	26.6	53.8	19.5
1989	117.61	32.25	62.14	23.22	100	27.4	52.8	19.7
1990	117.84	31.57	62.92	23.35	100	26.8	53.4	19.8
1991	118.96	31.41	63.04	24.51	100	26.4	53.0	20.6
1992	118.19	30.20	61.99	26.00	100	25.6	52.4	22.0
1993	118.37	29.08	62.96	26.33	100	24.6	53.2	22.2
1994	116.74	27.84	61.58	27.32	100	23.8	52.7	23.4
1995	118.01	23.96	55.52	38.53	100	20.3	47.0	32.6
1996	116.51	23.05	61.52	31.94	100	19.8	52.8	27.4
1997	112.56	23.73	58.27	30.56	100	21.1	51.8	27.1
1998	111.80	24.04	55.21	32.55	100	21.5	49.4	29.1
1999	115.00	24.11	54.88	36.01	100	21.0	47.7	31.3
2000	111.55	22.68	53.67	35.20	100	20.3	48.1	31.6
2001	119.33	20.55	59.71	39.07	100	17.2	50.0	32.7
2002	123.33	19.84	62.59	40.90	100	16.1	50.7	33.2
2003	132.88	18.03	70.91	43.94	100	13.2	53.5	33.1
2004	148.11	16.73	81.80	49.57	100	11.3	55.2	33.5
2005	148.55	14.56	80.81	53.18	100	9.8	54.4	35.8
2006	149.48	12.56	83.26	53.66	100	8.4	55.7	35.9
2007	156.23	11.87	87.96	56.40	100	7.6	56.3	36.1
2008	164.24	11.33	93.45	59.45	100	6.9	56.9	36.2
2009	170.09	11.06	96.10	62.93	100	6.5	56.5	37.0
2010	186.92	10.65	104.68	71.59	100	5.7	56.0	38.3
2011	193.55	9.60	107.97	75.98	100	5.0	55.8	39.3

6-3　主要年份城镇非私营单位在岗职工人数和工资情况
THE NUMBER AND THE WAGES OF FULLY EMPLOYED STAFF AND WORKERS OF URBAN NON-PRIVATE ENTITIES IN MAIN YEARS

年份 Year	年底在岗职工人数（万人） Number of Fully Employed Staff and Workers by the End of Year (10000 persons)	在岗职工工资总额（万元） Total Wages of Fully Employed Staff and Workers (10000 yuan)	在岗职工年平均工资（元） Average Annual Wage of Fully Employed Staff and Workers (yuan)	年份 Year	年底在岗职工人数（万人） Number of Fully Employed Staff and Workers by the End of Year (10000 persons)	在岗职工工资总额（万元） Total Wages of Fully Employed Staff and Workers (10000 yuan)	在岗职工年平均工资（元） Average Annual Wage of Fully Employed Staff and Workers (yuan)
1949	3.91	1472	376	1989	55.12	112962	2052
1952	6.44	3077	508	1990	56.17	128994	2333
1957	11.03	4854	573	1991	56.14	144208	2558
1962	16.51	7942	531	1992	56.15	178846	3147
1965	18.51	8266	572	1993	57.53	242714	4216
1970	13.45	9988	499	1994	55.52	325767	5887
1971	24.83	12021	512	1995	54.42	386820	7098
1972	26.03	12895	500	1996	53.70	430388	7984
1973	26.44	13423	507	1997	49.69	456656	8594
1974	27.21	13836	512	1998	46.67	455656	9570
1975	28.35	14341	517	1999	44.75	479067	10514
1976	30.26	14899	508	2000	40.39	489699	11542
1977	31.94	15343	493	2001	37.66	518441	13108
1978	36.63	19255	534	2002	35.90	552293	14907
1979	39.14	22002	580	2003	34.67	607812	17259
1980	40.99	27169	690	2004	34.84	698249	19985
1981	42.61	28835	697	2005	35.11	785656	22990
1982	44.24	32000	737	2006	35.47	928432	26553
1983	46.31	34859	764	2007	35.51	1076918	30413
1984	47.97	45634	973	2008	35.92	1253405	34834
1985	50.27	58411	1196	2009	35.97	1410417	39220
1986	51.89	71936	1417	2010	36.70	1615042	44214
1987	53.80	83035	1588	2011	38.07	2271309	49755
1988	55.44	102877	1902				

注：根据国家统计局规定，从2011年起，在岗职工工资中包括了用人单位使用的劳务派遣人员工资。

Note: In accordance with the provisions of the National Bureau of Statistics, from 2011 onwards,the wages of persons employed include the salaries of assigned personnel employed by the employers.

6-4 分地区城镇非私营单位从业人员（2011 年底）
NUMBER OF EMPLOYED PERSONS OF URBAN NON-PRIVATE ENTITIES BY REGION (END OF 2011)

单位：人（person）

指标	Item	全市 Whole Municipality	其中 of which 市区 Urban Area	溧阳市 Liyang City	金坛市 Jintan City
总计	**Total**	**501182**	**388684**	**57518**	**54980**
#女性	Female	196857	145534	24075	27248
按企业、事业、机关分	**Grouped by Character of the Units**				
企业	Enterprises	374133	296807	37499	39827
事业	Institutions	92247	67773	13328	11146
机关	Government Agencies	34802	24104	6691	4007
按登记注册类型分	**Grouped by Type of Registration**				
内资	Domestic-funded	388309	301985	50587	35737
国有	State-owned	152061	112677	23558	15826
集体	Collective-owned	13218	9790	754	2674
股份合作	Share-holding Cooperative	9249	4750	2342	2157
联营	Joint Ownership	1415	878	537	
有限责任公司	Limited Liability Corporations	102723	71835	19365	11523
股份有限公司	Share-holding Corporations Ltd.	84768	80152	2703	1913
其他	Others	24875	21903	1328	1644
港澳台商投资	Investment from Hongkong, Macao and Taiwan	61938	51283	2498	8157
外商投资	Foreign Investment	50935	35416	4433	11086
按国民经济行业分	**Grouped by Economic Sector**				
农林牧渔业	Farming,Forestry,Animal Husbandry and Fishery	1094	445	476	173
采矿业	Mining	395			395
制造业	Manufacturing	206796	155726	21521	29549
电力、燃气及水的生产和供应业	Production and Supply of Electricity, Gas and Water	7235	5694	980	561
建筑业	Construction	75541	66947	5527	3067
交通运输、仓储和邮政业	Transportation , Storage and Post	19788	15764	2347	1677
信息传输、计算机服务和软件业	Information Transformation, Computer Service and Software	4253	3483	475	295
批发和零售业	Wholesale and Retail Trade	17011	13409	2537	1065
住宿和餐饮业	Accommodation and Catering Services	6154	3732	2258	164
金融业	Banking	18373	16531	1011	831
房地产业	Real Estate Industry	4547	3760	316	471
租赁和商务服务业	Rent and Business Services	6565	3888	603	2074
科学研究、技术服务和地质勘查业	Scientific Research and Technology Service and Geologic Examination	8745	8271	183	291
水利、环境和公共设施管理业	Water Conservancy, Environment and Public Facilities Management	9729	6707	1499	1523
居民服务和其他服务业	Neighborhood Services and Other Services	364	285	57	22
教育	Education	47302	34499	7420	5383
卫生、社会保障和社会福利业	Hygiene, Social Security and Social Welfare	26576	20219	3304	3053
文化、体育和娱乐业	Culture, Sports and Entertainment	3377	3066	168	143
公共管理和社会组织	Public Administration and Social Organizations	37337	26258	6836	4243

注：根据国家统计局规定，从2011年起，从业人员中包含了劳务派遣人员。
Note：In accordance with the provisions of the National Bureau of Statistics, from 2011 onwards, the persons employed contain the assigned personnel.

6-5　分地区城镇非私营单位从业人员工资总额（2011 年）
TOTAL LABOR REWARD OF PERSONS EMPLOYED BY URBAN NON- PRIVATE ENTITIES BY REGION（2011）

单位：万元（10000 yuan）

指　标	Item	全　市 Whole Municipality	其　中 of which 市　区 Urban Area	溧阳市 Liyang City	金坛市 Jintan City
总　计	**Total**	**2331723**	**1886155**	**234836**	**210732**
按企业、事业、机关分	**Grouped by Character of the Units**				
企　业	Enterprises	1486682	1245816	118316	122550
事　业	Institutions	582429	451200	69983	61247
机　关	Government Agencies	262612	189140	46538	26934
按登记注册类型分	**Grouped by Type of Registration**				
内　资	Domestic-funded	1889577	1515710	217858	156009
国　有	State-owned	1015866	777723	141763	96380
集　体	Collective-owned	58893	46936	3247	8710
股份合作	Share-holding Cooperative	36770	24916	5315	6540
联　营	Joint Ownership	4809	3536	1273	
有限责任公司	Limited Liability Corporations	394367	308274	54710	31383
股份有限公司	Share-holding Corporations Ltd.	296778	278959	8295	9524
其　他	Others	82095	75367	3256	3472
港澳台商投资	Investment from Hongkong, Macao and Taiwan	228265	196901	7265	24099
外商投资	Foreign Investment	213880	173544	9712	30624
按国民经济行业分	**Grouped by Economic Sector**				
农林牧渔业	Farming,Forestry,Animal Husbandry and Fishery	5076	2468	2165	443
采矿业	Mining	2219	594		1625
制造业	Manufacturing	814751	669411	58946	86395
电力、燃气及水的生产和供应业	Production and Supply of Electricity, Gas and Water	57600	44228	8735	4637
建筑业	Construction	125729	100940	17493	7297
交通运输、仓储和邮政业	Transportation , Storage and Post	85946	72421	8925	4600
信息传输、计算机服务和软件业	Information Transformation, Computer Service and Software	30427	25704	3491	1232
批发和零售业	Wholesale and Retail Trade	75728	63722	7584	4423
住宿和餐饮业	Accommodation and Catering Services	17198	11633	5241	323
金融业	Banking	201388	188145	5720	7522
房地产业	Real Estate Industry	18049	14243	1624	2183
租赁和商务服务业	Rent & Business Services	24618	17626	2112	4880
科学研究、技术服务和地质勘查业	Scientific Research and Technology Service and Geologic Examination	56849	53413	1250	2186
水利、环境和公共设施管理业	Water Conservancy, Environment and Public Facilities Management	32584	23020	5557	4007
居民服务和其他服务业	Neighborhood Services and Other Services	2172	1785	242	145
教　育	Education	321159	244444	42135	34580
卫生、社会保障和社会福利业	Hygiene, Social Security and Social Welfare	165443	134642	15647	15153
文化、体育和娱乐业	Culture, Sports and Entertainment	21681	20674	494	514
公共管理和社会组织	Public Administration and Social Organizations	273106	197043	47475	28588

注：根据国家统计局规定，从2011年起，从业人员工资中包含了劳务派遣人员工资。

Note：In accordance with the provisions of the National Bureau of Statistics, from 2011 onwards,the wages of persons employed include the salaries of assigned personnel .

6-6 分地区城镇非私营单位从业人员平均工资（2011 年）
AVERAGE WAGE OF EMPLOYED PERSONS OF URBAN NON- PRIVATE ENTITIES BY REGION（2011）

单位：元（yuan）

指标	Item	全市 Whole Municipality	其中 of which 市区 Urban Area	溧阳市 Liyang City	金坛市 Jintan City
总计	**Total**	**49267**	**50652**	**41033**	**38191**
按企业、事业、机关分	**Grouped by Character of the Units**				
企业	Enterprises	42830	44019	31757	30572
事业	Institutions	63576	67113	52634	55217
机关	Government Agencies	76077	79281	69866	67319
按登记注册类型分	**Grouped by Type of Registration**				
内资	Domestic-funded	52471	55355	43184	43517
国有	State-owned	67106	68560	60764	61275
集体	Collective-owned	43660	46826	42054	31906
股份合作	Share-holding Cooperative	39627	34020	22482	28188
联营	Joint Ownership	35361	41648	24916	
有限责任公司	Limited Liability Corporations	38452	39725	28059	27284
股份有限公司	Share-holding Corporations Ltd.	50277	50939	30848	49707
其他	Others	35672	37435	25339	21004
港澳台商投资	Investment from Hongkong, Macao and Taiwan	36702	37333	30642	29314
外商投资	Foreign Investment	41955	45846	22018	27569
按国民经济行业分	**Grouped by Economic Sector**				
农林牧渔业	Farming,Forestry,Animal Husbandry and Fishery	46352	49749	45473	25607
采矿业	Mining	41043			41043
制造业	Manufacturing	39283	39830	27740	29038
电力、燃气及水的生产和供应业	Production and Supply of Electricity, Gas and Water	78442	75747	85975	83850
建筑业	Construction	25836	25443	30402	22534
交通运输、仓储和邮政业	Transportation , Storage and Post	42238	43922	37883	28309
信息传输、计算机服务和软件业	Information Transformation, Computer Service and Software	72792	75379	73497	41746
批发和零售业	Wholesale and Retail Trade	44082	46188	29856	41493
住宿和餐饮业	Accommodation and Catering Services	28648	27639	24108	19588
金融业	Banking	111857	112458	57200	90197
房地产业	Real Estate Industry	40451	38609	51227	47862
租赁和商务服务业	Rent & Business Services	38381	43587	35370	24062
科学研究、技术服务和地质勘查业	Scientific Research and Technology Service and Geologic Examination	68916	68601	68295	78079
水利、环境和公共设施管理业	Water Conservancy, Environment and Public Facilities Management	33963	34969	37373	26291
居民服务和其他服务业	Neighborhood Services and Other Services	60158	63294	42421	65909
教育	Education	68361	71364	57617	63871
卫生、社会保障和社会福利业	Hygiene, Social Security and Social Welfare	63045	67362	47808	50832
文化、体育和娱乐业	Culture, Sports and Entertainment	65581	68751	31465	36176
公共管理和社会组织	Public Administration and Social Organizations	73699	75742	69745	67504

注：根据国家统计局规定，从2011年起，从业人员工资中包含了劳务派遣人员工资。

Note: In accordance with the provisions of the National Bureau of Statistics, from 2011 onwards,the wages of persons employed include the salaries of assigned personnel employed by the employers.

6-7 分地区城镇非私营单位在岗职工人数（2011 年底）
NUMBER OF ON-POST STAFF AND WORKERS OF URBAN NON-PRIVATE ENTITIES BY REGION（END OF 2011）

单位：人 (person)

指 标	Item	全 市 Whole Municipality	其中 of which 市 区 Urban Area	溧阳市 Liyang City	金坛市 Jintan City
总 计	**Total**	**380678**	**274967**	**54317**	**51394**
按企业、事业、机关分	**Grouped by Character of the Units**				
企 业	Enterprises	264736	191966	35500	37270
事 业	Institutions	82822	60112	12444	10266
机 关	Government Agencies	33120	22889	6373	3858
按登记注册类型分	**Grouped by Type of Registration**				
内 资	Domestic-funded	292711	212913	47603	32195
国 有	State-owned	138469	101768	21685	15016
集 体	Collective-owned	10904	8400	569	1935
股份合作	Share-holding Cooperative	8447	3960	2342	2145
联 营	Joint Ownership	1169	633	536	
有限责任公司	Limited Liability Corporations	84157	54384	18785	10988
股份有限公司	Share-holding Corporations Ltd.	29958	25875	2427	1656
其 他	Others	19607	17893	1259	455
港澳台商投资	Investment from Hongkong, Macao and Taiwan	44640	34220	2281	8139
外商投资	Foreign Investment	43327	27834	4433	11060
按国民经济行业分	**Grouped by Economic Sector**				
农林牧渔业	Farming,Forestry,Animal Husbandry and Fishery	977	332	472	173
采矿业	Mining	395			395
制造业	Manufacturing	175943	125450	21291	29202
电力、燃气及水的生产和供应业	Production and Supply of Electricity, Gas and Water	6824	5515	862	447
建筑业	Construction	14474	7272	5309	1893
交通运输、仓储和邮政业	Transportation , Storage and Post	15825	12501	1834	1490
信息传输、计算机服务和软件业	Information Transformation, Computer Service and Software	2416	1918	288	210
批发和零售业	Wholesale and Retail Trade	13032	10245	2122	665
住宿和餐饮业	Accommodation and Catering Services	5660	3340	2160	160
金融业	Banking	13900	12332	887	681
房地产业	Real Estate Industry	3912	3208	316	388
租赁和商务服务业	Rent & Business Services	5311	2664	592	2055
科学研究、技术服务和地质勘查业	Scientific Research and Technology Service and Geologic Examination	7906	7496	178	232
水利、环境和公共设施管理业	Water Conservancy, Environment and Public Facilities Management	7871	5528	1491	852
居民服务和其他服务业	Neighborhood Services and Other Services	294	215	57	22
教 育	Education	44553	32289	6903	5361
卫生、社会保障和社会福利业	Hygiene, Social Security and Social Welfare	22989	17119	2912	2958
文化、体育和娱乐业	Culture, Sports and Entertainment	2975	2690	159	126
公共管理和社会组织	Public Administration and Social Organizations	35421	24853	6484	4084

6-8 分地区城镇非私营单位在岗职工工资总额（2011 年）
TOTAL WAGES OF ON-POST STAFF AND WORKERS OF URBAN NON-PRIVATE ENTITIES BY REGION（2011）

单位：万元（10000 yuan）

指 标	Item	全 市 Whole Municipality	其中 of which 市 区 Urban Area	溧阳市 Liyang City	金坛市 Jintan City
总 计	Total	**2271309**	**1836974**	**227653**	**206682**
按企业、事业、机关分	**Grouped by Character of the Units**				
企 业	Enterprises	1441063	1206791	114303	119969
事 业	Institutions	570009	442086	67788	60135
机 关	Government Agencies	260238	188098	45562	26578
按登记注册类型分	**Grouped by Type of Registration**				
内 资	Domestic-funded	1839808	1477869	210803	151135
国 有	State-owned	1002447	768798	138155	95494
集 体	Collective-owned	55864	44783	3199	7882
股份合作	Share-holding Cooperative	36304	24474	5315	6516
联 营	Joint Ownership	4788	3516	1272	
有限责任公司	Limited Liability Corporations	377614	295140	51968	30506
股份有限公司	Share-holding Corporations Ltd.	283321	266175	7686	9460
其 他	Others	79470	74985	3209	1277
港澳台商投资	Investment from Hongkong, Macao and Taiwan	226346	195142	7137	24067
外商投资	Foreign Investment	205156	163963	9712	31481
按国民经济行业分	**Grouped by Economic Sector**				
农林牧渔业	Farming,Forestry,Animal Husbandry and Fishery	5042	2445	2155	443
采矿业	Mining	2219	594		1625
制造业	Manufacturing	801081	655701	58673	86708
电力、燃气及水的生产和供应业	Production and Supply of Electricity, Gas and Water	56940	43594	8710	4637
建筑业	Construction	115023	94894	15063	5067
交通运输、仓储和邮政业	Transportation , Storage and Post	84923	71689	8661	4573
信息传输、计算机服务和软件业	Information Transformation, Computer Service and Software	30164	25697	3460	1008
批发和零售业	Wholesale and Retail Trade	71571	60352	6891	4328
住宿和餐饮业	Accommodation and Catering Services	16754	11293	5143	317
金融业	Banking	189454	176296	5715	7443
房地产业	Real Estate Industry	16838	13216	1624	1998
租赁和商务服务业	Rent & Business Services	24028	17091	2085	4853
科学研究、技术服务和地质勘查业	Scientific Research and Technology Service and Geologic Examination	55310	51926	1237	2147
水利、环境和公共设施管理业	Water Conservancy, Environment and Public Facilities Management	30319	21771	5291	3258
居民服务和其他服务业	Neighborhood Services and Other Services	2126	1739	242	145
教 育	Education	316339	240732	41034	34573
卫生、社会保障和社会福利业	Hygiene, Social Security and Social Welfare	161526	131878	14787	14861
文化、体育和娱乐业	Culture, Sports and Entertainment	21346	20386	482	478
公共管理和社会组织	Public Administration and Social Organizations	270305	195682	46402	28221

注：根据国家统计局规定，从2011年起，在岗职工工资中包含了劳务派遣人员的工资。

Note：In accordance with the provisions of the National Bureau of Statistics, from 2011 onwards,the wages of persons employed include the salaries of assigned personnel employed by the employers.

6-9　分地区城镇非私营单位在岗职工平均工资（2011 年）
AVERAGE WAGE OF ON-POST STAFF AND WORKERS OF URBAN NON-PRIVATE ENTITIES BY REGION（2011）

单位：元（yuan）

指　标	Item	全　市 Whole Municipality	其中 of which 市　区 Urban Area	溧阳市 Liyang City	金坛市 Jintan City
总　计	**Total**	**49755**	**52622**	**41551**	**39273**
按企业、事业、机关分	**Grouped by Character of the Units**				
企　业	Enterprises	42886	44470	31813	31233
事　业	Institutions	65803	68558	54716	58270
机　关	Government Agencies	76975	86889	70616	68220
按登记注册类型分	**Grouped by Type of Registration**				
内　资	Domestic-funded	53460	58790	43864	45307
国　有	State-owned	68289	70109	62426	61824
集　体	Collective-owned	47063	49187	42485	38507
股份合作	Share-holding Cooperative	39816	34545	22482	28231
联　营	Joint Ownership	35757	42410	24941	
有限责任公司	Limited Liability Corporations	38838	40467	27899	27453
股份有限公司	Share-holding Corporations Ltd.	50256	52342	31771	50078
其　他	Others	37096	40318	25586	22966
港澳台商投资	Investment from Hongkong, Macao and Taiwan	36605	37642	30764	29375
外商投资	Foreign Investment	40614	43742	22018	28422
按国民经济行业分	**Grouped by Economic Sector**				
农林牧渔业	Farming,Forestry,Animal Husbandry and Fishery	46645	50358	45646	25607
采矿业	Mining	41043			41043
制造业	Manufacturing	39000	39699	27761	29423
电力、燃气及水的生产和供应业	Production and Supply of Electricity, Gas and Water	78952	72868	87888	83850
建筑业	Construction	25681	30291	29827	23845
交通运输、仓储和邮政业	Transportation , Storage and Post	42647	45789	38821	28405
信息传输、计算机服务和软件业	Information Transformation, Computer Service and Software	73733	75433	73774	46860
批发和零售业	Wholesale and Retail Trade	45249	46337	30970	43108
住宿和餐饮业	Accommodation and Catering Services	29036	32011	24317	19696
金融业	Banking	118564	125417	57324	91551
房地产业	Real Estate Industry	43351	41495	51227	52291
租赁和商务服务业	Rent & Business Services	38237	42185	35215	24107
科学研究、技术服务和地质勘查业	Scientific Research and Technology Service and Geologic Examination	71129	70879	69494	78938
水利、环境和公共设施管理业	Water Conservancy, Environment and Public Facilities Management	37297	42006	38281	37705
居民服务和其他服务业	Neighborhood Services and Other Services	61797	65623	42421	65909
教　育	Education	69993	72962	59221	63906
卫生、社会保障和社会福利业	Hygiene, Social Security and Social Welfare	64507	67491	50347	51441
文化、体育和娱乐业	Culture, Sports and Entertainment	66874	69888	32561	37638
公共管理和社会组织	Public Administration and Social Organizations	74680	82905	70692	68348

注：根据国家统计局规定，从2011年起，在岗职工工资中包含了劳务派遣人员的工资。

Note：In accordance with the provisions of the National Bureau of Statistics, from 2011 onwards,the wages of persons employed include the salaries of assigned personnel by the employers.

6-10 分地区城镇非私营单位从业人员和工资（2011 年）
THE PERSONS EMPLOYED BY AND THE WAGES OFFERED BY URBAN NON-PRIVATE ENTITIES BY REGION（2011）

地 区	Region	年底从业人员人数（人） Number of Persons Employed at Year-end (person)	年底在岗职工人数（人） umber of Fully Employed Staff and Workers by the End of Year (person)	从业人员工资总额（万元） Total Wages of Persons Employed (10000 yuan)
全 市	**Whole Municipality**	**501182**	**380678**	**2331723**
市 区	Urban Area	388684	274967	1886156
武进区	Wujin Distric	158442	77713	648644
新北区	New District	61260	53267	361752
天宁区	Tianning District	95353	80042	506883
钟楼区	Zhonglou District	54919	46768	270743
戚墅堰区	Qishuyan District	18710	17177	98134
溧阳市	Liyang City	57518	54317	234836
金坛市	JintanCity	54980	51394	210732

6-10 续表 1 continued 1

地 区	Region	在岗职工工资总额（万元） Total Wages of Fully Employed Staff and Workers (10000 yuan)	从业人员平均工资（元） Average Wage of Persons Employed (yuan)	在岗职工平均工资（元） Average Wages of Staff and Workers with Post (yuan)
全 市	**Whole Municipality**	**2271309**	**49267**	**49755**
市 区	Urban Area	1836974	50652	52622
武进区	Wujin Distric	642445	46345	49060
新北区	New District	352290	57863	57315
天宁区	Tianning District	493084	55314	55759
钟楼区	Zhonglou District	252801	49764	50530
戚墅堰区	Qishuyan District	96354	52557	52918
溧阳市	Liyang City	227653	41033	41551
金坛市	JintanCity	206682	38191	39273

注：根据国家统计局规定，从2011年起，从业人员中包含了劳务派遣人员，在岗职工工资中包含了劳务派遣人员的工资。
Note：In accordance with the provisions of the National Bureau of Statistics, from 2011 onwards, the persons employed contain the assigned personnel, the wages of persons employed include the salaries of assigned personnel.

6-11　分地区城镇就业和失业变动情况（2011 年）
URBAN EMPLOMENT AND UNEMPLOYMENT CHANGE BY REGION（2011）

单位：人 (person)

指 标	Item	全 市 Whole Municipality	其 中 of which		
			市 区 Urban Area	溧阳市 Liyang City	金坛市 Jintan City
上年末结转失业人数	Number of Unemployed Persons Carried Forward at Previous Year-end	31454	25869	3095	2490
本年新登记失业人数	Number of Newly Registered Unemployed Persons at This Year	87152	79138	3837	4177
#女　性	Female	46013	42394	1651	1968
#由就业转失业人数	Number of Employed Persons Changed to Unemployed	58790	53992	2523	2275
本年失业人员就业数	Number of Employment of Former Unemployed Persons	84142	76676	3570	3896
#女　性	Female	44787	41421	1554	1812
年末实有登记失业人数	Actual Registered Unemployed Persons at Year-end	32650	26813	3362	2475
#女　性	Female	14418	11877	1431	1110
#由就业转失业人数	Long-term Unemployed Persons	8451	4617	2417	1417
登记失业率 (%)	Registered Unemployment Rate (%)	2.6	2.8	2.0	2.0

6-12　失业人员安置情况（2007-2011 年）
UNEMPLOYED PERSONS ALLOCATION （2007-2011）

单位：人 (person)

指 标	Item	2007	2008	2009	2010	2011
当年登记失业人数	Number of Registered Unem ployed Persons at This Year	45278	56683	48063	67464	87152
当年已安置就业人数	Number of Arranged Empl oyed Persons at This Year	44424	52651	48649	65387	84142
年末实有登记失业人数	Actual Number of Registered Unemployed Persons at Year-end	31060	32777	30811	31454	32650
登记失业率 (%)	Registered Unemployment Rate (%)	3.2	2.9	2.7	2.6	2.6

7

CHAPTER 7

物价指数

PRICE INDEX

常州统计年鉴

7 物价指数
PRICE INDEX

2011年主要统计指标
MAJOR STATISTICAL INDICATORS OF 2011

市区居民消费价格指数（以上年价格为100）	Consumer Price Index of Urban Residents (Preceding Year=100)	105.0
#食　品	Food	111.7
市区商品零售价格指数（以上年价格为100）	Retail Price Index of Urban Commodities (Preceding Year=100)	104.4
#食　品	Food	111.5

7-1　市区居民消费价格指数（1984-2011 年，以上年价格为 100）
CONSUMER PRICE INDEX OF URBAN RESIDENTS（1984-2011, PRECEDING YEAR=100）

年　份 Year	居民消费价格指数 Consumer Price Index	其　中 食品类 Food	其　中 of which 粮　食 Grain	肉禽及其制品 Meat and Poultry	水产品 Aquatic Products	菜　类 Vegetables	其中 of which 鲜　菜 Fresh Vegetables	衣着类 Clothing
1984	102.6	103.9	99.9	105.3	127.9		101.2	99.5
1985	112.9	119.0	100.7	118.1	148.5		160.7	100.1
1986	106.1	108.5	98.4	111.4	102.3		116.9	101.0
1987	116.2	112.9	104.1	115.5	118.1		128.2	108.0
1988	123.3	130.2	102.2	135.3	129.3		153.0	120.3
1989	116.1	112.9	101.2	115.5	119.9		98.3	125.6
1990	104.2	102.3	101.8	101.2	102.7		105.9	110.0
1991	108.4	111.3	155.9	97.9	107.4		139.8	105.6
1992	108.2	109.9	159.2	103.0	112.1		99.7	103.5
1993	121.7	123.0	153.1	112.6	142.0		138.8	111.6
1994	122.4	131.1	159.0	140.9	119.1	134.8	137.2	115.3
1995	114.9	117.9	129.1	122.9	115.6	121.0	122.8	118.0
1996	110.2	108.9	107.4	105.6	105.0	131.7	133.7	114.1
1997	101.9	98.7	83.6	105.3	97.1	94.6	93.1	102.1
1998	101.6	97.8	101.7	90.5	92.6	105.2	105.7	101.5
1999	98.3	94.0	97.7	84.9	90.6	95.3	94.8	97.8
2000	99.5	95.5	80.5	96.1	95.2	110.4	110.9	95.3
2001	100.1	97.4	91.4	97.4	95.3	93.3	92.0	94.4
2002	98.5	97.8	96.1	97.7	93.0	111.1	109.7	99.5
2003	100.7	102.8	102.8	104.6	98.9	110.5	111.4	97.4
2004	104.3	113.2	140.2	122.1	119.2	93.8	93.3	98.5
2005	102.8	104.7	99.7	106.2	101.3	107.7	108.5	97.1
2006	101.8	104.7	103.9	99.2	108.2	108.0	108.9	99.7
2007	103.3	110.4	104.2	125.1	111.8	116.4	117.1	100.4
2008	105.2	112.3	113.9	121.1	112.6	104.7	103.6	102.4
2009	99.5	101.3	106.9	91.0	102.0	115.8	116.9	102.6
2010	103.4	107.4	119.8	101.5	114.3	114.8	115.3	102.4
2011	105.0	111.7	116.0	121.6	113.9	107.6	106.6	101.6

of which								
家庭设备及用品类	医疗保健类	交通和通讯工具类	娱乐教育文化用品类	居住类	服务项目类	其中 of which		
						学杂保育费	修理及其他服务费	医疗保健服务
Household Appliances	Health Care	Means of Transportation and Commun-ication	Recreational, Educational and Cultural Goods	Housing	Service	Tuition and Children Care	Repair and Other Services	Medical and Health Care Services
98.6	106.3		99.7		104.3	116.4	106.9	100.0
101.0	102.4		100.5		109.8	127.3	118.1	100.0
102.6	100.8		101.5		106.6	104.4	113.5	102.3
106.9	104.9		103.2		108.5	100.0	115.4	105.4
111.0	117.5		107.7		117.6	100.4	133.7	100.0
114.7	112.2		121.3		115.7	148.3	123.4	100.0
101.3	101.0		97.2		114.1	102.7	109.6	332.4
102.1	101.5		96.1		111.5	100.0	115.4	100.0
103.7	109.6		90.4		121.1	148.0	103.2	100.0
112.2	108.9		102.3		140.3	130.1	148.2	231.5
111.8	103.3	105.7	109.6	113.5	117.6	117.1	120.0	114.4
105.3	103.9	103.8	105.8	111.9	121.6	128.7	123.8	100.0
101.6	108.7	97.2	113.0	126.0	112.3	115.7	100.4	101.4
101.9	102.1	100.1	103.6	109.7	113.2	127.3	100.2	100.1
95.9	98.7	100.5	101.5	117.7	112.8	109.2	108.3	138.7
98.4	102.4	102.7	98.0	106.5	108.5	122.1	100.9	118.9
99.7	101.8	97.6	101.7	103.8	111.7	128.7	100.0	108.8
98.5	101.6	97.6	112.8	99.7	110.5	138.5		116.9
97.5	100.3	98.2	97.5	100.7	99.5	102.3		100.0
93.9	98.2	98.9	99.4	103.7	101.1	103.7		100.0
98.3	93.6	100.2	99.2	103.3	100.8	100.0		100.0
100.2	100.2	99.7	103.6	106.5	104.9	112.5		101.0
101.6	101.1	99.3	96.2	106.3	101.8	99.0		103.4
101.4	100.9	96.8	96.2	104.2	99.4	97.5		100.0
103.8	102.0	99.2	97.9	106.5	102.0	101.1		100.0
101.3	100.4	94.9	98.6	97.9	99.5	100.0		100.3
101.8	101.5	100.1	99.7	104.1	102.2	100.1		102.1
106.3	102.4	100.0	101.5	104.4	103.0	100.7		102.4

7-2　市区商品零售价格指数（1984-2011 年，以上年价格为 100）
RETAIL PRICE INDEX OF URBAN COMMODITIES（1984-2011, PRECEDING YEAR=100）

年 份 Year	商品零售价格指数 Retail Price Index of commodities	其 中							
		食品类 Food	其 中 of which				饮 料 烟酒类 Beverages, Tobacco and Liquor	服 装 鞋帽类 Clothing, Shoes and Hats	纺织品类 Textiles
			粮 食 Grain	肉禽蛋 Meat,Poultry and Eggs	水产品 Aquatic Products	鲜 菜 Fresh Vegetables			
1984	102.5	103.9	99.9	105.3	127.9	101.2	99.3	99.6	99.2
1985	113.2	119.0	100.7	118.1	148.5	160.7	100.8	100.1	100.0
1986	106.1	108.5	98.4	114.4	102.3	116.9	101.9	100.8	101.3
1987	110.4	112.9	104.1	115.5	118.1	128.2	107.2	109.8	104.2
1988	123.8	130.2	102.2	135.3	129.3	153.0	124.1	120.9	118.9
1989	116.1	112.9	101.2	115.5	119.9	98.3	109.9	124.6	128.4
1990	103.4	102.3	101.8	101.2	102.7	105.9	97.6	109.8	110.5
1991	108.1	111.3	155.9	97.9	107.4	139.8	104.8	106.1	103.4
1992	107.0	109.9	159.2	103.0	112.1	99.7	111.3	104.3	101.3
1993	119.9	123.0	153.1	112.6	142.0	138.8	107.8	114.4	100.8
1994	118.9	134.9	154.7	135.6	121.2	137.6	108.2	118.3	111.6
1995	112.8	123.2	130.1	125.0	115.4	127.6	108.1	119.0	113.4
1996	107.8	109.4	111.8	105.7	105.4	132.2	107.8	117.8	112.4
1997	100.2	97.0	82.3	101.6	97.8	93.5	97.7	102.8	105.8
1998	98.8	98.4	101.6	93.4	93.1	106.3	99.1	102.7	100.7
1999	97.3	93.3	98.0	85.5	91.5	95.3	99.6	98.6	99.6
2000	98.0	94.0	80.6	94.3	95.7	110.4	95.9	97.2	94.1
2001	97.3	98.6	105.5	99.2	94.2	94.7	98.3	90.8	90.3
2002	99.0	99.3	97.2	99.0	94.2	105.6	94.2	100.8	106.0
2003	100.8	103.0	103.3	105.0	98.9	111.4	105.0	98.0	98.3
2004	103.7	114.0	139.2	123.9	119.5	92.8	101.6	97.3	100.0
2005	101.3	104.7	99.8	105.9	101.3	109.1	101.3	96.0	100.8
2006	100.6	104.4	102.9	98.6	108.2	108.9	97.3	97.0	99.9
2007	102.4	110.6	103.3	125.8	111.7	117.1	101.1	100.1	102.2
2008	104.7	112.6	113.9	121.8	111.8	103.6	103.9	102.7	103.7
2009	99.6	101.8	107.1	92.7	101.7	116.9	101.5	103.2	101.9
2010	102.7	107.8	120.0	100.8	114.1	115.3	100.5	102.5	109.5
2011	104.4	111.5	116.0	120.3	114.2	106.6	103.9	103.4	132.1

of which									
中西药品类 Traditional Chinese and Western Medicines	化妆品类 Cosmetics	书报杂志类 Newspapers and Magazines	文化体育用品类 Cultural and Sports Goods	日用品类 Articles for Daily Use	家用电器类 Household Appliances	首饰类 Jewelry	燃料类 Fuels	建筑装璜材料类 Building Decoration Materials	机电产品类 Mechanical and Electrical Products
106.3		100.0	99.5	100.5	98.4		100.0		
102.4		116.3	101.7	103.4	99.2		100.0		
100.8		125.4	106.9	102.1	101.3		100.0		
104.9		100.0	115.9	112.4	100.3		100.0		
117.5		116.2	108.2	115.7	107.7		100.0	127.8	
112.2		198.4	112.6	117.9	118.5		100.0	120.6	
101.0		110.9	109.5	107.4	96.2		161.9	101.7	
101.5		100.3	101.6	102.5	96.5		143.9	100.3	
109.6		108.1	100.7	105.8	91.4		141.8	100.8	
108.9		105.9	105.4	113.4	104.5		201.9	125.8	
103.7	133.0	135.2	107.4	114.0	105.9	114.2	124.5	103.5	
103.3	109.4	126.8	103.9	109.0	100.9	99.6	107.9	100.1	92.6
106.9	102.1	138.1	102.1	106.5	99.6	99.0	111.8	99.1	94.9
102.0	101.2	116.4	99.2	102.8	100.0	100.7	103.7	102.7	93.3
98.8	104.1	115.7	98.0	100.5	89.8	91.7	102.6	99.9	97.4
102.2	101.8	102.5	99.0	100.1	97.7	94.2	99.7	101.2	99.5
101.7	98.8	108.4	99.8	101.2	98.5	109.0	118.1	97.0	98.1
99.6	91.0	110.5	95.6	98.9	98.1	93.7	100.9	95.6	96.7
93.3	100.3	95.4	99.1	99.6	100.0	101.8	99.7	102.0	96.5
98.2	102.3	99.6	99.3	99.9	93.7	118.6	112.0	101.1	
92.2	100.7	100.2	100.2	100.6	94.8	114.2	107.6	104.6	
99.6	101.8	100.4	95.6	101.4	96.9	105.3	111.4	106.0	
98.3	100.1	96.6	98.4	101.4	94.0	119.1	110.9	111.4	
100.0	99.6	97.2	95.9	100.6	98.0	105.2	102.5	109.3	
102.1	99.7	105.0	93.7	105.0	98.0	110.6	109.7	107.8	
100.2	100.3	124.5	92.2	101.6	94.5	98.5	88.9	98.4	
97.7	101.6	101.6	101.2	101.8	93.7	108.0	111.0	108.0	
101.9	95.9	100.7	95.4	104.5	102.7	117.0	108.6	105.8	

7-3　市区居民消费价格指数（2011 年，以上年价格为 100）
CONSUMER PRICE INDEX OF URBAN RESIDENTS（2011, PRECEDING YEAR=100）

指　标	Item	2011
居民消费价格指数	**Residents Consumer Price Index**	**105.0**
服务项目价格指数	Price index of Service	103.0
消费品价格指数	Price index of Consumer Goods	106.2
食　品	Food	111.7
#粮　食	Grain	116.0
肉禽及其制品	Meat and Poultry	121.6
水产品	Aquatic Products	113.9
鲜　菜	Fresh Vegetables	106.6
烟酒及用品	Tobacco and Liquor and Articles	103.7
烟　草	Tobacco	99.9
酒	Liquor	115.3
吸烟饮酒用品	Smoking and Drinking Articals	120.2
衣　着	Clothing	101.6
服　装	Garments	101.1
衣着材料	Clothing Material	115.2
鞋袜帽	Shoes,Socks and Caps	102.6
衣着加工服务	Clothing Making Services	100.2
家庭设备用品及服务	Household Appliances and Services	106.3
耐用消费品	Durable Consumer Goods	106.2
室内装饰品	Interior Decorations	100.1
床上用品	Bed Articles	124.9
家庭日用杂品	Daily Use Household Articles	101.3
家庭服务及加工维修服务	Household Services,Processing and Repairing Services	105.7
医疗保健及个人用品	Health Care and Personal Articles	102.4
医疗保健	Medicine and Healthcare	102.0
个人用品及服务	Individual Articals and Services	102.9
交通和通讯	Transportation and Communication	100.0
交　通	Transportation	101.2
通　信	Communication	96.5
娱乐教育文化用品及服务	Recreational,Educational and Cultural Goods and Services	101.5
文娱用耐用消费品及服务	Durable Consumer Goods for Recreational Use and Services	92.2
教　育	Education	100.8
文化娱乐用品	Cultural and Recreational Articles	104.0
旅游及外出	Tour and External Business	106.0
居　住	Housing	104.4
建房及装修材料	Building Materials	105.3
租　房	Rent	103.6
自有住房	Housing	105.2
水、电、燃料	Water,Electricity and Fuels	102.5

7-4 市区商品零售价格指数（2011 年，以上年价格为 100）
RETAIL PRICE INDEX OF URBAN COMMODITIES（2011, PRECEDING YEAR=100）

指 标	Item	2011
商品零售价格指数	**Retail Price Index of commodities**	**104.4**
食 品	Food	111.5
#粮 食	Grain	116.0
淀粉及薯类	Starches and Tubers	108.6
干豆类及豆制品	Bean and Its Products	102.5
油 脂	Oil or Fat	115.2
肉禽及其制品	Meat, Poultry and Related Product	120.3
蛋	Eggs	114.3
水产品	Aquatic Products	114.2
菜	Vegetables	107.6
#鲜 菜	Fresh Vegetables	106.6
调味品	Flavoring	106.9
#糖	Carbohydrate	106.7
干鲜瓜果	Dried and Fresh Fruits and Melons	123.4
糕点饼干面包	Cake，Biscuit and Brad	113.1
奶及奶制品	Milk and Its Products	110.8
在外用膳食品	Out Ward Dinner	104.7
其它食品	Others Foods	110.2
饮料烟酒	Beverages,Tobacco and Liquor	103.9
服装鞋帽	Clothing,Shoes and Hats	103.4
纺织品	Textiles	132.1
家用电器及音像器材	Household Appliances and Acoutic and Visual Equipment	102.7
文化办公用品	Cultural Stationery	96.0
日用品	Articles for Daily Use	104.5
体育娱乐用品	Sports and Entertainment Articles	95.4
交通、通信用品	Tansportation and Telecommunication Facilities	94.9
家 具	Furniture	103.1
化妆品	Cosmetics	95.9
金银珠宝	Jewellery	117.0
中西药品及医疗保健用品	Chinese and Western Medicine and Medical care Articles	101.9
书报杂志及电子出版物	Newspaper, Magazine & Electronic Publication	100.7
燃 料	Fuels	108.6
建筑材料及五金电料	Construction Materials & Hardware Materials	105.8

7-5　市区分月主要农副产品价格（2011 年）
MAIN AGRICULTURAL AND SIDELINE PRODUCTS IN URBAN AREA BY MONTH（2011）

品　种	Name	规格等级	Specification and Grade	1 月 Jan.	2 月 Feb.
粳　米	Polished Rice	特　一	Special First Grade	5.50	5.50
植物油	Vegetable Oil	豆　油	Soybean Oil	11.34	11.34
猪　肉	Pork	去骨后腿肉	Thigh Meat without Bone	22.35	23.52
鸡	Chicken	活草鸡	Live Chicken	20.04	23.32
鲜　蛋	Fresh Eggs	新鲜完整	Fresh and Whole	9.47	9.50
鲢　鱼	Silver Carp	1.0千克以上	Above 1.0 Kilogram	11.31	11.76
鲫　鱼	Crucian	活200克左右	Live and Weight about 200 Gram	13.18	13.47
虾	Shrimps	活河虾	Live Shimps	115.99	119.66
大白菜	Chinese Cabbage	一　等	First Grade	1.81	1.86
油　菜	Rape	一　等	First Grade	1.40	1.79
芹　菜	Celery	一　等	First Grade	5.52	7.38
黄　瓜	Cucumber	一　等	First Grade	6.04	8.58
西红柿	Tomato	一　等	First Grade	6.88	8.91
萝　卜	Radish	一　等	First Grade	2.03	2.32
青　椒	Green Pepper	一　等	First Grade	7.28	11.35
生　姜	Ginger	一　等	First Grade	11.36	10.98
豆　芽	Bean Sprout	一　等	First Grade	3.51	3.95
苹　果	Apples	一　级	First Grade	9.78	10.25
梨	Pears	一　级	First Grade	5.59	6.17
香　蕉	Bananas	一　级	First Grade	5.79	6.55

单位：元/千克（yuan/kg）

3月 Mar.	4月 Apr.	5月 May	6月 June	7月 July	8月 Aug.	9月 Sept.	10月 Oct.	11月 Nov.	12月 Dec.
5.76	5.84	6.22	6.14	5.70	5.67	5.86	5.48	5.58	5.75
11.13	11.23	11.24	11.24	11.33	11.30	11.30	11.54	11.85	11.28
23.67	23.30	24.45	28.16	30.24	30.02	30.63	30.04	29.09	28.08
21.61	21.04	21.46	21.78	21.48	22.00	22.12	22.25	21.80	21.71
8.82	8.63	8.99	9.65	9.62	10.26	11.00	10.12	9.28	9.13
12.17	12.59	14.50	15.67	16.54	15.26	15.14	13.75	12.87	12.73
12.79	12.70	14.33	17.30	18.69	19.36	17.49	15.81	14.41	14.06
125.18	137.69	88.22	75.46	97.54	169.39	170.06	123.13	118.98	115.29
1.56	1.52	1.81	3.15	4.63	3.18	3.18	3.20	2.02	1.63
1.59	3.68	5.45	6.67	6.16	6.72	7.78	3.58	1.88	1.88
5.90	4.60	5.40	7.13	7.62	8.37	10.39	7.21	5.75	5.82
6.62	4.92	4.72	4.99	5.08	5.06	5.74	5.33	5.22	6.75
7.40	6.32	5.77	5.11	5.90	6.15	6.02	6.62	6.24	7.22
2.17	2.06	2.10	2.11	2.56	2.67	2.68	2.81	2.03	1.81
11.78	10.61	7.79	7.09	6.63	6.51	6.76	7.13	7.62	7.87
10.43	10.17	9.66	9.19	8.90	8.61	8.37	8.02	7.24	6.99
3.70	3.69	3.70	3.69	3.70	3.90	3.90	3.90	3.90	3.90
9.92	9.98	10.22	10.11	9.83	9.26	8.81	8.72	9.16	9.18
6.12	6.62	7.38	8.28	8.51	8.31	6.62	5.45	5.69	5.73
7.53	8.81	8.30	5.56	4.20	4.32	5.75	6.09	6.94	7.00

8
CHAPTER 8

人民生活

PEOPLE' S LIVELIHOOD

常州统计年鉴

8 人民生活 PEOPLE'S LIVELIHOOD

2011年主要统计指标 MAJOR STATISTICAL INDICATORS OF 2011

城市居民人均可支配收入	Per Capita Disposable Income of Urban Residents	29829元	(yuan)
比上年增长	Over the Previous Year	13.6%	
城市居民人均消费性支出	Per Capita Consuming Expenditures of Urban Residents	18893元	(yuan)
比上年增长	Over the Previous Year	10.3%	
农民人均纯收入	Per Capita Net Income of Rural Residents	14838元	(yuan)
比上年增长	Over the Previous Year	17.4%	
农村居民人均生活消费支出	Living Expenditure of Rural Residents (yuan)	11208元	(yuan)
比上年增长	Over the Previous Year	13.1%	

8-1 市区居民家庭基本情况（1984-2011 年）
BASIC INDICATORS OF URBAN HOUSEHOLDS（1984-2011）

年 份 Year	调查户数（户） Households Surveyed (household)	户均家庭人口（人） Number of Persons Per Household (person)	户均就业人口（人） Number of Employed Persons Per Household (person)	每一就业者负担人口（人） Persons Supported by Each Employee (person)	人均可支配收入（元） Per Capita Disposable Income (yuan)	人均现住房屋使用面积（平方米） Per Capita Subsidiary Usable Floor Space(sq.m)	恩格尔系数（%） Engel Coefficient (%)	基尼系数 Gini Coefficient
1984	100	3.58	2.37	1.51	701	10.06	56.8	
1985	100	3.33	2.07	1.61	889	11.59	56.1	0.148
1986	100	3.29	2.02	1.63	1089	12.07	54.0	0.136
1987	100	3.21	1.88	1.71	1236	12.49	54.0	0.146
1988	100	3.17	1.92	1.65	1417	12.12	53.0	0.149
1989	100	3.12	1.87	1.66	1559	12.99	59.0	0.134
1990	100	3.06	1.81	1.69	1769	13.22	61.6	0.144
1991	100	2.98	1.67	1.78	1996	13.51	61.0	0.125
1992	100	2.91	1.72	1.69	2509	14.03	59.0	0.141
1993	100	3.02	1.75	1.73	3195	13.70	56.0	0.178
1994	100	3.13	1.88	1.66	4617	15.60	55.0	0.149
1995	100	3.04	1.73	1.76	5632	15.04	54.9	0.137
1996	100	3.00	1.67	1.80	6743	15.65	50.0	0.134
1997	100	3.01	1.46	2.06	6853	15.25	46.0	0.179
1998	100	2.96	1.49	1.99	7107	15.55	52.0	0.209
1999	100	2.97	1.50	1.98	7874	15.87	44.0	0.219
2000	200	2.93	3.07	1.91	8540	15.19	40.1	0.246
2001	200	2.91	1.48	1.96	9406	16.23	36.9	0.253
2002	200	2.89	1.56	1.85	9933	17.44	36.8	0.280
2003	300	2.86	1.47	1.95	11303	20.35	36.2	0.279
2004	300	2.85	1.46	1.95	12867	20.65	37.2	0.314
2005	300	2.89	1.51	1.91	14589	21.04	35.9	0.293
2006	300	2.83	1.49	1.90	16649	21.49	35.7	0.332
2007	300	2.80	1.46	1.92	19089	21.77	35.0	0.323
2008	300	2.85	1.47	1.94	21592	24.38	33.8	0.309
2009	300	2.81	1.46	1.92	23751	24.69	33.7	0.306
2010	300	2.80	1.48	1.89	26269	24.91	32.7	0.319
2011	300	2.73	1.31	2.08	29829	26.11	35.8	0.299

注：“每一就业者负担人口”包括就业者本人,下同。
Note：“Persons Supported by Each Employee” includes the employee himself,the same below.

8-2 市区居民家庭人均消费支出情况（1984-2011 年）
PER CAPITA LIVING EXPENDITURE OF URBAN HOUSEHOLDS（1984-2011）

单位：元（yuan）

年　份 Year	人均消费支　出 Per Capita Living Expenditure	其　中 of which							
		食　品 Food	衣　着 Clothing	设备用品及服务 Facilities, Articles and Services	医疗保健 Medicine and Medical Services	交通与通讯 Transport, Post and Communication Services	文教娱乐服务 Recreation, Education and Cultural Services	居　住 Residence	杂项商品及服务 Miscellaneous Commodities and Services
1984	595	338	90	33	9	17	42	44	22
1985	746	419	112	46	11	19	54	56	28
1986	918	499	136	63	15	24	71	74	36
1987	1059	576	137	74	18	30	89	93	43
1988	1359	715	178	93	23	46	122	123	59
1989	1469	860	154	87	24	48	117	117	63
1990	1498	922	167	75	22	44	101	112	54
1991	1705	1046	210	83	28	49	110	123	56
1992	2000	1170	254	169	28	25	132	138	83
1993	2456	1377	308	199	36	50	195	205	87
1994	3503	1910	400	218	65	109	328	343	131
1995	4426	2429	462	253	61	208	431	379	203
1996	4946	2469	633	293	113	234	437	435	331
1997	5442	2506	620	379	145	265	510	764	253
1998	5282	2722	368	417	196	240	525	591	225
1999	6107	2658	398	461	514	305	610	850	312
2000	6759	2710	536	708	411	396	826	746	425
2001	7526	2777	495	958	513	728	722	867	466
2002	7973	2933	587	553	644	661	1394	876	326
2003	8944	3240	689	579	791	1052	1411	816	365
2004	9878	3673	680	856	676	1181	1387	1042	384
2005	10718	3848	1041	696	815	1309	1481	1063	464
2006	12503	4467	1072	911	782	1616	1637	1541	476
2007	13789	4824	1193	750	1005	2586	1657	1289	486
2008	14967	5056	1510	1027	1284	1970	2020	1519	581
2009	15961	5379	1615	987	1055	2831	2327	1078	690
2010	17124	5603	1629	1136	1108	2928	2574	1408	737
2011	18893	6760	1754	1299	1409	2957	2962	1250	502

8-3 主要年份市区居民家庭收支情况 INCOME AND EXPENSE CONDITION OF URBAN HOUSEHOLDS IN MAIN YEARS

指标	Item	1990	1995	2000	2005	2011
调查户数（户）	**Number of Household Surveyed (household)**	**100**	**100**	**200**	**300**	**300**
户均家庭人口（人）	**Average Household Size (person)**	**3.06**	**3.04**	**2.93**	**2.89**	**2.73**
有收入者人数	Number of People with Income	2.24	2.34	2.22	2.19	2.04
# 离退休人数	Number of Retired People	0.43	0.60	0.69	0.62	0.64
无收入者人数	Number of People without Income	0.82	0.70	0.70	0.70	0.69
人均家庭总收入（元）	**Per Capita Family Income (yuan)**	**1782**	**5636**	**8577**	**15820**	**32744**
# 可支配收入	Disposable Income	1769	5632	8540	14589	29829
最低收入户（占10%）	Lowest Income (Make up 10%)	1075	3868	2901	5089	10191
低收入户（占10%）	Low Income (Make up 10%)	1295	3991	4984	7434	14802
中等偏下收入户（占20%）	Medium-Low Income (Make up 20%)	1524	4619	6428	9910	20691
中等收入户（占20%）	Medium Income (Make up 20%)	1722	5219	7901	12620	27187
中等偏上收入户（占20%）	Medium-High Income (Make up 20%)	2026	6285	10448	16097	34858
高收入户（占10%）	High Income (Make up 10%)	2290	7290	13254	21405	46343
最高收入户（占10%）	Highest Income (Make up 10%)	2964	8575	17430	39873	71498
人均家庭总支出（元）	**Per Capita Family Expenditure (yuan)**	**1590**	**4785**	**8453**	**16551**	**25915**
# 消费性支出	Expenditure for Consumption	1498	4426	6759	10718	18893
最低收入户（占10%）	Lowest Income (Make up 10%)	1058	3645	2829	5049	9091
低收入户（占10%）	Low Income (Make up 10%)	957	3798	4886	6315	12627
中等偏下收入户（占20%）	Medium-Low Income (Make up 20%)	1278	3711	5453	8455	15292
中等收入户（占20%）	Medium Income (Make up 20%)	1544	4427	6546	10124	18303
中等偏上收入户（占20%）	Medium-High Income (Make up 20%)	1716	5030	7455	10635	23767
高收入户（占10%）	High Income (Make up 10%)	1928	4911	8381	14234	22891
最高收入户（占10%）	Highest Income (Make up 10%)	2264	5330	14292	26323	33626
购房与建房支出	Expenditure on Housing Purchas and Construction				3140	1073
人均借贷支出（元）	**Per Capita Debit and Credit Expenditures (yuan)**	**375**	**1496**	**2871**	**5803**	**13555**
# 存入储蓄款	Deposit Money in Bank	316	1447	2532	4199	12328
购买有价证券	Buy Valuable Negotiable Securities	7	1	10	0.2	

8-4　市区居民家庭人口分组（2011 年）
POPULATION OF URBAN HOUSEHOLDS（2011）

指　标	Item	总平均 Average	最低收入组（占10%） Lowest Income Households（Make up 10%）
调查户数（户）	**Number of Household Surveyed (household)**	**300**	**30**
家庭人口	**Household Population (person)**	**2.73**	**3.13**
有收入者人数	Number of Persons with Income	2.04	1.74
就业人数	Number of Persons Employed	1.31	0.83
国有经济单位职工	Workers and Staff of State Capital Involved Enterprises	0.26	0.03
城镇集体经济单位职工	Workers and Staff of Township Collective Capital Involved Enterprises	0.05	0.03
其他各种经济类型单位职工	Workers and Staff of Other Ownership Enterprises	0.53	0.31
个体经营者	Self-employed Individuals	0.11	0.03
个体被雇者	Employed Individuals	0.24	0.31
离退休再就业者	Reemployed Retirees	0.06	
其他就业者	Other Employment	0.07	0.11
离退休人数	Number of Retired Persons	0.64	0.54
其他有收入者人数	Number of Other People with Income	0.10	0.38
无收入者人数	Number of Persons without Income	0.69	1.39
平均每一就业者负担人数	**Number of Persons Supported by Each Employee**	**2.08**	**3.77**
期末家庭人口	**Household Population at Year-end**	**2.70**	**2.97**
附:非家庭人口在家用餐人次	Number of Non-family Members who frequently have dinner in the Family	12.90	4.18

单位：人（person）

按收入水平分组 Grouped by Level of Income							
其中 of which # 更低收入组（占5%） Poor Households (Make up 5%)	低收入组（占10%） Low Income Households (Make up 10%)	中等偏下组（占20%） Lower Middle Income Households (Make up 20%)	中等收入组（占20%） Middle Income Households (Make up 20%)	中等偏上组（占20%） Upper Middle Income Households (Make up 20%)	高收入组（占10%） High Income Households (Make up 10%)	最高收入组（占10%） Highest Income Households (Make up 10%)	其中 of which # 更高收入组（占5%） Higher Income Households (Make up 5%)
15	**30**	**60**	**60**	**60**	**30**	**30**	**15**
2.74	**2.95**	**2.75**	**2.73**	**2.62**	**2.47**	**2.53**	**2.60**
1.38	**2.00**	**2.04**	**2.25**	**2.05**	**2.05**	**1.95**	**1.87**
0.63	1.24	1.24	1.36	1.43	1.63	1.36	1.46
	0.17	0.12	0.20	0.38	0.53	0.44	0.40
0.07	0.03	0.07	0.03	0.08		0.03	0.07
0.07	0.26	0.57	0.65	0.56	0.56	0.62	0.74
0.07	0.07	0.02	0.15	0.15	0.17	0.17	0.07
0.28	0.48	0.33	0.19	0.14	0.20	0.07	0.13
	0.06	0.02	0.07	0.11	0.13	0.03	0.05
0.15	0.17	0.11	0.07		0.03		
0.27	0.54	0.77	0.84	0.59	0.41	0.45	0.28
0.48	0.22	0.02	0.05	0.03	0.01	0.14	0.13
1.37	0.95	0.72	0.49	0.57	0.42	0.57	0.73
4.35	**2.38**	**2.22**	**2.01**	**1.83**	**1.52**	**1.86**	**1.78**
2.67	**3.03**	**2.73**	**2.62**	**2.55**	**2.27**	**2.93**	**2.67**
6.13	7.83	12.54	9.25	16.84	23.44	16.34	18.92

8-5　市区居民家庭人均收支情况（2011 年）
PER CAPITA INCOME OF URBAN RESIDENTS AND EXPENDITURE CONDITION（2011）

指　标	Item	总平均 Average	最低收入组（占10%） Lowest Income Households (Make up 10%)
期初手存现金	**Cash on Hand at Beginning of Year**	**828.18**	**602.59**
家庭总收入	**Total Family Income**	**32744.04**	**11333.40**
# 可支配收入	Including: Disposable Income	29828.63	10191.19
工薪收入	Income from Wages and Salaries	20783.88	6096.48
工资及补贴收入	Wages and Subsidies Income	20545.84	5694.25
其他劳动收入	Other Labor Income	238.04	402.23
经营净收入	Operating Net Income	2556.53	507.66
财产性收入	Property Income	1346.18	354.52
利息收入	Interest Income	185.15	88.77
股息与红利收入	Divident and Bonus Income	34.77	
保险收益	Insurance Yield		
其它投资收入	Other Investment Income	551.51	
出租房屋收入	Housing Rent Income	574.63	265.74
其它财产性收入	Other Property Income	0.12	
转移性收入	Transfer Income	8057.46	4374.74
养老金或离退休金	Pension or Retirement Pay	6566.26	2981.15
社会救济收入	Income from Social Relief	112.77	651.64
辞退金	Dismissal Compensation	84.11	
保险收入	Insurance Income	20.85	
# 失业保险金	Including: Unemployment Insurance Money	8.87	
赡养收入	Income from Support	280.68	203.19
捐赠收入	Income from Donation	568.83	276.32
提取住房公积金	Withdraw Public Accumulation Fund for Housing Construction	72.74	
记帐补贴	Charge Account Subsidy	209.14	194.26
其他转移性收入	Other Transfer Income	138.94	68.19
出售财物收入	**Income from Property Sold**	**163.63**	**3.26**
借贷收入	**Debit and Credit Income**	**6500.59**	**2094.79**
提取储蓄存款	Withdraw Savings Deposits	5974.69	2080.85
借入款	Loan	100.93	13.94
收回借出款	Recover Loan	18.90	
收回储蓄性保险本	Recover Savings Insurance Capital		
住房贷款	Bank Loan for Housing Purchasing	403.93	
其它贷款	Other Loans	2.14	

单位：元（yuan）

按收入水平分组 Grouped by Level of Income							
其中 of which # 更低收入组（占5%） Poor Households (Make up 5%)	低收入组（占10%） Low Income Households (Make up 10%)	中等偏下组（占20%） Lower Middle Income Households (Make up 20%)	中等收入组（占20%） Middle Income Households (Make up 20%)	中等偏上组（占20%） Upper Middle Income Households (Make up 20%)	高收入组（占10%） High Income Households (Make up 10%)	最高收入组（占10%） Highest Income Households (Make up 10%)	其中 of which # 更高收入组（占5%） Higher Income Households (Make up 5%)
604.49	**713.64**	**701.15**	**802.44**	**1001.78**	**1022.02**	**1026.38**	**872.92**
9362.13	**16512.18**	**22926.89**	**29763.75**	**38730.45**	**50632.93**	**76932.38**	**89969.46**
8077.47	14801.63	20691.00	27186.66	34858.28	46343.22	71497.54	83744.50
4354.40	9879.75	15160.62	17779.59	25347.48	34167.08	48432.67	61264.98
3613.99	9637.15	15160.37	17616.74	25211.24	34048.17	47377.43	61034.21
740.40	242.60	0.25	162.85	136.24	118.92	1055.24	230.77
1159.19	983.52	515.60	2709.60	3100.83	5894.74	6684.39	2961.54
276.24	462.23	417.85	572.46	1055.56	636.61	8785.91	14943.70
19.23	86.17	103.03	102.02	238.91	323.64	539.67	699.21
		55.24		106.86	12.97	20.29	38.46
						6107.01	11574.62
257.00	376.06	259.58	470.43	709.16	300.00	2118.94	2631.41
				0.63			
3572.31	5186.67	6832.82	8702.10	9226.58	9934.49	13029.41	10799.24
1720.86	4129.52	6019.95	7718.08	7303.27	7930.16	9703.28	5493.56
1219.77	297.12	16.20	9.84			6.76	12.82
				26.72		873.82	1656.15
		4.91		61.65		87.43	165.70
		4.91				87.43	165.70
82.59	208.11	185.98	153.70	700.26	317.57	20.29	
324.87	264.82	352.02	392.71	720.34	848.65	1572.04	2492.31
			16.41		374.46	393.69	746.15
217.65	193.85	213.67	206.84	214.04	211.49	228.64	221.03
6.56	93.25	40.08	189.02	200.30	252.16	143.46	11.52
7.43	**3.59**	**2.31**	**5.86**	**3.82**	**11.11**	**1765.91**	**3334.37**
1480.57	**4100.22**	**3523.16**	**4776.68**	**8295.90**	**7437.84**	**20610.37**	**34378.21**
1479.35	3959.21	3508.60	4776.68	7956.46	7095.95	16078.24	25916.67
1.21	22.62			339.44	341.89		
	118.39					67.64	
		3.78				4464.49	8461.54
		10.77					

8-5 续表 continued

指　标	Item	总平均 Average	最低收入组（占10%） Lowest Income Households (Make up 10%)
家庭总支出	**Total Expenditures of Households**	**25914.61**	**11227.96**
消费支出	Consumption Expenditure	18893.11	9090.53
#服务性消费支出	Expenditure on Service	5258.40	2108.87
购房与建房支出	Expenditure on Housing Purchas and Construction	1072.82	
购　房	Housing Purchase	1072.82	
转移性支出	Transfer Expenditure	3285.25	1123.88
交纳的个人收入税	Personal Income Tax	251.61	2.49
捐赠支出	Expenditure on Donation	2077.02	935.48
购买彩票	Lottery Purchase	15.95	6.00
赡养支出	Expenditure on Support	667.09	156.38
#在外就学子女费用	Expenditure on Children Study Outside	342.09	
各种非储蓄性保险支出	Non-savings Insurance Expenditure	198.67	21.22
#车辆保险支出	Expenditure on Automobile Insurance	137.30	
其他转移性支出	Other Transfer Expenditure	74.91	2.30
社会保障支出	Expenditure on Social Security	2454.66	945.47
个人交纳的养老基金	Pension Fund Paid by Individual	1033.88	490.05
个人交纳的住房公积金	Public Accumulation Fund for Housing Construction Paid by Individual	968.29	180.69
个人交纳的医疗基金	Medical Treatment Fund Paid by Individual	346.22	207.06
个人交纳的失业基金	Unemployment Fund Paid by Individual	68.05	44.04
其他社会保障支出	Other Expenditure on Social Security	38.23	23.63
借贷支出	**Debit and Credit expenditure**	**13555.09**	**2165.21**
存入储蓄款	Savings Deposits	12327.62	2018.09
借出款	Lending	64.14	5.32
归还借款	Return Loan	152.72	19.15
储蓄性保险支出	Expenditure on Savings Insurance	176.20	37.55
购买有价证券	Valuable Securities Purchasing		
其它投资支出	Other Investment Expenditures	0.71	
归还住房贷款	Return Loan for Housing Purchase	822.29	85.11
归还汽车贷款	Car Loan Repayment		
其他借贷支出	Other Debit and Credit Expenditure	2.86	
期末手存现金	**Cash on Hand at Year-end**	**787.06**	**653.15**

单位：元（yuan）

按收入水平分组 Grouped by Level of Income							
其中 of which #更低收入组（占5%） Poor Households (Make up 5%)	低收入组（占10%） Low Income Households (Make up 10%)	中等偏下组（占20%） Lower Middle Income Households (Make up 20%)	中等收入组（占20%） Middle Income Households (Make up 20%)	中等偏上组（占20%） Upper Middle Income Households (Make up 20%)	高收入组（占10%） High Income Households (Make up 10%)	最高收入组（占10%） Highest Income Households (Make up 10%)	其中 of which #更高收入组（占5%） Higher Income Households (Make up 5%)
9520.29	**15469.77**	**19641.26**	**23252.68**	**31920.15**	**31879.43**	**57999.70**	**79240.74**
7949.21	12627.14	15291.55	18302.72	23767.40	22891.48	33626.13	43135.66
1974.58	3837.32	3738.63	5097.63	6266.20	7418.66	10342.94	13727.10
					379.82	11499.44	21794.87
					379.82	11499.44	21794.87
504.07	1312.99	2182.01	2628.18	4899.80	4624.09	7486.60	7858.88
	31.68	55.13	175.59	550.16	240.89	803.63	912.78
380.28	965.50	1018.92	1843.57	3050.72	3489.46	4205.60	3791.38
0.87	3.42	8.26	5.48	45.71	1.09	34.86	36.10
99.60	275.40	966.94	436.92	625.78	740.00	1657.58	2416.21
	216.14	326.50	154.06	381.08	444.05	1198.88	1639.28
23.32	26.35	105.60	133.35	357.65	126.09	712.86	653.41
		62.12	87.53	251.82	47.30	597.33	628.67
	10.64	27.16	33.26	269.77	26.55	72.05	49.01
1067.01	1485.01	1967.10	2194.66	3107.98	3837.33	4402.58	5091.16
600.16	857.23	1027.38	993.42	1174.45	1254.49	1518.61	1976.51
121.26	300.20	501.94	807.76	1418.14	1993.78	2162.97	2420.69
238.70	302.74	359.95	323.89	363.00	428.56	476.55	605.98
54.53	24.28	50.20	57.04	98.55	126.96	90.43	81.75
52.35	0.57	27.64	12.55	53.83	33.55	154.00	6.23
1231.58	**5127.19**	**6753.85**	**11291.28**	**15318.73**	**26271.44**	**41673.89**	**48758.00**
1219.43	4578.32	5799.59	10142.69	14450.73	25042.13	36709.51	42743.59
12.15		67.52	180.54	37.72		67.64	
	226.20	68.75	180.54	50.29		730.55	
	183.33	96.79	185.93	101.82	243.58	589.82	896.09
		3.56					
	139.34	717.30	601.58	619.82	985.73	3576.36	5118.32
		0.34		14.36			
712.62	**765.80**	**765.40**	**814.45**	**823.35**	**953.03**	**727.18**	**609.88**

8-6　市区居民家庭人均消费支出情况（2011 年）
PER CAPITA LIVING EXPENDITURES OF URBAN HOUSEHOLDS（2011）

指　标	Item	总平均 Average	最低收入组（占10%） Lowest Income Households (Make up 10%)
消费支出	**Consumption Expenditures**	**18893.11**	**9090.53**
#服务性消费支出	Expenditure on Service	5258.40	2108.87
食　品	**Food**	**6759.91**	**4318.69**
粮油类	Grain and Edible Oil	697.05	594.91
粮　食	Grain	440.10	373.36
淀粉及薯类	Starches and Tubers	46.40	41.56
干豆类及豆制品	Beans and Bean Products	96.32	76.41
油脂类	Oil and Fat	114.22	103.58
肉禽蛋水产品类	Meat, Poultry, Eggs and Aquatic Products	1846.17	1440.26
肉　类	Meat	884.92	708.01
禽　类	Poultry	308.91	235.16
蛋　类	Eggs	116.94	105.22
水产品类	Aquantic Products	535.39	391.88
蔬菜类	Vegetables	682.57	624.81
鲜　菜	Fresh Vegetables	631.42	585.23
干　菜	Dried Vegetables	30.04	24.10
菜制品	Vegetables Product	21.11	15.48
调味品	Condiments	66.60	52.19
糖烟酒饮料类	Sugar, Cigarette, Wine and Beverage	800.37	360.82
糖　类	Sugar	52.53	23.02
烟草类	Tobacco	488.28	241.09
酒　类	Liquor	164.96	53.74
饮　料	Beverages	94.60	42.96
干鲜瓜果类	Dried and Fresh Melons and Fruits	573.95	284.60
鲜　果	Fresh Fruits	329.60	160.21
鲜　瓜	Fresh Melons	42.7	22.17
其它干鲜瓜果类及制品	Other Dried and Fresh Melons and Fruits and Products	201.65	102.22
糕点、奶及奶制品	Cake, Milk and Dairy Products	408.30	184.67
糕　点	Cake	130.04	50.35
奶及奶制品	Milk and Dairy Products	278.26	134.32
其他食品	Other Food	128.67	37.40
饮食服务	Catering service	1556.22	739.03
食品加工服务费	Service Fee of Food Processing	5.86	2.96
在外饮食	Eating outside	1550.36	736.07
衣　着	**Clothing**	**1753.66**	**602.86**
服　装	Garments	1321.15	429.59
衣着材料	Clothing Materials	33.50	37.35
鞋　类	Footware	324.94	102.52

单位：元（yuan）

按收入水平分组 Grouped by Level of Income							
其中 of which #更低收入组（占5%） Poor Households (Make up 5%)	低收入组（占10%） Low Income Households (Make up 10%)	中等偏下组（占20%） Lower Middle Income Households (Make up 20%)	中等收入组（占20%） Middle Income Households (Make up 20%)	中等偏上组（占20%） Upper Middle Income Households (Make up 20%)	高收入组（占10%） High Income Households (Make up 10%)	最高收入组（占10%） Highest Income Households (Make up 10%)	其中 of which #更高收入组（占5%） Higher Income Households (Make up 5%)
7949.21	**12627.14**	**15291.55**	**18302.72**	**23767.40**	**22891.48**	**33626.13**	**43135.66**
1974.58	3837.32	3738.63	5097.63	6266.20	7418.66	10342.94	13727.10
4071.38	**4640.55**	**6467.66**	**7005.30**	**7423.57**	**7276.81**	**10546.21**	**12282.15**
602.04	617.93	717.76	788.62	666.43	703.43	729.55	659.42
382.50	399.81	457.22	497.59	417.73	425.94	468.55	453.15
44.65	36.44	47.48	51.71	45.48	57.43	41.10	41.46
70.80	77.30	94.02	111.86	95.26	123.61	89.48	72.11
104.09	104.38	119.04	127.46	107.96	96.46	130.41	92.70
1263.87	1522.92	1867.27	2036.73	1927.27	1869.06	2076.73	1891.62
636.82	733.96	892.01	976.89	922.49	940.64	931.51	853.78
205.96	269.11	337.14	309.05	316.68	357.51	322.44	228.71
95.88	94.02	125.24	131.87	122.26	106.90	106.06	110.19
325.20	425.82	512.90	618.92	565.84	464.01	716.72	698.93
663.21	557.22	653.39	756.01	688.08	683.13	792.77	795.98
620.04	518.49	600.11	689.76	635.01	637.12	949.68	746.54
22.79	21.58	28.21	39.87	31.36	27.76	29.04	36.25
20.39	17.15	25.06	26.39	21.71	18.25	14.05	13.19
43.23	50.31	62.25	84.56	69.72	68.51	65.00	54.83
347.25	510.85	861.89	766.17	970.97	739.71	1340.48	1913.05
22.62	41.61	49.78	55.74	79.39	46.52	50.22	44.59
257.66	334.58	545.23	498.17	599.06	383.48	705.20	965.24
35.14	71.49	152.63	117.56	206.81	174.23	452.53	718.28
31.84	63.17	114.25	94.70	85.70	135.48	132.53	184.94
232.70	385.49	507.98	619.57	644.00	609.64	1023.77	1310.93
121.38	205.48	289.23	366.45	352.69	343.55	635.97	785.89
21.18	29.59	47.04	48.05	39.34	42.13	70.68	82.22
90.15	150.41	171.71	205.06	251.97	223.96	317.12	442.82
177.59	339.32	366.07	427.80	485.70	426.21	639.99	725.28
51.00	94.99	121.63	129.97	156.59	154.71	210.16	160.63
126.59	244.33	244.45	297.83	329.10	271.50	429.83	564.64
31.55	63.66	95.18	136.02	196.58	160.90	201.39	242.50
709.93	592.86	1335.86	1389.83	1774.84	2016.22	3676.54	4688.54
0.90	1.82	6.84	7.35	7.80	8.21	2.34	
709.03	591.04	1329.02	1382.48	1767.04	2008.01	3674.20	4688.54
560.29	**1134.48**	**1285.79**	**1664.70**	**2045.24**	**2693.30**	**3620.79**	**4453.06**
442.86	760.00	964.14	1231.88	1537.68	2115.37	2852.55	3599.70
15.78	56.56	15.32	53.51	32.15	17.58	14.99	15.21
71.91	235.34	244.26	321.89	390.64	467.06	615.98	679.13

8-6 续表　continued

指　标	Item	总平均 Average	最低收入组（占10%） Lowest Income Households (Make up 10%)
其他衣着用品	Other Clothing Supplies	55.80	28.39
衣着加工服务费	Clothing Processing and Service Fees	18.28	5.00
家庭设备用品及服务	**Household Facilities, Articles and Service**	**1298.92**	**626.59**
耐用消费品	Durable Consumer Goods	480.76	230.22
室内装饰品	Room Decorations	16.20	5.11
床上用品	Bed Articles	137.20	24.07
家庭日用杂品	Household Articles for Daily Use	518.85	348.33
家具材料	Furniture Materials	0.21	
家庭服务	Household Services	145.71	18.86
医疗保健	**Medicine and Medical Services**	**1409.01**	**873.91**
医疗器具	Medical Appliance	13.38	0.01
保健器具	Health Care Articles	9.35	2.50
药品费	Medcial Expenses	604.02	485.68
滋补保健品	Tonics	241.94	39.88
医疗费	Health Care Service	516.71	340.80
其　他	Others	23.61	5.04
交通和通讯	**Transportation and Communications**	**2957.23**	**778.50**
交　通	Traffic	2251.50	431.24
家庭交通工具	Family Traffic Facility	937.45	74.26
车辆用燃料及零配件	Vehicles Applied Fuel and Fittings	769.70	204.80
交通工具服务支出	Expenditure on Vehicles Service	307.62	80.45
交通费	Traffic Fare	236.73	71.74
通　信	Post and Telecommunication	705.73	347.26
通信工具	Telecommunication Facilities	162.34	24.94
通信服务	Communication Service	543.38	322.32
教育文化娱乐服务	**Entertainment and Culture and Education Service**	**2961.62**	**933.91**
文化娱乐用品	Stationery and Recreational Articles	698.55	220.77
文化娱乐服务	Cultural and Recreational Service	1103.14	228.63
教　育	Education	1159.93	484.51
居　住	**Residence**	**1250.41**	**677.62**
住　房	Residential Housing	439.17	127.83
水电燃料及其他	Water, Electricity and Others	708.00	515.80
居住服务费	Residence Service Expenses	103.24	33.99
杂项商品和服务	**Miscellaneous Commodities and Service**	**502.35**	**278.45**
杂项商品	Miscellaneous Commodities	321.13	164.17
服　务	Service	181.22	114.28

单位：元（yuan）

按收入水平分组 Grouped by Level of Income							
其中 of which # 更低收入组（占5%） Poor Households (Make up 5%)	低收入组（占10%） Low Income Households (Make up 10%)	中等偏下组（占20%） Lower Middle Income Households (Make up 20%)	中等收入组（占20%） Middle Income Households (Make up 20%)	中等偏上组（占20%） Upper Middle Income Households (Make up 20%)	高收入组（占10%） High Income Households (Make up 10%)	最高收入组（占10%） Highest Income Households (Make up 10%)	其中 of which # 更高收入组（占5%） Higher Income Households (Make up 5%)
25.11	57.90	43.17	46.67	70.33	74.15	86.84	112.8
4.63	24.68	18.90	10.75	14.44	19.14	50.44	46.23
460.70	**536.58**	**902.92**	**1130.29**	**1792.97**	**2130.95**	**2421.51**	**2755.25**
112.42	78.25	283.38	339.24	924.83	1025.63	532.77	717.97
	1.47	8.08	10.13	9.68	86.49	23.11	43.79
18.32	45.01	88.75	203.85	181.64	126.35	263.48	129.24
321.73	375.86	455.87	442.76	611.45	550.89	985.21	1202.16
		0.37	0.69				
8.24	35.98	66.47	133.62	65.36	341.59	616.94	662.08
779.43	**2444.80**	**1129.45**	**1658.85**	**1240.94**	**1269.49**	**1406.37**	**1517.7**
	0.36	12.28	30.52	21.92	3.48	1.34	
		2.29	9.17	22.42	7.61	18.83	17.79
366.14	982.87	482.67	682.65	584.17	591.98	446.80	506.27
32.20	130.36	190.89	292.74	269.71	245.67	567.23	541.50
381.10	1321.89	435.34	576.79	320.91	410.72	349.06	451.82
	9.32	5.99	66.97	21.81	10.03	23.11	0.31
560.93	**1015.76**	**2100.84**	**2502.77**	**5259.84**	**2336.91**	**6624.75**	**9946.73**
143.38	474.50	1517.49	1754.60	4436.85	1521.02	5454.80	8431.71
5.59	94.98	563.40	737.20	2357.56	30.80	2168.85	4110.62
39.94	154.71	616.53	610.21	1159.07	999.90	1851.37	2292.14
54.27	23.93	180.12	197.65	515.70	249.09	1074.87	1548.33
43.58	200.87	157.43	209.54	404.52	241.23	359.71	480.62
417.55	541.27	583.35	748.17	823.00	815.89	1169.95	1515.02
51.50	67.35	86.85	151.80	223.98	173.47	497.03	854.76
366.06	473.91	496.51	596.37	599.02	642.42	672.92	660.26
851.07	**1582.54**	**1931.72**	**2726.41**	**3840.65**	**4374.00**	**6682.71**	**9455.29**
128.47	505.28	516.01	440.28	966.01	744.92	1898.25	2755.77
89.30	396.95	454.46	1191.96	1423.92	1572.35	3129.87	4376.9
633.31	680.31	961.25	1094.17	1450.72	2056.72	1654.59	2322.63
590.64	**924.79**	**1125.85**	**1180.24**	**1573.00**	**2142.87**	**1212.85**	**1338.29**
	411.25	304.97	324.63	638.55	1266.12	164.81	290.44
574.53	492.22	718.64	748.66	773.01	800.61	863.06	821.77
16.11	21.32	102.24	106.95	161.44	76.14	184.98	226.08
74.77	**347.65**	**347.32**	**434.16**	**591.19**	**667.15**	**1110.94**	**1387.2**
34.07	170.63	226.61	260.04	433.22	396.95	729.30	846.17
40.70	177.03	120.70	174.12	157.98	270.20	381.64	541.03

8-7　市区居民家庭不同收入水平收支情况（2011 年）
INCOME AND EXPENDITURE CONDITIONS OF DIFFERENT INCOME LEVELS OF URBAN HOUSEHOLDS (2011)

指标	Item	合计 Total	按人均每月可支配收入分组 200以下 Below 200	200～400	400～600
调查户数（户）	**Number of Households Surveyed (household)**	**300.00**	**1.17**	**2.83**	**6.83**
平均每户家庭人口数（人）	**Average Household Size (person)**	**2.73**	**2.29**	**2.71**	**2.93**
就业人口数	Number of Persons Employed	1.31	0.36	0.53	0.59
#国有集体职工人数	Number of staff and Workers in Stateowned and Collective-owned Units	0.26			0.06
期初手存现金（元）	**Cash on Hand at Beginning of Year (yuan)**	**828.18**	**696.54**	**630.48**	**657.98**
家庭总收入（元）	**Total Family Income (yuan)**	**32744.04**	**3265.50**	**5605.43**	**7366.09**
#可支配收入	Disposable Income	29828.63	1168.50	4043.14	5948.46
#工薪收入	Income from Wagers and Salaries	20783.88	2324.25	2560.43	2610.40
经营净收入	Operating Net Income	2556.53		568.70	747.15
财产性收入	Income from Property	1346.18	502.50	61.30	43.95
转移性收入	Transfer Income	8057.46	438.75	2415.00	3964.59
借贷收入（元）	**Debit and Credit Income (yuan)**	**6500.59**	**2550.00**	**1108.70**	**3240.50**
家庭总支出（元）	**Total Family Expenditure (yuan)**	**25914.61**	**7940.37**	**6422.28**	**10587.73**
消费性支出	Consumption Expenditure	18893.11	5498.37	4329.12	9031.40
食　品	Foodstuff	6759.91	3618.45	2149.29	3742.69
#粮油类	Grain and Edible Oil	697.05	753.60	385.02	584.59
肉禽蛋水产品类	Meat, Poultry and Aquatic Products	1846.17	1165.02	798.55	1048.31
蔬菜类	Vegetables	682.57	808.86	504.25	511.86
调味品	Condiments	66.60	52.05	31.40	49.25
糖烟酒饮料类	Sugar, Cigarette, Wine and Beverage	800.37	301.39	70.08	351.69
干鲜瓜果类	Reserved or Fresh Fruits	573.95	234.20	107.43	240.34
糕点、奶及奶制品	Cakes, Milk and Milk Products	408.30	224.06	71.80	199.30
其他食品	Other Foods	128.67	1.76	20.92	18.79
饮食服务	Catering service	1556.22	77.51	159.83	738.58
#食品加工服务费	Service Fee of Food Processing	5.86		1.70	0.10
在外饮食	Eating outside	1550.36	77.51	158.14	738.48
衣　着	Clothing	1753.66	369.64	255.67	749.58
#服　装	Garments	1321.10	214.88	216.68	608.28

Per Capita Monthly Disposable Income by Group								
600 ~ 800	800 ~ 1000	1000 ~ 1500	1500 ~ 2000	2000 ~ 2500	2500 ~ 3000	3000 ~ 4000	4000 ~ 5000	5000以上 Over 5000
11.25	**16.42**	**50.92**	**64.75**	**48.08**	**30.17**	**30.00**	**14.92**	**22.33**
3.30	**3.31**	**2.94**	**2.69**	**2.56**	**2.54**	**2.53**	**2.47**	**2.68**
1.39	1.11	1.44	1.28	1.26	1.33	1.37	1.34	1.57
0.14	0.13	0.17	0.18	0.28	0.43	0.37	0.36	0.48
563.40	**717.55**	**715.28**	**826.23**	**991.20**	**833.19**	**1012.22**	**1000.15**	**1110.83**
10519.64	**12275.46**	**17177.91**	**23416.85**	**29473.68**	**36163.12**	**44391.01**	**56553.31**	**117734.97**
8531.27	10688.12	14917.78	20908.40	26533.71	32525.12	40699.08	53203.34	112126.62
7886.66	7059.62	12108.61	14420.37	18753.11	22212.81	26911.85	31796.14	78616.90
480.27	479.08	846.16	1270.56	1626.49	2891.18	4194.84	7273.06	11283.85
113.77	413.07	429.16	283.15	365.18	703.37	1445.75	2719.67	10874.42
2038.93	4323.69	3793.98	7442.77	8728.90	10355.76	11838.57	14764.44	16959.79
3597.30	**3188.36**	**4403.31**	**3708.21**	**5464.86**	**10128.10**	**10055.60**	**9439.82**	**17328.20**
12763.15	**13385.51**	**18288.52**	**19840.96**	**26031.34**	**32814.81**	**34904.70**	**38495.32**	**62220.30**
9908.84	11074.14	14673.87	15550.11	20256.50	25389.89	23728.15	26603.28	35716.15
4644.34	4641.34	5669.89	6121.70	7560.87	7947.59	7789.77	8803.69	10591.17
473.09	588.40	665.85	660.57	812.94	739.24	824.90	769.65	700.02
1378.62	1640.62	1663.96	1805.11	2029.90	2174.18	1998.95	2360.50	2008.77
545.12	607.58	588.58	666.36	747.68	798.18	767.36	835.88	708.90
39.76	60.07	58.42	58.13	80.07	88.16	75.45	83.53	69.07
472.77	384.75	675.04	708.83	983.34	1002.11	819.50	950.25	1469.54
276.76	282.47	443.38	507.41	661.76	593.67	703.36	757.07	1250.37
225.95	256.96	393.88	366.18	447.87	551.93	500.31	516.70	486.35
55.55	54.75	89.31	130.85	139.33	168.12	196.99	118.48	236.28
1176.73	765.73	1091.49	1218.26	1657.98	1831.98	1902.95	2411.64	3661.86
1.70	0.62	3.03	5.24	7.52	9.31	16.30	3.81	5.08
1175.03	765.10	1088.46	1213.02	1650.46	1822.67	1886.65	2407.83	3656.78
956.76	951.55	1249.48	1520.08	1829.71	2115.23	2450.16	2656.52	3424.66
749.60	674.33	934.78	1059.54	1383.52	1619.11	1924.77	2204.85	2617.84

8-7 续表 continued

指 标	Item	合 计 Total	按人均每月可支配收入分组 200以下 Below 200	200～400	400～600
衣着材料	Clothing Materials	33.50		0.65	15.90
鞋 类	Footwear	324.94	116.25	32.28	96.35
其它衣着用品	Other Clothing Items	55.80	36.64	5.79	24.00
衣着加工服务费	Tailoring and Laundering Service Fees	18.28	1.88	0.26	5.05
家庭设备用品及服务	Household Facilities, Articles and Services	1298.92	129.45	245.87	397.01
耐用消费品	Durable Consumption Goods	480.76		11.74	63.99
室内装饰品	Indoor Decoration	16.20			
床上用品	Bedding	137.20	29.63	11.09	9.50
家庭日用杂品	Home Supplies	518.85	99.83	217.83	315.62
家具材料	Furniture Material	0.21			
家庭服务	Household Services	145.71		5.22	7.90
医疗保健	Medical Care	1409.01	673.73	307.34	2079.36
# 医疗器具	Medical Appliance	13.38			
保健器具	Health Care Articles	9.35			
药品费	Medcial Expenses	604.02	634.35	167.72	784.86
滋补保健品	Tonics	241.94	22.50	16.30	11.46
医疗费	Health Care Service	516.71	16.88	123.32	1282.55
其 他	Others	23.61			0.49
交通和通讯	Transportation and Communications	2957.23	177.63	274.68	662.72
# 交 通	Transportation	2251.50	33.00	76.04	450.82
通 信	Communications	705.73	144.63	198.64	211.90
教育文化娱乐服务	Recreation Education and Cultural Services	2961.62	19.35	541.92	688.54
# 文化娱乐用品	Stationery and Recreational Articles	698.55	13.46	41.96	82.98
文化娱乐服务	Cultural and Recreational Service	1103.14	0.75	67.17	118.00
教 育	Education	1159.93	5.14	432.78	487.56
居 住	Residence	1250.41	468.92	499.03	621.44
# 住 房	Residential Housing	439.17			55.00
水电燃料及其他	Water, Electricity and Others	708.00	405.17	499.03	529.38
居住服务费	Residence Service Expenses	103.24	63.75		37.06
杂项商品和服务	Miscellaneous Commodities and Services	502.35	41.21	55.32	90.07
# 杂项商品	Miscellaneous Commodities	321.13	11.96	27.27	48.24
服 务	Services	181.22	29.25	28.04	41.83
借贷支出（元）	**Debit and Credit Expenditure (yuan)**	**13555.09**		**652.17**	**550.00**
期末手存现金（元）	**Cash on Hand At Year-end (yuan)**	**787.06**	**208.26**	**748.88**	**777.45**

Per Capita Monthly Disposable Income by Group								
600 ~ 800	800 ~ 1000	1000 ~ 1500	1500 ~ 2000	2000 ~ 2500	2500 ~ 3000	3000 ~ 4000	4000 ~ 5000	5000以上 Over 5000
22.98	33.40	32.67	55.97	33.24	30.45	18.87	10.26	26.29
154.81	214.10	224.81	339.97	319.61	388.02	430.31	375.69	622.78
25.73	48.12	39.85	49.05	72.46	65.54	48.91	56.00	117.47
3.64	8.60	17.36	15.55	20.88	12.12	27.30	9.72	40.28
486.07	690.72	1011.18	955.95	1292.86	1965.88	1386.40	2141.45	3096.82
113.23	161.84	272.72	310.03	517.74	1086.81	510.03	513.18	1330.71
		8.65	7.32	0.16	96.84	9.49		42.51
20.55	118.59	204.05	72.41	96.78	85.27	92.59	303.47	417.15
300.03	358.16	471.21	473.99	530.89	564.71	659.71	586.65	869.05
		0.40						1.92
52.26	52.13	54.15	92.20	147.30	132.26	114.58	738.15	435.46
1427.45	1533.81	983.35	1162.50	1533.86	1138.68	1901.82	2013.33	2131.00
0.85	0.01	0.66	29.38	17.01		41.97	0.08	7.15
	0.64	3.81	3.05	13.71	38.04	4.67	15.67	16.55
556.88	834.23	470.30	498.69	606.23	331.70	788.00	806.29	1054.81
57.55	116.61	139.20	169.29	377.51	345.39	305.42	453.71	436.32
779.01	573.35	360.51	445.58	486.39	406.58	686.02	729.41	582.86
33.17	8.97	8.87	16.51	33.01	16.97	75.73	8.16	33.31
705.34	1081.53	2700.86	1698.85	3160.95	5107.03	3978.27	4707.41	6073.91
333.04	689.94	2088.75	1000.40	2417.44	4298.76	3169.38	3654.00	4924.00
372.30	391.59	612.12	698.46	743.51	808.27	808.90	1053.41	1149.91
927.88	1149.89	1918.64	2375.63	2955.79	4239.67	4507.08	4346.03	6998.74
246.41	332.77	577.46	586.19	709.61	831.03	915.70	796.07	1746.02
147.89	173.69	538.51	957.77	1097.47	2203.53	1381.37	1990.62	2612.53
533.58	643.43	802.66	831.67	1148.71	1205.11	2210.01	1559.35	2640.20
588.62	829.52	806.46	1251.40	1388.73	2369.02	1017.07	1337.70	2035.16
33.57	270.87	157.98	459.58	436.49	1399.44	106.07	283.03	995.35
507.40	495.80	603.26	750.23	757.56	783.96	774.90	937.89	845.52
47.65	62.84	45.22	41.59	194.67	185.63	136.09	116.77	194.30
172.36	195.77	334.01	464.00	533.72	506.78	697.58	597.15	1364.70
102.35	103.13	179.23	291.30	382.92	365.69	411.26	322.21	943.93
70.02	92.64	154.78	172.70	150.80	141.09	286.32	274.95	420.76
1277.66	**2190.93**	**3300.35**	**7112.62**	**8831.85**	**13226.30**	**20071.76**	**27636.38**	**75744.14**
552.69	**524.72**	**748.44**	**855.26**	**823.58**	**818.66**	**769.24**	**902.15**	**841.09**

8-8　主要年份市区居民主要消费品人均消费量
PER CAPITA CONSUMPTION ON MAJOR CONSUMER GOODS OF URBAN RESIDENTS IN MAIN YEARS

指　标	Item	1995	2000	2005	2010	2011
大　米（千克）	Rice (kg)	82.61	55.59	50.51	43.62	49.83
食用植物油（千克）	Edible Vegetable Oil (kg)	7.69	7.58	8.88	6.23	7.64
猪　肉（千克）	Pork (kg)	23.82	18.17	20.6	18.03	23.24
牛　肉（千克）	Beef (kg)	0.58	0.98	0.88	1.74	2.24
羊　肉（千克）	Mutton (kg)	0.19	0.19	0.15	0.18	0.32
鸡（千克）	Chieken (kg)	6.33	5.32	5.31	5.57	7.14
鸭（千克）	Duck (kg)	0.34	0.40	1.75	1.35	2.06
鲜　蛋（千克）	Eggs (kg)	22.32	11.34	9.87	9.63	10.14
鱼（千克）	Aquantic Products (kg)	3.27	5.18	11.01	11.82	13.44
虾（千克）	Shrimp (kg)	1.60	3.37	3.86	3.11	3.85
鲜　菜（千克）	Fresh Vegetables (kg)	123.73	114.10	107.53	113.68	120.82
白　酒（千克）	Liquor (kg)	1.43	1.51	1.02	1.08	1.22
果　酒（千克）	Wine (kg)	0.25	0.11	0.27	0.35	0.38
啤　酒（千克）	Beer (kg)	6.70	5.77	6.07	3.20	4.09
碳酸饮料（千克）	Carbonated Drinks (kg)	1.52	1.55	2.38	0.96	0.82
糕　点（千克）	Cakes (kg)	3.03	3.08	4.94	7.33	9.21
茶　叶（千克）	Tea (kg)	0.20	0.23	0.16	0.17	0.34
水　果（千克）	Fruits (kg)	13.66	22.14	55.71	51.86	46.20
鲜乳品及酸奶（千克）	Fresh Milk and Yogurt (kg)	4.36	21.51	31.64	26.78	28.65
生活用水（立方米）	Household Water Consumption (cubic meters)	34.27	38.83	33.96	37.23	48.55
生活用电（千瓦时）	Household Power Consumption (kwh)	230.85	339.66	549.52	702.34	732.89
液化石油气（千卡）	Liquified Petroleum Gas (kc)	38.25	26.76	17.45	8.06	8.36
管道煤气（立方米）	Pipeline Gas (cubic meters)	22.92	57.77	37.92	45.12	53.04

8-9 市区每百户居民家庭年末耐用消费品拥有量（2006-2011 年）
NUMBER OF DURABLE CONSUMER GOODS OWNED PER 100 URBAN HOUSEHOLDS AT YEAR-END（2006-2011）

指 标	Item	2006	2007	2008	2009	2010	2011
摩托车（辆）	Motorcycle (unit)	45.67	45.85	23.33	22.33	21.67	10.00
助力车（辆）	Scooter (unit)	52.00	56.81	64.00	70.00	74.67	66.33
家用汽车（辆）	Family Car (unit)	5.33	7.97	13.00	16.00	19.67	27.67
洗衣机（台）	Washing Machine (unit)	100.33	100.33	102.33	103.33	103.67	101.67
电冰箱（台,含冰柜）	Refrigerator (unit，Include Freezer)	94.33	95.68	101.00	102.67	104.00	98.00
彩色电视机（台）	Color TV Set (unit)	171.00	172.09	189.33	191.00	195.33	188.00
家用电脑（台）	Family Computer (unit)	58.00	62.46	71.67	75.00	82.67	95.00
组合音响（套）	Hi-Fi Stereo Component System (unit)	32.67	34.22	37.67	38.67	39.33	32.67
摄像机（架）	Pickup Camera (unit)	3.67	3.65	6.00	7.00	7.33	11.33
照相机（架）	Camera (unit)	46.67	48.50	60.33	61.00	65.00	55.00
钢琴（架）	Piano (set)	2.33	2.33	4.00	4.67	5.67	3.67
其他中高档乐器（件）	Other Medium and High Class Music Instruments (unit)	3.33	2.99	7.67	7.67	8.00	3.33
微波炉（台）	Microwave Oven (unit)	90.00	91.03	94.33	96.00	96.67	93.67
空调器（台）	Air Conditioner (unit)	150.33	153.82	186.67	192.67	199.00	213.67
淋浴热水器（台）	Shower Heater (unit)	87.00	89.37	95.67	98.33	101.33	99.67
消毒碗柜（台）	Disinfectant Cupboard (unit)	5.33	5.32	12.00	12.33	12.67	7.67
洗碗机（台）	Dishwasher (unit)	0.67	0.66	0.67	0.67	0.67	0.67
健身器材（套）	Healthy Equipment (unit)	5.67	4.98	6.33	6.33	6.67	5.00
普通电话（部）	Telephone (set)	142.00	97.67	92.00	91.67	91.67	82.00
移动电话（部）	Mobile Telephone (set)	132.67	181.40	195.00	204.33	211.00	192.00

注：2007年起移动电话中包含小灵通，2007年以前小灵通包含在普通电话中。
Note： The Little Smart has been included in the mobile telephone since the year of 2007, and it was included in the ordinary telephone before 2007.

8-10　农民家庭基本情况（1985-2011 年）
BASIC CONDITIONS OF RURAL HOUSEHOLDS（1985-2011）

年　份 Year	调查户数（户） Households Surveyed (household)	农民人均纯收入（元） Per Capita Net Income of Rural Residents (yuan)	农民人均生活消费支出（元） Per Capita Living Expenditure of Rural Residents (yuan)	每户整半劳动力（人） Number of Able-bodied and Semi-able-Bodied Laboerers Per Household (yuan)	每一劳动力负担人口（人） Number of Persons Supported by Each Laborer (person)	人均住房面积（平方米） Per Capita Living Space (sq.m)	户均住房面积（平方米） Living Space Per Household (sq.m)	恩格尔系数（%） Engel Coefficient (%)
1985	340	618	563	2.74	1.55	21.03	89.49	49.7
1986	340	777	697	2.74	1.55	22.33	93.08	44.8
1987	340	855	782	2.76	1.51	23.89	99.42	44.3
1988	340	1108	1161	2.78	1.47	25.72	105.24	42.1
1989	340	1301	1305	2.75	1.42	29.74	116.26	49.0
1990	340	1401	1231	2.74	1.43	31.66	123.92	49.5
1991	320	1318	1205	2.71	1.44	32.69	127.39	53.1
1992	320	1588	1442	2.70	1.41	33.46	127.04	50.0
1993	280	2041	1762	2.36	1.37	32.66	120.73	45.8
1994	280	2707	2259	2.74	1.35	33.78	124.99	49.7
1995	280	3397	2952	2.54	1.32	35.90	129.48	49.9
1996	300	4172	3598	2.51	1.39	38.81	135.59	45.5
1997	300	4216	3754	2.50	1.38	37.27	128.82	49.6
1998	280	4289	3045	2.42	1.41	36.97	126.62	46.6
1999	280	4313	3316	2.37	1.44	42.04	143.83	41.0
2000	300	4430	3243	2.30	1.44	49.27	162.75	43.1
2001	300	4719	3277	2.40	1.38	48.18	159.17	43.9
2002	410	5138	3698	2.42	1.40	54.20	182.30	40.4
2003	410	5550	3953	2.43	1.38	55.90	185.70	40.1
2004	410	6235	4793	2.42	1.38	55.70	186.40	42.0
2005	510	7002	5712	2.37	1.42	56.20	186.80	39.8
2006	510	8001	6518	2.41	1.38	58.27	193.54	37.7
2007	510	9033	7400	2.39	1.38	57.70	190.20	38.0
2008	380	10171	8128	2.37	1.37	58.73	191.50	37.7
2009	380	11198	8843	2.39	1.37	59.48	192.21	36.2
2010	380	12637	9924	2.39	1.34	58.40	187.49	35.1
2011	520	14838	11208	2.42	1.45	61.52	190.17	35.5

注：“每一劳动力负担人口”包括就业者本人,下同。
Note：“Persons Supported by Each Laborer” includes the laborer himself, the same below.

8-11 分地区农民家庭基本情况（2011 年）
BASIC CONDITIONS OF RURAL HOUSEHOLDS BY REGION（2011）

指 标	Item	全 市 Whole Municipality	其中 of which 溧阳市 Liyang City	金坛市 Jintan City
调查户数（户）	**Number of Households Surveyed (household)**	**520**	**150**	**100**
调查人数（人）	**Number of Residents Surveyed (person)**			
常住人口	Number of Permanent Residents in the Households Surveyed	1616	450	315
户均常住人口	Average Number of Permanent Residents Per household	3.11	3.00	2.63
户均整、半劳动力	Average Number of Able-bodied and Semi-able-bodied Laborers Per Household	2.42	2.40	2.23
户均非农业劳动力	Average Number of Non-agricultual Laborers Per Household	1.84	2.00	1.50
平均每一劳动力负担人数	Average Number of Persons Supported by a Laborer	1.45	0.50	1.28
人均总收入（元）	**Per Capita Total Incom (yuan)**	**17565**	**17196**	**18508**
工资性收入	Wage Income	9770	7539	9108
家庭经营收入	Household Business Income	5507	8100	7528
转移性收入	Transfer Income	1459	1203	1049
财产性收入	Property Income	829	353	823
人均纯收入	Per Capita Net Income	14838	13505	13812
人均总支出（元）	**Per Capita Total Expenditure (yuan)**	**15065**	**17320**	**17603**
家庭经营费用支出	Household Business Expenditure	2133	2769	4337
购置生产用固定资产支出	Expenditure On Productive Fixed Assets	62	42	231
税费支出	Expenditure for Taxes	6	4	1
生活消费支出	Living Expenditure	11208	12839	10758
# 食品支出	Food	3976	4537	3876
食品消费品支出	Food Consumption Goods	3207	3167	3490
食品消费服务性支出	Food Consumption Services	769	1370	386
衣 着	Clothing	801	1140	591
居 住	Residence	1340	1377	1092

8-11　续表　continued

指　标	Item	全　市 Whole Municipality	其中 of which 溧阳市 Liyang City	金坛市 Jintan City
家庭设备、用品及服务	Household Facilities, Articles and Services	699	789	846
医疗保健	Medicine and Medicinal Services	893	799	839
交通和通信	Transportation and Communications	1411	1639	1319
文教娱乐用品及服务	Cultural, Education and Recreation Articles and Services	1810	2327	1923
其它商品和服务	Other Commodities and Services	279	230	272
财产性支出	Property Expenditure	1		
转移性支出	Transfer Expenditure	1652	1667	2252
期末人均手存现金（元）	**Per Capita Cash in Hand at Year-end (yuan)**	**2097**	**849**	**2840**
期末人均存款（元）	**Per Capita Savings Deposits at Year-end (yuan)**	**12703**	**13540**	**15548**
农民家庭住房情况	**Housing Conditions of Rural Residential Buildings**			
户均使用面积（平方米）	Average Floor Space of Residential Buildings Per Household (sq.m)	190.17	143.00	129.00
住房价值（元/人）	Value of Residential Buildings (yuan/person)	49416	33735	19059
人均使用住房面积（平方米）	Per Capita Floor Space of Residential Buildings (sq.m)	61.52	48.00	49.00
# 钢筋混泥土结构面积	Reinforced Concrete Structure	45.23	43.25	46.22
砖木结构面积	Brick and Wood Structure	15.57	4.42	2.69
农民家庭居住条件	**Living Conditions of Peasant Households**			
使用水冲式厕所户数的比重（%）	Proportion of Households with Dry latrines (%)	91.5	88.3	100.0
使用空调户数的比重（%）	Proportion of Households with Air Conditioning (%)	84.9	82.1	97.6
使用燃气户数的比重（%）	Proportion of Households with Gas	83.5	71.1	97.6
饮用自来水户数的比重（%）	Proportion of Households with Tap Water	94.6	94.6	100.0
通水泥或柏油路面户数的比重（%）	Proportion of Households Nearby Roads Paved with Cement or Asphalt	88.7	88.3	100.0

8-12 不同收入组农村居民家庭基本情况（2011 年）
BASIC CONDITIONS OF RURAL HOUSEHOLDS GROUPED BY INCOME（2011）

指 标	Item	低收入户 Low Income Households	中低收入户 Medium Low Income	中等收入户 Medium Income Households	中高收入户 Upper-Medium Income Households	高收入户 High Income Households
平均每户常住人口（人）	Average Number of Permanent Residents Per Household (person)	3.32	3.57	3.71	3.32	3.14
平均每户整、半劳动力（人）	Average Number of Able-bodied and Semi-able-bodied Laborers Per Household (person)	2.34	2.61	2.70	2.42	2.29
平均每个劳动力负担人口（人）	Average Number of People Supported by a Laborer (person)	1.40	1.57	1.62	1.45	1.37
人均总收入（元）	**Per Capita Total Income (yuan)**	**8896**	**13002**	**16139**	**19473**	**32123**
工资性收入	Wage Income	4037	7922	9296	14033	18679
家庭经营收入	Household Business Income	3065	3265	4497	2601	9405
转移性收入	Transfer Income	1358	1428	1778	1791	1464
财产性收入	Property Income	437	387	569	1047	2575
人均纯收入（元）	Per Capita Net Income	6252	11193	14352	18275	27589
人均总支出（元）	**Per Capita Total Expenditure (yuan)**	**10981**	**11793**	**13019**	**12255**	**23889**
人均生活消费支出（元）	Per Capita Living Expenditure (yuan)	7648	8813	10430	9821	16749
食 品	Food	3173	3473	3543	3984	4748
衣 着	Clothing	441	560	669	693	1008
居 住	Residence	729	479	1263	804	3527
家庭设备用品及服务	Household Facilities, Articles and Services	352	426	914	643	981
交通和通讯	Transportation and Communications	665	1341	1327	998	2378
文化教育娱乐用品及服务	Cultural, Educational and Recreational Products and Services	1076	1175	1573	1620	2736
医疗保健	Medicine and Medical Services	1091	1052	811	827	883
其他商品和服务	Other Commodities and Services	122	307	330	253	487
人均生活消费现金支出（元）	Per Capita Consumption Paid in Cash (yuan)	7280	8467	10081	9566	16444
食 品	Food	2805	3128	3194	3729	4443
衣 着	Clothing	441	560	669	693	1008
居 住	Residence	729	479	1263	804	3527
家庭设备用品及服务	Household Facilities, Products and Services	352	426	914	643	981
交通和通讯	Transportation and Communications	665	1341	1327	998	2378
文化教育娱乐用品及服务	Cultural, Educational and Recreational Products and Services	1076	1175	1573	1620	2736
医疗保健	Medicine and Medical Services	1091	1052	811	827	883
其他商品和服务	Other Commodities and Services	122	307	330	253	487

8-13　分地区农民家庭主要消费品人均消费量（2011 年）
PER CAPITA CONSUMPTION OF MAJOR CONSUMER GOODS OF RURAL HOUSEHOLDS BY REGION（2011）

单位：千克 (kg)

指　标	Item	全　市 Whole Municipality	其中 of which 溧阳市 Liyang City	金坛市 Jintan City
粮　食	Grain	147.66	151.57	189.37
#谷 物	Corn	143.12	147.66	176.30
#小　麦	Wheat	12.91	10.45	22.09
稻　谷	Rice	129.19	136.95	151.10
薯　类	Tubers	0.69	0.17	2.50
豆　类	Beans	3.85	3.74	10.58
油脂类	Edible Oil	5.37	3.44	2.67
#植物油	Vegetable Oil	5.26	3.25	2.63
豆制品	Bean Products	6.15	4.28	8.98
蔬菜及菜制品	Vegetables &Related Products	106.52	73.30	125.89
鲜　菜	Fresh Vegetables	103.16	70.91	120.85
干　菜	Dried Food	0.62	0.99	0.94
鲜　菌	Fresh Mushroom	1.23	0.58	1.25
瓜　类	Melons	7.40	9.88	7.87
水果类	Fruits	12.73	9.51	13.41
肉禽及其制品	Meats，Poultry and Related Products	32.50	35.23	43.78
#猪　肉	Pork	17.92	27.74	24.44
牛　肉	Beef	1.15	0.85	0.75
羊　肉	Mutton	0.35	0.65	0.30
家　禽	Poultry	7.96	12.93	9.30
蛋类及蛋制品	Eggs & Related Products	6.76	15.32	8.66
奶和奶制品	Milk & Related Products	7.99	6.99	9.71
水产品	Aquatic Products	18.75	17.91	39.96
食　糖	Sugar	1.40	0.90	2.13
酒	Liquor	14.26	14.42	16.64
#白　酒	Liquor	4.79	8.87	7.11
啤　酒	Beer	6.97	5.43	7.72

8-14 每百户农民家庭年末耐用消费品拥有量（2011 年）
NUMBER OF DURABLE CONSUMER GOODS OWNED PER 100 RURAL HOUSEHOLDS AT YEAR-END（2011）

指 标	Item	全 市 Whole Municipality	其 中 of which 溧阳市 Liyang City	金坛市 Jintan City
自行车（辆）	Bicycle (unit)	213.20	105.33	174.00
摩托车（辆）	Motorcycle (coach)	79.24	46.00	44.00
家用汽车（辆）	Famliy Car (unit)	16.06	7.33	2.00
电　话（部）	Telephone Set (unit)	118.95	96.67	85.00
移动电话（部）	Mobile Telephone Sets (unit)	270.38	170.00	182.00
电视机（台）	TV Set (unit)	213.56	128.67	143.00
#彩　电	Color TV Set	213.56	128.67	143.00
摄像机（台）	Pickup Camera (unit)	5.20	6.70	1.00
影碟机（架）	Video Disc Player (unit)	31.20	16.67	21.00
照相机（架）	Camera (unit)	31.20	4.67	20.00
洗衣机（台）	Washing Machine (unit)	131.20	90.67	100.00
电冰箱（台）	Refrigerator (unit)	132.20	94.67	98.00
抽排油烟机（台）	Smoke Absorber (unit)	98.80	42.67	63.00
微波炉（台）	Microwave Oven (unit)	130.00	58.67	63.00
吸尘器（台）	Dust Catcher (unit)	10.40	8.00	8.00
淋浴热水器（台）	Shower Heater (unit)	129.63	97.33	94.00
家用电脑（台）	Computer (unit)	69.86	39.33	33.00
空调器（台）	Air Conditioner (unit)	175.96	102.67	95.00

注：全市农村住户抽样调查样本数为520户，其中溧阳市150户、金坛市100户。

Note：The sample number of rural residential household investigation in the whole year totalled 520 households,including 150 households from Liyang and 100 households from Jintan.

9

CHAPTER 9

固定资产投资

INVESTMENT IN FIXED ASSETS

常州统计年鉴

9 固定资产投资 INVESTMENT IN FIXED ASSETS

2011 年主要统计指标 MAJOR STATISTICAL INDICATORS OF 2011

全社会固定资产投资完成额	Total Investment in Fixed Assets	2338.94 亿元	(100 million yuan)
比上年增长	Over the Previous Year	20.0%	
在建项目个数	Number of projects under Construction	3942 个	(unit)
比上年增长	Over the Previous Year	-9.4%	
民间投资	Nongovernmental Investment	1705.13 亿元	(100 million yuan)
比上年增长	Over the Previous Year	25.0%	
公共基础设施投资	Public Infrastralture Investment	295.86 亿元	(100 million yuan)
比上年增长	Over the Previous Year	-13.1%	
工业投资	Transformation and Renovation Investment	1293.43 亿元	(100 million yuan)
比上年增长	Over the Previous Year	19.7%	
第三产业投资	Investment in Tertiary Industry	1033.09 亿元	(100 million yuan)
比上年增长	Over the Previous Year	20.7%	
房地产开发投资	Real Estate Investment	565.91 亿元	(100 million yuan)
比上年增长	Over the Previous Year	33.2%	

9-1　历年全社会固定资产投资完成额
TOTAL INVESTMENT IN FIXED ASSETS OVER THE YEARS

单位：万元（10000 yuan）

年 份 Year	全 市 Whole Municipality	其中 of which 市 区 Urban Area	年 份 Year	全 市 Whole Municipality	其中 of which 市 区 Urban Area
1949	31	24	1981	24198	30321
1950	129	105	1982	36336	46289
1951	148	94	1983	31428	43426
1952	456	257	1984	60334	53083
1953	494	394	1985	104735	93054
1954	557	431	1986	161834	127213
1955	829	659	1987	201796	156071
1956	1323	1032	1988	259486	201601
1957	964	654	1989	212533	163734
1958	6490	5657	1990	227093	170921
1959	8246	7390	1991	309921	237860
1960	11184	10223	1992	443866	355392
1961	3189	2975	1993	879129	706406
1962	1198	913	1994	964621	777442
1963	1070	825	1995	1150612	852333
1964	1714	1454	1996	1242072	922999
1965	1279	1060	1997	1319585	1009095
1966	1537	1238	1998	1401110	1066040
1967	793	578	1999	1448908	1117208
1968	749	555	2000	1634262	1268963
1969	1397	1037	2001	1906854	1509623
1970	2398	1823	2002	2500118	1977105
1971	3411	3075	2003	4465944	3583446
1972	4944	4219	2004	5886129	4730966
1973	5900	4832	2005	7698021	6097516
1974	3994	3486	2006	9515629	7386948
1975	3490	3119	2007	12039417	9327048
1976	3528	3194	2008	14481662	11028826
1977	3093	2634	2009	17047690	13340391
1978	8852	7553	2010	21035519	16489817
1979	13203	11327	2011	23389418	18211797
1980	23699	26313			

9-2 固定资产投资完成额（1985-2011 年）
REALIZED INVESTMENT IN FIXED ASSETS（1985-2011）

单位：万元（10000 yuan）

年 份 Year	全社会固定资产投资总额 Total Investmetn in Fixed Assets	其 中 of which 第一产业 Primary Industry	第二产业 Secondary Industry	其中 of which 工业投资 Industrial Investment	第三产业投资 Investment in Tertiary Industry	公共基础设施投资 Public Infrastralture Investment	民间投资 Civil Investment
1985	104735	952	62475	61503	41308		
1986	161834	3732	98907	98383	59195		
1987	201796	1499	142569	165828	57728		
1988	259486	1244	190533	189871	67709		
1989	212533	2932	170954	170860	38647		
1990	227093	4642	160225	159955	62226	17820	95088
1991	309921	2789	256344	225608	50788	24629	94167
1992	443866	3176	332873	331741	107817	34729	76327
1993	879129	1309	528769	499487	349051	91302	199902
1994	964621	4889	509772	453869	449960	140547	262832
1995	1150612	9776	559360	548978	581476	153314	295241
1996	1242072	6088	6041467	597020	631817	278333	375196
1997	1319585	19848	568241	559112	731496	308134	475233
1998	1401110	34000	536977	526974	830133	453150	479621
1999	1448908	55225	528263	520078	865420	547041	753172
2000	1634262	49771	604813	593913	979678	532296	888199
2001	1906854	53626	837711	830062	1015517	628214	1078742
2002	2500118	29619	1252088	1237465	1218411	699987	1445567
2003	4465944	20138	2591293	2508342	1854513	1262439	2666795
2004	5886129	5643	3451340	3425615	2429146	1597078	3533558
2005	7698021	11902	4648555	4597843	3037564	2042125	4798730
2006	9515629	20219	5653538	5629015	3841872	1857842	6307633
2007	12039417	6455	6870313	6808672	5162649	2284530	7987997
2008	14481662	29965	8391957	8315442	6059740	2428248	9626044
2009	17047690	39949	9788147	9710508	7219594	3555953	11469166
2010	21035519	73876	11865093	11804077	9096550	3403292	14816856
2011	23389418	100341	12958199	12934251	10330878	2958588	17051330

注：公共基础设施投资指电力、燃气、水的生产和供应业；交通运输、仓储和邮政业；电信、广播电视和卫星传输服务业；水利、环境和公共设施管理业；教育、卫生、社会保障和社会福利业；文化、体育、娱乐等行业的投资。

Note：Public infrastructure investment refers to the investment in production and supply of electricity, gas and water; transportation, storage and postal industries; telecommunications, radio and television and satellite transmission services; water conservancy, environment and public facility management industries; education, health, social security and social welfare; and culture, sports, entertainment industries and so on.

9-3　房地产开发主要指标（1990-2011 年）
MAJOR INDICATORS OF REAL ESTATE DEVELOPMENT（1990-2011）

单位：万元、万平方米（10000 yuan、10000 sq.m）

年份 Year	房地产开发投资额 Investment in Real Estate Development	商品房屋施工面积 Construction Area of Commodity Housing	其中 of which 住宅 Residence	商品房屋竣工面积 Completion Area of Commodity Housing	其中 of which 住宅 Residence	商品房屋销售面积 Sales Area of Commodity Housing	其中 of which 住宅 Residence
1990	9384	34.15	30.86	19.38	16.78		
1991	18274	61.87	54.58	28.53	23.51	16.91	
1992	34620	125.50	107.98	40.27	34.59	24.32	
1993	106860	206.39	175.07	99.08	82.86	44.95	
1994	157903	316.28	175.64	144.78	113.07	61.19	
1995	184684	258.48	181.05	120.28	101.41	70.74	61.20
1996	153586	248.16	163.46	134.28	104.96	80.78	72.65
1997	187827	241.81	161.21	121.65	88.20	93.16	85.64
1998	223200	315.52	234.31	132.77	104.08	103.61	93.67
1999	255026	346.92	288.73	169.31	143.19	135.36	123.15
2000	299834	407.39	343.75	204.02	160.96	149.26	133.59
2001	321709	487.47	398.14	192.98	169.51	172.85	162.39
2002	410169	526.05	439.66	268.79	226.74	248.61	223.82
2003	527754	645.00	489.23	249.17	190.56	205.91	170.48
2004	978955	991.33	744.99	250.33	187.75	236.56	196.68
2005	1142730	1246.07	953.78	520.72	397.84	422.53	363.29
2006	1710416	1706.26	1350.55	397.78	297.58	479.12	407.89
2007	2250453	2190.26	1700.02	616.25	486.21	579.49	514.52
2008	3089162	2577.34	1844.19	685.14	541.65	504.49	425.53
2009	3062037	2748.89	1995.22	749.81	547.12	922.64	802.50
2010	4469606	3208.11	2192.84	732.50	486.98	915.75	775.14
2011	5659063	3926.82	2712.48	682.22	472.38	661.12	537.94

9-4 全社会固定资产投资完成额（2011 年）TOTAL INVESTMENT IN FIXED ASSETS（2011）

单位：万元（10000 yuan）

指标	Item	合计 Total	其中 of which 城镇投资 Urban Investment	农村投资 Rural Investment	房地产投资 Real Estate Investment
投资总额	**Total Investment**	**23389418**	**11574529**	**6155826**	**5659063**
按地区分	**Grouped by Region**				
市　区	Urban Area	18211797	8790296	4354596	5066905
武进区	Wujin District	7157326	2764478	3079039	1313809
新北区	Xinbei District	4771925	2328652	1275557	1167716
天宁区	Tianning District	2360547	909100		1451447
钟楼区	Zhonglou District	2278615	1380727		897888
戚墅堰区	Qishuyan District	585209	349164		236045
溧阳市	Liyang City	3111597	1609229	1165784	336584
金坛市	Jintan City	2066024	1175004	635446	255574
按构成分	**Grouped by Use of funds**				
建筑工程	Construction	11493010	5049678	2990487	3452845
安装工程	Installation	1348184	754174	200829	393181
设备工器具购置	Purchase of Equipment and Investment	7802831	5068269	2582385	152177
其他费用	Others	2745393	702408	382125	1660860
按产业性质分	**Grouped by Industries**				
第一产业	Primary Industry	100341	5880	94461	
第二产业	Secondary Industry	12958199	7891249	5066950	
第三产业	Tertiary Industry	10330878	3677400	994415	5659063
按建设性质分	**Grouped by Type of Construction**				
新　建	New Construction	6510140	4306875	2203265	
扩　建	Expansion	6718986	3767656	2951330	
改　建	Reconstruction	2650694	2348009	302685	
其　它	Others	7509598	1151989	698546	5659063
按经济类型分	**Grouped by Economic Types**				
国有及国有控股企业	State-owned and State Holding Enterprises	2604900	2132789	295071	177040

9-4 续表 1　Continued 1

单位：万元（10000 yuan）

指　标	Item	合　计 Total	其中 of which 城镇投资 Urban Investment	农村投资 Rural Investment	房地产投资 Real Estate Investment
非国有投资	Non State-owned Investment	20784518	9441740	5860755	5482023
民间投资	Civil Investment	17051330	7407775	5501718	4141837
外商及港澳台商投资	Foreign Merchants & Hong Kong, Macao and Taiwan	3733188	2033965	359037	1340186
按登记注册类型分	**Grouped by Registration Status**				
内　资	Domestically-Funded	19540442	9471566	5749999	4318877
国　有	State-owned	2548463	2098994	294271	155198
集　体	Collective-owned	988256	421686	485795	80775
股份合作	Share-holding Cooperative	60534	13916	46618	
集体联营	State-owned Joint Operation	54580	54580		
国有独资公司	State-funded Corporations	52056	30214		21842
其它有限责任公司	Other Limited Liability Corporations	7662894	2976976	2705291	1980627
股份有限公司	Share-holding Corporations Ltd.	378074	223458	31141	123475
私　营	Private	7513415	3532822	2030398	1950195
其　他	Others	282170	118920	156485	6765
港澳台商投资	Investment from Hong Kong, Macao and Taiwan	2028790	886244	63031	1079515
合资经营	Joint-Venture	894596	209121	8987	676488
合作经营	Cooperative	10023		10023	
独资经营	Sole Investment	1012066	659123	44021	308922
股份有限公司	Share-holding Corporations Ltd.	112105	18000		94105
外商投资	Enterprises withForeign Investment	1704398	1147721	296006	260671
合资经营	Joint Ventures	441477	245180	73647	122650
合作经营	Cooperative	10913	2913	8000	
独资经营	Sole Investment	1223600	871220	214359	138021
股份有限公司	Share-holding Corporations Ltd.	28408	28408		

9-4 续表 2 Continued 2

单位：万元（10000 yuan）

指 标	Item	合 计 Total	其中 of which 城镇投资 Urban Investment	农村投资 Rural Investment	房地产投资 Real Estate Investment
个体经营	Individual	115788	68998	46790	
个体户	Self-employed Individuals	71569	66081	5488	
按国民经济行业分	**Grouped by Sector**				
农林牧渔业	Farming,Forestry,Animal Husbandry and Fishery	100341	5880	94461	
采矿业	Mining	19560	8120	11440	
制造业	Manufacturing	12468286	7441349	5026937	
电力、燃气及水的生产和供应业	Production and Supply of Electricity, Gas and Water	446405	417832	28573	
建筑业	Construction	23948	23948		
交通运输、仓储和邮政业	Transportation,Storage and Post	594237	541105	53132	
信息传输、计算机服务和软件业	Information Transformation, Computer Service and Software	225149	225149		
批发和零售业	Wholesale and Retail Trade	413474	379689	33785	
住宿和餐饮业	Accommodation and Catering Services	276020	250753	25267	
房地产业	Real Estate Industry	6487914	479233	349618	5659063
租赁和商务服务业	Rent and Business Services	218630	180740	37890	
科学研究、技术服务和地质勘查业	Scientific Research, Technology Service and Geologic Prospecting	69456	62206	7250	
水利、环境和公共设施管理业	Water Conservancy, Environment and Public Facilities Management	1231448	928408	303040	
居民服务和其他服务业	Neighborhood Services and Other Services	86066	75566	10500	
教 育	Education	178514	89164	89350	
卫生、社会保障和社会福利业	Hygiene, Social Security and Social Welfare	129308	110152	19156	
文化、体育和娱乐业	Culture, Sports and Entertainment	235312	210435	24877	
公共管理和社会组织	Public Administration and Social Organizations	136979	102429	34550	

9-5　市区全社会固定资产投资完成额（2011 年）
URBAN FIXED ASSETS INVESTMENT（2011）

单位：万元（10000 yuan）

指 标	Item	合 计 Total	其中 of which 城镇投资 Urban Investment	农村投资 Rural Investment	房地产投资 Real Estate Investment
市区投资总额	**Urban Fixed Assets Investmant**	**18211797**	**8790296**	**4354596**	**5066905**
按登记注册类型分	**Grouped by Registration Status**				
内　资	Domestically-Funded	14632309	6793825	4066237	3772247
国　有	State-owned	2391955	2051576	209577	130802
集　体	Collective-owned	922290	414736	426779	80775
股份合作	Share-holding Cooperative	60534	13916	46618	
集体联营	Collective-owned Joint Operation	54580	54580		
国有独资公司	State-funded Corporations	30214	30214		
其它有限责任公司	Other Limited Liability Corporations	6008894	1713917	2406626	1888351
股份有限公司	Share-holding Corporations Ltd.	336880	206558	11900	118422
私　营	Private	4603244	2193657	855690	1553897
其　他	Others	223718	114671	109047	
港澳台商投资	Investment from Hong Kong, Macao and Taiwan	1964132	868234	27210	1068688
合资经营	Joint-Venture	877036	197411	4437	675188
合作经营	Cooperative	9500		9500	
独资经营	Sole Investment	965491	652823	13273	299395
股份有限公司	Share-holding Corporations Ltd.	112105	18000		94105
外商投资	Enterprises with Foreign Investment	1504418	1060199	218249	225970
合资经营	Joint Ventures	365815	212728	43037	110050
合作经营	Cooperative	10913	2913	8000	
独资经营	Sole Investment	1102742	819610	167212	115920
股份有限公司	Share-holding Corporations Ltd.	24948	24948		

9-5 续表 Continued

单位：万元（10000 yuan）

指 标	Item	合 计 Total	其中 of which 城镇投资 Urban Investment	农村投资 Rural Investment	房地产投资 Real Estate Investment
个体经营	Individual	110938	68038	42900	
个体户	Self-employed Individuals	66719	65121	1598	
按国民经济行业分	**Grouped by Sector**				
农林牧渔业	Farming,Forestry,Animal Husbandry and Fishery	72298	3900	68398	
制造业	Manufacturing	8614638	5081538	3533100	
电力、燃气及水的生产和供应业	Production and Supply of Electricity, Gas and Water	396674	386301	10373	
建筑业	Construction	23948	23948		
交通运输、仓储和邮政业	Transportation,Storage and Post	492462	449130	43332	
信息传输、计算机服务和软件业	Information Transformation, Computer Service and Software	225149	225149		
批发和零售业	Wholesale and Retail Trade	282971	253076	29895	
住宿和餐饮业	Accommodation and Catering Services	211239	205939	5300	
房地产业	Real Estate Industry	5866646	479223	320518	5066905
租赁和商务服务业	Rent and Business Services	166340	143540	22800	
科学研究、技术服务和地质勘查业	Scientific Research, Technology Service and Geologic Prospecting	69456	62206	7250	
水利、环境和公共设施管理业	Water Conservancy, Environment and Public Facilities Management	1048922	876293	172629	
居民服务和其他服务业	Neighborhood Services and Other Services	68972	67172	1800	
教 育	Education	151409	69164	82245	
卫生、社会保障和社会福利业	Hygiene, Social Security and Social Welfare	116208	110152	6056	
文化、体育和娱乐业	Culture, Sports and Entertainment	219115	208765	10350	
公共管理和社会组织	Public Administration and Social Organizations	136979	102429	34550	

9-6　工业各行业固定资产投资完成额（2007-2011 年）
INVESTMENTS IN FIXED ASSETS OF INDUSTRIAL TRADES（2007-2011）

单位：万元（10000 yuan）

	行　业 Sector	2007	2008	2009	2010	2011
农副食品加工业	Food Processing	51655	52101	45828	36415	66205
食品制造业	Food Production	39127	53668	45130	55107	70471
饮料制造业	Beverage Production	26740	20713	11730	12247	6482
纺织业	Textile Industry	616452	454522	384132	461616	415170
纺织服装、鞋、帽制造业	Textile, Garments, Shoes and Hat Processing	239901	205791	193291	198810	162591
皮革、毛皮、羽毛（绒）及其制品业	Leather, Furs, Down and Related Products	18414	33864	19820	15880	51171
木材加工及木、竹、藤、棕、草制品业	Timber Processing, Bamboo, Cane, Palm Fiber and Straw Products	93249	70861	75384	128629	113098
家具制造业	Furniture Manufacturing	23732	15987	25894	30836	16609
造纸及纸制品业	Papermaking and Paper Products	39604	84855	53865	94955	182001
印刷业和记录媒介的复制	Printing and Record Medium Reproduction	27141	31073	27993	52951	52625
文教体育用品制造业	Cultural, Educational and Sports Goods	20990	26255	11642	17107	23295
石油加工、炼焦及核燃料加工业	Petroleum Processing, Coking and Nuclear Fuel Processing	7804	10042	30590	14858	15753
化学原料及化学制品制造业	Raw Chemical Materials and Chemica Products	645992	780437	744878	895765	1206272
医药制造业	Medical and Pharmaceutical Products	82635	119074	148663	197173	185697
化学纤维制造业	Chemical Fiber	12664	20544	49331	81250	172298
橡胶制品业	Rubber Products	41568	36311	29574	52310	43861
塑料制品业	Plastic Products	145291	189085	266627	262414	202640
非金属矿物制品业	Nonmetal Mineral Products	315776	377265	407444	539413	499780
黑色金属冶炼及压延加工业	Smelting and Pressing of Ferrous Metals	269123	348926	296750	717011	550312
有色金属冶炼及压延加工业	Smelting and Pressing of Nonferrous Metals	101082	87593	183536	231155	188913
金属制品业	Metal Products	407146	365376	684044	647018	558154
通用设备制造业	General Equipment Manufacturing	825839	1151480	1274211	1516640	1351766
专用设备制造业	For Special Purposes Equipment Manufacturing	424991	489444	722373	1274905	1005850
交通运输设备制造业	Transport Equipment Manufacturing	398240	577179	650485	770273	751683
电气机械及器材制造业	Electric Equipment and Machinery	744560	847316	1073544	1543245	1831450
通信设备、计算机及其他电子设备制造	Communication, Computer and Other Electronic Equipment	538383	968336	918553	1143509	1993648
仪器仪表及文化、办公用机械制造业	Instruments, Meters, Cultural and Office Machinery	140517	153807	164436	106249	503693
工艺品及其他制造业	Artcraft and Other Manufacturing	181136	101031	394562	254689	221489
电力、燃气及水的生产和供应业	Production and Supply of Electric Power and Thermal Power	301604	567805	721824	392494	446405

9-7 全社会新增固定资产（2011 年）
TOTAL NEWLY INCREASED FIXED ASSETS（2011）

单位：万元（10000 yuan）

指标	Item	新增固定资产 Newly Increased Fixed Assets	其中 of which 城镇投资 Urban Investment	农村投资 Rural Investment	房地产投资 Real Estate Investment
总计	**Total**	**15516734**	**8952612**	**4499729**	**2064393**
市区	Urban Area	11697747	6640242	3397664	1659841
溧阳市	Liyang City	2264985	1404873	660872	199240
金坛市	Jintan City	1554002	907497	441193	205312
按登记注册类型分	**Grouped by Registration Status**				
内资	Domestically-Funded	13500704	7592763	4233200	1674741
国有	State-owned	1954400	1666257	211871	76272
集体	Collective-owned	692443	305765	361148	25530
股份合作	Share-holding Cooperative	42131	5534	36597	
集体联营	Collective-owned Joint Operation	46410	46410		
国有独资公司	State-funded Corporations	11947	11947		
其它有限责任公司	Other Limited Liability Corporations	5314446	2551876	2087148	675422
股份有限公司	Share-holding Corporations Ltd.	371392	266001	17360	88031
私营	Private	4867345	2661687	1396172	809486
其他	Others	200190	77286	122904	
港澳台商投资	Investment from Hong Kong, Macao and Taiwan	713388	510613	46463	156312
合资经营	Joint-Venture	153334	56975	9153	87206
合作经营	Cooperative	6023		6023	
独资经营	Sole Investment	519505	453638	31287	34580
股份有限公司	Share-holding Corporations Ltd.	34526			34526
外商投资	Enterprises with Foreign Investment	1230169	810151	186678	233340
合资经营	Joint Ventures	294609	207669	59787	27153
合作经营	Cooperative	10557	2557	8000	
独资经营	Sole Investment	922002	596924	118891	206187
股份有限公司	Share-holding Corporations Ltd.	3001	3001		

9-7 续表　Continued　　　　单位：万元（10000 yuan）

指　标	Item	新增固定资产 Newly Increased Fixed Assets	其中 of which 城镇投资 Urban Investment	农村投资 Rural Investment	房地产投资 Real Estate Investment
个体经营	Individual	72473	39085	33388	
个体户	Self-employed Individuals	41573	36185	5388	
按国民经济行业分	**Grouped by Sector**				
农林牧渔业	Farming,Forestry,Animal Husbandry and Fishery	18155	1605	16550	
采矿业	Mining	15020	8120	6900	
制造业	Manufacturing	9304192	5560365	3743827	
电力、燃气及水的生产和供应业	Production and Supply of Electricity, Gas and Water	292187	274335	17852	
建筑业	Construction	17888	17888		
交通运输、仓储和邮政业	Transportation,Storage and Post	611432	578790	32642	
信息传输、计算机服务和软件业	Information Transformation, Computer Service and Software	146122	146122		
批发和零售业	Wholesale and Retail Trade	384166	370436	13730	
住宿和餐饮业	Accommodation and Catering Services	191818	175451	16367	
房地产业	Real Estate Industry	2669141	335380	269368	2064393
租赁和商务服务业	Rent and Business Services	135682	110260	25422	
科学研究、技术服务和地质勘查业	Scientific Research, Technology Service and Geologic Prospecting	16045	8795	7250	
水利、环境和公共设施管理业	Water Conservancy, Environment and Public Facilities Management	1183465	942434	241031	
居民服务和其他服务业	Neighborhood Services and Other Services	79300	69300	10000	
教　育	Education	102065	70135	31930	
卫生、社会保障和社会福利业	Hygiene, Social Security and Social Welfare	48235	40434	7801	
文化、体育和娱乐业	Culture, Sports and Entertainment	138527	119618	18909	
公共管理和社会组织	Public Administration and Social Organizations	123315	89165	34150	

9-8 市区全社会新增固定资产（2011 年）
NEWLY INCREASED FIXED ASSETS IN URBAN AREA（2011）

单位：万元（10000 yuan）

指 标	Item	新增固定资产 Newly Increased Fixed Assets	其中 of which 城镇投资 Urban Investment	农村投资 Rural Investment	房地产投资 Real Estate Investment
总 计	**Total**	**11697747**	**6640242**	**3397664**	**1659841**
按登记注册类型分	**Grouped by Registration Status**				
内 资	Domestically-Funded	9882895	5366623	3226107	1290165
国 有	State-owned	1830311	1642307	151461	36543
集 体	Collective-owned	650821	298815	326476	25530
股份合作	Share-holding Cooperative	42131	5534	36597	
集体联营	Collective-owned Joint Operation	46410	46410		
国有独资公司	State-funded Corporations	11947	11947		
其它有限责任公司	Other Limited Liability Corporations	3882309	1351654	1928620	602035
股份有限公司	Share-holding Corporations Ltd.	332592	250601	12210	69781
私 营	Private	2920034	1685319	678439	556276
其 他	Others	166340	74036	92304	
港澳台商投资	Investment from Hong Kong, Macao and Taiwan	663972	493903	16557	153512
合资经营	Joint-Venture	138824	45265	6353	87206
合作经营	Cooperative	5500		5500	
独资经营	Sole Investment	485122	448638	4704	31780
股份有限公司	Share-holding Corporations Ltd.	34526			34526
外商投资	Enterprises withForeign Investment	1083257	741591	125502	216164
合资经营	Joint Ventures	247550	190719	29678	27153
合作经营	Cooperative	10557	2557	8000	
独资经营	Sole Investment	822149	545314	87824	189011
股份有限公司	Share-holding Corporations Ltd.	3001	3001		
个体经营	Individual	67623	38125	29498	
个体户	Self-employed Individuals	36723	35225	1498	

9-8 续表　Continued　　　　单位：万元（10000 yuan）

指　标	Item	新增固定资产 Newly Increased Fixed Assets	其中 of which 城镇投资 Urban Investment	农村投资 Rural Investment	房地产投资 Real Estate Investment
按国民经济行业分	**Grouped by Sector**				
农林牧渔业	Farming,Forestry,Animal Husbandry and Fishery	4750		4750	
制造业	Manufacturing	6330895	3501762	2829133	
电力、燃气及水的生产和供应业	Production and Supply of Electricity, Gas and Water	274723	264651	10072	
建筑业	Construction	17888	17888		
交通运输、仓储和邮政业	Transportation,Storage and Post	520007	491365	28642	
信息传输、计算机服务和软件业	Information Transformation, Computer Service and Software	146122	146122		
批发和零售业	Wholesale and Retail Trade	284333	274493	9840	
住宿和餐饮业	Accommodation and Catering Services	171761	166561	5200	
房地产业	Real Estate Industry	2244789	335380	249568	1659841
租赁和商务服务业	Rent and Business Services	127080	108280	18800	
科学研究、技术服务和地质勘查业	Scientific Research, Technology Service and Geologic Prospecting	16045	8795	7250	
水利、环境和公共设施管理业	Water Conservancy, Environment and Public Facilities Management	1080102	927114	152988	
居民服务和其他服务业	Neighborhood Services and Other Services	62706	60906	1800	
教　育	Education	83235	55135	28100	
卫生、社会保障和社会福利业	Hygiene, Social Security and Social Welfare	43434	40434	3000	
文化、体育和娱乐业	Culture, Sports and Entertainment	126583	118212	8371	
公共管理和社会组织	Public Administration and Social Organizations	123315	89165	34150	

9-9 全社会固定资产投资效果（2011 年）
EFFECT OF INVESTMENT IN FIXED ASSETS（2011）

指 标	Item	合 计 Total	其中 of which 城镇投资 Urban Investment	农村投资 Rural Investment	房地产投资 Real Estate Investment
施工项目数（个）	Projects under Construction (unit)	3942	2162	1780	
# 本年新开工	Beginning Projects in this Year	2639	1432	1207	
本年建成投产项目数（个）	Number of Projects Completed (unit)	2856	1510	1346	
项目建成投产率（%）	Rate of Projects Completed and Put into Use (%)	72.5	69.8	75.6	
计划总投资（万元）	Plan of General Investment (10000 yuan)	57930613	24142529	9972045	23816039
本年完成投资（万元）	Completed Investment Value this year (10000 yuan)	23389418	11574529	6155826	5659063
建设周期（年）	Construction Cycle (year)	1.5	1.3	1.4	2.7
本年新增固定资产（万元）	Newly Increased Fixed Assets this year (10000 yuan)	15516734	8952612	4499729	2064393
固定资产交付使用率（%）	Rate of Fixed Assets Put into Use (%)	66.3	77.3	73.1	36.5
本年施工房屋面积（万平方米）	Floor Space of Buildings under Construction this year (10000 sq.km)	6935	1591	1428	3916
本年竣工房屋面积（万平方米）	Floor Space of Buildings Completed this year (10000 sq.km)	2616	849	1126	641
房屋竣工率（%）	Rate of Buildings Completed (%)	37.7	53.4	78.9	16.4

9-10　市区全社会固定资产投资效果（2011 年）
EFFECT OF INVESTMENT IN FIXED ASSETS OF URBAN AREA（2011）

指　标	Item	合　计 Total	其中 of which 城镇投资 Urban Investment	农村投资 Rural Investment	房地产投资 Real Estate Investment
施工项目数（个）	Projects under Construction (unit)	2809	1548	1261	
# 本年新开工	Beginning Projects in this Year	1767	908	859	
本年建成投产项目数（个）	Number of Projects Completed (unit)	2273	1155	1118	
项目建成投产率（%）	Rate of Projects Completed and Put into Use (%)	80.92	74.61	88.66	
计划总投资（万元）	Plan of General Investment (10000 yuan)	45958048	18274183	6473091	21210774
本年完成投资（万元）	Completed Investment Value this year (10000 yuan)	18211797	8790296	4354596	5066905
建设周期（年）	Construction Cycle (year)	1.6	1.3	1.3	3.1
本年新增固定资产（万元）	Newly Increased Fixed Assets this year (10000 yuan)	11697747	6640242	3397664	1659841
固定资产交付使用率（%）	Rate of Fixed Assets Put into Use (%)	64.2	75.5	78.0	32.8
本年施工房屋面积（万平方米）	Floor Space of Buildings under Construction this year (10000 sq.km)	5795	1231	1248	3316
本年竣工房屋面积（万平方米）	Floor Space of Buildings Completed this year (10000 sq.km)	2143	633	1014	496
房屋竣工率（%）	Rate of Buildings Completed (%)	37.0	51.4	81.3	15.0

9-11 全社会固定资产投资资金来源（2011 年）
FUND RESOURCES OF FIXED ASSETS INVESTMENT（2011）

单位：万元（10000 yuan）

指 标	Item	合 计 Total	其中 of which 城镇投资 Urban Investment	农村投资 Rural Investment	房地产投资 Real Estate Investment
资金来源总计	**Total Capital ources**	**26613909**	**11160107**	**6132128**	**9321674**
上年末结余资金	Balance of Last Year	2097226	90138	94505	1912583
本年资金来源	Total Funds of This Year	24516683	11069969	6037623	7409091
国家预算内资金	State Budgetary Appropriation	117992	97634	20358	
国内贷款	Domestic Loans	2671982	1144239	371231	1156512
利用外资	Foreign Investment	1091443	816867	152970	121606
# 外商直接投资	Foreign Direct Investment	628258	419662	93790	114806
自筹资金	Fundraising	15231287	8184975	5278821	1767491
其他资金来源	Other Fund Resources	5403979	826254	214243	4363482
附：本年各项应付款	**Accounts Payable of This Year**	**3363559**	**1126856**	**657685**	**1579018**
# 工程款	Funds of Projects	1662626	550167	204079	908380

9-12 市区全社会固定资产投资资金来源（2011 年）
FUND RESOURCES OF FIXED ASSETS INVESTMENT IN URBAN AREA（2011）

单位：万元（10000 yuan）

指 标	Item	合 计 Total	其中 of which 城镇投资 Urban Investment	农村投资 Rural Investment	房地产投资 Real Estate Investment
资金来源总计	**Total Capital Sources**	**20948445**	**8333314**	**4296020**	**8319111**
上年末结余资金	Balance of Last Year	1891130	89538	94505	1707087
本年资金来源	Total Funds of This Year	19057315	8243776	4201515	6612024
国家预算内资金	State Budgetary Appropriation	92084	92084		
国内贷款	Domestic Loans	1948297	697571	191914	1058812
利用外资	Foreign Investment	979731	747137	114564	118030
# 外商直接投资	Foreign Direct Investment	532546	349932	71384	111230
自筹资金	Fundraising	11260257	5902366	3688132	1669759
其他资金来源	Other Fund Resources	4776946	804618	206905	3765423
附：本年各项应付款	**Accounts Payable of This Year**	**2882888**	**1088364**	**560177**	**1234347**
# 工程款	Funds of Projects	1422346	520442	156031	745873

9-13 房地产开发企业经营情况（2011 年）
MANAGEMENT OF REAL ESTATE DEVELOPMENT ENTERPRISES（2011）

指标	Item	合计 Total	内资 Domestic Funded	国有 State-owned
开发企业个数（个）	**Number of Development Enterprises (unit)**	**419**	**348**	**10**
#亏损数	Number of Loss	190	163	5
经营情况（万元）	**Management Condition (10000 yuan)**			
实收资本	Paid-up Capital	4832822	2783662	101157
资产总计	Total Assets	21678757	16612258	507764
累计折旧	Accumulated Depreciation of Fixed Assets	136055	109579	5565
#本年折旧	Depreciation of This Year	32021	24962	192
负债总计	Total Liabilities	15851098	12936239	375197
所有者权益	Owner's Equity	5827659	3676019	132566
主营业务收入	Operating Income	5671278	4266076	159165
土地转让收入	Income from Land Transferred	81727	81727	0
商品房屋销售收入	Income from Commercial Houses Sold	5530457	4143476	158740
房屋出租收入	Housing Rental Income	6496	4339	0
其他收入	Other Incomes	52599	36534	425
主营业务成本	Operational Cost	4354138	3286484	127963
销售费用	Sales Expenses	153073	109603	1080
主营业务税金及附加	Business Tax and Extra Charges	432763	326782	14406
主营业务利润	Major Business Profits	884378	652810	16795
其他业务利润	Other Business Profits	26735	18587	152
管理费用	Management Expenses finance Charge	222476	176477	4546
财务费用	finance Charge	49340	37442	-916
投资收益	Income from Investment	34538	34163	-28
营业利润	Operating Surpius	514388	375664	12225
营业外收入	Nonbusiness Income	17670	17034	326
营业外支出	Nonbusiness Income	24262	20699	280
利润总额	Total Profits	506509	370739	12246
土地开发及购置（平方米）	**Land Area (sq.m)**			
待开发土地面积	Land Space Needed to Development	5225279	3612979	78352
本年购置土地面积	Land Space Purchases of This Year	2045117	1661937	66930
其他指标	**Other Indices**			
全部从业人员年平均数（人）	Annual Average Number of Staff and Workers (person)	11480	9440	216
本年应付职工薪酬（万元）	Total Amount of Payroll Payable this Year (10000 yuan)	87167	66874	1692

注：本年应付职工薪酬为贷方累计发生额。
Note：The total amount of either payroll payable this year refers to the accumulated amount of credit.

其中 of which									
集 体 Collective-owned	国有独资公司 State-owned Companies	其他有限责任公司 Limited liability Corpora-tion	股份有限公司 Share-holding Corporation Ltd	私营独资 Private	私营有限责任公司 Private Limited Liability Corporation	私营股份有限公司 Private Company Limited by Shares	其 他 Others	港澳台商投资 Investment from Hongkong,Macao andTaiwan	外商投资 Foreign Investment
2	**1**	**120**	**12**	**5**	**194**	**1**	**3**	**47**	**24**
1	1	56	4		93	1	2	20	7
12000	38500	1337299	302736	30800	931790	5180	24200	1520193	528966
204480	72945	8150648	1195268	359989	5869761	39611	211792	3765645	1300854
7	11	29150	12093	818	59082	520	2333	18085	8390
2	10	8701	2459	374	12063	150	1011	4010	3049
191646	35142	6300011	853189	327642	4641148	38173	174090	2183618	731242
12835	37802	1850637	342079	32347	1228613	1438	37703	1582027	569613
50173		1867405	245761	88144	1841327	4025	10077	1123698	281505
		50418	1523		29786				
50168		1791216	241776	88144	1802797	4025	6611	1107163	279818
		786	2441		1112			470	1687
5		24985	21		7633		3466	16064	
44112		1391924	206105	71403	1434315	4080	6582	882700	184953
55		53902	5101	1886	46978	56	545	35333	8137
2556		144433	21935	6524	134781	323	1825	75968	30014
3505		331049	17720	10217	272231	-378	1671	165030	66538
3		15711	73		2648			6817	1332
278	590	70558	16642	2669	77978	364	2853	28463	17536
533	1	7576	4845	83	25366	-7	-38	11152	746
		11858	15874	5	6454			11	364
2642	-591	224738	7182	5582	126367	-791	-1690	96910	41815
57		9127	3373	142	3399		610	315	322
35		9963	1586	101	8508	47	179	2951	612
2664	-591	221092	8217	5602	123608	-838	-1259	94245	41525
220603		1891484	117344	40346	1264850			1556550	55750
		916582	75844	59180	543401			316130	67050
39	39	3358	517	150	4978	25	118	1484	556
105	228	28627	6729	789	27815	100	791	15832	4462

9-14　市区房地产开发企业经营情况（2011 年）
MANAGEMENT OF REAL ESTATE DEVELOPMENT ENTERPRISES IN URBAN AREA（2011）

指 标	Item	合 计 Total	内 资 Domestic Funded	国 有 State-owned
开发企业个数（个）	**Number of Development Enterprises (unit)**	**314**	**258**	**8**
#亏损数	Number of Loss	151	128	4
经营情况（万元）	Management Condition (10000 yuan)			
实收资本	Paid-up Capital	4462672	2486635	76077
资产总计	Total Assets	19108863	14277884	400361
累计折旧	Accumulated Depreciation of Fixed Assets	105330	85805	2691
#本年折旧	Depreciation of This Year	22246	16751	68
负债总计	Total Liabilities	13745408	10971725	294968
所有者权益	Owner's Equity	5363455	3306159	105392
主营业务收入	Operating Income	4906346	3579760	139754
土地转让收入	Income from Land Transferred	81727	81727	
商品房屋销售收入	Income from Commercial Houses Sold	4771989	3462638	139329
房屋出租收入	Housing Rental Income	5133	3962	
其他收入	Other Incomes	47498	31434	425
主营业务成本	Operational Cost	3745259	2732506	112602
销售费用	Sales Expenses	133824	91902	880
主营业务税金及附加	Business Tax and Extra Charges	375698	275038	12497
主营业务利润	Major Business Profits	785388	572216	14656
其他业务利润	Other Businescs Profits	24248	16115	-73
管理费用	Management Expenses	183067	141978	3581
财务费用	Finance Charge	39249	28508	-957
投资收益	Income from Investment	32627	32253	-28
营业利润	Operating Surpius	479811	351882	11065
营业外收入	Nonbusiness Income	14731	14365	80
营业外支出	Nonbusiness Income	20745	17510	106
利润总额	Total Profits	472523	347491	11015
土地开发及购置（平方米）	Land Area (sq.m)			
待开发土地面积	Land Space Needed to Development	4425090	3024604	78352
本年购置土地面积	Land Space Purchases of This Year	1673225	1374645	66930
其他指标	Other Indices			
全部从业人员年平均数（人）	Annual Average Number of Staff and Workers (person)	8944	7301	161
本年应付职工薪酬（万元）	Total Amount of Payroll Payable this Year (10000 yuan)	75036	57411	1351

注：本年应付职工薪酬为贷方累计发生额。
Note：The total amount of either payroll payable this year refers to the accumulated amount of credit.

其中 of which							港澳台商投资 Investment from Hongkong,Macao and Taiwan	外商投资 Foreign Investment
集体 Collective-owned	其他有限责任公司 Limited liability Corporation	股份有限公司 Share-holding Corporation Ltd	私营独资 Private	私营有限责任公司 Private Limited Liability Corporation	私营股份有限公司 Private Company Limited by Shares	其他 Others		
1	**105**	**10**	**4**	**127**	**1**	**2**	**37**	**19**
	51	4		66	1	2	16	7
10000	1282203	297536	28800	782640	5180	4200	1477861	498176
154771	7523523	1136315	317680	4593976	39611	111648	3622665	1208315
7	24753	11959	718	42824	520	2333	13059	6466
2	4825	2441	289	7965	150	1011	2996	2499
143098	5719030	802860	287578	3581069	38173	104950	2091773	681911
11674	1804493	333455	30103	1012907	1438	6698	1530892	526404
38195	1705285	207902	79069	1398279	4025	7251	1086114	240471
	50418	1523		29786				
38190	1629807	203917	79069	1361690	4025	6611	1069595	239756
	590	2441		931			455	716
5	24470	21		5872		641	16064	
31828	1259039	173237	64400	1081326	4080	5995	855487	157266
55	51467	4634	1692	32572	56	545	34049	7873
2501	132769	19051	5743	101682	323	473	73694	26966
3866	313477	15615	8926	215271	-378	784	156933	56239
3	15697	73		415			6827	1306
202	61349	15997	1908	56293	364	2284	25202	15887
533	6083	4840	80	17941	-7	-6	9964	777
	11862	15874	5	4540			11	364
3079	220303	6193	5249	108825	-791	-2040	94557	33372
57	8627	3373	142	2080		5	271	95
35	9055	644	93	7371	47	159	2919	315
3100	216475	8182	5276	106475	-838	-2194	91880	33152
110603	1792026	80144	40346	923133			1364023	36463
	916582	23676		367457			231530	67050
20	3050	484	112	3367	25	82	1201	442
60	27057	6622	577	20926	100	717	13731	3894

9-15 房地产开发企业房屋建设情况（2011 年）
CONSTRUCTION OF BUILDINGS DEVELOPED BY REAL ESTATE COMPANIES（2011）

指 标	Item	施工面积（万平方米）Floor Space under Construction (10000 sq.m)	其中 of which #本年新开工 Floor Space Started This Year	竣工面积（万平方米）Floor Space Completed (10000 sq.m)	竣工价值（万元）Value Completed (10000 yuan)
总 计	**Total**	**3926.82**	**1451.09**	**682.22**	**1756036**
#溧阳市	Liyang City	330.60	164.19	73.09	205398
金坛市	Jintan City	271.81	121.24	76.87	154283
按经济成份分	**By Economic Sector**				
国 有	State-owned	111.17	38.35	23.94	41861
集 体	Collective-owned	8.89	2.06	7.20	25530
其 它	Others	3806.76	1410.67	651.08	1688645
按用途分	**By Use**				
住 宅	Residential Buildings	2712.48	1019.63	472.38	1204534
#别墅、高档公寓	Villas, Top Grade Apartments	183.39	90.57	17.20	79039
办公楼	Office Buildings	178.68	89.07	34.33	106939
商业营业用房	Buildings for Business Use	533.62	154.69	85.65	242869
其 他	Others	502.04	187.70	89.86	201694

9-16 市区房地产开发企业房屋建设情况（2011 年）
CONSTRUCTION OF BUILDINGS DEVELOPED BY REAL ESTATE COMPANIES IN URBAN AREA（2011）

指 标	Item	施工面积（万平方米）Floor Space under Construction (10000 sq.m)	其中 of which #本年新开工 Floor Space Started This Year	竣工面积（万平方米）Floor Space Completed (10000 sq.m)	竣工价值（万元）Value Completed (10000 yuan)
总 计	**Total**	**3324.41**	**1165.66**	**532.27**	**1396355**
按经济成份分	**By Economic Sector**				
国 有	State-owned	89.79	21.85	7.69	16543
集 体	Collective-owned	8.89	2.06	7.20	25530
其 它	Others	3225.73	1141.75	517.38	1354282
按用途分	**By Use**				
住 宅	Residential Buildings	2267.75	801.23	358.34	933830
#别墅、高档公寓	Villas, Top Grade Apartments	177.24	87.08	15.23	75034
办公楼	Office Buildings	176.19	88.83	34.09	106391
商业营业用房	Buildings for Business Use	423.74	108.63	63.87	180711
其 他	Others	456.74	166.98	75.97	175423

9-17 房地产开发企业商品房销售和出租情况（2011 年）
SOLD AND LEASEDCOMMODITY HOUSES OF REAL ESTATE DEVELOPMENT COMPANIES（2011）

指 标	Item	销售面积（万平方米）Actually Sales (10000sq.m)	其 中 of which 现 房 Existing house	期 房 Future marketable housing	待售面积（万平方米）Needed to sales (10000sq.m)
总 计	**Total**	**661.12**	**104.37**	**556.75**	**179.00**
# 溧阳市	Liyang City	60.90	8.21	52.69	12.49
金坛市	Jintan City	62.63	11.48	51.15	40.22
按经济成份分	**By Economic Sector**				
国 有	State-owned	14.58	1.69	12.89	10.32
集 体	Collective-owned	8.48	7.21	1.27	0.12
其 它	Others	638.07	95.47	542.60	168.56
按用途分	**By Use**				
住 宅	Residential Buildings	537.94	57.24	480.69	61.19
# 别墅、高档公寓	Villas, Top Grade Apartments	43.43	4.29	39.14	12.08
办公楼	Office Buildings	28.28	10.24	18.04	21.00
商业营业用房	Buildings for Business Use	81.82	30.11	51.72	59.14
其 他	Others	13.08	6.78	6.30	37.67

9-17 续表 Continued

指 标	Item	销售额（万元）Total Actually (10000 yuan)	其 中 of which 现 房 Existing house	期 房 Future marketable housing	出租面积（万平方米）Rent (10000sq.m)
总 计	**Total**	**4852285**	**507903**	**4344382**	**25.96**
# 溧阳市	Liyang City	433275	61526	371749	14.09
金坛市	Jintan City	309406	42940	266466	3.88
按经济成份分	**By Economic Sector**				
国 有	State-owned	62943	4541	58402	0.45
集 体	Collective-owned	38190	32548	5642	
其 它	Others	4751152	470814	4280338	25.51
按用途分	**By Use**				
住 宅	Residential Buildings	3686619	241610	3445009	
# 别墅、高档公寓	Villas, Top Grade Apartments	550539	44600	505939	
办公楼	Office Buildings	213443	55340	158103	2.85
商业营业用房	Buildings for Business Use	903063	188175	714888	21.87
其 他	Others	49160	22778	26382	1.24

9-18　市区房地产开发企业商品房销售和出租情况（2011 年）
COMMODITY HOUSES OF REAL ESTATE DEVELOPMENT COMPANIESSOLD AND LEASED IN URBAN AREA（2011）

指　标	Item	销售面积（万平方米）Actually Sales (10000sq.m)	其　中 of which 现　房 Existing house	期　房 Future marketable housing	待售面积（万平方米）Needed to sales (10000sq.m)
总　计	**Total**	**537.59**	**84.68**	**452.91**	**126.29**
按经济成份分	**By Economic Sector**				
国　有	State-owned	6.27		6.27	
集　体	Collective-owned	8.48	7.21	1.27	0.12
其　它	Others	522.85	77.47	445.38	126.17
按用途分	**By Use**				
住　宅	Residential Buildings	441.50	49.38	392.12	42.38
# 别墅、高档公寓	Villas, Top Grade Apartments	41.34	3.24	38.10	8.55
办公楼	Office Buildings	25.70	8.33	17.37	19.33
商业营业用房	Buildings for Business Use	61.81	22.01	39.80	34.80
其　他	Others	8.59	4.96	3.63	29.78

9-18 续表　Continued

指　标	Item	销售额（万元）Total Actually (10000 yuan)	其　中 of which 现　房 Existing house	期　房 Future marketable housing	出租面积（万平方米）Rent (10000sq.m)
总　计	**Total**	**4109604**	**403437**	**3706167**	**8.00**
按经济成份分	**By Economic Sector**				
国　有	State-owned	44637		44637	
集　体	Collective-owned	38190	32548	5642	
其　它	Others	4026777	370889	3655888	8.00
按用途分	**By Use**				
住　宅	Residential Buildings	3152544	206163	2946381	
# 别墅、高档公寓	Villas, Top Grade Apartments	527557	33406	494151	
办公楼	Office Buildings	199622	43119	156503	2.85
商业营业用房	Buildings for Business Use	724005	137802	586203	3.91
其　他	Others	33433	16353	17080	1.24

10

CHAPTER 10

农 业

AGRICULTURE

常州统计年鉴

10 农 业 AGRICULTURE

2011 年主要统计指标
MAJOR STATISTICAL INDICATORS OF 2011

年底乡村实有从业人员	Number of Persons Employed In Rural Area at Year-end	132.81 万人	(10000 persons)
比上年增长	Over the Previous Year	-0.9%	
农林牧渔业总产值	Total Output value of Farming,Forestry,Animal Husbandry and Fishing	194.68 亿元	(100 million yuan)
比上年增长	Over the Previous Year	11.8%	
粮食总产量	Total Output of Grain	115.19 万吨	(10000 tons)
比上年增长	Over the Previous Year	0.0%	
油料总产量	Total Output of Oil-Bearing	3.20 万吨	(10000 tons)
比上年增长	Over the Previous Year	-20.0%	

10-1 分地区农林牧渔业总产值（1978-2011 年）
GROSS OUTPUT VALUE OF FARMING, FORESTRY, ANIMAL HUSBANDARY AND FISHERY BY REGION（1978-2011）

按现价计算 At Current Prices　　单位：亿元（100 million yuan）

年 份 Year	全 市 Whole Municipality	其 中 of which		
		市 区 Urban Area	溧阳市 Liyang City	金坛市 Jintan City
1978	6.96	3.75	1.96	1.25
1979	8.13	4.00	2.15	1.89
1980	8.12	3.89	2.54	1.69
1981	8.14	3.99	2.48	1.67
1982	9.66	4.75	2.85	2.06
1983	10.08	5.04	2.95	2.09
1984	13.71	6.97	4.08	2.66
1985	15.10	8.08	4.27	2.75
1986	17.42	9.63	4.39	3.40
1987	19.17	10.19	5.00	3.98
1988	25.01	13.07	6.79	5.16
1989	26.87	14.40	6.76	5.70
1990	29.06	15.48	7.52	6.06
1991	27.78	16.22	6.46	5.10
1992	35.22	19.59	8.03	7.60
1993	45.95	26.05	10.65	9.25
1994	63.64	34.30	16.43	12.91
1995	74.74	39.34	20.02	15.39
1996	87.28	44.98	24.13	18.16
1997	82.16	43.64	21.45	17.07
1998	84.01	43.96	22.15	17.90
1999	83.67	42.77	22.37	18.54
2000	85.88	43.81	22.06	20.01
2001	89.37	44.94	23.21	21.22
2002	92.67	45.89	24.53	22.25
2003	90.63	42.62	24.52	23.50
2004	99.42	46.03	27.16	26.23
2005	104.10	47.90	28.64	27.55
2006	101.99	46.65	27.74	27.60
2007	108.87	49.16	30.41	29.30
2008	149.77	69.60	45.11	35.06
2009	160.77	73.91	49.59	37.27
2010	174.08	78.39	54.57	41.12
2011	194.68	86.69	62.02	45.97

注：2006年至2008年数据依据第二次农业普查数据作相应调整。
Note: The data from year 2006 to year 2008 was adjusted in accordance with the date of the second agricultural census.

10-2 主要年份年末耕地面积
YEAR-END AREA UNDER CULTIVATION IN MAIN YEARS

单位：千公顷（1000 hectares）

年 份 Year	全 市 Whole Municipality	其 中 of which 市 区 Urban Area	溧阳市 Liyang City	金坛市 Jintan City
1949	232.64	109.47	73.15	50.01
1952	235.41	108.91	75.53	50.97
1957	231.09	106.19	75.25	49.89
1962	217.05	98.03	72.94	46.08
1965	218.25	103.29	68.86	46.10
1970	209.59	100.90	65.61	43.08
1975	212.21	103.31	65.55	43.36
1978	210.15	100.84	65.36	43.95
1979	209.67	100.47	65.29	43.92
1980	209.13	100.24	65.23	43.66
1981	208.91	100.13	65.16	43.61
1982	206.73	98.09	65.06	43.57
1983	207.14	98.61	64.99	43.54
1984	206.79	98.38	64.93	43.49
1985	206.57	98.25	64.87	43.45
1986	206.16	98.08	64.68	43.40
1987	206.05	98.04	64.65	43.36
1988	205.31	97.38	64.63	43.31
1989	204.97	97.19	64.50	43.28
1990	204.54	97.01	64.34	43.19
1991	204.27	96.86	64.26	43.15
1992	203.60	96.59	63.94	43.07
1993	203.23	96.42	63.80	43.01
1994	202.42	95.81	63.68	42.93
1995	200.88	94.80	63.44	42.64
1996	205.35	90.16	68.99	46.19
1997	204.99	80.57	68.87	46.23
1998	204.70	80.29	68.87	46.25
1999	204.81	89.31	69.19	46.32
2000	204.25	88.75	69.15	46.35
2001	202.63	87.03	69.23	46.37
2002	199.97	84.93	68.91	46.13
2003	197.67	82.78	68.64	46.25
2004	178.09	66.14	66.89	45.06
2005	176.32	64.27	66.83	45.22
2006	161.81	60.58	62.24	38.99
2007	161.09	59.89	62.34	38.86
2008	161.09	59.32	62.60	39.17
2009	148.13	60.37	55.83	31.93
2010	150.39	59.25	57.64	33.50
2011	150.00	58.60	57.59	33.81

注：2011年末耕地面积为初步统计数据。
Note：The arable land calculated in the end of 2011 was based on the preliminary statistics.

10-3 主要年份粮食总产量
TOTAL OUTPUT OF GRAIN IN MAIN YEARS

单位：万吨（10000 tons）

年 份 Year	全 市 Whole Municipality	其 中 of which 市 区 Urban Area	溧阳市 Liyang City	金坛市 Jintan City
1949	57.89	34.54	11.86	11.48
1952	78.41	42.77	19.87	15.77
1957	71.52	37.60	18.34	15.57
1962	74.80	44.49	15.45	14.86
1965	116.93	65.31	29.20	22.43
1970	114.48	61.81	29.11	23.56
1975	121.23	68.96	30.90	21.37
1978	150.25	81.96	40.03	28.26
1979	154.07	81.35	43.61	29.11
1980	139.42	75.25	37.38	26.79
1981	132.79	71.57	37.23	23.98
1982	157.60	84.85	43.84	28.91
1983	164.73	85.76	48.47	30.49
1984	177.75	91.79	53.12	32.84
1985	153.34	80.46	44.50	28.39
1986	162.13	85.82	45.09	31.22
1987	151.45	81.42	42.92	29.80
1988	157.63	85.37	41.56	30.70
1989	160.60	85.87	43.17	31.55
1990	164.50	89.07	41.98	33.46
1991	138.39	77.55	35.15	25.70
1992	158.62	88.06	40.53	30.02
1993	154.24	82.17	40.52	31.56
1994	144.79	77.74	37.07	29.98
1995	159.57	81.30	43.55	34.72
1996	166.37	83.73	46.03	36.61
1997	170.77	85.47	48.39	36.92
1998	153.28	72.02	47.82	33.43
1999	154.83	76.13	46.00	32.70
2000	136.22	66.11	41.87	28.24
2001	126.14	57.32	41.89	26.94
2002	122.86	53.78	42.96	26.11
2003	103.54	42.49	38.53	22.52
2004	106.08	41.43	40.96	23.69
2005	98.06	39.28	36.61	22.17
2006	95.25	36.30	36.87	22.08
2007	94.84	31.91	40.96	21.97
2008	113.35	36.84	49.41	27.10
2009	114.18	36.37	49.78	28.03
2010	115.16	34.22	52.72	28.22
2011	115.19	32.34	54.47	28.38

注：2006、2007年数据依据第二次农业普查数据作相应调整。
Note: Data of year 2006 and 2007 are adjusted in accordance with the data of the second agricultural census.

10-4 主要年份棉花总产量
TOTAL OUTPUT OF COTTON IN MAIN YEARS

单位：吨（ton）

年 份 Year	全 市 Whole Municipality	其中 of which 市 区 Urban Area	溧阳市 Liyang City	金坛市 Jintan City
1949	261	195		66
1952	390	301		89
1957	50	4		46
1962	1		1	
1965	112	42	19	51
1970	34	27		7
1975	503		1	502
1978	2045		366	1679
1979	3274		482	2792
1980	5509		1831	3678
1981	10495	104	3366	7025
1982	11615	594	3457	7564
1983	11973	914	2937	8122
1984	12860	1198	3729	7933
1985	7240	559	2444	4237
1986	3464	227	1591	1646
1987	2954	252	1518	1184
1988	3325	215	1819	1291
1989	2259	125	1273	861
1990	2255	78	1193	984
1991	1956	86	1170	700
1992	2840	74	2031	735
1993	1828	27	1497	304
1994	1050		913	137
1995	1276		1086	190
1996	936		758	181
1997	1114		924	190
1998	1150		902	248
1999	589		388	201
2000	764		544	220
2001	708		348	360
2002	637		406	231
2003	305		182	123
2004	368		236	132
2005	298		185	113
2006	303		241	62
2007	283		204	79
2008	484		406	78
2009	454		332	120
2010	506		451	55
2011	491		457	34

注：2006、2007年数依据第二次农业普查数据作相应调整。
Note：Data of year 2006 and 2007 are adjusted in accordance with the data of the second agricultural census.

10-5 主要年份油料总产量
TOTAL OUTPUT OF OIL-BEARING CROPS IN MAIN YEARS

单位：吨（ton）

年 份 Year	全 市 Whole Municipality	其 中 of which 市 区 Urban Area	溧阳市 Liyang City	金坛市 Jintan City
1949	4455	1250	1244	1961
1952	5027	936	3538	553
1957	4146	550	3130	466
1962	2154	233	1414	507
1965	2493	118	1795	580
1970	7195	2969	2209	2017
1975	10586	4962	3382	2242
1978	13515	4713	6046	2756
1979	14894	5028	7040	2826
1980	17724	5747	9473	2504
1981	27590	9895	12578	5117
1982	52438	13308	31780	7350
1983	38895	10578	22205	6112
1984	38175	10080	22780	5315
1985	69961	13383	43870	12708
1986	55603	12017	32795	10791
1987	57063	11526	35544	9993
1988	46657	10347	27518	8792
1989	54054	10341	33295	10418
1990	63899	11710	38899	13290
1991	53931	10879	31126	11926
1992	68040	10594	42774	14672
1993	61498	10114	26942	24442
1994	51683	10610	29530	11543
1995	72786	12068	41895	18823
1996	70526	12793	38632	19101
1997	66204	11240	37689	17275
1998	35932	5154	21286	9492
1999	72421	9981	42509	19931
2000	91629	17412	53102	21115
2001	86994	15027	52238	19729
2002	73015	10270	45111	17634
2003	72586	8954	47360	16272
2004	85537	8725	59109	17703
2005	85960	8489	60469	17002
2006	76904	7074	56485	13345
2007	51326	4868	35198	11260
2008	52575	4316	38703	9556
2009	51608	4513	36561	10534
2010	40035	3922	26411	9702
2011	32048	3138	20710	8200

注：2006、2007年数依据第二次农业普查数据作相应调整。
Note: Data of year 2006 and 2007 are adjusted in accordance with the data of the second agricultural census.

10-6 主要年份人均占有主要农产品产量
PER CAPTIA OUTPUT OF MAJOR FARM PRODUCTS IN MAIN YEARS

单位：千克 / 人（kg/person）

年 份 Year	粮 食 Grain	油 料 Oil-bearing Crops	蚕 茧 Silkworm Cocoons	茶 叶 Tea	水 果 Fruit	猪 肉 Pork	水产品 Aquatic Products
1952	427.68	2.74	1.30	0.01	1.30		4.06
1957	351.09	2.04	0.68	0.01	1.60		4.96
1965	485.63	1.04	0.40	0.14	0.86		4.26
1970	429.06	2.70	1.08	0.36	0.94		3.76
1975	425.84	3.72	0.87	0.47	0.85		4.48
1978	516.31	4.64	0.61	0.47	1.01		4.49
1980	471.14	5.99	0.76	0.54	1.93	23.64	4.85
1985	499.71	22.80	1.78	0.89	2.79	19.64	9.22
1986	523.43	17.95	2.04	0.96	2.96	19.17	12.01
1987	492.13	18.22	2.05	1.09	3.42	19.32	13.00
1988	497.16	14.12	2.38	1.20	3.93	19.86	15.73
1989	499.29	16.81	2.77	1.17	3.38	20.13	13.81
1990	506.40	19.67	2.69	1.15	2.98	21.55	16.36
1991	423.38	16.50	2.64	1.03	2.95	22.44	11.44
1992	482.75	20.71	2.88	1.13	3.07	23.77	15.69
1993	468.36	18.67	3.38	1.24	4.17	23.98	21.14
1994	436.85	15.59	3.54	1.20	6.08	25.31	24.27
1995	478.25	21.82	3.01	0.76	6.81	26.97	27.15
1996	492.88	20.89	1.47	0.72	6.49	25.94	29.16
1997	503.41	19.52	1.51	0.80	6.32	17.47	27.57
1998	450.83	10.60	1.43	0.79	7.10	18.32	31.11
1999	455.78	21.32	1.28	0.81	7.92	17.56	32.16
2000	398.90	26.83	1.41	0.79	8.68	18.83	32.51
2001	369.40	25.47	1.53	0.77	10.55	19.83	33.80
2002	357.92	21.27	1.47	0.78	10.79	19.51	35.08
2003	299.06	20.97	1.30	0.78	17.30	21.30	36.02
2004	303.99	24.51	1.26	0.76	17.41	19.16	36.48
2005	278.88	24.45	0.81	0.79	19.13	18.46	37.03
2006	268.56	21.68	0.92	0.82	16.88	19.05	37.13
2007	265.37	14.36	0.68	0.93	20.69	16.52	37.83
2008	315.96	14.66	0.46	1.06	27.14	17.78	39.63
2009	317.33	14.34	0.20	1.09	23.12	17.40	39.13
2010	319.17	11.10	0.19	0.96	27.60	16.57	41.00
2011	317.45	8.83	0.14	0.95	25.61	16.74	45.31

注：2006、2007年数依据第二次农业普查数据作相应调整。
Note：Data of year 2006 and 2007 are adjusted in accordance with the data of the second agricultural census.

10-7　主要年份农村经济主要指标
MAJOR ECONOMIC INDICATORS OF AGRICULTURE IN MAIN YEARS

指　标	Item	1980	1985	1990	1995	2000	2005	2011
农业机械总动力（万千瓦）	Total Power of Agricultural Machinery (10000 kw)	81.49	105.65	116.92	137.19	167.67	162.03	155.25
农林牧渔业总产值（亿元）	Total Output Value of Farming,Forestry, Animal Husbandry and Fishery (100 million yuan)	7.08	13.35	29.06	74.74	85.88	104.10	194.68
# 农业产值	Value of Farming	5.33	9.30	15.95	44.65	51.37	50.14	107.78
林业产值	Value of Forestry	0.06	0.14	0.17	0.51	0.88	1.24	1.48
牧业产值	Value of Animal Hubandry	1.51	3.10	8.28	17.52	12.97	18.74	32.19
渔业产值	Value of Fishery	0.18	0.81	2.60	12.06	20.66	29.01	44.56
粮食产量（万吨）	Total Output of Grain (10000 tons)	139.42	153.34	164.50	159.57	136.22	98.06	115.19
棉花产量（吨）	Total Output of Cotton (ton)	5509	7240	2255	1276	764	298	491
油料产量（吨）	Total Output of Oil-bearing Grops (ton)	17724	69961	63899	72786	91629	85960	32048
水产品产量（吨）	Output of Aquatic Products (ton)	14353	26848	53149	90571	111188	130198	164421
蚕茧产量（吨）	Output of Silkworm Cocoons (ton)	2272	5476	8726	10055	4815	2843	544
水果产量（吨）	Output of Fruits (ton)	5723	8551	9670	22716	29639	67275	92918
茶叶产量（吨）	Output of Tea (ton)	1585	2727	3730	2550	2680	2762	3449

10-8　主要年份农村经济主要指标增长速度
GROWTH RATE OF MAJOR INDICATORS OF AGRICULTURAL ECONOMY IN MAIN YEARS

单位：%

指　标	Item	2011 年比下列各年增长 Growth Rate of 2011 over Following Years						
		1980	1985	1990	1995	2000	2005	2010
农业机械总动力	Total Power of Agricultural Machinery	90.5	46.9	32.8	13.2	-7.4	-4.2	3.4
农林牧渔业总产值	Total Output Value of Farming,Forestry, Animal Husbandry and Fishery	26.5倍	13.6倍	5.7倍	1.6倍	1.3倍	87.0	11.8
# 农业产值	Value of Farming	19.2倍	10.6倍	5.8倍	1.4倍	1.1倍	1.2倍	13.4
林业产值	Value of Forestry	23.7倍	9.6倍	7.7倍	1.9倍	68.2	19.4	17.5
牧业产值	Value of Animal Hubandry	20.3倍	9.4倍	2.9倍	83.7	1.5倍	71.8	17.4
渔业产值	Value of Fishery	246.6倍	54.0倍	16.1倍	2.7倍	1.2倍	53.6	5.2
粮食产量	Total Output of Grain	-17.4	-24.9	-30.0	-27.8	-15.4	17.5	0.0
油料产量	Total Output of Oil-bearing Grops	80.8	-54.2	-49.8	-56.0	-65.0	-62.7	-20.0
水产品产量	Output of Aquatic Products	10.5倍	5.1倍	2.1倍	81.5	47.9	26.3	11.1
蚕茧产量	Output of Silkworm Cocoons	-76.1	-90.1	-93.8	-94.6	-88.7	-80.9	-18.9
水果产量	Output of Fruits	15.2倍	9.9倍	8.6倍	3.1倍	2.1倍	38.1	-6.7
茶叶产量	Output of Tea	1.2倍	26.5	-7.5	35.2	28.6	24.9	-0.4

10-9 主要年份农村基本情况
FUNDAMENTAL CONDITION OF VILLAGE IN MAIN YEARS

	指 标 Item	1990	1995	2000	2005	2011
农村基层组织（个）	**Village Units (unit)**					
镇政府	Town Governments	32	73	70	73	37
村民委员会	Number of Villagers' Committees	1933	1924	1909	1101	775
村民小组	Villager Group	21557	21638	21485	17999	16821
乡村户数、人口数	Households and Rural Population					
总户数（万户）	Number of Households (10000 households)	74.68	76.80	80.41	79.98	78.00
总人口（万人）	Rural Population(10000 persons)	242.34	239.14	236.86	235.30	235.68
乡村实有从业人员（万人）	**Number of Rural Laborers (10000 persons)**	**135.80**	**136.31**	**128.67**	**126.86**	**132.81**
按性别分	Grouped by Sex					
男劳动力	Male	70.50	70.77	66.66	66.02	70.13
女劳动力	Female	65.30	65.54	62.01	60.84	62.68
按行业分	**Grouped by Sector**					
农林牧渔业	Farming, Forestry, Animal Husbandry and Fishery	65.45	54.65	51.03	32.21	26.02
# 种植业	Planting	59.15	47.29	43.98	26.11	20.40
工 业	Industry	37.58	42.88	36.98	48.35	58.45
建筑业	Construction	11.22	12.86	13.54	15.89	16.88
交通运输、仓储、邮电通信业	Transport, Storage, Post and Telecommunications	4.18	5.23	5.27	5.91	5.48
批发零售贸易餐饮业	Wholesale and Retail Trade, Catering Service	2.71	3.92	5.67	7.91	6.93
金融保险业	Banking and Insurance	0.10	0.11	0.17	0.49	0.83
房地产、社会服务业	Real Estate and Social Services	0.49	0.39	0.72	1.42	1.60
卫生、体育和社会福利业	Health Care, Sporting and Social Welfare	0.41	0.41	0.39	0.42	0.62
教育、文化艺术和广电业	Culture, Education and Arts, Radio, Film and Television	0.60	0.47	0.38	0.48	0.61
科研和综合技术服务业	Scientific Research and Polytechnical Services	0.08	0.07	0.14	0.16	0.21
乡经济组织管理业	Rural Economic Management	0.74	0.94	0.87	0.58	0.34
其他行业	Others	12.24	14.38	13.51	13.04	14.84

10-10　分地区农业现代化情况（2011 年）
STATISTICS ON AGRICULTURAL MODERNIZATION BY REGION（2011）

指 标	Item	全 市 Whole Municipality	武进区 Wujin District
农业机械情况	**Statistics on Agricultural Machinery**		
机耕地面积（千公顷）	Area Ploughed by Tractors (1000 hectares)	167.69	30.90
#占耕地面积（%）	Percentage of Coverage Area under Cultivation (%)	111.79	74.63
机播面积（千公顷）	Seeded Area by Tractors (1000 hectares)	139.30	26.27
机械植保面积（千公顷）	Plant Protection Area by Tractors (1000 hectares)	154.80	27.33
机收面积（千公顷）	Harvest Area by Tractors (1000 hectares)	150.79	26.66
机械脱粒粮食（万吨）	Amount of Shelling by Thresher (10000 tons)	104.00	38.60
农村电气化情况	**Electrization in Rural Area**		
农村用电量（万千瓦小时）	Electricity Consumed in Rural Area (10000 kwh)	1515809	782568
农村化学化情况	**Chemification Conditions of Village**		
化肥施用量（折纯量，吨）	Consumption of Chemical Fertilizer (ton)	65298	8571
#氮　肥	Nitrogenous Fertilizer	38839	5052
磷　肥	Phosphate Fertilizer	2282	461
钾　肥	Potash Fertilizer	1100	248
复合肥	Compound Fertilizer	23077	2810
农药使用量（吨）	Consumption of Agricultural Chemical Pesticide (ton)	3647	812
农用薄膜使用量（吨）	Consumption of Agricultural Film (ton)	2575	830
#地膜使用量（吨）	Consumption of Mulching Film (ton)	1051	303
地膜覆盖面积（公顷）	Area of Coverage of Mulching Film (hectare)	5938	1062
农用柴油（吨）	Agricultural Diesel Oil (ton)	25164	8914
通汽车村数（个）	**Number of Villages with Traffic Service (unit)**	**775**	**247**
自来水受益村数（个）	**Number of Villages with Access to Tap Water (unit)**	**775**	**247**

其中 of which					
新北区 Xinbei District	天宁区 Tianning District	钟楼区 Zhonglou District	戚墅堰区 Qishuyan District	溧阳市 Liyang City	金坛市 Jintan City
22.30				77.09	37.40
135.15				133.74	111.64
17.53				64.76	30.75
19.36				65.27	42.84
22.20				66.32	35.61
0.15				44.00	21.25
12737	46374	98612	14921	394593	166004
10107	8		99	23616	22897
7155	8		59	15368	11237
301			15	1477	28
412			13	384	44
2279			12	6388	11588
510	2		2	1458	863
210	3		6	849	677
110	1		2	431	204
389	61		28	3592	806
2402			23	8962	4863
119	**27**	**42**	**9**	**175**	**156**
119	**27**	**42**	**9**	**175**	**156**

10-11　分地区农村基本情况（2011 年底）
FUNDAMENTAL CONDITION OF VILLAGE BY REGION（END OF 2011）

指　标	Item	全　市 Whole Municipality	武进区 Wujin District
农村基层组织情况（个）	**Village Units (unit)**		
镇政府	Town Governments	37	14
村民委员会	Number of Villagers' Committees	755	247
村民小组	Villager Group	16821	6715
乡村户数、人口	**Households and Rural Population**		
乡村总户数（万户）	Number of Households (10000 households)	78.00	24.79
乡村总人口（万人）	Rural Population (10000 persons)	235.68	76.72
乡村实有从业人员数（万人）	**Number of Rural Laborers (10000 persons)**	**132.81**	**44.60**
按性别分	Grouped by Sex		
男劳动力	Male	70.13	23.22
女劳动力	Female	62.68	21.38
按行业分	Grouped by Sector		
农林牧渔业	Farming, Forestry, Animal Husbandry and Fishery	26.02	9.25
# 种植业	Planting	20.40	7.69
工　业	Industry	58.45	22.13
建筑业	Construction	16.88	2.23
交通运输、仓储、邮电通信业	Transport, Storage, Post and Telecommunications	5.48	1.77
批发零售贸易餐饮业	Wholesale and Retail Trade, Catering Service	6.93	2.00
金融保险业	Banking and Insurance	0.83	0.15
房地产、社会服务业	Real Estate and Social Services	1.60	0.73
卫生、体育和社会福利业	Health Care, Sporting and Social Welfare	0.62	0.13
教育、文化艺术和广电业	Culture, Education and Arts, Radio, Film and Television	0.61	0.17
科研和综合技术服务业	Scientific Research and Polytechnical Services	0.21	0.03
乡经济组织管理业	Rural Economic Management	0.34	0.07
其他行业	Others	14.84	5.94

其中 of which					
新北区 Xinbei District	天宁区 Tianning District	钟楼区 Zhonglou District	戚墅堰区 Qishuyan District	溧阳市 Liyang City	金坛市 Jintan City
6				10	7
119	27	42	9	175	156
2532	256	510	219	4959	1630
10.91	3.54	3.66	1.00	19.88	14.22
38.20	10.85	10.53	2.98	60.16	36.24
21.31	**6.75**	**5.72**	**2.00**	**31.90**	**20.53**
11.21	3.55	2.94	1.07	16.73	11.41
10.10	3.20	2.78	0.93	15.17	9.12
2.49	0.06	0.02	0.11	8.62	5.47
2.21	0.05		0.07	6.24	4.14
11.51	5.27	3.13	1.26	8.11	7.04
1.31	0.14	0.13	0.12	8.63	4.32
0.71	0.17	0.16	0.04	1.74	0.89
1.13	0.38	0.58	0.12	1.73	0.99
0.13	0.07	0.06	0.05	0.32	0.05
0.14	0.10	0.07	0.09	0.19	0.28
0.11	0.06	0.09	0.01	0.13	0.09
0.15	0.04	0.05	0.01	0.11	0.08
0.01	0.01	0.01		0.09	0.06
0.05	0.03	0.06	0.01	0.07	0.05
3.57	0.42	1.36	0.18	2.16	1.21

10-12 分地区农林牧渔业总产值（2011 年）
OUTPUT VALUE OF FARMING, FORESTRY, ANIMAL HUSBANDRY AND FISHERY BY REGION（2011）

指 标	Item	全 市 Whole Municipality	武进区 Wujin District
总 计	**Total**	**1946793**	**653581**
农业产值	**Output Value of Farming**	**1077873**	**412487**
谷物及其他作物	Grain and Other Crop	351714	53171
蔬菜园艺作物	Vegetable and Horticultural Crop	548442	300663
水果、坚果、饮料和香料作物	Fruit, Nut, Beverage and Aromatic Crop	177235	58653
林业产值	**Output Value of Forestry**	**14764**	**1471**
林木培养和种植	Forest Cultivation and Planting	7494	1418
林产品	Forest Products	782	
竹木采运	Bamboo and Wood Cuttingand Transportation	6488	53
牧业产值	**Output Value of Animal Husbandry**	**321894**	**109287**
牲 畜	Livestock	13253	2919
家 禽	Poultry	195381	63432
猪的饲养	Pig Breeding	107457	42173
捕 猎	Hunting	139	
其它畜牧业	Others	5664	763
渔业产值	**Output Value of Fishery**	**445621**	**94324**
内陆水域产品	Lnland Waters Aquatic Products	445621	94324
#养 殖	Artificial Culture	422466	86175
#贝 类	Shellfish	4571	230
其 他	Others	6463	1802
农林牧渔服务业	**Services**	**86641**	**36012**

单位：万元（10000 yuan）

其　中　of　which					
新北区 Xinbei District	天宁区 Tianning District	钟楼区 Zhonglou District	戚墅堰区 Qishuyan District	溧阳市 Liyang City	金坛市 Jintan City
207490	**1382**	**3900**	**470**	**620239**	**459731**
127236	**1233**		**470**	**338974**	**197473**
40330			250	169876	88087
83562	1233		220	81946	80818
3344				86992	28246
1092				**9137**	**3064**
937				2734	2405
26				619	137
129				5748	522
38849		**3900**		**64405**	**105453**
1195		3900		3105	2134
20368				34463	77118
15889				24859	24536
					139
1397				1978	1526
32932	**149**			**188106**	**130110**
32932				188106	130110
28954				185096	122092
1348				1007	1986
1821					2840
7381				**19617**	**23631**

10-13　农林牧渔业增加值（2011 年）
VALUE ADDED OF FARMING, FORESTRY, ANIMAL HUSBANDARY AND FISHERY（2011）

指　标	Item	总产值（万元）Gross Output Value (10000 yuan)	其中 of which 中间消耗 Depreciation	增加值 Value-Added	增加值率(%) Value-adding Rate(%)
总　计	**Total**	**1946793**	**829011**	**1117782**	**57.4**
农　业	Farming	1077873	381612	696261	64.6
林　业	Forestry	14764	7541	7233	49.0
牧　业	Animal Husbandry	321894	206269	115625	35.9
渔　业	Fishery	445621	205334	240287	53.9
农林牧渔服务业	Services	86641	28255	58386	67.4

10-14　分地区农林牧渔业增加值（2011 年）
VALUE ADDED OF FARMING, FORESTRY, ANIMAL HUSBANDARY AND FISHERY BY REGION（2011）

单位：万元（10000 yuan）

地　区	Region	增加值 Value-Added	其中 of which 农　业 Farming	林　业 Forestry	牧　业 Animal Husbandry	渔　业 Fishery	农林牧渔服务业 Services
全　市	**Whole Municipality**	**1117782**	**696261**	**7223**	**115625**	**240287**	**58386**
市　区	Urban Area	527505	363093	1583	59910	74786	28133
武进区	Wujin District	406515	280219	928	44530	56798	24040
新北区	New District	118682	81861	655	14130	17943	4093
天宁区	Tianning District	846	801			45	
钟楼区	Zhonglou District	1250			1250		
戚墅堰区	Qishuyan District	212	212				
溧阳市	Liyang City	344908	208253	3439	21275	96445	15496
金坛市	Jintan City	245369	124915	2201	34440	69056	14757

10-15 分地区农业机械拥有情况（2011 年底）
POSSESSION OF AGRICULTURAL MACHINERY BY REGION（END OF 2011）

指 标	Item	全 市 Whole Municipality	其中 of which 武进区 Wujin District	新北区 Xinbei District	溧阳市 Liyang City	金坛市 Jintan City
农业机械总动力（万千瓦）	**Total Power of Agricultural Machinery (10000 kw)**	**155.25**	**53.80**	**10.08**	**51.06**	**40.31**
拖拉机及配套机械	**Tractors and Subsidiary Machinery**					
大中型拖拉机（台）	Large and Medium Tractors (unit)	2520	1062	306	668	484
#轮式拖拉机	Roller Tractors	2520	1062	306	668	484
小型拖拉机（台）	Mini-tractors (unit)	20708	5313	1625	8343	5427
种植业机械	**Machinery of Farm Production**					
机引犁（台）	Trailed Tractor Plow (unit)	13377	3816	698	6152	2711
农用排灌动力机械（台）	Machinery for Agricultural Drainage and Irrigation (unit)	26395	5720	1048	13563	6064
机动喷雾（粉）机（台）	Motorized Duster (unit)	18064	5087	1500	6520	4957
联合收割机（台）	Combined Harvesters (unit)	1940	1057	172	372	339
机动脱粒机（台）	Threshing and Drying Machine (unit)	40347	25228	2977	2472	9670
农副产品加工机械	**Machinery of Agricultural and Sideline Products Processing**					
农副产品加工动力（台）	Machinery of Agricultural and Sideline Products Processing (unit)	13400	2315	869	4332	5884
#柴油机	Diesel Engines	2392	348	219	736	1089
电动机	Motor	10461	1967	650	3049	4795
农副产品加工作业机械（台）	Operation Machinery of Agricultural and Sideline Products Processing (unit)	10058	2207	869	3738	3244
畜牧业机械	**Machinery of Livestock Husbandry**					
饲料粉碎机（台）	Fodder Grinder (unit)	1754		814	393	547
林果机械（台）	**Forestry and Fruit Industry Machinery (unit)**	**135**	**44**		**26**	**65**
渔业机械（台）	**Machinery of Fishery (unit)**	**47326**	**16656**	**356**	**23825**	**6489**
农田基本建设机械（台）	**Machinery of Farmland Fundamental Construction (unit)**	**5773**	**354**	**144**	**4808**	**467**

10-16 分地区农村经济收益分配（2011 年）
RURAL ECONOMIC PROFIT DISTRIBUTION BY REGION（2011）

指 标	Item	全 市 Whole Municipality	武进区 Wujin District
经济总收入	**Total Economic Income**	**79408187**	**34856454**
农 业	Agriculture	900109	314823
# 种植业	Planting	867417	314682
林 业	Forestry	32424	1477
牧 业	Animal Husbandry	381612	117086
渔 业	Fishery	517360	137524
工 业	Industry	68901429	32316752
建筑业	Construction	2240407	475991
运输业	Transportation	655967	231467
贸易餐饮业	Trade and Catering Services	1997457	710167
服务业	Services	1009841	259215
其 他	Other Income	2771581	291954
经济总费用	**Total Economic Expenses**	**68949160**	**30443334**
# 生产费用	Production Expenses	58028114	26981441
管理费用	Management Expenses	6468310	2716587
经济净收入	**Net Economic Income**	**10459028**	**4413120**
投资收益	**Profit from Investment**	**70299**	**38823**
农民外出劳务收入	**Labor Service Income of Farmers from Outside**	**453848**	**82985**
可分配收入总额	**Total Disposable Income**	**10983174**	**4534927**
国家税金	State Tax	2683364	1095336
上交有关部门	Turn Over to Relevant Departments	873444	508134
外来投资分利	Bonus of Investment from Outside	469754	63476
外来人员带走劳务收入	Labor Service Payment to Persons from Outside	1243456	546441
企业各项留利	Reserved by Enterprises	2291805	975382
乡村集体所得	Earnings of Town and Township Collective	210703	122597
农民经营所得	Farmers' Eargings	3210649	1223560
农民从集体再分配收入	**Redistributed Earnings to Farmers from Collectives**	**281983**	**155895**
农民所得	**Farmers' Earnings**	**3492632**	**1379455**
每人平均（元）	Per Capita（yuan）	15220	15623

单位：万元（10000 yuan）

其中 of which					
新北区 Xinbei District	天宁区 Tianning District	钟楼区 Zhonglou District	戚墅堰区 Qishuyan District	溧阳市 Liyang City	金坛市 Jintan City
15295249	**907394**	**4104134**	**1794482**	**15321867**	**7128607**
44338	500	1928	1203	286603	250715
41558	350	1928	916	270335	237649
3783				10167	16997
35345			164	92628	136388
15805			368	165201	198462
12572729	431390	3547173	1736496	13057146	5239743
73773	47223	55861	12864	986685	588011
51969	980	84227	5297	130860	151167
394624	91180	328478	17355	165842	289812
49456	73288	78311	10740	364912	173920
2053427	262833	8156	9995	61823	83393
13602619	**826739**	**3934393**	**1478762**	**12832026**	**5831287**
10929033	578105	2704229	1077379	10817659	4940268
749516	232150	474554	90032	1665564	539908
1692630	**80655**	**169741**	**315720**	**2489841**	**1297321**
3273	**2015**	**3571**	**611**	**20000**	**2006**
93931	**1325**	**8007**	**5851**	**88738**	**173010**
1789834	**83995**	**181319**	**322182**	**2598579**	**1472338**
438988	16780	71043	128875	533292	399050
99371	14295	4147	9380	153059	85058
57248	1950	25010	3298	241979	76793
221102	20080	18153	32250	269100	136329
390814	13380	24873	106202	525852	255302
40391	3600	1855	14874	19850	7536
541921	13910	36238	27303	855447	512270
49473	**4480**	**14022**	**2669**	**25420**	**30025**
591393	**18390**	**50260**	**29972**	**880867**	**542295**
15000	13136	15706	15858	14886	15026

10-17 分地区农作物播种面积（2011 年）
SOWN AREA OF FARM CROPS BY REGION（2011）

单位：千公顷（1000 hectares）

指标	Item	全市 Whole Municipality	其中 of which 武进区 Wujin District	新北区 Xinbei District	天宁区 Tianning District	戚墅堰区 Qishuyan District	溧阳市 Liyang City	金坛市 Jintan City
农作物总播种面积	**Total Sown Area**	**226.22**	**46.70**	**26.69**	**0.13**	**0.30**	**95.51**	**56.89**
粮食作物	**Grain Crops**	**159.51**	**25.96**	**21.31**		**0.15**	**71.80**	**40.29**
夏收粮食	Summer Grain	65.97	11.31	10.50		0.03	27.36	16.77
谷 物	Cereal	63.98	11.01	10.43		0.03	26.36	16.15
小 麦	Wheat	63.53	10.95	10.19		0.03	26.36	16.00
元 麦	Hullless Barley	0.25	0.01	0.24				
大 麦	Barley	0.20	0.05	0.15				
秋收粮食	Autumn Grain	93.54	14.65	10.81		0.12	44.44	23.52
谷 物	Autumn Cereal	86.22	13.44	9.91		0.12	41.77	20.98
#稻 谷	Rice	84.23	13.41	9.80		0.12	40.42	20.48
中 稻	Middle-season Rice	2.87					2.71	0.16
单季晚稻	Single Harvest Late Rice	81.36	13.41	9.80		0.12	37.71	20.32
玉 米	Corn	1.93	0.03	0.05			1.35	0.50
豆 类	Beans	4.78	0.83	0.75			1.61	1.59
#大 豆	Soybeans	4.30	0.83	0.73			1.31	1.43
薯 类	Tubers	2.54	0.38	0.15			1.06	0.95
油 料	**Oil-bearing Crops**	**17.07**	**0.85**	**0.75**		**0.03**	**10.92**	**4.52**
#油菜籽	Rapeseeds	15.56	0.77	0.66		0.03	9.96	4.14
棉 花	**Cotton**	**0.58**					**0.55**	**0.03**
麻 类	**Fiber Crops**	**0.01**						**0.01**
糖 料	**Sugar Crops**	**0.09**		**0.01**			**0.07**	**0.01**
药 材	**Crude Drugs**	**0.06**					**0.03**	**0.03**
蔬 菜	**Vegetable**	**27.15**	**9.36**	**3.49**	**0.13**	**0.12**	**8.38**	**5.67**
瓜果类	**Melon Crops**	**3.68**	**0.75**	**0.16**			**2.07**	**0.70**
其他农作物	**Other Farm Crops**	**18.70**	**9.78**	**0.97**			**1.69**	**5.63**
#青饲料	Green Fodder	1.96	0.28	0.10			0.84	0.74
绿 肥	Green Manure	1.13	0.04				0.65	0.44

10-18 分地区农产品总产量（2011 年）
TOTAL YIELD OF FARM CROPS BY REGION（2011）

单位：吨（ton）

指标	Item	全市 Whole Municipality	其中 of which 武进区 Wujin District	新北区 Xinbei District	戚墅堰区 Qishuyan District	溧阳市 Liyang City	金坛市 Jintan City
粮食作物	**Grain Crops**	**1151896**	**181137**	**141011**	**1201**	**544735**	**283812**
夏收粮食	Summer Grain	315502	49535	46994	97	139326	79550
谷物	Cereal	311462	48915	46850	97	137151	78449
小麦	Wheat	309866	48668	46041	97	137151	77909
元麦	Hullless Barley	841	32	809			
大麦	Barley	755	215				540
秋收粮食	Autumn Grain	836394	131602	94017	1104	405409	204262
谷物	Cereal	807121	127031	91759	1104	391704	195523
#稻谷	Rice	793360	126839	90970		381676	192771
中稻	Middle-season Rice	26641				25172	1469
单季晚稻	Single Harvest Late Rice	766719	126839	90970	1104	356504	191302
玉米	Corn	13435	192	463		11028	2752
豆类	Beans	13877	2720	1517		5776	3846
#大豆	Soybeans	12632	2720	1480		4880	3552
薯类	Tubers	15396	1851	741		7929	4875
油料	**Oil-bearing Crops**	**32048**	**1647**	**1435**	**56**	**20710**	**8200**
#油菜籽	Rapeseeds	29013	1500	1294	56	18649	7514
棉花	**Cotton**	**491**				**457**	**34**
麻类	**Fiber Crops**	**28**					**28**
糖料	**Sugar Crops**	**5596**		**700**		**4865**	**31**

10-19 分地区农产品单产（2011 年）
YIELD OF FARM CROPS PER HECTARE BY REGION（2011）

单位：公斤 / 公顷（kg/hectare）

指 标	Item	全 市 Whole Municipality	其中 of which 武进区 Wujin District	新北区 Xinbei District	戚墅堰区 Qishuyan District	溧阳市 Liyang City	金坛市 Jintan City
粮食作物	**Grain Crops**	**7221**	**6978**	**6617**	**8007**	**7587**	**7044**
夏收粮食	Summer Grain	4783	4380	4476	3233	5092	4744
谷 物	Cereal	4868	4443	4492	3233	5203	4858
小 麦	Wheat	4877	4445	4518	3233	5203	4869
元 麦	Hullless Barley	3364	3200	3371			
大 麦	Barley	3775	4300				3600
秋收粮食	Autumn Grain	8942	8983	8697	9200	9123	8685
谷 物	Cereal	9361	9425	9259	9200	9378	9319
#稻 谷	Rice	9419	9459	9283	9200	9443	9413
中 稻	Middle-season Rice	9283				9289	9181
单季晚稻	Single Harvest Late Rice	9424	9459	9283	9200	9454	9414
玉 米	Corn	6961	6400	9260		7428	5504
豆 类	Beans	2903	3277	2023		3588	2430
#大 豆	Soybeans	2938	3277	2027		3725	2482
薯 类	Tubers	6061	4871	4940		7929	4875
油 料	**Oil-bearing Crops**	**1995**	**1838**	**1913**	**1867**	**2147**	**1805**
#油菜籽	Rapeseeds	1865	1948	1961	1867	1872	1815
棉 花	**Cotton**	**847**				**831**	**1133**
麻 类	**Fiber Crops**	**2800**					**2800**
糖 料	**Sugar Crops**	**62178**		**70000**		**69500**	**3100**

10-20 分地区畜牧业生产情况（2011 年）
STATISTICS ON LIVESTOCK HUSBANDRY BY REGION（2011 ）

指 标	Item	全 市 Whole Municipality	其中 of which 武进区 Wujin District	新北区 Xinbei District	钟楼区 Zhonglou District	溧阳市 Liyang City	金坛市 Jintan City
当年出栏数	**Slaughtered Livestock of the Year**						
牛（头）	Cattle and Buffaloes (head)	300				100	200
猪（万头）	Hogs (10000 heads)	84.72	30.56	14.30		18.01	21.84
羊（万只）	Sheep and Goats(10000 heads)	11.10	0.45	1.30		5.61	3.74
家 禽（万只）	Poultry (10000 heads)	4633.88	1823.45	270.00		571.00	1969.43
年末存栏数	**Livestock Being Raised at Year-end**						
牛（头）	Cattle and Buffaloes (head)	7100	3400	300	2000	1200	200
猪（万头）	Hogs (10000 heads)	47.51	15.65	6.80		7.52	17.54
羊（万只）	Sheep and Goats (10000 heads)	7.03	0.95	0.25		1.78	4.05
# 山 羊	Goats	7.03	0.95	0.25		1.78	4.05
家 禽（万只）	Poultry (10000 heads)	1270.22	428.36	86.30		245.00	510.56
产 量	**Output**						
肉 类（吨）	Meat (ton)	133977	52071	16014		22077	43815
# 猪牛羊肉	Pork,Beef and Mutton	62302	21482	11664		13187	15969
牛 肉	Beef	198				18	180
猪 肉	Pork	60742	21392	11514		12608	15228
羊 肉	Mutton	1362	90	150		561	561
禽 肉	Poultry	71194	30508	4350		8570	27766
牛 奶（吨）	Cow Milk (ton)	18898	9870	1000	7450	578	
蜂 蜜（吨）	Honey (ton)	166	106			57	3
禽 蛋（吨）	Poultry Eggs (ton)	34141	6845	4500		13098	9698

10-21 分地区林业、蚕茧、茶叶、水果生产情况（2011年）
STATISTICS ON FORESTRY, SILKWORM COCOONS, TEA AND FRUITS BY REGION (2011)

指 标	Item	全 市 Whole Municipality	其中 of which 武进区 Wujin District	新北区 Xinbei District	戚墅堰区 Qishuyan District	溧阳市 Liyang City	金坛市 Jintan City
林 业	**Forestry**						
当年造林面积（公顷）	Forestation Area at Current Year (hectare)	2427	709	254		768	695
木材产量（立方米）	Output of Timber (cu.m)	4325	190			2466	1669
蚕 桑	**Silkworm Cocoons and Mulberry**						
年末桑园面积（公顷）	Mulberry Field Area at Year-end (hectare)	1033				666.5	367
蚕茧产量（吨）	Output of Silkworm Cocoons (ton)	544				273	271
茶 叶	**Tea**						
年末茶园面积（公顷）	Tea Field Area at Year-end (hectare)	7778	271			4755	2752
茶叶产量（吨）	Output of Tea (ton)	3449	110			1987	1352
#红毛茶	Black Tea	5				3	2
绿毛茶	Green Tea	3264	110			1984	1170
其它茶	Other Tea	180					180
水 果	Fruits						
年末果园面积（公顷）	Area of Orchards at Year-end (hectare)	11102	4064	205	10	5543	1281
#桃 园	Peaches	2014	975	20		732	287
板栗园	Chinese chestnuts	4063				3930	133
梨 园	Pears	1152	586	81		299	187
葡萄园	Grapes	2882	2039	89	10	144	600
水果产量（吨）	Output of Fruits (ton)	92918	49592	3939	252	18701	20434
#桃	Peaches	23875	14225	500		4050	5100
板 栗	Chinese chestnuts	3280				2780	500
梨	Pears	19398	8248	1585		5765	3800
葡 萄	Grapes	36497	23052	1543	252	1850	9800

10-22 分地区淡水产品生产情况（2011 年）
STATISTICS ON FRESHWATER AQUATIC PRODUCTS BY REGION（2011）

指 标	Item	全 市 Whole Municipality	其中 of which 武进区 Wujin District	新北区 Xinbei District	天宁区 Tianning District	钟楼区 Tianning District	戚墅堰区 Qishuyan District	溧阳市 Liyang City	金坛市 Jintan City
淡水产品产量（吨）	**Output of Freshwater Aquatic Products (ton)**	**164421**	**54760**	**8420**	**98**	**105**	**37**	**63888**	**37113**
#鱼 类	Fish	127903	49613	8230	98	105	37	50286	19534
#青 鱼	Mackerel	9189	4667	738	7	8	2	3469	298
草 鱼	Grass Carp	21385	7608	2435	23	23	12	8968	2316
鲢 鱼	Silver Carp	22581	8496	2210	12	16	8	7026	4813
鲫 鱼	Crucian	28832	4997	1270	21	20	5	17180	5339
鳊 鱼	Bream	26215	17970	749	26	22	3	4565	2880
鳜 鱼	Mandarin Fish	2023	416	28				823	756
甲壳类	Crustacean	33835	4254	110				13206	16265
#河 蟹	River Crabs	25043	3490	34				9188	12331
青 虾	Shrimps	8615	738	22				4012	3843
鳖	Soft-shelled Turtle	892	328	70				11	483
珍 珠	Pearl	29						8	21
淡水养殖面积（公顷）	**Freshwater Raise Areas (hectares)**	**39259**	**8282**	**1200**	**14**	**12**	**25**	**13726**	**16000**
#特种养殖	Special Species Breeding	25598	3400	230				10213	11755
#池 塘	Pond	34106	7467	1000	14	12		13072	12541
湖 泊	Lake	3024	724					654	1646
水 库	Reservoir	533							533
河 沟	Brook	1596	91	200			25		1280

10-23　分镇、街道基本情况（2011 年）
BASIC STATISTICS ON TOWNS AND SUBDISTRICTS（2011）

镇、街道	Towhs and Subdistricts	总户数（户）Total Households (Household)	总人口（人）Total Population (person)	从业人员（人）Employment (person)	年底耕地面积（公顷）Cultivated Area Year-end (hectare)	农业机械总动力（千瓦）Total Agricultural Machinery Power (kw)	地区生产总值（万元）Gross Domestic Product (10000 yuan)
武进区	**Wujin District**						
湖塘镇	Hutang Town	95432	271372	122633	157	2538	1556356
牛塘镇	Niutang Town	26238	84435	40195	843	8925	767395
洛阳镇	Luoyang Town	26122	87472	55010	1760	22715	652580
遥观镇	Yaoguan Town	38767	112342	62434	704	9069	996424
横林镇	Henglin Town	30732	90650	46500	912	17363	725078
横山桥镇	Hengshanqiao Town	28548	83976	52306	1237	27237	927825
郑陆镇	Zhenlu Town	41018	113417	41024	2744	37838	766476
雪堰镇	Xueyan Town	35953	97552	48976	3343	73984	647707
前黄镇	Qianhuang Town	25255	78829	37760	3505	83131	550953
礼嘉镇	Lijia Town	15900	55590	31321	2247	48996	615719
邹区镇	Zhouqu Town	31987	96404	45649	2446	57052	883106
嘉泽镇	Jiaze Town	28886	85545	55176	4630	43057	420515
湟里镇	Huangli Town	26857	72898	38815	3509	36152	787547
奔牛镇	Benniu Town	19875	59553	31934	2394	23213	413346
新北区	**Xinbei District**						
龙虎塘街道	Longhutang Subdistrict	7480	25475	14780	61	90	331409
春江镇	Chunjiang Town	42274	142203	73611	4352	15113	1655139
新桥镇	Xinqiao Town	8026	26489	12398	691	9925	241808
薛家镇	Xuejia Town	13398	45692	22913	451	7500	657200
罗溪镇	Luoxi Town	15259	50222	24621	1625	20164	346400
西夏墅镇	Xixiashu Town	14946	50250	27125	2371	18140	223000
孟河镇	Menghe Town	27064	99004	44627	3748	17052	422891
三井街道	Sanjin Town	9411	28702	14739			529400
天宁区	**Tianning District**						
茶山街道	Chashan Subdistrict	8620	27797	14388		276	297775
雕庄街道	Diaozhuang Subdistrict	11352	35388	25169		58	1275209
红梅街道	Hongmei Subdistrict	4984	11221	6238		63	69985
青龙街道	Qinlong Subdistrict	12637	40107	27920	296	243	679532
钟楼区	**Zhonglou District**						
新闸镇	Xinzha Town	8774	31929	16328			750286
五星街道	Wuxing Subdistrict	21070	66769	45353			486502

其中 of which			乡镇企业营业收入总额（万元） Total Business Income of Township Enterprises (10000 yuan)	其中 of which		粮食总产量（吨） Total Output of Grain (ton)	乡镇财政收入（万元） Fiscal Revenue of Town and Township (10000 yuan)	储蓄存款余额（万元） Balance of Savings Deposits (10000 yuan)	农民人均纯收入（元） Per Capita Net Income of Rural Resident (yuan)
第一产业 Primary Industry	第二产业 Secondary Industry	第三产业 Tertiary Industry		# 乡镇企业净利润总额 Total Net Profit of Township Enterprises	出口产品交货额 Transaction Volume of Exported Products				
1779	863829	690748	3507879	102041	208685	137	222627	1516840	16914
12125	515919	239351	2738048	91879	300204	1356	62399	252901	16001
16062	461628	174890	2167401	75954	379670	8774	65366	329074	16705
4223	790557	201644	4358933	270289	531452	4671	141963	181023	16280
5707	483503	235868	2352553	65626	79274	5132	58980	438419	15528
9447	577902	340476	2693108	102338	120842	7803	75912	262758	16630
50256	404302	311918	1800156	76294	48939	19988	65085	278324	15088
28562	303855	315290	1749471	89284	7868	25197	71734	271550	16333
48470	269223	233260	1331300	37869	11227.8	39679	36913	265091	15530
18776	404928	192015	1886730	88648	202420	20079	49899	220462	15558
18161	368786	496159	1350212	47478	234918	8120	56326	180250	15280
70606	127419	222490	418566	8226	19842	366	34007	211900	15668
40850	460577	286120	2370620	30018	85262	1971	58558	125750	16078
15691	213561	184094	1025532	26466	6085	24638	39135	34837	15320
100	206093	125216	960116	39240	325018	40	62587	63940	16660
22615	1367311	265213	7775454	221524	667607	45057	148847	90761	14855
5023	161685	75100	708904	57957	190647	6014	51518	62256	16400
4800	557400	95000	2568849	100170	223396	5748	105947	112335	16178
10400	231000	105000	971357	49223	35669	17538	36000	92856	14361
7500	155800	59700	673173	27152	90811	23498	40040	90378	12400
18272	279000	125619	1090587	78245	35551	43842	48646	290138	13699
	410700	118700	2682283	154072	311548		152794	62300	17179
	182078	115697	1764500	64090			64590	37924	13785
	715886	559323	6691557	111857	305071		97445	29542	14015
	42370	27615	108685	2350	5729		38174	29650	12729
798	467356	211378	2839640	95376	31300		148663	48120	18850
	661738	88548	3008728	161875			57568	1002	14938
	289658	196844	1976973	46581	219492		69677	95461	14838

10-23　续表　Continued

镇、街道	Towhs and Subdistricts	总户数（户）Total Households (Household)	总人口（人）Total Population (person)	从业人员（人）Employment (person)	年底耕地面积（公顷）Cultivated Area Year-end (hectare)	农业机械总动力（千瓦）Total Agricultural Machinery Power (kw)	地区生产总值（万元）Gross Domestic Product (10000 yuan)
永红街道	Yonghong Subdistrict	8826	36850	17258			256520
北港街道	Beigang Subdistrict	6645	19276	10277			15779
西林街道	Xilin Subdistrict	8725	23264	13654		10605	192032
戚墅堰区	**Qishuyan District**						
丁堰镇	Dingyan Town	5395	26231	18172	132	1974	210608
潞城镇	Lucheng Town	7027	29638	19027	277	380	311200
溧阳市	**Liyang City**						
溧城镇	Licheng Town	80505	246464	169560	5773	24763	2223131
埭头镇	Litou Town	9286	27636	19223	2006	21791	214370
上黄镇	Shanghuang Town	9286	26275	13067	1822	32150	193102
戴埠镇	Daibu Town	18527	52167	31560	3684	23500	181355
天目湖镇	Tianmuhu Town	22920	72527	34538	5705	40886	306479
别桥镇	Bieqiao Town	23836	69925	43812	6554	59773	283531
上兴镇	Shangxing Town	27146	79561	38137	11319	63240	385302
竹箦镇	Zhuze Town	21448	62172	32512	6762	44920	177007
南渡镇	Nandu Town	25429	75612	39297	6784	49476	281072
社渚镇	Shezhu Town	23123	70416	39606	7754	57203	417597
金坛市	**Jintan City**						
金城镇	Jincheng Town	76260	190195	149375	7234	99142	996966
直溪镇	zhixi Town	25055	59491	41335	4285	43439	336035
朱林镇	Zhulin Town	14662	37770	25436	3257	31547	170097
薛埠镇	Xuebu Town	26067	67632	48929	6515	85750	317120
指前镇	Zhiqian Town	14300	40821	24815	3038	36032	136931
儒林镇	Rulin Town	13479	33001	16884	1580	41486	154170
尧塘镇	Yaoyang Town	22196	56673	39847	3429	51100	389219
开发区	Development Zone	24497	65892	46792	2603	12912	832179

其中 of which			乡镇企业营业收入总额（万元）Total Business Income of Township Enterprises (10000 yuan)	其中 of which		粮食总产量（吨）Total Output of Grain (ton)	乡镇财政收入（万元）Fiscal Revenue of Town and Township (10000 yuan)	储蓄存款余额（万元）Balance of Savings Deposits (10000 yuan)	农民人均纯收入（元）Per Capita Net Income of Rural Resident (yuan)
第一产业 Primary Industry	第二产业 Secondary Industry	第三产业 Tertiary Industry		#乡镇企业净利润总额 Total Net Profit of Township Enterprises	出口产品交货额 Transaction Volume of Exported Products				
	124512	132008	572803	45674	138201		50776	1852	15320
	9299	6480	387504	13887	4564		11895	58401	14474
	131832	60200	690295	13182	3482		23956	56893	15626
140	160020	50448	706496	60336	14779	237	47299	12000	15850
141	234246	76813	1086476	58754	10760	964	70540	12923	12387
44856	1550953	627322	11890285	414672	351020	51972	193840	237422	17441
10793	176077	27500	661631	22217	8642	17183	37797	42475	16022
31727	93970	67405	333784	13356	500	15652	18484	42000	17672
25120	90830	65405	410300	9508	1050	28917	22984	39560	14138
28621	167113	110745	752718	31373	45661	31050	45501	134100	15971
37842	161563	84126	387265	18964	14672	56684	16299	50729	13117
34533	249647	101122	1053242	59215	15662	97381	32366	76228	13138
27897	83830	65280	371148	21272	15740	61116	21288	82539	13729
30040	145061	105971	436137	9558	37233	69567	21341	33382	14244
37552	250103	129942	880669	94452	6580	101617	32939	104600	13477
58966	457800	480200	1576228	102070	234555	64407	100029	1548352	16628
31435	210000	94600	821068	100365	186286	46612	22801	92637	14738
22697	117300	30100	475645	53010	24042	34499	27221	60400	13856
37620	153500	126000	605772	41579	12860	46292	45342	83000	15200
26931	79700	30300	313917	33371	12008	32392	18747	43300	13577
26970	92000	35200	366598	41826	14515	13441	11691	49500	13806
29519	264000	95700	1028869	55813	442654	27370	54547	115120	15287
7279	630000	194900	2266089	182129	25668	18463	220704	33013	14386

11

CHAPTER 11

工 业

INDUSTRY

常州统计年鉴

11 工 业 INDUSTRY

2011 年主要统计指标
MAJOR STATISTICAL INDICATORS OF 2011

规模以上工业总产值	Total Output Value of Industry above Designated Size	8270.77 亿元	(100 million yuan)
比上年增长	Over the Previous Year	18.5%	
规模以上工业主营业务收入	Main Business Income of Industrial above Designated Size	8212.53 亿元	(100 million yuan)
比上年增长	Over the Previous Year	19.5%	
规模以上工业实现利税	Profits and Taxes of Industry above Designated Size	713.30 亿元	(100 million yuan)
比上年增长	Over the Previous Year	18.6%	
规模以上工业实现利润	Profit of Industry above Designated Size	468.43 亿元	(100 million yuan)
比上年增长	Over the Previous Year	15.7%	
规模以上工业总资产	Total Industrial Assets above Designated Size	6243.25 亿元	(100 million yuan)
比上年增长	Over the Previous Year	25.6%	

11-1 历年工业生产发展指数
INDICES OF GROSS INDUSTRIAL OUTPUT OVER THE YEARS

按可比价计算 1949=100 　　Calculated by comparable price：1949=100

年份 Year	全市 Whole Municipality	其中 of which #市区 Urban Area	年份 Year	全市 Whole Municipality	其中 of which #市区 Urban Area
1949	100.0	100.0	1981	4887.2	4765.6
1950	145.5	148.1	1982	5206.0	5023.9
1951	181.0	184.8	1983	5916.3	5712.2
1952	231.0	235.1	1984	7092.8	6745.8
1953	281.9	288.4	1985	9357.8	8807.2
1954	293.3	297.0	1986	10410.6	9688.6
1955	260.0	260.4	1987	12618.2	11457.3
1956	337.0	334.2	1988	15683.8	13769.0
1957	325.0	315.8	1989	16677.0	14582.2
1958	585.6	589.7	1990	18500.8	16280.5
1959	756.8	749.3	1991	21422.5	18847.3
1960	824.6	825.9	1992	27496.4	24117.3
1961	496.2	497.0	1993	38501.3	32980.7
1962	387.5	379.6	1994	47311.0	39967.6
1963	383.8	373.3	1995	53542.2	45391.8
1964	483.5	472.8	1996	64109.9	52915.2
1965	614.8	603.8	1997	63557.5	54208.9
1966	737.3	729.0	1998	61998.0	52938.4
1967	567.9	539.7	1999	69415.3	59018.4
1968	659.3	642.4	2000	76647.0	64689.3
1969	872.2	872.6	2001	86446.1	72835.6
1970	1161.9	1163.6	2002	102096.2	86752.5
1971	1431.8	1411.5	2003	130391.2	111681.7
1972	1667.0	1645.5	2004	146677.1	126836.9
1973	1963.5	1923.5	2005	178762.5	151521.9
1974	2047.4	2021.0	2006	219517.7	191379.5
1975	2305.4	2276.4	2007	266849.7	232001.2
1976	2531.8	2495.3	2008	292010.9	251498.2
1977	2890.9	2836.1	2009	358518.1	312735.6
1978	3208.7	3146.5	2010	329998.3	287947.2
1979	3632.7	3565.9	2011	305683.3	266768.9
1980	4409.7	4287.7			

11-2 历年规模以上工业企业主要经济指标
MAJOR ECONOMIC INDICATORS OF INDUSTRIAL ENTERPRISES ABOVE DESIGNATED SIZE OVER THE YEARS

单位：亿元（100 million yuan）

年份 Year	工业总产值 Gross Industrial Output Value	其中 of which #国有工业 State-owned	集体工业 Collective-owned	其他工业 Other Industries	主营业务收入 Main Business Income of Industrial	利税总额 Total Profits and Taxes	利润总额 Total Profits	固定资产原价 Original Value of Fixed Assets
1978	32.99	23.01	9.98					
1979	37.39	25.65	11.74					
1980	44.94	28.57	16.02	0.35				
1981	49.92	32.23	17.15	0.54				
1982	53.21	32.71	19.30	1.20	45.72	8.53	5.47	20.96
1983	60.45	35.30	22.17	2.98	51.14	9.69	6.47	24.64
1984	70.91	37.84	28.43	4.64	57.68	10.75	7.08	27.87
1985	89.62	42.52	40.94	6.16	75.01	14.14	9.26	33.41
1986	97.12	45.18	45.24	6.70	82.63	12.93	8.10	40.16
1987	118.20	51.26	57.91	9.03	103.18	14.33	9.07	49.73
1988	154.15	57.82	84.79	11.54	136.36	17.02	10.48	58.09
1989	179.47	71.09	93.11	15.27	151.55	15.44	7.99	68.26
1990	196.20	78.17	100.57	17.46	160.85	13.21	5.26	80.42
1991	220.70	79.98	112.50	28.22	199.51	11.81	2.58	95.17
1992	311.05	101.52	172.73	36.80	264.13	17.80	6.46	115.28
1993	464.02	129.02	272.32	62.68	399.13	24.64	9.63	145.96
1994	595.27	137.73	333.96	123.58	429.87	25.63	6.22	193.91
1995	579.62	143.96	312.42	123.24	542.82	34.65	11.83	252.19
1996	640.69	143.43	355.54	141.72	562.96	32.28	8.76	282.65
1997	615.36	127.14	316.39	171.83	558.17	31.29	7.69	314.77
1998	693.43	118.85	209.13	365.45	635.22	35.98	8.25	343.40
1999	769.93	116.83	216.86	436.24	718.07	46.05	16.31	378.43
2000	874.63	101.47	175.35	597.81	836.10	59.64	25.44	395.90
2001	1001.25	91.41	159.55	750.29	944.65	68.25	31.25	323.00
2002	1167.02	80.49	99.28	987.25	1135.55	86.03	45.89	508.89
2003	1527.28	69.63	75.56	1382.09	1510.77	114.41	65.62	584.71
2004	2127.20	49.40	89.49	1988.31	2064.71	136.24	82.49	697.26
2005	2504.19	70.11	76.92	2357.16	2459.56	161.84	96.23	796.70
2006	3293.77	55.51	103.00	3135.26	3243.79	228.91	142.26	992.68
2007	4253.90	71.30	120.60	4062.00	4171.08	301.73	188.78	1198.27
2008	5200.12	94.21	99.50	5006.41	5089.94	371.12	221.44	1370.82
2009	5982.91	63.95	26.76	5892.20	5868.05	450.07	276.77	1576.26
2010	7396.09	91.67	14.20	7290.21	7274.88	620.18	413.47	2219.00
2011	8270.77	100.80	5.80	8164.18	8212.53	713.30	468.43	2485.28

注：1、1978-1985年总产值为80不变价格，1986年开始为当年价格。
2、1978-1997 年规模以上工业口径为乡及乡以上全部独立核算工业企业，1998 至 2010 年为全部国有企业及年销售收入 500 万元以上工业企业，2011 年为主营业务收入 2000 万元以上的法人工业企业。

Note：1. The gross output value during year 1978 and 1985 is calculated at 1980 constant prices; while since year 1986, the gross output value has been calculated at current prices.
2. During year 1978 and 1997, the scaled industrial caliber involved industrial enterprises with wholly independent accounting;All the "state-owned companies and the industrial enterprises with annual main business income of 5 million yuan and above" cited from 1998 to 2010 has been altered to "corporate industrial enterprises with annual main business income of 20 million yuan and above".

11-3 规模以上工业企业主要经济指标（2011 年）
MAJOR ECONOMIC INDICATORS OF INDUSTRIAL ENTERPRISES ABOVE DESIGNATED SIZE（2011）

指 标	Item	企 业 单位数（个） Number of Enterpr-ises (unit)	其中 of which #亏损企业 Loss-incurring Enterprises	工 业 总产值 Gross Industrial Output Value	工业销售产值 Value of Industrial Products Sales
总 计	**Total**	**3638**	**335**	**82707703**	**81678390**
按地区分	**Grouped by Region**				
市 区	Urban Area	2955	290	64466417	63765893
武进区	Wujin District	1608	137	32237118	31614978
新北区	Xinbei District	765	104	16730067	16305935
天宁区	Tianning District	239	24	6381049	6446949
钟楼区	Zhonglou District	253	18	6715846	6928922
戚墅堰区	Qishuyan District	90	7	2402336	2469109
溧阳市	Liyang City	327	9	11372284	11213525
金坛市	Jintan City	356	36	6869002	6698973
按登记注册类型分	**Grouped by Registration Status**				
内 资	Domestic Investment	2904	224	54295394	53609305
#国 有	State-owned	17	2	1007972	1019470
集 体	Collective-owned	7		57972	57218
股份合作	Share-holding Cooperative	21	4	804716	800703
有限责任公司	Limited Liability Corporations	121	17	4492917	4415742
股份有限公司	Share-holding Corporations Ltd.	20		1739900	1729887
私 营	Private	2715	201	46166500	45561207
港澳台商投资	Investment from Hong Kong, Macao and Taiwan	287	41	9496647	9302468
合资经营	Joint-Venture	150	20	4646552	4599137
合作经营	Cooperative	10		197439	201333
独资经营	Sole Investment	119	20	3656343	3513719
股份有限公司	Share-holding Corporations Ltd.	8	1	996312	988279
外商投资	Foreign Investment	447	70	18915663	18766617
中外合资经营	Joint Ventures	187	20	10718684	10688121
中外合作经营	Cooperative Enterprises	20	1	325233	326199
外商独资	Sole Foreign Investment	231	49	7364753	7244049
股份有限公司	Share-holding Corporations Ltd.	9		506993	508248
按轻重工业分	**Grouped by Light and Heavy Industry**				
轻工业	Light Industry	1097	129	15478418	15223430
重工业	Heavy Industry	2541	206	67229285	66454960
按企业规模分	**Grouped by Size of Enterprises**				
大 型	Large-sized	92	4	29159406	28801480
中 型	Medium-sized	528	44	22308844	21967998
小 型	Small-sized	2944	274	30915652	30592669
微 型	Micro-sized	74	13	323801	316243

单位：万元（10000 yuan）

流动资产合计 Current Assets	其中 of which #应收帐款净额 Net Account Income	存货 Existing Stock	其中 of which #产成品 Manufac-tured Products	固定资产合计 Total Fixed Assets	固定资产原价合计 Total Original Value of Fixed Assets	累计折旧 Accumula-tive Deprecia-tion	资产总计 Total Assets
39565336	**12040022**	**8878910**	**3445752**	**15829759**	**24852758**	**10105702**	**62432484**
32262206	10115119	7632382	2952401	12541494	20367219	8813155	50602052
17192431	5411880	3946560	1386478	5815150	8452972	3129871	26109965
9051901	2906392	2283234	988048	3878690	7483416	3899314	14297901
2407228	557076	478180	188675	965047	1531853	580827	4165604
2358095	811110	592363	273420	1190842	1890287	883772	3726987
1252552	428661	332046	115780	691766	1008691	319372	2301595
4325665	1232719	748260	292414	2202039	2859393	742442	7356629
2977465	692185	498268	200938	1086227	1626146	550105	4473803
27180747	8225860	5794519	2195170	9923715	15275514	6145642	42316616
623191	170250	209612	41315	322750	603458	271273	1059352
22750	9967	3265	1718	17880	28386	10969	46466
258341	48421	98866	47290	99188	236902	138098	392560
1850871	533875	477837	184236	1358224	2188849	882926	3654832
1621198	308468	308117	151561	598727	922230	360116	2879047
22790920	7149765	4695128	1768654	7522675	11291047	4481855	34261038
4671118	1395955	1089027	423076	2127139	3659841	1650830	7562322
2386017	689727	608626	195759	1114709	1757953	696533	3809478
58575	19032	9776	3719	29394	48246	18852	90416
1848682	525578	380656	170850	821311	1619542	851802	3080814
377844	161618	89970	52747	161725	234101	83642	581614
7713471	2418208	1995364	827507	3778905	5917403	2309231	12553546
3565841	1026033	1033821	433098	1613553	2662236	1044186	5554833
89219	28622	21783	10596	146102	179577	47957	252142
3876061	1319291	890975	362576	1926659	2938361	1172141	6358677
182351	44262	48785	21237	92592	137229	44947	387894
6887854	1992005	1631750	674187	3036813	4632762	1770986	11427055
32677482	10048017	7247160	2771565	12792946	20219996	8334716	51005429
15241160	4651585	3206016	1169973	6192307	8990958	3249426	24493653
11264792	3058566	2842707	1190688	4593469	7727153	3478535	17737197
12863468	4272923	2804249	1074600	4998815	8059808	3368377	19916351
195917	56949	25938	10491	45168	74840	9364	285284

11-3 续表 Continued

指 标	Item	负债总计 Total Liabilities	其中 of which 流动负债合计 Total Current Liabilities	非流动负债合计 Total Non-current Liabilities	所有者权益 Owner's Equity	主营业务收入 Main Business Income
总 计	**Total**	**38042633**	**33822735**	**4000014**	**24389851**	**82125287**
按地区分	**Grouped by Region**					
市 区	Urban Area	30040306	27034163	2805772	20561746	64007053
武进区	Wujin District	15890987	14738154	1036911	10218979	31591749
新北区	Xinbei District	8362913	7080931	1237867	5934988	16364674
天宁区	Tianning District	2305323	2091934	179389	1860281	6456511
钟楼区	Zhonglou District	2178590	2062460	114939	1548397	6973831
戚墅堰区	Qishuyan District	1302494	1060686	236667	999102	2620287
溧阳市	Liyang City	5182888	4050446	1124641	2173741	11407595
金坛市	Jintan City	2819439	2738125	69601	1654365	6710639
按登记注册类型分	**Grouped by Registration Status**					
内 资	Domestic Investment	26264868	24346668	1750282	16051747	53867055
#国 有	State-owned	668752	603462	65285	390600	1062012
集 体	Collective-owned	32488	27576	4912	13977	58929
股份合作	Share-holding Cooperative	150519	146553	2953	242041	802747
有限责任公司	Limited Liability Corporations	2370862	1816564	548117	1283970	4462759
股份有限公司	Share-holding Corporations Ltd.	1196532	1137514	59018	1682515	1828275
私 营	Private	21838357	20607642	1069997	12422682	45628362
港澳台商投资	Investment from Hong Kong, Macao and Taiwan	4260631	3836377	404631	3301692	9362510
合资经营	Joint-Venture	2395273	2232984	152046	1414205	4593029
合作经营	Cooperative	57855	51801	1176	32561	203575
独资经营	Sole Investment	1490554	1319070	166984	1590260	3606954
股份有限公司	Share-holding Corporations Ltd.	316949	232523	84426	264666	958952
外商投资	Foreign Investment	7517134	5639690	1845101	5036412	18895722
中外合资经营	Joint Ventures	3737702	2698365	1036084	1817132	10806888
中外合作经营	Cooperative Enterprises	151954	95084	53998	100188	308807
外商独资	Sole Foreign Investment	3455673	2684248	749237	2903004	7249902
股份有限公司	Share-holding Corporations Ltd.	171805	161993	5782	216089	530125
按轻重工业分	**Grouped by Light and Heavy Industry**					
轻工业	Light Industry	6461936	5885566	490018	4965119	15157396
重工业	Heavy Industry	31580697	27937168	3509997	19424732	66967891
按企业规模分	**Grouped by Size of Enterprises**					
大 型	Large-sized	15015312	12608981	2399015	9478341	29217984
中 型	Medium-sized	10461632	9569184	844220	7275565	22187299
小 型	Small-sized	12381052	11461477	756347	7535298	30402011
微 型	Micro-sized	184637	183093	433	100647	317993

单位：万元（10000 yuan）

销售费用 Cost of Sales	管理费用 Cost of Management	财务费用 Finance Charge	营业利润 Business Profit	实现利税总额 Total Profits and Taxes	其中 of which 利润总额 Total Profits	其中 of which 主营业务税金及附加 Main Business Tax and Surcharges	其中 of which 应交增值税 Value Added Tax Payable	亏损企业亏损总额 Amount of Loss in Loss-incurring Enterprises	应付职工薪酬 Remuneration Payable to Employees
1403591	**2764070**	**1086011**	**5649164**	**7133017**	**4684335**	**259318**	**2172370**	**161533**	**4806423**
1133189	2329330	818667	4087977	5193843	3416100	197055	1566044	140308	4087569
417616	994251	450761	2041915	2443452	1560564	99837	781404	39956	2386511
388335	706540	212768	1044236	1388648	895487	47638	434640	79109	936962
155051	222800	62070	330253	453411	320031	19819	113331	12910	354630
122912	265248	54785	416917	561089	360219	19730	180254	5548	268590
49275	140491	38284	254656	347243	279800	10030	56415	2784	140876
150808	221431	168605	914352	1074966	648046	42033	383123	4369	402029
119594	213310	98739	646835	864208	620189	20230	223204	16856	316825
823779	1825886	783063	3493573	4463836	2853145	186252	1418819	77262	3060848
18783	71354	25839	49433	96777	51926	5164	39687	1601	83331
89	4225	331	5468	7607	5100	238	2269		4371
9281	17484	5225	42429	76997	34254	4366	38378	1158	57748
60921	176582	67412	312879	368352	259617	13808	92162	9964	233944
74909	100008	21557	190171	236291	191911	4608	39771		131146
659391	1455150	662606	2891100	3675338	2308240	158046	1206196	64540	2549546
163014	339711	108370	768357	1008269	750993	32538	224678	19541	742394
92433	187623	63027	403997	564050	408883	20937	134231	11375	280713
2081	6698	1843	12780	16200	11090	676	4434		8787
51335	120941	32212	315872	384376	295441	8476	80397	8057	296974
17165	24449	11289	35708	43643	35579	2448	5615	109	155919
416798	598473	194578	1387234	1660912	1080197	40528	528873	64730	1003182
219716	222642	95661	863345	926240	626368	23407	273464	19900	391397
4489	12202	5742	17336	29215	19359	872	8810	32	16335
186866	345592	88948	444596	639651	370990	15585	244936	44798	561745
5726	18038	4227	61957	65806	63480	664	1663		33705
369094	629229	185292	803445	1247480	817677	64696	362263	52372	1506952
1034497	2134841	900719	4845719	5885537	3866658	194621	1810107	109161	3299471
390358	805832	395254	2449082	2531775	1694439	86236	750546	3067	1918657
531575	889702	308911	1719402	2400652	1634242	86747	670045	45110	1531856
468007	1056979	378817	1477163	2191224	1352073	85771	747197	109685	1345468
13650	11557	3029	3518	9366	3581	564	4582	3672	10442

11-4 规模以上工业企业分行业主要经济指标（2011 年）
MAJOR ECONOMIC INDICATORS OF INDUSTRIAL ENTERPRISES ABOVE DESIGNATED SIZE BY SECTOR（2011）

指 标	Item	企业单位数（个）Number of Enterpr-ises (unit)	其中 of which #亏损企业 Loss-incurring Enter-prises	工业总产值 Gross Industrial Output Value
非金属矿采选业	Nonmetal Minerals Mining and Dressing	3		70808
农副食品加工业	Food Processing	14	6	176136
食品制造业	Food Production	13	3	111692
饮料制造业	Beverage Production	4		129634
纺织业	Textile Industry	373	46	4095281
纺织服装、鞋、帽制造业	Textile, Garments, Shoes and Hat Processing	139	9	2527843
皮革、毛皮、羽毛（绒）及其制品业	Leather, Furs, Down and Related Products	11	1	152343
木材加工及木、竹、藤、棕、草 制品业	Timber Processing, Bamboo, Cane, Palm Fiber and Straw Products	59	1	605897
家具制造业	Furniture Manufacturing	7		67547
造纸及纸制品业	Papermaking and Paper Products	40	2	307876
印刷业和记录媒介的复制	Printing and Record Medium Reproduction	26	3	206908
文教体育用品制造业	Cultural, Educational and Sports Goods	17	2	322113
石油加工、炼焦及核燃料加工业	Petroleum Processing, Coking and Nuclear Fuel Processing	13	2	340355
化学原料及化学制品制造业	Raw Chemical Materials and Chemica Products	403	34	11377995
医药制造业	Medical and Pharmaceutical Products	58	8	1255914
化学纤维制造业	Chemical Fiber	45	9	502728
橡胶制品业	Rubber Products	31	4	261083
塑料制品业	Plastic Products	108	13	817884
非金属矿物制品业	Nonmetal Mineral Products	152	8	3168331
黑色金属冶炼及压延加工业	Smelting and Pressing of Ferrous Metals	117	7	13193469
有色金属冶炼及压延加工业	Smelting and Pressing of Nonferrous Metals	104	11	4381085
金属制品业	Metal Products	168	19	2969253
通用设备制造业	General Equipment Manufacturing	442	32	4472775
专用设备制造业	For Special Purposes Equipment Manufacturing	292	18	5820299
交通运输设备制造业	Transport Equipment Manufacturing	203	10	4066454
电气机械及器材制造业	Electric Equipment and Machinery	460	56	13754758
通信设备、计算机及其他电子设备制造	Communication, Computer and Other Electronic Equipment	191	18	4074959
仪器仪表及文化、办公用机械制造业	Instruments, Meters, Cultural and Office Machinery	94	6	2058988
工艺品及其他制造业	Artcraft and Other Manufacturing	18	1	247161
废弃资源和废旧材料回收加工业	Recycling and Disposal of Waste	5		163536
电力、热力的生产和供应业	Production and Supply of Electric Power and Thermal Power	19	5	796712
燃气生产和供应业	Production and Supply of Gas	3		144882
水的生产和供应业	Production and Supply of Water	6	1	65005

单位：万元（10000 yuan）

工业销售产值 Value of Industrial Products Sales	流动资产合计 Current Assets	其中 of which: #应收帐款净额 Net Account Income	其中 of which: 存货 Existing Stock	其中 of which: #产成品 Manufac-tured Products	固定资产合计 Total Fixed Assets	固定资产原价合计 Total Original Value of Fixed Assets	累计折旧 Accumula-tive Deprecia-tion	资产总计 Total Assets
70740	86707	13645	2309	480	35786	71636	35850	124225
172616	85346	15587	28483	7614	45890	54711	11386	143233
108342	86089	18746	23136	16453	51890	73094	24357	148230
123424	41230	5573	15814	1854	38210	65478	27289	83982
4073972	1442398	388970	460741	214220	720070	1140104	467870	2721016
2520618	764081	209775	184265	49346	241624	433234	203100	1147339
145981	101638	12973	14756	4528	12438	19592	7217	116546
593687	187184	37126	74547	20347	42417	67905	28008	256031
67103	88139	4796	8344	1553	6608	10287	3739	163772
302050	200294	61682	41434	14545	64688	110821	49824	286233
206517	133350	40660	18780	5661	51003	96574	48321	199167
314636	103150	18159	33727	10290	56848	87147	34811	205849
342603	125764	27574	28185	5278	34486	38380	16349	167935
11095026	5089714	1309991	942663	394001	1987155	3876664	2124014	8380557
1195652	738623	162282	126821	59786	221666	351429	139203	1082670
493336	274780	83969	56975	29252	110059	169699	59428	427192
256628	168885	53783	28105	11655	62137	68023	20207	279404
794766	350671	115571	83637	33327	163111	250474	98149	553100
3149563	2023638	526313	234343	65688	937526	1445496	530416	3429736
13094951	5077742	1730305	1303622	521652	2443247	3095557	919937	8111289
4364002	1079759	259292	285913	108691	279841	485736	159093	1495795
2953065	1433567	431380	352258	155589	431871	658776	272742	2066858
4392852	2560607	787455	542048	206088	904080	1429132	611038	3901645
5799993	3595478	1101367	1180892	470015	1141282	2303818	1241072	5237398
4030894	2353483	787891	590091	202076	1086357	1486479	433010	3873807
13638729	7077567	2320336	1262903	535107	2073836	3292959	1313897	10014847
3978755	2259891	897940	449607	200081	996445	1316944	371157	3577202
2020468	1432533	471023	400145	89846	384337	553413	240318	2092585
232660	81610	21804	19215	9387	48593	72620	25922	158064
143426	58396	15788	14461	1204	24659	31837	2178	161001
793945	306653	96624	43134	4	734626	1163085	441418	1206003
144882	81350	6821	4842	137	99245	125063	26963	202639
62509	75021	4823	22719		297730	406593	117422	417138

11-4 续表 Continued

指标	Item	负债总计 Total Liabilities	其中 of which 流动负债合计 Total Current Liabilities	非流动负债合计 Total Non-current Liabilities	所有者权益 Owner's Equity
非金属矿采选业	Nonmetal Minerals Mining and Dressing	98071	98071		26154
农副食品加工业	Food Processing	104434	104317	117	38799
食品制造业	Food Production	93196	78945	13019	55033
饮料制造业	Beverage Production	50752	48134	1943	33230
纺织业	Textile Industry	1622956	1519716	64227	1098060
纺织服装、鞋、帽制造业	Textile, Garments, Shoes and Hat Processing	668923	593723	69995	478416
皮革、毛皮、羽毛（绒）及其制品业	Leather, Furs, Down and Related Products	93807	91759		22739
木材加工及木、竹、藤、棕、草制品业	Timber Processing, Bamboo, Cane, Palm Fiber and Straw Products	186023	169698	9603	70007
家具制造业	Furniture Manufacturing	141007	140935		22765
造纸及纸制品业	Papermaking and Paper Products	189323	179247	6086	96910
印刷业和记录媒介的复制	Printing and Record Medium Reproduction	155433	147587	5845	43734
文教体育用品制造业	Cultural, Educational and Sports Goods	105046	98051	6777	100803
石油加工、炼焦及核燃料加工业	Petroleum Processing, Coking and Nuclear Fuel Processing	118503	114291	2775	49432
化学原料及化学制品制造业	Raw Chemical Materials and Chemica Products	5440147	4986713	440299	2940410
医药制造业	Medical and Pharmaceutical Products	510324	488107	14424	572346
化学纤维制造业	Chemical Fiber	241241	227390	11278	185951
橡胶制品业	Rubber Products	112841	103253	4790	166563
塑料制品业	Plastic Products	344790	316439	23683	208310
非金属矿物制品业	Nonmetal Mineral Products	2256779	2105063	142677	1172957
黑色金属冶炼及压延加工业	Smelting and Pressing of Ferrous Metals	5311213	4226738	1073446	2800076
有色金属冶炼及压延加工业	Smelting and Pressing of Nonferrous Metals	982288	790967	188499	513507
金属制品业	Metal Products	1420136	1374131	38111	646722
通用设备制造业	General Equipment Manufacturing	2418217	2293482	101154	1483429
专用设备制造业	For Special Purposes Equipment Manufacturing	3110105	2878171	216907	2127293
交通运输设备制造业	Transport Equipment Manufacturing	2276425	2099419	175622	1597383
电气机械及器材制造业	Electric Equipment and Machinery	5436487	4836468	559887	4578360
通信设备、计算机及其他电子设备制造	Communication, Computer and Other Electronic Equipment	1780377	1520209	255526	1796824
仪器仪表及文化、办公用机械制造业	Instruments, Meters, Cultural and Office Machinery	1304651	1247579	50272	787934
工艺品及其他制造业	Artcraft and Other Manufacturing	97452	83367	14085	60612
废弃资源和废旧材料回收加工业	Recycling and Disposal of Waste	148822	82169	66204	12179
电力、热力的生产和供应业	Production and Supply of Electric Power and Thermal Power	806188	481977	322710	399815
燃气生产和供应业	Production and Supply of Gas	135349	117179	18170	67290
水的生产和供应业	Production and Supply of Water	281327	179441	101885	135811

单位：万元（10000 yuan）

主营业务收入 Main Business Income	销售费用 Cost of Sales	管理费用 Cost of Management	财务费用 Finance Charge	营业利润 Business Profit	实现利税总额 Total Profits and Taxes	其中 of which 利润总额 Total Profits	主营业务税金及附加 Main Business Tax and Surcharges	应交增值税 Value Added Tax Payable	亏损企业亏损总额 Amount of Loss in Loss-incurring Enterprises	应付职工薪酬 Remuneration Payable to Employees
74062	6423	6222	4765	7752	16996	8041	3387	5568		2431
170742	3477	3827	3314	5322	8088	4666	173	3249	2297	7042
107963	11136	5117	4366	-65	4685	1834	298	2084	1709	6783
118663	10562	5318	1342	6108	25224	8711	9909	6604		10198
4094648	39810	119773	48234	134823	228680	138631	10733	79103	15671	276692
2493689	47416	98706	19049	134908	214084	151991	9528	52521	1448	351766
149320	1583	3274	2263	9878	14035	8438	379	5185	21	18388
593753	19275	14776	3482	17241	32996	17221	1860	13916	20	29155
67557	1906	2763	674	974	2864	970	399	1495		3586
301977	5972	9424	8992	8591	17324	8305	840	8180	1115	16727
205744	3598	8665	4898	7776	13272	6799	581	5335	4021	19294
314870	6339	12688	4026	18530	25620	17352	1713	6555	128	34922
338411	3884	3534	2953	2842	7652	4906	478	2268	585	7940
11261113	177205	311477	127726	769729	951704	635145	28639	287564	18641	412443
1193800	94434	79685	14715	114257	173205	113664	6480	53021	2050	81108
489157	7553	14004	7125	20525	36174	21353	1443	12635	1705	31519
253842	5877	15253	2242	18794	26741	18290	798	7653	1520	27064
806171	18560	31644	9847	21889	42993	19086	2164	21743	4758	56971
3197239	66201	97482	109023	227323	429080	251750	16291	161032	1746	131348
13259489	35001	148939	168352	1007498	768562	436773	21768	310022	571	369732
4364470	21323	46940	32855	171419	212381	137799	8937	64671	5138	81153
2949824	50751	90094	43851	181631	224580	142532	11333	68868	6361	202578
4404984	89219	200576	63269	290529	369788	248621	12487	106851	13953	320854
5729673	172156	253184	59251	516835	650592	471360	18267	157429	11232	338446
4154192	80017	270414	47006	319662	440079	304418	21982	110407	18373	331853
13580505	285708	518659	173008	974869	1294624	838720	34812	419087	32638	845435
4010199	76987	207844	43566	302892	405964	313159	12534	79539	9432	547174
2037336	48860	128148	25623	220242	298635	215676	13021	69890	868	176724
228039	3167	8235	4164	7472	16760	8090	518	8153	173	16412
164546	787	4429	2667	2042	10454	2224	2090	6139		4691
801085	89	26161	35162	80506	112467	81333	4312	26529	5013	31214
145367	3655	6863	1197	31660	38272	32112	630	5530		6117
62854	4662	9956	7008	14710	18444	14365	535	3544	348	8666

11-5 规模以上民营工业企业主要经济指标（2011 年）
MAJOR ECONOMIC INDICATORS OF PRIVATE INDUSTRIAL ENTERPRISES ABOVE DESIGNATED SIZE（2011）

指 标	Item	企 业 单位数 （个） Number of Enterpr-ises (unit)	其中 of which # 亏损企业 Loss-incurring Enterprises	工 业 总产值 Gross Industrial Output Value
总 计	**Total**	**2853**	**218**	**51396292**
按地区分	**Grouped by Region**			
市 区	Urban Area	2322	185	40247074
武进区	Wujin District	1394	95	26201592
新北区	Xinbei District	504	47	6414503
天宁区	Tianning District	161	21	2714126
钟楼区	Zhonglou District	192	15	4163145
戚墅堰区	Qishuyan District	71	7	753709
溧阳市	Liyang City	276	8	6791652
金坛市	Jintan City	255	25	4357565
按轻重工业分	**Grouped by Light and Heavy Industry**			
轻工业	Light Industry	816	82	9180514
重工业	Heavy Industry	2037	136	42215778
按企业规模分	**Grouped by Size of Enterprises**			
大 型	Large-sized	53	1	17962643
中 型	Medium-sized	331	26	11632127
小 型	Small-sized	2404	183	21553852
微 型	Micro-sized	65	8	247670
按工业行业分	**Grouped by Sector**			
非金属矿采选业	Nonmetal Minerals Mining and Dressing	1		5056
农副食品加工业	Food Processing	13	6	132257
食品制造业	Food Production	9	1	57344
饮料制造业	Beverage Production	2		50225
纺织业	Textile Industry	305	35	2808127
纺织服装、鞋、帽制造业	Textile, Garments, Shoes and Hat Processing	68	6	1337451
皮革、毛皮、羽毛（绒）及其制品业	Leather, Furs, Down and Related Products	8	1	65633

单位：万元（10000 yuan）

工业销售产值 Value of Industrial Products Sales	流动资产合计 Current Assets	其中 of which			固定资产合计 Total Fixed Assets	固定资产原价合计 Total Original Value of Fixed Assets	累计折旧 Accumulative Depreciation	资产总计 Total Assets
		#应收帐款净额 Net Account Income	存货 Existing Stock	其中 of which #产成品 Manufactured Products				
50723333	**25372452**	**7747220**	**5319066**	**2034743**	**8562650**	**13118375**	**5371897**	**38402096**
39776827	20350624	6392547	4541099	1722034	6825795	10570003	4486922	30709127
25705921	13752018	4350006	3182041	1140441	4486713	6465484	2430613	20580634
6233477	3542050	1106520	742490	325984	1056101	2122588	1141924	5172555
2769248	1267601	327897	205332	73609	401409	614645	265606	2023210
4304242	1346937	474459	303892	142645	756484	1166257	568595	2228948
763939	442018	133665	107344	39355	125088	201030	80184	703780
6689718	3335643	983153	485474	191878	1224266	1721219	565351	5185236
4256788	1686186	371520	292494	120831	512589	827153	319624	2507733
9033906	3847774	1137838	925146	394390	1490504	2297638	908490	6041776
41689427	21524678	6609383	4393920	1640353	7072145	10820737	4463407	32360320
17790773	9994566	2904147	2086525	763294	3165430	4855438	2040944	14967355
11411607	6109894	1566288	1328537	550481	2268739	3489699	1394518	9639342
21279847	9128518	3237137	1888743	715055	3094808	4730642	1929332	13595275
241106	139474	39648	15261	5913	33673	42595	7103	200124
5056	555		258	42	223	582	359	2351
129780	72702	14333	20441	6583	36967	44468	10066	119016
56966	43222	8587	14689	11308	39498	51504	15110	84292
48846	17501	1189	1577	309	20182	34619	14436	39075
2786859	895245	279962	303710	133774	471571	758317	311960	1541079
1337189	358742	101575	80609	21323	151938	263014	118869	620410
62718	26847	5817	8020	1743	7622	12538	4979	35644

11-5 续表 1 Continued 1

指 标 Item		企业单位数（个）Number of Enterpr-ises (unit)	其中 of which #亏损企业 Loss-incurring Enterprises	工业总产值 Gross Industrial Output Value
木材加工及木、竹、藤、棕、草制品业	Timber Processing, Bamboo, Cane, Palm Fiber and Straw Products	53		421092
家具制造业	Furniture Manufacturing	6		57825
造纸及纸制品业	Papermaking and Paper Products	32	1	203036
印刷业和记录媒介的复制	Printing and Record Medium Reproduction	20	2	128563
文教体育用品制造业	Cultural, Educational and Sports Goods	11	1	140679
石油加工、炼焦及核燃料加工业	Petroleum Processing, Coking and Nuclear Fuel Processing	10	1	228414
化学原料及化学制品制造业	Raw Chemical Materials and Chemica Products	330	25	7932407
医药制造业	Medical and Pharmaceutical Products	42	5	874912
化学纤维制造业	Chemical Fiber	39	9	364127
橡胶制品业	Rubber Products	22	3	157159
塑料制品业	Plastic Products	86	7	560700
非金属矿物制品业	Nonmetal Mineral Products	130	5	2549333
黑色金属冶炼及压延加工业	Smelting and Pressing of Ferrous Metals	109	7	9018745
有色金属冶炼及压延加工业	Smelting and Pressing of Nonferrous Metals	89	6	2362811
金属制品业	Metal Products	141	14	2354588
通用设备制造业	General Equipment Manufacturing	371	19	3683528
专用设备制造业	For Special Purposes Equipment Manufacturing	227	8	2728643
交通运输设备制造业	Transport Equipment Manufacturing	155	4	2152840
电气机械及器材制造业	Electric Equipment and Machinery	355	39	8405767
通信设备、计算机及其他电子设备制造	Communication, Computer and Other Electronic Equipment	113	5	1123143
仪器仪表及文化、办公用机械制造业	Instruments, Meters, Cultural and Office Machinery	77	4	1018792
工艺品及其他制造业	Artcraft and Other Manufacturing	13	1	126603
废弃资源和废旧材料回收加工业	Recycling and Disposal of Waste	5		163536
电力、热力的生产和供应业	Production and Supply of Electric Power and Thermal Power	8	3	159019
燃气生产和供应业	Production and Supply of Gas	1		17121
水的生产和供应业	Production and Supply of Water	2		6819

单位：万元（10000 yuan）

工业销售产值 Value of Industrial Products Sales	流动资产合计 Current Assets	其中 of which #应收帐款净额 Net Account Income	存货 Existing Stock	其中 of which #产成品 Manufac-tured Products	固定资产合计 Total Fixed Assets	固定资产原价合计 Total Original Value of Fixed Assets	累计折旧 Accumula-tive Deprecia-tion	资产总计 Total Assets
414700	164175	31895	67991	19025	32450	52711	21614	213915
57381	86711	4796	7182	1427	4489	7743	3314	154658
196797	139100	45764	30679	8936	27101	50148	24426	172138
127793	99823	34611	14129	4702	38829	68362	32277	143984
133813	43999	12558	12125	2093	15726	27889	13508	68557
227675	39733	8501	16176	2301	25565	25953	11416	72912
7769298	3622032	997703	676397	288000	1128634	2109939	1120000	5740659
842762	489924	105905	73283	31754	121291	198938	81210	687805
355209	191312	53263	41976	22854	67156	104385	38466	283508
156585	109492	37239	15341	7729	32208	31291	11121	185395
544403	261880	82689	53846	19866	93173	146265	63637	385171
2552576	1750871	435176	190906	51309	774124	1203079	440847	2947782
8926271	4459387	1585789	1071161	407046	1667641	2228711	818948	6609749
2354335	595540	171308	180658	50549	133416	222565	101295	837603
2327487	1080701	349033	235830	99262	275054	452274	210594	1530274
3621799	2115462	665155	416883	162804	647936	1083721	492159	3155791
2684835	1653193	523860	482262	164678	626422	969728	382658	2510614
2093516	1415394	482080	267261	110173	435125	616923	203983	2099189
8357716	4233052	1259261	741616	306557	1058715	1468040	503565	5829565
1104273	517027	205911	112827	39877	185381	260941	87770	751157
1002804	666289	187869	140380	49512	222273	278802	107377	1017572
120432	69167	14364	16695	7867	41160	59550	20195	135070
143426	58396	15788	14461	1204	24659	31837	2178	161001
156092	74860	22197	5692		105796	190469	89671	190599
17121	16863	2202	3999	137	42605	49593	8132	59468
6819	3256	842	5		7723.3	13478.6	5756	16093

11-5 续表 2 Continued 2

指标	Item	负债总计 Total Liabilities	其中 of which 流动负债合计 Total Current Liabilities	其中 of which 非流动负债合计 Total Non-current Liabilities	所有者权益 Owner's Equity	主营业务收入 Main Business Income
总 计	**Total**	**23878158**	**22390836**	**1319409**	**14523938**	**50822121**
按地区分	**Grouped by Region**					
市 区	Urban Area	18779741	17556374	1073466	11929386	39788424
武进区	Wujin District	12941639	12063952	773192	7638995	25651598
新北区	Xinbei District	3139888	2960285	151391	2032668	6219698
天宁区	Tianning District	1118833	1049185	53786	904376	2764579
钟楼区	Zhonglou District	1294772	1209364	85378	934176	4307843
戚墅堰区	Qishuyan District	284609	273588	9718	419171	844706
溧阳市	Liyang City	3505227	3294016	204410	1680009	6757048
金坛市	Jintan City	1593190	1540446	41534	914543	4276649
按轻重工业分	**Grouped by Light and Heavy Industry**					
轻工业	Light Industry	3830531	3624982	143994	2211245	8977543
重工业	Heavy Industry	20047627	18765854	1175415	12312693	41844578
按企业规模分	**Grouped by Size of Enterprises**					
大 型	Large-sized	9168797	8622873	540608	5798558	17935508
中 型	Medium-sized	5642173	5204439	402295	3997169	11553565
小 型	Small-sized	8942068	8439834	376073	4653207	21089948
微 型	Micro-sized	125120	123691	433	75004	243101
按工业行业分	**Grouped by Sector**					
非金属矿采选业	Nonmetal Minerals Mining and Dressing	603	603		1748	5056
农副食品加工业	Food Processing	88739	88622	117	30277	129022
食品制造业	Food Production	52731	38480	13019	31560	55074
饮料制造业	Beverage Production	20236	20236		18839	48846
纺织业	Textile Industry	1072335	993892	47758	468745	2776065
纺织服装、鞋、帽制造业	Textile, Garments, Shoes and Hat Processing	349610	326395	22438	270800	1324541
皮革、毛皮、羽毛(绒)及其制品业	Leather, Furs, Down and Related Products	23835	21787		11809	64857

单位：万元（10000 yuan）

销售费用 Cost of Sales	管理费用 Cost of Management	财务费用 Finance Charge	营业利润 Business Profit	实现利税总额 Total Profits and Taxes	其中 of which 利润总额 Total Profits	主营业务税金及附加 Main Business Tax and Surcharges	应交增值税 Value Added Tax Payable	亏损企业亏损总额 Amount of Loss in Loss-incurring Enterprises	应付职工薪酬 Remuneration Payable to Employees
750681	**1639314**	**704385**	**3255922**	**4100228**	**2599366**	**172052**	**1325494**	**72658**	**2873759**
572632	1330651	540461	2348165	2862090	1798443	124430	935920	60108	2393306
304715	727670	391312	1542483	1800995	1080490	78341	640561	23208	1689519
138419	294295	84247	357830	440578	303733	19581	116905	18477	313480
41798	113774	29519	121541	175541	118658	10929	45804	11093	185478
72271	145467	31626	260489	359477	229182	12885	117120	4546	164858
15429	49446	3758	65822	85498	66380	2694	15529	2784	39972
110782	175160	111181	513655	703273	434299	35963	233011	3221	288979
67267	133502	52744	394103	534865	366624	11660	156563	9329	191473
162194	340974	121568	358989	603498	358546	34318	209870	26597	759922
588487	1298340	582817	2896933	3496730	2240820	137735	1115624	46061	2113836
236285	419652	231356	1498408	1398345	933607	59319	405420	35	978594
199939	475765	193697	747700	1152167	742363	47007	362798	20907	886529
310719	735549	277185	1005844	1541216	919164	65271	553613	49738	1000279
3738	8349	2148	3971	8499	4231	456	3664	1978	8357
	137	96	23	971	200	70	701		224
2293	3299	3212	1800	5339	1935	173	3231	2297	5937
2001	2830	3134	469	3690	2613	133	944	79	3820
3404	2548	1084	447	14279	4769	5837	3673		5110
22531	74666	33230	53486	115036	51312	7487	56238	14031	197963
20458	53011	11498	59282	85651	57620	4758	23273	576	179790
492	1563	942	5697	6451	4561	294	1563	21	5391

11-5 续表 3 Continued 3

指 标	Item	负债总计 Total Liabilities	其中 of which 流动负债合计 Total Current Liabilities	非流动负债合计 Total Non-current Liabilities	所有者权益 Owner's Equity	主营业务收入 Main Business Income
木材加工及木、竹、藤、棕、草制品业	Timber Processing, Bamboo, Cane, Palm Fiber and Straw Products	153053	137688	9602	60862	409202
家具制造业	Furniture Manufacturing	139665	139593		14993	57835
造纸及纸制品业	Papermaking and Paper Products	131543	129871	308	40595	197465
印刷业和记录媒介的复制	Printing and Record Medium Reproduction	121020	113175	5845	22963	130643
文教体育用品制造业	Cultural, Educational and Sports Goods	41432	40934	280	27125	133646
石油加工、炼焦及核燃料加工业	Petroleum Processing, Coking and Nuclear Fuel Processing	49055	45837	2693	23857	233947
化学原料及化学制品制造业	Raw Chemical Materials and Chemica Products	3814805	3677981	126049	1925854	7835619
医药制造业	Medical and Pharmaceutical Products	320903	312806	2449	366902	844577
化学纤维制造业	Chemical Fiber	180755	178184	1693	102753	351440
橡胶制品业	Rubber Products	72325	62760	4790	113070	156121
塑料制品业	Plastic Products	251935	242748	4519	133236	557695
非金属矿物制品业	Nonmetal Mineral Products	1975024	1853401	113585	972758	2580879
黑色金属冶炼及压延加工业	Smelting and Pressing of Ferrous Metals	4033334	3835758	186546	2576416	9003937
有色金属冶炼及压延加工业	Smelting and Pressing of Nonferrous Metals	548841	364789	181230	288762	2358271
金属制品业	Metal Products	1118825	1090906	22689	411449	2312167
通用设备制造业	General Equipment Manufacturing	2056899	1990239	50827	1098892	3632054
专用设备制造业	For Special Purposes Equipment Manufacturing	1545664	1464457	67394	964951	2660973
交通运输设备制造业	Transport Equipment Manufacturing	1183637	1091072	91180	915553	2114938
电气机械及器材制造业	Electric Equipment and Machinery	3048416	2813768	204875	2781150	8295319
通信设备、计算机及其他电子设备制造	Communication, Computer and Other Electronic Equipment	436314	425440	9803	314843	1093137
仪器仪表及文化、办公用机械制造业	Instruments, Meters, Cultural and Office Machinery	624844	574802	44502	392728	991416
工艺品及其他制造业	Artcraft and Other Manufacturing	88515	74430	14085	46556	118650
废弃资源和废旧材料回收加工业	Recycling and Disposal of Waste	148822	82169	66204	12179	164546
电力、热力的生产和供应业	Production and Supply of Electric Power and Thermal Power	124659	113032	10127	65940	160208
燃气生产和供应业	Production and Supply of Gas	48698	38728	9970	10770	17121
水的生产和供应业	Production and Supply of Water	11086	6254	4832	5007	6855

单位：万元（10000 yuan）

销售费用 Cost of Sales	管理费用 Cost of Management	财务费用 Finance Charge	营业利润 Business Profit	实现利税总额 Total Profits and Taxes	其中 of which 利润总额 Total Profits	主营业务税金及附加 Main Business Tax and Surcharges	应交增值税 Value Added Tax Payable	亏损企业亏损总额 Amount of Loss in Loss-incurring Enterprises	应付职工薪酬 Remuneration Payable to Employees
11626	8451	2790	11526	20357	11754	1639	6964		21256
1521	2397	696	969	2564	970	399	1195		2863
2338	6113	6700	3410	9495	3657	432	5405	1002	11667
2765	5191	3670	528	4691	1102	382	3207	1460	13010
3888	6978	1225	5983	9449	5787	804	2858	43	14097
1179	2334	1407	3393	3562	2407	132	1023	151	6887
128519	236756	95458	511174	652726	420235	24276	207859	11611	318198
24828	42622	11855	70229	100537	69928	3271	27298	1187	53657
3082	8776	4863	14937	27374	14993	993	10715	1705	24396
2815	9062	895	9698	15327	10397	568	4363	661	13294
10688	20690	8429	16313	30140	15277	1567	13296	1988	35598
38912	74331	93676	142184	318839	182488	12683	123668	1412	104365
27502	126077	128310	682089	500408	281361	18484	200563	571	307151
11987	32668	17347	126330	156811	105631	7958	43222	991	65486
37804	60803	36857	162842	200641	128875	10040	61644	2763	164489
70384	151799	54169	235383	287947	190075	10032	87221	5066	261071
73322	150316	32949	157228	231229	145710	12423	73043	2148	207873
51998	130500	23546	233076	305757	216260	12717	76780	1283	166128
151110	286013	89129	603353	748519	520828	24065	203145	17033	434148
12517	56824	9624	54647	93551	57807	3226	31831	365	130847
27175	62155	15118	72355	114570	72791	4393	37385	480	96006
2509	7301	3760	5134	11100	5891	410	4799	173	11064
787	4429	2667	2042	10454	2224	2090	6139		4691
5	7493	5800	7988	10174	8091	262	1529	3561	6706
242	808	90	1052	1811	1036	55	719		440
	376	162	859	781	781				136

11-6 规模以上三资工业企业主要经济指标（2011 年）
MAJOR ECONOMIC INDICATORS OF FOREIGN-FUNDED ENTERPRISES ABOVE DESIGNATED SIZE（2011）

指 标	Item	企 业 单位数（个）Number of Enterpr-ises (unit)	其中 of which #亏损企业 Loss-incurring Enterprises	工 业 总产值 Gross Industrial Output Value	工业销售产值 Value of Industrial Products Sales
总 计	**Total**	**734**	**111**	**28412309**	**28069085**
按地区分	**Grouped by Region**				
市 区	Urban Area	596	102	21747666	21518114
武进区	Wujin District	209	40	5970661	5845122
新北区	Xinbei District	248	57	9622023	9390567
天宁区	Tianning District	73	2	3418682	3444817
钟楼区	Zhonglou District	51	3	2024556	2074412
戚墅堰区	Qishuyan District	15		711743	763196
溧阳市	Liyang City	43	1	4340253	4297335
金坛市	Jintan City	95	8	2324390	2253636
按轻重工业分	**Grouped by Light and Heavy Industry**				
轻工业	Light Industry	271	45	6048961	5957751
重工业	Heavy Industry	463	66	22363348	22111334
按企业规模分	**Grouped by Size of Enterprises**				
大 型	Large-sized	33	3	9943339	9764746
中 型	Medium-sized	182	17	9913218	9800511
小 型	Small-sized	513	87	8523798	8473286
微 型	Micro-sized	6	4	31955	30542
按工业行业分	**Grouped by Sector**				
非金属矿采选业	Nonmetal Minerals Mining and Dressing	1		63091	63091
农副食品加工业	Food Processing	1		43879	42836
食品制造业	Food Production	3	1	25216	21605
饮料制造业	Beverage Production	2		79409	74578
纺织业	Textile Industry	67	11	1180558	1192088
纺织服装、鞋、帽制造业	Textile, Garments, Shoes and Hat Processing	69	3	1173348	1166293
皮革、毛皮、羽毛（绒）及其制品业	Leather, Furs, Down and Related Products	3		86710	83263

单位：万元（10000 yuan）

流动资产合计 Current Assets	其中 of which #应收帐款净额 Net Account Income	存货 Existing Stock	其中 of which #产成品 Manufac-tured Products	固定资产合计 Total Fixed Assets	固定资产原价合计 Total Original Value of Fixed Assets	累计折旧 Accumula-tive Deprecia-tion	资产总计 Total Assets
12384589	**3814162**	**3084391**	**1250582**	**5906044**	**9577245**	**3960060**	**20115869**
10423412	3298900	2657460	1079221	4531555	7927581	3667277	16532951
3409138	1057282	755105	240437	1305252	1960137	695065	5466793
5186232	1714093	1432214	633016	2423118	4721227	2515389	8331391
881812	196227	223290	92218	485123	751829	244536	1430130
621880	206845	167782	63154	262055	359412	128557	900776
324350	124453	79069	50396	56006	134977	83730	403862
824848	219460	229138	94597	862966	972413	121931	1836327
1136328	295803	197793	76765	511524	677251	170852	1746591
2721126	827044	662147	259446	1447705	2160383	781394	4591339
9663462	2987119	2422244	991137	4458339	7416862	3178666	15524530
4440001	1519796	892133	343063	2386938	3188887	911719	7516841
4527673	1356094	1358000	570570	2013051	3733955	1893424	7069845
3392828	933510	829821	334978	1496800	2644023	1153244	5494853
24087	4762	4438	1972	9256	10379	1673	34329
85587	13328	2045	437	34880	69511	34631	120467
12644	1254	8042	1031	8923	10243	1320	24217
28705	5127	7687	4852	10188	18936	8796	47573
23729	4383	14237	1545	18028	30860	12853	44907
372834	92659	123809	66700	189250	275507	106020	600467
389523	108156	103654	28022	83312	161684	82068	504739
74791	7156	6735	2785	4816	7054	2238	80902

11-6 续表 1 Continued 1

指 标	Item	企业单位数（个）Number of Enterpr-ises (unit)	其中 of which #亏损企业 Loss-incurring Enterprises	工业总产值 Gross Industrial Output Value	工业销售产值 Value of Industrial Products Sales
木材加工及木、竹、藤、棕、草制品业	Timber Processing, Bamboo, Cane, Palm Fiber and Straw Products	5	1	146943	141865
家具制造业	Furniture Manufacturing	1		9722	9722
造纸及纸制品业	Papermaking and Paper Products	8	1	104840	105253
印刷业和记录媒介的复制	Printing and Record Medium Reproduction	4	1	61561	61394
文教体育用品制造业	Cultural, Educational and Sports Goods	6	1	181434	180823
石油加工、炼焦及核燃料加工业	Petroleum Processing, Coking and Nuclear Fuel Processing	3	1	111941	114928
化学原料及化学制品制造业	Raw Chemical Materials and Chemica Products	67	9	3189128	3074647
医药制造业	Medical and Pharmaceutical Products	15	3	318844	297608
化学纤维制造业	Chemical Fiber	6		138601	138128
橡胶制品业	Rubber Products	9	1	103924	100043
塑料制品业	Plastic Products	22	6	257184	250363
非金属矿物制品业	Nonmetal Mineral Products	18	2	439999	416168
黑色金属冶炼及压延加工业	Smelting and Pressing of Ferrous Metals	8		4174724	4168680
有色金属冶炼及压延加工业	Smelting and Pressing of Nonferrous Metals	13	4	1925522	1922411
金属制品业	Metal Products	25	5	535728	542563
通用设备制造业	General Equipment Manufacturing	69	13	754905	738918
专用设备制造业	For Special Purposes Equipment Manufacturing	61	10	2891341	2914375
交通运输设备制造业	Transport Equipment Manufacturing	41	6	1070223	1090761
电气机械及器材制造业	Electric Equipment and Machinery	100	16	5053240	4975895
通信设备、计算机及其他电子设备制造	Communication, Computer and Other Electronic Equipment	77	13	2900971	2825355
仪器仪表及文化、办公用机械制造业	Instruments, Meters, Cultural and Office Machinery	16	2	1037896	1015585
工艺品及其他制造业	Artcraft and Other Manufacturing	5		120558	112227
电力、热力的生产和供应业	Production and Supply of Electric Power and Thermal Power	5	1	53997	53243
燃气生产和供应业	Production and Supply of Gas	2		127761	127761
水的生产和供应业	Production and Supply of Water	2		49113	46617

单位：万元（10000 yuan）

流动资产合计 Current Assets	其中 of which			固定资产合计 Total Fixed Assets	固定资产原价合计 Total Original Value of Fixed Assets	累计折旧 Accumula-tive Deprecia-tion	资产总计 Total Assets
	#应收帐款净额 Net Account Income	存货 Existing Stock	其中 of which #产成品 Manufac-tured Products				
22284	5213	6544	1316	9140	13819	5220	40564
1428		1162	126	2119	2544	425	9114
61194	15918	10755	5609	37587	60672	25398	114095
26449	5541	2601	278	6354	15649	9295	40259
59151	5601	21602	8197	41122	59258	21303	137292
86031	19073	12009	2977	8921	12427	4933	95023
1298564	290050	253164	102519	756276	1598781	934679	2358821
199476	52786	45473	22465	88662	130391	47605	329138
83467	30706	14999	6398	42904	65314	20961	143683
59393	16544	12763	3926	29928	36732	9085	94009
88791	32882	29791	13461	69938	104210	34512	167929
145845	67645	23293	5569	81206	122055	44617	243297
618355	144516	232461	114606	775606	866846	100990	1501540
467930	84298	99963	55470	141348	255320	55024	630035
286432	72515	82041	32919	136065	173138	51215	449361
434185	119541	118537	40958	249335	337386	116338	728062
1812165	516202	661874	294856	446950	1196680	794468	2514649
420304	140189	129679	43882	314712	430023	132669	810060
2642877	989848	453044	200072	925376	1622568	722998	3858573
1672002	665221	318583	147854	801276	1043143	281013	2734846
765814	282865	259627	40234	162028	274561	132927	1074511
12443	7439	2519	1520	7433	13071	5726	22994
27918	9125	2430		83449	115289	37924	113897
64487	4619	843		56640	75470	18830	143171
39791	3763	22427		282273	378105	103980	337674

11-6 续表 2 Continued 2

指标	Item	负债总计 Total Liabilities	其中 of which 流动负债合计 Total Current Liabilities	非流动负债合计 Total Non-current Liabilities	所有者权益 Owner's Equity	主营业务收入 Main Business Income
总 计	**Total**	**11777765**	**9476067**	**2249732**	**8338104**	**28258231**
按地区分	**Grouped by Region**					
市 区	Urban Area	9269346	7888613	1330269	7263605	21591685
武进区	Wujin District	2891273	2618278	261568	2575520	5875902
新北区	Xinbei District	4673091	3711959	945228	3658300	9446381
天宁区	Tianning District	932901	798495	116272	497229	3439972
钟楼区	Zhonglou District	552182	548798	2223	348595	2072586
戚墅堰区	Qishuyan District	219900	211084	4977	183962	756845
溧阳市	Liyang City	1437872	545476	891395	398455	4421121
金坛市	Jintan City	1070547	1041977	28068	676044	2245425
按轻重工业分	**Grouped by Light and Heavy Industry**					
轻工业	Light Industry	2349068	1989495	334777	2242271	5912189
重工业	Heavy Industry	9428697	7486572	1914955	6095833	22346042
按企业规模分	**Grouped by Size of Enterprises**					
大 型	Large-sized	4721598	3098088	1621510	2795243	9920314
中 型	Medium-sized	4109448	3747317	349342	2960397	9827636
小 型	Small-sized	2922470	2606528	278880	2572383	8479985
微 型	Micro-sized	24249	24134		10081	30296
按工业行业分	**Grouped by Sector**					
非金属矿采选业	Nonmetal Minerals Mining and Dressing	97021	97021		23446	66113
农副食品加工业	Food Processing	15695	15695		8522	41720
食品制造业	Food Production	28787	28787		18786	23118
饮料制造业	Beverage Production	30516	27898	1943	14391	69817
纺织业	Textile Industry	348232	332234	7669	252235	1186644
纺织服装、鞋、帽制造业	Textile, Garments, Shoes and Hat Processing	315581	263596	47557	189158	1152108
皮革、毛皮、羽毛（绒）及其制品业	Leather, Furs, Down and Related Products	69972	69972		10930	84463

单位：万元（10000 yuan）

销售费用 Cost of Sales	管理费用 Cost of Management	财务费用 Finance Charge	营业利润 Business Profit	实现利税总额 Total Profits and Taxes	其中 of which 利润总额 Total Profits	主营业务税金及附加 Main Business Tax and Surcharges	应交增值税 Value Added Tax Payable	亏损企业亏损总额 Amount of Loss in Loss-incurring Enterprises	应付职工薪酬 Remuneration Payable to Employees
579812	**938185**	**302948**	**2155591**	**2669181**	**1831189**	**73066**	**753551**	**84270**	**1745575**
505708	833613	218434	1542713	2032583	1403704	60502	559333	76254	1528167
111444	261602	57184	501869	644035	482401	21425	140165	14055	693627
236391	381909	108155	654748	885856	554401	25093	298143	60631	591724
101463	86311	29080	158417	205915	141770	7373	56691	564	149814
29112	80015	17329	122734	155357	102503	4502	47756	1003	69351
27299	23776	6686	104944	141420	122630	2109	16578		23650
33623	33999	45247	373261	327724	186691	4630	134638	1148	99401
40481	70573	39268	239617	308874	240794	7934	59580	6869	118007
187262	258532	60019	383444	557769	387532	28094	140064	25281	721473
392550	679653	242930	1772146	2111412	1443657	44972	613487	58989	1024102
132065	294891	130391	813042	937073	608208	19611	308698	3032	840474
299536	354509	91479	914138	1157310	834998	36306	278644	21525	585941
147713	287008	80545	429130	575217	388659	17109	166434	58166	318454
497	1776	535	-719	-418	-676	40	-225	1547	707
6423	6006	4656	7641	15549	7753	3075	4721		2046
1184	528	102	3522	2749	2731		18		1105
855	2039	1198	-616	-118	-633	97	-51	1484	2883
7158	2770	258	5661	10945	3942	4072	2931		5088
15778	33983	12014	46386	67309	43090	2462	21544	1640	69719
26453	42273	7424	68550	119616	88093	4542	26938	872	168485
1091	1711	1321	4181	7584	3877	85	3622		12997

11-6 续表 3 Continued 3

指 标	Item	负债总计 Total Liabilities	其中 of which 流动负债合计 Total Current Liabilities	其中 of which 非流动负债合计 Total Non-current Liabilities	所有者权益 Owner's Equity	主营业务收入 Main Business Income
木材加工及木、竹、藤、棕、草制品业	Timber Processing, Bamboo, Cane, Palm Fiber and Straw Products	32399	31439		8165	144229
家具制造业	Furniture Manufacturing	1342	1342		7772	9722
造纸及纸制品业	Papermaking and Paper Products	57780	49377	5778	56315	104512
印刷业和记录媒介的复制	Printing and Record Medium Reproduction	29003	29003		11257	58339
文教体育用品制造业	Cultural, Educational and Sports Goods	63614	57117	6497	73678	181225
石油加工、炼焦及核燃料加工业	Petroleum Processing, Coking and Nuclear Fuel Processing	69448	68454	82	25575	104464
化学原料及化学制品制造业	Raw Chemical Materials and Chemica Products	1441238	1158202	280677	917583	3171072
医药制造业	Medical and Pharmaceutical Products	179826	166033	11649	149311	294218
化学纤维制造业	Chemical Fiber	60486	49205	9585	83197	137717
橡胶制品业	Rubber Products	40516	40493		53493	97722
塑料制品业	Plastic Products	92855	73691	19164	75074	248477
非金属矿物制品业	Nonmetal Mineral Products	93927	91145	1782	149371	438940
黑色金属冶炼及压延加工业	Smelting and Pressing of Ferrous Metals	1277879	390979	886900	223661	4255553
有色金属冶炼及压延加工业	Smelting and Pressing of Nonferrous Metals	410941	406812	4128	219095	1913308
金属制品业	Metal Products	254695	240077	11955	194666	554589
通用设备制造业	General Equipment Manufacturing	351165	293091	50327	376897	740794
专用设备制造业	For Special Purposes Equipment Manufacturing	1435346	1295093	139039	1079302	2865784
交通运输设备制造业	Transport Equipment Manufacturing	451714	431271	20442	358347	1110365
电气机械及器材制造业	Electric Equipment and Machinery	2156762	1797300	349107	1701810	4993468
通信设备、计算机及其他电子设备制造	Communication, Computer and Other Electronic Equipment	1297498	1048204	245723	1437348	2826270
仪器仪表及文化、办公用机械制造业	Instruments, Meters, Cultural and Office Machinery	679549	672519	5770	394962	1043841
工艺品及其他制造业	Artcraft and Other Manufacturing	8937	8937		14056	109389
电力、热力的生产和供应业	Production and Supply of Electric Power and Thermal Power	71875	33169	38707	42022	55028
燃气生产和供应业	Production and Supply of Gas	86651	78451	8200	56520	128246
水的生产和供应业	Production and Supply of Water	226514	129461	97053	111160	46979

单位：万元（10000 yuan）

销售费用 Cost of Sales	管理费用 Cost of Management	财务费用 Finance Charge	营业利润 Business Profit	实现利税总额 Total Profits and Taxes	其中 of which 利润总额 Total Profits	主营业务税金及附加 Main Business Tax and Surcharges	应交增值税 Value Added Tax Payable	亏损企业亏损总额 Amount of Loss in Loss-incurring Enterprises	应付职工薪酬 Remuneration Payable to Employees
7600	6247	663	5107	11390	5059	199	6132	20	7402
385	366	-22	5	300			300		723
3635	3310	2292	5181	7829	4648	408	2774	113	5060
342	1603	1182	6326	6830	4723	120	1431	2561	4378
2451	5710	2801	12547	16171	11565	909	3697	85	20826
2705	1200	1546	-551	4090	2499	346	1245	434	1053
42873	59970	24233	241979	272012	195476	3395	73141	7031	83859
61522	30174	3195	27830	49537	27400	2487	19651	863	20375
4471	5229	2262	5588	8800	6360	450	1920		7123
3061	6191	1347	9096	11413	7893	230	3290	859	13769
7872	10953	1418	5576	12854	3809	597	8448	2771	21373
25172	17159	5066	72079	89520	56483	2843	30187	170	17712
7499	22863	40042	325410	268154	155412	3283	109459		62581
7864	13091	14904	43728	53536	30659	764	21140	4132	14551
9268	21734	7054	17712	20482	12898	1000	4819	3597	29850
17177	45918	8738	53442	77861	56841	2367	17443	8887	58282
92491	92864	23902	344340	397184	311532	5066	77103	9083	117858
20820	68287	5386	46694	64207	39963	5982	17246	17090	94613
117465	213311	77659	365459	524083	310881	9458	202220	12927	388922
56557	140547	33107	232558	297789	243338	8989	45419	9067	412948
21669	65881	10505	147851	184028	142848	8627	32553	387	80554
658	934	404	2338	5661	2199	108	3354		5348
18	2520	1392	5119	8198	5059	153	2986	199	1698
3413	6055	1107	30608	36461	31076	575	4810		5677
3885	6759	5793	14245	17156	13717	378	3061		6718

11-7 大中型工业企业主要经济指标（2011 年）
MAJOR ECONOMIC INDICATORS OF LARGE AND MEDIUM-SIZED ENTERPRISES（2011）

指 标	Item	企 业 单位数（个）Number of Enterpr-ises（unit）	其中 of which #亏损企业 Loss-incurring Enterprises	工 业 总产值 Gross Industrial Output Value	工业销售产值 Value of Industrial Products Sales
总 计	**Total**	**620**	**48**	**51468250**	**50769478**
按地区分	**Grouped by Region**				
市 区	Urban Area	487	41	39640299	39144808
# 武进区	Wujin District	271	23	22900944	22472861
溧阳市	Liyang City	60	1	8027710	7926455
金坛市	Jintan City	73	6	3800241	3698215
按登记注册类型分	**Grouped by Registration Status**				
内 资	Domestic Investment	405	28	31611693	31204220
国 有	State-owned	8		858497	866580
集 体	Collective-owned	1		15893	15910
股份合作	Share-holding Cooperative	3	1	677355	671325
有限责任公司	Limited Liability Corporations	28	3	2886388	2846860
股份有限公司	Share-holding Corporations Ltd.	15		1647608	1634121
私 营	Private	350	24	25525953	25169425
港澳台商投资	Investment from Hong Kong, Macao and Taiwan	91	5	7013527	6829163
合资经营	Joint-Venture	51	2	3452525	3413075
合作经营	Cooperative	2		76526	78844
独资经营	Sole Investment	33	2	2598705	2461138
股份有限公司	Share-holding Corporations Ltd.	5	1	885772	876106
外商投资	Foreign Investment	124	15	12843030	12736095
中外合资经营	Joint Ventures	56	5	7544412	7555336
中外合作经营	Cooperative Enterprises	3		55350	55158
外商独资	Sole Foreign Investment	60	10	4758155	4639594
股份有限公司	Share-holding Corporations Ltd.	5		485113	486007
按轻重工业分	**Grouped by Light and Heavy Industry**				
轻工业	Light Industry	221	24	8531509	8347459
重工业	Heavy Industry	399	24	42936741	42422019
按企业规模分	**Grouped by Size of Enterprises**				
大 型	Large-sized	92	4	29159406	28801480
中 型	Medium-sized	528	44	22308844	21967998

单位：万元（10000 yuan）

流动资产合计 Current Assets	其中 of which #应收帐款净额 Net Account Income	存货 Existing Stock	其中 of which #产成品 Manufactured Products	固定资产合计 Total Fixed Assets	固定资产原价合计 Total Original Value of Fixed Assets	累计折旧 Accumulative Depreciation	资产总计 Total Assets
26505951	**7710150**	**6048723**	**2360661**	**10785776**	**16718111**	**67279613**	**42230850**
21441774	6542125	5125523	2005829	8333220	13455813	58512944	33875281
12623545	3805046	2848931	978072	4217664	6112447	22914463	19162410
2943920	774121	572618	216379	1615175	2028122	4751707	5129221
2120257	393904	350583	138453	837382	1234176	4014962	3226347
17538277	4834260	3798590	1447028	6385788	9795269	39228188	27644163
522380	152046	191704	36588	280341	515541	2240687	902928
5700	4775	509	46	2445	5524	30794	8410
215541	32913	88034	44687	86560	213121	1267024	334907
1241319	307549	329595	138819	794206	1311792	5605522	2341644
1571786	292772	298950	146887	555987	897284	3522255	2784548
13981551	4044205	2889799	1080000	4666250	6852008	26561906	21271726
3610770	1090714	848906	335146	1642720	2512721	9808566	5807647
1928457	539543	501178	152971	917076	1327080	4594806	3074161
32608	9440	3346	766	10999	15218	42193	44231
1335574	402209	266819	135363	587641	983566	4451972	2217671
314131	139521	77563	46046	127004	186856	719595	471585
5356904	1785176	1401227	578487	2757268	4410121	18242859	8779040
2558276	787697	831532	333419	1334788	2209501	9135146	4132342
13558	2697	4106	1962	5916	6962	20748	21429
2621713	953371	523779	222639	1338918	2076598	8689731	4271706
163357	41411	41810	20468	77646	117060	397234	353563
4070397	1127005	954043	395172	1830774	2849411	11110367	6912141
22435555	6583145	5094681	1965489	8955002	13868700	56169246	35318709
15241160	4651585	3206016	1169973	6192307	8990958	32494261	24493653
11264792	3058566	2842707	1190688	4593469	7727153	34785352	17737197

11-7 续表 Continued

指标	Item	负债总计 Total Liabilities	其中 of which 流动负债合计 Total Current Liabilities	非流动负债合计 Total Non-current Liabilities	所有者权益 Owner's Equity	主营业务收入 Main Business Income
总 计	**Total**	**25476944**	**22178165**	**3243235**	**16753906**	**51405283**
按地区分	**Grouped by Region**					
市 区	Urban Area	19690497	17481484	2162632	14184785	39485189
#武进区	Wujin District	11485917	10713855	745032	7676493	22514267
溧阳市	Liyang City	3653668	2635707	1016961	1475553	8160751
金坛市	Jintan City	2132779	2060974	63642	1093568	3759343
按登记注册类型分	**Grouped by Registration Status**					
内 资	Domestic Investment	16645898	15332760	1272383	10998266	31657333
国 有	State-owned	597629	534669	62960	305299	924962
集 体	Collective-owned	5026	4946	80	3384	17233
股份合作	Share-holding Cooperative	111362	110551	810	223545	673276
有限责任公司	Limited Liability Corporations	1522812	1081441	436620	818832	2887436
股份有限公司	Share-holding Corporations Ltd.	1158278	1099660	58618	1626270	1728442
私 营	Private	13250791	12501492	713295	8020935	25425984
港澳台商投资	Investment from Hong Kong, Macao and Taiwan	3344937	3002417	333960	2462710	6864322
合资经营	Joint-Venture	1978402	1839979	129862	1095759	3409670
合作经营	Cooperative	26363	25790	574	17868	78822
独资经营	Sole Investment	1075814	951317	124498	1141856	2529333
股份有限公司	Share-holding Corporations Ltd.	264358	185332	79026	207227	846496
外商投资	Foreign Investment	5486110	3842988	1636892	3292930	12883628
中外合资经营	Joint Ventures	2853444	1830251	1021140	1278898	7669317
中外合作经营	Cooperative Enterprises	12089	12088		9340	53073
外商独资	Sole Foreign Investment	2472971	1853054	615742	1798734	4653528
股份有限公司	Share-holding Corporations Ltd.	147606	147595	10	205958	507711
按轻重工业分	**Grouped by Light and Heavy Industry**					
轻工业	Light Industry	3564897	3177953	368261	3347244	8330297
重工业	Heavy Industry	21912047	19000212	2874973	13406662	43074986
按企业规模分	**Grouped by Size of Enterprises**					
大 型	Large-sized	15015312	12608981	2399015	9478341	29217984
中 型	Medium-sized	10461632	9569184	844220	7275565	22187299

单位：万元（10000 yuan）

销售费用 Cost of Sales	管理费用 Cost of Management	财务费用 Finance Charge	营业利润 Business Profit	实现利税总额 Total Profits and Taxes	其中 of which 利润总额 Total Profits	 主营业务税金及附加 Main Business Tax and Surcharges	 应交增值税 Value Added Tax Payable	亏损企业亏损总额 Amount of Loss in Loss-incurring Enterprises	应付职工薪酬 Remuneration Payable to Employees
921933	**1695534**	**704165**	**4168484**	**4932427**	**3328681**	**172983**	**1420591**	**48177**	**3450513**
725352	1409476	514276	3056229	3618627	2450816	126543	1033417	38096	2974779
273046	640204	320675	1754360	1897752	1269832	72958	554961	11018	1824561
123348	148517	108899	735221	798330	501040	32477	263048	1148	264979
73234	137542	80990	377034	515470	376825	13963	124126	8933	210755
490331	1046133	482296	2441304	2838045	1885474	117065	833249	23620	2024098
15244	58650	25194	43639	82896	44619	4733	33545		74659
63	2826	28	390	1691	407	138	1146		2575
8569	13629	3828	37231	65767	28754	3718	33295	975	50262
35125	117341	36029	230555	241648	178946	9166	51280	3564	178361
72812	92939	20277	173982	218617	177525	4236	36856		126524
358520	760748	396940	1955507	2227426	1455223	95076	677127	19081	1591718
123341	246137	78722	634317	833027	636465	26271	170291	1107	622663
75471	140460	49036	353267	484144	360281	17604	106260	63	217534
893	2636	828	5863	5689	4433	461	795		4496
31825	83084	19618	243429	305211	239703	5924	59585	935	248292
15152	19957	9240	31758	37982	32048	2282	3652	109	152341
308260	403263	143148	1092864	1261356	806741	29646	417051	23450	803752
188498	156223	70163	722056	741551	504579	19235	215347	9521	315653
921	2000	485	214	1690	903	172	441		4697
114100	229701	69014	310196	454133	239233	9660	199886	13928	451497
4742	15339	3486	60398	63982	62026	579	1377		31906
243710	369358	96456	562732	833191	580059	44673	207105	22251	1115373
678223	1326176	607709	3605752	4099236	2748621	128310	1213485	25926	2335140
390358	805832	395254	2449082	2531775	1694439	86236	750546	3067	1918657
531575	889702	308911	1719402	2400652	1634242	86747	670045	45110	1531856

11-8 规模以上工业企业主要经济分析指标（2011 年） MAJOR ECONOMIC ANALYTICAL INDICATORS OF INDUSTRIAL ENTERPRISES ABOVE DESIGNATED SIZE（2011）

指 标	Item	工业产品销售率（%） Sales Ratio of Industrial products	工业成本费用利润率（%） Ratio of Profits to Industrial Cost
总 计	**Total**	**98.76**	**6.09**
按地区分	**Grouped by Region**		
市 区	Urban Area	98.91	5.66
武进区	Wujin District	98.07	5.22
新北区	Xinbei District	97.46	5.83
天宁区	Tianning District	101.03	5.20
钟楼区	Zhonglou District	103.17	5.49
戚墅堰区	Qishuyan District	102.78	11.74
溧阳市	Liyang City	98.60	6.15
金坛市	Jintan City	97.52	10.25
按登记注册类型分	**Grouped by Registration Status**		
内 资	Domestic Investment	98.74	5.61
国 有	State-owned	101.14	5.13
集 体	Collective-owned	98.70	9.49
股份合作	Share-holding Cooperative	99.50	4.48
有限责任公司	Limited Liability Corporations	98.28	6.19
股份有限公司	Share-holding Corporations Ltd.	99.42	11.62
私 营	Private	98.69	5.35
港澳台商投资	Investment from Hong Kong, Macao and Taiwan	97.96	8.73
合资经营	Joint-Venture	98.98	9.73
合作经营	Cooperative	101.97	5.80
独资经营	Sole Investment	96.10	8.98
股份有限公司	Share-holding Corporations Ltd.	99.19	3.85
外商投资	Foreign Investment	99.21	6.16
中外合资经营	Joint Ventures	99.71	6.28
中外合作经营	Cooperative Enterprises	100.30	6.70
外商独资	Sole Foreign Investment	98.36	5.45
股份有限公司	Share-holding Corporations Ltd.	100.25	13.52
按轻重工业分	**Grouped by Light and Heavy Industry**		
轻工业	Light Industry	98.35	5.71
重工业	Heavy Industry	98.85	6.17
按企业规模分	**Grouped by Size of Enterprises**		
大 型	Large-sizde	98.77	6.22
中 型	Medium-sized	98.47	7.97
小 型	Small-sized	98.96	4.68
微 型	Micro-sized	97.67	1.14

每百元固定资产原值实现利税（元） Profits and Taxes of Original Value of Fixed Assets Per One Hundred Yuan(yuan)	其 中 of which	平均每一从业人员（元） Per Person Employed (yuan)		
	#利 润 Profits	实现利税 Profits and Taxes	占有固定资产原值 Original Value of Fixed Assets	实现工业总产值 Gross Industrial Output Value Achieved
28.70	**18.85**	**82812**	**288533**	**960212**
25.50	16.77	73983	290119	918284
28.91	18.46	59724	206612	787957
18.56	11.97	87525	471673	1054480
29.60	20.89	73450	248150	1033686
29.68	19.06	115870	390362	1386884
34.43	27.74	144108	418613	996986
37.59	22.66	143218	380958	1515133
53.14	38.14	102566	192994	815225
29.22	18.68	75794	259370	921908
16.04	8.60	83486	520582	869541
26.80	17.97	71490	266788	544852
32.50	14.46	88168	271272	921465
16.83	11.86	94804	563352	1156359
25.62	20.81	94984	370716	699401
32.55	20.44	72984	224214	916760
27.55	20.52	79963	290252	753152
32.09	23.26	108290	337503	892075
33.58	22.99	80517	239790	981307
23.73	18.24	73200	308425	696314
18.64	15.20	22400	120156	511375
28.07	18.25	113520	404443	1292848
34.79	23.53	148545	426955	1719005
16.27	10.78	74585	458456	830312
21.77	12.63	84679	388991	974973
47.95	46.26	146204	304886	1126401
26.93	17.65	42681	158506	529580
29.11	19.12	103424	355316	1181387
28.16	18.85	100656	357454	1159291
31.07	21.15	88524	284938	822637
27.19	16.78	65309	240221	921436
12.51	4.79	30048	240102	1038822

11-9 规模以上工业企业分行业主要经济分析指标（2011 年）
MAJOR ECONOMIC ANALYTICAL INDICATORS OF INDUSTRIAL ENTERPRISES ABOVE DESIGNATED SIZE BY SECTOR（2011）

指 标	Item	工业产品销售率（%） Sales Ratio of Industrial products	工业成本费用利润率（%） Ratio of Profits to Industrial Cost
非金属矿采选业	Nonmetal Minerals Mining and Dressing	99.90	12.78
农副食品加工业	Food Processing	98.00	2.82
食品制造业	Food Production	97.00	1.69
饮料制造业	Beverage Production	95.21	8.49
纺织业	Textile Industry	99.48	3.50
纺织服装、鞋、帽制造业	Textile, Garments, Shoes and Hat Processing	99.71	6.48
皮革、毛皮、羽毛（绒）及其制品业	Leather, Furs, Down and Related Products	95.82	6.07
木材加工及木、竹、藤、棕、草制品业	Timber Processing, Bamboo, Cane, Palm Fiber and Straw Products	97.98	3.00
家具制造业	Furniture Manufacturing	99.34	1.47
造纸及纸制品业	Papermaking and Paper Products	98.11	2.85
印刷业和记录媒介的复制	Printing and Record Medium Reproduction	99.81	3.33
文教体育用品制造业	Cultural, Educational and Sports Goods	97.68	5.87
石油加工、炼焦及核燃料加工业	Petroleum Processing, Coking and Nuclear Fuel Processing	100.66	1.46
化学原料及化学制品制造业	Raw Chemical Materials and Chemica Products	97.51	6.02
医药制造业	Medical and Pharmaceutical Products	95.20	10.62
化学纤维制造业	Chemical Fiber	98.13	4.56
橡胶制品业	Rubber Products	98.29	7.75
塑料制品业	Plastic Products	97.17	2.44
非金属矿物制品业	Nonmetal Mineral Products	99.41	8.50
黑色金属冶炼及压延加工业	Smelting and Pressing of Ferrous Metals	99.25	3.46
有色金属冶炼及压延加工业	Smelting and Pressing of Nonferrous Metals	99.61	3.27
金属制品业	Metal Products	99.45	5.16
通用设备制造业	General Equipment Manufacturing	98.21	6.04
专用设备制造业	For Special Purposes Equipment Manufacturing	99.65	9.03
交通运输设备制造业	Transport Equipment Manufacturing	99.13	7.95
电气机械及器材制造业	Electric Equipment and Machinery	99.16	6.63
通信设备、计算机及其他电子设备制造	Communication, Computer and Other Electronic Equipment	97.64	8.45
仪器仪表及文化、办公用机械制造业	Instruments, Meters, Cultural and Office Machinery	98.13	11.91
工艺品及其他制造业	Artcraft and Other Manufacturing	94.13	3.73
废弃资源和废旧材料回收加工业	Recycling and Disposal of Waste	87.70	1.39
电力、热力的生产和供应业	Production and Supply of Electric Power and Thermal Power	99.65	10.98
燃气生产和供应业	Production and Supply of Gas	100.00	24.19
水的生产和供应业	Production and Supply of Water	96.16	22.30

每百元固定资产原值实现利税（元） Profits and Taxes of Original Value of Fixed Assets Per One Hundred Yuan(yuan)	其 中 of which	平均每一从业人员（元） Per Person Employed （yuan）		
	# 利 润 Profits	实现利税 Profits and Taxes	占有固定资产原值 Original Value of Fixed Assets	实现工业总产值 Gross Industrial Output Value Achieved
23.73	11.23	310715	1309609	1294479
14.78	8.53	53813	364009	1171897
6.41	2.51	24985	389833	595688
38.52	13.30	96164	249631	494220
20.06	12.16	37451	186713	670676
49.42	35.08	30554	61831	360775
71.63	43.07	31689	44236	343968
48.59	25.36	53168	109418	976309
27.84	9.43	29895	107378	705084
15.63	7.49	40139	256767	713337
13.74	7.04	32851	239045	512149
29.40	19.91	39678	134965	498859
19.94	12.78	71049	356356	3160212
24.55	16.38	132319	538987	1581925
49.29	32.34	110709	224627	802757
21.32	12.58	51274	240537	712583
39.31	26.89	40938	104138	399698
17.16	7.62	30780	179320	585541
29.68	17.42	167394	563920	1236036
24.83	14.11	162559	654742	2790556
43.72	28.37	137775	315106	2842092
34.09	21.64	55564	162991	734636
25.88	17.40	51233	198001	619687
28.24	20.46	104865	371338	938138
29.61	20.48	79478	268458	734401
39.31	25.47	97380	247693	1034620
30.83	23.78	44972	145888	451414
53.96	38.97	104279	193244	718970
23.08	11.14	44422	192473	655078
32.84	6.99	185679	565485	2904723
9.67	6.99	274443	2838178	1944148
30.60	25.68	535270	1749138	2026316
4.54	3.53	106923	2357061	376838

11-10 规模以上民营工业企业主要经济分析指标（2011 年） MAJOR ECONOMIC ANALYTICAL INDICATORS OF PRIVATE INDUSTRIAL ENTERPRISES ABOVE DESIGNATED SIZE（2011）

指 标	Item	工业产品销售率（%）Sales Ratio of Industrial products	工业成本费用利润率（%）Ratio of Profits to Industrial Cost
总 计	**Total**	**98.69**	**5.42**
按地区分	**Grouped by Region**		
市 区	Urban Area	98.83	4.75
武进区	Wujin District	98.11	4.41
新北区	Xinbei District	97.18	5.17
天宁区	Tianning District	102.03	4.50
钟楼区	Zhonglou District	103.39	5.66
戚墅堰区	Qishuyan District	101.36	8.46
溧阳市	Liyang City	98.50	6.91
金坛市	Jintan City	97.69	9.46
按轻重工业分	**Grouped by Light and Heavy Industry**		
轻工业	Light Industry	98.40	4.17
重工业	Heavy Industry	98.75	5.69
按企业规模分	**Grouped by Size of Enterprises**		
大 型	Large-sized	99.04	5.52
中 型	Medium-sized	98.10	6.87
小 型	Small-sized	98.73	4.59
微 型	Micro-sized	97.35	1.77
按工业行业分	**Grouped by Sector**		
非金属矿采选业	Nonmetal Minerals Mining and Dressing	100.00	4.02
农副食品加工业	Food Processing	98.13	1.52
食品制造业	Food Production	99.34	4.73
饮料制造业	Beverage Production	97.26	11.20
纺织业	Textile Industry	99.24	1.89
纺织服装、鞋、帽制造业	Textile, Garments, Shoes and Hat Processing	99.98	4.58
皮革、毛皮、羽毛（绒）及其制品业	Leather, Furs, Down and Related Products	95.56	7.75

每百元固定资产原值实现利税（元）Profits and Taxes of Original Value of Fixed Assets Per One Hundred Yuan (yuan)	其中 of which	平均每一从业人员（元）Per Person Employed（yuan）		
	#利润 Profits	实现利税 Profits and Taxes	占有固定资产原值 Original Value of Fixed Assets	实现工业总产值 Gross Industrial Output Value Achieved
31.26	**19.81**	**72934**	**233347**	**914227**
27.08	17.01	63282	233706	889875
27.86	16.71	59528	213701	866031
20.76	14.31	60133	289706	875497
28.56	19.31	49302	172629	762288
30.82	19.65	114937	372892	1331099
42.53	33.02	89227	209799	786588
40.86	25.23	126318	309155	1219875
64.66	44.32	98629	152527	803534
26.27	15.61	36274	138102	551806
32.32	20.71	88343	273381	1066564
28.80	19.23	103280	358618	1326704
33.02	21.27	70890	214714	715700
32.58	19.43	58883	180736	823474
19.95	9.93	33740	169096	983207
166.67	34.28	122848	73709	640025
12.01	4.35	41941	349313	1038940
7.16	5.07	39089	545590	607461
41.25	13.78	90950	220501	319904
15.17	6.77	26056	171759	636042
32.57	21.91	22939	70441	358201
51.45	36.38	41808	81258	425362

11-10 续表 Continued

指 标	Item	工业产品销售率（%）Sales Ratio of Industrial products	工业成本费用利润率（%）Ratio of Profits to Industrial Cost
木材加工及木、竹、藤、棕、草制品业	Timber Processing, Bamboo, Cane, Palm Fiber and Straw Products	98.48	2.97
家具制造业	Furniture Manufacturing	99.23	1.72
造纸及纸制品业	Papermaking and Paper Products	96.93	1.91
印刷业和记录媒介的复制	Printing and Record Medium Reproduction	99.40	0.85
文教体育用品制造业	Cultural, Educational and Sports Goods	95.12	4.56
石油加工、炼焦及核燃料加工业	Petroleum Processing, Coking and Nuclear Fuel Processing	99.68	1.04
化学原料及化学制品制造业	Raw Chemical Materials and Chemica Products	97.94	5.70
医药制造业	Medical and Pharmaceutical Products	96.33	9.12
化学纤维制造业	Chemical Fiber	97.55	4.45
橡胶制品业	Rubber Products	99.64	7.08
塑料制品业	Plastic Products	97.09	2.82
非金属矿物制品业	Nonmetal Mineral Products	100.13	7.50
黑色金属冶炼及压延加工业	Smelting and Pressing of Ferrous Metals	98.97	3.24
有色金属冶炼及压延加工业	Smelting and Pressing of Nonferrous Metals	99.64	4.71
金属制品业	Metal Products	98.85	6.02
通用设备制造业	General Equipment Manufacturing	98.32	5.59
专用设备制造业	For Special Purposes Equipment Manufacturing	98.39	5.80
交通运输设备制造业	Transport Equipment Manufacturing	97.24	11.57
电气机械及器材制造业	Electric Equipment and Machinery	99.43	6.73
通信设备、计算机及其他电子设备制造	Communication, Computer and Other Electronic Equipment	98.32	5.57
仪器仪表及文化、办公用机械制造业	Instruments, Meters, Cultural and Office Machinery	98.43	7.94
工艺品及其他制造业	Artcraft and Other Manufacturing	95.13	5.14
废弃资源和废旧材料回收加工业	Recycling and Disposal of Waste	87.70	1.39
电力、热力的生产和供应业	Production and Supply of Electric Power and Thermal Power	98.16	5.30
燃气生产和供应业	Production and Supply of Gas	100.00	6.47
水的生产和供应业	Production and Supply of Water	100.00	13.02

每百元固定资产原值实现利税（元）Profits and Taxes of Original Value of Fixed Assets Per One Hundred Yuan(yuan)	其 中 of which	平均每一从业人员（元） Per Person Employed（yuan）		
	#利 润 Profits	实现利税 Profits and Taxes	占有固定资产原值 Original Value of Fixed Assets	实现工业总产值 Gross Industrial Output Value Achieved
38.62	22.30	41851	108370	865733
33.11	12.53	31731	95827	715656
18.93	7.29	29542	156030	631724
6.86	1.61	15593	227266	427404
33.88	20.75	33819	99818	503504
13.73	9.27	39229	285822	2515573
30.94	19.92	116642	377044	1417514
50.54	35.15	93288	184595	811832
26.22	14.36	48501	184948	645157
48.98	33.23	43767	89351	448768
20.61	10.44	30652	148749	570223
26.50	15.17	152052	573742	1215763
22.45	12.62	125917	560809	2269380
70.46	47.46	123192	174849	1856243
44.36	28.49	58830	132612	690394
26.57	17.54	47915	180332	612941
23.84	15.03	53626	224896	632817
49.56	35.05	95717	193126	673942
50.99	35.48	90255	177013	1013549
35.85	22.15	36218	101022	434821
41.09	26.11	64106	155999	570049
18.64	9.89	42938	230366	489759
32.84	6.99	185679	565485	2904723
5.34	4.25	77845	1457299	1216673
3.65	2.09	148418	4065025	1403369
5.79	5.79	134655	2323897	1175690

11-11 规模以上三资工业企业主要经济分析指标（2011 年）
MAJOR ECONOMIC ANALYTICAL INDICATORS OF FOREIGN-FUNDED INDUSTRIAL ENTERPRISES ABOVE DESIGNATED SIZE（2011）

指 标	Item	工业产品销售率（%） Sales Ratio of Industrial products	工业成本费用利润率（%） Ratio of Profits to Industrial Cost
总 计	**Total**	**98.79**	**7.01**
按地区分	**Grouped by Region**		
市 区	Urban Area	98.94	6.99
武进区	Wujin District	97.90	8.98
新北区	Xinbei District	97.59	6.30
天宁区	Tianning District	100.76	4.27
钟楼区	Zhonglou District	102.46	5.26
戚墅堰区	Qishuyan District	107.23	18.87
溧阳市	Liyang City	99.01	4.62
金坛市	Jintan City	96.96	12.02
按轻重工业分	**Grouped by Light and Heavy Industry**		
轻工业	Light Industry	98.49	7.01
重工业	Heavy Industry	98.87	7.00
按企业规模分	**Grouped by Size of Enterprises**		
大 型	Large-sized	98.20	6.69
中 型	Medium-sized	98.86	9.34
小 型	Small-sized	99.41	4.82
微 型	Micro-sized	95.58	-2.18
按工业行业分	**Grouped by Sector**		
非金属矿采选业	Nonmetal Minerals Mining and Dressing	100.00	14.00
农副食品加工业	Food Processing	97.62	7.15
食品制造业	Food Production	85.68	-2.67
饮料制造业	Beverage Production	93.92	6.56
纺织业	Textile Industry	100.98	3.77
纺织服装、鞋、帽制造业	Textile, Garments, Shoes and Hat Processing	99.40	8.17
皮革、毛皮、羽毛（绒）及其制品业	Leather, Furs, Down and Related Products	96.02	4.83

每百元固定资产原值实现利税（元）Profits and Taxes of Original Value of Fixed Assets Per One Hundred Yuan(yuan)	其中 of which	平均每一从业人员（元）Per Person Employed（yuan）		
	#利润 Profits	实现利税 Profits and Taxes	占有固定资产原值 Original Value of Fixed Assets	实现工业总产值 Gross Industrial Output Value Achieved
27.87	**19.12**	**97987**	**351585**	**1043029**
25.64	17.71	89424	348775	956791
32.86	24.61	60912	185387	564698
18.76	11.74	108413	577796	1177568
27.39	18.86	94357	344512	1566550
43.23	28.52	124675	288430	1624714
104.77	90.85	253850	242284	1277586
33.70	19.20	199261	591240	2638933
45.61	35.55	107783	236330	811107
25.82	17.94	46318	179400	502309
28.47	19.46	138928	488019	1471476
29.39	19.07	91388	310996	969722
30.99	22.36	115128	371449	986154
21.76	14.70	83189	382383	1232725
-4.03	-6.51	-21557	535021	1647144
22.37	11.15	390678	1746508	1585201
26.84	26.66	119522	445348	1907783
-0.62	-3.35	-1293	206951	275587
35.47	12.77	103937	293063	754122
24.43	15.64	47115	192851	826374
73.98	54.48	37379	50525	366660
107.51	54.96	26279	24443	300450

11-11 续表 Continued

指 标	Item	工业产品销售率（%） Sales Ratio of Industrial products	工业成本费用利润率（%） Ratio of Profits to Industrial Cost
木材加工及木、竹、藤、棕、草制品业	Timber Processing, Bamboo, Cane, Palm Fiber and Straw Products	96.54	3.64
家具制造业	Furniture Manufacturing	100.00	
造纸及纸制品业	Papermaking and Paper Products	100.39	4.68
印刷业和记录媒介的复制	Printing and Record Medium Reproduction	99.73	8.03
文教体育用品制造业	Cultural, Educational and Sports Goods	99.66	6.85
石油加工、炼焦及核燃料加工业	Petroleum Processing, Coking and Nuclear Fuel Processing	102.67	2.39
化学原料及化学制品制造业	Raw Chemical Materials and Chemica Products	96.41	6.66
医药制造业	Medical and Pharmaceutical Products	93.34	10.34
化学纤维制造业	Chemical Fiber	99.66	4.86
橡胶制品业	Rubber Products	96.27	8.85
塑料制品业	Plastic Products	97.35	1.58
非金属矿物制品业	Nonmetal Mineral Products	94.58	15.49
黑色金属冶炼及压延加工业	Smelting and Pressing of Ferrous Metals	99.86	3.96
有色金属冶炼及压延加工业	Smelting and Pressing of Nonferrous Metals	99.84	1.63
金属制品业	Metal Products	101.28	2.40
通用设备制造业	General Equipment Manufacturing	97.88	8.30
专用设备制造业	For Special Purposes Equipment Manufacturing	100.80	12.34
交通运输设备制造业	Transport Equipment Manufacturing	101.92	3.75
电气机械及器材制造业	Electric Equipment and Machinery	98.47	6.71
通信设备、计算机及其他电子设备制造	Communication, Computer and Other Electronic Equipment	97.39	9.40
仪器仪表及文化、办公用机械制造业	Instruments, Meters, Cultural and Office Machinery	97.85	16.01
工艺品及其他制造业	Artcraft and Other Manufacturing	93.09	2.15
电力、热力的生产和供应业	Production and Supply of Electric Power and Thermal Power	98.60	10.15
燃气生产和供应业	Production and Supply of Gas	100.00	26.62
水的生产和供应业	Production and Supply of Water	94.92	28.21

每百元固定资产原值实现利税（元）Profits and Taxes of Original Value of Fixed Assets Per One Hundred Yuan (yuan)	其中 of which	平均每一从业人员（元） Per Person Employed（yuan）		
	#利润 Profits	实现利税 Profits and Taxes	占有固定资产原值 Original Value of Fixed Assets	实现工业总产值 Gross Industrial Output Value Achieved
82.42	36.61	95078	115354	1226569
11.79		20000	169600	648133
12.90	7.66	71047	550566	951363
43.65	30.18	93434	214075	842149
27.29	19.52	44147	161773	495316
32.91	20.11	242012	735320	6623716
17.01	12.23	189900	1116156	2226423
37.99	21.01	128802	339029	829028
13.47	9.74	62366	462892	982289
31.07	21.49	37668	121228	342984
12.33	3.66	31085	252018	621968
73.34	46.28	285641	389455	1403952
30.93	17.93	355736	1149967	5538239
20.97	12.01	216922	1034520	7801951
11.83	7.45	39988	338028	1045935
23.08	16.85	66730	289155	646988
33.19	26.03	232516	700550	1692624
14.93	9.29	44443	297656	740793
32.30	19.16	110776	342965	1068113
28.55	23.33	46540	163029	453383
67.03	52.03	171349	255643	966383
43.31	16.82	47651	110021	1014799
7.11	4.39	161700	2273943	1065030
48.31	41.18	614858	1272683	2154477
4.54	3.63	157103	3462501	449749

11-12 大中型工业企业主要经济分析指标（2011 年）
MAIN ECONOMIC ANALYTICAL INDICATORS OF LARGE AND MEDIUM-SIZED INDUSTRIAL ENTERPRISES（2011）

指 标	Item	工业产品销售率（%）Sales Ratio of Industrial products	工业成本费用利润率（%）Ratio of Profits to Industrial Cost
总 计	**Total**	**98.64**	**6.97**
按地区分	**Grouped by Region**		
市 区	Urban Area	98.75	6.64
#武进区	Wujin District	98.13	6.00
溧阳市	Liyang City	98.74	6.71
金坛市	Jintan City	97.32	11.14
按登记注册类型分	**Grouped by Registration Status**		
内 资	Domestic Investment	98.71	6.35
国 有	State-owned	100.94	5.09
集 体	Collective-owned	100.11	2.37
股份合作	Share-holding Cooperative	99.11	4.49
有限责任公司	Limited Liability Corporations	98.63	6.63
股份有限公司	Share-holding Corporations Ltd.	99.18	11.32
私 营	Private	98.60	6.09
港澳台商投资	Investment from Hong Kong, Macao and Taiwan	97.37	10.20
合资经营	Joint-Venture	98.86	11.75
合作经营	Cooperative	103.03	6.02
独资经营	Sole Investment	94.71	10.49
股份有限公司	Share-holding Corporations Ltd.	98.91	3.93
外商投资	Foreign Investment	99.17	6.84
中外合资经营	Joint Ventures	100.14	7.26
中外合作经营	Cooperative Enterprises	99.65	1.75
外商独资	Sole Foreign Investment	97.51	5.51
股份有限公司	Share-holding Corporations Ltd.	100.18	13.83
按轻重工业分	**Grouped by Light and Heavy Industry**		
轻工业	Light Industry	97.84	7.48
重工业	Heavy Industry	98.80	6.87
按企业规模分	**Grouped by Size of Enterprises**		
大 型	Large-sized	98.77	6.22
中 型	Medium-sized	98.47	7.97

每百元固定资产原值实现利税（元） Profits and Taxes of Original Value of Fixed Assets Per One Hundred Yuan (yuan)	其 中 of which	平均每一从业人员（元） Per Person Employed（yuan）		
	#利 润 Profits	实现利税 Profits and Taxes	占有固定资产原值 Original Value of Fixed Assets	实现工业总产值 Gross Industrial Output Value Achieved
29.50	**19.91**	**94362**	**319832**	**984633**
26.89	18.21	84238	313239	922790
31.05	20.77	72587	233794	875934
39.36	24.70	184961	469886	1859902
41.77	30.53	103129	246919	760307
28.97	19.25	88785	306434	988938
16.08	8.65	83523	519436	864984
30.60	7.37	32889	107469	309198
30.86	13.49	100931	327073	1039526
18.42	13.64	91927	499027	1098029
24.36	19.78	90540	371608	682352
32.51	21.24	88297	271619	1011871
33.15	25.33	84612	255220	712373
36.48	27.15	128505	352244	916397
37.38	29.13	61770	165236	830896
31.03	24.37	74302	239445	632642
20.33	17.15	20225	99497	471657
28.60	18.29	120578	421581	1227717
33.56	22.84	164873	491251	1677393
24.27	12.97	13740	56602	449998
21.87	11.52	83637	382445	876304
54.66	52.99	155901	285234	1182049
29.24	20.36	43771	149691	448194
29.56	19.82	123336	417277	1291867
28.16	18.85	100656	357454	1159291
31.07	21.15	88524	284938	822637

11-13 规模以上工业企业资本金构成（2011 年）
CAPITAL CONDITION OF INDUSTRIAL ENTERPRISES ABOVE DESIGNATED SIZE（2011）

指 标	Item	实收资本合计 Total Paid-up Capital
总 计	**Total**	**10978113**
按地区分	**Grouped by Region**	
市 区	Urban Area	9110203
武进区	Wujin District	4013165
新北区	Xinbei District	3263954
天宁区	Tianning District	716020
钟楼区	Zhonglou District	630080
戚墅堰区	Qishuyan District	486984
溧阳市	Liyang City	1167939
金坛市	Jintan City	699971
按登记注册类型分	**Grouped by Registration Status**	
内 资	Domestic Investment	6375316
国 有	State-owned	283091
集 体	Collective-owned	4926
股份合作	Share-holding Cooperative	62837
有限责任公司	Limited Liability Corporations	712781
股份有限公司	Share-holding Corporations Ltd.	417417
私 营	Private	4881156
港澳台商投资	Investment from Hong Kong, Macao and Taiwan	1593019
合资经营	Joint-Venture	621107
合作经营	Cooperative	20911
独资经营	Sole Investment	812135
股份有限公司	Share-holding Corporations Ltd.	138867
外商投资	Foreign Investment	3009777
中外合资经营	Joint Ventures	886524
中外合作经营	Cooperative Enterprises	55224
外商独资	Sole Foreign Investment	1999123
股份有限公司	Share-holding Corporations Ltd.	68907
按轻重工业分	**Grouped by Light and Heavy Industry**	
轻工业	Light Industry	2223924
重工业	Heavy Industry	8754188
按企业规模分	**Grouped by Size of Enterprises**	
大 型	Large-sized	3120238
中 型	Medium-sized	3223213
小 型	Small-sized	4560445
微 型	Micro-sized	74216

单位：万元（10000 yuan）

国家资本 National Capital	法人资本 Capital of Legal Person	集体资本 Collective-owned Capital	个人资本 Individual Capital	港澳台资本 Captial of Hongkong, Macao and Taiwan	外商资本 Foreign Capital
391562	**94300**	**3285900**	**3520264**	**1136383**	**2549704**
371562	74704	2635416	2724320	961215	2342987
10261	32229	1377858	1714449	467664	410705
30387	19462	692284	467373	371410	1683037
80024	9941	203961	218798	79753	123542
121798	4966	152032	247974	34626	68684
129092	8105	209280	75726	7761	57020
13000	13684	364528	551981	83949	140797
7000	5912	285956	243963	91219	65920
350224	67054	2434166	3356934	64236	102702
55530	2000	215562	10000		
	3838	1088			
	1385	25107	35466	282	598
196026	14092	419500	42527	23212	17425
91945	4069	138170	150098	10125	23011
4925	41670	1623432	3118843	30618	61669
15750	18116	366801	118714	1008410	65229
15750	12233	253185	108022	198694	33224
	5883	65489	1136	730510	9117
25588	9131	484933	44616	63737	2381773
25159	4235	344036	39920	40882	432292
	4467	31997	3410	33	15316
429	429	67332	1285	18175	1911474
93353	43160	505943	665521	374207	541740
298209	51140	2779957	2854743	762176	2007964
214697	20292	1171261	782180	265744	666064
130746	36222	905684	869391	431900	849271
45519	37786	1156378	1850965	438589	1031209
600		52577	17729	150	3160

11-14 规模以上工业企业分行业资本金构成（2011 年）
CAPITAL COMPOSITION OF INDUSTRIAL ENTERPRISES ABOVE DESIGNATED SIZE BY SECTOR（2011）

指 标	Item	实收资本合计 Total Paid-up Capital
非金属矿采选业	Nonmetal Minerals Mining and Dressing	10557
农副食品加工业	Food Processing	35211
食品制造业	Food Production	42266
饮料制造业	Beverage Production	40804
纺织业	Textile Industry	480868
纺织服装、鞋、帽制造业	Textile, Garments, Shoes and Hat Processing	198956
皮革、毛皮、羽毛（绒）及其制品业	Leather, Furs, Down and Related Products	13859
木材加工及木、竹、藤、棕、草制品业	Timber Processing, Bamboo, Cane, Palm Fiber and Straw Products	42652
家具制造业	Furniture Manufacturing	17675
造纸及纸制品业	Papermaking and Paper Products	57147
印刷业和记录媒介的复制	Printing and Record Medium Reproduction	30188
文教体育用品制造业	Cultural, Educational and Sports Goods	32691
石油加工、炼焦及核燃料加工业	Petroleum Processing, Coking and Nuclear Fuel Processing	27479
化学原料及化学制品制造业	Raw Chemical Materials and Chemica Products	1711233
医药制造业	Medical and Pharmaceutical Products	156698
化学纤维制造业	Chemical Fiber	64628
橡胶制品业	Rubber Products	59942
塑料制品业	Plastic Products	123536
非金属矿物制品业	Nonmetal Mineral Products	684360
黑色金属冶炼及压延加工业	Smelting and Pressing of Ferrous Metals	519698
有色金属冶炼及压延加工业	Smelting and Pressing of Nonferrous Metals	268641
金属制品业	Metal Products	381924
通用设备制造业	General Equipment Manufacturing	741329
专用设备制造业	For Special Purposes Equipment Manufacturing	1155595
交通运输设备制造业	Transport Equipment Manufacturing	913145
电气机械及器材制造业	Electric Equipment and Machinery	1842404
通信设备、计算机及其他电子设备制造	Communication, Computer and Other Electronic Equipment	604725
仪器仪表及文化、办公用机械制造业	Instruments, Meters, Cultural and Office Machinery	301405
工艺品及其他制造业	Artcraft and Other Manufacturing	41447
废弃资源和废旧材料回收加工业	Recycling and Disposal of Waste	7658
电力、热力的生产和供应业	Production and Supply of Electric Power and Thermal Power	277214
燃气生产和供应业	Production and Supply of Gas	27316
水的生产和供应业	Production and Supply of Water	64865

单位：万元（10000 yuan）

国家资本 National Capital	法人资本 Capital of Legal Person	集体资本 Collective-owned Capital	个人资本 Individual Capital	港澳台资本 Captial of Hongkong, Macao and Taiwan	外商资本 Foreign Capital
		500	10057		
	35	2550	25796	6831	
600		2818	20568		18280
	6400	9600	800		24004
55166	14547	76780	187581	96744	50050
109	6283	63641	66505	41632	20786
		3407	4640		5812
980		3000	34440	30	4203
			10562		7113
	200	17412	10136	16498	12902
3193	7166	3460	13749	2579	41
	2877	4168	14770	1639	9238
		840	10553	1249	14836
25977	3067	690574	386685	326174	278756
		53352	63094	11613	28638
	158	11680	30457	6953	15381
862	96	9828	20134	7100	21922
300	1164	35521	34809	16637	35105
20446	2604	214455	371116	11526	64212
	100	127357	339391	43835	9014
3619	900	67461	67730	3946	124986
	6193	86774	137394	11429	140134
17994	4976	196692	330268	22381	169018
65487	729	305872	289169	99762	394577
131800	6072	337230	200761	20113	217169
25356	8281	479314	558229	114055	657171
2885	5000	130573	108576	233582	124109
508	409	107265	125959	8747	58516
		6741	14546	154	20006
		6200	1458		
280	14795	213749	20112	16477	11801
8300		496	10220		8300
27700	2250	16590		14700	3625

11-15 规模以上工业主要产品产量（2011 年）
OUTPUT OF INDUSTRIAL ENTERPRISES ABOVE DESIGNATED SIZE（2011）

产品名称	Name of Products	全 市 Whole Municipality	其中 of which #市 区 Urban Area
原 盐（吨）	Crude Salt (ton)	2940086	
大 米（吨）	Grain (ton)	27104	
饲 料（吨）	Feedign Stuff (ton)	398426	59582
精制食用植物油（吨）	Purified Edible Vegetable Oil (ton)	6096	6096
饮料酒（千升）	Drinks (kilolitre)	409567	231118
#啤 酒	Beer	409567	231118
纱（万吨）	Yarn (10000 tons)	16	13
#棉 纱	Cotton Yarn	13	11
布（万米）	Cloth (10000 m)	96417	88885
#棉 布	Cotton Cloth	74927	74392
#牛仔布	Jean	19814	19814
印染布（万米）	Printing and Dyeing Cloth (10000 m)	27291	27291
服 装（万件）	Garment (10000 units)	39681	20839
复合木地板（万平方米）	Laminate Flooring (10000 m²)	10077	10077
纸制品（吨）	Paper Products (ton)	119814	107874
润滑油（吨）	Lubricants (ton)	246920	246920
硫 酸（折100%,吨）	Sulfuric Acid (100%, ton)	229380	229380
盐酸（含量31%以上,吨）	Hydrochloric Acid (content above 31%, ton)	96150	31089
烧碱（折100%,吨）	Caustic Soda (100%, ton)	250090	102241
化学农药原药（折有效成份100%，吨）	Chemical pesticide (Converted into effective components 100%,ton)	86023	33526

11-15 续表 1 Continued 1

产品名称	Name of Products	全 市 Whole Municipality	其中 of which #市 区 Urban Area
涂 料（吨）	Coating (ton)	188447	184393
初级形态的塑料（吨）	Primary-form Plastic (ton)	981539	981539
化学药品原药（吨）	Chemical Pesticide (ton)	1430	1430
化学纤维（吨）	Chemical Fiber (ton)	96872	66019
钢化玻璃（平方米）	Tempered Glass (square meter)	506453	506453
水泥熟料（万吨）	Cement Clinker (10000 tons)	1518	
水 泥（万吨）	Cement (10000 tons)	2337	114
生 铁（万吨）	Pig Iron (10000 tons)	816	609
粗 钢（万吨）	Raw Steel (10000 tons)	1004	803
钢 材（万吨）	Rolled-Steel (10000 tons)	1176	867
铁合金（万吨）	Ferroalloy (10000 tons)	11	11
单晶硅（吨）	Monocrystalline silicon (ton)	735107	
多晶硅（吨）	Polysilicon (ton)	93404	93404
金属集装箱（万立方米）	Metal Container (10000 m³)	595	595
金属切削机床（台）	Metal-Cutting Machine Tool (unit)	1377	1377
滚动轴承（万套）	Rolling Axle Bearing (10000 sets)	47688	42184
电动手提式工具（台）	Portable Electric Tools (set)	12600246	12397080
衡 器（秤,台）	Weighing Apparatus (set)	350852	350852
减速机（台）	Reducer (set)	534954	534954
挖掘机（台）	Mechanical Excavator(set)	16343	16343
装载机（台）	Shovel Loader (set)	5812	5812
金属冶炼设备（吨）	Melting Equipment (ton)	14997	14997

11-15 续表 2 Continued 2

产品名称	Name of Products	全 市 Whole Municipality	其中 of which #市 区 Urban Area
金属轧制设备（吨）	Metal Rolling Equipment (ton)	29599	29599
大中型拖拉机（台）	Large and Medium Size Tractor (set)	70162	70162
小型拖拉机（台）	Mini-tractors (unit)	106805	106805
铁路机车（辆）	Locomotive (unit)	218	218
汽 车（辆）	Motor Vehicles (City Buses,unit)	1190	1190
摩托车整车（万辆）	Finished Motorcycle(10000 units)	20	20
两轮脚踏自行车（万辆）	Bicycles (10000 units)	254	254
电动自行车（万辆）	Electric Bicycle (10000 units)	20	20
民用钢质船舶（载重吨）	Civil Steel Ship (deadweight tons) (DWT))	3542	
风力发电机组（千瓦）	Wind Turbine (kW)	55279	55279
交流电动机（千瓦）	AC Machine (kw)	520502	520502
变压器（兆伏安）	Transformer (MVA)	129528	62969
通信电缆（对千米）	Telecommunications Cable (pair,km)	133986	133986
电力电缆（千米）	Electric Cable (1000 m)	290429	139746
原电池（折R20 标准万只）	Primary battery (converted into R20 standard (10000 units)	63436	24552
太阳能电池（兆瓦）	Solar Cell (megawatt)	2017	1824
房间空气调节器（台）	Air Conditioners (unit)	146769	146769
GPS接收机（台）	GPS Receiver (unit)	87865	87865
半导体分立器件（万只）	Semiconduction Separating Part (10000 units)	1516074	1516074
彩色电视机（台）	Color TV Sets (unit)	291192	291192
激光视盘机（台）	Video-CD Players (unit)	428925	428925
光学仪器（台）	Optical Instruments (unit)	275680	275680
发电量（万千瓦时）	Power Generation (10000 kw.h)	1561584	1421924

12

CHAPTER 12

建筑业

CONSTRUCTION

常州统计年鉴

12 建 筑 业 CONSTRUCTION

2011 年主要统计指标
MAJOR STATISTICAL INDICATORS OF 2011

年底建筑业企业数（含劳务企业）	Number of Construction Enterprises (Including Labor Services Enterprises)	668 个	(unit)
# 施工总承包企业数	Number of Construction Contracting Enterprises	577 个	(unit)
建筑业企业总产值（含劳务企业）	Construction Enterprises Output Value (Including Labor Service Enterprises)	899.64 亿元	(100 million yuan)
比上年增长	Over the Previous Year	20.6%	
房屋建筑施工面积	Floor Space of Buildings Under Construction	7657.15 万平方米	(10000 sq.m)
比上年增长	Over the Previous Year	23.8%	
房屋建筑竣工面积	Floor Space of Buildings Completed	2831.52 万平方米	(10000 sq.m)
比上年增长	Over the Previous Year	6.5%	
计算劳动生产率的平均人数	Average Empolyees of Construction Indusry	360787 人	(person)
比上年增长	Over the Previous Year	13.0%	

12-1　分地区建筑业企业生产情况（2011 年）
STATISTICS ON CONSTRUCTION ENTERPRISES BY REGION（2011）

指　标	Item	全　市 Whole Municipality	其中 of which 市　区 Urban Area	溧阳市 Liyang City	金坛市 JintanCity
企业个数（不含劳务企业，个）	Number of Enterprises (Excluding Labor Enterprises, unit)	577	429	85	63
建筑业总产值（万元）	Gross Output Value of Construction (10000 yuan)	8838698	4007898	3533204	1297597
#装饰装修产值	Output of Decoration and Fitment	654206	571468	49525	33213
在外省完成的产值	Output Achieved out of Jiangsu Province	2187251	445470	1360602	381179
按构成分	Grouped by Use of funds				
建筑工程	Construction Projects	7816112	3713433	2824783	1277896
安装工程	Installation Projects	918985	238048	672508	8429
其它产值	Other Output Value	103601	56416	35912	11273
竣工产值（万元）	Output Value of Buildings Completed (10000 yuan)	675715	297790	266968	110957
房屋建筑施工面积（万平方米）	Floor Space of Buildings Under Construction (10000 sq.m)	7657.15	3784 .44	2600.73	1271.99
房屋建筑竣工面积（万平方米）	Floor Space of Buildings Completed (10000 sq.m)	2831.52	1216.01	931.81	683.69
#住　宅	Residential Buildings	1626.30	709.08	477.72	439.49
自有施工机械设备年末净值（万元）	Net Value of Existing Machinery and Equipment at Year-end (10000yuan)	282326	143048	108051	31228
自有机械设备年底总台数（台）	Number of Machinery and Equipment at Year-end (unit)	85334	27868	46013	11453
自有施工机械设备年底总功率（千瓦）	Total Power of Existing Machinery and Equipment (kw)	1672686	823478	650333	198875
平均从业人员（人）	Average Number of Staff of Calculating Labor Productivity (person)	415059	217833	147823	49403
计算建筑业劳动生产率的平均人数（人）	The Average Number of People for Calculation of the Labour Productivity in Construction Industry (person)	360787	190112	121842	48833

12-2 分行业建筑业企业生产情况（2011 年）
STATISTICS ON CONSTRUCTION ENTERPRISES BY SECTOR（2011）

指 标	Item	合 计 Total	房屋和土木工程建筑业 Building and Civil Engineering	建筑安装业 Installation	建筑装饰业 Decoration	其他建筑业 Others
企业个数（不含劳务企业，个）	Number of Enterprises (Excluding Labor Enterprises, unit)	577	296	79	143	59
建筑业总产值（万元）	Gross Output Value of Construction (10000 yuan)	8838698	7096411	973797	602844	165646
#装饰装修产值	Output of Decoration and Fitment	654206	76739	32742	541706	3019
在外省完成的产值	Output Achieved out of Jiangsu Province	2187251	1498811	487877	165597	34966
按构成分	Grouped by Use of funds					
建筑工程	Construction Projects	7816112	6845880	243352	596509	130372
安装工程	Installation Projects	918985	171001	723513	3779	20692
其它产值	Other Output Value	103601	79530	6932	2556	14583
竣工产值（万元）	Output Value of Buildings Completed (10000 yuan)	675715	520340	94512	45867	14996
房屋建筑施工面积（万平方米）	Floor Space of Buildings Under Construction (10000 sq.m)	7657.15	7559.49	92.99	4.67	
房屋建筑竣工面积（万平方米）	Floor Space of Buildings Completed (10000 sq.m)	2831.52	2795.80	35.72		
#住 宅	Residential Buildings	1626.30	1621.92	4.38		
自有施工机械设备年末净值（万元）	Net Value of Existing Machinery and Equipment at Year-end (10000yuan)	282326	241024	20313	13742	7247
自有机械设备年底总台数（台）	Number of Machinery and Equipment at Year-end (unit)	85334	63753	16116	4256	1209
自有施工机械设备年底总功率（千瓦）	Total Power of Existing Machinery and Equipment (kw)	1672686	1387229	193569	65102	26786
平均从业人员（人）	Average Number of Staff of Calculating Labor Productivity (person)	415059	333909	38611	36069	6470
计算建筑业劳动生产率的平均人数（人）	The Average Number of People for Calculation of the Labour Productivity in Construction Industry (person)	360787	289600	34877	28952	7358

12-3 分登记注册类型建筑业企业生产情况（2011 年）
STATISTICS ON CONSTRUCTION ENTERPRISES BY REGISTER STATUS（2011）

指 标	Item	合 计 Total	内资企业 Domestic Funded Enterprises
企业个数（不含劳务企业，个）	Number of Enterprises (Excluding Labor Enterprises, unit)	577	568
建筑业总产值（万元）	Gross Output Value of Construction (10000 yuan)	8838698	8787647
#装饰装修产值	Output of Decoration and Fitment	654206	632114
在外省完成的产值	Output Achieved out of Jiangsu Province	2187251	2169610
按构成分	**Grouped by Use of funds**		
建筑工程	Construction Projects	7816112	7773439
安装工程	Installation Projects	918985	910607
其它产值	Other Output Value	103601	103601
竣工产值（万元）	Output Value of Buildings Completed (10000 yuan)	675715	671777
房屋建筑施工面积（万平方米）	Floor Space of Buildings Under Construction (10000 sq.m)	7657.15	7640.14
房屋建筑竣工面积（万平方米）	Floor Space of Buildings Completed (10000 sq.m)	2831.52	2831.52
#住 宅	Residential Buildings	1626.30	1626.30
自有施工机械设备年末净值（万元）	Net Value of Existing Machinery and Equipment at Year-end(10000 yuan)	282326	280302
自有机械设备年底总台数（台）	Number of Machinery and Equipment at Year-end (unit)	85334	84581
自有施工机械设备年底总功率（千瓦）	Total Power of Existing Machinery and Equipment (kw)	1672686	1660806
平均从业人员（人）	Average Number of Staff of Calculating Labor Productivity (person)	415059	413181
计算建筑业劳动生产率的平均人数（人）	The Average Number of People for Calculation of the Labour Productivity in Construction Industry (person)	360787	358501

其中 of which					港澳台投资企业 Enterprises With Investment From HongKong, Macao and Taiwan
国有企业 State-owned Enterprises	集体企业 Collective-owned Enterprises	有限责任公司 Limited Liability Corporations	股份有限公司 Share-holding Corporations Ltd	私营企业 Private Enterprises	
7	3	55	4	499	9
77894	6376	1228736	24232	7450409	51051
	156	86792		545166	22092
8264		127544	3773	2030029	17642
77177	6376	1066968	24232	6598685	42673
716		143598		766293	8378
		18170		85432	
6310	693	93308	2147	569320	3938
9.76		1186.88		6443.50	17.01
0.61		405.43		2425.48	
		220.57		1405.72	
3526	1411	15958	5172	254234	2025
753	72	8217	255	75284	753
24845	4120	127147	19511	1485183	11880
3383	361	71564	776	337097	1878
3201	273	49016	976	305035	2286

12-4　分资质等级建筑业企业生产情况（2011 年）
STATISTICS ON CONSTRUCTION ENTERPRISES BY GRADE（2011）

指　标	Item	总　计 Total
企业个数（不含劳务企业，个）	Number of Enterprises (Excluding Labor Enterprises, unit)	577
建筑业总产值（万元）	Gross Output Value of Construction (10000 yuan)	8838698
# 装饰装修产值	Output of Decoration and Fitment	6542058
在外省完成的产值	Output Achieved out of Jiangsu Province	2187251
按构成分	**Grouped by Use of funds**	
建筑工程	Construction Projects	7816112
安装工程	Installation Projects	918985
其它产值	Other Output Value	103601
竣工产值（万元）	Output Value of Buildings Completed (10000 yuan)	6757153
房屋建筑施工面积（万平方米）	Floor Space of Buildings Under Construction (10000 sq.m)	7657.15
房屋建筑竣工面积（万平方米）	Floor Space of Buildings Completed (10000 sq.m)	2831.52
# 住　宅	Residential Buildings	1626.30
自有施工机械设备年末净值（万元）	Net Value of Existing Machinery and Equipment at Year-end (10000 yuan)	282326
自有机械设备年底总台数（台）	Number of Machinery and Equipment at Year-end (unit)	85334
自有施工机械设备年底总功率（千瓦）	Total Power of Existing Machinery and Equipment (kw)	1672686
平均从业人员（人）	Average Number of Staff of Calculating Labor Productivity (person)	415059
计算建筑业劳动生产率的平均人数（人）	The Average Number of People for Calculation of the Labour Productivity in Construction Industry (person)	360787

施工总承包 Contracted Construction	其中 of which 一级 First Grade	二级 Second Grade	三级及以下 Under Third Grade	专业承包 Professional Contracting	其中 of which 一级 First Grade	二级 Second Grade	三级及以下 Under Third Grade
257	28	93	136	320	28	83	209
7581640	3347860	3032996	1200785	1257058	513085	360800	383173
760035	500586	183984	75465	5782023	3728311	1306379	747333
1774110	943014	716572	114524	413141	212633	97028	103480
6811714	2779644	2923941	1108128	1004398	471988	226819	305591
687489	528673	73701	85114	231496	41097	120111	70289
82438	39543	35353	7542	21164		13871	7293
5742914	2510198	2182111	1050605	1014238	390823	312457	310959
7497.30	3263.27	3128.73	1105.30	159.85		12.90	146.95
2749.81	1069.95	1113.07	566.78	81.71		12.90	68.81
1603.41	644.28	679.92	279.21	22.89			22.89
228724	59704	96342	72679	53602	12981	16084	24538
69203	23593	34404	11206	16131	4717	5932	5482
1455774	537688	603516	314570	216912	72398	52661	91853
346444	136573	151616	58255	68615	34104	15392	19119
298571	110192	131863	56516	62216	23358	18248	20610

12-5 分地区建筑业企业财务状况（2011 年）
FINANCIAL CONDITIONS OF CONSTRUCTION ENTERPRISES BY REGION（2011）

单位：万元（10000 yuan）

指标	Item	全市 Whole Municipality	其中 of which 市区 Urban Area	溧阳市 Liyang City	金坛市 JintanCity
年末资产负债	**Asset and Liabilities at Year-end**				
年初存货	Opening Stock	1135426	767929	171396	196101
流动资产	Current Assets	5331403	3838752	923989	568662
固定资产	Fixed Assets	547664	314819	166474	66371
固定资产原价	Original Value of Fixed Assets	802679	501096	203550	98033
累计折旧	Accumulative Total Depreciation	312750	208741	63158	40851
#本年折旧	Depreciation Within the Year	51247	34826	8815	7606
在建工程	Projects Under Construction	42392	15349	21913	5130
资产合计	Total Assets	6249958	4355555	1174796	719607
流动负债	Liquid Liabilities	3856813	2811065	620169	425580
长期负债	Long-term Liabilities	117962	106051	8021	3890
负债合计	Total Liabilities	3974775	2917116	628189	429470
所有者权益	Owners' Equity	2275183	1438440	546606	290138
损益及分配	**Expenditure,Income and Distribution**				
营业收入	Business Income	7517227	3793505	2826841	896882
营业税金及附加	Business Tax and Surcharges	255151	123702	100455	30995
其他业务利润	Other Business Profit	14325	13520	359	446
管理费用	Management and Financial Expenditures	201479	126991	53833	20654
财务费用	Financial Costs	63952	44392	14195	5365
营业利润	Operating Surplus	323705	178033	108446	37225
利润总额	Total Profits	327447	180997	109280	37169
补充资料	**Supplementary Material**				
应付职工薪酬	Remuneration Payable to Employees	1191317	499830	544595	146892
应收工程款	Project Fund Payable	1379204	1029630	210669	138905
#竣工工程款	Completed Project Fund	707817	473706	133165	100946

注：本表统计范围不含劳务企业。
Note: The statistical rang of this table doesn't including Labour Service Enterprises.

12-6 分行业建筑业企业财务状况（2011 年）
FINANCIAL CONDITIONS OF CONSTRUCTION ENTERPRISES BY SECTOR（2011）

单位：万元（10000 yuan）

指 标	Item	合 计 Total	房屋和土木工程建筑业 Building and Civil Engineering	建 筑 安装业 Installation	建 筑 装饰业 Decoration	其 他 建筑业 Others
年末资产负债	**Asset and Liabilities at Year-end**					
年初存货	Opening Stock	1135426	949054	73268	86769	26335
流动资产	Current Assets	5331403	4241294	534283	446650	109176
固定资产	Fixed Assets	547664	443729	40696	41118	22120
固定资产原价	Original Value of Fixed Assets	802679	654674	55675	59725	32604
累计折旧	Accumulative Total Depreciation	312750	255495	20192	24609	12454
#本年折旧	Depreciation Within the Year	51247	39980	3547	4314	3406
在建工程	Projects Under Construction	42392	33840	2625	5611	316
资产合计	Total Assets	6249958	4964389	622241	513822	149506
流动负债	Liquid Liabilities	3856813	3033898	414805	335392	72719
长期负债	Long-term Liabilities	117962	110566	4182	1651	1563
负债合计	Total Liabilities	3974775	3144463	418987	337043	74282
所有者权益	Owners' Equity	2275183	1819926	203255	176779	75224
损益及分配	**Expenditure,Income and Distribution**					
营业收入	Business Income	7517227	5944439	875354	508774	188661
营业税金及附加	Business Tax and Surcharges	255151	202145	30172	17384	5450
其他业务利润	Other Business Profit	14325	8571	1180	4275	300
管理费用	Management and Financial Expenditures	201479	139290	30227	25284	6678
财务费用	Financial Costs	63952	57219	2206	3897	630
营业利润	Operating Surplus	323705	229371	52194	25988	16153
利润总额	Total Profits	327447	230220	52985	26954	17288
补充资料	**Supplementary Material**					
应付职工薪酬	Remuneration Payable to Employees	1191317	976689	131255	68019	15354
应收工程款	Project Fund Payable	1379204	1085021	147343	115056	31784
#竣工工程款	Completed Project Fund	707817	575446	64110	55307	12954

注：本表统计范围不含劳务企业。
Note： The statistical rang of this table doesn't including Labour Service Enterprises.

12-7 分登记注册类型建筑业企业财务状况（2011 年）
FINANCIAL CONDITIONS OF CONSTRUCTION ENTERPRISES BY REGISTER STATUS（2011）

指 标	Item	合 计 Total	内资企业 Domestic Funded Enterprises
年末资产负债	**Asset and Liabilities at Year-end**		
年初存货	Opening Stock	1135426	1129918
流动资产	Current Assets	5331403	5274071
固定资产	Fixed Assets	547664	538983
固定资产原价	Original Value of Fixed Assets	802679	792515
累计折旧	Accumulative Total Depreciation	312750	309892
# 本年折旧	Depreciation Within the Year	51247	50836
在建工程	Projects Under Construction	42392	41106
资产合计	Total Assets	6249958	6178607
流动负债	Liquid Liabilities	3856813	3826013
长期负债	Long-term Liabilities	117962	117962
负债合计	Total Liabilities	3974775	3943974
所有者权益	Owners' Equity	2275183	2234633
损益及分配	**Expenditure,Income and Distribution**		
营业收入	Business Income	7517227	7466640
营业税金及附加	Business Tax and Surcharges	255151	253584
其他业务利润	Other Business Profit	14325	14250
管理费用	Management and Financial Expenditures	201479	199832
财务费用	Financial Costs	63952	63531
营业利润	Operating Surplus	323705	319867
利润总额	Total Profits	327447	323685
补充资料	**Supplementary Material**		
应付职工薪酬	Remuneration Payable to Employees	1191317	1186027
应收工程款	Project Fund Payable	1379204	1354590
# 竣工工程款	Completed Project Fund	707817	703060

单位：万元（10000 yuan）

其中 of which					港澳台投资企业 Enterprises With Investment From HongKong, Macao and Taiwan
国有企业 State-owned Enterprises	集体企业 Collective-owned Enterprises	有限责任公司 Limited Liability Corporations	股份有限公司 Share-holding Corporations Ltd	私营企业 Private Enterprises	
19310	516	193080	13821	903191	5508
111353	11025	1165697	24623	3961374	57331
9037	1418	62598	5746	460184	8681
16734	2127	91296	8941	673418	10163
7696	708	32765	3196	265527	2858
914	68	4544	773	44537	410
		3777		37329	1286
183576	12443	1259316	31443	4691829	71351
127462	2770	861092	17107	2817581	30801
		92776		25186	
127462	2770	953868	17107	2842767	30801
56114	9673	305448	14336	1849062	40551
97609	6211	1032992	27707	6302120	50587
3236	210	33024	974	216140	1567
2645	453	3149	854	7148	75
3093	291	25562	951	169935	1647
96	8	6031	501	56895	421
3198	315	50181	1199	264973	3838
3217	315	50985	1199	267968	3762
7988	693	132300	2779	1042267	5291
27010	146	194807	1369	1131258	24614
21661		104002	451	576946	4758

12-8 分资质等级建筑业企业财务状况（2011 年）
FINANCIAL CONDITIONS OF CONSTRUCTION ENTERPRISES BY GRADE（2011）

指 标	Item	总 计 Total
年末资产负债	**Asset and Liabilities at Year-end**	
年初存货	Opening Stock	1135426
流动资产	Current Assets	5331403
固定资产	Fixed Assets	547664
固定资产原价	Original Value of Fixed Assets	802679
累计折旧	Accumulative Total Depreciation	312750
# 本年折旧	Depreciation Within the Year	51247
在建工程	Projects Under Construction	42392
资产合计	Total Assets	6249958
流动负债	Liquid Liabilities	3856813
长期负债	Long-term Liabilities	117962
负债合计	Total Liabilities	3974775
所有者权益	Owners' Equity	2275183
损益及分配	**Expenditure,Income and Distribution**	
营业收入	Business Income	7517227
营业税金及附加	Business Tax and Surcharges	255151
其他业务利润	Other Business Profit	14325
管理费用	Management and Financial Expenditures	201479
财务费用	Financial Costs	63952
营业利润	Operating Surplus	323705
利润总额	Total Profits	327447
补充资料	**Supplementary Material**	
应付职工薪酬	Remuneration Payable to Employees	1191317
应收工程款	Project Fund Payable	1379204
# 竣工工程款	Completed Project Fund	707817

注：本表统计范围不含劳务企业。
Note：The statistical rang of this table doesn't including Labour Service Enterprises.

单位：万元（10000 yuan）

施工总承包 Contracted Construction	其中 of which 一级 First Grade	二级 Second Grade	三级及以下 Under Third Grade	专业承包 Professional Contracting	其中 of which 一级 First Grade	二级 Second Grade	三级及以下 Under Third Grade
905855	287064	418454	200336	229571	80103	71428	78040
4160314	1312411	1674650	1173252	1171089	388387	329625	453077
418003	118114	171362	128528	129661	23675	55406	50580
614586	201531	254445	158610	188093	47748	78476	61869
237288	90037	95412	51839	75462	27863	29429	18170
35683	10827	14946	9909	15564	4567	6927	4069
30910	5917	8408	16584	11483	3780	2207	5495
4859298	1497298	1993181	1368819	1390661	433930	429880	526851
3051495	1040729	1275681	735085	805319	308624	249549	247145
103652	9219	7446	86986	14310	1177	5885	7248
3155146	1049948	1283127	822071	819629	309801	255434	254394
1704152	447350	710054	546748	571032	124128	174446	272458
6304579	2620494	2575822	1108264	1212648	446307	368917	397423
215624	89112	87577	38935	39527	15371	11503	12653
9155	2643	4549	1963	5170	1241	2341	1588
135943	41450	53543	40950	65536	17943	26337	21256
55526	19750	26806	8971	8426	3239	3550	1638
253715	84155	86563	82996	69990	20109	24575	25306
256142	87455	84431	84255	71305	20173	26089	25043
1040527	427281	450407	162839	150791	52148	44441	54202
1074563	380677	440185	253702	304641	87891	100771	115979
567984	203611	216035	148338	139834	39901	40241	59692

13

CHAPTER 13

交通运输　邮电通信

TRANSPORTATION,POST AND TELCOMMUNICATIONS

13 交通运输 邮电通信 TRANSPORTATION, POST AND TELECOMMUNICATIONS

2011 年主要统计指标 MAJOR STATISTICAL INDICATORS OF 2011

客运量	Passenger Traffic	15845 万人	(10000 persons)
比上年增长	Over the Previous Year	19.4%	
货运量	Freight Traffic	15644 万吨	(10000 tons)
比上年增长	Over the Previous Year	19.9%	
邮电业务收入	Revenue from Post & Telecommunication Services	59.95 亿元	(100 million yuan)
比上年增长	Over the Previous Year	7.6%	
年底本地网电话用户数	Number of Telephone Subscribers of Local Telephone Net	158.74 万户	(10000 households)
比上年增长	Over the Previous Year	-0.5%	
年底移动电话用户	Number of Mobile Phones Subscribers at Year-End	560.46 万户	(10000 households)
比上年增长	Over the Previous Year	11.8%	
年底互联网用户	Number of Internet Subscribers	107.79 户	(10000 households)
比上年增长	Over the Previous Year	21.3%	

13-1 主要年份客、货运量
TOTAL PASSENGER AND FREIGHT TRAFFIC IN MAIN YEARS

年份 Year	客运量（万人） Passenger Traffic (10000 persons)	其中 of which 铁路 Railways	民航 Civil Aviation	公路 Highways	水路 Waterways	货运量（万吨） Freight Traffic (10000 tons)	其中 of which 铁路 Railways	民航 Civil Aviation	公路 Highways	水路 Waterways
1949	192	41		41	110	96	2		17	78
1952	273	68		83	122	139	7		38	95
1957	535	69		170	296	168	13		24	131
1962	867	165		295	407	289	25		68	196
1965	712	110		438	164	405	20		111	274
1970	1005	125		618	262	498	28		131	339
1975	1837	180		1194	463	1072	47		319	706
1980	3071	245		2465	361	1839	51		621	1167
1981	3701	261		2917	523	1842	54		641	1147
1982	4074	282		3396	396	1926	59		679	1188
1983	4199	353		3563	283	2299	109		938	1251
1984	4373	429		3732	212	2880	117		1510	1253
1985	4373	488		3760	125	4351	128		2330	1893
1986	4389	511	1	3773	104	4836	135	0.02	2369	2332
1987	4958	544	2	4333	79	4612	132	0.05	2627	1853
1988	5259	647	3	4534	75	4983	126	0.06	3051	1806
1989	4877	395	3	4431	48	4812	131	0.06	3061	1620
1990	5048	585	3	4428	32	4375	126	0.06	2943	1306
1991	5361	579	3	4740	39	5998	136	0.05	4246	1616
1992	5372	639	5	4706	23	6266	162	0.12	3833	2271
1993	5492	700	6	4766	19	5987	158	0.10	3707	2121
1994	5336	697	10	4620	9	6173	162	0.20	3802	2209
1995	7270	734	7	6522	6	5804	187	0.10	3551	2065
1996	7099	570	12	6513	4	5917	127	0.15	3843	1947
1997	7687	490	27	7168	2	5246	193	0.45	3375	1677
1998	8042	492	23	7526	1	5167	193	0.50	3340	1634
1999	9216	550	22	8643	1	4909	222	0.50	3299	1388
2000	10196	557	19	9620	1	4696	223	0.60	3335	1137
2001	10507	566	13	9928		4830	240	0.30	3445	1144
2002	11216	603	15	10598		5140	246	0.30	3783	1111
2003	11413	577	16	10820		5437	254	0.30	4040	1143
2004	12679	682	24	11973		5648	361	0.40	4334	952
2005	15235	715	15	14505		6032	296	0.47	4950	786
2006	16719	741	20	15958		6855	298	0.42	5692	865
2007	19096	745	21	18330		8083	396	0.54	6710	976
2008	21018	818	34	20166		8729	258	0.54	7490	980
2009	24778	840	23	23837	78	11206	232	0.53	9839	1134
2010	29361	874	27	28380	80	13109	219	0.55	11600	1290
2011	15845	981	36	14733	95	15644	195	0.68	13936	1512

注：公路、水路客、货运量2011年以前年份数据为全社会口径，2011年为营业性口径。

Note: The statistical coverage of passenger and cargo by land and river throughput before 2011 refers to the whole society, which has been altered to business statistical data in 2011.

13-2 主要年份客、货运周转量
PASSENGER TRAFFIC AND FREIGHT TRAFFIC IN MAIN YEARS

年 份 Year	客运周转量（万人公里）Passenger-kilometers (10000 persons-km)	其 中 of which 公 路 Highways	水 路 Waterways	货运周转量（万吨公里）Freight Ton-kilometers (10000 tons-km)	其 中 of which 公 路 Highways	水 路 Waterways
1949	4327	610	3717	6037	40	5997
1952	5681	1235	4446	7559	84	7475
1957	10032	3153	6879	7997	68	7929
1962	20259	9859	10400	13965	1004	12961
1965	13336	9723	3613	19800	1660	18140
1970	22934	17776	5158	28970	3272	25698
1975	40465	33385	7080	73230	12065	61165
1980	68882	62748	6134	144838	27546	117292
1981	79911	70592	9319	151476	30279	121197
1982	90280	82680	7600	166308	32469	133839
1983	94294	88286	6008	209359	36518	172841
1984	107560	102404	5156	223855	47519	176336
1985	125797	121910	3887	220817	63970	156847
1986	136856	133160	3696	245502	70345	175157
1987	152028	148706	3322	262000	81134	180866
1988	164462	161268	3194	273096	99083	174013
1989	162072	159840	2232	265580	108727	156853
1990	168514	166596	1918	246937	111072	135865
1991	193806	191781	2025	287995	128732	159263
1992	223327	222135	1192	376867	133152	243715
1993	226534	225580	954	377914	154140	223774
1994	191495	190916	579	380862	154382	226480
1995	310456	309924	532	354690	139846	214844
1996	316737	316392	345	344144	138748	205396
1997	324783	324585	198	319055	142140	176915
1998	321356	321172	184	307452	135819	171633
1999	395343	395174	169	327542	148289	179253
2000	440379	440154	225	273472	145475	127997
2001	454239	454239		279312	150555	128757
2002	474890	474890		274835	151418	123417
2003	479180	479180		291913	164781	127132
2004	579976	579976		299376	187981	111395
2005	640944	640944		312269	220159	92110
2006	765984	765984		379974	267524	112450
2007	888260	888260		461815	328558	133257
2008	992311	992311		505902	369226	136676
2009	1286371	1286051	320	774413	596587	177826
2010	1541228	1540900	328	898400	698600	199800
2011	897763	897373	390	1098169	858887	239282

13-3 主要年份公路总里程
TOTAL LENGTH OF HIGHWAYS IN MAIN YEARS

单位：公里（km）

年 份 Year	公路总里程 Total Length of Highways	其中 of which					
		高速公路 Expressway	一级公路 First Class	二级公路 Second Class	三级公路 Third Class	四级公路 Fourth Class	等外公路 Substandard Highways
1949	179			45	17	116	1
1952	220			45	17	117	41
1957	312			60	53	138	61
1962	405			60	65	184	96
1965	442			60	69	217	96
1970	531			60	83	262	126
1975	659			60	101	351	147
1980	838			73	101	499	165
1981	862			73	101	523	165
1982	907			88	104	546	169
1983	940			90	97	590	163
1984	1020			95	130	628	167
1985	1044			102	140	635	167
1986	1106			134	155	650	167
1987	1183			155	201	660	167
1988	1215			162	232	654	167
1989	1215		5	185	233	628	164
1990	1215		5	192	263	613	142
1991	1226		5	230	308	615	68
1992	1227		5	236	337	588	61
1993	1228		5	249	348	573	53
1994	1230		5	299	362	511	53
1995	1241		41	311	348	500	41
1996	1296	43	33	338	346	483	53
1997	1313	43	77	319	342	479	53
1998	1344	43	122	315	339	472	53
1999	1384	43	140	313	374	471	43
2000	1384	43	144	321	362	471	43
2001	5165	43	200	457	910	2262	1293
2002	5232	43	250	467	926	2254	1292
2003	5404	60	297	532	987	2294	1234
2004	5999	117	336	736	1033	2694	1083
2005	5444	117	406	886	1266	1816	953
2006	5546	117	459	908	1247	2278	537
2007	6732	221	558	1095	1572	2763	523
2008	7185	221	809	1130	1229	3547	249
2009	7479	221	794	1167	1227	3849	221
2010	8348	221	855	1170	1282	4768	52
2011	8446	247	882	1179	1301	4784	52

13-4 公路和内河航道里程数（2011 年）
TOTAL LENGTH OF HIGHWAYS AND NAVIGABLE INLAND WATERWAYS（2011）

单位：公里（km）

指 标	Item	全 市 Whole Municipality	其中 of which 市 区 Urban Area
公路总里程	**Total Length of Highways**	**8446**	**4035**
# 高速公路	Expressway	247	130
一级公路	First Class	882	667
二级公路	Second Class	1179	580
三级公路	Third Class	1301	754
四级公路	Fourth Class	4784	1905
航道里程	**Length of Navigable Inland Waterways**	**1097**	**542**
# 通机动船里程	Length of Navigation of Motor Vessels	866	386

13-5 机动车辆数（2011 年）
NUMBER OF MOTOR VEHICLES（2011）

单位：辆（unit）

指 标	Item	合 计 Total	其中 of which 私 人 Private
民用汽车	**Civil Vehicles**	**560405**	**434436**
客 车	Passenger Vehicles	492548	412450
# 大 型	Large-scale	5805	20
中 型	Medium-sized	6495	2368
小 型	Compact car	467335	398439
微 型	Minicar	12913	11623
# 轿 车	Sedan	357154	309463
货 车	Freight Trucks	63582	21048
# 重 型	Heavy-duty	18407	3854
中 型	Medium-sized	16206	2558
轻 型	Pick-up Truck	28699	14453
微 型	Minicar	270	183
其他汽车	Other Motorcar	4275	938
摩托车	**Motorcycle**	**317421**	**315755**
# 普通摩托车	Ordinary Motorcycle	311833	310177
轻便摩托车	Scooter	5588	5578
挂 车	**Trailer**	**3329**	**428**
其他机动车	**Other Motor Vehicles**	**33**	**4**
附：机动车驾驶员人数（人）	**Number of Drivers of Motor Vehicles (person)**	**969900**	
# 汽车驾驶员人数	Number of Driver of Vehicles	778869	

13-6 分地区全社会客、货运量（2011 年）
TOTAL PASSENGER AND FREIGHT TRAFFIC BY REGION（2011）

指 标	Item	全 市 Whole Municipality	其 中 of which 市 区 Urban Area	溧阳市 Liyang City	金坛市 Jintan City
客运量（万人）	**Passenger Traffic (10000 Persons)**	**15845**	**11360**	**2665**	**1820**
铁 路	Railway	981	981		
公 路	Highway	14733	10343	2570	1820
民 航	Civil Aviation	36	36		
水 路	Waterway	95		95	
旅客周转量（万人公里）	**Passenger-kilometers (10000 persons-km)**	**897763**	**626071**	**161391**	**110301**
公 路	Highway	897373	626071	161001	110301
水 路	Waterway	390		390	
货运量（万吨）	**Freight Traffic (10000 tons)**	**15644**	**10668**	**2911**	**2065**
铁 路	Railway	195	195		
公 路	Highway	13936	10043	2546	1347
水 路	Waterway	1512	429	365	718
民 航	Civil Aviation	0.68	0.68		
货运周转量（万吨公里）	**Freight Ton-kilometers (10000 tons-km)**	**1098169**	**689303**	**212964**	**195902**
公 路	Highway	858887	619398	155665	83824
水 路	Waterway	239282	69905	57299	112078
港口货物吞吐量（万吨）	**Volume of Freight Handled in Ports (10000 tons)**	**9521**	**4894**	**3403**	**1224**

13-7 交通系统分地区客、货运量（2011 年）
PASSENGER AND FREIGHT TRAFFIC OF COMMUNICATIONS SYSTEM BY REGION（2011）

指 标	Item	全 市 Whole Municipality	其 中 of which 市 区 Urban Area	溧阳市 Liyang City	金坛市 Jintan City
客运量（万人）	**Passenger Traffic (10000 Persons)**	**6826**	**2200**	**3610**	**1016**
铁 路	Railway	981	981		
公 路	Highway	5809	1183	3610	1016
民 航	Aviation	36	36		
旅客周转量（万人公里）	**Passenger-kilometers (10000 persons-km)**	**286614**	**157694**	**79269**	**49651**
公 路	Highway	286614	157694	79269	49651
货运量（万吨）	**Freight Tranfic (10000 tons)**	**767**	**345**	**5**	**417**
铁 路	Railway	195	195		
公 路	Highway	143	138	5	
水 路	Waterway	428	11		417
民 航	Aviation	0.68	0.68		
货运周转量（万吨公里）	**Freight Ton-kilometers (10000 tons-km)**	**75007**	**5242**	**392**	**69373**
公 路	Highway	3198	2806	392	
水 路	Waterway	71809	2436		69373

13-8 历年邮电业务主要指标
MAJOR INDICATORS OF POST AND TELECOMMUNICATIONS OVER THE YEARS

年 份 Year	邮电局所数 (个) Number of Post and Telecommun-ications Offices (unit)	邮路单程长度 (公里) Lengh of Postal Routs (one way,km)	邮电业务总量 (万元) Business Volume of Post and Telecommunications (10000 yuan)	市话交换机容量 (门) Capacity of Urban Telephones Exchanges (line)
1952	261		235	1620
1953	282		266	1640
1954	263		266	1650
1955	213		259	1670
1956	210		284	1670
1957	201		302	1670
1958	249	4190	372	1830
1959	194	3999	525	2730
1960	204	3642	619	3030
1961	203	3012	600	3030
1962	189	2740	514	3020
1963	193	3776	513	3120
1964	194	6237	537	3180
1965	171	7579	567	3280
1966	171	7953	593	3280
1967	173	8330	531	3280
1968	173	8330	503	3280
1969	170	9311	589	3180
1970	241	8937	662	3180
1971	244	8452	669	3180
1972	238	9496	747	3250
1973	203	9629	792	4100
1974	204	10043	884	4250
1975	207	10217	928	4250
1976	207	10427	964	4250
1977	208	10076	1031	5250
1978	209	10029	1127	6250
1979	210	9948	1202	6420
1980	206	10108	1368	7420
1981	212	4554	1470	7850

13-8　续表　Continued

年 份 Year	邮电局所数 （个） Number of Post and Telecommun-ications Offices (unit)	邮路单程长度 （公里） Lengh of Postal Routs (one way,km)	邮电业务总量 （万元） Business Volume of Post and Telecommunications (10000 yuan)	市话交换机容量 （门） Capacity of Urban Telephones Exchanges (line)
1982	215	2854	1561	7400
1983	212	2762	1743	7400
1984	217	2788	1920	12350
1985	218	3078	2454	17200
1986	215	2065	2780	17200
1987	211	2233	3442	17200
1988	210	1892	4776	23000
1989	204	1889	6026	32000
1990	196	1881	7477	40500
1991	193	1715	10315	44000
1992	181	1790	16184	67500
1993	167	2226	27740	121300
1994	166	2516	43122	144000
1995	220	2502	56746	160000
1996	223	2419	77169	402000
1997	233	5509	107951	539609
1998	297	5776	131919	560375
1999	255	6297	175449	539108
2000	248	9401	284105	606730
2001	263	9799	192078	675348
2002	263	9799	247394	1142675
2003	375	9947	281939	1342600
2004	250	10129	318161	1332400
2005	250	10129	348747	1311800
2006	166	9045	391996	1712600
2007	166	10161	451700	2918700
2008	160	8995	505176	2975000
2009	190	7903	538059	2884424
2010	167	3740	574083	2844144
2011	151	4269	594741	3099600

注：1、从 2006 年起邮电局所数不包括电信网点数字；1952-2000 年邮电业务总量按 1990 年价格计算，2001 年起按 2000 年价格计算。
　　2、年末邮路单程长度不包括速递邮路单程长度。

Note：1、The number of post stations and offices excludes the number of telecommunication network offices since the year of 2006.The total business volumes of post and telecommunication from 1952 to 2000 have been calculated by the price of 1990, The figures from the year of 2001 have been calculated according to the price in 2000.
　　2、The one-way postal length by the end of year does not include the one-way length of postal express.

13-9 分地区邮政电信情况（2011 年）
POSTS AND TELECOMMUNCIATIONS BY REGION（2011）

指 标	Item	全 市 Whole Municipality	其中 of which 市 区 Urban Area	溧阳市 Liyang City	金坛市 Jintan City
年末邮政机构数（个）	**Number of Network Points of Post**	**151**	**87**	**37**	**27**
#邮政局	Post Offices	3	1	1	1
邮政支局	Post Branches	127	83	18	26
自办所	Self-Run Post Services	21	3	18	
年末邮路单程长度（公里）	**Lengh of Postal Routes (single way,km)**	**4268.9**	**3445.5**	**563.4**	**260**
农村投递线路（公里）	**Rural Delivery Routes (km)**	**13375**	**8666**	**2251**	**2458**
年末电话交换机总容量（万门）	**Total Capacity of Urban and Rural Telephone Exchanges (10000 lines)**	**309.96**	**225.34**	**44.94**	**39.68**
邮电业务收入（亿元）	**Total Business Volume of Post & Telecommunications (100 mitlion yuan)**	**59.95**	**47.69**	**6.96**	**5.3**
邮政业务收入	Total Business Volume of Post Services	5.99	4.44	0.82	0.73
通信业务收入	Total Business Volume of Communications Services	53.96	43.25	6.14	4.57
主要业务量	**Major Business Volume**				
函件（万件）	Number of Letters (10000 pcs)	7455.40	6392.45	564.88	498.07
特快专递（万件）	Pieces of Express Mail Services (10000 pcs)	62.48	49.42	6.9	6.16
包件（万件）	Pieces of Courier Services (10000 pcs)	8.69	6.90	0.30	1.49
汇票（万件）	Number of Bill of Exchange (10000 pcs)	97.70	62.81	21.91	12.98
集邮业务（万枚）	Business Volume of Philately (10000 pcs)	782.1	729.05	33.8	19.25
年末本地网电话用户数（万户）	**Number of Telephone Subscribers of Local Telephone Net (10000 households)**	**158.74**	**114.23**	**24.14**	**20.37**
城市电话用户	Urban Telephone Subscribers	77.15	58.92	9.73	8.50
#住 宅	Residential Telephone Subscribers	52.90	38.14	7.27	7.48
农村电话用户	Rural Telephone Subscribers	55.81	32.12	13.82	9.87
#住 宅	Residential Telephone Subscribers	24.89	7.95	10.56	6.39
无线市话用户	Wireless Urban Telephone Subscribers	8.96	6.05	0.77	2.14
年末移动电话用户数（万户）	**Number of Mobile Telephone Subscribers (10000 households)**	**560.46**	**423.80**	**78.15**	**58.52**
年末互联网用户（万户）	**Number of Internet Subscribers (10000 households)**	**107.79**	**85.63**	**12.31**	**9.84**
#宽带网用户	Widebband Network Subscribers	104.51	82.76	12.04	9.71

注：1、年末电话交换机总容量不包括无线市话，宽带网用户中含无线上网用户。
2、年末邮路单程长度不包括速递邮路单程长度。

Note：1、Total capacity of urban and rural telephone exchanges doesn’t including wireless urban telephone,internet subscribers include wireless internet subscribers.
2、The one-way postal length by the end of year does not include the one-way length of postal express.

14

CHAPTER 14

贸易　住宿餐饮业

TRADE,ACCOMMODATION AND CATERING TRADE

14 贸易 住宿餐饮业 TRADE, ACCOMMODATION AND CATERING TRADE

2011 年主要统计指标 MAJOR STATISTICAL INDICATORS OF 2011

社会消费品零售总额	Total Retail of Consumer Goods	1236.10 亿元	(100 million yuan)
比上年增长	Over the Previous Year	17.3%	
限额以上批发零售贸易业商品销售总额	Total Sales of Wholesale and Retail Trade above Designated Size	1898.9 亿元	(100 million yuan)
比上年增长	Over the Previous Year	4.0%	
超亿元商品交易市场成交额	Transaction Value of Trade Market of Goods	1623.08 亿元	(100 million yuan)
比上年增长	Over the Previous Year	21.4%	

14-1 历年分地区社会消费品零售总额
TOTAL RETAIL SALES OF CUNSUMER GOODS BY REGION OVER THE YEARS

单位：万元（10000 yuan）

年份 Year	全市 Whole Municipality	其中 of which 市区 Urban Area	溧阳市 Liyang City	金坛市 Jintan City	年份 Year	全市 Whole Municipality	其中 of which 市区 Urban Area	溧阳市 Liyang City	金坛市 Jintan City
1949	8102	5816	1389	897	1981	79614	48181	17532	13901
1950	9594	7076	1576	942	1982	89417	53600	20312	15505
1951	11884	8727	1869	1288	1983	108328	65763	22645	19920
1952	12572	8833	2215	1524	1984	129310	81806	25874	21630
1953	14109	9664	2685	1760	1985	181736	119591	35557	26588
1954	14814	10163	2813	1838	1986	202929	133243	39765	29921
1955	13435	9007	2773	1655	1987	248014	165286	46660	36068
1956	14622	9869	2927	1826	1988	323678	213641	61009	49028
1957	14603	10067	2725	1811	1989	363259	242555	63731	56973
1958	17975	12581	3279	2115	1990	381931	262148	66529	53254
1959	19734	14172	3220	2342	1991	436920	300243	76502	60175
1960	22434	16325	3589	2520	1992	558904	402730	97255	58919
1961	18873	13966	2794	2113	1993	782257	547972	132046	102239
1962	20377	14290	3541	2546	1994	1002394	673218	191109	138067
1963	18044	12217	3569	2258	1995	1317764	849886	285210	182668
1964	19142	12326	4055	2761	1996	1575902	1016554	330375	228973
1965	21379	13042	4857	3480	1997	1679581	1110655	334340	234586
1966	22577	13729	5002	3846	1998	1739300	1143964	341290	254046
1967	23951	14451	5329	4171	1999	1844235	1208355	364403	271477
1968	21685	12506	5356	3823	2000	2023126	1338778	391687	292661
1969	21764	11629	5945	4190	2001	2226101	1480205	425803	320093
1970	26295	14902	6897	4496	2002	2488005	1659780	469821	358404
1971	26512	14514	7461	4537	2003	2806470	1907533	494016	404921
1972	30343	17743	7551	5049	2004	3240528	2193610	581878	465040
1973	31821	17804	8376	5641	2005	4449415	3292101	652950	504364
1974	34606	20093	8639	5874	2006	5178307	3840209	753775	584323
1975	38450	23473	8692	6285	2007	6144075	4581050	881159	681866
1976	40233	24572	8951	6710	2008	7640631	5740836	1072741	827054
1977	44298	27330	9594	7374	2009	8915444	6745496	1218920	951028
1978	48236	28813	10881	8542	2010	10543943	7906496	1475388	1162058
1979	58116	34682	13371	10063	2011	12361038	9262314	1732009	1366715
1980	72740	42012	17880	12848					

注：2005 年至 2008 年数据已按照第二次经济普查结果重新进行了修订。
Note: The statistic data from year 2005 to year 2008 was adjusted in accordance with the second economic survey.

14-2 分地区社会消费品零售总额（2011 年）
TOTAL RETAIL SALES OF CONSUMER GOODS BY REGION（2011）

单位：万元（10000 yuan）

指 标	Item	全 市 Whole Municipality	其中 of which 市 区 Urban Area	溧阳市 Liyang City	金坛市 Jintan City
总 计	**Total**	**12361038**	**9262314**	**1732009**	**1366715**
# 个体经济	Self-employed Business	5352982	3366887	1082566	903529
按销售地区分	**Grouped by Sales Region**				
市的零售额	Retail Price in Urban Area	11542677	9187179	1103751	1251747
县以下的零售额	Retail Price Below Country Level	818361	75135	628257	114968
按行业分	**Grouped by Sector**				
批发零售贸易业	Wholesale,Retail Sales	11337847	8533811	1568213	1235823
住宿餐饮业	Accommodation Catering Trade	1023191	728504	163795	130892

14-3 分地区批发零售贸易业商品销售总额（2011 年）
TOTAL COMMODITIES SALES VOLUME OF WHOLESALE AND RETAIL TRADES BY REGION（2011）

单位：万元（10000 yuan）

指 标	Item	全 市 Whole Municipality	其中 of which 市 区 Urban Area	溧阳市 Liyang City	金坛市 Jintan City
总 计	**Total**	**44094812**	**39008547**	**2767801**	**2318465**
限额以上企业及个体	Enterprises and Individuals Above Designated Size	18989430	18095735	509342	384354
批 发	Wholesale	13475514	13109273	162888	203354
零 售	Retail	5513916	4986462	346454	181000
限额以下企业及个体	Enterprises and Individuals Below Designated Size	25105382	20912812	2258459	1934111
批 发	Wholesale	18067205	16633369	629515	804321
零 售	Retail	7038177	4279443	1628943	1129791

14-4 分地区住宿餐饮业营业额（2011 年）
SALES TURNOVER OF ACCOMMODATION & CATERING TRADE GROUPED BY REGION（2011）

单位：万元（10000 yuan）

指 标	Item	全 市 Whole Municipality	其中 of which 市 区 Urban Area	溧阳市 Liyang City	金坛市 Jintan City
总 计	**Total**	**1460777**	**1050373**	**251049**	**159354**
限额以上企业及个体	Enterprises and Individuals Above Designated Size	616025	496834	79513	39677
住 宿	Accommodation	189834	117575	59306	12954
餐 饮	Catering	426191	379260	20208	26723
限额以下企业及个体	Enterprises and Individuals Below Designated Size	844752	553539	171536	119677
住 宿	Accommodation	172921	107800	50971	14150
餐 饮	Catering	671831	445739	120565	105528

14-5 限额以上批发零售贸易企业商品销售总额（2011 年）
TOTAL SALES OF WHOLESALE AND RETAIL ENTERPRISES ABOVE DESIGNATED SIZE（2011）

指 标	Item	企业数（个）Number of Enterprises (unit)	销售额（万元）Total Sales (10000 yuan)	其中 of which 批发额 Wholesale	零售额 Retail Sales
总 计	**Total**	**800**	**17115727**	**12659236**	**4456491**
市 区	Urban Area	720	16416647	12305563	4111083
溧阳市	Liyang City	19	372799	153335	219463
金坛市	Jintan City	61	326282	200337	125944
#国有及国有控股	State-owned and State Holding Majority Shares	19	1392459	1152167	240292
按登记注册类型分组	**Group by Registration Status**				
内 资	Domestic Investment	783	16271135	12219690	4051445
国 有	State-owned	6	599264	553926	45338
股份合作	Share-holding Cooperative	5	96696	84495	12201
集 体	Collective-owned	3	425771	407142	18629
有限责任公司	Limited Liability Corporations	90	2749610	1991491	758119
股份有限公司	Share-holding Cooperative Ltd.	6	590566	268902	321663
私 营	Private	667	11779281	8892399	2886882
其 他	Others	6	29947	21335	8612
港澳台商投资	Hong Kong,Macao and Taiwan Funded	9	366560	188743	177817
外商投资	Foreign Investment	8	478033	250803	227229
批发贸易业	**Wholesale Trade**	**515**	**12428267**	**12267706**	**160561**
#国有及国有控股	State-owned and State Holding Majority Shares	10	1074311	1052440	21871
按登记注册类型分组	**Group by Registration Status**				
内 资	Domestic Investment	511	11988942	11828381	160561
国 有	State-owned	4	553106	553106	
集 体	Collective-owned	1	84495	84495	
股份合作	Share-holding Cooperative	1	406420	406420	
有限责任公司	Limited Liability Corporations	46	1943366	1886099	57267
股份有限公司	Share-holding Cooperative Ltd.	3	166438	162340	4099
私 营	Private	451	8812048	8714587	97461
其 他	Others	5	23070	21335	1735
港澳台商投资	Hong Kong,Macao and Taiwan Funded	3	188743	188743	
外商投资	Foreign Investment	1	250582	250582	
按主要行业分组	**Group by Sector**				
农畜产品批发	Wholesale of Agricultural and Animal Product	13	130523	125350	5173
食品、饮料及烟草制品批发	Wholesale of Food,Beverages and Tobaccos	25	783207	777446	5760
纺织、服装及日用品批发	Wholesale of Textile, Garments and Commodity	38	1042400	1037074	5326
医药及医疗器材批发	Wholesale of Medicine and Medical Appliance	7	221650	217546	4104
矿产品、建材及化工产品批发	Wholesale of Mineral Product, Building Material and Chemical Product	345	8416548	8322100	94447
机械设备、五金交电及电子产品批发	Wholesale of Machinery, Hardware and Eletronic Products	59	1068687	1023803	44884
贸易经纪与代理	Trade Broker and Agent	13	237271	237271	
其他批发	Others	15	527983	527116	868

14-5 续表 Continued

指 标	Item	企业数（个） Number of Enterprises (unit)	销售额（万元） Total Sales (10000 yuan)	其 中 of which 批发额 Wholesale	零售额 Retail Sales
零售贸易业	**Retail Trade**	**285**	**4687460**	**391530**	**4295930**
#国有及国有控股	State-owned and State Holding Majority Shares	9	318148	99727	218421
按登记注册类型分组	**Group by Registration Status**				
内 资	Domestic Investment	272	4282192	391309	3890884
国 有	State-owned	2	46158	820	45338
集 体	Collective-owned	4	12201		12201
股份合作	Share-holding Cooperative	2	19352	722	18629
有限责任公司	Limited Liability Corporations	44	806244	105392	700853
股份有限公司	Share-holding Cooperative Ltd.	3	424128	106563	317565
私 营	Private	216	2967233	177812	2789421
其 他	Others	1	6877		6877
港澳台商投资	Hong Kong,Macao and Taiwan Funded	6	177817		177817
外商投资	Foreign Investment	7	227451	221	227229
按主要行业分组	**Group by Sector**				
综合零售	Comprehensive Retail	49	1111361	4106	1107256
食品、饮料及烟草制品专门零售	Speicalized Retail of Food, Beverage and Tobacco	18	70361	2823	67538
纺织、服装及日用品专门零售	Specialized Retail of Textile, Garments and Commodity	13	56750	1243	55507
文化、体育用品及器材专门零售	Specialized Retail of Stationers Goods, Sports Goods and Apparatus	19	193424	34633	158790
医药及医疗器材专门零售	Specialized Retail of Medicine and Medical aappliance	14	539929	209200	330729
汽车、摩托车、燃料及零配件专门零售	Specialized Retail of Automobile, Motorcycle, Fuel and Fittings	120	2259728	115918	2143810
家用电器及电子产品专门零售	Specialized Retail of Household Appliance and Electronic Products	39	414810	12048	402762
五金、家具及室内装修材料专门零售	Specialized Retail of Hardware, Furniture and Interior Decoration Materials	4	14870	10486	4384
无店铺及其他零售	Retail without Shops and Other Retail	9	26227	1073	25154
按经营方式分组	**Group by Means of Operation**				
独立商店	Independent Store	223	3452149	236069	3216080
连锁商店总店	Head Office of Chain Store	12	412402	141	412261
连锁商店分店	Branch Store of Chain Store	21	409682	33245	376437
其 他	Others	29	413227	122076	291152
按零售业态分组	**Group by Retail Size**				
百货商店	Composite Store	19	500781	3744	497038
食杂店	Traditional Grocery Stores	1	1651		1651
超 市	Supermarket	13	129378	141	129238
大型超市	Large Supermarket	17	483814	221	483593
便利店	Convenience Stores	2	7416		7416
厂家直销中心	Factory Outlet Centers	4	230509	99267	131242
网上商店	Online stores	2	5200	206	4994
专业店	Specialized Store	143	1299161	67219	1231942
专卖店	Speciality Store	84	2029550	220733	1808817

14-6 限额以上个体批发零售贸易业商品销售总额（2011 年）
TOTAL SALES OF INDIVIDUAL WHOLESALE AND RETAIL ENTERPRISES ABOVE DESIGNATED SIZE（2011）

指 标	Item	企业数（个） Number of Enterprises (unit)	销售额（万元） Total Sales (10000 yuan)	其中 of which 批发额 Wholesale	零售额 Retail Sales
总 计	**Total**	**827**	**1873703**	**963021**	**910682**
市 区	Urban Area	636	1679088	950934	728154
溧阳市	Liyang City	115	136543	12087	124457
金坛市	Jintan City	76	58072		58072
批发贸易业	**Wholesale Trade**	**257**	**1047247**	**880962**	**166285**
按主要行业分组	**Group by Sector**				
农畜产品批发	Wholesale of Agricultural and Animal Product	27	128624	128624	
食品、饮料及烟草制品批发	Wholesale of Food,Beverages and Tobaccos	94	503710	450739	52971
纺织、服装及日用品批发	Wholesale of Textile, Garments and Commodity	80	262793	184854	77939
矿产品、建材及化工产品批发	Wholesale of Mineral Product, Building Material and Chemical Product	45	128853	93821	35032
机械设备、五金交电及电子产品批发	Wholesale of Machinery, Hardware and Eletronic Products	11	23267	22923	344
零售贸易业	**Retail Trade**	**570**	**826456**	**82059**	**744397**
按主要行业分组	**Group by Sector**				
综合零售	Comprehensive Retail	25	21624	813	20811
食品、饮料及烟草制品专门零售	Speicalized Retail of Food, Beverage and Tobacco	55	57273	7240	50033
纺织、服装及日用品专门零售	Specialized Retail of Textile, Garments and Commodity	42	112034	26292	85742
文化、体育用品及器材专门零售	Specialized Retail of Stationers Goods, Sports Goods and Apparatus	8	5055	40	5015
汽车、摩托车、燃料及零配件专门零售	Specialized Retail of Automobile, Motorcycle, Fuel and Fittings	35	42554	109	42445
家用电器及电子产品专门零售	Specialized Retail of Household Appliance and Electronic Products	12	11512		11512
五金、家具及室内装修材料专门零售	Specialized Retail of Hardware, Furniture and Interior Decoration Materials	350	543935	47566	496369
无店铺及其他零售	Retail without Shops and Other Retail	43	32470		32470
按经营方式分组	**Group by Means of Operation**				
独立商店	Independent Store	564	820850	82059	738792
连锁商店分店	Branch Store of Chain Store	1	1085		1085
其 他	Others	5	4521		4521
按零售业态分组	**Group by Retail Size**				
百货商店	Composite Store	36	39138	4510	34628
超 市	Supermarket	10	8428	438	7991
家居建材商店	Home Building Materials Stores	366	619340	66747	552593
食杂店	Traditional Grocery Stores	33	33119	6707	26412
专业店	Specialized Store	73	87954	2694	85259
专卖店	Speciality Store	5	2718	533	2185
厂家直销中心	Factory Outlet Centers	2	2109	430	1679
便利店	Convenience Stores	1	660		660
大型超市	Large Supermarket	1	520		520
自动售货亭	Automatic Kiosk	43	32470		32470

14-7 市区限额以上批发零售贸易企业商品销售总额（2011 年）
TOTAL SALES OF WHOLESALE AND RETAIL ENTERPRISES ABOVE DESIGNATED SIZE IN URBAN AREA（2011）

指 标	Item	企业数（个）Number of Enterprises (unit)	销售额（万元）Total Sales (10000 yuan)	其中 of which 批发额 Wholesale	零售额 Retail Sales
总 计	**Total**	**720**	**16416647**	**12305563**	**4111083**
#国有及国有控股	State-owned and State Holding Majority Shares	14	1362368	1134199	228170
按登记注册类型分组	**Group by Registration Status**				
内 资	Domestic Investment	705	15631752	11866017	3765735
国 有	State-owned	4	579799	535957	43842
集 体	Collective-owned	3	95319	84495	10824
股份合作	Share-holding Cooperative	2	425049	406420	18629
有限责任公司	Limited Liability Corporations	81	2719117	1981949	737168
股份有限公司	Share-holding Cooperative Ltd.	4	539360	225662	313698
私 营	Private	607	11257776	8616202	2641574
其 他	Others	4	15333	15333	
港澳台商投资	Hong Kong,Macao and Taiwan Funded	9	366560	188743	177817
外商投资	Foreign Investment	6	418335	250803	167531
批发贸易业	**Wholesale Trade**	**483**	**12072082**	**11918559**	**153523**
#国有及国有控股	State-owned and State Holding Majority Shares	8	1056343	1034472	21871
按登记注册类型分组	**Group by Registration Status**				
内 资	Domestic Investment	479	11632757	11479234	153523
国 有	State-owned	2	535137	535137	
集 体	Collective-owned	1	84495	84495	
股份合作	Share-holding Cooperative	1	406420	406420	
有限责任公司	Limited Liability Corporations	45	1933824	1876557	57267
股份有限公司	Share-holding Cooperative Ltd.	2	119099	119099	
私 营	Private	424	8538449	8442193	96256
其 他	Others	4	15333	15333	
港澳台商投资	Hong Kong,Macao and Taiwan Funded	3	188743	188743	
外商投资	Foreign Investment	1	250582	250582	
按主要行业分组	**Group by Sector**				
农畜产品批发	Wholesale of Agricultural and Animal Product	11	112554	107382	5173
食品、饮料及烟草制品批发	Wholesale of Food,Beverages and Tobaccos	24	777895	773340	4555
纺织、服装及日用品批发	Wholesale of Textile, Garments and Commodity	36	1020499	1015173	5326
医药及医疗器材批发	Wholesale of Medicine and Medical Appliance	5	164967	164961	6
矿产品、建材及化工产品批发	Wholesale of Mineral Product, Building Material and Chemical Product	329	8286161	8193448	92712
机械设备、五金交电及电子产品批发	Wholesale of Machinery, Hardware and Eletronic Products	55	1042915	998031	44884
贸易经纪与代理	Trade Braker and Agent	11	231121	231121	
其他批发	Others	12	435970	435103	868

14-7 续表 Continued

指 标	Item	企业数（个） Number of Enterprises (unit)	销售额（万元） Total Sales (10000 yuan)	其中 of which 批发额 Wholesale	零售额 Retail Sales
零售贸易业	**Retail Trade**	**237**	**4344565**	**387004**	**3957561**
#国有及国有控股	State-owned and State Holding Majority Shares	6	306026	99727	206299
按登记注册类型分组	**Group by Registration Status**				
内 资	Domestic Investment	226	3998996	386783	3612212
国 有	State-owned	2	44662	820	43842
集 体	Collective-owned	2	10824		10824
股份合作	Share-holding Cooperative	1	18629		18629
有限责任公司	Limited Liability Corporations	36	785294	105392	679902
股份有限公司	Share-holding Cooperative Ltd.	2	420261	106563	313698
私 营	Private	183	2719326	174009	2545318
港澳台商投资	Hong Kong,Macao and Taiwan Funded	6	177817		177817
外商投资	Foreign Investment	5	167753	221	167531
按主要行业分组	**Group by Sector**				
综合零售	Comprehensive Retail	36	910822	3383	907439
食品、饮料及烟草制品专门零售	Speicalized Retail of Food, Beverage and Tobacco	14	66013	2823	63190
纺织、服装及日用品专门零售	Specialized Retail of Textile, Garments and Commodity	13	56750	1243	55507
文化、体育用品及器材专门零售	Specialized Retail of Stationers Goods, Sports Goods and Apparatus	13	177399	34274	143125
医药及医疗器材专门零售	Specialized Retail of Medicine and Medical aappliance	12	535091	209200	325891
汽车、摩托车、燃料及零配件专门零售	Specialized Retail of Automobile, Motorcycle, Fuel and Fittings	105	2167328	112474	2054854
家用电器及电子产品专门零售	Specialized Retail of Household Appliance and Electronic Products	33	401958	12048	389910
五金、家具及室内装修材料专门零售	Specialized Retail of Hardware, Furniture and Interior Decoration Materials	4	14870	10486	4384
无店铺及其他零售	Retail without Shops and Other Retail	7	14334	1073	13261
按经营方式分组	**Group by Means of Operation**				
独立商店	Independent Store	186	3298439	234987	3063451
连锁商店总店	Head Office of Chain Store	10	404499	141	404358
连锁商店分店	Branch Store of Chain Store	14	231679	29801	201878
其 他	Others	27	409949	122076	287874
按零售业态分组	**Group by Retail Size**				
百货商店	Composite Store	14	436013	3021	432992
食杂店	Traditional Grocery Stores	1	1651		1651
超 市	Supermarket	9	120490	141	120349
大型超市	Large Supermarket	13	356931	221	356710
便利店	Convenience Stores	2	7416		7416
厂家直销中心	Factory Outlet Centers	3	228549	98907	129642
网上商店	Online stores	2	5200	206	4994
专业店	Specialized Store	112	1199499	67219	1132280
专卖店	Speciality Store	81	1988815	217290	1771526

14-8 市区限额以上个体批发零售贸易业商品销售总额（2011 年）
TOTAL SALES OF INDIVIDUAL WHOLESALE AND RETAIL ENTERPRISES ABOVE DESIGNATED SIZE IN URBAN AREA（2011）

指 标	Item	企业数（个） Number of Enterprises (unit)	销售额（万元） Total Sales (10000 yuan)	其中 of which 批发额 Wholesale	零售额 Retail Sales
总 计	**Total**	**636**	**1679088**	**950934**	**728154**
批发贸易业	**Wholesale Trade**	**253**	**1037191**	**871250**	**165941**
按主要行业分组	**Group by Sector**				
农畜产品批发	Wholesale of Agricultural and Animal Product	26	125092	125092	
食品、饮料及烟草制品批发	Wholesale of Food,Beverages and Tobaccos	94	503710	450739	52971
纺织、服装及日用品批发	Wholesale of Textile, Garments and Commodity	79	259728	181789	77939
矿产品、建材及化工产品批发	Wholesale of Mineral Product, Building Material and Chemical Product	44	128153	93121	35032
机械设备、五金交电及电子产品批发	Wholesale of Machinery, Hardware and Eletronic Products	10	20508	20508	
零售贸易业	**Retail Trade**	**383**	**641897**	**79684**	**562212**
按主要行业分组	**Group by Sector**				
综合零售	Comprehensive Retail	8	8648		8648
食品、饮料及烟草制品专门零售	Speicalized Retail of Food, Beverage and Tobacco	42	46941	5827	41114
纺织、服装及日用品专门零售	Specialized Retail of Textile, Garments and Commodity	40	110263	26292	83972
文化、体育用品及器材专门零售	Specialized Retail of Stationers Goods, Sports Goods and Apparatus	5	3377		3377
汽车、摩托车、燃料及零配件专门零售	Specialized Retail of Automobile, Motorcycle, Fuel and Fittings	32	38928		38928
家用电器及电子产品专门零售	Specialized Retail of Household Appliance and Electronic Products	4	3133		3133
五金、家具及室内装修材料专门零售	Specialized Retail of Hardware, Furniture and Interior Decoration Materials	252	430606	47566	383040
按经营方式分组	**Group by Means of Operation**				
独立商店	Independent Store	377	636291	79684	556607
连锁商店分店	Branch Store of Chain Store	1	1085		1085
其 他	Others	5	4521		4521
按零售业态分组	**Group by Retail Size**				
百货商店	Composite Store	20	25709	4135	21574
超 市	Supermarket	7	7111		7111
食杂店	Traditional Grocery Stores	24	25185	5827	19358
家居建材商店	Home Building Materials Stores	267	504813	66747	438066
专业店	Specialized Store	59	74272	2546	71726
专卖店	Speciality Store	2	1518		1518
厂家直销中心	Factory Outlet Centers	2	2109	430	1679
便利店	Convenience Stores	1	660		660
大型超市	Large Supermarket	1	520		520

14-9 限额以上批发零售贸易企业主要财务指标（2011 年）
MAIN FINANCIAL INDICATORS OF WHOLESALE AND RETAIL ENTERPRISES ABOVE DESIGNATED SIZE（2011）

指 标	Item	流动资产合计 Total Circulating Funds	固定资产原价 Original Value of Fixed Assets	资产总计 Total Assets	负债总计 Total Liabilities
总 计	**Total**	**4921710**	**682589**	**6068069**	**4723130**
市 区	Urban Area	4657213	615430	5661573	4389907
溧阳市	Liyang City	92793	26781	137651	113886
金坛市	Jintan City	171704	40377	268845	219338
# 国有及国有控股	State-owned and State Holding Majority Shares	487228	59602	534908	234851
按登记注册类型分组	**Group by Registration Status**				
内 资	Domestic Investment	4720997	620475	5797818	4507385
国 有	State-owned	313578	53561	349318	83938
集 体	Collective-owned	6133	146	6403	5231
股份合作	Share-holding Cooperative	43078	6512	53960	50345
有限责任公司	Limited Liability Corporations	756298	94101	901711	746946
股份有限公司	Share-holding Cooperative Ltd.	181556	60435	304220	198927
私 营	Private	3414519	403700	4173808	3416941
其 他	Others	5835	2021	8399	5057
港澳台商投资	Hong Kong,Macao and Taiwan Funded	109002	36718	154555	114849
外商投资	Foreign Investment	91711	25396	115696	100897
批发贸易业	**Wholesale Trade**	**3176645**	**258771**	**3701489**	**2818992**
# 国有及国有控股	State-owned and State Holding Majority Shares	353181	43218	384152	112838
按登记注册类型分组	**Group by Registration Status**				
内 资	Domestic Investment	3031231	252774	3543223	2710666
国 有	State-owned	301339	41975	329725	71464
集 体	Collective-owned	4005	4	4006	3763
股份合作	Share-holding Cooperative	39153	5635	48684	46008
有限责任公司	Limited Liability Corporations	444318	42201	533560	443722
股份有限公司	Share-holding Cooperative Ltd.	34147	377	74265	66291
私 营	Private	2204719	161234	2547683	2076506
其 他	Others	3549	1351	5301	2912
港澳台商投资	Hong Kong,Macao and Taiwan Funded	77421	3702	88732	43959
外商投资	Foreign Investment	67993	2295	69534	64367
按主要行业分组	**Group by Sector**				
农畜产品批发	Wholesale of Agricultural and Animal Product	53043	11233	66146	48725
食品、饮料及烟草制品批发	Wholesale of Food,Beverages and Tobaccos	374475	44520	405648	128818
纺织、服装及日用品批发	Wholesale of Textile, Garments and Commodity	252873	20000	279782	227585
医药及医疗器材批发	Wholesale of Medicine and Medical Appliance	156943	13934	283237	226091
矿产品、建材及化工产品批发	Wholesale of Mineral Product, Building Material and Chemical Product	1850277	141380	2127144	1738862
机械设备、五金交电及电子产品批发	Wholesale of Machinery, Hardware and Eletronic Products	340313	23071	387195	322987
贸易经纪与代理	Trade Broker and Agent	48215	3744	51277	42344
其他批发	Others	100506	889	101061	83580

单位：万元（10000 yuan）

所有者权益 Creditors Equity	实收资本 Total Capital Hold	其中 of which #国家资本 State Capital	营业收入 Business Revenues	其中 of which #主营业务收入 Major Business Revenues	主营业务成本 Major Business Cost	主营业务税金及附加 Major Business Taxes and Extra Charges	营业利润 Profits from Bus iness	利润总额 Total profits	本年应交增值税 Value Added Tax Payable	全部从业人员年平均人数（人） Annual Average Number of Employees(person)
1344939	**793474**	**12660**	**14900129**	**14824663**	**13983470**	**50743**	**160932**	**193740**	**163184**	**45871**
1271666	721641	12351	14281500	14213276	13426474	47384	154516	186077	151520	39481
23766	19225		335473	331625	304114	2519	7480	7222	5116	2723
49508	52608	309	283156	279762	252882	840	-1064	440	6548	3667
300057	29263	9661	1155205	1153410	1013005	25493	85207	86828	22359	1828
1290434	726387	12660	14194502	14134511	13370791	48116	153492	187710	145273	41577
265379	4243	4243	475529	475529	353560	25060	77088	79262	19610	1021
1172	1579		83614	83614	82591	26	519	458	287	45
3616	1212		363907	363907	356748	125	477	450	1049	171
154765	116411	5310	2414423	2392972	2283440	5103	17676	27432	32672	6490
105292	32075	1793	509694	503825	459306	1591	18042	18618	7345	2639
756867	568332	1030	10320657	10288049	9809934	16201	39803	61457	84225	31074
3343	2535	284	26679	26616	25212	10	-112	33	86	137
39706	46030		326932	314640	259083	1687	11420	11540	11982	2402
14799	21057		378695	375512	353596	940	-3980	-5511	5929	1892
882497	**507664**	**8316**	**10928123**	**10893133**	**10412607**	**38096**	**98678**	**118782**	**110941**	**18359**
271314	10220	8036	898746	898620	774522	25155	80261	81432	20925	849
832558	473716	8316	10530363	10506118	10065737	37088	83456	103269	102513	18067
258261	2742	2742	453186	453186	336999	24963	76285	77968	18969	755
244	1027		72969	72969	72596	12	275	256	107	6
2676	362		347367	347367	340946	114	428	401	959	136
89837	67311	5260	1718692	1718562	1671243	3514	5968	15576	25060	1139
7975	18000		142255	142255	136055	95	-3289	-3265	916	1582
471177	382739	30	7775246	7751171	7488291	8382	3762	12161	56426	14367
2389	1535	284	20648	20608	19606	9	28	172	76	82
44773	29648		172063	161319	123530	975	13555	13908	8157	282
5167	4299		225697	225697	223340	33	1667	1606	270	10
17421	15359	185	184697	184697	177839	2127	100	1578	143	322
276830	12752	2587	685839	685178	553276	25194	81420	82326	20100	1472
52196	26502		974939	962717	916752	408	3264	10877	12286	7058
57146	59753		191206	190461	174726	248	-3078	-2705	1515	2384
388283	342651	5010	7268225	7260019	7074236	3310	3353	-1129	26256	4946
64209	28598	534	939529	927476	849728	1514	20951	23302	11564	1659
8932	6270		228032	226928	218761	22	831	835	-762	250
17480	15778		455656	455656	447288	5273	-8163	3699	39840	268

14-9 续表 Continued

指 标	Item	流动资产合计 Total Circulating Funds	固定资产原价 Original Value of Fixed Assets	资产总计 Total Assets	负债总计 Total Liabilities
零售贸易业	**Retail Trade**	**1745065**	**423818**	**2366580**	**1904138**
#国有及国有控股	State-owned and State Holding Majority Shares	134048	16384	150756	122014
按登记注册类型分组	**Group by Registration Status**				
内 资	Domestic Investment	1689766	367701	2254595	1796719
国 有	State-owned	12239	11586	19592	12474
集 体	Collective-owned	2129	142	2397	1468
股份合作	Share-holding Cooperative	3925	877	5277	4336
有限责任公司	Limited Liability Corporations	311980	51900	368151	303224
股份有限公司	Share-holding Cooperative Ltd.	147409	60058	229955	132637
私 营	Private	1209800	242467	1626125	1340435
其 他	Others	2286	670	3099	2145
港澳台商投资	Hong Kong,Macao and Taiwan Funded	31581	33016	65824	70890
外商投资	Foreign Investment	23719	23101	46162	36529
按主要行业分组	**Group by Sector**				
综合零售	Comprehensive Retail	608371	232682	871506	753451
食品、饮料及烟草制品专门零售	Speicalized Retail of Food, Beverage and Tobacco	18789	2938	21822	13370
纺织、服装及日用品专门零售	Specialized Retail of Textile, Garments and Commodity	17803	1903	19280	13213
文化、体育用品及器材专门零售	Specialized Retail of Stationers Goods, Sports Goods and Apparatus	97581	23969	117169	72429
医药及医疗器材专门零售	Specialized Retail of Medicine and Medical Appliance	201138	10619	238623	163458
汽车、摩托车、燃料及零配件专门零售	Specialized Retail of Automobile, Motorcycle, Fuel and Fittings	664033	119409	926136	770687
家用电器及电子产品专门零售	Specialized Retail of Household Appliance and Electronic Products	126656	25113	152808	105713
五金、家具及室内装修材料专门零售	Specialized Retail of Hardware, Furniture and Interior Decoration Materials	3176	4555	5896	4426
无店铺及其他零售	Retail without Shops and Other Retail	7519	2629	13339	7392
按经营方式分组	**Group by Means of Operation**				
独立商店	Independent Store	1307535	331678	1811036	1464034
连锁商店总店	Head Office of Chain Store	120702	32955	152503	117708
连锁商店分店	Branch Store of Chain Store	131913	44153	189988	163820
其 他	Others	184916	15031	213054	158576
按零售业态分组	**Group by Retail Size**				
百货商店	Composite Store	372062	127860	530224	428959
食杂店	Traditional Grocery Stores	295	35	311	239
超 市	Supermarket	35958	15499	49770	47039
大型超市	Large Supermarket	196272	87881	283164	270483
便利店	Convenience Stores	6108	1751	10652	7113
网上商店	Online stores	1280	239	2956	1422
厂家直销中心	Factory Outlet Centers	113666	1577	121182	101951
专业店	Specialized Store	408034	89286	547258	410878
专卖店	Speciality Store	611390	99689	821064	636055

单位：万元（10000 yuan）

所有者权益 Creditors Equity	实收资本 Total Capital Hold	其中 of which #国家资本 State Capital	营业收入 Business Revenues	其中 of which #主营业务收入 Major Business Revenues	主营业务成本 Major Business Cost	主营业务税金及附加 Major Business Taxes and Extra Charges	营业利润 Profits from Business	利润总额 Total Profits	本年应交增值税 Value Added Tax Payable	全部从业人员年平均人数（人） Annual Average Number of Employees(person)
462442	**285810**	**4344**	**3972007**	**3931530**	**3570863**	**12647**	**62254**	**74958**	**52243**	**27512**
28742	19042	1625	256458	254790	238483	338	4946	5397	1434	979
457876	252671	4344	3664139	3628394	3305054	11028	70036	84441	42760	23510
7118	1501	1501	22343	22343	16561	97	803	1294	641	266
929	552		10645	10645	9995	14	244	201	180	39
940	850		16540	16540	15802	11	49	49	90	35
64927	49101	50	695731	674410	612197	1590	11708	11857	7611	5351
97318	14075	1793	367439	361570	323251	1497	21331	21882	6429	1057
285690	185594	1000	2545412	2536878	2321643	7819	36041	49296	27799	16707
954	1000		6031	6009	5606	1	-139	-139	10	55
-5066	16382		154869	153321	135553	711	-2135	-2367	3824	2120
9632	16757		152999	149815	130257	907	-5647	-7116	5659	1882
118056	96328	50	960358	930409	790971	6347	20851	20655	24433	12119
8452	6194		37424	37424	33102	70	1068	1053	582	546
6068	2296		50649	50649	44165	53	1231	1122	637	439
44740	8325	1575	157201	157025	129784	2730	12146	23527	2757	935
75166	28185	1719	463967	462442	434935	623	9581	10020	3256	2500
155450	115936	1000	1925059	1923550	1809900	1863	5256	5861	15003	8137
47094	22453		340980	334032	294808	919	12397	13116	5383	2401
1470	565		12316	12316	11909	14	-234	-44	31	113
5947	5530		24055	23684	21290	29	-41	-352	161	322
347002	221019	4220	2942909	2921697	2677621	7238	30557	31702	36826	18549
34795	9722		345135	338275	288717	1134	10774	13166	6646	3162
26167	21033	124	335213	326372	280171	3471	14714	13078	6892	4514
54478	34037		348749	345186	324355	804	6209	17012	1879	1287
101266	39792		438256	426828	354363	4150	27115	27523	10968	4296
72	50		1412	1412	1341	1	9	8	10	15
2731	3862	50	115540	110858	93379	373	-1214	-10	2214	2203
12681	50723		407491	393651	344343	1827	-4464	-6281	11269	5651
3539	2237		6339	6339	5146	24	-192	-190	208	176
1534	1508		4507	4507	4047	16	-287	-592	53	68
19231	16608		198903	197377	190248	168	3119	3292	303	419
136380	67759	1575	1055225	1047494	944387	3998	24205	26397	12758	7549
185009	103271	2719	1744335	1743064	1633610	2091	13963	24810	14460	7135

14-10 市区限额以上批发零售贸易企业主要财务指标（2011 年）
MAIN FINANCIAL INDICATORS OF WHOLESALE AND RETAIL ENTERPRISES ABOVE DESIGNATED SIZE IN URBAN AREA（2011）

指 标	Item	流动资产合计 Total Circulating Funds	固定资产原价 Original Value of Fixed Assets	资产总计 Total Assets	负债总计 Total Liabilities
总 计	**Total**	**4657213**	**615430**	**5661573**	**4389907**
#国有及国有控股	State-owned and State Holding Majority Shares	470059	51361	511358	211931
按登记注册类型分组	**Group by Registration Status**				
内 资	Domestic Investment	4468603	557908	5406465	4186331
国 有	State-owned	301835	48155	332453	66719
集 体	Collective-owned	4771	74	4804	3763
股份合作	Share-holding Cooperative	42831	6465	53696	50147
有限责任公司	Limited Liability Corporations	744357	91538	886323	735321
股份有限公司	Share-holding Cooperative Ltd.	157689	58639	239321	139583
私 营	Private	3215464	352185	3887136	3189572
其 他	Others	1654	853	2732	1226
港澳台商投资	Hong Kong,Macao and Taiwan Funded	109002	36718	154555	114849
外商投资	Foreign Investment	79608	20804	100553	88727
批发贸易业	**Wholesale Trade**	**3087434**	**243478**	**3550857**	**2688623**
#国有及国有控股	State-owned and State Holding Majority Shares	341437	37812	367288	95618
按登记注册类型分组	**Group by Registration Status**				
内 资	Domestic Investment	2942021	237481	3392591	2580297
国 有	State-owned	289596	36569	312861	54245
集 体	Collective-owned	4005	4	4006	3763
股份合作	Share-holding Cooperative	39153	5635	48684	46008
有限责任公司	Limited Liability Corporations	441621	42168	530852	442384
股份有限公司	Share-holding Cooperative Ltd.	11900	114	11954	8889
私 营	Private	2154091	152140	2481503	2023782
其 他	Others	1654	853	2732	1226
港澳台商投资	Hong Kong,Macao and Taiwan Funded	77421	3702	88732	43959
外商投资	Foreign Investment	67993	2295	69534	64367
按主要行业分组	**Group by Sector**				
农畜产品批发	Wholesale of Agricultural and Animal Product	41299	5827	49282	31506
食品、饮料及烟草制品批发	Wholesale of Food,Beverages and Tobaccos	371534	42287	400682	123990
纺织、服装及日用品批发	Wholesale of Textile, Garments and Commodity	249219	19857	275905	225263
文化、体育用品及器材批发	Wholesale of Cultural,Sports Equipments and Appliances				
医药及医疗器材批发	Wholesale of Medicine and Medical Appliance	128336	12762	213374	162096
矿产品、建材及化工产品批发	Wholesale of Mineral Product, Building Material and Chemical Product	1822952	135575	2087516	1710183
机械设备、五金交电及电子产品批发	Wholesale of Machinery, Hardware and Eletronic Products	335767	22678	382235	319688
贸易经纪与代理	Trade Broker and Agent	46805	3604	49787	41534
其他批发	Others	91523	887	92077	74363

单位：万元（10000 yuan）

所有者权益 Creditors Equity	实收资本 Total Capital Hold	其中 of which #国家资本 State Capital	营业收入 Business Revenues	其中 of which #主营业务收入 Major Business Revenues	主营业务成本 Major Business Cost	主营业务税金及附加 Major Business Taxes and Extra Charges	营业利润 Profits from Business	利润总额 Total Profits	本年应交增值税 Value Added Tax Payable	全部从业人员年平均人数（人） Annual Average Number of Employees(person)
1271666	**721641**	**12351**	**14281500**	**14213276**	**13426474**	**47384**	**154516**	**186077**	**151520**	**39481**
299427	28903	9352	1128285	1126652	988720	25444	85600	86362	22075	1500
1220134	655054	12351	13631646	13578898	12861328	45056	148622	180169	137398	35863
265734	4058	4058	457560	457560	335931	25059	78115	79224	19610	975
1041	1467		82437	82437	81474	24	540	479	276	29
3549	1162		363290	363290	356177	124	475	448	1042	150
151001	112878	5260	2387680	2366672	2260651	5027	17466	27456	32403	5897
99738	17001	1719	465931	460152	421499	1476	21361	21732	6460	1028
697565	517965	1030	9861644	9835682	9393358	13336	30564	50642	77532	27730
1506	523	284	13105	13105	12238	9	101	189	76	54
39706	46030		326932	314640	259083	1687	11420	11540	11982	2402
11826	20557		322922	319738	306063	641	-5527	-5633	2141	1216
862234	**483950**	**8131**	**10610801**	**10577116**	**10112886**	**36538**	**104061**	**121083**	**107344**	**16186**
271669	10035	7851	880778	880652	756894	25154	81289	81394	20925	803
812294	450002	8131	10213042	10190101	9766017	35530	88839	105569	98916	15894
258616	2557	2557	435217	435217	319371	24962	77312	77930	18969	709
244	1027		72969	72969	72596	12	275	256	107	6
2676	362		347367	347367	340946	114	428	401	959	136
88468	67061	5260	1710537	1710407	1663467	3514	5670	15255	25114	1136
3064	3000		101794	101794	100608		283	92	118	22
457722	375472	30	7532052	7509241	7256791	6919	4770	11446	53573	13831
1506	523	284	13105	13105	12238	9	101	189	76	54
44773	29648		172063	161319	123530	975	13555	13908	8157	282
5167	4299		225697	225697	223340	33	1667	1606	270	10
17776	15174		166728	166728	160211	2126	1127	1540	143	276
276692	12636	2587	681300	680639	549406	25187	81338	82287	20048	1421
50643	25502		953269	941048	895885	408	3047	10658	12281	6979
51278	44410		142410	141665	131343	147	648	801	672	800
377333	337201	5010	7154288	7146173	6968539	3178	2768	-2351	25150	4621
62546	28148	534	916282	905443	828507	1502	20592	22919	11519	1612
8253	5550		221882	220779	213125	22	827	831	-763	226
17715	15328		374643	374643	365869	3968	-6285	4398	38296	251

14-10 续表 Continued

指 标	Item	流动资产合计 Total Circulating Funds	固定资产原价 Original Value of Fixed Assets	资产总计 Total Assets	负债总计 Total Liabilities
零售贸易业	**Retail Trade**	**1569778**	**371953**	**2110716**	**1701284**
#国有及国有控股	State-owned and State Holding Majority Shares	128622	13550	144070	116312
按登记注册类型分组	**Group by Registration Status**				
内 资	Domestic Investment	1526582	320427	2013874	1606034
国 有	State-owned	12239	11586	19592	12474
集 体	Collective-owned	766	71	798	
股份合作	Share-holding Cooperative	3678	830	5012	4139
有限责任公司	Limited Liability Corporations	302736	49370	355471	292937
股份有限公司	Share-holding Cooperative Ltd.	145790	58525	227367	130694
私 营	Private	1061373	200045	1405633	1165790
港澳台商投资	Hong Kong,Macao and Taiwan Funded	31581	33016	65824	70890
外商投资	Foreign Investment	11616	18510	31019	24360
按主要行业分组	**Group by Sector**				
综合零售	Comprehensive Retail	472201	190853	667110	588367
食品、饮料及烟草制品专门零售	Speicalized Retail of Food, Beverage and Tobacco	16829	2668	19268	11833
纺织、服装及日用品专门零售	Specialized Retail of Textile, Garments and Commodity	17803	1903	19280	13213
文化、体育用品及器材专门零售	Specialized Retail of Stationers Goods, Sports Goods and Apparatus	89408	20827	107116	64253
医药及医疗器材专门零售	Specialized Retail of Medicine and Medical Appliance	199515	10350	236746	161726
汽车、摩托车、燃料及零配件专门零售	Specialized Retail of Automobile, Motorcycle, Fuel and Fittings	646402	114188	902205	751598
家用电器及电子产品专门零售	Specialized Retail of Household Appliance and Electronic Products	120367	24971	146445	102269
五金、家具及室内装修材料专门零售	Specialized Retail of Hardware, Furniture and Interior Decoration Materials	3176	4555	5896	4426
无店铺及其他零售	Retail without Shops and Other Retail	4078	1637	6649	3600
按经营方式分组	**Group by Means of Operation**				
独立商店	Independent Store	1186042	300799	1647143	1336514
连锁商店总店	Head Office of Chain Store	119039	31464	149453	114717
连锁商店分店	Branch Store of Chain Store	80226	24697	101527	91732
其 他	Others	184471	14993	212594	158321
按零售业态分组	**Group by Retail Size**				
百货商店	Composite Store	349315	115654	475582	387911
食杂店	Traditional Grocery Stores	295	35	311	239
超 市	Supermarket	33800	12878	45785	41469
大型超市	Large Supermarket	85007	60880	137394	152018
便利店	Convenience Stores	6108	1751	10652	7113
网上商店	Online stores	1280	239	2956	1422
厂家直销中心	Factory Outlet Centers	112694	1105	119489	100052
专业店	Specialized Store	374950	81866	503745	379162
专卖店	Speciality Store	606330	97545	814802	631899

单位：万元（10000 yuan）

所有者权益 Creditors Equity	实收资本 Total Capital Hold	其中 of which #国家资本 State Capital	营业收入 Business Revenues	其中 of which #主营业务收入 Major Business Revenues	主营业务成本 Major Business Cost	主营业务税金及附加 Major Business Taxes and Extra Charges	营业利润 Profits from Business	利润总额 Total Profits	本年应交增值税 Value Added Tax Payable	全部从业人员年平均人数（人） Annual Average Number of Employees(person)
409432	**237691**	**4220**	**3670699**	**3636160**	**3313588**	**10846**	**50455**	**64995**	**44176**	**23295**
27758	18868	1501	247508	246001	231826	290	4311	4969	1151	697
407840	205052	4220	3418604	3388797	3095311	9526	59783	74600	38482	19969
7118	1501	1501	22343	22343	16561	97	803	1294	641	266
798	440		9468	9468	8878	13	265	223	169	23
873	800		15922	15922	15231	10	47	47	83	14
62534	45818		677143	656265	597184	1514	11796	12201	7289	4761
96674	14001	1719	364137	358358	320891	1476	21079	21640	6342	1006
239843	142493	1000	2329591	2326441	2136567	6417	25794	39196	23959	13899
-5066	16382		154869	153321	135553	711	-2135	-2367	3824	2120
6659	16257		97225	94041	82724	608	-7193	-7238	1870	1206
78742	59722		777690	753458	641257	4816	10076	11413	17306	9317
7435	5439		33593	33593	30090	61	753	661	517	467
6068	2296		50649	50649	44165	53	1231	1122	637	439
42863	8017	1501	144537	144537	120093	2553	11651	23114	2404	600
75021	27835	1719	459832	458307	431415	614	9792	10294	3201	2298
150607	111067	1000	1849489	1848003	1738795	1808	4977	5812	14703	7639
44176	20003		329996	323071	284679	908	12320	13040	5295	2278
1470	565		12316	12316	11909	14	-234	-44	31	113
3050	2747		12597	12226	11183	21	-110	-416	82	144
310629	186783	4220	2812032	2792646	2562757	6703	28391	29747	32897	16675
34736	9117		338380	331520	282525	1124	11021	13412	6587	2972
9795	7858		174339	169609	146460	2219	4968	4955	2833	2394
54273	33933		345948	342385	321846	799	6076	16880	1860	1254
87671	26892		381164	371126	307846	3388	22710	23143	9065	3219
72	50		1412	1412	1341	1	9	8	10	15
4316	3157		107340	103015	86428	355	-732	589	2143	1928
-14624	27723		290116	280245	248098	1074	-11318	-11741	6115	4201
3539	2237		6339	6339	5146	24	-192	-190	208	176
1534	1508		4507	4507	4047	16	-287	-592	53	68
19437	16558		197228	195702	188686	167	3217	3390	296	408
124583	57395	1501	973074	965564	870680	3761	23783	26270	12077	6283
182904	102171	2719	1709521	1708249	1601317	2059	13264	24118	14209	6997

14-11　限额以上住宿餐饮企业主要情况（2011 年）
MAIN CONDITION OF ACCOMMODATION AND CATERING BUSINESS ABOVE DESIGNATED SIZE（2011）

指　标	Item	企业数（个） Number of Enterprises (unit)	年末餐饮营业面积（平方米） Operation Area of Catering At Year-end (sq.m)
总　计	**Total**	**149**	**676368**
市　区	Urban Area	107	501414
溧阳市	Liyang City	22	126374
金坛市	Jintan City	20	48580
#国有及国有控股	State-owned and State Holding Majority Shares	6	16178
按登记注册类型分组	**Group by Registration Status**		
内　资	Domestic Investment	139	613228
国　有	State-owned	5	15658
集　体	Collective-owned	2	500
股份合作	Cooperative	1	1298
有限责任公司	Limited Liability Corporations	10	44857
私　营	Private	120	548915
其　他	Others	1	2000
港澳台商投资	Hong Kong,Macao and Taiwan Funded	7	54733
外商投资	Foreign Investment	3	8407
住宿业	**Accommodation Trade**	**62**	**280153**
#国有及国有控股	State-owned and State Holding Majority Shares	6	16178
按登记注册类型分组	**Group by Registration Status**		
内　资	Domestic Investment	57	255567
国　有	State-owned	5	15658
集　体	Collective-owned	1	
有限责任公司	Limited Liability Corporations	4	20477
私　营	Private	47	219432
港澳台商投资	Hong Kong,Macao and Taiwan Funded	3	20086
外商投资	Foreign Investment	2	4500

营业收入（万元） Operational Revenues (10000 yuan)	其中 of which 客房收入 Room Rate Revenues	餐费收入 Catering Revenues	商品销售收入 Commodity Sales Revenues	其他收入 Other Revenues	床位数（张） Number of Beds (bed)	餐位数（位） Catering Seats Available (Seat)
477300	**90957**	**365210**	**6854**	**14279**	**21150**	**78396**
384532	65158	305166	3675	10534	14716	60804
66811	20732	41086	2489	2505	5011	12929
25956	5067	18958	691	1241	1423	4663
7350	2590	3265	943	552	1090	2330
397318	76200	302314	6785	12018	19051	73425
6637	2311	2944	943	440	993	2130
1237	981	149	16	91	350	30
381	94	288			64	300
41467	11703	27379	732	1654	2304	6050
346829	61113	270787	5095	9834	15340	64515
767		767				400
62664	11964	49266	8	1425	1769	3675
17318	2793	13629	61	836	330	1296
184521	**71647**	**96419**	**4892**	**11563**	**16575**	**28144**
7350	2590	3265	943	552	1090	2330
154750	59929	80307	4823	9691	14942	26596
6637	2311	2944	943	440	993	2130
940	877		1	62	200	
21697	7307	12329	589	1473	1346	2440
125475	49433	65035	3291	7717	12403	22026
22959	8925	12990	8	1036	1303	1398
6812	2793	3123	61	836	330	150

14-11 续表　Continued

指　标	Item	企业数（个）Number of Enterprises (unit)	年末餐饮营业面积（平方米）Operation Area of Catering At Year-end (sq.m)
按星级饭店分组	**Restaurants Grouped By Star Level**		
五　星	Five-star	6	71998
四　星	Four-star	16	115214
三　星	Three-star	16	49846
二　星	Two-star	4	2050
一　星	One-star	2	1650
其　他	Others	18	39395
餐饮业	**Catering Trade**	**87**	**396215**
按登记注册类型分组	**Group by Registration Status**		
内　资	Domestic Investment	82	357661
集　体	Collective-owned	1	500
股份合作	Cooperative	1	1298
有限责任公司	Limited Liability Corporations	6	24380
私　营	Private	73	329483
其　他	Others	1	2000
港澳台商投资	Hong Kong,Macao and Taiwan Funded	4	34647
外商投资	Foreign Investment	1	3907
按主要行业分组	**Group by Sector**		
正　餐	Dinner	80	295053
快　餐	Fast Food	5	99472
饮料及冷饮服务	Beverage and Cold Drinks		700
其他餐饮业	Others	2	990
按经营方式分组	**Group by Means of Operation**		
独立商店	Independent Store	78	250556
连锁商店总店	Head Office of Chain Store	3	113150
连锁商店分店	Branch Store of Chain Store	3	23822
其　他	Others	3	8687

营业收入（万元）Operational Revenues (10000 yuan)	其中 of which				床位数（张）Number of Beds (bed)	餐位数（位）Catering Seats Available (Seat)
	客房收入 Room Rate Revenues	餐费收入 Catering Revenues	商品销售收入 Commodity Sales Revenues	其他收入 Other Revenues		
57349	19036	33279	1857	3177	2749	6270
74453	29421	37650	1364	6018	4759	11026
17476	7489	8703	266	1018	3339	6195
3739	1670	1910	87	72	618	822
1997	1174	621		201	401	200
29507	12856	14255	1318	1078	4709	3631
292779	**19310**	**268790**	**1962**	**2716**	**4575**	**50252**
242568	16272	222007	1962	2327	4109	46829
297	103	149	15	29	150	30
381	94	288			64	300
19770	4395	15050	143	181	958	3610
221353	11680	205753	1804	2117	2937	42489
767		767				400
39704	3039	36277		389	466	2277
10507		10507				1146
155261	19310	131273	1962	2716	4575	42749
130460		130460				7007
1224		1224				70
5833		5833				426
139897	14780	121016	1936	2165	3792	39652
123616		123616				6744
12836	1270	11353	26	187	319	2534
16430	3261	12805		364	464	1322

14-12 限额以上个体住宿餐饮企业主要情况（2011 年）
MAIN CONDITION OF INDIVIDUAL ACCOMMODATION AND CATERING BUSINESS ABOVE DESIGNATED SIZE（2011）

指 标	Item	户数（户）Number of Enterprises (Unit)	从业人员数（人）Number of Employees (People)
总 计	**Total**	**215**	**10217**
市 区	Urban Area	162	9180
溧阳市	Liyang City	29	604
金坛市	Jintan City	24	433
住宿业	**Accommodation Trade**	**12**	**323**
按主要行业分组	**Group by Sector**		
旅游饭店	Tourist Hotel	3	59
一般旅馆	Regular Hotel	5	133
其他住宿服务	Other Accommodation	4	131
餐饮业	**Catering Trade**	**203**	**9894**
按主要行业分组	**Group by Sector**		
正 餐	Dinner	181	8847
快 餐	Fast Food	3	65
饮料及冷饮服务	Beverage and Cold Drinks	10	742
其他餐饮业	Others	9	240
按经营方式分组	**Group by Means of Operation**		
独立商店	Independent Store	196	9728
连锁商店分店	Branch Store of Chain Store	6	141
其 他	Others	1	25

营业收入（万元）Operational Revenues (10000 yuan)	其　中　of　which				床位数（张）Number of Beds (bed)	餐位数（位）Catering Seats Available (Seat)
	客房收入 Room Rate Revenues	餐费收入 Catering Revenues	商品销售收入 Commodity Sales Revenues	其他收入 Other Revenues		
138725	**5925**	**105288**	**27138**	**375**	**2476**	**49035**
112302	4280	81802	25881	340	1790	40855
12702	1462	9948	1258	35	646	3275
13721	183	13538			40	4905
5313	**2644**	**2444**	**83**	**143**	**754**	**1468**
1655	792	840	23		218	350
2367	715	1456	55	141	256	956
1292	1137	148	5	2	280	162
133412	**3281**	**102844**	**27055**	**232**	**1722**	**47567**
103290	3281	93957	5824	229	1722	43822
734		716	15	3		570
24214		2997	21217			1910
5174		5174				1265
130639	3082	100522	26902	132	1562	46251
2436	198	1985	153	100	160	1236
336		336				80

14-13 市区限额以上住宿餐饮企业主要情况（2011 年）
MAIN CONDITION OF ACCOMMODATION AND CATERING TRADE ABOVE DESIGNATED SIZE WITHIN CITY（2011）

指 标	Item	企业数（个）Number of Enterprises (unit)	年末餐饮营业面积（平方米）Operation Area of Catering At Year-end (sq.m)
总 计	**Total**	**107**	**501414**
#国有及国有控股	State-owned and State Holding Majority Shares	3	11860
按登记注册类型分组	**Group by Registration Status**		
内 资	Domestic Investment	100	450564
国 有	State-owned	3	11860
集 体	Collective-owned	1	
股份合作	Share-holding Cooperative	1	1298
有限责任公司	Limited Liability Corporations	7	38037
私 营	Private	87	397369
其 他	Others	1	2000
港澳台商投资	Hong Kong,Macao and Taiwan Funded	6	45733
外商投资	Foreign Investment	1	5117
住宿业	**Accommodation Trade**	**35**	**143598**
#国有及国有控股	State-owned and State Holding Majority Shares	3	11860
按登记注册类型分组	**Group by Registration Status**		
内 资	Domestic Investment	31	120512
国 有	State-owned	3	11860
集 体	Collective-owned	1	
有限责任公司	Limited Liability Corporations	2	14957
私 营	Private	25	93695
港澳台商投资	Hong Kong,Macao and Taiwan Funded	3	20086
外商投资	Foreign Investment	1	3000

营业收入（万元）Operational Revenues (10000 yuan)	其　中　of　which				床位数（张）Number of Beds (bed)	餐位数（位）Catering Seats Available (Seat)
	客房收入 Room Rate Revenues	餐费收入 Catering Revenues	商品销售收入 Commodity Sales Revenues	其他收入 Other Revenues		
384532	**65158**	**305166**	**3675**	**10534**	**14716**	**60804**
6019	2150	2520	938	411	745	1420
313253	51342	249947	3627	8337	12854	57169
6019	2150	2520	938	411	745	1420
940	877		1	62	200	
381	94	288			64	300
34036	10320	21759	566	1391	1905	5270
271110	37901	224613	2122	6473	9940	49779
767		767				400
61109	11843	47858	8	1401	1694	2875
10170	1974	7361	39	796	168	760
113939	**46624**	**56702**	**2300**	**8313**	**10712**	**15606**
6019	2150	2520	938	411	745	1420
85409	35725	40951	2253	6481	9241	14058
6019	2150	2520	938	411	745	1420
940	877		1	62	200	
16380	5934	8665	566	1216	1027	2240
62070	26764	29767	748	4792	7269	10398
22959	8925	12990	8	1036	1303	1398
5571	1974	2762	39	796	168	150

14-13 续表 Continued

指 标	Item	企业数（个）Number of Enterprises (unit)	年末餐饮营业面积（平方米）Operation Area of Catering At Year-end (sq.m)
按星级饭店分组	**Restaurants Grouped By Star Level**		
五 星	Five-star	2	21436
四 星	Four-star	7	66002
三 星	Three-star	10	32795
二 星	Two-star	2	650
一 星	One-star	2	1650
其 他	Others	12	21065
餐饮业	**Catering Trade**	**72**	**357816**
按登记注册类型分组	**Group by Registration Status**		
内 资	Domestic Investment	69	330052
股份合作	Cooperative	1	1298
有限责任公司	Limited Liability Corporations	5	23080
私 营	Private	62	303674
其 他	Others	1	2000
港澳台商投资	Hong Kong,Macao and Taiwan Funded	3	25647
外商投资	Foreign Investment		2117
按主要行业分组	**Group by Sector**		
正 餐	Dinner	67	258544
快 餐	Fast Food	4	97682
饮料及冷饮服务	Beverage and Cold Drinks		700
其他餐饮业	Others	1	890
按经营方式分组	**Group by Means of Operation**		
独立商店	Independent Store	64	213947
连锁商店总店	Head Office of Chain Store	3	113150
连锁商店分店	Branch Store of Chain Store	2	22032
其 他	Others	3	8687

营业收入（万元）Operational Revenues (10000 yuan)	其中 of which 客房收入 Room Rate Revenues	餐费收入 Catering Revenues	商品销售收入 Commodity Sales Revenues	其他收入 Other Revenues	床位数（张）Number of Beds (bed)	餐位数（位）Catering Seats Available (Seat)
27962	10748	15010	33	2171	1207	2070
46436	17639	23852	693	4252	2576	5748
12522	5384	6136	262	740	1975	3975
765	607	126	11	21	367	242
1997	1174	621		201	401	200
24258	11072	10958	1301	928	4186	3371
270593	**18535**	**248463**	**1374**	**2221**	**4004**	**45198**
227844	15618	208996	1374	1856	3613	43111
381	94	288			64	300
17656	4387	13095		175	878	3030
209040	11138	194847	1374	1681	2671	39381
767		767				400
38150	2917	34868		364	391	1477
4599		4599				610
139174	18535	117045	1374	2221	4004	38231
124553		124553				6471
1224		1224				70
5642		5642				426
123618	14005	106596	1348	1669	3221	35134
123616		123616				6744
6929	1270	5446	26	187	319	1998
16430	3261	12805		364	464	1322

14-14　市区限额以上个体住宿餐饮企业主要情况（2011 年）
MAIN CONDITION OF INDIVUDUAL ACCOMMODATION AND CATERING BUSINESS ABOVE DESIGNATED SIZE IN URBAN AREA（2011）

指　标	Item	户数（户）Number of Enterprises (unit)	从业人员数（人）Number of Employees (person)
总　计	**Total**	**162**	**9180**
住宿业	**Accommodation Trade**	**8**	**256**
按主要行业分组	**Group by Sector**		
旅游饭店	Tourist Hotel	1	18
一般旅馆	Regular Hotel	5	133
其他住宿服务	Other Accommodation	2	105
餐饮业	**Catering Trade**	**154**	**8924**
按主要行业分组	**Group by Sector**		
正　餐	Dinner	140	8052
快　餐	Fast Food	1	52
饮料及冷饮服务	Beverage and Cold Drinks	10	742
其他餐饮业	Others	3	78
按经营方式分组	**Group by Means of Operation**		
独立商店	Independent Store	147	8758
连锁商店分店	Branch Store of Chain Store	6	141
其　他	Others	1	25

营业收入（万元）Operational Revenues (10000 yuan)	其中 of which				床位数（张）Number of Beds (bed)	餐位数（位）Catering Seats Available (Seat)
	客房收入 Room Rate Revenues	餐费收入 Catering Revenues	商品销售收入 Commodity Sales Revenues	其他收入 Other Revenues		
112302	**4280**	**81802**	**25881**	**340**	**1790**	**40855**
3636	**1533**	**1903**	**60**	**141**	**478**	**1218**
663	319	344			82	150
2367	715	1456	55	141	256	956
606	498	103	5		140	112
108667	**2747**	**79899**	**25821**	**199**	**1312**	**39637**
82162	2747	74611	4604	199	1312	36777
424		424				320
24214		2997	21217			1910
1867		1867				630
105894	2549	77578	25668	99	1152	38321
2436	198	1985	153	100	160	1236
336		336				80

14-15 限额以上住宿餐饮企业财务指标（2011 年）
FINANCIAL INDEX OF ACCOMMODATION AND CATERING TRADE ABOVE DESIGNATED SIZE（2011）

指 标	Item	流动资产合计 Total Circulating Funds	固定资产原价 Original Value of Fixed Assets	资产总计 Total Assets	负债总计 Total Liabilities
总 计	**Total**	**201904**	**370324**	**569952**	**471601**
市 区	Urban Area	167537	271975	434116	369461
溧阳市	Liyang City	28520	68862	85693	66272
金坛市	Jintan City	5847	29487	50143	35868
#国有及国有控股	State-owned and State Holding Majority Shares	10158	16546	16570	6484
按登记注册类型分组	**Group by Registration Status**				
内 资	Domestic Investment	167616	339101	515248	417867
国 有	State-owned	9976	16498	16368	6299
集 体	Collective-owned	1204	833	1779	2324
股份合作	Cooperative	132	174	207	149
有限责任公司	Limited Liability Corporations	3199	52241	56576	36290
私 营	Private	153015	269278	440203	372750
其 他	Others	90	76	115	55
港澳台商投资	Hong Kong,Macao and Taiwan Funded	31892	14688	39974	41996
外商投资	Foreign Investment	2397	16536	14730	11739
住宿业	**Accommodation Trade**	**98899**	**281142**	**350771**	**303676**
#国有及国有控股	State-owned and State Holding Majority Shares	10158	16546	16570	6484
按登记注册类型分组	**Group by Registration Status**				
内 资	Domestic Investment	73225	256211	309432	260540
国 有	State-owned	9976	16498	16368	6299
集 体	Collective-owned	617	694	1145	1047
有限责任公司	Limited Liability Corporations	-586	50446	45361	25314
私 营	Private	63219	188572	246558	227880
港澳台商投资	Hong Kong,Macao and Taiwan Funded	23889	9013	28602	31649
外商投资	Foreign Investment	1785	15918	12737	11488

单位：万元（10000 yuan）

所有者权益 Creditors Equity	实收资本 Total Capital Hold	其中 of which #国家资本 State Capital	营业收入 Business Revenues	其中 of which #主营业务收入 Major Business Revenues	主营业务成本 Major Business Cost	主营业务税金及附加 Major Business Taxes and Extra Charges	营业利润 Profits from Business	利润总额 Total Profits	全部从业人员年平均人数（人） Annual Average Number of Employees (person)
98351	**146112**	**5794**	**452827**	**451511**	**186298**	**24534**	**7130**	**3760**	**30737**
64655	105044	4574	361944	361173	153397	19378	5990	5549	24911
19420	17942	1200	65480	65034	21399	3656	2281	1004	3713
14275	23125	20	25403	25303	11503	1500	-1140	-2793	2113
10087	2713	2713	7330	7308	2553	337	-262	-232	445
97381	130063	2713	380281	379154	157709	20481	2612	185	26603
10069	2693	2693	6617	6596	2305	301	-259	-225	383
-545	118		1174	1174	165	66	-100	-101	105
58	20		380	380	217	16	100	8	40
20286	48554	20	32564	32539	16440	1805	-3114	-3092	2201
67453	78648		338779	337698	138123	18251	5969	3580	23829
61	30		767	767	460	43	16	16	45
-2022	6934		61065	61065	22993	3426	3890	3894	3728
2991	9114	3081	11480	11292	5596	627	628	-319	406
47096	**93249**	**5794**	**166198**	**165537**	**57454**	**9149**	**-2514**	**-5458**	**9656**
10087	2713	2713	7330	7308	2553	337	-262	-232	445
48893	83671	2713	138229	137756	49413	7599	-4882	-6871	8778
10069	2693	2693	6617	6596	2305	301	-259	-225	383
98	98		877	877	13	49	-21	-21	63
20048	46874	20	13204	13204	7888	734	-2423	-2515	915
18678	34006		117531	117079	39208	6516	-2180	-4110	7417
-3046	970		21464	21464	4285	1200	2393	2385	608
1249	8608	3081	6505	6317	3755	349	-25	-972	270

14-15 续表 Continued

指 标	Item	流动资产合计 Total Circulating Funds	固定资产原价 Original Value of Fixed Assets	资产总计 Total Assets	负债总计 Total Liabilities
按星级饭店分组	**Restaurants Grouped By Star Level**				
五 星	Five-star	32916	99644	133539	125859
四 星	Four-star	19076	121682	97748	81548
三 星	Three-star	18229	29036	57131	47272
二 星	Two-star	326	3084	3279	4447
一 星	One-star	3522	5862	7098	5988
其 他	Others	24830	21834	51976	38563
餐饮业	**Catering Trade**	**103005**	**89182**	**219181**	**167926**
按登记注册类型分组	**Group by Registration Status**				
内 资	Domestic Investment	94391	82890	205815	157327
集 体	Collective-owned	587	139	634	1277
股份合作	Cooperative	132	174	207	149
有限责任公司	Limited Liability Corporations	3785	1795	11215	10977
私 营	Private	89796	80706	193645	144870
其 他	Others	90	76	115	55
港澳台商投资	Hong Kong,Macao and Taiwan Funded	8003	5675	11372	10347
外商投资	Foreign Investment	612	618	1994	252
按主要行业分组	**Group by Sector**				
正 餐	Dinner	71632	66789	159280	134446
快 餐	Fast Food	30836	21292	53996	29307
其他餐饮业	Others	537	1101	5904	4172
按经营方式分组	**Group by Means of Operation**				
独立商店	Independent Store	66878	64585	148145	126475
连锁商店总店	Head Office of Chain Store	28693	21158	53331	31158
连锁商店分店	Branch Store of Chain Store	3160	1259	5211	1881
其 他	Others	4274	2180	12494	8411

单位：万元（10000 yuan）

所有者权益 Creditors Equity	实收资本 Total Capital Hold	其中 of which	营业收入 Business Revenues	其中 of which	主营业务成本 Major Business Cost	主营业务税金及附加 Major Business Taxes and Extra Charges	营业利润 Profits from Business	利润总额 Total Profits	全部从业人员年平均人数（人）Annual Average Number of Employees（person）
		#国家资本 State Capital		#主营业务收入 Major Business Revenues					
7681	25808		55607	55291	14195	3106	-222	-1334	2279
16200	49232	3081	66185	65996	25294	3674	-188	-1620	3969
9860	9030	1663	17279	17164	5955	941	-1268	-1237	1317
-1168	375		3725	3725	1904	246	173	173	153
1110	1058		1997	1997	569	100	40	40	107
13413	7745	1050	21407	21365	9537	1082	-1050	-1479	1831
51255	**52863**		**286628**	**285974**	**128845**	**15385**	**9644**	**9218**	**21081**
48488	46392		242052	241398	108296	12882	7494	7056	17825
-643	20		297	297	152	16	-80	-80	42
58	20		380	380	217	16	100	8	40
238	1680		19360	19335	8553	1071	-691	-577	1286
48775	44642		221248	220619	98916	11736	8149	7690	16412
61	30		767	767	460	43	16	16	45
1024	5964		39601	39601	18708	2225	1497	1510	3120
1742	506		4975	4975	1841	279	653	653	136
24834	36756		154875	154242	71309	8599	126	-395	9776
24689	15556		126153	126153	53485	6471	9443	9552	11073
1732	550		5601	5579	4051	315	76	61	232
21669	35406		136986	136332	64995	7701	-1036	-1622	8951
22173	14800		123616	123616	53649	6244	8653	8829	10947
3329	2006		9596	9596	3366	529	690	691	425
4084	650		16430	16430	6836	912	1337	1320	758

14-16 市区限额以上住宿餐饮企业财务指标（2011 年）
FINANCIAL INDEX OF ACCOMMODATION AND CATERING TRADE ABOVE DESIGNATED SIZE WITHIN CITY（2011）

指 标	Item	流动资产合计 Total Circulating Funds	固定资产原价 Original Value of Fixed Assets	资产总计 Total Assets	负债总计 Total Liabilities
总 计	**Total**	**167537**	**271975**	**434116**	**369461**
# 国有及国有控股	State-owned and State Holding Majority Shares	9802	12870	15086	5220
按登记注册类型分组	**Group by Registration Status**				
内 资	Domestic Investment	135062	246447	384939	320044
国 有	State-owned	9802	12870	15086	5220
集 体	Collective-owned	617	694	1145	1047
股份合作	Cooperative	132	174	207	149
有限责任公司	Limited Liability Corporations	8504	46988	37132	28120
私 营	Private	115917	185644	331254	285453
其 他	Others	90	76	115	55
港澳台商投资	Hong Kong,Macao and Taiwan Funded	31620	14125	39150	41258
外商投资	Foreign Investment	855	11403	10027	8159
住宿业	**Accommodation Trade**	**74861**	**197757**	**241814**	**223887**
# 国有及国有控股	State-owned and State Holding Majority Shares	9802	12870	15086	5220
按登记注册类型分组	**Group by Registration Status**				
内 资	Domestic Investment	50117	177340	203185	184080
国 有	State-owned	9802	12870	15086	5220
集 体	Collective-owned	617	694	1145	1047
有限责任公司	Limited Liability Corporations	5459	45337	26684	17697
私 营	Private	34238	118439	160269	160116
港澳台商投资	Hong Kong,Macao and Taiwan Funded	23889	9013	28602	31649
外商投资	Foreign Investment	855	11403	10027	8159

单位：万元（10000 yuan）

所有者权益 Creditors Equity	实收资本 Total Capital Hold	其中 of which #国家资本 State Capital	营业收入 Business Revenues	其中 of which #主营业务收入 Major Business Revenues	主营业务成本 Major Business Cost	主营业务税金及附加 Major Business Taxes and Extra Charges	营业利润 Profits from Business	利润总额 Total Profits	全部从业人员年平均人数（人） Annual Average Number of Employees (person)
64655	**105044**	**4574**	**361944**	**361173**	**153397**	**19378**	**5990**	**5549**	**24911**
9866	**1493**	**1493**	**5999**	**5999**	**2100**	**268**	**67**	**102**	**307**
64896	91089	1493	297065	296483	127687	15748	2558	2117	21158
9866	1493	1493	5999	5999	2100	268	67	102	307
98	98		877	877	13	49	-21	-21	63
58	20		380	380	217	16	100	8	40
9012	32604		25791	25766	13409	1428	-1440	-1430	1713
45801	56844		263251	262694	111489	13945	3836	3443	18990
61	30		767	767	460	43	16	16	45
-2109	6847		59614	59614	22332	3345	3924	3929	3601
1868	7108	3081	5265	5076	3379	286	-492	-497	152
17927	**56530**	**4574**	**96056**	**95865**	**34747**	**5228**	**-3306**	**-3394**	**5311**
9866	1493	1493	5999	5999	2100	268	67	102	307
19105	48452	1493	69327	69325	27083	3741	-5207	-5282	4551
9866	1493	1493	5999	5999	2100	268	67	102	307
98	98		877	877	13	49	-21	-21	63
8987	30974		8135	8135	6049	452	-695	-787	485
154	15887		54316	54314	18921	2973	-4558	-4576	3696
-3046	970		21464	21464	4285	1200	2393	2385	608
1868	7108	3081	5265	5076	3379	286	-492	-497	152

14-16 续表　Continued

指　标	Item	流动资产合　计 Total Circulating Funds	固定资产原　价 Original Value of Fixed Assets	资产总计 Total Assets	负债总计 Total Liabilities
按星级饭店分组	**Restaurants Grouped By Star Level**				
五　星	Five-star	29088	50320	63885	77148
四　星	Four-star	10535	101508	77477	63181
三　星	Three-star	8878	18556	42649	38609
二　星	Two-star	60	3039	2975	4165
一　星	One-star	3522	5862	7098	5988
其　他	Others	22779	18471	47731	34796
餐饮业	**Catering Trade**	**92676**	**74219**	**192302**	**145574**
按登记注册类型分组	**Group by Registration Status**				
内　资	Domestic Investment	84946	69106	181755	135964
股份合作	Cooperative	132	174	207	149
有限责任公司	Limited Liability Corporations	3044	1651	10447	10423
私　营	Private	81679	67206	170985	125338
其　他	Others	90	76	115	55
港澳台商投资	Hong Kong,Macao and Taiwan Funded	7730	5112	10547	9610
按主要行业分组	**Group by Sector**				
正　餐	Dinner	61972	52489	134473	112361
快　餐	Fast Food	30224	20675	52002	29056
其他餐饮业	Others	480	1055	5827	4157
按经营方式分组	**Group by Means of Operation**				
独立商店	Independent Store	57160	50240	123260	104375
连锁商店总店	Head Office of Chain Store	28693	21158	53331	31158
连锁商店分店	Branch Store of Chain Store	2549	641	3217	1630
其　他	Others	4274	2180	12494	8411

所有者权益 Creditors Equity	实收资本 Total Capital Hold	其中 of which	营业收入 Business Revenues	其中 of which	主营业务成本 Major Business Cost	主营业务税金及附加 Major Business Taxes and Extra Charges	营业利润 Profits from Business	利润总额 Total Profits	全部从业人员年平均人数(人) Annual Average Number of Employees (person)
		#国家资本 State Capital		#主营业务收入 Major Business Revenues					
-13263	2728		26469	26469	5352	1532	568	535	899
14295	41412	3081	38464	38275	17195	2099	-1537	-1546	2043
4040	3941	463	12324	12324	4228	677	-549	-514	886
-1190	193		763	763	105	43	-293	-293	77
1110	1058		1997	1997	569	100	40	40	107
12935	7197	1030	16040	16038	7299	778	-1535	-1615	1299
46728	**48514**		**265888**	**265308**	**118650**	**14151**	**9296**	**8943**	**19600**
45791	42637		227738	227159	100604	12006	7765	7399	16607
58	20		380	380	217	16	100	8	40
25	1630		17656	17631	7360	976	-745	-643	1228
45647	40957		208935	208380	92568	10972	8395	8019	15294
61	30		767	767	460	43	16	16	45
938	5877		38150	38150	18046	2144	1531	1545	2993
22111	32964		139300	138721	63058	7653	430	-17	8463
22947	15050		121178	121178	51644	6192	8790	8900	10937
1670	500		5410	5410	3949	306	76	60	200
18885	31564		121221	120641	56641	6745	-732	-1244	7606
22173	14800		123616	123616	53649	6244	8653	8829	10947
1587	1500		4621	4621	1525	250	38	38	289
4084	650		16430	16430	6836	912	1337	1320	758

14-17 亿元商品交易市场基本情况（2011 年）
MARKETS WITH TRANSACTION VOLUME OVER 100 MILLION YUAN（2011）

指 标	Item	市场个数（个）Number of Markets (unit)	市场摊位总量（个）Number of Market Booth (unit)	摊位出租率（%）Occupancy Rate (%)	市场营业面积（平方米）Operation Area (sq.m)	商品成交总额(万元) Transaction Volume (10000 yuan)
总 计	**Total**	**59**	**40444**	**87.5**	**4287183**	**16230833**
按经营环境分	**By Operation Environment**					
露天式	Outdoor	6	2362	98.1	419675	1318046
封闭式	Close	42	30702	86.9	3039187	11237166
其 他	Other	11	7380	86.6	828321	3675621
按经营方式分	**By Operation Method**					
批 发	Wholesale	33	25724	83.5	3577879	14937027
零 售	Retail	26	14720	94.5	709304	1293806
按市场类别分	**By Market Type**					
综合市场	**Comprehensive Market**	**19**	**10990**	**92.0**	**436963**	**2117882**
生产资料综合市场	Production Materials Market	1	820	85.4	3000	45000
工业消费品综合市场	Industrial Consumable Market	2	2159	100.0	59360	821305
农产品综合市场	Farm and Side-line Products	14	6645	89.0	76008	405781
其他综合市场	Others	2	1366	97.7	298595	845795
专业市场	**Professional Market**	**40**	**29454**	**85.8**	**3850220**	**14112952**
生产资料市场	Markets of Means of Production	14	9493	74.3	1170111	6961497
农业生产用具市场	Agricultural Appliances Market	1	550	85.5	45857	57125
木材市场	Timber	3	3421	96.7	323550	584027
建材市场	Building Materials Market	3	475	99.8	325304	412740
化工材料及制品市场	Chemical Materials and Related Products Market	2	1712	54.1	221000	2840000
金属材料市场	Metal Materials Market	3	2127	42.1	232140	2775297
机械设备市场	Mechanical Equipment Market	2	1208	81.4	22260	292308
农产品市场	Agricultural Products Market	2	2198	100.0	432764	1879966
水产品市场	Aquatic Products Market	1	100	100.0	6780	40104
棉麻土畜、烟叶市场	Cotton Gunny Specialty Livestock and Tobacco Market	1	2098	100.0	425984	1839862

14-17 续表 Continued

指标	Item	市场个数（个） Number of Markets (unit)	市场摊位总量（个） Number of Market Booth (unit)	摊位出租率（%） Occupancy Rate (%)	市场营业面积（平方米） Operation Area (sq.m)	商品成交总额（万元） Transaction Volume (10000 yuan)
食品、饮料及烟酒市场	Foodstuff, Beverage, Cigarette & Wine	5	4355	72.4	884820	2308008
食品饮料市场	Food and Beverage Market	2	1220	45.6	365000	156854
茶叶市场	Tea Market	1	420	100.0	39960	23000
其他食品、饮料及烟酒市场	Others	2	2715	80.1	479860	2128154
纺织、服装、鞋帽市场	Textile, Garment, Shoes and Hat	2	3352	100.0	90000	282611
日用品及文化用品市场	Daily Necessities and Cultural Articles Market	3	2558	99.6	24448	142635
小商品市场	Small Commodities Market	2	2063	100.0	16448	128880
其他日用品及文化用品市场	Other Daily Products and Stationery Market	1	495	98.0	8000	13755
电器、通讯器材、电子设备市场	Appliance communication Equipment and Electronic Device Market	1	426	35.4	10000	11555
计算机及辅助设备市场	Computer and Component Market	1	426	35.4	10000	11555
家具、五金及装饰材料市场	Furniture, Hardware and Decorative Materials Market	10	4962	98.7	943077	1325154
家具市场	Furniture Market	4	1518	98.6	374236	208890
装饰材料市场	Decorative Materials Market	2	461	99.1	116200	202507
灯具市场	Lighting Fixtures Market	3	2433	100.0	360000	691457
五金材料市场	Hardware Materials Market	1	550	93.1	92641	222300
汽车、摩托车及零配件市场	Automobile, Motorcycle and Parts & Fittings Market	2	510	62.5	60000	213525
汽车市场	Automobile Market	1	60	98.3	15000	48496
机动车零配件市场	Auto Parts Market	1	450	57.8	45000	165029
花、鸟、鱼、虫市场	Flowers, Birds, Fish and Insects Market	1	1600	100.0	235000	988000
花卉市场	Flowers	1	1600	100.0	235000	988000

15

CHAPTER 15

个体　私营经济

INDIVIDUAL AND PRIVATE ECONOMY

15 个体　私营经济
INDIVIDUAL AND PRIVATE ECONOMY

2011 年主要统计指标
MAJOR STATISTICAL INDICATORS OF 2011

年底私营个体经济单位数	Number of Individual and Private Economy at Year-end	24.60 万户	(10000 units)
比上年增长	Over the Previous Year	9.5%	
年底私营个体企业注册资金	Registered Capital of Individual and Private Economy at Year-end	2240.68 亿元	(100 million yuan)
比上年增长	Over the Previous Year	32.7%	
年底私营个体企业从业人数	Number of Employees in Individual and Private Enterprises at Year-end	155.88 万人	(10000 persons)
比上年增长	Over the Previous Year	2.4%	

15-1 个体工商业户数（2007-2011 年） NUMBER OF SELF-EMPLOYED BUSINESS（2007-2011）

单位：户（unit）

指 标	Item	2007	2008	2009	2010	2011
总 计	**Total**	**123392**	**127837**	**143339**	**157532**	**170755**
按行业分	**Grouped By Sector**					
农林牧渔业	Farming,Forestry,Animal Husbandry and Fishery	556	604	747	902	1091
采矿业	Mining	30	24	16	16	12
制造业	Manufacturing	13777	13451	14756	17222	18999
电力、燃气及水的生产和供应业	Eletric Power, Gas and Tap Water Production and Supply	26	24	24	24	24
建筑业	Construction	134	172	207	250	280
交通运输、仓储和邮政业	Transportation, Storage and Post	1390	1290	1367	1441	1438
信息传输、计算机服务和软件业	Information Transmission, Computer Service and Software	382	400	457	467	504
批发零售贸易业	Wholesale and Retail Trade	81969	85490	94121	101239	108799
住宿和餐饮业	Accommodation and Catering Services	8886	9761	11459	12713	14435
金融业	Financial		5	4	4	4
房地产业	Real Estate	14	16	27	76	88
租赁和商务服务业	Lease and Commercial Service	820	867	1085	1368	1582
科学研究、技术服务和地质勘查业	Scientific Research, Technology Service and Geological Prospecting		36	38	47	48
水利、环境和公共设施管理业	Water Conservancy, Environment and Public Facility Management		16	14	14	16
居民服务和其他服务业	Residents Service and Other Service	14182	14703	17966	20441	21981
教 育	Education		17	23	19	34
卫生、社会保障和社会福利业	Healthcare, Social security and Social Welfare	64	67	79	93	107
文化、体育和娱乐业	Culture, Sport and Entertainment	991	889	944	1192	1308
其他行业	Other Sectors	171	5	5	4	5
按城乡分	**Grouped By City and Village**					
城 镇	Urban and Town	111270	117733	134185	148668	162106
农 村	Countryside	12122	10104	9154	8864	8649

15-2 个体工商户从业人数 （2007-2011 年） EMPLOYEES OF SELF-EMPLOYED BUSINESS （2007-2011）

单位 ：人（person）

指 标	Item	2007	2008	2009	2010	2011
总 计	**Total**	**231084**	**238031**	**268869**	**320352**	**331195**
按行业分	**Grouped By Sector**					
农林牧渔业	Farming,Forestry,Animal Husbandry and Fishery	1187	1403	1683	2156	2515
采矿业	Mining	233	181	60	87	77
制造业	Manufacturing	40328	40174	46794	66460	61101
电力、燃气及水的生产和供应业	Eletric power, Gas and Tap water production and Supply	67	60	67	62	63
建筑业	Construction	349	502	601	720	847
交通运输、仓储和邮政业	Transportation, Storage and Post	2471	2450	2664	2936	3163
信息传输、计算机服务和软件业	Information Transmission, Computer Service and Software	751	724	729	711	730
批发零售贸易业	Wholesale and Retail Trade	129843	133787	145491	158715	166909
住宿和餐饮业	Accommodation and Catering Services	24441	26567	32580	38121	41747
金融业	Financial		6	5	5	5
房地产业	Real Estate	30	33	40	104	125
租赁和商务服务业	Lease and Commercial Service	1620	1653	2001	2562	2947
科学研究、技术服务和地质勘查业	Scientific Research, Technology Service and Geological Prospecting		74	71	104	97
水利、环境和公共设施管理业	Water Conservancy, Environment and Public Facility Management		34	35	41	45
居民服务和其他服务业	Residents Service and Other Service	27124	27988	33402	44199	46991
教 育	Education		44	51	46	88
卫生、社会保障和社会福利业	Healthcare, Social Security and Social Welfare	183	184	175	234	317
文化、体育和娱乐业	Culture, Sport and Entertainment	2155	2160	2412	3083	3419
其他行业	Other Sectors	302	7	8	6	9
按城乡分	**Grouped By City and Village**					
城 镇	Urban and Town	207325	217329	250889	302914	314801
农 村	Countryside	23759	20702	17980	17438	16394

15-3 分地区年底个体工商业户数（2011 年）
NUMBER OF SELF-EMPLOYED BUSINESS AT YEAR-END BY REGION（2011）

单位：户（unit）

指标	Item	全市 Whole Municipality	其中 of which 市区 Urban Area	溧阳市 Liyang City	金坛市 Jintan City
总计	**Total**	**170755**	**130964**	**23739**	**16052**
按行业分	**Grouped By Sector**				
农林牧渔业	Farming, Forestry, Animal Husbandry and Fishery	1091	554	404	133
采矿业	Mining	12	4	3	5
制造业	Manufacturing	18999	14651	2275	2073
电力、燃气及水的生产和供应业	Eletric Power, Gas and Tap water Production and Supply	24	14	7	3
建筑业	Construction	280	171	59	50
交通运输、仓储和邮政业	Transportation, Storage and Post	1438	1033	130	275
信息传输、计算机服务和软件业	Information Transmission, Computer Service and Software	504	252	228	24
批发零售贸易业	Wholesale and Retail Trade	108799	83128	15733	9938
住宿和餐饮业	Accommodation and Catering Services	14435	11265	1922	1248
金融业	Financial	4		4	
房地产业	Real Estate	88	21	66	1
租赁和商务服务业	Lease and Commercial Service	1582	1050	335	197
科学研究、技术服务和地质勘查业	Scientific Research, Technology Service and Geological Prospecting	48	30	10	8
水利、环境和公共设施管理业	Water Conservancy, Environment and Public Facility Management	16	9	3	4
居民服务和其他服务业	Residents Service and Other Service	21981	17653	2409	1919
教育	Education	34	28	5	1
卫生、社会保障和社会福利业	Healthcare, Social Security and Social Welfare	107	88	11	8
文化、体育和娱乐业	Culture, Sport and Entertainment	1308	1011	133	164
其他行业	Other Sectors	5	2	2	1
按城乡分	**Grouped By City and Village**				
城镇	Urban and Town	162106	130300	19515	12291
农林牧渔业	Farming, Forestry, Animal Husbandry and Fishery	785	542	166	77
采矿业	Mining	7	4		3
制造业	Manufacturing	17649	14527	1708	1414
电力、燃气及水的生产和供应业	Eletric power, Gas and Tap Water Production and Supply	22	14	5	3
建筑业	Construction	265	171	53	41

15-3 续表 Continued

单位：户（unit）

指 标	Item	全 市 Whole Municipality	其 中 of which 市 区 Urban Area	溧阳市 Liyang City	金坛市 Jintan City
交通运输、仓储和邮政业	Transportation, Storage and Post	1345	1033	104	208
信息传输、计算机服务和软件业	Information Transmission, Computer Service and Software	499	250	227	22
批发零售贸易业	Wholesale and Retail Trade	103221	82680	12988	7553
住宿和餐饮业	Accommodation and Catering Services	13929	11243	1647	1039
金融业	Financial	4		4	
房地产业	Real Eestate	88	21	66	1
租赁和商务服务业	Lease and Commercial Service	1558	1047	324	187
科学研究、技术服务和地质勘查业	Scientific Research, Technology Service and Geological Prospecting	47	30	10	7
水利、环境和公共设施管理业	Water Conservancy, Environment and Public Facility Management	13	9	2	2
居民服务和其他服务业	Residents Service and Other Service	21245	17602	2065	1578
教 育	Education	34	28	5	1
卫生、社会保障和社会福利业	Healthcare, Social Security and Social Welfare	107	88	11	8
文化、体育和娱乐业	Culture, Sport and Entertainment	1284	1009	128	147
其他行业	Other Sectors	4	2	2	
农 村	Countryside	8649	668	4221	3760
农林牧渔业	Farming, Forestry, Animal Husbandry and Fishery	306	12	238	56
采矿业	Mining and Quarrying	5	3		2
制造业	Manufacturing	1350	124	567	659
电力、燃气及水的生产和供应业	Eletric Power, Gas and Tap Water Production and Supply	2		2	
建筑业	Construction	15		6	9
交通运输、仓储和邮政业	Transportation, Storage and Post	93		26	67
信息传输、计算机服务和软件业	Information Transmission, Computer Service and Software	5	2	1	2
批发零售贸易业	Wholesale and Retail Trade	5578	448	2745	2385
住宿和餐饮业	Catering Trade	506	22	275	209
租赁和商务服务业	Lease and Commercial Service	24	3	11	10
科学研究、技术服务和地质勘查业	Scientific Research, Technology Service and Geological Prospecting	1			1
水利、环境和公共设施管理业	Water Conservancy, Environment and Public Facility Management	3		1	2
居民服务和其他服务业	Residents Service and Other Service	736	51	344	341
文化、体育和娱乐业	Culture, Sport and Entertainment	24	2	5	17
其他行业	Other Sectors	1	1		

15-4 分地区年底个体工商户从业人数（2011 年）
NUMBER OF EMPLOYEES IN SELF-EMPLOYED BUSINESS AT YEAR-END BY REGION（2011）

单位：人（person）

指 标	Item	全 市 Whole Municipality	其中 of which 市 区 Urban Area	溧阳市 Liyang City	金坛市 Jintan City
总 计	**Total**	**331195**	**251948**	**47063**	**32184**
按行业分	**Grouped By Sector**				
农林牧渔业	Farming,Forestry,Animal Husbandry and Fishery	2515	1191	930	394
采矿业	Mining	77	12	52	13
制造业	Manufacturing	61101	45241	8482	7378
电力、燃气及水的生产和供应业	Eletric power, Gas and Tap Water Production and Supply	63	29	19	15
建筑业	Construction	847	522	168	157
交通运输、仓储和邮政业	Transportation, Storage and Post	3163	2582	268	313
信息传输、计算机服务和软件业	Information Transmission, Computer Service and Software	730	433	255	42
批发零售贸易业	Wholesale and Retail Trade	166909	126179	24479	16251
住宿和餐饮业	Accommodation and Catering Services	41747	32571	6083	3093
金融业	Financial	5		5	
房地产业	Real Estate	125	36	87	2
租赁和商务服务业	Lease and Commercial Service	2947	1982	619	346
科学研究、技术服务和地质勘查业	Scientific Research, Technology Service and Geological Prospecting	97	62	17	18
水利、环境和公共设施管理业	Water Conservancy, Environment and Public Facility Management	45	27	7	11
居民服务和其他服务业	Residents Service and Other Service	46991	38211	5067	3713
教 育	Education	88	73	13	2
卫生、社会保障和社会福利业	Healthcare, Social Security and Social Welfare	317	237	25	55
文化、体育和娱乐业	Culture, Sport and Entertainment	3419	2555	484	380
其他行业	Other Sectors	9	5	3	1
按城乡分	**Grouped By City and Village**				
城 镇	Urban and Town	314801	250729	38663	25409
农林牧渔业	Farming, Forestry, Animal Husbandry and Fishery	2515	1862	431	222
采矿业	Mining	77	69		8
制造业	Manufacturing	61101	49892	5831	5378
电力、燃气及水的生产和供应业	Eletric Power, Gas and Tap Water Production and Supply	63	34	14	15
建筑业	Construction	847	573	149	125

15-4 续表 Continued

单位：人（person）

指 标	Item	全 市 Whole Municipality	其中 of which 市 区 Urban Area	溧阳市 Liyang City	金坛市 Jintan City
交通运输、仓储和邮政业	Transportation, Storage and Post	3037	2582	218	237
信息传输、计算机服务和软件业	Information Transmission, Computer Service and Software	721	431	253	37
批发零售贸易业	Wholesale and Retail Trade	158967	125509	20606	12852
住宿和餐饮业	Accommodation and Catering Services	40506	32402	5457	2647
金融业	Financial	5		5	
房地产业	Real Eestate	125	36	87	2
租赁和商务服务业	Lease and Commercial Service	2907	1979	602	326
科学研究、技术服务和地质勘查业	Scientific Research, Technology Service and Geological Prospecting	96	62	17	17
水利、环境和公共设施管理业	Water Conservancy, Environment and Public Facility Management	39	27	6	6
居民服务和其他服务业	Residents Service and Other Service	45724	38130	4471	3123
教 育	Education	88	73	13	2
卫生、社会保障和社会福利业	Healthcare, Social Security and Social Welfare	317	237	25	55
文化、体育和娱乐业	Culture, Sport and Entertainment	3384	2552	475	357
其他行业	Other Sectors	8	5	3	
农 村	Countryside	16394	1272	8348	6774
农林牧渔业	Farming, Forestry, Animal Husbandry and Fishery	686	15	499	172
采矿业	Mining and Quarrying	57	52		5
制造业	Manufacturing	4927	276	2651	2000
电力、燃气及水的生产和供应业	Eletric Power, Gas and Tap Water Production and Supply	5		5	
建筑业	Construction	51		19	32
交通运输、仓储和邮政业	Transportation, Storage and Post	126		50	76
信息传输、计算机服务和软件业	Information Transmission, Computer Service and Software	9	2	2	5
批发零售贸易业	Wholesale and Retail Trade	7942	670	3873	3399
住宿和餐饮业	Catering Trade	1241	169	626	446
租赁和商务服务业	Lease and Commercial Service	40	3	17	20
科学研究、技术服务和地质勘查业	Scientific Research, Technology Service and Geological Prospecting	1			1
水利、环境和公共设施管理业	Water Conservancy, Environment and Public Facility Management	6		1	5
居民服务和其他服务业	Residents Service and Other Service	1267	81	596	590
文化、体育和娱乐业	Culture, Sport and Entertainment	35	3	9	23
其他行业	Other Sectors	1	1		

15-5 私营企业单位数（2007-2011 年）
NUMBER OF PRIVATE ENTERPRISES（2007-2011）

单位：户（unit）

指标	Item	2007	2008	2009	2010	2011
总计	**Total**	**48169**	**56828**	**59659**	**67203**	**75216**
按行业分	**Grouped By Sector**					
农林牧渔业	Farming, Forestry, Animal Husbandry and Fishery	407	456	455	538	655
采矿业	Mining	52	54	41	39	37
制造业	Manufacturing	26545	28305	28819	31044	33130
电力、燃气及水的生产和供应业	Eletric Ppower, Gas and Tap Water Production and Supply	74	105	108	111	111
建筑业	Construction	1595	2166	2369	2866	3360
交通运输、仓储和邮政业	Transportation, Storage and Post	676	846	891	1007	1137
信息传输、计算机服务和软件业	Information transmission, Computer service and Software	1059	1110	1176	1299	1366
批发零售贸易业	Wholesale and Retail Trade	12018	16456	17489	20296	23243
住宿和餐饮业	Accommodation and Catering Services	353	534	563	592	624
金融业	Financial		54	65	72	93
房地产业	Real Eestate	752	1118	1235	1449	1651
租赁和商务服务业	Lease and Commercial Service	2216	2640	2971	3654	4556
科学研究、技术服务和地质勘查业	Scientific Research, Technology Service and Geological Prospecting		1166	1625	2295	3225
水利、环境和公共设施管理业	Water Conservancy, Environment and Public Facility Management		129	143	157	169
居民服务和其他服务业	Residents Service and Other Service	1104	1354	1366	1441	1482
教育	Education		16	24	32	41
卫生、社会保障和社会福利业	Healthcare, Social Security and Social Welfare	21	23	23	29	26
文化、体育和娱乐业	Culture, Sport and Entertainment	270	296	296	282	310
其他行业	Other Sectors	1027				
按城乡分	**Grouped By City and Village**					
城镇	Urban and Town	44749	54237	57272	64910	72423
农林牧渔业	Farming, Forestry, Animal Husbandry and Fishery	274	331	347	419	485
采矿业	Mining	11	15	17	18	12
制造业	Manufacturing	24149	26638	27268	29589	31512
电力、燃气及水的生产和供应业	Eletric Power, Gas and Tap Water Production and Supply	55	89	92	97	99
建筑业	Construction	1507	2091	2296	2788	3261

15-5　续表　Continued　　　　单位：户（unit）

指　标	Item	2007	2008	2009	2010	2011
交通运输、仓储和邮政业	Transportation, Storage and Post	643	816	866	983	1098
信息传输、计算机服务和软件业	Information Transmission, Computer Service and Software	1025	1080	1146	1270	1336
批发零售贸易业	Wholesale and Retail Trade	11596	16049	17120	19927	22701
住宿和餐饮业	Accommodation and Catering Services	338	521	550	580	611
金融业	Financial		54	65	72	91
房地产业	Real Estate	727	1096	1215	1433	1623
租赁和商务服务业	Lease and Commercial Service	2145	2588	2922	3601	4491
科学研究、技术服务和地质勘查业	Scientific Research, Technology Service and Geological Prospecting		1147	1609	2275	3159
水利、环境和公共设施管理业	Water Conservancy, Environment and Public Facility Management		119	134	145	154
居民服务和其他服务业	Residents Service and other Service	1009	1273	1287	1373	1416
教　育	Education		16	24	32	41
卫生、社会保障和社会福利业	Healthcare, Social Security and Social Welfare	20	22	22	28	25
文化、体育和娱乐业	Culture, Sport and Entertainment	262	292	292	280	308
其他行业	Other Sectors	988				
农　村	Countryside	3420	2591	2387	2293	2793
农林牧渔业	Farming, Forestry, Animal Husbandry and Fishery	133	125	108	119	170
采矿业	Mining and Quarrying	41	39	24	21	25
制造业	Manufacturing	2396	1667	1551	1455	1618
电力、燃气及水的生产和供应业	Eletric Power, Gas and Tap Water Production and Supply	19	16	16	14	12
建筑业	Construction	88	75	73	78	99
交通运输、仓储和邮政业	Transportation, Storage and post	33	30	25	24	39
信息传输、计算机服务和软件业	Information Transmission, Computer Service and Software	34	30	30	29	30
批发零售贸易业	Wholesale and Retail Trade	422	407	369	369	542
住宿和餐饮业	Accommodation and Catering Services	15	13	13	12	13
金融业	Financial					2
房地产业	Real Estate	25	22	20	16	28
租赁和商务服务业	Lease and Commercial Service	71	52	49	53	65
科学研究、技术服务和地质勘查业	Scientific Research, Technology Service and Geological Prospecting		19	16	20	66
水利、环境和公共设施管理业	Water Conservancy, Environment and Public Facility Management		10	9	12	15
居民服务和其他服务业	Residents Service and Other Service	95	81	79	68	66
卫生、社会保障和社会福利业	Healthcare, Social Security and Social Welfare	1	1	1	1	1
文化、体育和娱乐业	Culture, Sport and Entertainment	8	4	4	2	2
其他行业	Other Sectors	39				

15-6 分地区年底私营企业单位数（2011 年）
NUMBER OF PRIVATE ENTERPRISES AT YEAR-END BY REGION（2011）

单位：户（unit）

指标	Item	全市 Whole Municipality	其中 of which 市区 Urban Area	溧阳市 Liyang City	金坛市 Jintan City
总计	**Total**	**75216**	**64240**	**5529**	**5447**
按行业分	**Grouped By Sector**				
农林牧渔业	Farming, Forestry, Animal Husbandry and Fishery	655	236	240	179
采矿业	Mining	37	2	26	9
制造业	Manufacturing	33130	27990	2116	3024
电力、燃气及水的生产和供应业	Eletric Power, Gas and Tap Water Production and Supply	111	72	24	15
建筑业	Construction	3360	2731	366	263
交通运输、仓储和邮政业	Transportation, Storage and Post	1137	953	123	61
信息传输、计算机服务和软件业	Information Transmission, Computer Service and Software	1366	1205	105	56
批发零售贸易业	Wholesale and Retail Trade	23243	20601	1700	942
住宿和餐饮业	Accommodation and Catering Services	624	533	63	28
金融业	Financial	93	70	19	4
房地产业	Real Estate	1651	1383	180	88
租赁和商务服务业	Lease and Commercial Service	4556	3918	338	300
科学研究、技术服务和地质勘查业	Scientific Research, Technology Service and Geological Prospecting	3225	2809	157	259
水利、环境和公共设施管理业	Water Conservancy, Environment and Public Facility Management	169	128	14	27
居民服务和其他服务业	Residents Service and Other Service	1482	1261	46	175
教育	Education	41	35	3	3
卫生、社会保障和社会福利业	Healthcare, Social Security and Social Welfare	26	26		
文化、体育和娱乐业	Culture, Sport and Entertainment	310	287	9	14
按城乡分	**Grouped By City and Village**				
城镇	Urban and Town	72423	63831	4145	4447
农林牧渔业	Farming, Forestry, Animal Husbandry and Fishery	485	235	107	143
采矿业	Mining	12	2	5	5
制造业	Manufacturing	31512	27762	1480	2270
电力、燃气及水的生产和供应业	Eletric Power, Gas and Tap Water Production and Supply	99	71	18	10
建筑业	Construction	3261	2719	313	229

15-6 续表 Continued　　　　单位：户（unit）

指标	Item	全市 Whole Municipality	其中 of which 市区 Urban Area	溧阳市 Liyang City	金坛市 Jintan City
交通运输、仓储和邮政业	Transportation, Storage and Post	1098	948	98	52
信息传输、计算机服务和软件业	Information Transmission, Computer Service and Software	1336	1197	94	45
批发零售贸易业	Wholesale and Retail Trade	22701	20501	1328	872
住宿和餐饮业	Accommodation and Catering Services	611	530	58	23
金融业	Financial	91	70	17	4
房地产业	Real Estate	1623	1377	162	84
租赁和商务服务业	Lease and Commercial Service	4491	3900	303	288
科学研究、技术服务和地质勘查业	Scientific Research, Technology Service and Geological Prospecting	3159	2803	102	254
水利、环境和公共设施管理业	Water Conservancy, Environment and Public Facility Management	154	125	9	20
居民服务和其他服务业	Residents Service and Oother Service	1416	1245	39	132
教　育	Education	41	35	3	3
卫生、社会保障和社会福利业	Healthcare, Social Security and Social Welfare	25	25		
文化、体育和娱乐业	Culture, Sport and Entertainment	308	286	9	13
其他行业	Other Sectors				
农　村	Countryside	2793	409	1384	1000
农林牧渔业	Farming, Forestry, Animal Husbandry and Fishery	170	1	133	36
采矿业	Mining and Quarrying	25	0	21	4
制造业	Manufacturing	1618	228	636	754
电力、燃气及水的生产和供应业	Eletric Power, Gas and Tap Water Production and Supply	12	1	6	5
建筑业	Construction	99	12	53	34
交通运输、仓储和邮政业	Transportation, Storage and Post	39	5	25	9
信息传输、计算机服务和软件业	Information Transmission, Computer Service and Software	30	8	11	11
批发零售贸易业	Wholesale and Retail Trade	542	100	372	70
住宿和餐饮业	Accommodation and Catering Services	13	3	5	5
金融业	Financial	2		2	
房地产业	Real Estate	28	6	18	4
租赁和商务服务业	Lease and Commercial Service	65	18	35	12
科学研究、技术服务和地质勘查业	Scientific Research, Technology Service and Geological Prospecting	66	6	55	5
水利、环境和公共设施管理业	Water Conservancy, Environment and Public Facility Management	15	3	5	7
居民服务和其他服务业	Residents Service and Other Service	66	16	7	43
卫生、社会保障和社会福利业	Healthcare, Social Security and Social Welfare	1	1		
文化、体育和娱乐业	Culture, Sport and Entertainment	2	1		1

15-7 私营企业从业人数（2007-2011 年）
EMPLOYEES OF PRIVATE ENTERPRISES（2007-2011）

单位：人（person）

指标	Item	2007	2008	2009	2010	2011
总计	**Total**	**894654**	**1069125**	**1109882**	**1201563**	**1227556**
按行业分	**Grouped By Sector**					
农林牧渔业	Farming, Forestry, Animal Husbandry and Fishery	7456	6818	5847	7568	8667
采矿业	Mining	1039	1188	981	874	848
制造业	Manufacturing	596157	688938	692579	728323	725189
电力、燃气及水的生产和供应业	Eletric power, Gas and Tap Water Production and Supply	2196	2691	2370	2092	2294
建筑业	Construction	84355	108822	139444	144368	145280
交通运输、仓储和邮政业	Transportation, Storage and Post	11619	15366	15159	16411	16817
信息传输、计算机服务和软件业	Information Transmission, Computer Service and Software	7164	7781	7711	9297	9725
批发零售贸易业	Wholesale and Retail Trade	104608	136975	140132	152998	165493
住宿和餐饮业	Accommodation and Catering Services	14370	16317	15530	17825	16946
金融业	Financial		475	488	618	753
房地产业	Real Estate	11207	13660	15006	18385	23585
租赁和商务服务业	Lease and Commercial Service	20552	24080	25705	33909	42342
科学研究、技术服务和地质勘查业	Scientific Research, Technology Service and Geological Prospecting		16533	21695	29212	38542
水利、环境和公共设施管理业	Water Conservancy, Environment and Public Facility Management		2930	3742	4578	5501
居民服务和其他服务业	Residents Service and Other Service	17270	23300	20093	31688	21697
教 育	Education		397	228	322	432
卫生、社会保障和社会福利业	Healthcare, Social Security and Social Welfare	421	615	747	862	830
文化、体育和娱乐业	Culture, Sport and Entertainment	1845	2239	2425	2233	2615
其他行业	Other Sectors	14395				
按城乡分	**Grouped By City and Village**					
城 镇	Urban and Town	798190	970583	1029844	1109193	1137554
农林牧渔业	Farming, Forestry, Animal Husbandry and Fishery	5388	4665	4338	5876	6724
采矿业	Mining	255	333	311	299	216
制造业	Manufacturing	533408	627446	637567	677986	674096
电力、燃气及水的生产和供应业	Eletric power, Ggas and Tap Water Production and Supply	1874	2422	2062	1890	2046
建筑业	Construction	69435	89947	127118	116880	121464

15-7 续表 Continued 单位：人（person）

指 标	Item	2007	2008	2009	2010	2011
交通运输、仓储和邮政业	Transportation, Storage and Post	11360	14821	14825	15800	15924
信息传输、计算机服务和软件业	Information Transmission, Computer Service and Software	6924	7602	7550	9080	9552
批发零售贸易业	Wholesale and Retail Trade	98810	132455	135383	148135	159538
住宿和餐饮业	Accommodation and Catering Services	13582	15685	15203	17081	16283
金融业	Financial		475	488	618	729
房地产业	Real Eestate	10971	13413	14784	18172	23215
租赁和商务服务业	Lease and Commercial Service	19964	23591	24850	33299	41644
科学研究、技术服务和地质勘查业	Scientific Research, Technology Service and Geological Prospecting		16227	21381	28865	37574
水利、环境和公共设施管理业	Water Conservancy, Environment and Public Facility Management		2351	3479	4148	4959
居民服务和其他服务业	Residents Service and Other Service	11094	16023	17228	27741	19822
教 育	Education		397	228	322	432
卫生、社会保障和社会福利业	Healthcare, Social Security and Social Welfare	418	512	645	774	727
文化、体育和娱乐业	Culture, Sport and Entertainment	1800	2218	2404	2227	2609
其他行业	Other Sectors	12907				
农 村	Countryside	96464	98542	80038	92370	90002
农林牧渔业	Farming, Forestry, Animal Husbandry and Fishery	2068	2153	1509	1692	1943
采矿业	Mining and Quarrying	784	855	670	575	632
制造业	Manufacturing	62749	61492	55012	50337	51093
电力、燃气及水的生产和供应业	Eletric power, Gas and Tap Water Production and Supply	322	269	308	202	248
建筑业	Construction	14920	18875	12326	27488	23816
交通运输、仓储和邮政业	Transportation, Storage and Post	259	545	334	611	893
信息传输、计算机服务和软件业	Information Transmission, Computer Service and Software	240	179	161	217	173
批发零售贸易业	Wholesale and Retail Trade	5798	4520	4749	4863	5955
住宿和餐饮业	Accommodation and Catering Services	788	632	327	744	663
金融业	Financial					24
房地产业	Real Estate	236	247	222	213	370
租赁和商务服务业	Lease and Commercial Service	588	489	855	610	698
科学研究、技术服务和地质勘查业	Scientific Research, Technology Service and Geological Prospecting		306	314	347	968
水利、环境和公共设施管理业	Water Conservancy, Environment and Public Facility Management		579	263	430	542
居民服务和其他服务业	Residents Service and Other Service	6176	7277	2865	3947	1875
卫生、社会保障和社会福利业	Healthcare, Social Security and Social Welfare	3	103	102	88	103
文化、体育和娱乐业	Culture, Sport and Entertainment	45	21	21	6	6
其他行业	Other Sectors	1488				

15-8 分地区年底私营企业从业人数（2011 年）
NUMBER OF EMPLOYEES IN PRIVATE ENTERPRISES AT YEAR-END BY REGION (2011)

单位：人（person）

指标	Item	全市 Whole Municipality	其中 of which 市区 Urban Area	溧阳市 Liyang City	金坛市 Jintan City
总计	**Total**	**1227556**	**914521**	**168239**	**144796**
按行业分	**Grouped By Sector**				
农林牧渔业	Farming, Forestry, Animal Husbandry and Fishery	8667	3069	3274	2324
采矿业	Mining	848	9	757	82
制造业	Manufacturing	725189	567719	79499	77971
电力、燃气及水的生产和供应业	Eletric power, Gas and Tap Water Production and Ssupply	2294	695	1195	404
建筑业	Construction	145280	70534	49795	24951
交通运输、仓储和邮政业	Transportation, Storage and Post	16817	12023	2699	2095
信息传输、计算机服务和软件业	Information Transmission, Computer Service and sSoftware	9725	8655	603	467
批发零售贸易业	Wholesale and Retail Trade	165493	138499	15924	11070
住宿和餐饮业	Accommodation and Catering Services	16946	12059	3631	1256
金融业	Financial	753	542	182	29
房地产业	Real Estate	23585	19037	2715	1833
租赁和商务服务业	Lease and Commercial Service	42342	30517	4341	7484
科学研究、技术服务和地质勘查业	Scientific Research, Technology Service and Geological Prospecting	38542	31189	2303	5050
水利、环境和公共设施管理业	Water Conservancy, Environment and Public Facility Management	5501	4635	228	638
居民服务和其他服务业	Residents Service and Other Service	21697	12091	912	8694
教育	Education	432	267	79	86
卫生、社会保障和社会福利业	Healthcare, Social Security and Social Welfare	830	830		
文化、体育和娱乐业	Culture, Sport and Entertainment	2615	2151	102	362
按城乡分	**Grouped By City and Village**				
城镇	Urban and Town	1137554	901292	122842	113420
农林牧渔业	Farming, Forestry, Animal Husbandry and Fishery	6724	3067	1725	1932
采矿业	Mining	216	9	150	57
制造业	Manufacturing	674096	556906	59481	57709
电力、燃气及水的生产和供应业	Eletric Power, Gas and Tap Water Production and Supply	2046	695	989	362
建筑业	Construction	121464	70426	32513	18525

15-8 续表 Continued

单位：人（person）

指 标	Item	全 市 Whole Municipality	其中 of which 市 区 Urban Area	溧阳市 Liyang City	金坛市 Jintan City
交通运输、仓储和邮政业	Transportation, Storage and Post	15924	11989	2279	1656
信息传输、计算机服务和软件业	Information Transmission, Computer Service and Software	9552	8572	549	431
批发零售贸易业	Wholesale and Retail Trade	159538	137337	12557	9644
住宿和餐饮业	Accommodation and Catering Services	16283	11664	3520	1099
金融业	Financial	729	542	158	29
房地产业	Real Estate	23215	18969	2467	1779
租赁和商务服务业	Lease and Commercial Service	41644	30371	3868	7405
科学研究、技术服务和地质勘查业	Scientific Research, Technology Service and Geological Prospecting	37574	31105	1498	4971
水利、环境和公共设施管理业	Water Conservancy, Environment and Public Facility Management	4959	4591	94	274
居民服务和其他服务业	Residents Service and Oother Service	19822	11907	813	7102
教 育	Education	432	267	79	86
卫生、社会保障和社会福利业	Healthcare, Social Security and Social Welfare	727	727		
文化、体育和娱乐业	Culture, Sport and Entertainment	2609	2148	102	359
农 村	Countryside	90002	13229	45397	31376
农林牧渔业	Farming, Forestry, Animal Husbandry and Fishery	1943	2	1549	392
采矿业	Mining and Quarrying	632		607	25
制造业	Manufacturing	51093	10813	20018	20262
电力、燃气及水的生产和供应业	Eletric Power, Gas and Tap Water Production and Supply	248		206	42
建筑业	Construction	23816	108	17282	6426
交通运输、仓储和邮政业	Transportation, Storage and Post	893	34	420	439
信息传输、计算机服务和软件业	Information Transmission, Computer Service and Software	173	83	54	36
批发零售贸易业	Wholesale and Retail Trade	5955	1162	3367	1426
住宿和餐饮业	Accommodation and Catering Services	663	395	111	157
金融业	Financial	24		24	
房地产业	Real Estate	370	68	248	54
租赁和商务服务业	Lease and Commercial Service	698	146	473	79
科学研究、技术服务和地质勘查业	Scientific Research, Technology Service and Geological Prospecting	968	84	805	79
水利、环境和公共设施管理业	Water Conservancy, Environment and Public Facility Management	542	44	134	364
居民服务和其他服务业	Residents Service and Other Service	1875	184	99	1592
卫生、社会保障和社会福利业	Healthcare, Social Security and Social Welfare	103	103		
文化、体育和娱乐业	Culture, Sport and Entertainment	6	3		3

15-9 私营企业注册资金（2007-2011 年）
REGISTERED CAPITAL OF PRIVATE ENTERPRISES（2007-2011）

单位：万元（10000 yuan）

指 标	Item	2007	2008	2009	2010	2011
总 计	**Total**	**8529858**	**10003083**	**12022022**	**16287776**	**21700710**
按行业分	**Grouped By Sector**					
农林牧渔业	Farming, Forestry, Animal Husbandry and Fishery	72970	89319	121979	168834	201584
采矿业	Mining	6889	7079	5956	15346	57676
制造业	Manufacturing	4351658	4975212	5708863	6977454	8632281
电力、燃气及水的生产和供应业	Eletric Power, Gas and Tap Water Production and Supply	109117	103632	83229	86885	104011
建筑业	Construction	750470	917578	1121064	1398813	1740843
交通运输、仓储和邮政业	Transportation, Storage and Post	91024	95507	121210	219490	269088
信息传输、计算机服务和软件业	Information Transmission, Computer Service and Coftware	76726	92245	98640	119747	131031
批发零售贸易业	Wholesale and Retail Trade	1452804	1682814	2007386	2978205	4037756
住宿和餐饮业	Accommodation and Catering Services	52232	52510	63056	76110	101969
金融业	Financial		69353	104463	280863	632329
房地产业	Real Estate	722848	825595	1089217	1607127	2004212
租赁和商务服务业	Lease and Commercial Service	431386	620068	886031	1408317	2254121
科学研究、技术服务和地质勘查业	Scientific Research, Technology Service and Geological Prospecting		242135	376745	685571	1230856
水利、环境和公共设施管理业	Water Conservancy, Environment and Public Facility Management		45425	50397	68476	80894
居民服务和其他服务业	Residents Service and Other Service	145549	159847	155939	164803	178806
教 育	Education		629	1295	1398	1588
卫生、社会保障和社会福利业	Healthcare, Social security and Social Welfare	4438	4518	5788	7638	7388
文化、体育和娱乐业	Culture, Sport and Entertainment	15869	19615	20765	22700	34276
其他行业	Other Sectors	245878				
按城乡分	**Grouped By City and Village**					
城 镇	Urban and Town	7832264	9398173	11365074	15572241	20208846
农林牧渔业	Farming, Forestry, Animal Husbandry and Fishery	52417	66319	94281	137841	161045
采矿业	Mining	1673	2171	1961	1746	31676
制造业	Manufacturing	3919082	4602511	5305306	6546856	7831215
电力、燃气及水的生产和供应业	Eletric Power, Gas and Tap Water Production and Supply	92722	87365	66962	76678	92445
建筑业	Construction	677475	850084	1040695	1304083	1614344

15-9 续表 Continued

单位：万元（10000 yuan）

指 标	Item	2007	2008	2009	2010	2011
交通运输、仓储和邮政业	Transportation, Storage and Post	87957	92072	115520	213760	259607
信息传输、计算机服务和软件业	Information Transmission, Computer Service and Software	71985	89594	96251	117368	129092
批发零售贸易业	Wholesale and Retail Trade	1370606	1611305	1935364	2903541	3777665
住宿和餐饮业	Accommodation and Catering Services	49099	49897	60433	73497	96241
金融业	Financial		69353	104463	280863	562329
房地产业	Real Estate	700857	814164	1077786	1596226	1980181
租赁和商务服务业	Lease and Commercial Sservice	419063	611113	875878	1396135	2220761
科学研究、技术服务和地质勘查业	Scientific Research, Technology Service and Geological Prospecting		240042	374032	680758	1176214
水利、环境和公共设施管理业	Water Conservancy, Environment and Public Facility Management		40221	45313	58872	66654
居民服务和其他服务业	Residents Service and Other Service	133119	147874	144058	153323	167166
教 育	Education		629	1295	1398	1588
卫生、社会保障和社会福利业	Healthcare, Social Security and Social Welfare	3838	3918	4788	6638	6388
文化、体育和娱乐业	Culture, Sport and Entertainment	15715	19539	20689	22660	34236
其他行业	Other Sectors	236656				
农 村	Countryside	697594	604909	656948	715535	1491864
农林牧渔业	Farming, Forestry, Animal Husbandry and Fishery	20553	23001	27698	30994	40540
采矿业	Mining and Quarrying	5216	4908	3995	13600	26000
制造业	Manufacturing	432576	372700	403556	430599	801066
电力、燃气及水的生产和供应业	Eletric Power, Gas and Tap Water Production and Supply	16395	16267	16267	10207	11567
建筑业	Construction	72995	67494	80369	94730	126500
交通运输、仓储和邮政业	Transportation, Storage and Post	3067	3435	5690	5730	9481
信息传输、计算机服务和软件业	Information Transmission, Computer Service and Software	4741	2651	2389	2379	1939
批发零售贸易业	Wholesale and Retail Trade	82198	71509	72023	74664	260091
住宿和餐饮业	Accommodation and Catering Services	3133	2613	2623	2613	5728
金融业	Financial					70000
房地产业	Real Estate	21991	11431	11431	10901	24031
租赁和商务服务业	Lease and Commercial Service	12323	8955	10154	12182	33360
科学研究、技术服务和地质勘查业	Scientific Research, Technology Service and Geological Prospecting		2093	2713	4813	54642
水利、环境和公共设施管理业	Water Conservancy, Environment and Public Facility Management		5204	5084	9604	14240
居民服务和其他服务业	Residents Service and Other Service	12430	11973	11881	11480	11640
卫生、社会保障和社会福利业	Healthcare, Eocial Security and Eocial Welfare	600	600	1000	1000	1000
文化、体育和娱乐业	Culture, Sport and Entertainment	154	76	76	40	40
其他行业	Other Sectors	9222				

16

CHAPTER 16

对外经济　旅游

FOREIGN ECONOMY AND TOURISM

常州统计年鉴

16 对外经济　旅游 FOREIGN ECONOMY AND TOURISM

2011 年主要统计指标 MAJOR STATISTICAL INDICATORS OF 2011

进出口总额	Total Imports and Exports	286.35 亿美元	(USD 100 million)
比上年增长	Over the Previous Year	28.5%	
出口总额	Total Exports	193.61 亿美元	(USD 100 million)
比上年增长	Over the Previous Year	24.4%	
新签外资项目数	Number of Signed Contracts	308 个	(unit)
比上年增长	Over the Previous Year	-5.8%	
协议（合同）外资金额	Contracted Foreign Capital	46.32 亿美元	(USD 100 million)
比上年增长	Over the Previous Year	-2.3%	
实际利用外资金额	Foreign Capital Actually Used	30.52 亿美元	(USD 100 million)
比上年增长	Over the Previous Year	14.3%	
国家及省级开发区	Number of State and Provincial Development Zones	10 个	(unit)
# 国家级开发区	State Development Zone	1 个	(unit)
接待国际旅游者人数	Number of International Tourists	41.31 万人次	(10000 persons-times)
比上年增长	Over the Previous Year	15.1%	

16-1 主要年份对外经济指标 MAJOR INDICATORS OF FOREIGN TRADE AND ECONOMIC COOPERATION IN MAJOR YEARS

单位：万美元（USD 10000）

年 份 Year	进出口总额 Total Import and Export	其中 of which 进口 Import	出口 Export	协议（合同）外资金额 Amount of Foreign Capital in the Signed Agreements and Contracts	实际利用外资金额 Amount of Foreign Capital Actually Utilized	新签对外承包劳务合同额 Amount of Newly Signed Foreign Contracted Labor Contract	对外承包劳务营业额 Business Value of Foreign Contracted Labor
1982						110	9
1985	128		128	3617	1455	581	567
1990	6153	1180	4973	1751	666	433	73
1991	11520	2279	9241	9002	2384	1432	599
1992	20188	2516	17672	36897	8557	3842	1619
1993	38847	6047	32800	62412	14440	3076	1408
1994	64564	8101	56463	52882	27772	2859	1843
1995	99315	22371	76944	88728	32858	4568	3817
1996	135493	35261	100232	99906	51764	7448	6623
1997	168431	45457	122974	107417	56639	7321	6849
1998	159380	28345	131035	82327	55681	8630	7544
1999	192723	65056	127667	90158	62569	9424	8309
2000	282208	96174	186034	100285	70006	12480	9409
2001	325884	109306	216577	117625	62192	10275	7644
2002	391831	126244	265587	122132	56102	13997	9837
2003	525126	172170	352956	205376	85522	16189	12371
2004	690551	218920	471631	218671	58000	20432	14594
2005	833364	220936	612428	285100	73120	26010	20561
2006	1044213	255109	789104	329575	125145	40695	26479
2007	1322596	338192	984404	440087	183481	51694	32618
2008	1762893	438540	1324353	340952	204002	52231	37175
2009	1507929	421284	1086645	422114	226129	52280	41082
2010	2227750	671944	1555806	474203	267000	57685	46913
2011	2863464	927380	1936084	463196	305238	58005	49505

注：1、从 1999 年起进出口为海关数。
2、从 2001 年起新签对外承包劳务合同额、营业额为经贸部口径。
3、从 2002 年起协议合同外资金额、实际利用外资金额为新口径，即协议注册外资额、注册外资实际到帐额。
4、从 2004 年起实际利用外资金额为有验资报告的实际到帐注册外资数。

Note: 1.The indices of import and export are the statistical figures of the customs since 1999.
2.Since the year of 2001, the amount of newly signed foreign contracted labor contracts and the business value of foreign contracted labor belong to the statistical figures of the Ministry of Foreign Trade and Cooperation.
3.The amount of foreign capital in signed agreements and contracts and foreign capital actually utilized are based on new statistical specifications since 2002,Namely the actual paid up amount of contracted foreign capital and registered foreign capital.
4.The amount of foreign capital actually utilized since 2004 has been included in capital verification report.

16-2 分地区对外经济主要指标（2011 年）
MAJOR INDICATORS OF FOREIGN TRADE AND ECONOMIC COOPERATION BY REGION（2011）

指标	Item	全市 Whole Municipality	其中 of which 市区 Urban Area	溧阳市 Liyang City	金坛市 Jintan City
进出口总额（万美元）	**Total Import and Export (USD 10000)**	**2863464**	**2557208**	**104062**	**202194**
对外贸易公司	Foreign Trade Corporation	252948	245859	4390	2699
自营生产企业	Self-supporting Manufacturing Enterprises	973946	891664	37678	44604
三资企业	Three Types of Foreign-funded Enterprises	1636570	1419685	61994	154891
出　口	**Export**	**1936084**	**1685526**	**89063**	**161495**
对外贸易公司	Foreign Trade Corporation	230640	224947	3140	2553
自营生产企业	Self-supporting Manufacturing Enterprises	666953	600831	28930	37192
三资企业	Three Types of Foreign-funded Enterprises	1038491	859748	56993	121750
进　口	**Import**	**927380**	**871682**	**14999**	**40699**
对外贸易公司	Foreign Trade Corporation	22308	20912	1250	146
自营生产企业	Self-supporting Manufacturing Enterprises	306993	290833	8748	7412
三资企业	Three Types of Foreign-funded Enterprises	598079	559937	5001	33141
新签外商直接投资项目（个）	**Newly Signed Foreign Capital Project (unit)**	**308**	**219**	**46**	**43**
三资企业	Three Types of Foreign-funded Enterprises	308	219	46	43
港、澳、台商投资企业	Enterprises with Investment from Hongkong, Macao and Taiwan	128	81	26	21
外商投资企业	Enterprises with Foreign Investment	180	138	20	22

16-2 续表 Continued

指标	Item	全市 Whole Municipality	其中 of which 市区 Urban Area	溧阳市 Liyang City	金坛市 Jintan City
协议（合同）外资（万美元）	**Amount of Foreign Capital in the Newly Signed Agreements (USD 10000)**	**463196**	**332034**	**67589**	**63573**
三资企业	Three Types of Foreign-funded Enterprises	463196	332034	67589	63573
港、澳、台商投资企业	Enterprises with Investment from Hongkong, Macao and Taiwan	286395	203066	43779	39550
外商投资企业	Enterprises with Foreign Investment	176801	128968	23810	24023
实际到帐注册外资（万美元）	**Foreign Capital Actually Utilized (USD 10000)**	**305238**			
期末实有外商投资企业数（个）	**Number of Foreign-funded Enterprises at Year-end (unit)**	**2758**	**2123**	**265**	**370**
新签对外承包工程和劳务合作	**Newly Signed Foreign Contracted Projects and Labor Cooperation**				
项目个数（个）	Number of Project (unit)	303	255	41	7
合同金额（万美元）	Amount of Contracts (USD 10000)	58005	33986	7422	16597
营业额（万美元）	Business Value (USD 10000)	49505	27720	6600	15185
派出人数（人）	Number of Persons Sent Abroad (person)	2176	163	659	1354
期末在外人数（人）	Number of Persons Abroad (person)	3977	1214	1487	1276
新批海外投资企业	**Newly Approved Enterprises with Overseas Investment**				
本年新签海外投资企业（个）	Accumulated Number of Enterprises with Overseas Investment under Operation (unit)	49	44		5
本年海外投资开业企业（个）	Accumulated Number of Enterprises with Overseas Investment under Operation (unit)	40	36		4
本年中方协议投资总额（万美元）	Total Contractual Investment from Chinese Investors during this year (USD 10000)	44457	29147		15310

注：1、从 2001 年起新签对外承包工程和劳务合作指标为经贸部口径。
2、从 2002 年起新签协议外资和实际利用外资为新口径，即协议注册外资额、注册外资实际到帐额。
3、从 2004 年起实际利用外资金额为有验资报告的实际到帐注册外资数。

Notes：1.The newly signed Contracted Projects Overseas and Labor Cooperation Indicators from the year of 2001 come from the statistical data of the Ministry of Foreign Trade and Economic Cooperation.
2. The amount of foreign capital in signed agreements and contracts and foreign capital actually utilized are based on new statistical specifications since 2002,Namely the actual paid up amount of contracted foreign capital and registered foreign capital.
3.The amount of foreign capital actually utilized since 2004 has been included in capital verification report.

16-3 按贸易方式和产品类别分的外贸进出口商品总额（2007-2011 年）
TOTAL VALUE OF IMPORTS AND EXPORTS BY TRADE AND DIFFERENT PRODUCTS（2007-2011）

单位：万美元（USD 10000）

指标	Items	2007	2008	2009	2010	2011
进口总额	**Total Value of Imports**	**338192**	**438540**	**421284**	**671944**	**927380**
# 高新技术产品	High and New Technological Products	28562	34525	25310	102608	149083
按贸易方式分	**Grouped by Trade**					
# 一般贸易	Original Trade	170708	238199	274993	428833	592868
来料加工装配贸易	Processing and Assembling Trade Provided with Raw Material	13375	12959	13860	12729	10927
进料加工贸易	Raw Material Input Processing Trade	108897	130344	101016	151752	194032
外商投资企业投资设备	Goods as Invested for Import Equipments	31926	41830	17235	33606	76196
按产品类别分	**Grouped by Different Products**					
# 化工产品	Chemicals and Related Products	72925	112292	81495	119721	161721
纺织服装	Textile Materials and Products	27221	26786	23240	36626	52904
机电产品	Electrical and Mechanical Products	148907	168704	182595	315480	425225
出口总额	**Total Value of Exports**	**984404**	**1324353**	**1086645**	**1555806**	**1936084**
# 高新技术产品	High and New Technological Products	90150	198794	158996	368401	410518
按贸易方式分	**Grouped by Trade**					
# 一般贸易	Original Trade	740096	949515	768604	1091793	1376255
来料加工装配贸易	Processing and Assembling Trade Provided with Raw Material	21526	23893	23050	24555	22715
进料加工贸易	Raw Material Input Processing Trade	222530	350863	291921	434304	529221
按产品类别分	**Grouped by Different Products**					
# 化工产品	Chemicals and Related Products	91966	110416	99953	136707	179065
纺织服装	Textile Materials and Products	224456	253957	242653	304682	375169
机电产品	Electrical and Mechanical Products	491651	721909	558068	870062	1033688

16-4 分国别或地区进出口总额（2011 年）
TOTAL IMPORTS AND EXPORTS BY COUNTRY OR REGION（2011）

单位：万美元（USD 10000）

国别或地区	Region	进出口总额 Total Import and Export	其中 of which 出口 Export	进口 Import
总 计	**Total**	**2863464**	**1936084**	**927380**
亚 洲	**Asia**	**1250471**	**730452**	**520019**
#香 港	Hongkong	76840	62558	14282
日 本	Japan	404282	183635	220647
韩 国	Korea,Rep.	173472	55399	118073
台 湾	Taiwan	77988	25208	52780
非 洲	**Africa**	**73374**	**65354**	**8020**
欧 洲	**Europe**	**792015**	**594364**	**197652**
#英 国	United Kindom	44515	39959	4556
德 国	Germany	211542	121561	89981
法 国	France	47098	40099	6999
俄罗斯	Russia	49179	42650	6529
拉丁美洲	**Latin America**	**148630**	**108406**	**40224**
北美洲	**North America**	**472101**	**388101**	**84000**
#美 国	United States	422185	354437	67748
大洋洲	**Oceania**	**126036**	**48680**	**77357**
#澳大利亚	Australia	121319	44097	77222

16-5　外商直接投资情况（2011 年）
FOREIGN INVESTMENT CONDITIONS（2011）

指　标	Item	新签项目个数(个) Number ofNewly Signed Agreements (unit)	协议外资金额(万美元) Amount of Contractual Foreign Captial (USD 10000)	年底外商投资企业数(个) Number of Foreign Investment Enterprises at Year-end (unit)
总　计	**Total**	**308**	**463196**	**2758**
按企业登记注册类型分	**Grouped by Type of Registration**			
合资经营企业	Joint Venture	85	85975	1154
合作经营企业	Cooperative	1	619	81
独资经营企业	Sole Investment	222	374997	1511
股份有限公司	Share-holding Corporations Ltd.		1605	12
按国民经济行业分	**Grouped by Sector**			
农林牧渔业	Farming,Forestry,Animal Husbandry and Fishery	15	7203	40
采矿业	Mining	1	940	3
制造业	Manufacturing	192	322696	2102
#纺织业	Textile Industry	2	3474	177
纺织服装、鞋、帽制造业	Textile, Garments, Shoes and Hat Processing	6	3505	244
化学原料及化学制品制造业	Raw Chemical Materials and Chemical Products	9	24002	115
医药制造业	Medical and Pharmaceutical Products	1	235	26
通用设备制造业	General Equipment Manufacturing	39	71579	188
专用设备制造业	For Special Purposes Equipment Manufacturing	15	27428	221
交通运输设备制造业	Transport Equipment Manufacturing	15	21955	123
电气机械及器材制造业	Electric Equipment and Machinery	39	84561	227
通信设备、计算机及其他电子设备制造	Communication, Computer and Other Electronic Equipment	25	28139	214
电力、煤气及水的生产和供应业	Production and Supply of Electric Power, Steam and Water	4	900	23
建筑业	Construction	2	109	10
交通运输、仓储及邮政业	Transportation, Storage and Post	6	10078	13
信息传输、计算机服务和软件业	Information Transmission, Computer Service and Software Industries	9	1209	26
批发和零售业	Wholesale and Retail Trade	36	32224	106

16-5 续表 Continued

指 标	Item	新签项目个数(个) Number ofNewly Signed Agreements (unit)	协议外资金额(万美元) Amount of Contractual Foreign Captial (USD 10000)	年底外商投资企业数(个) Number of Foreign Investment Enterprises at Year-end (unit)
住宿和餐饮业	Hoteling and Eateries	2	588	21
房地产业	Real Estate	4	66619	117
租赁和商务服务业	Lease hold and Business in Services	12	8609	52
科学研究、技术服务和地质勘查业	Scientific Research, Technology Service and Geological Prospecting	23	9231	236
水利、环境和公共设施管理业	Management Industry of Water Conservancy, Environment and Public Facilities			2
居民服务和其他服务业	Neighborhood Services and Other Services	1	-200	4
文化、体育和娱乐业	Culture, Sports and Entertainment	1	2990	3
按投资国别、地区分	**Grouped by Country and Region**			
亚 洲	**Asia**	**196**	**371261**	**1792**
#香 港	Hongkong	102	262664	948
台 湾	Taiwan	26	23731	244
新加坡	Singapore	10	22543	84
日 本	Japan	41	40206	312
韩 国	Korea	5	3273	97
非 洲	**Africa**	**10**	**14019**	**39**
#塞舌尔	Seychelle	7	10376	13
南 非	South-Africa			7
欧 洲	**Europe**	**35**	**27348**	**244**
#英 国	United Kindom	7	5050	48
德 国	Germany	8	732	57
法 国	France	2	411	21
意大利	Italy	2	2947	20
西班牙	Spain	1	758.6	18
瑞 士	Switzerland	2	225	15
拉丁美洲	**Latin America**	**6**	**-626**	**121**
#巴巴多斯	Barbados		990	4
开曼群岛	CaymanIslands		-6228	12
英属维尔京群岛	British West Indies	3	2437	95
北美洲	**North America**	**47**	**16903**	**392**
#加拿大	Canada	11	8009	89
美 国	United States	36	8894	303
大洋洲	**Oceania**	**17**	**15402**	**103**
#澳大利亚	Australia	11	11320	74
新西兰	New Zealand	2	1745	12
萨摩亚	Samoa	4	1837	15

16-6 分国别外国人过夜人数（2011 年）
NUMBER OF FOREIGN TOURISTS STAYING OVERNIGHT BY COUNTRY（2011）

单位：人次（person-time）

指 标	Item	全 市 Whole Municipality	其 中 of which 市 区 Urban Area	溧阳市 Liyang City	金坛市 Jintan City
总 计	**Total**	**359823**	**343511**	**9379**	**6933**
日 本	Japan	90052	85298	1905	2849
韩 国	Korea	16419	15423	352	644
印度尼西亚	Indonesia	1996	1860	128	8
马来西亚	Malaysia	6072	5635	421	16
新加坡	Singapore	7739	7426	185	128
泰 国	Thailand	4033	3794	229	10
印 度	India	6781	6595	137	49
英 国	United Kindom	9986	9019	187	780
法 国	France	8001	7293	455	253
德 国	Germany	44290	42666	590	1034
意大利	Italy	8204	7897	275	32
瑞 士	Switzerland	8196	7973	183	40
瑞 典	Sweden	2133	1998	95	40
俄罗斯	Russia	4321	4247	34	40
西班牙	Spain	1975	1834	125	16
美 国	United States	53020	52226	540	254
加拿大	Canada	10661	10361	239	61
澳大利亚	Australia	8615	8426	142	47
新西兰	New Zealand	668	556	15	97
其它国家	Others	66661	62984	3142	535

16-7 分地区旅游人数和收入（2011 年）
NUMBER OF TOURISTS AND ERANINGS FROM TOURISM BY REGION（2011）

指 标	Item	全 市 Whole Municipality	其中 of which 市 区 Urban Area	溧阳市 Liyang City	金坛市 Jintan City
旅游总人数（万人次）	**Number of Tourists (10000 persons-times)**	**3402.19**	**1999.03**	**901.31**	**501.85**
国内旅游人数	Number of Dometic Tourists	3360.88	1959.55	900.22	501.11
入境旅游人数	Number of International Tourists	41.31	39.48	1.09	0.74
旅游总收入	**Total Earnings from Tourism**	**425.90**	**289.58**	**86.37**	**49.95**
国内旅游收入（亿元）	Domestic Tourism (100 million yuan)	398.52	263.44	85.56	49.52
旅游创汇（万美元）	International Tourism (USD 10000)	42138	40238	1200	700
旅游景区（点）	**Scenic Spots**				
接待游客（万人次）	Number of Tourists (10000 persons-times)	7080	5164	1266	650
营业收入（万元）	Foreign Exchange Income (10000 yuan)	243174	135912	99544	7718

16-8 分地区国际旅游人数和收入（2011 年）
TOTAL NUMBER OF INTERNATIONAL TOURISTS AND ERANINGS FROM INTERNATIONAL TOURISM BY REGION（2011）

指 标	Item	全 市 Whole Municipality	其中 of which 市 区 Urban Area	溧阳市 Liyang City	金坛市 Jintan City
国际旅游接待人数（人次）	**Number of International Tourists (person-time)**	**413101**	**394782**	**10928**	**7391**
外国人	Foreigners	359823	343511	9379	6933
香 港	Hongkong	19673	19073	395	205
澳 门	Macao	1376	1193	183	
台 湾	Taiwan	32229	31006	970	253
国际旅游接待天数（人天）	**Number of International Tourists (person-day)**	**2253648**	**2155770**	**65017**	**32861**
外国人	Foreigners	1733408	1650940	53796	28672
香 港	Hongkong	148288	143027	3357	1904
澳 门	Macao	2620	1729	891	
台 湾	Taiwan	369332	360074	6973	2285
旅游创汇（万美元）	**Foreign Exchange Earings of Tourism (USD 10000)**	**42138**	**40238**	**1200**	**700**

16-9 主要旅游区（点）情况（2011 年）
MAIN SCENIC SPOTS（2011）

名　称 Name	接待人数（万人次） Persons Reception (10000 persons-times)	营业收入（万元） Business Income (10000 yuan)	地　址 Address	联系电话 Contact Telephone Number	邮政编码 Post Code
中华恐龙园 China Dinosaur Park	386.36	44967	常州新区长江东路1号 No. 1 East Changjing Rd. New District, Changzhou	85106668	213022
天宁禅寺 Tianning Temple	41.05	1942	常州延陵东路636号 No. 636 East Yanling Rd., Changzhou	88111447	213003
亚细亚影视城 Asia Flim Town	230.48	4619	常州怀德中路21号 No.21 Middle Huide Rd., Changzhou	86608965	213003
红梅公园 Red Plum Park	7510.00	2459	常州罗汉路1号 No. 1 Luohan Rd., Changzhou	88108020	213003
东坡公园 Dongpo Park	38.40	18	常州延陵东路水门桥堍 Shuimen Bridge, East Yanling Rd., Changzhou	88815005	213003
瞿秋白纪念馆 Qu Qiubai Memorial	50.86		常州延陵西路102号 No.102 West Yanling Rd., Changzhou	86636909	213003
张太雷纪念馆 Zhang Tailei Memorial	17.70		常州清凉路子和里3号 No. 3 Ziheli Qingliang Rd., Changzhou	88813757	213003
武进横山风景旅游区 Wujin Hengshan Scenic Spot	81.12	146	武进区横山桥镇 Hengshanqiao Town,Wujin District	88605967	213119
武进艺林园 Wujin Horticulture Garden	29.83	736	武进区夏溪镇厚余街 Huoyu St., Xiaxi Town, Wujin District	83681109	213146
溧阳天目湖旅游度假区 Liyang Tianmu Lake Tourism and Vacation Zone	413.12	68044	溧阳市天目湖镇 Tianmu Lake Town, Liyang City	87980388	213333
溧阳南山竹海旅游度假区 Liyang South Mount and Bamboo Sea Tourism Vacation Zone	221.42	6855	溧阳市横涧镇 Hengjian Town, Liyang City	87935088	213333
金坛茅山风景名胜区 Jintan Maoshan Scenic Spot	159.14	2405	金坛市茅东林场西侧 West of Maodong Forestry Center, Jintan City	82669388	213200
金坛华罗庚公园 Jintan Hua Luogeng Park	117.11	240	金坛市市府路38号 No. 38 Shifu Rd., Jintan City	82822957	213200
金坛城南风景区 Jintan Chengnan Scenic Spot	159.14	2405	金坛市金城镇 Jincheng Town, Jintan City	82823427	213200
青枫公园 Qingfeng Park	275.50	158	常州钟楼区星港大道 Xinggang Boulevard, Zhonglou District, Changzhou	88156617	213200
春秋淹城遗址旅游区 Tourist Resort of Yancheng Remains of Spring and Autumn Period	290.50	22677	常州市武进区武宜南路588号 No.588 South Wuyi Road, Wujin District, Changzhou	86318622	213161

16-10 旅游涉外饭店、宾馆情况（2011 年底）
FOREIGN-CONCERNED HOTEL AND RESTAURANT CONDITIONS（END OF 2011）

名 称 Name	星级标准 Standard		地 址 Address	联系电话 Contact Telephone Number	客房数（间） Number of Guest Room (room)	客房出租率(%) Room Occupancy Rate (%)
常州大酒店	五星	Five-star	常州市延陵西路65号	88109988	391	64.83
常州富都大酒店有限公司	五星	Five-star	新区通江大道398号	85168888	378	70.82
江苏天目湖宾馆有限公司	五星	Five-star	溧阳市天目湖旅游度假区	87168888	171	56.36
溧阳宾馆有限公司	五星	Five-star	溧阳市西大街118号	87222777	290	69.23
溧阳市天目湖国际饭店有限公司	五星	Five-star	溧阳市天目湖旅游度假区	87989999	304	53.44
常州市和平假日大饭店有限公司	四星	Four-star	常州市和平南路151号	88163388	172	81.64
常州阳光国际大酒店有限公司	四星	Four-star	常州市怀德中路45号	86606888	333	63.53
常州市明都大饭店管理有限公司	四星	Four-star	常州市和平北路39号	88118888	236	71.34
江苏中天凤凰集团有限公司中天凤凰大酒店	四星	Four-star	常州市新区通江大道555号	86187888	162	76.14
溧阳市天目湖华天度假村有限公司	四星	Four-star	溧阳市天目湖旅游度假区	87980999	203	46.43
溧阳市天目湖静泊山庄有限公司	四星	Four-star	溧阳天目湖旅游度假区内	87169999	159	35.81
溧阳假日酒店有限公司	四星	Four-star	溧阳罗湾路99号	87199999	145	68.09
常州万豪花都国际大酒店	四星	Four-star	常州晋陵北路168号	88222222	184	57.35
常州新都大酒店	四星	Four-star	北环路17号	85577888	126	63.84
常州九洲环宇商务广场管理有限公司	四星	Four-star	关河东路38号	85228820	110	75.22
常州香树湾花园酒店有限公司	四星	Four-star	新北区汉江路2号	85118900	121	84.92
常州电力燃料有限公司海阳大酒店	四星	Four-star	通江大道371号	88516778	118	77.42
金坛颐丰大酒店有限公司	四星	Four-star	金坛市丹阳门中路188号	82796666	66	73.84
常州锦江国际大酒店有限公司	四星	Four-star	新北区通江中路769号	85198888	261	77.97
金坛市九九宾馆有限公司	四星	Four-star	金坛市横街16-18号	82838899	81	74.19
金坛樱花大酒店有限公司	四星	Four-star	金坛西门大街88号	82396666	110	47.46
常州金色南都国际大酒店有限公司	四星	Four-star	武进区湖塘环府路58号	86319588	70	85.8
常州国安大酒店有限公司	四星	Four-star	常州小河沿1号	85221688	116	68.94
溧阳市公路运输有限公司皇廷国际大酒店	四星	Four-star	溧阳市燕山中路9号	83106888	145	65.83
常州湟里金鼎国际大酒店有限公司	四星	Four-star	武进区湟里镇金鼎路8号	83349898	147	50.22
溧阳市天目湖水悦山庄	三星	Three-star	溧阳市天目湖旅游度假区	87167888	129	23.88
常州市长兴楼饭店有限公司	三星	Three-star	常州市邮电路8号	86631888	101	0
常州市武进区新苑宾馆有限公司	三星	Three-star	武进湖塘环府路	86312888	160	62.56

16-10 续表　Continued

名 称 Name	星级标准 Standard		地 址 Address	联系电话 Contact Telephone Number	客房数（间） Number of Guest Room (room)	客房出租率(%) Room Occupancy Rate (%)
新锦江假日酒店	三星	Three-star	常州市新丰街14号	88101710	188	66.73
国瑞宾馆	三星	Three-star	武进横山桥镇	88603888	150	47.41
武进兰新大饭店	三星	Three-star	武进湖塘新常漕路12号	86569888	99	39.14
溧阳市江南大酒店	三星	Three-star	溧阳市平陵中路268号	87217987	102	67.94
金坛市南天宾馆	三星	Three-star	金坛市东环二路1—1号	82337900	32	54.56
溧阳市望湖岭山庄	三星	Three-star	溧阳市天目湖旅游度假区	87982785	56	34.60
溧阳市天目水庐宾馆	三星	Three-star	溧阳市天目湖旅游度假区	87981798	69	50.14
武进金龙大酒店	三星	Three-star	武进湖塘人民路1号	86550978	86	76.72
溧阳虹枫美食休闲度假村	三星	Three-star	溧阳天目湖旅游度假区内	87167718	243	51.99
宫苑宾馆	三星	Three-star	常州市延陵西路85号	86602606	106	72.93
溧阳云海宾馆	三星	Three-star	溧阳燕山路33号	87179666	92	57.83
亚细亚明星宾馆	三星	Three-star	怀德中路21号	86608965	54	38.35
常州馨雅楼宾馆	三星	Three-star	戚机厂工房1区1号	85052122	116	62.15
常瑞宾馆	三星	Three-star	常州市浦南路8号	86183888	126	59.41
椿庭楼宾馆	三星	Three-star	常州市局前街27号	88152222	99	52.20
常州鸣凰大酒店	三星	Three-star	武进湖塘鸣西路89号	86531577	49	54.13
武进锦海城市大酒店	三星	Three-star	常州市会馆浜路11号	86856577	82	72.08
金坛市九龙宾馆	三星	Three-star	金坛市东环二路39号	82399000	68	80.28
常州苏南枫泽山庄大酒店	三星	Three-star	武进夏溪章庄	88368077	50	36.08
文笔山庄	二星	Two-star	常州市武青路146号	88159999	53	0.00
金坛华电宾馆	二星	Two-star	金坛市北门大街111号	82812801	49	32.63
银星宾馆	二星	Two-star	常州市公园路2号	86613331	41	0.00
溧阳市交通大酒店	二星	Two-star	溧阳市西大街142号	87225188	79	45.36
溧阳市翠竹园宾馆	二星	Two-star	溧阳市天目湖旅游度假区	87980358	127	51.59
金坛市凯利大酒店	二星	Two-star	金坛市丹阳门北路2号	82851000	50	39.63
溧阳天目湖大酒店	二星	Two-star	溧阳天目湖镇	87980396	31	49.98
武进假日酒店	准评星	Units Qualified for Star Levels	武进区延政中路33号	86313888	280	55.11
常州金陵江南大饭店	准评星	Units Qualified for Star Levels	新北区通江路466号	85119988	165	69.40

16-11 开发区建设情况（2011 年）
CONSTRUCTION OF THE DEVELOPMENT ZONES（2011）

指 标	Item	合 计 Total	常州高新技术产业开发区 Changzhou High and New Technology Industries Development Zone	江苏省武进高新技术产业园区 Wujin Hi-tech Industrial Zone Jiangsu
年底开发区开发面积（平方公里）	Area of Development Zones at Year-end (sq.km)	149.92	38.00	23.30
本年全社会固定资产投资（亿元）	Total Investment in Fixed Assets at This Year (100 million yuan)	1280.47	477.61	162.10
本年批准外商投资企业（个）	Approved Foreign-funded Enterprises in Current Year (unit)	271	71	87
本年新签协议注册外资（万美元）	Accumulated Contractual Foreign Capital of Approved Enterprises at This Year (USD 10000)	404108	135088	74647
本年实际到帐注册外资（万美元）	Accumulated Actual Foreign Investment at This Year (USD 10000)	265072	100042	52067
本年建成外商投资企业投产开业（个）	Foreign-funded Enterprises Completed in Current Year Starting Operation (unit)	66	16	7
业务总收入（亿元）	Total Business Income (100 million yuan)	9304.73	3602.24	1921.12
#工业产品销售收入	Sales Revenue from Industrial Products	6709.83	2112.82	1278.45
地方一般预算收入（亿元）	Local budgetary revenue (100 million Yuan)	197.63	73.02	30.43

注：各开发区包括进区企业。
Note： All development zones include the enterprises settled down in the zone.

江苏省武进经济开发区 Wujin Economic Development Zone Jiangsu	江苏省金坛经济开发区 Jintan Economic Development Zone, Jiangsu	江苏省溧阳经济开发区 Liyang Economic Development Zone, Jiangsu	江苏省常州天宁经济开发区 Tianning Economic Development Zone, Changzhou, Jiangsu	江苏省常州钟楼经济开发区 Zhonglou Economic Development Zone, Changzhou, Jiangsu	江苏省常州戚墅堰经济开发区 Qishuyan Economic Development Zone, Changzhou, Jiangsu	天目湖旅游度假区 Tianmu Lake Tourist Resort
10.70	15.00	14.00	19.80	12.70	5.92	10.50
45.37	95.81	130.39	145.38	141.86	40.96	40.99
16	32	32	13	11	5	4
23768	40213	46717	31747	26308	17109	8511
14056	23688	29911	25373	15061	973	3901
7	11	9	3	5	6	2
157.32	707.46	1377.81	1079.30	698.08	274.91	116.49
118.17	536.67	1117.97	701.15	573.45	195.88	75.27
4.65	13.80	23.90	30.13	13.08	5.99	2.63

17

CHAPTER 17

常州统计年鉴

能源消费

CONSUMPTION OF ENERGY

17 能源消费
CONSUMPTION OF ENERGY

2011 年主要统计指标
MAJOR STATISTICAL INDICATORS OF 2011

全社会用电量	Total Electriccity Consumed	331.66亿千瓦时	(100 million kw.h)
比上年增长	Over the Previous Year	13.9%	
工业用电量	Industrial Electricity Consumption	267.21亿千瓦时	(100 million kw.h)
比上年增长	Over the Previous Year	15.3%	
城乡居民生活用电量	Electricity Consumption by Urban and Rural Residents	28.04亿千瓦时	(100 million kw.h)
比上年增长	Over the Previous Year	1.9%	
规模以上工业企业生产综合能源消费量	Production of the Comprehensive energy Consumption of Industrial Enterprises above Designated Size	1475.73万吨	(10000 tons)
比上年增长	Over the Previous Year	7.7%	

17-1 全社会用电量（1980-2011 年）
TOTAL ELECTRICITY CONSUMPTION（1980-2011）

单位：万千瓦时（10000 kw.h）

年 份 Year	全社会用电量 Total Electricity Consumption	其中 of which #农林牧渔水利业 Farming, Forestry, Animal Husbandry, Fishery and Water Conservancy	工 业 Industry	交通运输、邮电通信业 Transportation, Post and Telecommuni-cations Services	城乡居民生活 Electricity Consumption by of Urban and Rural Residents
1980	134387	27134	102715	459	4079
1981	144076	33226	105738	375	4737
1982	155004	35467	113498	293	5746
1983	166728	41084	119095	321	6228
1984	180092	45608	126691	291	7502
1985	195387	54628	131151	287	9321
1986	226192	27971	183961	778	7059
1987	253060	28737	207018	340	9549
1988	268665	31616	214548	921	12346
1989	270752	32965	213121	1322	14256
1990	293370	38930	223449	1709	17283
1991	330885	42703	250208	3915	18973
1992	378832	47382	286052	2024	25103
1993	424120	51949	310357	2627	33968
1994	483755	57671	342772	3287	46000
1995	522521	60136	362325	3726	57620
1996	557030	63478	381807	4248	62910
1997	586748	71269	391600	5735	68439
1998	601148	72676	391733	6975	77286
1999	641191	79090	421049	7435	78497
2000	743453	87042	492989	7924	97199
2001	813527	96264	542864	8812	108352
2002	988809	112040	686011	10134	110380
2003	1269745	142175	915670	12391	118145
2004	1522392	164706	1107854	15586	128541
2005	1826605	34748	1452046	36287	149200
2006	2126844	23952	1749992	16396	172817
2007	2306172	17285	1908046	12272	186762
2008	2373291	17634	1920858	15038	213800
2009	2554100	18246	2054113	15913	229934
2010	2911875	21420	2318221	23790	275163
2011	3316562	22438	2672080	32690	280418

注：本表按当年口径统计，1986年行业用电分类按调整口径统计，1991年以前交通运输、邮电通信业仅指交通运输业，2006年以后的交通运输、邮电通信业指交通运输、仓储和邮政业。

Notes: This form is in compliance with the specification of this year. The statistic data of the electricity consumption by sectors in 1986 was based upon the regulatory specification. The transportation, post and telecommunications had only indicated the transportation before 1991, After 2006, transportation, post and telecommunications refers to transportation, storage and postal industry.

17-2 全社会分月用电量（2011 年）
TOTAL ELECTRICITY CONSUMPTION BY MONTH（2011）

单位：万千瓦时（10000 kw.h）

月 份 Month		全社会用电量 Total Electricity Consumption	其 中 of witch	
			#工 业 Industry	城乡居民生活用电 Electricity Consumption by of Urban and Rural Residents
总 计	**Total**	**3316562**	**2672080**	**280418**
第一季度	First Quarter	757350	595382	72699
1		264788	216123	19999
2		197410	142731	25044
3		295152	236528	27656
第二季度	Second Quarter	839042	701656	60383
4		274553	226679	23321
5		289240	244150	19059
6		275249	230827	18003
第三季度	Third Quarter	918210	725525	84748
7		321522	265747	20747
8		313736	245069	29553
9		282952	214709	34448
第四季度	Fourth Quarter	801960	649517	62588
10		261237	204484	25004
11		248483	204660	19106
12		292240	240373	18478

17-3 分地区全社会用电量（2011 年）
TOTAL ELECTRICITY CONSUMPTION BY REGION（2011）

单位：万千瓦时（10000 kw.h）

指 标	Item	全 市 Whole Municipality	其中 of witch 市 区 Urban Area	溧阳市 Liyang City	金坛市 Jintan City
总 计	**Total**	**3316562**	**2408214**	**565572**	**342776**
农林渔牧业	Farming, Forestry, Animal Husbandry and Fishery	22438	10026	5407	7005
农 业	Agriculture	3440	1214	1303	923
林 业	Forestry	476	300	117	59
畜牧业	Animal Husbandry	3378	1270	279	1829
渔 业	Fishery	6639	1771	2510	2358
农、林、牧、渔服务业	Farming,Forestry, Animal Husbandry and Fishery	8505	5471	1198	1836
#排 灌	Irrigation and Drainage	6100	3843	982	1275
工 业	Industry	2672080	1899324	488742	284014
采矿业	Mining	765		765	
制造业	Manufacturing	2378358	1683094	446786	248478
食品、饮料和烟草制造业	Production of Food ,Beverages and Tobacco	17858	11708	3932	2218
纺织业	Textiles	245761	222611	11962	11188
造纸及纸制品业	Papermaking and Paper Production	13202	11039	1195	968
石油加工、炼焦及核燃料加工业	Petroleum Processing, Coking and Nuclear Fuel Processing	708	685	21	2
化学原料及化学制品制造业	Raw Chemical Materials and Chemica Production	216381	123030	15771	77580
医药制造业	Medical and Pharmaceutical Production	20176	13207	2644	4325
化学纤维制造业	Chemical Fiber	19724	15526	734	3464
橡胶和塑料制品业	Rubber and Plastic Production	126559	114919	4111	7529
非金属矿物制品业	Nonmetal Mineral Production	339470	49280	206343	83847
黑色金属冶炼及压延加工业	Smelting and Pressing of Ferrous Metals	516973	377510	119248	20215
有色金属冶炼及压延加工业	Smelting and Pressing of Nonferrous Metals	40258	31105	1760	7393

17-3 续表 continued

单位：万千瓦时（10000 kwh）

指 标	Item	全 市 Whole Municipality	其中 of witch 市 区 Urban Area	溧阳市 Liyang City	金坛市 Jintan City
金属制品业	Metal Products	187229	153404	28449	5376
通用及专用设备制造业	Universal & Special Equipments Manufacturing	265744	227385	30178	8181
交通运输、电气、电子设备制造业	Electronic and Transportation Equipment	280511	257621	15500	7390
其他工业	Other Industry	87804	74064	4938	8802
电力、燃气及水的生产和供应业	Production and Supply of Electric Power, Gas and Water	292957	216230	41191	35536
电力、热力的生产和供应业	Production and Supply of Electric Power and Thermal Power	266148	198934	38978	28236
燃气生产和供应业	Production and Supply of Gas	7622	1781	500	5341
自来水生产和供应业	Production and Supply of Running Water	19187	15515	1713	1959
建筑业	Construction	28679	22291	4313	2075
交通运输、仓储和邮政业	Communication and Transportation, Storage and Post Industry	32690	30627	1081	982
商业、住宿和餐饮业	Commerce, Accommodation and Catering Industry	100236	78670	13639	7927
信息传输、计算机服务和软件业	Information transmission, computer service and software	14318	10839	2147	1332
金融、房地产、租赁和商务、居民服务和其他服务业	Finance, Real Estate, Renting and Business, Residents Services and Other Services	67498	59511	4639	3348
卫生、社会保障和社会福利事业	Health Care,Social Security and Social Welfare	14190	11244	1327	1619
教育、文化体育和娱乐业	Education,Culture Sports and Recreation	31283	27503	1923	1857
科学研究、技术服务和地质堪查业	Scientific Research,Polytechnical Services and Geological Exploration	2611	2402	91	118
公共管理和社会组织、国际组织	Public Administration and Social or International Organizations	17876	13970	2065	1841
水利、环境和公共设施管理业	Water, Environment and Public Facilities	32245	29021	2189	1035
城乡居民生活用电	Electricity Consumption by Urban and Rura Residents	280418	212786	38009	29623
农 村	Villiage	158820	117825	23723	17272
城 市	City	121598	94961	14286	12351

17-4 规模以上工业企业分行业生产综合能源消费量（2011 年）
COMPREHENSIVE ENERGY CONSUMPTION IN PRODUCTION OF ABOVE-SCALE INDUSTRIAL ENTERPRISES BY SECTOR（2011）

指 标	Item	企业单位数（个）Number of Enterprises(unit)	综合能源消费量（吨标准煤）Comprehensive Energy Consumption (tce)
总 计	**Total**	**3366**	**14757356**
按地区分	**Grouped by Region**		
市 区	Urban Area	2714	9794568
#武进区	Wujin District	1430	5929114
溧阳市	Liyang City	313	4193258
金坛市	Jintan City	339	769531
按行业分	**Grouped by Sector**		
黑色金属矿采选业	Ferrous Metal Mining and Dressing		
非金属矿采选业	Nonmetal Minerals Mining and Dressing	4	107385
农副食品加工业	Food Processing	14	5512
食品制造业	Food Production	14	20538
饮料制造业	Beverage Production	4	12900
纺织业	Textile Industry	353	583781
纺织服装、鞋、帽制造业	Textile, Garments, Shoes and Hat Processing	143	75137
皮革、毛皮、羽毛（绒）及其制品业	Leather, Furs, Down and Related Products	13	1964
木材加工及木、竹、藤、棕、草制品业	Timber Processing, Bamboo, Cane, Palm Fiber and Straw Products	67	22379
家具制造业	Furniture Manufacturing	12	1849
造纸及纸制品业	Papermaking and Paper Products	42	42020
印刷业和记录媒介的复制	Printing and Record Medium Reproduction	26	4271
文教体育用品制造业	Cultural, Educational and Sports Goods	14	4667
石油加工、炼焦及核燃料加工业	Petroleum Processing, Coking and Nuclear Fuel Processing	17	4015
化学原料及化学制品制造业	Raw Chemical Materials and Chemical Products	343	1012505
医药制造业	Medical and Pharmaceutical Products	49	96547
化学纤维制造业	Chemical Fiber	27	38035
橡胶制品业	Rubber Products	41	20249
塑料制品业	Plastic Products	118	55363
非金属矿物制品业	Nonmetal Mineral Products	148	2435264
黑色金属冶炼及压延加工业	Smelting and Pressing of Ferrous Metals	107	6533090
有色金属冶炼及压延加工业	Smelting and Pressing of Nonferrous Metals	103	139825
金属制品业	Metal Products	165	146367
通用设备制造业	General Equipment Manufacturing	431	275821
专用设备制造业	For Special Purposes Equipment Manufacturing	256	221734
交通运输设备制造业	Transport Equipment Manufacturing	200	132709
电气机械及器材制造业	Electric Equipment and Machinery	399	249557
通信设备、计算机及其他电子设备制造	Communication, Computer and Other Electronic Equipment	174	187013
仪器仪表及文化、办公用机械制造业	Instruments, Meters, Cultural and Office Machinery	39	4075
工艺品及其他制造业	Artcraft and Other Manufacturing	11	2920
废弃资源和废旧材料回收	Recycling and Disposal of Waste	4	913
电力、热力的生产和供应业	Production and Supply of Electric Power and Thermal Power	19	2300981
燃气生产和供应业	Production and Supply of Gas	3	1303
水的生产和供应业	Production and Supply of Water	6	16667

17-5 年耗能 5000 吨标煤及以上工业企业生产综合能源消费量（2011 年）
COMPREHENSIVE ENERGY CONSUMPTION IN PRODUTTION OF INDUSTRIAL ENTERPRISES WITH ANNUAL CONSUMPTION OF 5000 TCE AND ABOVE（2011）

指 标	Item	企业单位数（个）Number of Enterpr-ises(unit)	综合能源消费量（吨标准煤）Comprehensive Energy Consumption (tce)
总 计	**Total**	**166**	**13074571**
按地区分	**Grouped by Region**		
市 区	Urban Area	117	8443868
# 武进区	Wujin District	51	5224062
溧阳市	Liyang City	33	4020586
金坛市	Jintan City	16	610118
按行业分	**Grouped by Sector**		
非金属矿采选业	Nonmetal Minerals Mining and Dressing	1	105214
食品制造业	Food Production	1	8489
饮料制造业	Beverage Production	1	10540
纺织业	Textile Industry	30	319644
纺织服装、鞋、帽制造业	Textile, Garments, Shoes and Hat Processing	2	23476
造纸及纸制品业	Papermaking and Paper Products	1	22077
化学原料及化学制品制造业	Raw Chemical Materials and Chemical Products	29	786321
医药制造业	Medical and Pharmaceutical Products	5	58939
化学纤维制造业	Chemical Fiber	1	6402
塑料制品业	Plastic Products	1	6252
非金属矿物制品业	Nonmetal Mineral Products	12	2329875
黑色金属冶炼及压延加工业	Smelting and Pressing of Ferrous Metals	20	6449499
有色金属冶炼及压延加工业	Smelting and Pressing of Nonferrous Metals	5	70529
金属制品业	Metal Products	4	67957
通用设备制造业	General Equipment Manufacturing	10	100935
专用设备制造业	For Special Purposes Equipment Manufacturing	11	139879
交通运输设备制造业	Transport Equipment Manufacturing	2	48181
电气机械及器材制造业	Electric Equipment and Machinery	7	104016
通信设备、计算机及其他电子设备制造	Communication, Computer and Other Electronic Equipment	5	109304
电力、热力的生产和供应业	Production and Supply of Electric Power and Thermal Power	17	2297017
水的生产和供应业	Production and Supply of Water	1	10027

17-6 规模以上工业企业分行业主要能源品种消费量（2011 年）
ENERGY CONSUMPTION OF MAIN VARIETIES OF ABOVE-SCALE INDUSTRIAL ENTERPRISES BY SECTOR（2011）

指 标	Item	原 煤（吨）Raw Coal (ton)
总 计	**Total**	**9948081**
按地区分	**Grouped by Region**	
市 区	Urban Area	6724094
# 武进区	Wujin District	1694553
溧阳市	Liyang City	2517242
金坛市	Jintan City	706746
按行业分	**Grouped by Sector**	
黑色金属矿采选业	Ferrous Metal Mining and Dressing	
非金属矿采选业	Nonmetal Minerals Mining and Dressing	
农副食品加工业	Food Processing	2594
食品制造业	Food Production	11405
饮料制造业	Beverage Production	11780
纺织业	Textile Industry	65182
纺织服装、鞋、帽制造业	Textile, Garments, Shoes and Hat Processing	35951
皮革、毛皮、羽毛（绒）及其制品业	Leather, Furs, Down and Related Products	261
木材加工及木、竹、藤、棕、草制品业	Timber Processing, Bamboo, Cane, Palm Fiber and Straw Products	4766
家具制造业	Furniture Manufacturing	364
造纸及纸制品业	Papermaking and Paper Products	12145
印刷业和记录媒介的复制	Printing and Record Medium Reproduction	1623
文教体育用品制造业	Cultural, Educational and Sports Goods	1193
石油加工、炼焦及核燃料加工业	Petroleum Processing, Coking and Nuclear Fuel Processing	1624
化学原料及化学制品制造业	Raw Chemical Materials and Chemical Products	553921
医药制造业	Medical and Pharmaceutical Products	47253
化学纤维制造业	Chemical Fiber	12360
橡胶制品业	Rubber Products	7875
塑料制品业	Plastic Products	11293
非金属矿物制品业	Nonmetal Mineral Products	2292900
黑色金属冶炼及压延加工业	Smelting and Pressing of Ferrous Metals	797046
有色金属冶炼及压延加工业	Smelting and Pressing of Nonferrous Metals	32526
金属制品业	Metal Products	75025
通用设备制造业	General Equipment Manufacturing	32840
专用设备制造业	For Special Purposes Equipment Manufacturing	71194
交通运输设备制造业	Transport Equipment Manufacturing	2165
电气机械及器材制造业	Electric Equipment and Machinery	22260
通信设备、计算机及其他电子设备制造	Communication, Computer and Other Electronic Equipment	7385
仪器仪表及文化、办公用机械制造业	Instruments, Meters, Cultural and Office Machinery	20
工艺品及其他制造业	Artcraft and Other Manufacturing	33
电力、热力的生产和供应业	Production and Supply of Electric Power and Thermal Power	5833097
燃气生产和供应业	Production and Supply of Gas	
水的生产和供应业	Production and Supply of Water	

洗精煤 (吨) Fien Coal (ton)	焦　炭 (吨) Coke (ton)	天然气 (万立方米) Natural Gas (10000 cubicmeters)	汽　油 (吨) Gasoline (ton)	煤　油 (吨) Kerosene (ton)	柴　油 (吨) Diesel Oil (ton)	燃料油 (吨) Fuel Oil (ton)	液化石油气 (吨) LPG (ton)	热　力 (百万千焦) Heat (1million kilojoule)
1801203	**4528972**	**107890**	**47011**	**1590**	**76936**	**2796**	**5971**	**25569576**
874264	3407247	101590	43001	1386	68089	2632	5272	21724737
874243	3250748	13202	11069	487	21733	99	791	5654946
922265	1115718	5535	428	101	1958			391241
4674	6007	765	3582	103	6889	164	699	3453599
					278			2892262
		22	135		11			24510
		205	1476	13	25		10	107553
			78		10	541		1257
2450		1776	2246	87	1652		118	9875280
726	10	387	915	7	584	157	50	544090
			54		41		2	
			579		311	20		
			24		18			
498			319		810	1025		504090
			239		71			
			66		139		168	
		150	52					
2749	780	5363	6088	396	4223	336	299	7751352
		186	2791		598			859593
	448	196	206		83		13	
	385	20	1760		436	4	9	41625
		299	845	2	918			68460
503785	3107	3856	1531	31	22175	610	1150	56443
1284968	4452137	3489	387		6264		165	2155381
	1880	3684	1126	55	2042		555	78392
	4961	633	2527	55	2573	11	329	8400
5126	57488	696	5008	247	8469	92	549	23635
201	5523	3441	4318	2	4937		272	107961
	419	1132	4457	591	13575		1990	435031
701	1834	5426	6840	55	4752		272	32000
		712	2083	50	562			466
			504		139		20	
			78		86			
		76213	29		1072			1796
		2	120		21			
			131		62			

17-7 年耗能 5000 吨标煤及以上工业企业主要能源品种消费量（2011 年）
ENERGY CONSUMPTION OF MAIN VARIETIES OF INDUSTRIAL ENTERPRISES WITH ANNUAL CONSUMPTION OF 5000 TCE AND ABOVE（2011）

指 标	Item	原 煤（吨）Raw Coal (ton)
总 计	**Total**	**9543620**
按地区分	**Grouped by Region**	
市 区	Urban Area	6479728
# 武进区	Wujin District	1503826
溧阳市	Liyang City	2431783
金坛市	Jintan City	632109
按行业分	**Grouped by Sector**	
非金属矿采选业	Nonmetal Minerals Mining and Dressing	
食品制造业	Food Production	11405
饮料制造业	Beverage Production	11780
纺织业	Textile Industry	27212
纺织服装、鞋、帽制造业	Textile, Garments, Shoes and Hat Processing	15378
造纸及纸制品业	Papermaking and Paper Products	
化学原料及化学制品制造业	Raw Chemical Materials and Chemical Products	449054
医药制造业	Medical and Pharmaceutical Products	32282
化学纤维制造业	Chemical Fiber	7572
塑料制品业	Plastic Products	
非金属矿物制品业	Nonmetal Mineral Products	2268184
黑色金属冶炼及压延加工业	Smelting and Pressing of Ferrous Metals	729170
有色金属冶炼及压延加工业	Smelting and Pressing of Nonferrous Metals	9808
金属制品业	Metal Products	61033
通用设备制造业	General Equipment Manufacturing	10059
专用设备制造业	For Special Purposes Equipment Manufacturing	67648
交通运输设备制造业	Transport Equipment Manufacturing	66
电气机械及器材制造业	Electric Equipment and Machinery	9572
通信设备、计算机及其他电子设备制造	Communication, Computer and Other Electronic Equipment	300
电力、热力的生产和供应业	Production and Supply of Electric Power and Thermal Power	5833097
水的生产和供应业	Production and Supply of Water	

洗精煤 (吨) Fien Coal (ton)	焦 炭 (吨) Coke (ton)	天然气 (万立方米) Natural Gas (10000 cubicmeters)	汽 油 (吨) Gasoline (ton)	煤 油 (吨) Kerosene (ton)	柴 油 (吨) Diesel Oil (ton)	燃料油 (吨) Fuel Oil (ton)	液化石油气 (吨) LPG (ton)	热 力 (百万千焦) Heat (1million kilojoule)
1793803	**4486347**	**99757**	**2515**	**42**	**24292**	**333**	**2284**	**20181386**
871538	3382120	93953	1745	30	21571	333	2284	16771997
871538	3232408	8176	661		6417		264	3917802
922265	1103822	5317	56	12	606			279140
	405	487	714		2115			3130249
								2862616
			7		13			
			28					
		574	466		252		115	6864738
			83		98			245433
			24		61			450103
		4652	153		656	333		6481056
			132		393			607839
		178						
503785		3645	7		251			
1284968	4450787	3149	147		6106		165	2155381
		2833	32		85			9990
	3396	176	25		189			
5050	28364	248	424	20	2334			23635
	3697	2961	34	2	1064		219	82338
	82	171	221	20	11497		1785	384461
	21	4723	64		147			12000
		233	528		20			
		76213	29		1072			1796
			113		55			

18
CHAPTER 18

财政 金融 保险

PUBLIC FINANCE, BANKING AND INSURANCE

常州统计年鉴

18 财政 金融 保险
PUBLIC FINANCE, BANKING AND INSURANCE

2011 年主要统计指标
MAJOR STATISTICAL INDICATORS OF 2011

地方一般预算收入	Budgetary Revenue of Local Government	350.88亿元	(100 million yuan)
比上年增长	Over the Previous Year	22.6%	
一般预算财政支出	Budgetary Expenditure	361.81亿元	(100 million yuan)
比上年增长	Over the Previous Year	28.6%	
年底金融机构本外币存款余额	Balance of Domestic and Foreign Currency Deposits in Financial Institutions at Year-end	5028.88亿元	(100 million yuan)
比上年增长	Over the Previous Year	7.6%	
年底金融机构人民币存款余额	RMB Deposits Balance of Banking Institutions at Year-end	4902.15亿元	(100 million yuan)
比上年增长	Over the Previous Year	7.7%	
年底城乡居民本外币储蓄存款余额	Balance of Domestic and Foreign Currency Savings Deposits of Urban and Rural Residents at Year-end	2171.20亿元	(100 million yuan)
比上年增长	Over the Previous Year	7.3%	
年底城乡居民人民币储蓄存款余额	RMB Urban and Rural Saving Deposits Balance at Year-end	2157.39亿元	(100 million yuan)
比上年增长	Over the Previous Year	7.4%	
年底金融机构本外币贷款余额	Balance of Domestic and Foreign Currency Loans in Financial Institutions at Year-end	3505.80亿元	(100 million yuan)
比上年增长	Over the Previous Year	13.2%	
年底金融机构人民币贷款余额	RMB Loans Balance of Banking Institutions at Year-end	3406.35亿元	(100 million yuan)
比上年增长	Over the Previous Year	13.1%	

18-1 历年财政总收入、财政支出
TOTAL FINANCIAL REVENUE AND FINANCIAL EXPENDITURE OVER THE YEARS

单位：万元（10000 yuan）

年份 Year	财政总收入 Financial Revenue	其中 of which #市区 Urban Area	财政支出 Financial Expenditure	其中 of which #市区 Urban Area
1949	1209	861	17	17
1950	2664	1974	207	93
1951	3885	3074	357	254
1952	5155	4129	741	538
1953	6258	4886	854	591
1954	6956	5500	1033	750
1955	6338	5084	957	678
1956	7146	5900	1431	993
1957	7813	6602	2025	1557
1958	18880	17106	7633	6408
1959	18662	17008	3048	2065
1960	18853	17106	2766	1563
1961	11878	10729	2041	1279
1962	8694	7503	1915	1341
1963	9551	8280	1977	1441
1964	13225	11873	2306	1634
1965	16044	14639	2533	1832
1966	20250	18886	2674	1880
1967	12603	11205	2574	1793
1968	13793	12354	2411	1641
1969	21562	20027	4376	3419
1970	31837	29958	3917	2706
1971	33681	31894	6148	4888
1972	37363	35414	6843	5382
1973	43564	40973	6180	4860
1974	44651	42029	6162	4394
1975	49437	46665	5470	3992
1976	52558	49769	6359	4561
1977	57904	54827	6843	4970
1978	62128	58560	9259	6583
1979	62364	58983	13585	8481
1980	66960	63122	11603	8293
1981	72163	67767	10615	7837
1982	70139	65046	13109	9805
1983	73628	67892	16885	12799
1984	80543	77320	21601	16794
1985	100364	92691	25231	19660
1986	103337	94451	31333	24513
1987	109850	99516	32565	25238
1988	115680	103528	38331	29560
1989	126680	113446	47647	36535
1990	130953	116644	51082	38698
1991	117190	103734	55849	41716
1992	136516	119384	59228	43719
1993	198857	171003	99387	74698
1994	246778	210378	114387	86228
1995	285043	239948	133252	101585
1996	343032	289773	153820	116570
1997	401779	337700	193880	150801
1998	450937	376665	224114	176498
1999	492092	415554	257172	202273
2000	602271	507742	325043	259763
2001	753317	633537	414753	331521
2002	1029032	866120	610099	495583
2003	1361047	1136921	847597	690368
2004	1447666	1181910	1048820	1181910
2005	2204491	1821223	1402776	1126903
2006	2772705	2269853	1710373	1341912
2007	4143811	3399957	2743954	2192203
2008	5426800	4536087	3844112	3178717
2009	6817200	5737600	5208061	4297952
2010	8416700	7101100	6382050	5291309
2011	9777913	8102756	7430767	6050417

注：2002年7月起财政收入包括行政性收费收入、基金收入。
Note: The financial revenue includes the incomes from administrative charge and funds since July 2002.

18-2 分地区地方一般预算收入、支出（1997-2011 年） GENERAL BUDGETARY REVENUE AND EXPENDITURE BY REGION（1997-2011 年）

单位：万元（10000 yuan）

年份 Year	地方一般预算收入 Local Government Budgetary Revenue	其中 of which 市区 Urban Area	溧阳市 Liyang City	金坛市 Jintan City	年份 Year	地方一般预算支出 Ordinary Budgetary Expenditure	其中 of which 市区 Urban Area	溧阳市 Liyang City	金坛市 Jintan City
1997	189210	157949	17173	14088	1997	186742	144839	23756	18147
1998	222536	185568	19889	17079	1998	219440	172644	26428	20368
1999	251712	210724	21946	19042	1999	254124	199993	30822	23309
2000	322524	270430	28035	24059	2000	318283	254115	36046	28122
2001	420961	351387	36968	32606	2001	411581	329178	45098	37305
2002	461972	386364	40399	35209	2002	518223	418456	53993	45774
2003	566729	473538	52977	40214	2003	630490	514181	67521	48788
2004	673407	556044	68201	49162	2004	756627	611906	87767	56954
2005	949905	791432	91088	67385	2005	978458	797957	109280	71221
2006	1188818	984472	118008	86338	2006	1176965	945667	135700	95598
2007	1580688	1305365	162588	112735	2007	1546367	1250226	175098	121043
2008	1851888	1527880	196188	127820	2008	1866796	1510855	218523	137418
2009	2158888	1786378	231688	140822	2009	2187465	1715610	284866	186989
2010	2861788	2391480	290028	180280	2010	2814401	2258104	334681	221616
2011	3508800	2906762	371280	230758	2011	3618123	2877736	443228	297159

18-3 分地区金融机构人民币存、贷款余额（1990-2011 年）
DEPOSIT AND LOAN BALANCE OF FINANCIAL INSTITUTIONS BY REGION（1990-2011 年）

单位:亿元（100 million yuan）

年 份 Year	存款余额 Deposits Balance	其中 of which 市 区 Urban Area	溧阳市 Liyang City	金坛市 Jintan City	年 份 Year	贷款余额 Loans Balance	其中 of which 市 区 Urban Area	溧阳市 Liyang City	金坛市 Jintan City
1990	59.37	46.24	7.50	5.63	1990	74.24	58.52	8.98	6.74
1991	81.35	64.79	9.64	6.92	1991	93.10	73.94	10.95	8.21
1992	104.84	83.34	12.83	8.67	1992	112.46	89.96	13.27	9.23
1993	127.73	101.60	17.06	9.07	1993	132.16	105.84	15.81	10.51
1994	192.71	158.68	21.74	12.29	1994	180.48	148.54	19.31	12.63
1995	257.61	205.93	32.12	19.56	1995	211.88	170.12	25.43	16.33
1996	308.89	251.34	35.73	21.82	1996	237.04	192.43	26.71	17.90
1997	403.16	329.26	44.15	29.75	1997	304.83	242.25	36.05	26.53
1998	479.80	387.49	56.17	36.14	1998	342.13	272.79	39.93	29.41
1999	560.03	454.81	62.86	42.36	1999	369.06	298.86	40.39	29.80
2000	629.36	511.00	69.00	49.36	2000	389.26	324.19	39.52	25.55
2001	735.25	596.55	79.78	58.92	2001	444.54	376.32	40.08	28.14
2002	904.71	738.30	95.75	70.66	2002	559.85	476.15	46.97	36.69
2003	1170.56	964.37	117.88	88.31	2003	799.14	683.11	66.72	49.31
2004	1362.22	1129.93	134.10	98.19	2004	956.38	835.85	70.05	50.48
2005	1649.61	1375.25	159.62	114.74	2005	1113.25	966.84	87.90	58.51
2006	1974.05	1644.73	190.81	138.51	2006	1348.60	1164.62	108.67	75.31
2007	2263.84	1893.65	216.59	153.58	2007	1590.11	1349.12	140.68	100.30
2008	2819.42	2348.91	281.79	188.72	2008	1851.69	1550.76	181.86	119.09
2009	3765.91	3141.89	382.84	241.18	2009	2513.97	2100.23	256.02	157.71
2010	4550.47	3800.47	454.64	295.37	2010	3011.67	2518.92	299.11	193.64
2011	4902.15	4024.70	541.80	335.65	2011	3406.35	2817.27	361.26	227.81

18-4 历年城乡居民储蓄存款余额
URBAN AND RURAL SAVINGS DEPOSITS BALANCE OVER THE YEARS

单位：万元（10000 yuan）

年份 Year	城乡居民储蓄存款余额 Urban and Rural Savings Deposits Balance	其中 of which 市区 Urban Area	城镇居民 Urban Residents	年份 Year	城乡居民储蓄存款余额 Urban and Rural Savings Deposits Balance	其中 of which 市区 Urban Area	城镇居民 Urban Residents
1949	8	8	8	1981	20123	15454	12691
1950	59	57	59	1982	26767	20211	16633
1951	280	239	280	1983	36154	26686	20056
1952	598	544	552	1984	48512	34826	26338
1953	734	664	722	1985	67304	48969	41172
1954	913	782	850	1986	92511	67526	56958
1955	970	833	879	1987	134174	96557	83406
1956	1256	1070	1103	1988	157915	117394	102727
1957	1666	1329	1276	1989	230962	170915	157210
1958	1580	1400	1410	1990	342914	254479	232416
1959	2267	1945	1914	1991	462939	348651	323615
1960	2333	2013	2032	1992	568704	429591	401502
1961	2281	1951	1906	1993	673404	496160	488279
1962	1594	1410	1376	1994	909347	675495	668914
1963	1968	1719	1664	1995	1286526	969196	963142
1964	2662	2311	2098	1996	1726519	1321397	1319672
1965	2829	2453	2287	1997	2246590	1733748	1707923
1966	3144	2737	2517	1998	2841400	2324026	2216275
1967	2974	2658	2496	1999	3326100	2522385	2639503
1968	2981	2477	2137	2000	3555700	2681100	2816500
1969	2503	2059	1903	2001	4126500	3099500	3296800
1970	2566	2197	2040	2002	4999400	3798700	4076300
1971	3236	2621	2370	2003	6229200	4783000	5114000
1972	3577	2975	2711	2004	7243600	5609100	5970800
1973	4313	3520	3194	2005	8653900	6718200	7789175
1974	4530	3803	3523	2006	10140100	6947139	9183439
1975	4960	4148	3851	2007	10921400	8514100	9863400
1976	5137	4317	4023	2008	14312100	11181700	11802900
1977	5928	4942	4508	2009	17562400	13727400	14560300
1978	7182	6008	5347	2010	20092400	15672600	16602600
1979	12032	9256	7631	2011	21573900	16740100	17676800
1980	16337	12704	10175				

18-5 分地区财政总收入（2011 年）
TOTAL FINANCIAL REVENUE BY REGION（2011）

单位：万元（10000 yuan）

指 标	Item	全 市 Whole Municipality	其中 of which 市 区 Urban Area	溧阳市 Liyang City	金坛市 Jintan City
总 计	**Total**	**9777913**	**8102756**	**1003276**	**671881**
中央收入	Revenue of Central Government	2442029	1992949	265226	183854
增值税 (75%)	Value-added Tax (75%)	1456734	1196463	158822	101449
消费税	Consumption Tax	36566	31600	4735	231
企业所得税 (60%)	Corporate Income Tax (60%)	661061	542536	75473	43052
个人所得税 (60%)	Individual Income Tax (60%)	287668	222350	26196	39122
地方一般预算收入	Local Government Budgetary Revenue	3508800	2906762	371280	230758
税收收入	Tax Revenue	2808293	2307986	308154	192153
# 增值税 (25%)	Value-added Tax (25%)	485570	398813	52941	33816
营业税	Operation Tax	741059	610865	87979	42215
企业所得税(40%)	Enterprise's Income Tax (40%)	440707	361691	50315	28701
个人所得税 (40%)	Individual Income Tax (40%)	191779	148234	17464	26081
资源税	Resources Tax	8059		4235	3824
城市维护建设税	Tax on Urban Construction and Maintenance	189769	153242	22910	13617
房产税	Tax on Real Estates	94597	78448	9537	6612
印花税	Stamp Tax	52109	42694	6066	3349
城镇土地使用税	Tax on Use of Urban Land	135343	114920	13855	6568
土地增值税	Land Value Added Tax	169583	146048	17313	6222
车船税	Vehicle and Vessel Usage Tax	15825	13211	1487	1127
耕地占用税	Tax on the Occupancy of Cultivated Land	31473	19583	4008	7882
契 税	Contract Tax	252420	220237	20044	12139
非税收入	Non-tax Revenue	700507	598776	63126	38605
专项收入	pecial Revenue	107695	81706	17959	8030
行政性收费收入	Income From Administrative Fees	207561	167001	26255	14305
罚没收入	Fine and Confiscatory Revenue	52066	37830	9800	4436
国有资本经营收入	Revenue from State-owned Assets	57195	47645		9550
财政基金收入	Fund Revenue	3827084	3203045	366770	257269

18-6 分地区财政支出（2011 年）
FINANCIAL EXPENDITURE BY REGION （2011）

单位：万元（10000 yuan）

指 标	Item	全 市 Whole Municipality	其中 of which 市 区 Urban Area	溧阳市 Liyang City	金坛市 Jintan City
总 计	**Total**	**7430767**	**6050417**	**822616**	**557734**
一般预算支出	Ordinary Budgetary Expenditure	3618123	2877736	443228	297159
#一般公共服务	General Public Services	386701	293921	51439	41341
国 防	National Defense	21727	17048	3309	1370
公共安全	Public Security	209798	166757	25012	18029
教 育	Education	549170	399456	90871	58843
科学技术	Science and Technology	125299	106306	10130	8863
文化体育与传媒	Culture, Sports and Media	58648	43726	10348	4574
社会保障和就业	Social Security and Employment	363633	297412	38907	27314
医疗卫生	Medical Treatment and Health	196910	148032	27729	21149
环境保护	Environmental Protection	158404	93479	48315	16610
城乡社区事务	Urban and Rural Community Affairs	680141	624419	37226	18496
农林水事务	Agriculture, Forestry and Water Affairs	256631	159097	61992	35542
交通运输	Traffic and Transportation	121176	107198	9853	4125
资源勘探电力信息等事务	Resource Exploration and Power Information	84945	78949	3225	2771
商业服务业等事务	Business and Services	72628	57034	8459	7135
金融监管等事务	Financial Regulation	10278	6022	3095	1161
国土资源气象等事务	Land, Resources and Weather	29367	13873	5126	10368
住房保障支出	Housing Security Expenditure	108031	87294	3850	16887
粮油物资储备管理事务	Food, Oil and Material Reserves Management	4091	1608	2280	203
其 他	Others	180545	176105	2062	2378
财政基金支出	Fund Expenditure	3812644	3172681	379388	260575

18-7 五区财政收支（2011 年）
FINANCIAL REVENUE AND EXPENDITURE OF FIVE DISTRICTS（2011）

单位：万元（10000 yuan）

指 标	Item	武进区 wujin District	新北区 Xinbei District	天宁区 Tianning District	钟楼区 Zhonglou District	戚墅堰区 Qishuyan District
财政收入	**Financial Revenue**	**3155600**	**2041074**	**617644**	**532072**	**189743**
中央收入	Revenue of Central Government	800053	589225	246817	188294	92892
地方一般预算收入	Local Government Budgetary Revenue	1052800	730151	356735	312913	85500
税收收入	Tax Revenue	849509	636263	323008	259160	79299
# 增值税	Value-added Tax	175061	112120	46850	33051	22600
营业税	Operation Tax	177600	160363	122524	101503	15960
企业所得税	Enterprise's Income Tax	129424	126270	50894	38592	11649
个人所得税	Individual Income Tax	53355	37394	19504	19025	5077
城市维护建设税	Tax on Urban Construction and Maintenance	53461	40606	22571	15930	8092
房产税	Tax on Real Estates	28909	20760	10767	10461	2906
印花税	Stamp Tax	16528	13098	5581	3714	1547
契 税	Contract Tax	107141	47748	11	11	3
非税收入	Non-tax Revenue	203291	93888	33727	53753	6201
财政基金收入	Fund Revenue	1302747	721698	14092	30865	11351
财政支出	**Financial Expenditure**	**2323383**	**1121522**	**162124**	**205776**	**59973**
一般预算支出	Ordinary Budgetary Expenditure	1058968	387740	151791	177230	49638
# 一般公共服务	General Public Services	76844	46819	25556	22843	9796
国 防	National Defense	8061	1	650	167	384
公共安全	Public Security	38762	11393	8558	4289	2572
教 育	Education	151924	60885	28003	28240	8072
科学技术	Science and Technology	38670	27710	5736	10539	1430
文化体育与传媒	Culture, Sports and Media	15608	2606	950	711	189
社会保障和就业	Social Security and Employment	56003	66234	24242	23856	8738
医疗卫生	Medical Treatment and Health	45422	23876	7100	7637	2206
环境保护	Environmental Protection	44777	10846	1573	1378	748
城乡社区事务	Urban and Rural Community Affairs	403292	64731	15004	62564	9514
农林水事务	Agriculture, Forestry and Water Affairs	95491	16863	24413	4764	2235
交通运输	Traffic and Transportation	31352	10			3
商业服务业等事务	Business and Services	9477	2920	3944	5538	833
住房保障支出	Housing Security Expenditure	6941	5	2	4	3
其 他	Others	36344	52841	6060	4700	2915
财政基金支出	Fund Expenditure	1264415	733782	10333	28546	10335

18-8 分地区金融机构信贷收支情况（2011 年）
CREDIT FUNDS BALANCE OF FINANCIAL INSTITUTIONS GROUPED BY REGION（2011）

单位：亿元（100 million yuan）

指 标	Item	全 市 Whole Municipality	其中 of which 市 区 Urban Ared	溧阳市 Liyang City	金坛市 Jintan City
金融机构存贷款余额（本外币）	**Balance of Deposits and Loans in Financial Institutions (Domestic and Foreign Currency)**				
各项存款余额	Balance of Deposits	5020.88	4126.43	549.25	345.20
# 个人存款	Svings Deposits	2208.05	1717.97	289.11	200.97
# 储蓄存款	Savings Deposits	2171.20	1686.00	287.44	197.77
各项贷款余额	Balance of Loans	3505.80	2907.92	365.87	232.01
金融机构存贷款余额（人民币）	**Balance of Deposits and Loans in Financial Institutions (RMB)**				
各项存款余额	Balance of Deposits	4902.15	4024.70	541.80	335.65
# 企业存款	Deposits of Enterprises	2605.90	2226.90	246.71	132.30
个人存款	Svings Deposits	2193.53	1705.28	288.24	200.01
# 储蓄存款	Savings Deposits	2157.39	1674.01	286.58	196.81
各项贷款余额	Balance of Loans	3406.35	2817.27	361.26	227.81
短期贷款	Short-term Loans	1839.97	1497.30	220.60	122.07
# 个人贷款及透支	Personal Loan and Overdraft	167.89	112.59	36.63	18.66
# 个人消费贷款	Personal Consumption and Overdraft	21.89	19.14	1.40	1.35
单位贷款及透支	Unit Loan and Overdraft	1504.61	1247.11	168.68	88.82
# 经营贷款	Operating Loans	1474.26	1219.49	166.82	87.96
固定资产贷款	Fixed Asset Loans	30.29	27.57	1.86	0.87
银团贷款	Syndicated Loans	1.50	0.20		1.30
贸易融资	Trade Financing	165.97	137.40	15.29	13.29
中长期贷款	Medium-term and Long-term Loans	1482.51	1246.63	134.11	101.77
# 个人贷款及透支	Personal Loan and Overdraft	575.96	485.07	49.17	41.72
# 个人消费贷款	Personal Consumption and Overdraft	483.56	409.06	39.40	35.10
单位贷款及透支	Unit Loan and Overdraft	830.24	699.34	78.04	52.86
# 经营贷款	Operating Loans	96.93	73.39	11.39	12.15
固定资产贷款	Fixed Asset Loans	733.31	625.94	66.66	40.71
银团贷款	Syndicated Loans	67.81	53.73	6.90	7.19
票据融资	Bill Financing	82.92	72.42	6.55	3.95

18-9 分地区金融机构外汇信贷收支情况（2011 年）
CREDIT FUNDS BALANCE IN FOREIGN CURRENCIES OF FINANCIAL INSTITUTIONS GROUPED BY REGION（2011）

单位：万美元（USD 10000）

项 目	Item	全 市 Whole Municipality	其中 of which 市 区 Urban Area	溧阳市 Liyang City	金坛市 Jintan City
金融机构外币存款余额	**Deposits Balance in Foreign Currencies of Banking Institutions**	**188437**	**161451**	**11836**	**15150**
# 企业存款	Deposits of Enterprises	164253	140178	10455	13620
个人存款	Svings Deposits	23038	20141	1373	1525
# 储蓄存款	Savings Deposits	21927	19034	1369	1523
金融机构外币贷款余额	**Loans Balance in Foreign Currencies of Banking Institutions**	**157841**	**143868**	**7319**	**6654**
短期贷款	Short-term Loans	152861	138925	7319	6617
中长期贷款	Medium-term and Long-term Loans	4979	4942		37
贸易融资	Export and Import Trade Financing	135459	121523	7319	6617

18-10 证券交易情况（2011 年）
TRADING SUMMARY FOR SECURITIES（2011）

单位：亿元（100 million yuan）

项 目	Item	全 市 Whole Municipality
证券交易总额（亿元）	Total Transaction Volume of Securities (100 million yuan)	4839.06
A 股	A Shares	4767.51
B 股	B Shares	11.72
基 金	Funds	52.99
债 券	Bonds	6.84
资金帐户总数（万户）	Total Capital Accounts (10000 households)	53.48

18-11 分地区保险业务情况（2011 年） BASIC STATISTICS ON INSURANCE BY REGION（2011）

单位：万元（10000 yuan）

指标	Item	全市 Whole Municipality	其中 of which 市区 Urban Area	溧阳市 Liyang City	金坛市 Jintan City
财产险	**Property Insurance**				
承保金额	Insurance Value	107935288	95432862	7074740	5427686
企业财产险	Enterprise Property Insurance	30245767	26381260	2428628	1435879
机动车辆险	Motor Vehicle Insurance	24129614	19466554	2718442	1944618
货物运输险	Freight Transport Insurance	11185033	10492231	194398	498404
工程险	Project Liability Insurance	1301141	1242510	13346	45285
家庭财产险	Family Property Insurance	1749373	1212768	505367	31238
责任险	Liability Insurance	26272309	24786891	514333	971085
其它险	Other Insurance	13052051	11850648	700226	501177
保费收入	Premium Income	296454	245930	30729	19795
企业财产险	Enterprise Property Insurance	27566	23760	2146	1660
机动车辆险	Motor Vehicle Insurance	233579	195287	23195	15097
货物运输险	Freight Transport Insurance	6052	4785	898	369
工程险	Project Liability Insurance	1158	1059	66	33
家庭财产险	Family Property Insurance	1655	979	662	14
责任险	Liability Insurance	8718	7300	886	532
其它险	Other Insurance	17726	12760	2876	2090
赔付支出	Indemnity Experditur	145493	118536	16201	10756
企业财产险	Enterprise Property Insurance	12700	10630	1477	593
机动车辆险	Motor Vehicle Insurance	123428	100512	13605	9311
货物运输险	Freight Transport Insurance	1249	1046	141	62
工程险	Project Liability Insurance	149	148	1	
家庭财产险	Family Property Insurance	450	365	80	5
责任险	Liability Insurance	3103	2542	409	152
其它险	Other Insurance	4414	3293	488	633
人寿险	**Life Insurance**				
保费收入	Premium Income	696377	587350	53649	55378
意外伤害险	Personal and Accident Insurance	13741	10825	1903	1013
健康险	Health Insurance	11531	10531	448	552
人寿险	Life Insurance	671105	565994	51298	53813
赔付支出	Indemnity Experditur	20244	16847	1634	1763
意外伤害险	Personal and Accident Insurance	4357	3788	389	180
健康险	Health Insurance	6346	5740	300	306
人寿险	Life Insurance	9541	7319	945	1277

18-12 分地区企业职工基本养老保险情况（2011 年）
BASIC CONDITIONS OF PENSION INSURANCE OF ENTERPRISES' STAFF AND WORKERS GROUPED BY REGION（2011）

指 标	Item	全 市 Whole Municipality	其中 of which 市 区 Urban Area	溧阳市 Liyang City	金坛市 Jintan City
参保单位数（个）	Number of Units Covered by Insurance (unit)	42769	36269	4015	2485
参保职工人数（人）	Number of Employees Covered by Insurance (person)	1137507	890036	137240	110231
领取养老保险金人数（人）	Number of People Receiving Pension Insurance (person)	310901	260103	31646	19152
基金总收入（万元）	General Fund Revenue (10000 yuan)	756439	594705	106557	55177
#基本养老保险费	Basic Pension Insurance Premiums	697759	544146	100317	53296
基金总支出（万元）	General Fund Expenditure (1000 yuan)	596045	508052	51983	36010
#基本养老金	Basic Pension	558182	477172	47940	33070

18-13 分地区城乡居民社会养老保险情况（2011 年）
BASIC CONDITIONS OF THE URBAN AND RURAL SOCIAL PENSION INSURANCE GROUPED BY REGION（2011）

指 标	Item	全 市 Whole Municipality	其中 of which 市 区 Urban Area	溧阳市 Liyang City	金坛市 Jintan City
参保缴费人数（万人）	Number of People with Pension Insurance (10000 persons)	49.60	20.84	15.80	12.96
领取养老金人数（人）	Number of Pensioners (person)	410572	224020	104020	82532
基金总收入（万元）	General Fund Revenue (10000 yuan)	112313	70431	23575	18307
基金总支出（万元）	General Fund Expenditure (10000 yuan)	69801	53132	8996	7673

18-14 分地区基本医疗保险情况（2011 年）
BASIC CONDITIONS OF MEDICAL INSURANCE GROUPED BY REGION（2011）

指 标	Item	全 市 Whole Municipality	其中 of which 市 区 Urban Area	溧阳市 Liyang City	金坛市 Jintan City
参保人数（人）	Number of Persons Coverd by Insurance (person)	1490834	1199506	161868	129460
在职职工	Employed Staff and Workers	1128579	901191	124263	103125
退休人员	Retirees	362255	298315	37605	26335
基金总收入（万元）	General Fund Revenue (10000 yuan)	284730	238525	25218	20987
#统筹账户	Pool Account	166507	141231	13254	12022
基金总支出（万元）	General Fund Expenditure (10000 yuan)	230006	192037	21047	16922
#统筹账户	Pool Account	133791	112978	10637	10176

18-15 分地区失业保险情况（2011 年）
BASIC CONDITIONS OF UNEMPLOYMENT INSURANCE GROUPED BY REGION（2011）

指 标	Item	全 市 Whole Municipality	其中 of which 市 区 Urban Area	溧阳市 Liyang City	金坛市 Jintan City
参保人数（人）	Number of People Covered by Insurance (person)	889415	700033	103262	86120
领取失业保险金人数（人）	Number of People Receiving Unemployment Insurance (person)	38486	32101	2364	4021
基金总收入（万元）	General Fund Revenue (10000 yuan)	70984	60618	5464	4902
基金总支出（万元）	General Fund Expenditure (10000 yuan)	49679	47094	1056	1529

18-16 分地区工伤保险情况（2011 年）
BASIC CONDITIONS OF WORK-RELATED INJURY INSURANCE GROUPED BY REGION（2011）

指 标	Item	全 市 Whole Municipality	其中 of which 市 区 Urban Area	溧阳市 Liyang City	金坛市 Jintan City
参保人数（人）	Number of People Covered by Insurance (person)	885381	691947	87312	106122
基金总收入（万元）	General Fund Revenue (10000 yuan)	18685	13652	2025	3008
基金总支出（万元）	General Fund Expenditure (10000 yuan)	19226	13785	2756	2685
当年享受工伤保险待遇人次（人次）	Number of People Receiving Work-Related Injury Insurance (person-time)	6575	3932	1095	1548

18-17 分地区生育保险情况（2011 年）
BASIC CONDITIONS OF MATERNITY INSURANCE GROUPED BY REGION（2011）

指 标	Item	全 市 Whole Municipality	其中 of which 市 区 Urban Area	溧阳市 Liyang City	金坛市 Jintan City
参保人数（人）	Number of People Covered by Insurance (person)	802433	672882	56266	73285
基金总收入（万元）	General Fund Revenue (10000 yuan)	16644	14276	926	1442
基金总支出（万元）	General Fund Expenditure (10000 yuan)	8830	7853	330	647
当年享受生育保险待遇人次（人次）	Number of People Receiving Maternity Insurance (person-time)	15181	13576	540	1065

19

CHAPTER 19

企业调查

ENTERPRISES SURVEY

常州统计年鉴

19 企业调查
ENTERPRISES SURVEY

2011 年主要统计指标
MAJOR STATISTICAL INDICATORS OF 2011

企业家信心指数	Index of Enterpreneur's confidencd	
一季度	the First Quarter	130.0
二季度	the Second Quarter	130.4
三季度	the Third Quarter	121.3
四季度	the Fourth Quarter	110.0
企业综合经营景气指数	Index of General Operating Situation of Enterprises	
一季度	the First Quarter	126.3
二季度	the Second Quarter	129.0
三季度	the Third Quarter	126.2
四季度	the Fourth Quarter	116.4

19-1 企业家信心指数（2011 年）
INDEX OF ENTREPRENEUR'S CONFIDENCE（2011）

指 标	Item	一季度 the First Quarter	二季度 the Second Quarter	三季度 the Third Quarter	四季度 the Fourth Quarter
企业家信心指数	**Index of Entrepreneus Confidence**	**130.0**	**130.4**	**121.3**	**110.0**
按登记注册类型分	**Grouped by Registration Status**				
#国　有	State-owned	128.8	135.5	116.3	110.1
集　体	Collective-owned	133.3	133.3	133.3	133.3
股份合作	Share-holding Cooperative	33.3	33.3	33.3	33.3
联　营	Joint Ownership	100.0	100.0	100.0	100.0
有限责任公司	Limited Liability Corporations	121.1	123.3	115.8	99.6
股份有限公司	Share-holding Corporations Ltd.	146.3	144.3	127.5	122.6
私　营	Private	137.2	137.2	118.4	116.3
港澳台投资	Investment from Hong Kong, Macao and Taiwan	139.3	117.3	129.1	114.1
外商投资	Foreign Investment	167.5	132.3	112.9	113.6
按行业分	**Grouped by Sector**				
工　业	Industry	128.7	129.6	113.5	99.9
建筑业	Constuction	148.8	135.6	141.1	138.5
交通、仓储和邮政业	Transportation,Storage,Post and Telecommunication	100.0	105.9	100.0	94.1
批发和零售业	Wholesale and Retail Trade and Catering Services	140.4	142.9	138.1	132.6
房地产业	Real Estate	109.0	97.8	86.7	64.5
社会服务业	Social Services	132.0	136.0	140.0	132.0
信息传输、计算机服务和软件业	Information Transmission,Computer Services and Software Industries	137.5	137.5	137.5	125.0
住宿和餐饮业	Accommodation and Catering	136.0	136.0	128.0	112.0
按规模分	**Grouped by Size of Enterprises**				
大　型	Large-sized	136.2	156.4	108.7	78.1
中　型	Medium-sized	131.3	128.6	115.8	106.7
小　型	Small-sized	122.5	120.3	121.1	109.5
按特定企业群体分	**Grouped by Special Enterprises Group**				
#上市公司	Public enlisted company	181.6	135.2	131.9	148.8
国有控股企业	State Controlled Enterprises	135.9	143.2	115.8	121.1

19-2 企业综合经营景气指数（2011 年）
INDEX OF GENERAL OPERATING SITUATION OF ENTERPRISES（2011）

指 标	Item	一季度 the First Quarter	二季度 the Second Quarter	三季度 the Third Quarter	四季度 the Fourth Quarter
企业综合经营景气指数	**Index of General Operating Situation of Enterprises**	**126.3**	**129.0**	**126.2**	**116.4**
按登记注册类型分	**Grouped by Registration Status**				
#国 有	State-owned	135.1	141.7	141.3	110.1
集 体	Collective-owned	100.0	66.7	66.7	100.0
股份合作	Share-holding Cooperative	100.0	100.0	66.7	
联 营	Joint Ownership	100.0	100.0	100.0	100.0
有限责任公司	Limited Liability Corporations	120.0	123.6	121.3	105.0
股份有限公司	Share-holding Corporations Ltd.	131.7	133.9	130.7	136.5
私 营	Private	127.9	139.4	134.9	132.6
港澳台投资	Investment from Hong Kong, Macao and Taiwan	129.1	133.2	139.1	144.1
外商投资	Foreign Investment	146.5	140.5	97.1	102.5
按行业分	**Grouped by Sector**				
工 业	Industry	121.9	129.7	123.8	107.3
建筑业	Constuction	143.2	135.6	133.4	133.4
交通、仓储和邮政业	Transportation,Storage,Post and Telecommunication	105.9	100.0	94.1	82.4
批发和零售业	Wholesale and Retail Trade and Catering Services	152.7	148.8	140.2	142.3
房地产业	Real Estate	125.6	125.6	123.5	75.6
社会服务业	Social Services	124.0	120.0	128.0	140.0
信息传输、计算机服务和软件业	Information Transmission,Computer Services and Software Industrises	100.0	100.0	137.5	100.0
住宿和餐饮业	Accommodation and Catering	128.0	140.0	132.0	128.0
按规模分	**Grouped by Size of Enterprises**				
大 型	Large-sized	128.8	132.5	114.1	79.5
中 型	Medium-sized	131.3	138.4	131.6	119.4
小 型	Small-sized	117.1	117.2	119.5	112.6
按特定企业群体分	**Grouped by Special Enterprises Group**				
#上市公司	Public enlisted company	157.4	121.7	132.1	162.1
国有控股企业	State Controlled Enterprises	136.0	149.2	140.0	127.7
按观察指标分	**Grouped by Indices of Observation**				
生产总量	Total Yield	102.8	127.6	120.5	110.2
盈利（亏损）变化	Profit (loss) changes	104.1	109.9	106.6	104.6
流动资金	Circulating Funds	93.6	90.7	90.4	79.4
货款拖欠	Loan Defaulted	92.8	91.8	91.8	88.8
劳动力需求	Labor Demanded	131.8	130.3	121.0	113.6
固定资产投资	Investment in fixed assets	104.9	115.8	116.7	110.4

20

CHAPTER 20

城市建设　环境保护

URBAN CONSTRUCTION AND ENVIRONMENTAL PROTECTION

20 城市建设　环境保护 URBAN CONSTRUCTION AND ENVIRONMENTAL PROTECTION

2011 年主要统计指标 MAJOR STATISTICAL INDICATORS OF 2011

城区人口密度	Urban Population Density	3572 人 / 平方公里	(person/sq.km)
城区实有道路面积	Area of Existing Road in Urban District	3230 万平方米	(10000 sq.m)
城区人均公园绿地面积	Per Capita Green Area of Parks in Urban District	12.41 平方米	(sq.m)
城区出租车营运数量	Number of Taxi in Operation in Urban Area	2542 辆	(coach)
城区燃气普及率	Gas Penetration Rate in Urban District	99.1%	

20-1　市区城市公用事业基本情况（1978-2011 年）
BASIC STATISTICS ON URBAN PUBLIC UTILITIES（1978-2011）

年　份 Year	建成区面积 (平方公里) Developed Area (sq.km)	年末实有铺装道路长度(公里) Length of Roads at Year-end(km)	年末实有铺装道路面积(万平方米) Area of Paved Roads at Year-end (10000 sq.m)	城市下水道总长度(公里) Total Length of Urban Sewerage Drain(km)	园林绿地面积 (公顷) Parkes,Gardens and Green Areas (hectare)	其中 of which # 公园绿地面积 (公顷) Green Space of Park (hectare)
1978	24.44	98	83	140	145	54
1979	26.80	102	86	145	150	55
1980	27.85	105	89	150	161	56
1981	28.98	109	90	155	171	59
1982	29.58	119	93	161	174	61
1983	31.00	124	103	190	177	64
1984	32.52	127	108	195	272	68
1985	34.30	121	104	225	275	71
1986	35.10	198	154	231	283	76
1987	35.90	320	263	284	294	80
1988	37.20	326	273	289	310	99
1989	37.80	332	279	229	322	107
1990	39.00	336	296	231	343	121
1991	39.60	354	312	238	364	137
1992	41.10	355	314	260	389	147
1993	54.80	415	359	271	920	223
1994	57.40	449	432	312	947	233
1995	60.60	483	450	698	1067	283
1996	65.00	559	606	714	1105	301
1997	67.00	593	662	736	1188	357
1998	68.14	648	713	818	1300	412
1999	68.14	671	777	894	1378	440
2000	68.95	697	868	929	1441	458
2001	70.95	821	1024	1040	1509	500
2002	90.50	2497	2907	1544	4779	1101
2003	92.28	3828	3563	2414	4813	1193
2004	98.50	3548	3772	2775	5213	1433
2005	104.31	3584	3954	2918	5529	1568
2006	107.58	1349	2158	2366	4037	1333
2007	112.50	1551	2247	2918	6057	1389
2008	120.51	1565	2606	3223	6468	1450
2009	133.90	1656	2809	3458	6773	1561
2010	153.05	1753	3023	3627	7222	1632
2011	173.15	1811	3230	3807	7535	1704

注：1、本表数据按当年行政区划统计；从1995年起，供水总量中不包括单位自备水量。
　　2、由于建设局统计口径发生变化，2006年起均为城区口径，同时公共绿地面积调整为公园绿地面积。
　　3、自2010年起年末实有公共汽车营运车辆统计口径调整为市区口径。

Note：1、The data in the tabal were calculated according to the administrative division of that year;Since 1995,the total volume of water supply excludes the volume oh self-prepared water supply by units.
　　2、Due to the change of statistic coverage of municipal construction authorities, the data were calculated as per statistic coverage of urban area since the year of 2006, meanwhile, public green area was adjusted as green area of park.
　　3、Since 2010, the actual number of buses in operation by the end of year has been calculated as per statistical coverage of urban areas.

供水总量(万立方米) Total Annual Volume of Water Supply (10000 m^3)	年末实有公共汽车营运车辆(辆) Number of Operating Public Transport Vehicles at Year-end (coach)	全年公共汽车客运总数(万人次) Total Number of Annual Passengers Despatched by Public Transport Vehicles (10000 persons/time)	年末实有出租汽车营运车辆(辆) Number of Operating Taxies at Year-end (coach)	管道燃气供气总量(万立方米) Total Pipe Natural Gas Supply (10000 m^3)	液化气供气总量(吨) Total Liquefied of Gas Supply(ton)
20578	117	7184			
20876	133	9706			
21219	147	10862		109	
21385	157	11023		143	
21881	167	10907		115	
22911	182	10171		224	
24332	205	10119		333	
25759	227	11271		515	
26611	217	11082	92	996	2386
26878	209	10762	116	1058	2798
27050	211	10519	131	1157	4161
24871	208	10290	136	1415	3757
25994	232	9482	137	1601	5469
26066	244	9632	146	1655	10556
28353	254	10201	290	1654	22877
26240	283	9129	356	1667	20802
25789	297	8354	419	1729	22940
11257	307	8704	592	1783	24662
11491	348	8768	1029	2624	28995
14870	371	9199	1209	3224	28923
15310	1415	11490	1173	3533	33405
15291	1423	12624	1564	3846	35443
16631	1572	14616	1443	4256	38827
20123	1703	14865	1442	4502	43835
31431	1651	14195	1442	5058	92852
30517	1804	15523	1442	5898	87464
30965	2065	18089	1642	5694	77510
32384	2105	21829	1842	8030	80800
20940	1608	18940	1842	14892	42115
23636	1779	25973	2142	26943	37025
23220	1788	33150	2142	31298	26656
23633	1934	35583	2142	33444	23532
21981	2518	38948	2542	48099	11037
21664	2600	40717	2542	52355	8182

20-2　主要年份市区城市设施水平
URBAN CIVIL FACILITIES IN MAIN YEARS

指　标	Item	2000	2005	2010	2011
人均日生活用水量（升）	Per Capita Daily Consumption of Tap Water for Rrsidential Use (liter)	224.2	181.6	238.7	229.9
自来水普及率（%）	Percentage of Population with Access to Tap Water (%)	100.0	92.7	100.0	100.0
每万人拥有公交车辆（标台）	Average Public Service Vehicles per 10000 Persons (coach)	15.6	9.0	13.1	14.3
燃气普及率（%）	Percentage of Population with Access to Fuel Gas (%)	99.8	92.0	99.0	99.1
人均拥有道路面积（平方米）	Per Capita Area of Roads (sq.m)	10.7	17.9	22.9	23.5
污水处理率（%）	Rate of Sewerage Disposal(%)	69.0	86.8	89.8	91.7
人均公园绿地面积（平方米）	Per Capita Green Area of Parks (sq.m)	5.6	7.1	12.4	12.4
建成区绿化覆盖率（%）	Rate of the Green Space in Constructed Areas (%)	31.7	38.8	42.2	42.2
生活垃圾无害化处理率（%）	Rate of No Harm Disposal of Living Garbage (%)	50.5	92.1	100.0	100.0

20-3　分地区城市建设用地情况（2011 年）
LAND USE OF URBAN CONSTRUCTION BY REGION（2011）

单位：平方公里 (sq.km)

指　标	Item	市　区 Urban Area	溧阳市 Liyang City	金坛市 Jintan City
建成区面积	Area of Constructed Regions	173.15	23.11	22.10
城市建设用地面积	Floor space of Urban Constructed Area	173.15	23.04	21.82
# 居住用地	Residential Area	47.66	7.38	7.31
公共设施用地	Public Utility Area	17.00	2.40	2.45
工业用地	Industrial Area	42.61	6.06	4.42
仓储用地	Storage and Warehouse	3.07	0.23	0.40
对外交通用地	Space for Transportation	7.76	2.22	1.67
道路广场用地	Space for Road and Squares	21.21	2.22	2.69
市政公用设施用地	Space for Public Facilities	5.64	0.99	0.91

20-4 分地区城市市政设施情况（2011 年）
URBAN CIVIL FACILITIES BY REGION（2011）

指 标	Item	市 区 Urban Area	溧阳市 Liyang City	金坛市 Jintan City
实有道路长度（公里）	Length of Roads (km)	1811	212	222
实有道路面积（万平方米）	Area of Roads (10000 sq.m)	3230	353	288
桥梁数（座）	Number of Bridges (unit)	1000	51	41
排水管道长度（公里）	Length of Sewage Pipelines (km)	3807	303	294
污水日处理能力（万立方米）	Capacity of Sewage Disposal (10000 m^3)	99	5	7
防洪堤长度（公里）	Length of Anti-Flood Diker (km)	1929		9
路灯盏数（千盏）	Street Lamps (1000 sets)	163	10	18

20-5 分地区城市园林绿化情况（2011 年）
URBAN PARKS, GARDENS AND GREEN AREAS BY REGION（2011）

指 标	Item	市 区 Urban Area	溧阳市 Liyang City	金坛市 Jintan City
园林绿地面积（公顷）	Parkes,Gardens and Green Areas (hectare)	7535	1126	921
公园绿地面积（公顷）	Green Space of Park (hectare)	1704	181	212
建成区绿化覆盖面积（公顷）	Green Space in Constucted Areas (hectare)	7302	957	896
人均公园绿地面积（平方米）	Per Capita Green Area of Park (sq.m)	12.4	9.4	12.3
建成区绿地率（%）	Rate of the Green Space in Constructed Areas (%)	38.4	38.4	36.7
建成区绿化覆盖率（%）	Rate of the Green Space in Constructed Areas (%)	42.2	41.4	40.7
城市公园个数（个）	Urban Parks (unit)	25	6	5
公园面积（公顷）	Park Area (hectare)	520	128	128

20-6　分地区城市公共汽车、出租汽车情况（2011 年）
URBAN PUBLIC SERVICE VEHICLES AND TAXIES BY REGION（2011）

指　标	Item	市　区 Urban Area	溧阳市 Liyang City	金坛市 Jintan City
公共汽车	**Public Service Vehicles**			
年底营运车辆数（辆）	Number in Operation at Year-end (coach)	2600	136	66
年底营运线路网长度（公里）	Length of Operating Route Net at Year-end (km)	3138	167	217
客运总量（万人次）	Total volume of travellers (10000 Persons/times)	40717	2200	775
每万人拥有公交车辆（标台）	Average Public Service Vehicles per 10000 Persons (coach)	14.3	5.4	4.4
出租汽车	**Taxies**			
营运车辆（辆）	Operation Vehicles (coach)	2542	335	279

20-7　分地区城市自来水情况（2011 年）
URBAN TAP WATER CONDITION BY REGION（2011）

指　标	Item	市　区 Urban Area	溧阳市 Liyang City	金坛市 Jintan City
自来水综合生产能力（万立方米 / 日）	General Production Capacity of Water Treatment Plant (10000 m^3 /day)	157.5	10.0	5.0
供水管道长度（公里）	Length of Water Supply Piplines (km)	8882	536	939
供水总量（万立方米）	Total Water Supply (10000 m^3)	21664	1962	2460
# 生产用水量	Water for Production	6719	879	836
生活用水量	Water for Livelihood	11521	909	1032
用水人口（万人）	Population with Access to Tap Water (10000 persons)	137.30	19.21	17.30
人均日生活用水量（升）	Per Capita Daily Comsumption of Tap Water for Livelihood (litre)	229.90	129.66	163.43
自来水普及率（%）	Percentage of Population with Access to Tap Water (%)	100.0	100.0	100.0

20-8 分地区城市燃气情况（2011 年） URBAN GAS SUPPLY BY REGION（2011）

指 标	Item	市 区 Urban Area	溧阳市 Liyang City	金坛市 Jintan City
天然气	**Natural Gas**			
燃气管道长度（公里）	Length of natural gas pipelines (km)	3918	275	399
供气总量（万立方米）	Total Gas Supply (10000 m^3)	52355	6268	6900
#家庭用量	Consumption for Residential Use	9766	515	1017
用气户数（户）	Total Number of Residents with Access to Gas (household)	496861	39557	43500
#家庭用户	Households Consumers	479358	38850	43249
用气人口（万人）	Total Population with Access to Gas (10000 persons)	131.58	13.50	12.10
天然气汽车加气站（座）	Natural Gas Filling Stations for Automobiles (unit)	9	2	1
液化石油气	**Liquefied Petroleum Gas**			
供气总量（吨）	Total Gas Supply (ton)	8182	4369	5900
#家庭用量	Consumption for Residential Use	2615	2584	2493
用气户数（户）	Total Number of Residents with Access to Gas (household)	17155	16393	31000
#家庭用户	Households Consumers	15755	16023	24350
用气人口（万人）	Total Population with Access to Gas (10000 persons)	4.48	5.56	5.20
燃气普及率（%）	**Percentage of Population with Access to Fuel Gas (%)**	**99.1**	**99.2**	**100.0**

20-9 分地区城市环境卫生情况（2011 年） URBAN ENVIRONMENT SANITATION BY REGION（2011）

指 标	Item	市 区 Urban Area	溧阳市 Liyang City	金坛市 Jintan City
实际清扫面积（万平方米）	Actually Cleaned Area (10000 sq.m)	2431	232	337
生活垃圾清运量（万吨）	Volume of Residential Garbage Disposal (10000 tons)	54.95	5.91	5.55
粪便清运量（万吨）	Clearing of Excrement and Urine (10000 tons)	0.74	0.13	0.99
公共厕所（座）	Public Lavatories (unit)	801	51	74
环卫机械数（台）	Environmental Sanitation Equipment (unit)	289	57	161

20-10 市区城市生态自然环境情况（2007-2011 年）
URBAN ECOLOGICAL NATURAL ENVIRONMENT（2007-2011）

指 标	Item	2007	2008	2009	2010	2011
园林绿化	**Parks,Gardens and Green Areas**					
园林绿地面积（公顷）	Parkes,Gardens and Green Areas (hectare)	6057	6468	6773	7222	7535
公园绿地面积（公顷）	Green Space of Park (hectare)	1389	1450	1561	1632	1704
建成区绿化覆盖面积（公顷）	Green Space in Constucted Areas (hectare)	4680	5076	5640	6451	7302
建成区绿化覆盖率（%）	Rate of Green Space in Constructed Areas (%)	41.6	42.1	42.1	42.2	42.2
人均公园绿地面积（平方米）	Per Capita Green Area of Park (sq.m)	11.35	12.12	12.20	12.35	12.41
城市公园个数（个）	Urban Parks (unit)	21	21	24	25	25
公园面积（公顷）	Park Area (hectare)	458	465	489	520	520
水、空气和噪声情况	**Water, Air and Noise**					
城市集中式饮用水源地水质达标率（%）	Rate up to the Standards of Water Quality for Urban Potable Water Sources (%)	100.0	100.0	100.0	100.0	100.0
空气污染指数小于100天数占全年天数的比例（%）	Proportion of Days with Air Pollution Index less than 100 to Whole Year (%)	85.2	86.1	91.5	91.5	92.1
区域环境噪声平均值（分贝）	Average Value of Noise in Whole Area (dB)	55.0	55.0	54.7	54.4	54.7
交通干线噪声平均值（分贝）	Average Value of Noise Along Main Traffic Artery (dB)	66.8	67.0	67.8	67.4	67.3
生活垃圾无害化处理	**Harmless Disposal of Household Garbage**					
垃圾清运量（万吨）	Wastes Transported (10000 Tons)	43.50	46.64	49.16	51.99	54.95
垃圾无害化处理量（万吨）	Volume of Garbage Disposal (10000 ton)	43.48	46.64	49.16	51.99	54.95
生活垃圾无害化处理率（%）	Rate of Harmless Disposal of Household Garbage (%)	100.0	100.0	100.0	100.0	100.0

20-11 环境保护情况（1986-2011 年）
ENVIRONMENTAL PROTECTION（1986-2011）

年 份 Year	工业废水排放总量（万吨） Total Volume of Industrial Wastewater Discharged (10000 tons)	工业废水中 COD 排放总量（吨） Total Volume of COD in Industrial Wastewater Discharged (ton)	工业废气中二氧化硫排放总量（吨） Total Volume of Sulphur Dioxide Emission in Industrial Waste Gas (ton)	工业废气中烟尘排放总量（吨） Total Volume of Soot Emission in Industrial Waste Gas (ton)	工业废气中粉尘排放总量（吨） Total Volume of Dust Emission in Industrial Waste Gas (ton)
1986	20681	64856	42527	49395	32500
1987	22647	51396	41072	38406	27800
1988	22386	43617	46968	37395	33700
1989	20546	35879	56252	56307	32700
1990	20439	30508	56099	55662	43400
1991	21455	28797	73472	62014	25700
1992	18697	31121	75671	57791	19200
1993	12070	27998	45906	26704	19000
1994	10931	22308	55355	28196	31300
1995	11489	22865	55971	25282	34300
1996	10523	15979	57236	28991	65900
1997	11193	26763	74320	35814	104600
1998	10183	17436	51476	26563	30300
1999	16455	19873	47409	33895	48700
2000	14728	16436	39042	30798	41200
2001	27086	29903	48242	17590	46400
2002	23912	29289	45133	19329	41447
2003	24071	30015	45722	15375	43986
2004	23082	43018	62958	28086	54602
2005	32519	51579	86215	35804	61091
2006	27300	36215	82930	31465	59396
2007	31875	30944	72243	29496	52085
2008	32601	28273	66656	25392	14904
2009	35942	26354	62255	24917	11299
2010	37715	24827	48000	19582	10784
2011	17371	9416	43734	38563	

注：从2011年起工业废气中烟尘、粉尘排放总量合并成烟（粉）尘排放量。
Note: The Total Dust and Powder Emissions in Industrial Emissions was combined as Smoke (Powder) Dust Emissions starting from 2011.

20-12　分地区环境保护情况（2011 年）
ENVIRONMENTAL PROTECTION BY REGION（2011）

指　标	Item	全　市 Whole Municipality	其中 of which 市　区 Urban Area	溧阳市 Liyang City	金坛市 Jintan City
废水排放	**Wastewater Discharged**				
工业废水排放总量（万吨）	Total Volume of Industrial Wastewater Discharged (10000 tons)	17371	14138	2041	1192
废水中化学需氧量排放量（吨）	Volume of Chemical Oxygen Demand in Wastwater Discharged (ton)	9416	7539	1184	693
废水中氨氮排放量（吨）	Ammonia Emissions from Wastewater (ton)	512	379	95	38
废气排放	**Waste Gas**				
工业废气排放总量（万标立方米）	Total Volume of Industrial Waste Gas Emission (10000 Nm^3)	36977677	31667106	3350629	1959912
二氧化硫（吨）	Volume of Sulphur Dioxide Emission (ton)	43734	32062	8982	2690
氮氧化物（吨）	Nitrogen Oxides (ton)	85823	51558	28502	5762
烟（粉）（吨）	Smoke (Powder) Dust Emissions (ton)	38563	27096	7901	3566
工业固体废物	**Industrail Solid Wastes**				
工业固体废物产生量（万吨）	Volume of Industrial Solid Wastes Produced (10000 tons)	623.79	530.00	77.07	16.72
工业固体废物综合利用量（万吨）	Volume of Industrial Solid Wastes Utilized (10000 tons)	611.12	518.12	76.29	16.71
工业固体废物处置量（万吨）	Volume of Industrial Solid Wastes Treated (10000 tons)	12.67	11.88	0.78	0.01
工业固体废物综合利用率（%）	Percentage of Industrial Solid Wastes Utilized (%)	98.0	97.8	99.00	99.9
环境建设	**Environmental Construction**				
自然保护区覆盖率（%）	Coverage Rate of Nature Reserves (%)	1.56	0.00	4.45	1.00

21
CHAPTER 21

科技 教育 文化

SCIENCE,TECHNOLOGY, EDUCATION AND CULTURE

21 科技 教育 文化
SCINECE & TECHNOLOGY EDUCATION AND CULTURE

2011 年主要统计指标
MAJOR STATISTICAL INDICATORS OF 2011

普通高等学校数	Number of Institutions of Higher Education	9 所	(unit)
普通高等学校在校学生数	Students Enrollment of Institutions of Higher Education	12.39 万人	(10000 persons)
普通中学数	Regular Secondary Schools	162 所	(unit)
普通中学在校学生数	Student Enrollment of Regular Secondary Schools	17.76 万人	(10000 persons)
小学学校数	Primary Schools	186 所	(unit)
小学学校在校学生数	Student Enrollment of Primary Schools	22.90 万人	(10000 persons)
年底公共图书馆	Number of Public Libraries	4 个	(unit)
电视台数	Number of Television Stations	4 座	(unit)
广播电台数	Number of Broadcasting Stations	4 座	(unit)

21-1　科研开发基本情况（2007-2011 年）
BASIC STATISTICS OF SCIENCE RESEARCH DEVELOPMENT（2007-2011）

指　标	Item	2007	2008	2009	2010	2011
机构数（个）	**Number of Institutes (unit)**	**20**	**19**	**19**	**18**	**17**
从业人数（人）	**Number of Employed Persons (person)**	**2747**	**2982**	**2970**	**3375**	**3741**
# 从事科技活动人数	Number of Personnel Engaged in Science and Technology	1184	1237	1335	1338	1496
# 从事 R&D 人员数	Number of Personnel Engaged in R&D	530	529	969	914	964
# 课题活动人数	Number of Persons Engaged in Subject Activity	631	588	612	864	893
经费收入总额（万元）	**Total Funds Income (10000 yuan)**	**174300**	**176534**	**194707**	**292888**	**301408**
# 政府资金	Government Funds	1966	2262	3881	2119	3316
技术性收入	Technological Income	7863	5978	7538	8449	11809
经营收入	Operating Income	148472	161701	175634	270125	279966
经费支出总额（万元）	**Total Expenditure (10000 yuan)**	**105586**	**106906**	**153210**	**190045**	**237057**
# R&D 经费支出	Expenditure on Research and Development	6319	5255	13688	17853	24310
# 购置科研仪器设备	Purchasing Scientific Research Instruments and Equipments	205	1282	1439	1956	4715
发表科技论文（篇）	**Number of Published Scientific and Technological Thesis (piece)**	**149**	**114**	**126**	**128**	**197**

21-2 国家级、省级科技计划数（2011 年）
NUMBER OF SCIENTIFIC AND TECHNOLOGICAL PLANS AT STATE LEVEL OR PROVINCE LEVEL（2011）

计划名称	Name of Plan	合计（项）Total (Unit)	其中 of which 国家级 State Level	省级 Province Level	总投资（亿元）Total Investment (100 million yuan)	上级拨款（万元）Higher Organizations Appropriations (10000 yuan)	其中 of which 国家 State	省 Province
国家863计划	National 863 Plan	2	2			1452	1452	
国家科技支撑计划	National Science & Technology Pillar Program	6	6			4172	4172	
科技型中小企业技术创新基金	Technology Innovation Funds for Scientific and Technical Type Small and Medium Enterprises	65	65			4571	4571	
国家农业科技成果转化资金	National Agricultural Scientific and Technological Achievements Transformation Funds	1	1			60	60	
国家重大科技专项	Major National Science and Technology Projects	5	5			4717	4717	
国家国际科技合作	National and International Scientific and Technological Cooperation	5	5			3135	3135	
国家火炬计划	National Torch Plan	33	33			660	660	
国家重点新产品计划	National Key New Product Plan	23	23			390	390	
省科技支撑计划（工业）	Provincial Scientific and Technological Support Plan (Industry)	22		22	2.04	1830		1830
省科技支撑计划（农业）	Provincial Scientific and Technological Support Plan (Agriculture)	8		8	0.16	230		230
省科技支撑计划（社会发展）	Provincial Scientific and Technological Support Plan (Social Development)	19		19	0.76	400		400
省科技支撑计划（重要技术标准）	Provincial Scientific and Technological Support Plan (Key Technology Standards)	3		3		140		140
省工程技术研究中心	Provincial Engineering and Technology Reaearch Center	15		15				
省国际科技合作计划	International Scientific and Technologic Cooperation Plan	5		5		170		170
省基础研究计划	Provincial Fundamental Research Plan	37		37		354		354
省科技成果转化专项资金	Special Fund for Scientific and Technological Achievements Transfer	16		16	15.93	13560		13560
省知识产权战略推进计划	Provincial Promotion Plan of Intellectual Property Rights Strategy	5		5	0.09	180		180
省专利实施计划	Provincial Patent Implementation Plan	2		2	0.07	45		45
省软科学研究	Provincial Soft Science Research	1		1		2		2
省科技创新资金	Provincial Science & Technology Innovation Capital	15		15		375		375
省企业重大研发机构	Provincial Major Enterprise R&D Institutions	1		1	3.00	300		300
省产学研联合创新资金	Provincial Industry-University Joint Innovation Fund	14		14	2.53	2375		2375
省科技公共服务平台	Provincial Science & Technology Public Service Platform				1.18	800		800
省企业院士工作站	Provincial Enterprise Academician Workstations	2		2	0.29	200		200
省科技创新团队项目	Provincial Technology Innovation Team Projects	1		1	2.40	1500		1500

注：本表项目数和上级拨款为当年新上项目数及新上项目的上级拨款总额。

Note：The number of projects and appropriation from higher authorities in this table shall be the number of new projects and total appropriations of the current year.

21-3　市级科技计划项目情况（2011 年）
SCIENTIFIC AND TECHNOLOGICAL PLAN AT CITY LEVEL（2011）

单位：万元（10000 yuan）

项目名称	Name of Project	项数（项）Number of Project (unit)	科技拨款 Scientific and Technological appropriations
农业科技	Agricultural Science and Technology	45	720
工业科技	Industrial Science and Technology	474	6249
社会发展科技	Social Development Science and Technology	74	921
软课题	Research Task	32	80

注：本表未包括指导性计划。
Note: This table doesn't include guidance plans.

21-4　科技进步获奖情况（2011 年）
STATISTICS ON PRIZE OF ADVANCE OF SCIENCE AND TECHNOLOGY（2011）

单位：项（unit）

奖励级别	Prize Grade	合计 Total	其中 of which		
			一等奖 First Prize	二等奖 Second Prize	三等奖 Third Prize
国家级	State Level	2		2	
省　级	Provincial Level	18	1	5	12
市　级	City Level	79	7	21	51

21-5　分地区专利申请及授权情况（2011 年）
STATISTICS ON PATENT APPLICATIONS EXAMINED AND GRANTED BY REGION（2011）

单位：项（unit）

指　标	Item	合　计 Total	其中 of which		
			市　区 Urban Area	溧阳市 Liyang City	金坛市 Jintan City
专利申请量	**Number of Patent Applications Examined**	**23413**	**17573**	**3224**	**2616**
发明专利	Patent for Invention	6125	4862	838	425
实用新型专利	Practical New-type Patent	9694	8533	765	396
外观专利	Appearance Patent	7580	4164	1621	1795
专利授权量	**Number of Patent Authorizations Granted**	**11390**	**8884**	**2058**	**448**
发明专利	Patent for Invention	744	656	49	39
实用新型专利	Practical New-type Patent	6496	5907	317	272
外观专利	Appearance Patent	4142	2313	1692	137

21-6 分地区政府科技拨款数（2011 年）
GOVERNMENT APPROPRIATION OF SCIENCE AND TECHNOLOGY BY REGION (2011)

单位：万元（10000 yuan）

指 标	Item	全 市 Whole Municipality	其中 of which 市 区 Urban Area	溧阳市 Liyang City	金坛市 Jintan City
总 计	**Total**	**156988**	**137994**	**10130**	**8864**
科学技术管理事务	Scientific & Technical Management Affairs	2189	1589	380	220
基础研究	Basic Research	695	695		
应用研究	Applied Research	1702	1032	670	
技术研究与开发	Technology Research and Development	47498	32516	7080	7902
科技条件与服务	Scientific & Technical Conditions and Service	20305	19535	440	330
社会科学	Social Science	1874	1874		
科学技术普及	Science & Technology Popularization	1437	962	301	174
科技交流与合作	Science and Technology Exchange and Cooperation	3517	3517		
科技重大专项	Special science and Technology Major	7712	7712		
其他科学技术支出	Other Expenditure For Science & Technology	70059	68562	1259	238

21-7 分地区高新技术企业情况（2011 年）
STATISTICS ON HIGH AND NEW TECHNOLOGY ENTERPRISES BY REGION (2011)

指 标	Item	全 市 Whole Municipality	其中 of which 市 区 Urban Area	溧阳市 Liyang City	金坛市 Jintan City
年末高新技术企业数（家）	Number of High and New Technology Enterprises at Year-end (unit)	618	548	34	36
# 当年确认数	Confirmed Number at Current Year	165	149	7	9
企业总产值（亿元）	Gross Output Value of Enterprises (100 million yuan)	1871 .30	1563 .30	191	117
新技术产品产值（亿元）	Output Value of New Technological Products (100 million yuan)	918.50	771.50	88	59
出口创汇总额（亿美元）	Total Exports (USD 100 million)	69.30	58.70	2.10	8.50
利税总额（亿元）	Total Amount of Pre-tax (100 million yuan)	194.20	161 .27	19.57	13.36
研究与开发经费（亿元）	Research and Development Funds (100 million yuan)	81.20	70 .02	6.90	4.28
职工总数（万人）	Number of staff and workers (10000 persons)	18 .12	15.75	1.17	1.20

21-8　分地区高新技术产品情况（2011 年）
STATISTICS ON HIGH AND NEW TECHNOLOGICAL PRODUCTS BY REGION（2011）

指标	Item	全市 Whole Municipality	其中 of which 市区 Urban Area	溧阳市 Liyang City	金坛市 Jintan City
省级高新技术产品累计数（只）	Accumulated Number of High and New Technological Products at Provincial Level (unit)	2440	2057	270	113
当年经省确认的高新技术产品数（只）	Number of High and New Technological Products Confirmed by the Province at This Year (unit)	779	673	76	30

21-9　技术（市场）贸易情况（2011 年）
STATISTICS ON TECHNOLOGY (MARKET) TRADE（2011）

指标	Item	全市 Whole Municipality
网上登记技术合同（项）	Number of Online Registered Technology Contracts (unit)	1817
网上登记技术合同成交金额（万元）	Business Volume of Online Registered Technology Contracts (10000 yuan)	137310

21-10　科技企业孵化器、加速器情况（2011 年）
STATISTICS ON SCIENTIFIC AND TECHNOLOGICAL ENTERPRISE INCUBATORS AND ACCELERATORS（2011）

指标	Item	全市 Whole Municipality	其中 of which 市区 Urban Area	溧阳市 Liyang City	金坛市 Jintan City
孵化器个数（个）	Number of Incubators and Accelerators（unit）	49	44	3	2
#省级以上	Provincial Level and Above	28	24	2	2
场地面积（万平方米）	Site Area（10000 square meters）	364	338	12	14
#省级以上	Provincial Level and Above	248	226	8	14
本年在孵企业数（家）	Number of Entered Enterprises（unit）	3610	3299	201	110
#省级以上	Provincial Level and Above	3120	2856	154	110
在孵企业总收入（万元）	Gross Income of Entered Enterprises（10000 yuan）	508260	474025	26820	7415
#省级以上	Provincial Level and Above	470180	438445	24320	7415
在孵企业从业人员数（人）	Persons Employed in Entered Enterprises（person）	39207	36132	2094	981
累计毕业企业数（家）	Accumulated Number of Incubated Enterprises （unit）	712	641	51	20
#当年毕业企业数	Number of Incubated Enterprises at Current Year	145	131	8	6

21-11 分地区规模以上工业企业科技活动情况（2011 年）
SCIENTIFIC AND TECHNOLOGICAL ACTIVITIES OF ABOVE-SCALE INDUSTRIAL ENTERPRISES BY REGION（2011）

指 标	Item	全 市 Whole Municipality	其中 of which 市 区 Urban Area	溧阳市 Liyang City	金坛市 Jintan City
企业基本情况	**Statistics on Industrial Enterprises**				
有 R&D 活动企业数（个）	Number of Enterprises Having R&D Activities (unit)	956	777	96	83
有 R&D 活动企业所占比重（%）	Percentage of Enterprises Having R&D Activities to Total Number of Enterprises (%)	26.3	26.3	29.4	23.3
R&D 活动情况	**Statistics on R&D Activities**				
R&D 人员（人）	Total Number of R&D Personnel (person)	35942	29599	4184	2159
R&D 经费内部支出（万元）	Intramural Expenditure on R&D (10000 yuan)	794012	609749	103229	81034
R&D 项目数（项）	Total Number of R&D Projects(unit)	3591	2759	398	434
企业办科技机构情况	**Scientific and Technological Institutions Run by Enterprises**				
企业办科技机构数（个）	Number of Scientific and Technological Institutions Run by Enterprises(unit)	907	713	64	130
机构科技活动人员（人）	Number of Scientific and Technological Personnel in Technological Institutions (person)	30576	26556	2062	1958
# 博士生	Ph.D. Owners	431	324	63	44
硕士生	Master's Degree Owners	2054	1753	180	121
新产品开发及生产情况	**Statitstics on New Product Development and Production**				
新产品开发项目数（个）	Number of New Products (unit)	4550	3627	454	469
新产品开发经费支出（万元）	Expenditure on New Product Development (10000 yuan)	1097660	874366	127047	96247
新产品产值（万元）	Output Value of New Products (10000 yuan)	12558702	10789902	1057858	710942
新产品销售收入（万元）	Sales Income of New Products (10000 yuan)	12501176	10765355	1056139	679682
# 新产品出口	Export	2865919	2392457	63023	410439
专利情况	**Statistics on Patent**				
专利申请数（件）	Patent Applications (piece)	7224	6173	547	504
# 发明专利	Inventions	2047	1518	247	282
有效发明专利数（件）	Number of Patents In Force (piece)	2542	2087	273	182
技术改造和技术获取情况	**Technical Innovation and Technology Acquisition**				
引进国外技术经费支出（万元）	Appropriation Expenditure on Foreign Technology Introduction (10000 yuan)	24721	22400	1278	1043
引进技术的消化吸收经费支出（万元）	Expenditure on Introduced Technology Absorption (10000 yuan)	18979	15185	2799	995
购买国内技术经费支出（万元）	Expenditure on Purchasing Domestic Technology (10000 yuan)	19949	15428	4020	501
技术改造经费支出（万元）	Appropriation Expenditure on Technical Inovation (10000 yuan)	1776675	1578115	122561	75999

21-12　分地区大中型工业企业科技活动情况（2011 年）
SCIENTIFIC AND TECHNOLOGICAL ACTIVITIES OF LARGE AND MEDIUM INDUSTRIAL ENTERPRISES BY REGION（2011）

指 标	Item	全 市 Whole Municipality	其中 of which 市 区 Urban Area	溧阳市 Liyang City	金坛市 Jintan City
企业基本情况	**Statistics on Industrial Enterprises**				
有 R&D 活动企业数（个）	Number of Enterprises Having R&D Activities (unit)	374	304	35	35
有 R&D 活动企业所占比重（%）	Percentage of Enterprises Having R&D Activities to Total Number of Enterprises (%)	59.7	61.5	59.3	48.0
R&D 活动情况	**Statistics on R&D Activities**				
R&D 人员（人）	Total Number of R&D Personnel (person)	24620	20431	2896	1293
R&D 经费内部支出（万元）	Intramural Expenditure on R&D (10000 yuan)	565007	431129	76758	57120
R&D 项目数（项）	Total Number of R&D Projects (unit)	1815	1390	225	200
企业办科技机构情况	**Scientific and Technological Institutions Run by Enterprises**				
企业办科技机构数（个）	Number of Scientific and Technological Institutions Run by Enterprises(unit)	477	356	40	81
机构科技活动人员（人）	Number of Scientific and Technological Personnel In Technological Institutions (person)	22224	19259	1640	1325
# 博士生	Ph.D. Owners	256	195	36	25
硕士生	Master's Degree Owners	1518	1289	145	84
新产品开发及生产情况	**Statitstics on New Product Development and Production**				
新产品开发项目数（个）	Number of New Products (unit)	2276	1803	270	203
新产品开发经费支出（万元）	Expenditure on New Product Development (10000 yuan)	794804	628119	99981	66704
新产品产值（万元）	Output Value of New Products (10000 yuan)	10725343	9106627	946281	672435
新产品销售收入（万元）	Sales Income of New Products (10000 yuan)	10689732	9103610	944232	641890
# 新产品出口	Export	2667891	2202336	62961	402594
专利情况	**Statistics on Patent**				
专利申请数（件）	Patent Applications (piece)	3953	3315	313	325
# 发明专利	Inventions	1125	781	157	187
有效发明专利数（件）	Number of Patents In Force (piece)	1108	804	170	134
技术改造和技术获取情况	**Technical Innovation and Technology Acquisition**				
引进国外技术经费支出（万元）	Appropriation Expenditure on Foreign Technology Introduction (10000 yuan)	15872	13811	1278	783
引进技术的消化吸收经费支出（万元）	Expenditure on Introduced Technology Absorption (10000 yuan)	14271	12273	1153	845
购买国内技术经费支出（万元）	Expenditure on Purchasing Domestic Technology (10000 yuan)	15123	11893	2730	500
技术改造经费支出（万元）	Appropriation Expenditure on Technical Inovation (10000 yuan)	1123332	970768	89336	63228

21-13 历年各类学校数
NUMBER OF SCHOOLS BY TYPE OVER THE YEARS

单位：所（unit）

年 份 Year	合 计 Total	其中 of which			
		# 普通高等院校 Institutions of Higher Education	普通中等专业学校 Specialized Secondary Schools	普通中学 Regular Secondary Schools	小 学 Primary Schools
1949	1666		3	54	1607
1950	1865		4	52	1807
1951	1983		5	54	1923
1952	2076		5	55	2015
1953	2033		3	55	1974
1954	2017		2	58	1956
1955	2003		2	59	1941
1956	2281		3	66	2211
1957	2138		2	68	2067
1958	2862	4	9	110	2465
1959	2921	3	9	116	2634
1960	2651	3	10	123	2367
1961	2436	2	6	116	2217
1962	2391		2	117	2245
1963	2348		2	116	2199
1964	3181		2	115	2974
1965	3726		2	103	3322
1966	3252		5	117	2855
1967	3038		5	120	2636
1968	2907		5	129	2467
1969	2615		4	183	2380
1970	2649		4	192	2445
1971	2712		5	308	2390
1972	2736		6	333	2390
1973	2769		6	300	2457
1974	2638		7	345	2281
1975	2641		8	427	2201
1976	2691		7	635	2043
1977	2612		7	632	1967
1978	2477		8	509	1952
1979	2466		10	478	1968

21-13　续表　Continued　　单位：所（unit）

年 份 Year	合 计 Total	其中 of which #普通高等院校 Institutions of Higher Education	普通中等专业学校 Specialized Secondary Schools	普通中学 Regular Secondary Schools	小 学 Primary Schools
1980	2490		13	360	2104
1981	2386	2	12	266	2093
1982	2400	2	11	282	2092
1983	2369	2	11	278	2061
1984	2294	2	14	282	1974
1985	2253	3	14	275	1933
1986	2212	3	15	270	1895
1987	2176	3	16	266	1862
1988	2136	3	16	260	1830
1989	2072	3	16	248	1776
1990	2021	3	16	235	1736
1991	1955	3	17	219	1678
1992	1822	3	16	212	1550
1993	1758	3	16	205	1497
1994	1633	3	16	199	1374
1995	1597	3	17	201	1332
1996	1448	3	17	193	1189
1997	1228	3	17	184	978
1998	1018	3	17	178	771
1999	927	3	17	176	683
2000	816	3	14	174	581
2001	736	5	12	177	498
2002	681	8	8	177	450
2003	550	8	8	174	327
2004	528	9	8	173	307
2005	499	9	7	172	284
2006	468	9	8	172	252
2007	446	9	8	169	234
2008	430	9	8	168	221
2009	408	9	8	166	206
2010	388	9	12	163	190
2011	384	9	13	162	186

21-14 历年在校学生数
NUMBER OF STUDENTS OVER THE YEARS

单位：人（person）

年份 Year	合计 Total	其中 of which # 普通高等院校 Institutions of Higher Education	普通中等专业学校 Specialized Secondary Schools	普通中学 Regular Secondary Schools	小学 Primary Schools
1949	154997		586	13223	140949
1950	158060		855	12568	144402
1951	186276		1404	16334	168353
1952	260160		1919	25587	221884
1953	270719		923	28973	230248
1954	264525		740	31813	231904
1955	284551		726	34113	249646
1956	311969		1243	30826	279829
1957	321017		1010	44123	275815
1958	416767	1069	2099	53013	338334
1959	436537	855	2991	59030	351695
1960	475975	1004	4614	65497	380691
1961	424200	1037	3487	61509	347389
1962	361579		1406	50482	306269
1963	353245		571	47779	301894
1964	412149		213	50043	355244
1965	447588		468	5225	372321
1966	464351		1027	74009	382302
1967	441394		1113	69817	364815
1968	450651		890	60215	360821
1969	500982		479	95506	403911
1970	446826			90659	352914
1971	497600			102324	391535
1972	558081		625	134911	419129
1973	549911		1220	124534	422645
1974	574459		1785	128937	442630
1975	601646		1725	159492	439205
1976	614776		464	193235	419580
1977	645041		1203	261068	381334
1978	598917	434	1980	215461	379391
1979	561234	542	2962	185704	369719

21-14　续表　Continued　　　　单位：人（person）

年 份 Year	合 计 Total	其中 of which # 普通高等院校 Institutions of Higher Education	普通中等专业学校 Specialized Secondary Schools	普通中学 Regular Secondary Schools	小 学 Primary Schools
1980	539645	481	3064	173164	360399
1981	513322	1312	3686	161621	343001
1982	492065	1036	3878	158452	324956
1983	486181	1240	5100	161380	312593
1984	487492	2059	6655	155577	314954
1985	491522	3161	9717	148865	319954
1986	493492	4044	12462	150555	313588
1987	483933	4578	13657	150979	301508
1988	476768	4839	14024	147573	296839
1989	468608	5079	14777	146394	289683
1990	461007	5085	15715	149037	277043
1991	453827	5190	15616	153409	262497
1992	452175	5469	16799	157068	253370
1993	460296	8897	20868	153547	255823
1994	478422	10908	26562	155908	261261
1995	501879	11644	33885	158586	271583
1996	526262	12182	42918	157074	289272
1997	542890	13156	49260	149390	305431
1998	550361	14251	52981	146903	312446
1999	561141	15120	53704	159995	309019
2000	571011	20013	49925	182332	300091
2001	584831	26668	49267	203570	287717
2002	603213	35159	52535	221258	273755
2003	622271	53059	50887	229845	263522
2004	642190	73862	51821	228206	255632
2005	648778	95396	48848	220718	244589
2006	648373	107742	46247	215938	234874
2007	643540	119131	39477	211346	229781
2008	630821	123174	36448	205966	224181
2009	614813	125468	34523	199351	216791
2010	603938	122802	36029	188436	221533
2011	600423	123947	38231	177639	229035

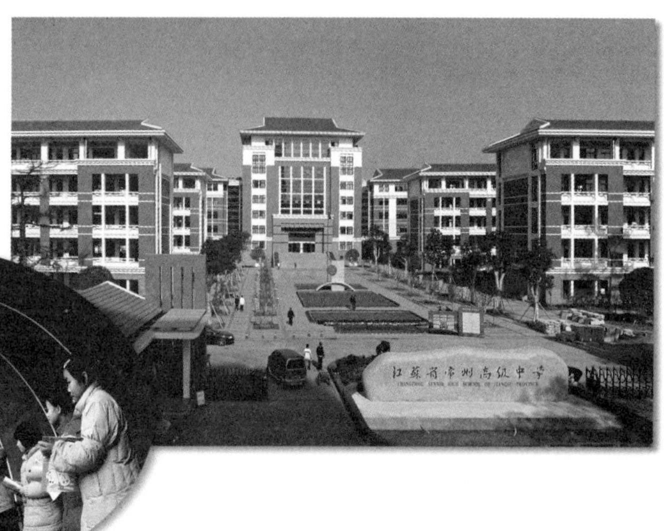

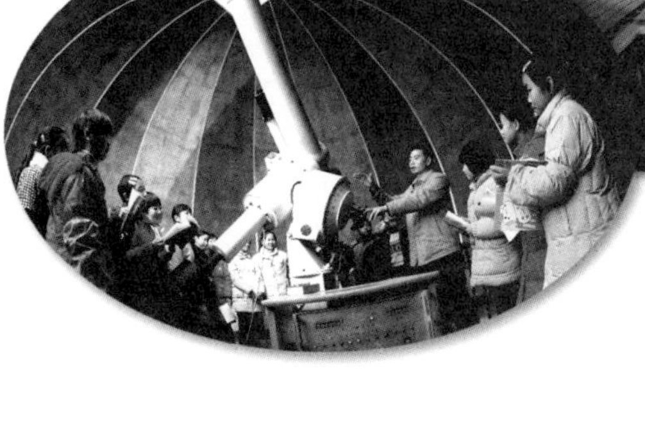

22-1 续表 Continued

年 份 Year	机构数（个） Institutions (unit)	其中 of which #医院（含妇保院）、卫生院 Hospitals (include Women-Children Health Care Hospitals) and Health Care Centers	床位数（张） Beds (bed)	其中 of which #医院（含妇保院）、卫生院 Hospitals (include Women-Children Health Care Hospitals) and Health Care Centers	卫生技术人员（人） Medical Technical Personnel (person)	其中 of which #医生 Doctors
1980	803	159	8422	7337	8615	3238
1981	814	161	9553	7864	9178	3749
1982	823	162	9474	7775	9711	4039
1983	802	160	9773	7937	9759	4198
1984	827	161	9282	7839	10061	4384
1985	831	162	9405	7993	10458	4437
1986	841	162	9883	8505	10957	4586
1987	859	163	10054	8734	11397	4570
1988	913	163	9996	8979	12098	5268
1989	881	163	10253	9313	12539	5923
1990	890	163	10460	9495	12942	6144
1991	880	163	10454	9538	13470	6345
1992	873	159	10607	9693	13695	6511
1993	855	160	11190	9992	13971	6411
1994	855	161	11138	10000	14580	6973
1995	855	161	11566	10339	14963	7073
1996	855	162	11268	10893	15538	7520
1997	833	161	11273	10843	16031	7567
1998	833	161	11223	10813	16405	7685
1999	824	161	11213	10803	16495	7680
2000	782	117	11143	10730	16731	7779
2001	769	114	11393	11030	16743	7737
2002	620	111	11842	11613	15242	6424
2003	625	111	12135	11687	15597	6592
2004	611	109	12352	11932	15707	6586
2005	1269	113	12474	11734	17859	8356
2006	1180	116	13247	12207	18414	8570
2007	1173	111	14696	14100	18091	8323
2008	1261	99	15113	14242	19795	8725
2009	1089	100	16170	15278	20244	9512
2010	1103	93	16701	15263	21921	9962
2011	1101	94	16936	15589	22877	10376

注：1、2002年起卫生技术人员包含领取医师执业证书和注册护士证书的人数以及药师（士）、技师（士）、其他卫技人员;
2、2005年起机构数的统计口径调整为含村级卫生室;
3、2008年起，规范城市社区和乡村卫生机构统计口径后，卫生院机构数有所减少。

Note: 1. Since year 2002, the medical technical personnel has been including Physician Practice Certificate holders, Registered Nurse Certificate holders, pharmacists, technicians and other medical technical personnel.
2. Since year 2005, the statistics of institution numbers has been including village health stations.
3. Since year 2008, the scope of statistics of health service institutions in urban communities and villages has been regulated, which caused the reduction of health service institutions.

22-2 分地区卫生事业机构数（2011 年底）
NUMBER OF HEALTH SERVICE INSTITUTIONS BY REGION（END OF 2011）

单位：个（unit）

指标	Item	全市 Whole Municipality	其中 of which 市区 Urban Area	溧阳市 Liyang City	金坛市 Jintan City
总　计	**Total**	**1101**	**710**	**215**	**176**
医　院	Hospitals	30	14	11	5
非营利性医院	Non-profitmaking Hospitals	20	12	4	4
#综合医院	Polyclinics	11	5	3	3
中医医院	Hospitals for Maternity and Child Care	4	2	1	1
儿童医院	Children's Hospitals	1	1		
营利性医院	profitmaking Hospitals	10	2	7	1
卫生院、社区卫生服务中心（站）	Health Center and Community Health Service Center (Station)	209	161	20	28
门诊部	Outpatient Department	12	10		2
疗养院	Sanatoriums	1	1		
急救中心	First-aid Center	2	1		1
采供血机构	Flood Extraction and Supply Organizations	3	1	1	1
妇幼保健院（所、站）	Maternity and Child Care Centers (Office, Station)	8	6	1	1
专科疾病防治院（所、站）	Specialized Disease Prevention and Cure Hospitals (Office,Station)	2	1	1	
疾病预防控制中心（防疫站）	Disease Prevention and Control Centers (Epidemic Prevention Station)	8	6	1	1
卫生监督所	Sanitation Supervise Offices	6	4	1	1
医学科学研究机构	Institutions of Medical Sciences Research	2	2		
医学在职培训机构	On-the-job Training Institute of The Hospital	4	2	1	1
其他卫生机构	Other Health Institutions	7	7		
诊所、卫生保健所、医务室机构	Clinics, Health Care Centers and Medical Institutions	343	270	44	29
村卫生室	Village Health Station	464	224	134	106

22-3 分地区卫生机构床位和人员数（2011 年底）
HEALTH INSTITUTIONS, BEDS AND PERSONS ENGAGED BY REGION (END OF 2011)

指 标	Item	全 市 Whole Municipality	其中 of which 市 区 Urban Area	溧阳市 Liyang City	金坛市 Jintan City
床位数（张）	**Number of Beds(bed)**	**16936**	**12730**	**2361**	**1845**
#医院（含妇保院）床位	Number of Hospital Beds (Including Those of Women's and Children's Hospitals)	11249	8460	1482	1307
卫生院床位	Number of Rural Township Hospital Beds	4340	3126	836	378
人员数（人）	**Personnel (person)**	**26809**	**19602**	**4255**	**2952**
卫生技术人员	Medical Technical Personnel	22877	16790	3500	2587
#医 生	Doctors	10376	7167	1851	1358
#执业（助理）医师	Practicing (Assistant) Doctors	8361	6074	1326	961
注册护士	Certified Junior Nurses	8550	6534	1196	820
药师（士）	Pharmacists	1197	883	159	155
技师（士）	Technicians	1077	761	171	145
其他卫生技术人员	Other Medical Technical Personnel	2484	2028	248	208
其他技术人员	Other Technical Personnel	994	732	92	170
管理人员	Managerial Personnel	1098	925	137	36
工勤技能人员	Personnel with Professional Qualification Serving at Government and State-owned Enterprises	1823	1151	513	159

22-4 分地区乡卫生院运营情况（2011 年）
STATISTICS ON HOSPITALS AT AND ABOVE COUNTY LEVEL BY REGION（2011）

指 标	Item	全 市 Whole Municipality	其中 of which 市 区 Urban Area	溧阳市 Liyang City	金坛市 Jintan City
机构数（个）	Number of Medical Institution (unit)	62	33	18	11
诊疗人次（万人次）	Number of Persons Diagnosed and Treated (10000 person-times)	551.48	390.27	71.50	89.71
#门诊人次	Number of Outpatients	506.79	355.71	66.92	84.16
急诊人次	Number of Persons Received Emergency Treatment	40.14	31.93	2.82	5.39
健康检查（万人）	Health Examination (10000 persons)	27.68	15.59	8.55	3.54
出院人数（人）	Number of Patients Left Hospitals (person)	96760	61097	27872	7791
治愈人数	Number of Cured Patients	35004	18825	11600	4579
好转人数	Number of Patients Improved	45896	29727	13299	2870
未愈人数	Number of Un-cured Patients	4276	3420	780	76
死亡人数	Number of Deceased	23	17		6
其 他	Others	11561	9108	2193	260
治愈率（%）	Cure Rate (%)	48.12	43.64	49.49	62.11
好转率（%）	Improvement Rate (%)	47.43	50.27	47.71	36.84
病死率（%）	Case-fatality Rate (%)	0.02	0.02	0.00	0.08
年末实有床位数（张）	Number of Beds at Year-end (bed)	4340	3126	836	378
病床周转次数（次）	Number of Turnover of Hospital Beds (time)	24	18	36	24
病床工作日（日）	Number of Days Per Bed in Use (day)	165	121	253	204
病床使用率（%）	Untilization Rate of Beds (%)	45.10	33.15	69.26	55.85
出院者平均住院日（日）	Average of Hospitalization Period (day)	7	7	6	8

22-5 分地区医院运营情况（2011 年）
STATISTICS ON HOSPITALS OPERATION BY REGION（2011）

指 标	Item	全 市 Whole Municipality	其中 of which 市 区 Urban Area	溧阳市 Liyang City	金坛市 Jintan City
医院（妇保院）（个）	Hospitals (Including Those of Women's and Children's Hospitals) (unit)	32	15	12	5
诊疗人次（万人次）	Number of Persons Diagnosed and Treated (10000 person-times)	913.91	741.06	95.31	77.54
#门诊人次	Number of Outpatients	706.99	572.47	80.38	54.14
急诊人次	Number of Persons Received Emergency Treatment	132.40	111.32	10.16	10.92
健康检查（万人）	Health Examination (10000 persons)	58.03	41.45	8.14	8.44
出院人数（人）	Number of Patients Left Hospitals (person)	345341	265771	44997	34573
治愈人数	Number of Cured Patients	111714	87625	14420	9669
好转人数	Number of Patients Improved	179269	135937	23419	19913
未愈人数	Number of Un-cured Patients	8674	5548	1837	1289
死亡人数	Number of Deceased	1099	882	107	110
其 他	Others	45681	35042	7047	3592
治愈率（%）	Cure Rate (%)	60.00	44.69	60.39	38.36
好转率（%）	Improvement Rate (%)	38.37	53.30	37.12	57.60
病死率（%）	Case-fatality Rate (%)	0.18	0.38	0.15	0.32
年末实有医院（含妇保院）床位数（张）	Number of Beds of Hospitals (include Women-Children Health Care Hospitals) by the End of Year (Bed)	11249	8460	1482	1307
病床周转次数（次）	Number of Turnover of Hospital Beds (time)	38	37	42	30
病床工作日（日）	Number of Days Per Bed in Use (day)	381	386	368	410
病床使用率（%）	Untilization Rate of Beds (%)	103.35	105.75	100.87	112.22
出院者平均住院日（日）	Average of Hospitalization Period (day)	11	11	9	13

22-6 分地区妇幼保健发展情况（2011 年）
STATISTICS ON HEALTH CARE FOR WOMEN AND CHILDREN BY REGION（2011）

指 标	Item	全 市 Whole Municipality	其中 of which 市 区 Urban Area	溧阳市 Liyang City	金坛市 Jintan City
婴儿死亡率（男，‰）	Death Rate of Infant (Boy，‰)	2.80	2.53	3.00	4.21
婴儿死亡率（女，‰）	Death Rate of Infant (Girl，‰)	2.81	3.09	1.83	2.83
5岁以下儿童死亡率（男，‰）	Death Rate of Child under 5 Years Old (Boy，‰)	4.22	3.79	4.36	6.84
5岁以下儿童死亡率（女，‰）	Death Rate of Child under 6 Years Old (Girl，‰)	3.79	4.15	2.75	3.40
围产儿死亡率（‰）	Death Rate of Perinatal Infant (‰)	5.70	6.54	3.88	2.57
新生儿疾病筛查率（%）	Rate of Selected Examination of Newborn Diseases (%)	97.59	97.67	97.20	97.74
新生儿出生缺陷发生率（‰）	Incidence of Congenital Anomalies of Newborn (‰)	6.08	7.24	3.16	2.34
7岁以下儿童保健管理率（%）	Rate of Health Care for Children under 7 Years Old (%)	98.87	98.49	99.94	99.02
5岁以下儿童中重度营养不良患病率（%）	Morbidity Rate of Moderate and Serious Malnutri-tion of Children under 5 Years (%)	0.25	1.80	0.54	0.16
孕产妇死亡率（1/10万）	Death Rate of Pregnant Women and Lying-in Women (1/100 thousand)	2.89	4.17		
妇女病普查率（%）	Rate of General Survey of Women's Disease (%)	93.71	95.69	91.22	92.68
孕产妇保健管理率（%）	System Management Rate of Pregnant Women and Lying-in Women (%)	99.72	99.95	98.78	100
住院分娩率（%）	Hospitalized Parturition Rate (%)	100	100	100	100
婚前医学检查率（%）	Antenuptial Medical Examination Ratio (%)	94.97	96.16	90.19	95.05
托幼机构卫生保健合格率（%）	Qualification Rate of Health-care in Nursery (%)	100	100	100	100

22-7 分地区体育事业情况（2011 年）
STATISTICS ON SPORTS CAUSE BY REGION（2011）

指标	Item	全市 Whole Municipality	其中 of which 市区 Urban Area	溧阳市 Liyang City	金坛市 Jintan City
运动会	**Sports Meets**				
举办县级以上运动会次数（含单项）（次）	Number of Sports Meets Held at and above County Level (Including Individual Events) (time)	68	47	10	11
参加县级以上运动会人数（含单项）（人）	Number of Athletes Participating Sports Meets at and above County Level(Including Individual Events) (person)	8355	5480	1275	1600
等级运动员发展人数（人）	**Number of Athletes Developed in Grades (person)**	**275**	**216**	**38**	**21**
#女性	Female	94	76	12	6
等级裁判员发展人数（人）	**Number of Referees Developed in Grades (person)**	**217**	**199**	**14**	**4**
#女性	Female	100	91	9	
公共体育运动场地	**Public Stadiums and Gymnasiums**				
体育场地个数（个）	Number of Stadiums and Gymnasiums (unit)	25	19	2	4
体育场	Stadiums	8	6	1	1
体育馆	Gymnasiums	10	8		2
室内外游泳池	Indoor and Outdoor Swimming Pools	7	5	1	1

注：等级运动员发展人数中不含三级运动员。
Note: The number of sportspersons with grade under development excludes those third grades.

22-8 参加体育竞赛获奖数（2011 年）
NUMBER OF PRIZES WON IN SPORTS GAMES（2011）

单位：枚（unit）

指标	Item	金牌 Gold Medals	银牌 Silver Medals	铜牌 Bronze Medals
总计	**Total**	**70.5**	**55**	**54**
参加国际比赛获奖数	Number of Prizes Won in International Sports Games	3	2	2
参加全国比赛获奖数	Number of Prizes Won in National Sports Games	19		
参加全省比赛获奖数	Number of Prizes Won in Provinical Sports Games	48.5	53	52

23

CHAPTER 23

民政 司法 其他

CIVIL ADMINISTRATION JUDICATURE AND OTHERS

常州统计年鉴

23 民政 司法 其他
CIVIL ADMINISTRATION JUDICATURE AND OTHERS

2011 年主要统计指标
MAJOR STATISTICAL INDICATORS OF 2011

社会福利院数	Socail Welfare Institutions	2个	(unit)
精神病福利院数	Psychotics Welfare Institutions	1个	(unit)
老年福利机构数	Aged People's Homes	92个	(unit)
社会福利院床位数	Beds of Socail Welfare Institutions	805张	(bed)
精神病福利院床位数	Beds of Psychotics Welfare Institutions	792张	(bed)
老年福利机构床位数	Beds of Aged People's Homes	14453张	(bed)
律师事务所	Lawyer Offices	83个	(unit)
专职律师数	Full-time Lawyers	865人	(person)
公证处数	Notary Public Offices	5个	(unit)
办理公证件数	Notarized Documents	34032件	(case)
人民调解委员会数	People's Mediation Committees	1803个	(unit)
调解民间纠纷数	Civil Disputes Mediated	26102件	(case)

23-1　分地区社会福利事业情况（2011 年底）
BASIC STATISTICS ON SOCIAL WELFARE BY REGION（END OF 2011）

指　标	Item	全　市 Whole Municipality	其中 of which 市　区 Urban Area	溧阳市 Liyang City	金坛市 Jintan City
社会福利院	Social Welfare Homes				
院　数（个）	Number of Homes (unit)	2	2		
年底职工人数（人）	Number of Staff and Workers at Year-end (person)	142	142		
年底床位数（张）	Number of Beds at Year-end (bed)	805	805		
年底在院人数（人）	Number of Persons Housed at Year-end (person)	623	623		
#老　人	Elders	414	414		
精神病福利院	Mental Homes				
院　数（个）	Number of Homes (unit)	1	1		
年底职工人数（人）	Number of Staff and Workers at Year-end (person)	237	237		
年底床位数（张）	Number of Beds at Year-end (bed)	792	792		
年底在院人数（人）	Number of Persons Housed at Year-end (person)	792	792		
老年福利机构	Elderly Welfare Unit				
单位数（个）	Number of Unit (unit)	92	57	18	17
年底职工人数（人）	Number of Staff and Workers at Year-end (person)	1084	612	273	199
年底床位数（张）	Number of Beds at Year-end (bed)	14453	8438	3565	2450
年底在院人数（人）	Number of Persons Housed at Year-end (person)	9070	4526	2773	1771
#老　人	Elders	8994	4474	2773	1747

23-2　分地区集体社会福利企业情况（2011 年）
STATISTICS ON COLLECTIVE SOCIAL WELFARE ENTERPRISES BY REGION（2011）

指　标	Item	全　市 Whole Municipality	其中 of which 市　区 Urban Area	溧阳市 Liyang City	金坛市 Jintan City
单位数（个）	Number of Units（unit）	282	189	38	55
职工人数（人）	Number of Staff & Workers（person）	30930	20223	5608	5099
销售收入（亿元）	Sales Income（100 million yuan）	225.0	208.0	5.0	12.0
利润总额（亿元）	Total Profits（100 million yuan）	10.6	6.0	4.6	

23-3 分地区居民最低生活保障情况（2011 年底）
STATISTICS ON LOWEST COST-OF-LIVING WELFARE FOR RESIDENTS BY REGION（END OF 2011）

指 标	Item	全 市 Whole Municipality	其 中 of which 市 区 Urban Area	溧阳市 Liyang City	金坛市 Jintan City
城镇居民最低生活保障人数（人）	**Number of Urban Residents Receiving Lowest Cost-of-living Welfare (person)**	**20439**	**17039**	**1789**	**1611**
# 在职人员	Persons Employed	1046	1006	14	26
老年人	Elderly	2992	2214	393	385
城镇居民最低生活保障家庭数（户）	Number of Urban Households Receiving Lowest Cost-of-living Welfare (Household)	10891	9009	913	969
农村居民最低生活保障人数（人）	Number of Rural Residents Receiving Lowest Cost-of-living Welfare (person)	36273	14975	11879	9419
农村居民最低生活保障家庭数（户）	Number of Rural Households Receiving Lowest Cost-of-living Welfare (Household)	19392	8048	6003	5341

23-4 分地区优抚对象享受优待抚恤情况（2011 年底）
STATISTICS ON PERSONS RECEIVING PERIODICAL COMPENSATION AND SUBSIDIES BY REGION（END OF 2011 ）

单位：人（person）

指 标	Item	全 市 Whole Municipality	其 中 of which 市 区 Urban Area	溧阳市 Liyang City	金坛市 Jintan City
抚恤、补助优抚对象人数	Number of People Subject to Pension, Subsidy and Special Care	19457	7887	6632	4938
优抚对象定期抚恤人数	Number of Persons Receiving Periodical Compen-sation	598	235	159	204
烈士家属	Family Members of Martyrs	291	129	84	78
牺牲军人家属	Family Members of Sacrificed Servicemen	99	43	16	40
病故军人家属	Family Members of Deceased Servicemen	208	63	59	86
优抚对象定期补助人数	Number of Persons Receiving Periodical Subsidies	16516	6428	5779	4309
# 在乡复员军人	Servicemen Demobilized before Nov. 1,1954 in Rural Area	2741	752	939	1050

23-5 分地区城镇社区服务和农村服务网络（2011 年底）
URBAN COMMUNITY SERVICES AND RURAL SERVICE NETWORK BY REGION（END OF 2011）

指 标	Item	全 市 Whole Municipality	其中 of which 市 区 Urban Area	溧阳市 Liyang City	金坛市 Jintan City
城镇社区服务	**Urban Community Service**				
城镇社区服务设施数（个）	Number of Urban Community Service Facilities (unit)	795	459	155	181
从业人员数（人）	Number of Persons Engaged (person)	5823	1848	3125	850
#安置下岗人员	Laid-off Persons Arrangement	1336	200	736	400
便民利民服务网点（个）	Number of Convenient Service Points for Civilian (unit)	3209	1106	216	1887
社区服务志愿者组织（个）	Number of Volunteers Organizations of Urban Community Service (unit)	2702	2207	265	230
社区服务志愿者人数（人）	Number of Persons Supported by Urban Community Service (person)	193879	176363	3516	14000
建立农村社会保障网络的乡镇数（个）	**Number of Towns and Townships Established Rural Social Security Network (unit)**	**37**	**20**	**10**	**7**

23-6 分地区婚姻登记情况（2011 年）
BASIC STATISTICS ON MARRIAGE REGISTRATION BY REGION（2011）

指 标	Item	全 市 Whole Municipality	其中 of which 市 区 Urban Area	溧阳市 Liyang City	金坛市 Jintan City
结婚登记数（对）	Marriage Legally Registered (couple)	38945	24003	8781	6161
初 婚（人）	First Marriages (person)	63833	36577	16818	10438
再 婚（人）	Remarriages (person)	14057	11429	744	1884
离婚登记数（对）	Legally Registered Divorces (couple)	8186	5266	1802	1118

23-7 律师、公证、调解工作情况（2011 年）
STATISTICS ON LAWYERS, NOTARIZATION AND MEDIATION（2011）

指　标	Item	全　市 Whole Municipality	其中 of which #市　区 Urban Area
律师工作	**Lawyers**		
律师事务所（个）	Number of Law Offices (unit)	83	67
取得律师资格（人）	Persons with Lawyer's Qualification (person)	897	748
专职律师	Full-time Lawyers	865	716
兼职律师	Part-time Lawyers	32	32
聘请担任常年法律顾问单位（个）	Number of Units with Permanent Legal advisors (unit)	4883	4062
民事诉讼代理（件）	Agent of Civil Cases (case)	15694	11505
刑事诉讼辩护及代理（件）	Defender and Agent of Criminal Cases (case)	2241	1826
行政诉讼代理（件）	Agent of Administrative Action (case)	256	185
非诉讼法律事务（件）	Agent of Non-litigious Legal Affairs (case)	2221	1933
法律咨询（件）	Agent of Legal Advisory services (case)	15260	8801
代写法律事务文书（件）	Agent of Legal Documents Written on Behalf of Clients (case)	1255	1139
公证工作	**Notarization**		
公证处（个）	Number of Notary Offices (unit)	5	3
公证人员（人）	Notarial Personnel (person)	65	50
#公证员（一、二、三、四级）	Notaries (Grade1, 2,3,4)	31	23
公证员助理	Assistant Notaries	19	15
办理公证件数（件）	Number of Notarial Documents Issued (case)	34032	28220
国内民事	Domestic Civil Relations	16628	13349
国内经济	Domestic Economic Affairs	5718	5410
涉外及港澳台公证	Foreign-related and Hongkong,Macao and Taiwan Notarization	11686	9461
人民调解工作	**People's Mediation**		
专职司法助理员（名）	Number of Full-time Judical assistants (person)	340	254
人民调解委员会（个）	Number of People's Mediation Committees (unit)	1803	931
调解人员数（人）	Number of Mediators (person)	10412	4632
调解民间纠纷数（件）	Number of Civil Disputes Mediated (case)	26102	19002

23-8 国内公证文书分类情况（2007-2011 年）
DOMESTIC NOTARIAL DOCUMENT BY TYPE（2007-2011）

单位：件（unit）

指 标	Item	2007	2008	2009	2010	2011
总 计	**Total**	**26295**	**27560**	**21295**	**23722**	**22346**
经济公证	Notarized Documents on Economic Affairs	4373	3957	6818	7459	5718
#购 销	Purchases and Sales of products	2	2		2	12
拍 卖	Auctions		2			
贷 款	Loans	145	145	37	29	49
招标、投标	Bidding	199	257	291	357	507
劳务合同	Labor Contracts	3	2			
建筑工程承包	Construction Project Contracts					
农林牧渔业承包	Farming,Forestry,Animal Husbandry,Sideline Production and Fishery Contracts				1	
财产租赁	Property Leases	1	3			
企业租赁	Enterprises Leases	2				
其他经济合同	Other Business Contracts	189	647	934	421	347
法人（代表人）资格	Legal Person(agent)Identification	10	16	14	25	48
法人委托书	Legal Person Trust deeds	1556	1279	1918	2066	1807
民事公证	Notarized Documents on Civil Relations	11437	12321	14477	16263	16628
#继承权	Rights of Inheritance	2795	2578	3577	3210	2990
遗 嘱	Testaments	331	334	362	250	260
产 权	Property Rights					
亲属关系	Kinship Confirmation	32	38	59	108	221
房屋买卖	Purchases and Sales of House	131	189	231	220	318
房屋租赁	House Leases	2	5	15	3	23
遗赠抚养协议	Donations and Family Fostering	2	3	12	2	3
委托书	Trust Deeds	2880	4087	5114	1725	1031
赠与书	Presentaton Documents	1036	814	550	6902	6924
声明书	Declarations	1082	918	959	623	942
现场监督	Field Supervision	108	501	39	664	606

23-9 涉外及涉港澳台公证文书分类情况（2007-2011 年）
FOREIGN AND HONG KONG, MACAO AND TAIWAN NOTARIAL DOCUMENT BY TYPE（2007-2011）

单位：件（unit）

指 标	Item	2007	2008	2009	2010	2011
总 计	**Total**	**10480**	**11282**	**11485**	**12802**	**11686**
出 生	Births	1187	1635	2075	1745	1481
学 历	Schooling	950	1129	1066	1187	903
经 历	Personal Histories	137	86	115	119	125
生存、居住	Survial and Residence	4	24	17	362	391
死 亡	Deaths	10	28	18	13	112
收养子女	Children Adoption	1	1			
亲属关系	Family Relationship	903	975	1006	1237	964
婚姻状况	Marriages	354	463	441	796	689
委托书	Trust Deeds	150	159	201	220	331
声明书	Declarations	223	221	179	233	193
受、未受刑事处分	Criminal Records and Uncriminal Records	1124	1448	1253	2153	1263
文本相符	Confirmation of Copies & Photo-Offest Copies to Originals	2671	2608	2156	2486	2217
其 他	Others	2766	1105	2958	2251	3017

23-10 调解民事纠纷分类情况（2007-2011 年）
STATISTICS ON CIVIL DISPUTES MEDIATED BY TYPE（2007-2011）

单位：件（unit）

指 标	Item	2007	2008	2009	2010	2011
总 计	**Total**	**20474**	**24116**	**20783**	**21831**	**16230**
婚 姻	Marriages	5054	4053	3409	3370	3465
房屋宅基地	Housing And Housing Sites	1649	1210	344	466	621
生产经营	Business	630	239	1480	854	225
邻 里	Neighbor Disputes	5108	5146	4227	3887	4114
损害赔偿	Compensation for Damages	1177	768	3087	3468	4084
其 他	Others	6856	12700	8236	9786	3721

23-11 分地区道路、船舶交通事故及火灾情况（2011 年）
STATISTICS ON HIGHWAYS,WATERWAY TRAFFIC ACCIDENTS AND FIRES BY REGION（2011）

指 标	Item	全 市 Whole Munici pality	其中 of which 市 区 Urban Area	溧阳市 Liyang City	金坛市 Jintan City
道路交通事故	**Road Accidents**				
发生起数（起）	Number of Traffic Accident (case)	1348	990	207	151
死亡人数（人）	Number of Death (person)	273	196	45	32
受伤人数（人）	Number of Injuries (person)	1417	981	260	176
损失折款（万元）	Losses Coverted into Cash (10000 yuan)	303	161	102	40
船舶交通事故	**Waterway Accidents**				
发生起数（起）	Number of Traffic Accident (case)	—	—	—	—
损失折款（万元）	Losses Coverted into Cash (10000 yuan)	—	—	—	—
火灾事故	**Fires**				
发生起数（起）	Number of Traffic Accident (case)	396	299	64	33
死亡人数（人）	Number of Death (person)	5	3	1	1
受伤人数（人）	Number of Injuries (person)	—	—	—	—
损失折款（万元）	Losses Coverted into Cash (10000 yuan)	658	458	73	127

23-12 主要年份住房公积金情况
STATEMENT OF PUBLIC ACCUMULATION FUND FOR HOUSING CONSTRUCTION IN MAIN YEARS

年 份 Year	缴存人数(人) Number of Paypable Persons (person)	缴存比例 (%) Payment proportion (%)	人均月缴存额 (元) Per capita monthly payment amount (yuan)	缴存金额 (万元) Payment Amount (10000 yuan)	提取金额 (万元) Withdrawed Amount (10000 yuan)
1992	278000	10	14	2929	103
1995	323230	10	37	8775	854
2000	334997	12-14	121	39759	11750
2001	316781	14-16	142	49727	18076
2002	321151	14-16	192	59676	28973
2003	311722	16-24	264	80298	34153
2004	303994	20-24	330	106998	45344
2005	313772	20-24	384	132568	46627
2006	322824	20-24	437	163392	83478
2007	344071	20-24	510	196771	113598
2008	373059	20-24	587	250796	125442
2009	370396	20-24	616	275505	189093
2010	430171	20-24	627	323831	204934
2011	485392	20-24	732	405620	216913

23-12 续表 Continued

年 份 Year	缴存余额 (万元) Payment Balance (10000 yuan)	个人贷款发放户数 (户) Number of Household with loan (houshold)	个人贷款发放金额 (万元) Amount of Loans (10000 yuan)	个人贷款回收金额 (万元) Individual Loan Repayment Amount (10000 yuan)	个人贷款逾期率 (%) Overdue Rate of Loans (%)	提取廉租房补充资金总额(万元) Accumulated Amount of Withdrawn Supplementory Financing to Low Rent Houses(10000 yuan)
1992	2825					
1995	23229	5	15			
2000	134776	4241	26742	6940	0.050	
2001	168577	4242	32886	11603	0.050	5003
2002	210625	6510	65839	20259	0.050	6669
2003	259442	6869	85740	32594	0.030	8505
2004	325051	7213	111401	57474	0.020	9503
2005	410992	8472	150552	64320	0.010	10694
2006	500853	12071	212077	84107	0.004	12410
2007	584026	12647	225062	101970	0.000	14349
2008	709381	10132	184035	100529	0.001	18510
2009	795793	12350	264884	140548	0	23000
2010	914690	10185	239414	143443	0	27541
2011	1103397	11272	286306	144702	0	35856

23-13 分地区住房公积金情况（2011 年）
CONDITION OF PUBLIC ACCUMULATION FUND FOR HOUSING CONSTRUCTION (HOUSING FUND) BY REGION（2011）

指 标	Item	全 市 Whole Municipality	其中 of which 市 区 Urban Area	溧阳市 Liyang City	金坛市 Jintan City
住房公积金缴存	**Payment of Housing Fund**				
应缴单位（个）	Work Unit Payable (Unit)	12292	10855	698	739
当年新开户单位（个）	New Account-opening Unit (Unit)	2557	2340	97	120
缴存人数（人）	Number of Paypable Persons (person)	485392	410049	41084	34259
当年新开户人数（人）	Number of New Account-opening Persons (person)	114317	99162	7729	7426
缴存金额（万元）	Payment Amount (10000 yuan)	405620	345602	34954	25064
缴存余额（万元）	Payment Balance (10000 yuan)	1103397	918278	106888	78231
累计缴存金额（万元）	Accumulated Payment Amount (10000 yuan)	2241589	1916491	177557	147541
住房公积金提取	**Withdrawal of Housing Fund**				
提取人数（人）	Number of Person Withdrawed Fund (person)	117716	102274	8114	7328
#转帐还贷提取	Withdrawal for Transfer Account and Repay Loan	80441	69045	6011	5385
提取金额（万元）	Withdrawed Amount (10000 yuan)	216912	185357	17252	14303
#转帐还贷提取	Withdrawal for Transfer Account and Repay Loan	125306	108940	8320	8046
累计提取金额（万元）	Accumulated Withdrawed Amount (10000 yuan)	1138192	998213	70670	69309
住房公积金个人贷款	**Housing fund for Individual Loan**				
贷款户数（户）	Number of Household with loan (household)	11272	9345	981	946
贷款金额（万元）	Amount of Loans (10000 yuan)	286306	238216	24985	23105
平均贷款年数（年）	Average Loan Term (year)	14	15	13	13
平均贷款金额（万元）	Average Loan Amount (10000 yuan)	25.40	25.55	25.47	24.42
贷款余额（万元）	Balance of Loans (10000 yuan)	1003919	837878	89642	76399
贷款逾期率（%）	Overdue Rate of Loans (%)	0.000	0.000	0.000	0.000
累计贷款金额（万元）	Accumulated Amount of Loans (10000 yuan)	1904728	1594919	161909	147900
住房公积金运用	**Application of Housing Fund**				
廉租房补充资金（万元）	Supplementary Fund of Bargain Tenement (10000 yuan)	8261	7048	617	596
资金使用率（%）	Fund Utility Rate (%)	91.01	91.28	83.87	97.66
个人贷款比率（%）	Individual Loan Ratio (%)	90.98	91.24	83.87	97.66

附　录

APPENDIX

附录 1　全国经济社会发展主要指标（2011 年）
MAJOR INDEX IN THE DEVELOPING OF SOCIETY AND ECONOMY IN CHINA（2011）

指标	Item	2011	比上年增减（%）Increase/Decrease over the previous year (%)
年末总人口（万人）	Total Population By the End of the Year (10000 persons)	134735	0.5
农民工总量（万人）	Total Number of Peasant Workers (10000 persons)	25278	4.4
#外出农民工	Migrant Workers from Rural Areas	15863	3.4
年末城镇登记失业率（%）	Registred Unemployment rate by the end of the Year (%)	4.1	平 equal
国内生产总值（亿元）	GDP (100 million yuan)	471564	9.2
第一产业	Primary Industry	47712	4.5
第二产业	Secondary Industry	220592	10.6
工　业	Industry	188572	10.7
建筑业	Construction	32020	10.0
第三产业	Tertiary Industry	203260	8.9
全社会固定资产投资总额（亿元）	Total Investment in Fixed Assets (100 million yuan)	311022	23.6
#城　镇	Urban	301933	23.8
第一产业	Primary Industry	6792	25.0
第二产业	Secondary Industry	132263	27.3
第三产业	Tertiary Industry	162877	21.1
#农　户	Peasant household	9089	15.3
#房地产开发	Real Estate Development	61740	27.9
货物运输总量（亿吨）	Total Freight Traffic (100 million tons)	369	13.7
货物周转量（亿吨公里）	Total Volume of Cargo Transported (100 million tons kilometers)	159014	12.1
旅客运输总量（亿人）	Total Passenger Traffic (100 million persons)	352	7.6
旅客周转量（亿人公里）	Total Volume of Passenger Transported (100 million persons kilometers)	30936	10.9
邮电业务总量（亿元）	Business Volume of Post and Telecommunications (100 million yuan)	13379	16.5
电话普及率（部/百人）	Popularized Rate of Telephone (set/100 persons)	94.9	8.4部 8.4(sets)

附录1 续表 Appendix 1 Continued

指标	Item	2011	比上年增减（%） Increase/Decrease over the previous year (%)
互联网普及率（%）	Internet Penetration Rate (%)	38.3	4.0个百分点 4.0 percentage points
社会消费品零售总额（亿元）	Total Volume of Social Consumption Retail Sale (100 million yuan)	183919	17.1
按消费形态分	Group by Consumption Patterns		
商品零售额	Retail Sales	163284	17.2
餐饮收入额	Revenue of Restaurant and Catering	20635	16.9
居民消费价格指数（上年=100）	Consumption Price Index of Residents (preceding year=100)	105.4	5.4个百分点 5.4 percentage points
进出口总额（亿美元）	Gross Value of Export and Import (USD 100 million)	36421	22.5
出 口	Export	18986	20.3
进 口	Import	17435	24.9
实际外商直接投资（亿美元）	Actual Foreign Direct Investment (USD 100 million)	1160	9.7
金融机构本外币存款余额（亿元）	Total Deposit of Financiai Departments (100 million yuan)	826701	13.5
#城乡居民储蓄存款余额	Deposit By Urban and Rural Residents	351957	15.5
#人民币余额	Balance of RMB	348046	15.7
金融机构本外币贷款余额（亿元）	Total Loans of Financial Departments (100 million yuan)	581893	15.9
财政总收入（亿元）	Gross Finance Revenue (100 million yuan)	103740	24.8
财政支出（亿元）	Finance Expenditure (100 million yuan)	108930	21.2
城镇居民人均可支配收入（元）	Per Capita Disposable Income of Urban Residents (yuan)	21810	8.4
农民人均纯收入（元）	Per Capita Net Income of Rural Residents (yuan)	6977	11.4
城镇居民家庭恩格尔系数（%）	Engel Coefficient of Urban Households (%)	36.3	0.6个百分点 0.6percentage points
农村居民家庭恩格尔系数（%）	Engel Coefficient of Rural Households (%)	40.4	-0.7个百分点 -0.7percentage points
普通高等学校本专科在校学生（万人）	Students in Regular Institutions of Higher Education(10000 persons)	2308.5	3.4
科学研究与试验发展（R&D）经费支出（亿元）	Appropriation Expenditure on Science Research and Development (100 million yuan)	8610	21.9
申请专利件数（万件）	Number of Patent Applications Examined(10000 units)	163.3	33.6

附录 2　全国主要工农业产品产量（2011 年）
OUTPUT OF MAJOR INDUSTRIAL AND AGRICULTURAL PRODUCTS（2011）

产品名称	Name of Products	2011	比上年增减（%）Increase/Decrease over the previous year (%)
农产品产量（万吨）	**Output of Agricultural Products (10000 tons)**		
粮　食	Grain	57121	4.5
夏　粮	Summer Grain	12627	2.5
早　稻	Early Season Rice	3276	4.5
秋　粮	Autumn Grain	41218	5.1
油　料	Oil-bearing Crops	3279	1.5
棉　花	Cotton	660	10.7
糖　料	Sugar Crops	12520	4.3
烤　烟	Tabacco	287	5.1
茶　叶	Tea	162	9.9
肉类总产量	Total Output of Meat	7957	0.4
水产品产量	Total Output of Aquatic Products	5600	4.2
工业产品产量	Output Of Industrial Products		
纱（万吨）	Yarn (10000 tons)	2900	6.7
布（亿米）	Cloth (100 million meters)	837	4.6
化　纤（万吨）	Chemical Fibre (10000 tons)	3390	9.7
成品糖（万吨）	Finished Sugar (10000 tons)	1187.4	6.2
卷　烟（亿支）	Cigarette (100 million pieces)	24474.0	3.0
彩色电视机（万台）	Colour TV (10000 units)	12231.4	3.4
家用电冰箱（万台）	Household Refrigerator (10000 units)	8699.2	19.2
房间空调器（万台）	Household Air-conditioner (10000 units)	13912.5	27.8
一次能源生产总量（亿吨标准煤）	Total Output of Primary Energy (100 million tons of SCE)	31.8	7.0
原　煤（亿吨）	Coal (100 million tons)	35.2	8.7
原　油（亿吨）	Crude Oil (100 million tons)	2.04	0.3
天然气（亿立方米）	Natural Gas (100 million cu.m)	1030.6	8.7
发电量（亿千瓦时）	Electricity (100 million kw.h)	47000.7	11.7
粗　钢（万吨）	Steel (10000 tons)	68388.3	7.3
钢　材（万吨）	Steel Products (10000 tons)	88258.2	9.9
十种有色金属（万吨）	10 Kinds of Nonferrous Metals (10000 tons)	3434.0	10.0
# 精炼铜（铜）	Refined Copper (copper)	517.9	12.9
电解铝	Electrolytic Aluminum	1767.7	12.1
氧化铝（万吨）	Alumina (10000 tons)	3417.2	18.1
水　泥（亿吨）	Cement (100 million tons)	20.9	10.8
硫　酸（万吨）	Sulfuric Acid (10000 tons)	7466.4	5.3
纯　碱（万吨）	Soda Ash (10000 tons)	2308.2	13.4
烧　碱（万吨）	Caustic Soda (10000 tons)	2466.2	10.7
乙　烯（万吨）	Ethene (10000 tons)	1527.5	7.5
化　肥（折100%,万吨）	Chemical Fertilizer (10000 tons)	6217.2	-1.9
发电设备（万千瓦）	Electricity Generation Equiments (10000 kw)	14410.4	11.9
汽　车（万辆）	Motor Vehicles (10000 coaches)	1841.6	0.8
# 轿　车	Cars	1012.7	5.8
大中型拖拉机（万台）	Tractors (10000 units)	40.2	19.3
集成电路（亿块）	Integrated Citcuit (100 million pcs)	719.6	10.3
程控交换机（万线）	Distance Exchange and Transmitting Machine (10000 lines)	3034.0	-3.3
移动通信手持机（万部）	Mobile Telephone (10000 units)	113257.6	13.5
微型电子计算机（万部）	Micro-computers (10000 units)	32036.7	30.3

附录 3 江苏省经济社会发展主要指标（2011 年）
MAJOR INDEX IN THE DEVELOPING OF SOCIETY AND ECONOMY IN JIANGSU PROVINCE（2011）

指标	Item	2011	比上年增减（%） Increase/Decrease over the previous year (%)
年末城镇登记失业率（%）	Registred Unemployment rate by the end of the Year (%)	3.22	0.06个百分点 0.06percentage points
地区生产总值（亿元）	GDP (100 million yuan)	49110.3	11.0
第一产业	Primary Industry	3064.8	4.0
第二产业	Secondary Industry	25023.8	11.7
第三产业	Tertiary Industry	20842.2	11.1
规模以上工业增加值（亿元）	Added Value of Industry (100million yuan)	25034.8	13.8
#国有及国有控股企业	State-owned and State Share-holding Enterprises	1534.9	10.3
集体企业	Collective Enterprises	276.6	5.3
股份制企业	Joint-share Enterprises	11715.7	13.9
外商及港澳台投资企业	Enterprises with Investment from Foreign, Hong Kong, Macao and Taiwan.	10206.6	13.8
工业企业实现利税总额（亿元）	Pre-tax Profit realized By Industrial Enterprises (100 million yuan)	10622.4	24.8
工业企业实现利润总额（亿元）	Gross Profit realized By Industrial Enterprises (100 million yuan)	6850.4	24.3
工业产品销售率（%）	Sales Rate of Industrial Products (%)	98.59	平 equal
建筑业总产值（亿元）	Gross Output Value of Construction	15122.7	21.9
全社会固定资产投资总额（亿元）	Total Investment in Fixed Assets (100 million yuan)	26693.8	21.2
第一产业	Primary Industry	155.2	17.8
第二产业	Secondary Industry	13929.2	20.9
第三产业	Tertiary Industry	12215.0	22.2
#房地产开发	Real Estate Development	5552.7	29.2

注：工业增加值和效益指标值为主营业务收入2000万元及以上的法人工业企业。

Note：The added value of industry and profit index refers to the number of the Corporate industrial enterprises with annual main business income of 20 million yuan and above.

附录3 续表 Appendix 3 Continued

指标	Item	2011	比上年增减（%） Increase/Decrease over the previous year (%)
货物周转量（亿吨公里）	Total Volume of Cargo Transported (100 million tons kilometers)	7514.0	22.9
旅客周转量（亿人公里）	Total Volume of Passenger Transported (100 million persons kilometers)	1777.8	10.8
电话普及率（部/百人）	Popularized Rate of Telephone (set/100 persons)	115	6部 6(sets)
社会消费品零售总额（亿元）	Total Volume of Social Consumption Retail Sale (100 million yuan)	15988.4	17.5
居民消费价格指数（上年=100）	Consumption Price Index of Residents (preceding year=100)	105.3	5.3个百分点 5.3percentage points
商品零售价格指数（上年=100）	Retail Price Index (preceding year=100)	104.6	4.6个百分点 4.6percentage points
进出口总额（亿美元）	Gross Value of Export and Import (USD 100 million)	5397.6	15.9
出 口	Export	3126.2	15.6
进 口	Import	2271.4	16.3
协议外商直接投资（亿美元）	Negotiated Foreign Direct Investment (USD 100 million)	595.5	4.8
实际外商直接投资（亿美元）	Actual Foreign Direct Investment (USD 100 million)	321.3	12.8
金融机构人民币存款余额（亿元）	RMB Deposits Balance of Financial Departments (100 million yuan)	65723.6	11.4
#单位存款	Deposits of Enterprises	37300	平 equal
储蓄存款	Savings Deposits	25914.7	11.1
金融机构人民币贷款余额（亿元）	RMB Loans Balance of Financial Departments (100 million yuan)	47868.3	13.6
财政总收入（亿元）	Gross Finance Revenue (100 million yuan)	14119.9	20.2
#地方一般预算收入	Local General Budgetary Revenue	5147.9	26.2
地方一般预算支出（亿元）	Local General Budgetary Expenditure (100 million yuan)	6221.7	26.6
城镇居民人均可支配收入（元）	Per Capita Disposable Income of Urban Residents (yuan)	26341	14.8
农民人均纯收入（元）	Per Capita Income of Rural Residents (yuan)	10805	18.5
城镇居民家庭恩格尔系数（%）	Engel Coefficient of Urban Households (%)	36.1	-0.4个百分点 -0.4 percentage points
农村居民家庭恩格尔系数（%）	Engel Coefficient of Rural Households (%)	38.5	0.4个百分点 0.4percentage points
普通高校在校学生（万人）	Students in Ordinary High Schools (10000 persons)	165.9	0.6
科学研究与试验发展（R&D）经费支出（亿元）	Appropriation Expenditure on Science Research and Development (100 million yuan)	1070	2.2
申请专利件数（万件）	Number of Patent Applications Examined(10000 units)	34.8	47.7
报纸出版量（亿份）	Total Volume of Newspaper Issued (100 million copies)	28.4	4.8

附录 4 江苏省主要工农业产品产量（2011 年）
OUTPUT OF MAJOR INDUSTRIAL AND AGRICULTURAL PRODUCTS IN JIANGSU PROVINCE（2011）

产品名称	Name of Products	2011	比上年增减（%）Increase/Decrease over the previous year (%)
农产品产量（万吨）	**Output of Agricultural Products (10000 tons)**		
粮 食	Grain	3307.8	2.2
棉 花	Cotton	24.7	-5.4
油 料	Oil-bearing Crops	144.1	-5.2
# 油菜籽	Rapeseeds	105.2	-6.4
花 生	Peanut	37.0	-1.9
蚕 茧	Silkworm Cocoons	7.0	-11.2
茶 叶	Tea	1.5	-0.9
水 果	Fruits	745.3	0.9
肉 类	Meat	375.9	2.5
禽 蛋	Poultry Eggs	194.9	2.2
牛 奶	Cow Milk	59.2	3.3
水产品	Aquatic Products	475.9	3.4
工业产品产量	**Output Of Industrial Products**		
纱（万吨）	Yarn (10000 tons)	411.2	0.7
布（亿米）	Cloth (100 million meters)	67.7	6.6
化 纤（万吨）	Chemical Fibre (10000 tons)	1123.8	10.5
卷 烟（亿支）	Cigarette (100 million pieces)	991.1	3.3
彩色电视机（万部）	Colour TV (10000 units)	1476.9	-10.1
家用电冰箱（万台）	Household Refrigerator (10000 units)	1194.8	48.0
房间空调器（万台）	Household Air-conditioner (10000 units)	509.5	-5.1
原 煤（万吨）	Coal (10000 tons)	2100.3	-0.8
原 油（万吨）	Crude Oil (10000 tons)	189	1.6
发电量（亿千瓦时）	Electricity (100 Million kw.h)	3755.6	10.8
粗 钢（万吨）	Crude Steel (10000 tons)	6838.8	9.8
钢 材（万吨）	Steel Products (10000 tons)	9994	9.4
十种有色金属（万吨）	10 Kinds of Nonferrous Metals (10000 tons)	67.1	18.9
水 泥（万吨）	Cement (10000 tons)	14899.7	2.8
硫 酸（万吨）	Sulfuric Acid (10000 tons)	488.1	7.6
纯 碱（万吨）	Soda Ash (10000 tons)	318.9	19.4
乙 烯（万吨）	Ethene (10000 tons)	153.9	26.7
化 肥（折100%,万吨）	Chemical Fertilizer (10000 tons)	243.7	2.8
汽 车（万辆）	Motor Vehicles (10000 coaches)	80.4	10.2
# 轿 车（万辆）	Cars (10000 coaches)	38.4	22.2
发电设备（万千瓦）	Electricity Generation Equiments (10000 kw)	779.8	23.8
集成电路（亿块）	Integrated Citcuit (100 million pcs)	224.8	2.0
程控交换机（万线）	Distance Exchange and Transmitting Machine (10000 lines)	6.1	66.1
微型电子计算机（万部）	Micro-computers (10000 units)	9916.2	8.1
移动通讯基站设备（信道）	Mobile Communication Devices (Channels)	1570774	145.1

附录 5 江苏省市、县主要经济指标 (2011 年)

MAJOR ECONOMY INDICATORS OF CITIES AND COUNTIES OF JIANGSU PROVINCE (2011)

指 标	Item	南京市 Nanjing City	溧水县 Lishui County	高淳县 Gaochun County
年末总人口（万人）	Year-end Population (10000 persons)	636.36	41.7	43.1
年末常住人口（万人）	Year-end permanent population (10000 persons)	810.91	41.93	41.93
土地面积（平方公里）	Area of Land (sq.km)	6587	1064	790
国内生产总值（亿元）	Gross Domestic Products (100 million yuan)	6145.52	303.77	302.82
第一产业	Primary Industry	164.28	26.01	27.09
第二产业	Secondary Industry	2760.84	188.59	171.09
#工 业	Industry	2390.51	159.79	137.00
第三产业	Tertiary Industry	3220.41	89.19	104.64
人均地区生产总值（元）	Per Capita GDP (yuan)	76263	72257	72338
固定资产投资完成额（亿元）	Investment in Fixed Assets (100 million yuan)	3757.25	185.61	74.10
地方一般预算收入（亿元）	Local General Budgetary Revenue (100 million yuan)	635.00	25.00	18.00
地方一般预算支出（亿元）	Local General Budgetary Expenditure (100 million yuan)	666.21	31.55	27.30
年底金融机构存款余额（亿元）	Balance of Deposits of Financial Institutions at Year-end (100 million yuan)	13945.92	175.79	148.12
#储蓄存款	Savings Deposits	3910.20	89.74	82.53
年底金融机构贷款余额（亿元）	Balance of Loans of Financial Institutions at Year-end (100 million yuan)	11132.09	132.64	133.20
规模以上工业企业主要指标	**Major Economic Indicators of Industrial Enterprises Above Designated Size**			
工业总产值（亿元）	Gross Industrial Output Value (100 million yuan)	10354.65	503.59	478.70
主营业务收入（亿元）	Main Business Income (100 million yuan)	10472.31	492.85	493.10
利润总额（亿元）	Total Profits (100 million yuan)	594.40	48.95	37.89
利税总额（亿元）	Total Profits and Taxes (100 million yuan)	1192.54	74.96	60.55
工业用电量（亿千瓦时）	Industrial Electricity Consumption (100 million kw.h)	256.84	10.50	3.91
社会消费品零售总额（亿元）	Total Retail Sales of Consumer Goods (100 million yuan)	2697.10	85.53	100.06
进出口总额（亿美元）	Total Imports (USD 100 million)	573.46	3.60	3.41
#出 口	Exports	308.68	3.21	3.07
实际利用外资（亿美元）	Foreign Capital Actually Utilized(USD 100 million)	35.66	1.23	0.61
城镇居民人均可支配收入（元）	Per Capita Disposable Income of Urban Residents (yuan)	31100	28016	29284
城镇居民人均消费支出（元）	Per Capita Consuming Expenditures of Urban Residents (yuan)	20098	16304	17410
农民人均纯收入（元）	Per Capita Net Income of Rural Residents (yuan)	13108	12716	13142
农民人均生活消费支出（元）	Per Capita Living Expenditure of Rural Residents (yuan)	9956	9913	9572

注：城市居民人均可支配收入、城市居民人均消费性支出数据为全市口径。

Note: The data of per capita disposable income and per capita nonproductive expenditure of urban residents is subject to the municipal caliber.

附录 5　续表 1

指　标	Item	无锡市 Wuxi City	江阴市 Jiangyin City	宜兴市 Yixing City
年末总人口（万人）	Year-end Population (10000 persons)	467.96	120.88	107.61
年末常住人口（万人）	Year-end permanent population (10000 persons)	643.22	161.64	124.37
土地面积（平方公里）	Area of Land (sq.km)	4627	987	1997
国内生产总值（亿元）	Gross Domestic Products (100 million yuan)	6880.15	2335.87	980.39
第一产业	Primary Industry	122.98	43.02	42.48
第二产业	Secondary Industry	3728.12	1354.31	536.02
#工　业	Industry	3463.12	1306.00	474.60
第三产业	Tertiary Industry	3029.05	938.54	401.89
人均地区生产总值（元）	Per Capita GDP (yuan)	107437	145456	79080
固定资产投资完成额（亿元）	Investment in Fixed Assets (100 million yuan)	3135.03	711.92	412.20
地方一般预算收入（亿元）	Local General Budgetary Revenue (100 million yuan)	615.00	153.37	71.20
地方一般预算支出（亿元）	Local General Budgetary Expenditure (100 million yuan)	592.67	136.44	75.70
年底金融机构存款余额（亿元）	Balance of Deposits of Financial Institutions at Year-end (100 million yuan)	9372.69	2193.35	1291.78
#储蓄存款	Savings Deposits	3312.38	699.23	546.81
年底金融机构贷款余额（亿元）	Balance of Loans of Financial Institutions at Year-end (100 million yuan)	6883.44	1640.94	938.50
规模以上工业企业主要指标	**Major Economic Indicators of Industrial Enterprises Above Designated Size**			
工业总产值（亿元）	Gross Industrial Output Value (100 million yuan)	14568.38	5953.02	2501.19
主营业务收入（亿元）	Main Business Income (100 million yuan)	14567.14	5970.02	2433.18
利润总额（亿元）	Total Profits (100 million yuan)	1149.38	513.63	139.38
利税总额（亿元）	Total Profits and Taxes (100 million yuan)	1523.07	718.70	195.91
工业用电量（亿千瓦时）	Industrial Electricity Consumption (100 million kw.h)	476.28	211.77	72.18
社会消费品零售总额（亿元）	Total Retail Sales of Consumer Goods (100 million yuan)	2142.02	451.92	325.54
进出口总额（亿美元）	Total Imports (USD 100 million)	724.63	209.05	47.63
#出　口	Exports	423.11	118.89	31.12
实际利用外资（亿美元）	Foreign Capital Actually Utilized (USD 100 million)	35.05	7.21	3.57
城镇居民人均可支配收入（元）	Per Capita Disposable Income of Urban Residents (yuan)	31638	34888	29494
城镇居民人均消费支出（元）	Per Capita Consuming Expenditures of Urban Residents (yuan)	19780	22425	16438
农民人均纯收入（元）	Per Capita Net Income of Rural Residents (yuan)	16438	17460	14949
农民人均生活消费支出（元）	Per Capita Living Expenditure of Rural Residents (yuan)	11239	10606	11010

注：城市居民人均可支配收入、城市居民人均消费性支出数据为全市口径。
Note: The data of per capita disposable income and per capita nonproductive expenditure of urban residents is subject to the municipal caliber.

Appendix 5 Continued 1

徐州市 Xuzhou City	丰县 Feng County	沛县 Pei County	睢宁县 Shuining County	新沂市 Xiyi City	邳州市 Pizhou City	常州市 Changzhou City	溧阳市 Liyang City	金坛市 Jintan City
976.66	115.08	127.12	135.46	104.70	178.63	362.86	78.73	55.15
857.26	95.51	111.97	103.16	91.34	144.01	464.97	75.58	55.53
11259	1446	1349	1767	1571	2088	4372	1535	976
3551.65	190.61	376.98	252.36	301.37	448.86	3580.99	503.78	365.10
334.54	40.28	59.80	50.90	42.14	69.92	111.78	34.49	24.08
1777.04	86.98	181.09	109.35	129.94	198.50	1950.84	283.92	203.94
1509.82	61.46	146.89	87.06	110.21	161.93	1768.91	257.58	180.56
1440.07	63.35	136.09	92.11	129.29	180.44	1518.37	185.37	137.08
41407	19867	33335	24366	32861	30972	77485	66934	65944
2201.03	101.07	211.91	121.21	189.64	230.83	2223.26	311.16	206.60
318.42	19.66	31.90	20.20	26.51	35.08	350.88	37.13	23.08
454.24	40.40	50.79	42.39	43.18	53.45	361.81	44.32	29.72
2980.99	145.62	246.49	186.86	158.03	205.33	4902.15	541.80	335.65
1495.42	103.88	161.52	128.20	97.85	135.53	2157.39	288.24	196.81
1734.84	84.88	89.28	98.26	130.48	149.84	3406.35	361.26	227.81
6950.65	221.28	788.07	380.46	604.30	1049.04	8270.77	1137.23	686.90
6940.76	216.43	773.69	375.25	601.44	1050.09	8212.53	1140.76	671.06
643.54	18.40	56.53	42.87	45.36	98.81	468.43	64.80	62.02
1123.70	33.12	105.54	61.61	78.58	171.33	713.30	107.50	86.42
225.91	5.51	21.15	13.43	29.64	17.05	267.21	48.87	28.40
1141.89	59.38	107.49	73.75	71.81	98.37	1236.10	173.20	136.67
63.10	1.11	2.88	3.56	2.83	10.13	286.35	10.41	20.22
41.59	1.04	2.84	2.25	2.25	9.79	193.61	8.91	16.15
14.66	0.42	1.07	1.05	0.66	1.67	30.52	4.01	4.01
19206	14261	16910	14465	15508	18083	29559	26418	28087
12450	10219	11366	9524	13384	9827	19126	18081	18528
9490	8642	10001	8384	8643	9931	14838	13505	13812
5973	6288	7587	4987	5766	5188	11207	12839	10758

附录 5 续表 2

指 标	Item	苏州市 Suzhou City	常熟市 Changshu City	张家港市 Zhangjiagang City
年末总人口（万人）	Year-end Population (10000 persons)	642.33	106.72	90.79
年末常住人口（万人）	Year-end permanent population (10000 persons)	1051.87	151.22	125.22
土地面积（平方公里）	Area of Land (sq.km)	8488	1094	990
国内生产总值（亿元）	Gross Domestic Products (100 million yuan)	10716.99	1710.45	1860.28
第一产业	Primary Industry	177.75	33.65	25.03
第二产业	Secondary Industry	5957.74	938.07	1098.01
#工 业	Industry	5555.33	898.40	1057.20
第三产业	Tertiary Industry	4581.50	738.73	737.24
人均地区生产总值（元）	Per Capita GDP (yuan)	102129	113133	148727
固定资产投资完成额（亿元）	Investment in Fixed Assets (100 million yuan)	4279.98	492.83	532.56
地方一般预算收入（亿元）	Local General Budgetary Revenue (100 million yuan)	1100.88	122.50	142.32
地方一般预算支出（亿元）	Local General Budgetary Expenditure (100 million yuan)	1002.63	115.02	132.77
年底金融机构存款余额（亿元）	Balance of Deposits of Financial Institutions at Year-end (100 million yuan)	15180.78	1815.87	1857.34
#储蓄存款	Savings Deposits	5078.59	823.57	665.62
年底金融机构贷款余额（亿元）	Balance of Loans of Financial Institutions at Year-end (100 million yuan)	11873.89	1319.15	1309.15
规模以上工业企业主要指标	**Major Economic Indicators of Industrial Enterprises Above Designated Size**			
工业总产值（亿元）	Gross Industrial Output Value (100 million yuan)	27778.75	3251.66	4461.91
主营业务收入（亿元）	Main Business Income (100 million yuan)	27578.16	3184.39	4688.83
利润总额（亿元）	Total Profits (100 million yuan)	1484.73	186.02	197.12
利税总额（亿元）	Total Profits and Taxes (100 million yuan)	2029.38	237.79	296.02
工业用电量（亿千瓦时）	Industrial Electricity Consumption (100 million kw.h)	946.19	119.94	243.12
社会消费品零售总额（亿元）	Total Retail Sales of Consumer Goods (100 million yuan)	2829.58	426.26	316.46
进出口总额（亿美元）	Total Imports (USD 100 million)	3008.63	198.04	334.32
#出 口	Exports	1672.33	135.46	120.93
实际利用外资（亿美元）	Foreign Capital Actually Utilized (USD 100 million)	90.16	9.02	9.02
城镇居民人均可支配收入（元）	Per Capita Disposable Income of Urban Residents (yuan)	34617	35041	35128
城镇居民人均消费支出（元）	Per Capita Consuming Expenditures of Urban Residents (yuan)	22330	22280	23829
农民人均纯收入（元）	Per Capita Net Income of Rural Residents (yuan)	17226	17289	17252
农民人均生活消费支出（元）	Per Capita Living Expenditure of Rural Residents (yuan)	12485	13162	12977

注：城市居民人均可支配收入、城市居民人均消费性支出数据为全市口径。
Note: The data of per capita disposable income and per capita nonproductive expenditure of urban residents is subject to the municipal caliber.

Appendix 5 Continued 2

昆山市 Gunshan City	吴江市 Wujiang City	太仓市 Taichang City	南通市 Nantong City	海安县 Haian County	如东县 Rudong County	启东市 Qidong County	如皋市 Rugao City	海门市 Haimeng City
72.36	80.18	47.04	764.88	93.72	104.75	112.41	142.26	99.99
165.87	127.75	71.41	728.91	86.60	99.07	96.76	126.20	90.27
932	1238	823	8001	1108	1733	1208	1492	939
2432.25	1192.28	867.53	4080.22	429.52	425.45	520.17	520.67	590.33
22.17	30.97	30.88	287.21	42.94	50.50	55.96	46.99	41.39
1510.06	699.48	485.72	2221.48	228.01	223.13	277.11	288.82	348.22
1437.06	663.52	459.30	1840.41	186.16	180.66	219.19	245.03	284.61
900.02	461.83	350.93	1571.53	158.57	151.82	187.11	184.86	200.71
147186	93417	121656	56005	49598	42843	53629	41178	65226
642.57	504.84	386.25	2378.36	260.12	250.75	302.99	272.02	300.66
200.22	112.88	85.41	373.69	28.51	25.39	44.07	45.63	42.35
174.58	108.06	80.51	419.45	43.09	42.41	53.27	60.54	47.65
2075.19	1550.66	890.23	5502.08	556.67	423.07	572.40	597.06	608.72
684.00	555.66	325.41	3052.30	356.46	296.74	406.11	370.40	409.30
1443.06	1213.33	749.49	3285.40	362.23	213.54	322.78	291.54	340.16
7282.21	2993.67	1706.25	8679.82	1071.86	1045.32	1036.53	1157.30	1201.98
7207.49	3018.09	1687.26	8432.59	1014.26	1020.99	1007.61	1118.31	1219.01
412.55	179.55	96.65	694.85	88.81	90.50	95.08	60.87	133.02
511.25	239.65	143.51	1017.50	119.28	127.95	139.03	96.72	196.55
143.25	168.85	66.78	212.15	28.79	24.15	14.88	29.31	21.02
420.98	263.65	167.17	1493.27	157.00	174.58	198.53	198.65	204.93
855.30	224.04	121.64	257.75	12.39	12.58	24.91	30.42	15.84
533.38	115.80	53.57	180.12	10.27	10.07	18.28	18.77	11.38
17.50	9.02	8.10	21.66	1.59	2.95	3.83	4.76	1.13
35190	35212	34887	25094	23775	23773	23889	23028	26339
24212	22231	23124	15613	14241	15747	15164	13452	16555
17374	17150	17201	11730	11216	10786	12535	10312	13453
13955	11307	11094	8510	8483	8563	9018	6959	9685

附录 5 续表 3

指 标	Item	连云港市 Lianyun-gang City	赣榆县 Guanyu County	东海县 Donghai County
年末总人口（万人）	Year-end Population (10000 persons)	505.18	114.07	116.24
年末常住人口（万人）	Year-end permanent population (10000 persons)	438.61	94.56	94.76
土地面积（平方公里）	Area of Land (sq.km)	7615	1514	2037
国内生产总值（亿元）	Gross Domestic Products (100 million yuan)	1410.52	283.07	245.67
第一产业	Primary Industry	204.11	43.43	45.42
第二产业	Secondary Industry	654.28	144.44	116.44
#工 业	Industry	517.82	110.87	99.86
第三产业	Tertiary Industry	552.13	95.20	83.81
人均地区生产总值（元）	Per Capita GDP (yuan)	32119	29846	25845
固定资产投资完成额（亿元）	Investment in Fixed Assets (100 million yuan)	1043.19	168.03	157.66
地方一般预算收入（亿元）	Local General Budgetary Revenue (100 million yuan)	180.08	23.81	23.50
地方一般预算支出（亿元）	Local General Budgetary Expenditure (100 million yuan)	274.63	44.63	43.35
年底金融机构存款余额（亿元）	Balance of Deposits of Financial Institutions at Year-end (100 million yuan)	1367.85	158.42	165.84
#储蓄存款	Savings Deposits	623.23	102.84	103.31
年底金融机构贷款余额（亿元）	Balance of Loans of Financial Institutions at Year-end (100 million yuan)	1011.18	117.63	110.02
规模以上工业企业主要指标	**Major Economic Indicators of Industrial Enterprises Above Designated Size**			
工业总产值（亿元）	Gross Industrial Output Value (100 million yuan)	2630.52	595.06	364.75
主营业务收入（亿元）	Main Business Income (100 million yuan)	2601.67	592.21	357.18
利润总额（亿元）	Total Profits (100 million yuan)	190.10	37.54	23.91
利税总额（亿元）	Total Profits and Taxes (100 million yuan)	299.95	64.20	37.75
工业用电量（亿千瓦时）	Industrial Electricity Consumption (100 million kw.h)	69.84	17.13	12.31
社会消费品零售总额（亿元）	Total Retail Sales of Consumer Goods (100 million yuan)	500.23	92.53	89.66
进出口总额（亿美元）	Total Imports (USD 100 million)	68.98	2.63	2.88
#出 口	Exports	37.36	2.10	2.19
实际利用外资（亿美元）	Foreign Capital Actually Utilized (USD 100 million)	6.10	0.57	0.76
城镇居民人均可支配收入（元）	Per Capita Disposable Income of Urban Residents (yuan)	18433	17240	17380
城镇居民人均消费支出（元）	Per Capita Consuming Expenditures of Urban Residents (yuan)	11473	10249	10420
农民人均纯收入（元）	Per Capita Net Income of Rural Residents (yuan)	8434	9068	8701
农民人均生活消费支出（元）	Per Capita Living Expenditure of Rural Residents (yuan)	5498	5686	5754

注：城市居民人均可支配收入、城市居民人均消费性支出数据为全市口径。
Note：The data of per capita disposable income and per capita nonproductive expenditure of urban residents is subject to the municipal caliber.

Appendix 5 Continued 3

灌云县 Guanyun County	灌南县 Guannan County	淮安市 Huaian City	涟水县 Lianshui County	洪泽县 Hongze County	盱眙县 Xuyu County	金湖县 Jinhu County	盐城市 Yancheng City	响水县 Xiangshui County
101.82	77.52	543.24	110.34	38.32	77.47	35.71	820.70	61.57
81.81	61.93	480.34	84.72	33.14	65.20	32.98	723.74	50.68
1840	1025	10072	1676	1394	2497	1394	16972	1461
192.22	182.33	1690.00	194.54	133.83	191.19	121.96	2771.33	161.16
44.29	34.33	223.46	47.43	22.07	35.79	20.10	416.83	32.50
90.29	91.38	794.18	76.78	59.16	84.17	50.92	1306.26	79.62
68.97	77.53	661.15	59.29	49.22	65.56	43.91	1111.50	71.03
57.64	56.62	672.36	70.33	52.60	71.23	50.94	1048.24	49.04
23496	29358	35181	22793	40690	29158	37469	38222	31697
136.94	135.86	1020.60	113.37	74.68	141.26	69.57	1586.98	116.33
21.61	22.22	204.63	20.28	14.85	20.11	13.00	269.04	17.01
35.91	37.67	296.68	38.55	23.28	36.36	22.42	407.22	26.24
126.24	72.86	1310.00	151.61	83.92	140.46	105.39	2320.16	93.17
73.41	50.00	678.92	86.72	41.73	72.32	61.88	1264.37	51.40
82.87	54.89	991.69	89.76	67.37	104.49	81.15	1558.64	75.42
303.36	319.54	2940.09	291.46	261.86	335.49	224.21	4360.08	322.66
300.27	314.83	2918.90	292.42	259.42	333.89	221.30	4355.32	319.16
22.33	14.77	150.21	15.31	19.80	12.03	13.19	269.17	28.45
29.91	30.71	299.68	24.39	27.41	20.74	17.91	508.98	38.20
4.39	11.91	92.09	7.73	11.84	8.14	6.89	132.29	15.13
68.12	48.18	547.85	53.34	49.34	52.15	46.37	895.09	37.20
2.92	1.28	28.54	2.06	0.72	1.17	1.60	52.45	4.39
2.71	1.08	18.39	1.75	0.66	0.79	1.56	29.78	3.34
0.16	0.16	16.20	2.10	1.59	2.12	1.51	16.88	1.05
14047	16394	18510	16018	19219	19690	19535	19414	16112
8528	9429	13188	12732	12934	12657	11455	13188	12881
7839	7451	8645	8043	9532	8807	9336	10511	8673
4468	5407	5904	5499	5632	4793	7196	6142	5313

附录 5 续表 4

指 标	Item	滨海县 Binhai County	阜宁县 Huning County	射阳县 Sheyang County
年末总人口（万人）	Year-end Population (10000 persons)	120.05	110.37	97.37
年末常住人口（万人）	Year-end permanent population (10000 persons)	95.07	84.07	89.52
土地面积（平方公里）	Area of Land (sq.km)	1915	1439	2855
国内生产总值（亿元）	Gross Domestic Products (100 million yuan)	238.00	244.09	287.98
第一产业	Primary Industry	45.41	42.30	63.66
第二产业	Secondary Industry	104.34	117.14	117.78
#工 业	Industry	87.91	87.42	106.92
第三产业	Tertiary Industry	88.25	84.65	106.54
人均地区生产总值（元）	Per Capita GDP (yuan)	24948	28978	32131
固定资产投资完成额（亿元）	Investment in Fixed Assets (100 million yuan)	152.59	132.57	138.77
地方一般预算收入（亿元）	Local General Budgetary Revenue (100 million yuan)	20.77	23.14	19.01
地方一般预算支出（亿元）	Local General Budgetary Expenditure (100 million yuan)	38.36	41.04	35.83
年底金融机构存款余额（亿元）	Balance of Deposits of Financial Institutions at Year-end (100 million yuan)	138.52	181.94	181.28
#储蓄存款	Savings Deposits	81.42	116.10	112.32
年底金融机构贷款余额（亿元）	Balance of Loans of Financial Institutions at Year-end (100 million yuan)	95.98	126.19	133.35
规模以上工业企业主要指标	**Major Economic Indicators of Industrial Enterprises Above Designated Size**			
工业总产值（亿元）	Gross Industrial Output Value (100 million yuan)	341.54	338.37	375.99
主营业务收入（亿元）	Main Business Income (100 million yuan)	330.44	339.69	372.66
利润总额（亿元）	Total Profits (100 million yuan)	20.74	13.97	14.25
利税总额（亿元）	Total Profits and Taxes (100 million yuan)	37.94	29.66	28.50
工业用电量（亿千瓦时）	Industrial Electricity Consumption (100 million kw.h)	12.68	18.78	8.93
社会消费品零售总额（亿元）	Total Retail Sales of Consumer Goods (100 million yuan)	61.66	72.40	97.02
进出口总额（亿美元）	Total Imports (USD 100 million)	1.60	2.28	1.69
#出 口	Exports	1.49	1.77	1.08
实际利用外资（亿美元）	Foreign Capital Actually Utilized (USD 100 million)	1.36	1.51	1.26
城镇居民人均可支配收入（元）	Per Capita Disposable Income of Urban Residents (yuan)	16879	16153	17129
城镇居民人均消费支出（元）	Per Capita Consuming Expenditures of Urban Residents (yuan)	9982	11979	13353
农民人均纯收入（元）	Per Capita Net Income of Rural Residents (yuan)	9197	9299	10377
农民人均生活消费支出（元）	Per Capita Living Expenditure of Rural Residents (yuan)	5004	4884	5455

注：城市居民人均可支配收入、城市居民人均消费性支出数据为全市口径。
Note: The data of per capita disposable income and per capita nonproductive expenditure of urban residents is subject to the municipal caliber.

Appendix 5 Continued 4

建湖县 Jianhu County	东台市 Dongtai City	大丰市 Dafeng City	扬州市 Yangzhou City	宝应县 Baoying County	仪征市 Yizheng City	高邮市 Gaoyou City	镇江市 Zhenjiang City
80.49	113.40	72.53	460.05	91.42	56.62	82.06	271.86
74.00	98.79	70.33	446.30	75.20	56.20	74.00	313.43
1160	3221	3059	6591	1462	857	1922	3847
288.77	447.92	346.96	2630.30	291.53	333.41	302.50	2311.45
38.51	71.49	57.90	184.54	49.75	17.71	50.47	100.77
138.02	205.43	153.39	1427.87	139.45	196.19	145.63	1272.39
119.25	181.19	131.51	1240.87	112.35	173.69	119.13	1175.63
112.24	171.00	135.67	1017.89	102.33	119.51	106.40	938.29
38966	45293	49218	58950	38754	59214	40746	73983
145.62	228.31	177.09	1475.43	160.15	205.74	196.37	1226.94
28.25	35.92	30.07	218.08	34.39	20.58	25.95	181.90
44.58	53.70	41.44	264.37	42.99	32.30	27.41	202.90
198.26	375.08	296.13	2818.31	296.05	255.80	221.90	2431.84
133.34	267.01	166.02	1427.87	161.25	172.22	143.13	1108.83
138.70	209.78	165.07	1718.03	156.14	142.80	137.53	1787.42
412.08	569.91	419.43	6772.79	570.92	944.67	750.38	5207.67
407.19	557.65	417.02	6563.35	546.82	940.25	744.85	5040.45
24.78	30.21	21.28	517.25	29.21	77.69	63.12	468.23
46.71	56.81	39.87	841.64	50.34	112.27	95.72	301.58
9.83	25.12	17.10	122.04	8.33	21.38	13.79	148.95
94.63	139.29	95.85	853.74	92.68	99.79	96.34	664.07
2.17	3.82	5.82	101.40	5.67	8.31	3.84	100.75
2.02	3.50	3.88	73.20	4.14	4.64	3.12	56.19
1.36	2.65	2.65	21.03	1.72	2.92	1.56	18.08
18774	21093	19851	22835	16848	23675	20078	26637
12276	13164	12522	14757	10889	14715	13373	15518
10358	12056	11941	11217	10327	10826	10449	12825
6168	6869	7404	7791	7354	7942	7341	9136

附录 5　续表 5

指　标	Item	丹阳市 Danyang City	扬中市 Yangzhong City	句容市 Jurong City
年末总人口（万人）	Year-end Population (10000 persons)	81.29	28.01	58.91
年末常住人口（万人）	Year-end permanent population (10000 persons)	96.76	33.78	61.91
土地面积（平方公里）	Area of Land (sq.km)	1047	331	1387
国内生产总值（亿元）	Gross Domestic Products (100 million yuan)	724.90	300.05	291.89
第一产业	Primary Industry	38.80	10.01	27.56
第二产业	Secondary Industry	400.20	171.82	157.86
#工　业	Industry	383.54	165.68	144.68
第三产业	Tertiary Industry	285.90	118.22	106.47
人均地区生产总值（元）	Per Capita GDP (yuan)	75189	89194	47147
固定资产投资完成额（亿元）	Investment in Fixed Assets (100 million yuan)	231.68	120.01	142.85
地方一般预算收入（亿元）	Local General Budgetary Revenue (100 million yuan)	41.13	19.60	20.50
地方一般预算支出（亿元）	Local General Budgetary Expenditure (100 million yuan)	43.64	22.18	30.92
年底金融机构存款余额（亿元）	Balance of Deposits of Financial Institutions at Year-end (100 million yuan)	590.26	296.74	262.61
#储蓄存款	Savings Deposits	313.96	164.55	146.42
年底金融机构贷款余额（亿元）	Balance of Loans of Financial Institutions at Year-end (100 million yuan)	465.18	195.82	166.86
规模以上工业企业主要指标	**Major Economic Indicators of Industrial Enterprises Above Designated Size**			
工业总产值（亿元）	Gross Industrial Output Value (100 million yuan)	1604.94	729.66	715.08
主营业务收入（亿元）	Main Business Income (100 million yuan)	1569.01	695.94	705.95
利润总额（亿元）	Total Profits (100 million yuan)	68.26	48.89	33.55
利税总额（亿元）	Total Profits and Taxes (100 million yuan)	105.27	77.48	66.98
工业用电量（亿千瓦时）	Industrial Electricity Consumption (100 million kw.h)	45.59	10.31	14.09
社会消费品零售总额（亿元）	Total Retail Sales of Consumer Goods (100 million yuan)	173.77	77.50	80.98
进出口总额（亿美元）	Total Imports (USD 100 million)	23.45	8.86	5.33
#出　口	Exports	18.25	3.50	3.85
实际利用外资（亿美元）	Foreign Capital Actually Utilized (USD 100 million)	2.69	1.92	4.44
城镇居民人均可支配收入（元）	Per Capita Disposable Income of Urban Residents (yuan)	26631	29595	26264
城镇居民人均消费支出（元）	Per Capita Consuming Expenditures of Urban Residents (yuan)	13985	16198	15014
农民人均纯收入（元）	Per Capita Net Income of Rural Residents (yuan)	13426	14692	11692
农民人均生活消费支出（元）	Per Capita Living Expenditure of Rural Residents (yuan)	10358	9209	7855

注：城市居民人均可支配收入、城市居民人均消费性支出数据为全市口径。
Note：The data of per capita disposable income and per capita nonproductive expenditure of urban residents is subject to the municipal caliber.

Appendix 5 Continued 5

泰州市 Taizhou City	兴化市 Xinghua City	靖江市 Jingjiang City	泰兴市 Taixing City	姜堰市 Jiangyan City	宿迁市 Suqian City	沭阳县 Shuyang County	泗阳县 Siyang County	泗洪县 Sihong County
507.12	157.3	67.15	120.21	79.45	555.05	186.45	103.32	102.55
462.60	125.43	68.54	107.51	72.98	476.64	154.70	84.30	91.60
5787	2395	656	1170	928	8555	2298	1418	2731
2422.61	459.47	538.98	486.39	364.08	1320.83	410.45	238.18	226.05
175.11	74.18	17.41	39.23	28.89	209.72	65.86	42.50	44.60
1308.21	202.83	306.25	264.88	192.17	614.48	185.57	119.27	93.70
1132.27	175.77	283.96	230.79	158.31	502.57	160.80	98.30	74.15
939.29	182.46	215.32	182.28	143.02	496.63	159.02	76.41	87.75
52396	36639	78683	45268	49908	27839	26583	28458	24748
1197.65	155.01	232.05	213.78	178.16	788.97	205.90	141.84	121.91
218.00	25.56	48.68	27.90	22.19	120.98	37.28	17.33	14.88
262.02	49.36	41.50	41.88	30.56	221.24	64.11	35.46	35.72
2592.95	346.47	559.05	388.01	372.08	997.81	237.22	167.15	144.45
1307.77	234.88	261.87	250.63	218.77	497.50	150.45	94.89	81.53
1725.34	231.88	352.84	228.01	265.13	760.00	178.05	123.63	120.68
5813.13	773.26	1227.02	1072.55	736.22	1522.30	428.26	280.25	193.49
5672.88	766.10	1180.45	1060.02	701.22	1498.37	421.28	280.18	189.05
438.02	44.41	99.01	84.78	51.25	190.53	49.61	22.27	34.53
711.56	78.08	139.34	143.59	80.92	262.11	67.60	30.14	47.34
155.13	44.91	30.29	30.25	20.88	66.04	18.95	5.57	5.27
651.17	100.12	109.13	126.67	108.28	336.26	93.72	55.48	56.53
110.88	5.99	43.57	17.79	6.91	20.70	2.72	4.63	2.68
74.78	4.65	30.21	9.31	5.92	17.13	2.22	4.49	2.62
14.17	1.14	3.02	2.21	1.28	1.90	0.43	0.36	0.21
23597	21480	25580	23391	23746	14972	15127	14553	14002
14415	12493	15928	14531	13739	10634	11244	9117	11149
11046	10439	12116	11047	10802	8344	8383	8379	8189
8046	6932	11022	7296	7851	5838	6251	6211	4261

附录 6 长江三角洲地区各城市主要经济指标（2011 年）
MAIN ECONOMIC INDICATORS BY CITY IN THE YANGSE RIVER DELTA（2011）

指 标	Item	上海市 Shanghai City	南京市 Nanjing City	无锡市 Wuxi City
土地面积（平方公里）	Area of Land (sq.km)	6341	6587	4627
年末户籍人口（万人）	Year-end Population (10000 persons)	1419.36	636.36	467.96
年末常住人口（万人）	Year-end permanent population (10000 persons)	2347.46	810.91	643.22
地区生产总值（亿元）	Gross Domestic Products (100 million yuan)	19195.69	6145.52	6880.15
第一产业	Primary Industry	124.94	164.28	122.98
第二产业	Secondary Industry	7927.89	2760.84	3728.12
#工 业	Industy	7208.59	2390.51	3463.12
第三产业	Tertiary Industry	11142.86	3220.41	3029.05
人均地区生产总值（元）	Per Capita GDP (yuan)	82560	76263	107437
规模以上工业总产值（亿元）	Total Output Value of Industry above Designated Size (100 million yuan)	31987.44	10354.65	14568.38
社会消费品零售总额（亿元）	Total Retail of Consumer Goods (100 million yuan)	6814.80	2697.10	2142.02
固定资产投资完成额（亿元）	Investment in Fixed Assets (100 million yuan)	5067.09	3757.25	3169.18
#房地产投资	Real Estate Investment	2170.31	871.43	877.78
进出口总额（亿美元）	Total Imports and Exports(USD 100 million)	4374.36	573.46	724.63
#出 口	Exports	2097.89	308.68	423.11
实际利用外资金额（亿美元）	Foreign Capital Actually Used (USD 100 million)	126.01	35.66	35.05
地方一般预算收入（亿元）	Local General Budgetary Revenue (100 million yuan)	3429.83	635.00	615.00
地方一般预算支出（亿元）	Local General Budgetary Expenditure (100 million yuan)	3914.88	666.21	592.67
金融机构本外币存款余额（亿元）	Deposits Balance in Foreign Currencies of Banking Institutions (100 million yuan)	58186.48	14241.99	9722.44
#储蓄存款	Savings Deposits	17288.45	3968.03	3340.09
金融机构本外币贷款余额（亿元）	Loans Balance in Foreign Currencies of Banking Institutions (100 million yuan)	37196.79	11723.52	7279.81
城市居民人均可支配收入（元）	Per Capita Disposable Income of Urban Residents (yuan)	36230	31100	31638
城市居民人均消费性支出（元）	Per Capita Consuming Expenditures of Urban Residents (yuan)	25102	20098	19780
农民人均纯收入（元）	Per Capita Net Income of Rural Residents (yuan)	15644	13108	16438
农民人均生活消费支出（元）	Per Capita Living Expenditure of Rural Residents (yuan)	11272	9956	11239
全社会用电量（亿千瓦时）	Total Electriccity Consumed (100 million kw.h)	1339.62	399.74	580.60
#工 业	Industrial	805.76	256.84	476.28

注：城市居民人均可支配收入、城市居民人均消费性支出数据为全市口径。
Note：The data of per capita disposable income and per capita nonproductive expenditure of urban residents is subject to the municipal caliber.

常州市 Changzhou City	苏州市 Shanghai City	南通市 Nantong City	扬州市 Yangzhou City	镇江市 zhenjiang City	泰州市 Taizhou City	杭州市 Hangzhou City	宁波市 Ningbo City	嘉兴市 Jiaxing City	湖州市 Huzhou City
4372	8488	8001	6591	3847	5787	16596	9816	3915	5818
362.86	642.33	764.88	460.05	271.86	507.12	695.71	576.40	343.05	261.05
464.97	1051.87	728.91	446.30	313.43	462.60	873.80	762.80	453.10	289.90
3580.99	10716.99	4080.22	2630.30	2311.45	2422.61	7019.06	6010.48	2677.09	1520.06
111.78	177.75	287.21	184.54	100.77	175.11	236.77	255.76	142.80	116.22
1950.84	5957.74	2221.48	1427.87	1272.39	1308.21	3323.79	3335.37	1537.26	817.71
1768.91	5555.33	1840.41	1240.87	1175.63	1132.27	2944.00	3004.84	1378.15	729.48
1518.37	4581.50	1571.53	1017.89	938.29	939.29	3458.50	2419.35	997.03	586.13
77485	102129	56005	58950	73983	52396	80478	78884	59256	52477
8270.77	27778.75	8679.82	6772.79	5207.67	5813.13	12352.92	12044.77	5763.36	2890.05
1236.10	2829.58	1493.27	853.74	664.07	651.17	2548.36	2018.90	948.57	609.89
2223.26	4279.98	2378.36	1475.43	1226.94	1197.65	3100.02	2392.91	1488.27	804.67
565.91	1199.13	379.96	198.46	137.98	228.26	1302.72	756.87	383.37	184.68
286.35	3008.63	257.75	101.40	100.73	110.88	639.72	981.88	284.84	86.62
193.61	1672.33	180.12	73.20	56.19	74.78	415.21	608.32	192.72	73.56
30.52	90.16	21.66	21.03	18.08	14.17	47.22	28.12	17.21	9.40
350.88	1100.88	373.69	218.08	181.90	218.00	785.15	657.55	226.40	122.12
361.81	1002.63	419.45	264.37	202.90	262.02	747.51	750.72	240.61	151.73
5020.88	16004.17	5614.60	2860.65	2474.45	2632.69	18396.57	10659.27	4168.17	2102.05
2171.20	5126.89	3068.10	1435.27	1115.64	1311.60	5547.48	3696.28	1880.45	954.44
3505.80	12776.25	3408.64	1751.50	1835.50	1804.45	16573.74	10676.84	3212.74	1712.17
29559	34617	25094	22835	26637	23597	32434	34058	31520	29367
19126	22330	15613	14757	15518	14415	21404	21779	19535	18166
14838	17226	11730	11217	12825	11046	15245	16518	16707	15381
11207	12485	8510	7791	9136	8046	12125	11253	10707	10093
331.66	1131.63	280.77	167.22	184.09	195.68	575.28	505.30	327.91	157.56
267.21	946.19	212.15	122.04	148.95	155.13	399.60	388.62	271.30	122.57

附录 6 续表 Appendix 6 continued

指 标	Item	绍兴市 Shao xing City	舟山市 Zhoushan City	台州市 Taizhou City
土地面积（平方公里）	Area of Land (sq.km)	8256	1440	9411
年末户籍人口（万人）	Year-end Population (10000 persons)	440.01	96.99	586.79
年末常住人口（万人）	Year-end permanent population (10000 persons)	493.40	113.70	599.90
地区生产总值（亿元）	Gross Domestic Products (100 million yuan)	3332.00	772.75	2754.41
第一产业	Primary Industry	172.10	76.04	189.25
第二产业	Secondary Industry	1834.34	349.16	1390.72
#工 业	Industy	1632.35	267.28	1253.40
第三产业	Tertiary Industry	1325.56	347.55	1174.45
人均地区生产总值（元）	Per Capita GDP (yuan)	67676	68434	46011
规模以上工业总产值（亿元）	Total Output Value of Industry above Designated Size (100 million yuan)	7932.68	1105.03	3448.45
社会消费品零售总额（亿元）	Total Retail of Consumer Goods (100 million yuan)	1006.75	251.71	1132.37
固定资产投资完成额（亿元）	Investment in Fixed Assets (100 million yuan)	1426.26	476.09	1007.81
#房地产投资	Real Estate Investment	403.24	116.79	319.16
进出口总额（亿美元）	Total Imports and Exports(USD 100 million)	335.05	132.64	205.04
#出 口	Exports	259.86	74.73	170.35
实际利用外资金额（亿美元）	Foreign Capital Actually Used (USD 100 million)	8.05	1.08	1.43
地方一般预算收入（亿元）	Local General Budgetary Revenue (100 million yuan)	239.69	76.48	200.12
地方一般预算支出（亿元）	Local General Budgetary Expenditure (100 million yuan)	253.31	148.10	265.53
金融机构本外币存款余额（亿元）	Deposits Balance in Foreign Currencies of Banking Institutions (100 million yuan)	5510.14	1314.97	3998.90
#储蓄存款	Savings Deposits	2227.67	461.30	2068.79
金融机构本外币贷款余额（亿元）	Loans Balance in Foreign Currencies of Banking Institutions (100 million yuan)	4463.09	1162.66	3470.76
城市居民人均可支配收入（元）	Per Capita Disposable Income of Urban Residents (yuan)	33273	30496	30490
城市居民人均消费性支出（元）	Per Capita Consuming Expenditures of Urban Residents (yuan)	20353	19183	19808
农民人均纯收入（元）	Per Capita Net Income of Rural Residents (yuan)	15861	16608	13108
农民人均生活消费支出（元）	Per Capita Living Expenditure of Rural Residents (yuan)	10073	12124	9491
全社会用电量（亿千瓦时）	Total Electriccity Consumed (100 million kw.h)	324.60	42.90	221.98
#工 业	Industrial	268.68	25.05	157.03

注：城市居民人均可支配收入、城市居民人均消费性支出数据为全市口径。
Note：The data of per capita disposable income and per capita nonproductive expenditure of urban residents is subject to the municipal caliber.

附录 7　主要统计指标解释

1. 地区生产总值　指一个国家（地区）所有常住单位在一定时期内生产活动的最终成果。国内生产总值有三种表现形态，即价值形态、收入形态和产品形态。从价值形态看，它是所有常住单位在一定时期内所生产的全部货物和服务价值超过同期投入的全部非固定资产货物和服务价值的差额，即所有常住单位的增加值之和；从收入形态看，它是所有常住单位在一定时期内所创造并分配给常住单位和非常住单位的初次分配收入之和；从产品形态看，它是最终使用的货物和服务减去进口货物和服务。在实际核算中，国内生产总值的三种表现形态表现为三种计算方法，即生产法、收入法和支出法。三种方法分别从不同的方面反映地区生产总值及其构成。

2. 可比价格　指对不同时期的价值进行对比时，扣除了价格变动的因素，以确切反映物量的变化情况。按可比价格计算的方法有两种：一是直接按产品产量乘不变价格计算；二是用物价指数换算。

3. 不变价格　指以同类产品某年的平均价格作为固定价格，用于计算各年的产品价值。按不变价格计算的产品价值消除了价格变动因素，不同时期对比可以反映生产的发展速度。新中国成立后，随着工农业产品价格水平的变化，国家统计局先后五次制定了全国统一的工业产品不变价格和农业产品不变价格。从1952年到1957年使用1952年工（农）业产品不变价格，从1957年到1970年使用1957年不变价格，从1971年到1980年使用1970年不变价格，从1981年到1990年使用1980年不变价格，从1991年开始使用1990年不变价格。

4. 各个计划时期　各个计划“时期”代表的年份如下：恢复时期为1950-1952年；第一个五年计划时期（简称“一五”时期）为1953-1957年；第二个五年计划时期（简称“二五”时期）为1958-1962年；调整时期为1963-1965年；第三个五年计划时期（简称“三五”时期）为1966-1970年；第四个五年计划时期（简称“四五”时期）为1971-1975年；第五个五年计划时期（简称“五五”时期）为1976-1980年；第六个五年计划时期（简称“六五”时期）为1981-1985年；第七个五年计划时期（简称“七五”时期）为1986-1990年；第八个五年计划时期（简称“八五”时期）为1991-1995年；第九个五年计划时期（简称“九五”时期）为1996-2000年；第十个五年计划时期（简称“十五”时期）从2001-2005年；第十一个五年计划时期（简称“十一五”时期）为2006-2010年；第十二个五年计划时期（简称“十二五”时期）为2011-2015年。

5. 平均增长速度　指某种现象在一个较长时期中逐年增长的平均速度。其计算方法有两种：一是习惯上经常使用的“水平法”，又称几何水平法，是以间隔期最后一年的水平同基期水平对比来计算平均每年增长（或下降）速度；二是“累计法”，又称代数平均法或方程法，是以间隔期内各年水平的总和同基期水平对比来计算平均每年增长（或下降）速度。在一般正常情况下，两种方法计算的数值比较接近，但在经济发展不平衡，出现大起大落时，该两个数值差别较大。

本《年鉴》内所列的平均每年的增长速度，均用“水平法”计算。从某年到某年平均每年增长速度的年份，均不包括基期年在内。如改革开放33年以来的平均每年增长速度是以1978年为基期计算的，则写为1979-2011年平均每年增长速度，其余类推。

6. 企业（单位）登记注册类型　是以在工商行政管理机关登记注册的各类企业为划分对象，以工商行政管理部门对企业登记注册的类型为依据，将企业登记注册类型分为内资企业、港澳台商投资企业和外商投资企业三大类。内资企业包括国有企业、集体企业、股份合作企业、联营企业、有限责任公司、股份有限公司、私营公司和其他企业;港澳台商投资企业和外商投资企业分别包括合资经营企业、合作经营企业、独资经营企业和股份有限公司。对不在工商行政管理部门进行登记注册的行政机关、事业单位和社会团体，主要按其经费来源和管理方式进行划分。

7. 国有企业　指企业全部资产归国家所有，并按《中华人民共和国企业法人登记管理条例》规定登记注册的非公司制经济组织。不包括有限责任公司中的国有独资公司。

8. 集体企业　指企业资产归集体所有，并按《中华人民共和国企业法人登记管理条例》规定登记注册的经济组织。

9. 股份合作企业　指以合作制为基础，由企业职工共同出资入股，吸收一定比例的社会资产投资组建，实行自主经营，自负盈亏，共同劳动，民主管理，按劳分配与按股分红相结合的一种集体经济组织。

10. 联营企业　指两个及两个以上相同或不同所有制性质的企业法人或事业单位法人，按自愿、平等、互利的原则，共同投资组成的经济组织。联营企业包括国有联营企业、集体联营企业、国有与集体联营企业和其他联营企业。

11. 有限责任公司　指根据《中华人民共和国公司登记管理条例》规定登记注册，由两个以上、五十个以下的股东共同出资，每个股东以其所认缴的出资额对公司承担有限责任，公司以其全部资产对其债务承担责任的经济组织。有限责任公司包括国有独资公司以及其他有限责任公司。

12. 股份有限公司　指根据《中华人民共和国公司登记管理条例》规定登记注册，其全部注册资本由等额股份构成并通过发行股票筹集资本，股东以其认购的股份对公司承担有限责任，公司以其全部资产对其债务承担责任的经济组织。

13. 私营企业　指由自然人投资设立或由自然人控股，以雇佣劳动为基础的营利性经济组织。包括按照《公司法》、《合伙企业法》、《私营企业暂行条例》规定登记注册的私营有限责任公司、私营股份有限公司、私营合伙企业和私营独资企业。

14. 其他企业　指上述企业之外的其他内资经济组织。

15. 港、澳、台投资企业　指港、澳、台地区投资者参照中华人民共和国有关涉外经济的法律、法规，以合资、合作或独资的形式在祖国大陆举办的企业。包括合资经营企业、合作经营企业和独资企业。

16. 外商投资企业 指外国投资者根据中华人民共和国有关涉外经济的法律、法规，以合资、合作或独资的形式在中国大陆境内开办的企业。包括中外合资经营企业、中外合作经营企业和外资企业。

17. 三次产业 根据社会生产活动历史发展的顺序对产业结构的划分，产品直接取自自然界的部门称为第一产业，对初级产品进行再加工的部门称为第二产业，为生产和消费提供各种服务的部门称为第三产业。它是世界上通用的产业结构分类，但各国的划分不尽一致。我国的三次产业划分是：

第一产业：农林牧渔业（包括农业、林业、畜牧业、渔业和农林牧渔服务业）。

第二产业：工业（包括采掘工业、制造业、自来水、电力、蒸汽、热水、煤气）和建筑业。

第三产业：除第一、第二产业以外的其他各业。

18. 人口数 指一定时点、一定地区范围内的有生命的个人的总和。年度统计的年末人口数是指每年12月31日24时的常住人口数。不包括户籍不在本市的外来人数。

19. 出生率（又称粗出生率） 指在一定时期内（通常为一年）出生的人数与同期平均人数（或期中人数）比率，一般用千分率表示。计算公式：

出生率=年出生人数/年平均人数×1000‰

出生人数是指活产婴儿，即胎儿脱离母体时（不管怀孕月数），有过呼吸或其他生命现象。

目前出生率的计算，在市级有公安的户籍口径、计生委的常住人口统计口径；国家、省级还有年度人口抽样调查公布口径等。本年鉴用的为公安口径出生数，包括补报往年出生数在内。

年平均人数是年初、年底人口数的平均数，也可用年中人口数代替。

20. 死亡率（又称粗死亡率） 指在一定时期内（通常为一年）一定地区的死亡人数与同期平均人数（或期中人数）之比，一般用千分率表示。计算公式：

死亡率=年死亡人数/年平均人数×1000‰

21. 人口自然增长率 指在一定时期内（通常为一年）人口自然增加数（出生人数减死亡人数）与该时期内平均人数（或期中人数）之比，一般用行千分率表示。计算公式：

人口自然增长率=（本年出生人数-本年死亡人数）/年平均人数×1000‰

人口自然增长率=人口出生率—人口死亡率

22. 人口预期寿命 指在一定年龄组死亡率水平下，对某一确定的年龄日后平均还能继续生存的年数（或该年龄组未来的平均预期寿命）。

23. 从业人员 指从事一定社会劳动并取得劳动报酬或经营收入的人员。包括：（1）国有、集体、其他经济类型中的全部在岗职工和其他从业人员；（2）城镇私营及个体劳动者；（3）农村社会劳动者。

各单位的从业人员是指在各级国家机关、政党机关、社会团体及企业、事业单位中工作，取得工资或其他形式的劳动报酬的全部人员。包括：在岗职工、再就业的离退休人员、在各单位中工作的外方人员和港澳台方人员、兼职人员、借用的外单位人员和第二职业者。不包括离开本单位仍保留劳动关系的职工。

24. 职 工 指在内资（国有、集体、股份合作、联营、有限责任公司、股份有限公司）单位、港澳台投资单位和外商投资单位及其附属机构工作，并由其支付工资的在岗人员以及不在岗但劳动关系在本单位的离岗人员。

25. 在岗职工 指在本单位工作并由单位支付工资的人员，以及有工作岗位，但由于学习、病伤产假等原因暂未工作，仍由单位支付工资的人员。

26. 离岗职工 指由于各种原因，已经离开本人的生产或工作岗位，并已不在本单位从事其他工作，但仍与用人单位保留劳动关系的职工。

27. 从业人员工资总额 指各单位在一定时期内直接支付给本单位全部从业人员的劳动报酬总额。包括在岗职工工资总额、劳务派遣人员工资总额和其他从业人员工资总额三部分。

28. 在岗职工工资总额 指各单位在一定时期内直接支付给本单位全部在岗职工的劳动报酬总额。

工资总额的计算原则应以直接支付给职工的全部劳动报酬为根据。各单位支付给职工的劳动报酬以及其他根据有关规定支付的工资，不论是计入成本的还是不计入成本的，不论是按国家规定列入计征奖金税项目的，还是未列入计征奖金税项目的，不论是以货币形式支付的还是以实物形式支付的，均包括在工资总额内。

29. 在岗职工平均工资 指各单位的在岗职工在一定时期内平均每人所得的货币工资额。它表明一定时期内职工工资收入高低程度，是反映职工工资水平的主要指标。计算公式为：

在岗职工平均工资=报告期实际支付的全部在岗职工工资总额/报告期全部在岗职工平均人数

30. 城镇登记失业人员 指在劳动年龄（16周岁至退休年龄）内，有劳动能力，有就业要求，处于无业状态，并在公共就业人才服务机构进行失业登记的城镇人员。

31.居民消费价格指数 居民消费价格，指城乡居民支付生活消费品和服务项目消费的价格，是社会产品和服务项目的最终价格，同人民生活密切相关，在整个国民经济价格体系中具有极为重要的地位。居民消费价格指数，就是指反映一定时期内居民消费价格变动趋势和变动程度的相对数。

32.商品零售价格指数 商品零售价格，指工业、商业、餐饮业和其他零售企业向城乡居民、机关团体出售生活消费品和办公用品的价格。商品零售价格指数，就是指反映一定时期内商品零售价格变动趋势和变动程度的相对数。

33.服务项目价格指数 指居民非商品服务性支出的相对数。服务项目包括：电信费、邮费、交通费、洗理美容费、文娱费、学杂保育费、修理及其他服务费、医疗保险服务费8个大类。

34.城镇居民家庭就业人口 指城镇居民从事社会劳动并取得劳动报酬或经营收入的人口。就业人口包括通过国家统筹规划和指导由劳动部门介绍就业，自愿组织起来就业和自谋职业等方式，在国有单位、集体单位、中外合资、中外合作、外资在华独资的企业事业单位和私营企业单位工作或从事个体劳动的有固定性职业或临时性职业的人口。被聘用或留用的离休人员也记入就业人口。它是反映城镇居民的就业情况，计算就业面、负担系数的资料之一。

35. 城镇居民家庭总收入 指调查户中生活在一起的所有家庭成员在调查期得到的工薪收入、经营净收入、财产性收入、转移性收入的总和,不包括出售财物和借贷收入。收入以实际发生数额为准。无论收入是补发还是预发，只要是调查期得到的都应如实计算，不作分摊。

财产性收入指家庭拥有的动产（如银行存款、有价证券）、不动产（如房屋、车辆、土地、收藏品等）所获得的收入。包括出让财产使用权所获得的利息、租金、专利收入；财产营运所获得的红利收入、财产增值收益等。

转移性收入指国家、单位、社会团体对居民家庭的各种转移支付和居民家庭间的收入转移。包括政府对个人收入转移的离退休金、失业救济金、赔偿等；单位对个人收入转移的辞退金、保险索赔、住房公积金、家庭间的赠送和赡养等。

36. 城镇居民家庭可支配收入 指调查户可用于最终消费支出和其他非义务性支出以及储蓄的总和,即居民家庭可用于自由支配的收入。计算公式为：可支配收入＝家庭总收入-交纳个人所得税-个人交纳的社会保障支出-记帐补贴。

37. 家庭总支出 指家庭除借贷支出以外的全部实际支出。包括消费性支出、购房建房支出、转移性支出、财产性支出、社会保障支出。支出统计是以实际购得的商品或服务的总价值填报，不论其付款方式是一次性付清、分期付款，还是赊购，只要商品或服务已被消费就要按其总价值计量。如果采用分期付款或赊购形式，则要在借贷收入类相应的项目填入实付款与总的应付款的差额。

38. 城镇居民家庭消费支出 指被调查的城镇居民家庭用于日常生活的全部支出，包括食品、衣着、家庭设备用品及服务、医疗保健、交通和通信、教育文化娱乐服务、居住、杂项商品和服务八大类。包括用于赠送的商品或服务。

39. 农村居民家庭纯收入 指农村常住居民家庭总收入中，扣除从事生产和非生产经营费用支出、缴纳税款和上交承包集体任务金额以后剩余的，可直接用于进行生产性、非生产性建设投资、生活消费和积蓄的那一部分收入。它是反映农民家庭实际收入水平的综合性主要指标。农民家庭纯收入，既包括从事生产性和非生产性的经营收入，又包括取自在外人口寄回带回和国家财政救济、各种补贴等非经营性收入，还包括自产自用的实物收入。但不包括向银行、信用社和向亲友借款等属于借贷性的收入。

40. 农村居民家庭整半劳动力 指农村常住居民家庭成员中有劳动能力并经常参加实际劳动的人员。是生产的基本要素指标之一，是发展生产增加农民家庭收入的重要源泉。按规定，农村男18周岁至50周岁、女18周岁至45周岁为整劳动力；男16周岁到17周岁、51周岁到60周岁，女16周岁到17周岁、46周岁至55周岁为半劳动力。农民家庭整半劳动力，既包括在上述规定劳动年龄内和劳动年龄以外有劳动能力并经常参加实际劳动的男女整半劳动力，也包括农民家庭常住人员中属于职工的劳动力。但不包括在劳动年龄内已丧失劳动能力的人员。

41. 农村居民家庭生活消费支出 指农村常住居民家庭年内用于日常生活的全部开支。它是用来反映和研究农民家庭实际生活消费水平高低的重要指标。包括用于吃、穿、住、烧、用等生活消费品开支和文化、生活服务费用开支两大部分。

42. 全社会固定资产投资 固定资产投资是社会固定资产再生产的主要手段。固定资产投资额是以货币表现的建造和购置固定资产活动的工作量，它是反映固定资产投资规模、速度、比例关系和使用方向的综合性指标。全社会固定资产投资包括各种经济类型的投资，其投资总额分为：城镇投资、房地产开发投资、农村投资。

43. 房地产开发投资 指各种登记注册类型的房地产开发公司、商品房建设公司及其他房地产开发单位统一开发的包括统代建、拆迁还建的住宅、厂房、仓库、饭店、宾馆、度假村、写字楼、办公楼等房屋建筑物和配套的服务设施、土地开发工程（如道路、给水、排水、供电、供热、通讯、平整场地等基础设施工程）的投资。还包括非房地产企业实际从事房地产开发或经营活动，不包括单纯的土地交易活动。

44. 固定资产投资的资金来源 根据固定资产投资的资金来源不同，分为上年末结余资金、本年资金来源。其中本年资金来源又分为国家预算内资金、国内贷款、债券、利用外资、自筹资金和其他资金来源6种。

45. 固定资产投资按构成分 固定资产投资活动按其工作内容和实现方式分为建筑工程，安装工程，设备、工具、器具购置，其他费用4个部分。

46. 新增固定资产 指通过投资活动所形成的新的固定资产价值。包括已经建成投入生产或交付使用的工程价值和达到固定资产标准的设备、工具、器具的价值及有关应摊入的费用。它是以价值形式表示的固定资产投资成果的综合性指标，可以综合反映不同时期、不同部门、不同地区的固定资产投资成果。

47. 固定资产交付使用率 指在一定时期所增固定资产与同期完成投资额的比率。它是反映各个时期固定资产动用速度，衡量建设过程中投资改革的一个综合性指标。

48. 施工项目 指报告期内曾进行建筑或安装工程施工活动的建设项目。包括报告期内新开工项目、报告期以前开工跨入报告期继续施工的项目以及报告期施过工并在报告期内全部建成投产或停缓建的项目。

49. 全部建成投产项目 工业项目是指设计文件规定形成生产能力的主体工程及其相应配套的辅助设施全部建成，经负荷试运转，证明具备生产设计规定合格产品的条件，并经过验收鉴定合格或达到竣工验收标准，与生产性工程配套的生产福利设施可以满足近期正常生产的需要，正式移交生产的建设项目。非工业项目是指设计文件规定的主体工程和相应的配套工程全部建成，能够发挥设计规定的全部效益，经验收鉴定合格或达到竣工验收标准，正式移交使用的建设项目。

50. 房屋建筑面积 指从房屋外墙线算起的各层平面面积的总和，包括房屋结构（如柱、墙）占用的面积和地下室面积。多层建筑按各自然层面积总和计算，包括房屋内的楼隔层、突出墙面的眺望间、门斗、有柱雨罩的面积。不包括突出墙面结构的构件、艺术装饰等所占的面积，如台阶等。凹阳台，挑阳台按其水平投影面积一半计算建筑面积。

51. 房屋施工面积 指在报告期内施工的全部房屋（包括地下室、半地下室以及配套房屋）建筑面积。包括本期新开工的面积和上年开工跨入本期继续施工的房屋面积，以及上期已停建在本期恢复施工的房屋面积。本期竣工和本期施工后又停建缓建的房屋面积仍包括在施工面积中，多层建筑应填各层建筑面积之和。

52. 房屋竣工面积 指在报告期内房屋建筑按照设计要求已全部完工，达到住人和使用条件，经验收鉴定合格或达到竣工验收标准，可正式移交使用的各栋房屋建筑面积的总和。

53. 住宅面积 指施工和竣工房屋建筑面积中供居住用的施工房屋建筑面积。

54. 农林牧渔业总产值 是以货币表现的农、林、牧、渔业全部产品的总量和对农林牧渔业生产活动进行的各种支持性服务活动的价值。它反映一定时期内农林牧渔业生产的总规模和总成果。农、林、牧、渔业的统计范围是：

（1）农业 包括农作物种植业和其他农业。

农作物种植业包括谷物、豆类、薯类、棉花、油料、糖料、麻类、烟叶、蔬菜、药材、瓜类和其他农作物的种植以及茶园、桑园、果园的生产经营。

其他农业包括采集野生植物的果实、纤维、树胶、树脂、油料以及柴草、野生药材、菌类等及农民家庭兼营的商品性工业。

（2）林业 包括林木的栽培（不包括茶园、桑园和果园的栽培、管理和收获等活动）、林产品的采集和村及村以下合作经济组织和农户的竹木采伐。

（3）牧业 包括除渔业养殖以外的一切动物饲养和放牧以及野生动物的捕猎和饲养。

（4）渔业 包括水生动物和海藻类植物的养殖和捕捞。

（5）农林牧渔服务业 包括灌溉服务、农产品初级加工服务、其他农业服务、林业服务、兽医服务、其他畜牧服务、渔业服务业等。

55. 粮食产量 指全社会的粮食产量。包括国有经济经营的、集体统一经营的和农民家庭经营的粮食产量，还包括工矿企业家属办的农场和其他生产单位的产量。（粮食除包括稻谷、小麦、玉米、高粱、谷子及其他杂粮外，还包括薯类和豆类）。1989年以前全国粮食产量数据主要靠全面报表取得，1989年开始使用抽样调查数据。

56. 油料产量 指全部油料作物的生产量。包括花生、油菜籽、芝麻、向日葵籽、胡麻籽（亚麻籽）和其他油料。不包括大豆，也不包括木本油料和野生油料。花生以带壳干花生计算。

57. 水产品产量 指人工养殖的水产品和天然生长的水产品捕捞量，包括海水的鱼类、虾蟹类、贝类和藻类以及内陆水域的鱼类、虾蟹类和贝类，不包括淡水生植物。

58. 猪、牛、羊肉产量 指当年出栏并已屠宰后除去头蹄下水后带骨肉的重量（即胴体重）。

59. 耕地面积 指可以用来种植农作物、经常进行耕锄的田地，除包括熟地、当年新开荒地、连续撂荒未满三年的耕地和当年的休闲地（轮歇地）外，还包括以种植农作物为主并附带种植桑树、茶树、果树和其他林木的土地，以及沿海、沿湖地区已围垦利用的“海涂”、“湖田”等面积。但不包括属于专业性的桑园、茶园、果园、果木苗圃、林地、芦苇地、天然或人工草地面积。

60. 农作物播种面积 指实际播种或移植有农作物的面积。凡是实际种植有农作物的面积，不论种植在耕地上还是种植在非耕地上，均包括在农作物播种面积中，同时还包括因遭灾而重新改种和补种的农作物面积。目前，农作物播种面积主要包括粮食、油料、棉花、麻类、糖料、烟叶、药材、蔬菜、瓜类和其他农作物等十大类。

61. 有效灌溉面积 指具有一定的水源，地块比较平稳，灌溉工程或设备已经配套，在一般年景下当年能够进行正常灌溉耕地面积。在一般情况下，该面积应等于灌溉工程或设备已经配套，能够进行正常灌溉的水田和水源地面积之和。

62. 农用化肥使用量 指本年内实际用于农业生产的化肥数量，包括氮肥、磷肥、钾肥和复合肥。并要求按折纯量计算数量。折纯量指氮肥、磷肥、钾肥分别按氮、五氧化二磷、钾的100%成分进行折纯后的数量，复合肥按其所含主要成分折算的。

63. 农业机械总动力 指主要用于农、林、牧、渔业的各种动力机械的动力总和。包括耕作机械、排灌机械、收获机械、农产品加工机械、运输机械、植物保护机械、牧业机械、林业机械、渔业机械和其他农业机械[内燃机按引擎马力折成瓦（特）计算，电动机按功率折成瓦（特）计算]。不包括专门用于乡、镇、村、组办工业、基本建设、非农业运输、科学试验和教学等非农业生产方面用的动力机械与作业机械。但从事农副产品初级加工的村户工业的机械动力统计在内。

64. **期初（末）畜禽存栏数** 指本期期初（末）农村各种合作经济组织和国营农场、农民个人、机关、团体、学校、工矿企业、部队等单位以及城镇居民饲养的大牲畜、猪、羊、家禽等畜禽的存栏数。从1997年起，猪及家禽调查方法，由全面调查改为抽样调查。

65. **工　业** 指从事自然资源的开采，对采掘品和农产品进行加工和再加工的物质生产部门。具体包括：（1）对自然资源的开采，如采矿、晒盐、森林采伐等（但不包括禽兽捕猎和水产捕捞）；（2）对农副产品的加工、再加工，如粮油加工、食品加工、轧花、缫丝、纺织、制革等；（3）对采掘品的加工、再加工，如炼铁、炼钢、化工生产、石油加工、机器制造、木材加工等，以及电力、自来水、煤气的生产和供应等；（4）对工业品的修理、翻新，如机器设备的修理、交通运输工具（包括小卧车）的修理等。

66. **轻工业** 指主要提供生活消费品和制作手工工具的工业。另一定义为：指生产消费资料的工业。包括：（1）以农产品为原料的。如棉、毛、麻、丝的纺织及缝纫，皮革及其制品，纸浆及造纸，食品制造等工业；（2）以非农产品为原料的。如日用金属、日用化工、日用玻璃、日用陶瓷、化学纤维及其织品、火柴、生活用木制品等工业。轻工业产品大部分是生产消费品，一部分作为原料和半成品用于生产，如化学纤维、工业用布、纸张、盐等。

67. **重工业** 指为国民经济各部门提供物质技术基础的主要生产资料的工业。按其生产性质和产品用途，可以分为下列三类：（1）采掘（伐）工业，是指对自然资源的开采，包括石油开采、煤炭开采、金属矿开采、非金属矿开采和木材采伐等工业；（2）原材料工业，是指向国民经济各部门提供基本材料、动力和燃料的工业。包括金属冶炼及加工、炼焦及焦炭化学、化工原料、水泥、人造板以及电力、石油和煤炭加工等工业；（3）加工工业，是指对工业原材料进行再加工制造的工业。包括装备国民经济各部门的机械设备制造工业、金属结构、水泥制品等工业，以及为农业提供的生产资料如化肥、农药等工业。

根据上述划分原则，修理业中以重工业产品为修理作业对象的划为重工业，反之划为轻工业。

68. **工业总产值** 指工业企业在报告期内生产的以货币形式表现的工业最终产品和提供工业劳务活动的总价值量。包括：生产的成品价值、对外加工费收入、自制半成品在制品期末期初差额价值。

69. **工业销售产值** 指以货币表现的工业企业在一定时期内销售的本企业生产的工业产品总量。包括已销售的成品、半成品价值，对外提供的工业性作业价值和对本单位基本建设部门、生活福利部门等提供的产品和工业性作业及自制设备的价值。已销售的成品、半成品不论是本期生产的、还是上期生产的，只要是本期销售出去的均包括在内。对外提供的工业性作业是指企业按合同对外提供的工业性劳务。企业为本单位基本建设部门、生活福利部门等提供的产品和工业性作业及自制设备也应视同销售，这部分也作为销售统计。

工业销售产值的计算范围、计算价格和计算方法与工业总产值一致，但两者计算的基础不同；工业销售产值计算的基础是产品销售总量，工业总产值计算的基础是工业产品生产总量。

70. **应收账款** 指企业因销售商品、提供劳务等经营活动，应向购货单位或接受劳务单位收取的款项，主要包括企业销售商品或提供劳务等应向有关债务人收取的价款及代购货单位垫付的包装费、运杂费等。

71. **实收资本** 指企业各投资者实际投入的资本（或股本）总额，包括货币、实物、无形资产等各种形式的投入。按投资主体可分为国家资本、集体资本、法人资本、个人资本、港澳台资本和外商资本。

72. **资产总计** 指企业过去的交易或者事项形成的、由企业拥有或者控制的、预期会给企业带来经济利益的资源。

73. **流动资产合计** 资产满足以下条件之一应归为流动资产：（1）预计在一个正常营业周期中变现、出售或耗用，主要包括存货、应收账款等；（2）主要为交易目的而持有；（3）预计在资产负债表日起一年内（含一年）变现；（4）自资产负债日起一年内，交换其他资产或清偿负债的能力不受限制的现金或现金等价物。

74. **固定资产合计** 指企业为生产商品、提供劳务、出租或经营管理而持有的，使用寿命超过一个会计年度的有形资产。

75. **固定资产原价** 指固定资产的成本，包括企业在购置、自行建造、安装、改建、扩建、技术改造某项固定资产时所发生的全部支出总额。

76. **累计折旧** 指企业在报告期末提取的历年固定资产折旧累计数。

77. **本年折旧** 指企业在报告期内提取的固定资产折旧合计数。根据会计“财务状况变动表”中“固定资产折旧”项的数值填报。

78. **负债合计** 指企业过去的交易或者事项形成的，预期会导致经济利益流出企业的现时义务。负债一般按偿还期长短分为流动负债和非流动负债。

79. **流动负债合计** 负债满足下列条件之一的应归为流动负债：（1）预计在一个正常营业周期中清偿；（2）主要为交易目的而持有；（3）自资产负债表日起一年内到期应予清偿；（4）企业无权自主地将清偿推迟至资产负债表日后一年以上。包括短期借款、应付票据、应付账款、应付职工薪酬、应交税费等项目。

80. **非流动负债** 指流动负债之外的负债。包括长期借款、应付债券等。根据会计“资产负债表”中“非流动负债合计”项目的期末余额数填报。

81. **所有者权益合计** 指企业资产扣除负债后由所有者享有的剩余权益。公司的所有者权益又称股东权益。包括实收资本、资本公积、盈余公积、未分配利润等。

82. **主营业务收入** 指企业确认的销售商品、提供劳务等主营业务的收入。

83. **主营业务税金及附加** 指企业经营主要业务应负担的营业税、消费税、城市维护建设税、教育费附加等。

84. **利税总额** 指企业产品销售税金及附加、应交增值税和利润总额之和。

85. **工业成本费用利润率** 该指标反映工业投入的生产成本及费用的经济效益，同时也反映企业降低成本所取得的经济效益。计算公式为：

工业成本费用利润率=利润总额/成本费用总额

86. **工业产品销售率** 该指标反映工业产品已实现销售的程度，是分析工业产销衔接情况、研究工业产品满足社会需求的指标。计算公式为：

工业产品销售率＝（现价工业销售产值/现价工业总产值）×100%

87. **建筑业总产值** 是以货币表现的建筑业企业在一定时期内生产的建筑业产品和服务的总和。建筑业总产值包括三部份内容：

① 建筑工程产值：指列入建筑工程预算内的各种工程价值。

② 设备安装工程产值：指设备安装工程价值。

③ 其他产值：指房屋构筑物修理产值、非标准设备制造产值、总包企业向分包企业收取的管理费以及不能明确划分的施工活动所完成的产值。

88.**竣工产值** 一般是以单位工程为对象,当该工程按照设计所规定的工程内容全部完成,达到了设计规定的交工条件,经有关部门检查验收鉴定合格的单位工程价值工程,即为竣工产值。竣工产值包括范围应是报告期内竣工单位工程从开工到竣工的全部自行完成的价值，如果一个单位工程跨两个年度施工,其竣工价值应当包括上年度完成的价值。有些大型单位工程，如大型厂房、高级宾馆、各种管道、公路、铁路等，能够分跨、分层、分段施工并按合同规定，能够分开交付使用的，可以分开计算竣工产值。竣工产值不包括附属辅助企业或内部核算的其他单位为外单位生产和服务的价值。

89.**房屋建筑施工面积** 指报告期内施过工的全部房屋建筑面积，它包括本期新开工的面积、上期跨入本期继续施工的房屋面积、上期停缓建在本期恢复工的房屋面积、本期竣工的房屋面积以及本期施工后又停缓建的房屋面积。

90.**房屋建筑竣工面积** 指在报告期内房屋建筑按照设计要求已全部完工，达到了使用条件，经检查验收鉴定合格的房屋建筑面积。计算房屋竣工面积，必须严格执行房屋竣工验收标准。对民用建筑来讲，一般应按设计要求在土建工程和房屋本身附属的水、卫、气、暖等工程已经完工，通风、电梯等设备已安装完毕，做到水通、灯亮、经验收鉴定合格，并正式交付使用单位后，才能计算竣工面积。对于工业及科研单位等生产性房屋建筑：一般应按设计要求在土建工程（包括水、暖、电、卫、通风）及属于房屋组成部分的生活间、操作间等已经完成，经验收合格后才计算竣工面积。只差安装工艺设备、管线工程的亦可以计算竣工面积。

91. **自有机械设备年底总台数** 指归本企业（或单位）所有，属于本企业固定资产的生产性机械设备年末总台数。包括施工机械、生产设备、运输设备以及其他设备。

92. **自有施工机械设备年底总功率** 指本企业（或单位）自有施工机械、生产设备、运输设备以及其他设备等列为在册固定资产的生产性机械设备年末总功率，按设定能力或查定能力计算。包括机械本身的动力和为该机械服务的单独动力设备，如电动机等。计量单位用千瓦，动力换算可按1马力＝0.735千瓦折合成千瓦数。电焊机、变压器、锅炉不计算动力。

93. **工程结算收入** 指企业（或单位）按承包工程实现的工程价款结算收入，以及向发包单位收取的除工程价款以外的按规定列作营业收入的各种款项，如临时设施费、劳动保险费、施工机械调迁费等以及向发包单位收取的各种索赔款。

94. **工程结算利润** 指已结算工程实现的利润。如为亏损以“-”号表示。其计算公式为：

工程结算利润＝工程结算收入-工程结算成本-工程结算税金及附加。

95. **公路里程** 指在一定时期内实际达到《公路工程技术标准JTJ0l—88》规定的等级公路，并经公路主管部门正式验收交付使用的公路里程数。其计算单位为：KM。它包括大中城市的郊区公路以及通过小城镇街道部分的公路里程，也包括桥梁、渡口的长度，但不包括大中城市的街道、厂矿、林区生产用道和农业生产用道的里程。两条或多条公路共同经由同一路段，只计算一次，不得重复计算里程长度。公路里程是反映公路建设发展规模的重要指标，也是计算运输网密度等指标的基础资料。

96. **内河航道里程** 也称“内河通航里程”，是反映内河水运网规模、水平和发展情况的主要指标，是指在一定时期内，能通航运输船舶及排筏的天然河流、湖泊水库、运河及通航渠道的长度。包括全年季节性通航累计三个月以上的航道，但不包括仅供零散流放竹、木排的河道。

97. **货（客）运量** 指在一定时期内，各运输部门实际运送的货物（旅客）数量。是反映运输业为国民经济和人民生活服务的数量指标，也是制定和检查运输生产计划，研究运输发展规模和速度的重要指标。货运按吨计算，客运按人计算。货物不论运输距离长短，货物类别，均按实际重量统计；旅客不论行程远近或票价多少，均按一人一次作为客运量统计。半价票、小孩票也按一人统计。

98. **货物（旅客）周转量** 指在一定时期内，由各种运输工具运送的货物（旅客）数量与其相应运输距离的乘积之总和，是反映运输业生产总成果的重要指标，也是编制和检查运输生产计划，计算运输效率、劳动生产率以及核算运输单位成本的主要基础资料。通常以吨公里和人公里为计算单位。计算货物周转量通常按发出站与到达站之间的最短距离，也就是计费距离计算。

99. **邮电业务总量** 指以价值量形式表现的邮电通信企业为社会提供各类邮电通信服务的总数量。邮电业务量按专业分类包括函件、包件、汇票、报刊发行、邮政快件、特快专递、集邮、固定电话、出租电路、移动电话、分组交换数据通信、出租代维等。计算方法为各类产品乘以相应的平均单价（不变价）之和，再加上出租电路和设备、代用户维护电话交换机和线路等的服务收入。

100. **移动电话用户** 是指通过移动电话交换机进入移动电话网、占用移动电话号码的电话用户。用户数量以报告期末在移动电话营业部门实际办理登记手续进入移动电话网的户数进行计算，一部移动电话统计为一户。

101. **英特网用户数** 指办理登记手续且已接入国际互联网的用户数，包括局域网、城域网和广域网，包括拨号上网用户和专线上网用户。

102. **社会消费品零售总额** 指各种经济类型的批发零售贸易业、住宿餐饮业和其他行业对城乡居民和社会集团的消费品零售额总和。这个指标反映通过各种商品流通渠道向居民和社会集团供应的生活消费品来满足他们生活需要，是研究人民生活、社会消费品购买力、货币流通等问题的重要指标。

103. **批发零售贸易业** 指不直接从事商品的生产，而是从工农业生产者或从商品流通企业购进商品，不做任何加工，或只做简单的加工（如清洗、整理、分类、包装等），通过转卖以获取经济利益的单位。

104. **住宿业** 指有偿为顾客提供临时住宿的服务活动。

105. **餐饮业** 指在一定的场所内，以烹饪、调制等手段，向购买者提供各种主要供现场消费的食品、饮料，并且所提供的这种服务要大于所提供的其他服务（如娱乐）的单位。

106. **限额以上批发企业** 指年主营业务收入在2000万元及以上的批发贸易企业。

107. **限额以上零售企业** 指年主营业务收入在500万元及以上的零售企业。

108. **限额以上餐饮企业** 指年主营业务收入在200万元及以上的餐饮企业。

109. **商品销售总额** 指对本企业以外的单位和个人出售的商品（包括售给本单位消费用的商品）金额。这个指标反映批发零售贸易企业在国内市场上销售商品以及出口商品的总量。包括：（1）售给城乡居民和社会集团消费的商品；（2）售给工业、农业等各行业作为生产、经营使用的商品；（3）售给批发零售贸易业作为转卖或加工后转卖的商品；（4）对国（境）外直接出口的商品。

110. **商品交易市场成交额** 指在消费品市场与生产资料市场买卖双方（包括农民、非农业居民、机关、团体、工商企业、个体商贩）成交的全部商品金额，是反映商品交易市场规模的综合性指标。

111. **私营企业注册资本** 指私营企业办理开业登记，或变更登记时核准的资金数，不包括银行贷款。

112. **个体工商业户数** 指已经领取《营业执照》或《临时营业执照》的个体工商户的数量。

113. **个体工商业从业人员** 指经过工商行政管理部门核准的、参加经营活动并领取报酬的所有人员，包括个体经营者本人、帮手、学徒等。

114. **个体工商业注册资金** 指申请登记或变更登记时核准的资金。

115. **利用外资** 指我国各级政府、部门、企业和其他经济组织通过对外借款、吸收外商直接投资以及用其他方式筹措的境外现汇、设备、技术等。

116. **外商直接投资** 是指外国企业和经济组织或个人（包括华侨、港澳台胞以及我国在境外注册的企业）按我国有关政策、法规，用现汇、实物、技术等在中国大陆开办外商独资企业、与中国大陆的企业或经济组织共同举办中外合资经营企业、合作经营企业或者合作开发资源的投资（包括外商投资收益的再投资）以及经政府有关部门批准的项目投资总额内，企业从境外借入的资金。

117. **对外承包工程** 包括各对外承包公司以招标议标承包方式承揽的下列业务（1）承包国外工程建设项目。（2）承包我国对外经援项目。（3）承包我国驻外机构的工程建设项目。（4）与外国承包公司合营或联合承包工程项目时我国公司分包部分。（5）以服务成果向业主收费的技术服务项目（包括承担地形地貌测绘；地质资源勘探与普查；建设区域规划；提供设计文件、图纸、生产工艺技术资料和工程技术经济咨询；工程项目的可行性考察、研究和评估；进行技术指导和培训人员等）。（6）对外承包兼营的房屋开发业务。对外承包工程的营业额是以货币表现的本期内完成的对外承包工程的工作量，包括以前年度签订的合同和本年度新签订的合同在报告期完成的工作量。

118. **对外劳务合作** 指以收取工资的形式向业主或承包商提供技术和劳动服务的活动。我国对外承包公司在境外开办的合营企业，中国公司同时又提供劳务的，其劳务部分也纳入劳务合作统计。劳务合作营业额按报告期内向雇主提交的结算数（包括工资、加班费和奖金等）统计。

119. **国际旅游人数** 指来中国大陆参观、访问、旅行、探亲、访友、休养、考察、参加会议和从事经济、科技、文化、教育、体育、宗教等活动的外国人、华侨、港澳和台湾同胞的人数。不包括外国在我国的常驻机构，如使领馆、通讯社、企业办事处的工作人员；来我国常住的外国专家、留学生以及在岸逗留不过夜人员。

120. **全社会用电量** 指全年用电的总量，按用户的用电性质分为：“农村用电”、工业用电”、“交通运输用电”和“城乡居民生活用电”等，各类用电中均包括电力企业售给本市用户的电量、自备电厂自发自用电量（包括余热发电量）和自备电厂售给附近用户的电量以及趸售电量。

121. **工业企业能源消费量** 指工业企业在生产过程中作为燃料、原材料、动力、辅助材料使用的能源、工艺用能及非生产用能。

122. **财政总收入** 指国家财政参与社会产品分配所取得的收入，包括一般预算收入和基金预算收入。一般预算收入主要包括：

（1）各项税收，包括增值税、消费税、营业税、企业所得税、个人所得税、资源税、固定资产投资方向调节税、城市维护建设税、房产税、印花税、土地增值税、城镇土地使用税、关税、契税和耕地占用税等。

（2）行政性收费收入，指按规定纳入预算管理的行政性收费收入。

（3）专项收入，包括排污费收入、水资源费收入、教育费附加收入等。

（4）其他收入，包括基本建设贷款归还收入、基本建设收入、捐赠收入等。基金预算收入主要包括工业交通部门基金收入、社会保险基金收入、土地有偿使用收入、政府住房基金收入等。

123. 财政支出 指国家财政将筹集起来的资金进行分配使用的数额。以满足经济建设和各项事业的需要，主要包括：

（1）一般公共服务：反映政府提供一般公共服务的支出。

（2）国防：反映政府用于现役部队、国防后备力量、国防动员等方面的支出。

（3）公共安全：反映政府维护社会公共安全方面的支出。

（4）教育：反映政府教育事务支出。

（5）科学技术：反映用于科学技术方面的支出。

（6）文化体育与传媒：反映政府在文化、文物、体育、广播影视、新闻出版等方面的支出。

（7）社会保障和就业：反映政府在社会保障与就业方面的支出。

（8）医疗卫生：反映政府医疗卫生方面的支出。

（9）环境保护：反映政府环境保护支出。

（10）城乡社区事务：反映政府城乡社区事务支出。

（11）农林水事务：反映政府农林水事务支出。

（12）交通运输：反映政府交通运输方面的支出。

（13）工业商业金融等事务：反映政府工业、商业、金融等事务支出。

（14）其他支出：反映不能划分到上述功能科目的其他政府支出。

124. 中央财政收入和地方财政收入 指按财政体制划分的中央本级收入和地方本级收入。1994年税制及财政体制改革以后，属于中央财政的收入包括关税，消费税，海关代征的进口货物增值税，铁路运输企业、国有银行、国有邮政企业所得税，铁道营业税，金融保险营业税（中央），海洋石油资源税，车辆购置税（费）等；属于地方一般预算的收入包括一般营业税，固定资产投资方向调节税，房产税，城镇土地使用税，土地增值税，车船使用税，屠宰税，耕地占用税，契税等；属于中央和地方共享的收入主要有：增值税，企业所得税，城市维护建设税，个人所得税，印花税等。需要指出的是，由于近几年来中央收入和地方收入的分配方式、比例发生了较大的调整，因此，历年的数据不完全可比。

125. 存　款 指企业、机关、团体或居民根据可以收回的原则，把货币资金存入银行或其他信用机构保管并取得一定利息的一种信用活动形式。根据存款对象的不同可划分为企业存款、财政存款、机关团体存款、基本建设存款、城镇储蓄存款、农村存款等项目。它是银行信贷资金的主要来源。

126. 城乡储蓄存款余额 城乡储蓄存款，包括城镇居民储蓄存款和农民个人储蓄存款两部分，不包括居民的手存现金和工矿企业、部队、机关团体等集团存款。城乡居民储蓄存款余额指城乡居民存入银行及农村信用社储蓄的时点数（存入数扣除取出数的余额），如月末、季末或年末数额。

127. 贷　款 指银行或其他信用机构根据必须归还的原则，按一定利率，为企业、个人等提供资金的一种信用活动形式。我国银行贷款，分流动资金贷款、固定资产贷款、城乡个体工商户贷款以及农户贷款等科目。

128. 承保额（保险金额） 指保险人对被保险人负担损失补偿或约定给付的金额。它是保险合同上的最高责任额，也是计算保费的依据。

129. 保费（保险费） 指保险人根据保险合同的有关规定，为被保险人取得因约定危险事故发生所造成的经济损失补偿（或给付）权利，付给保险人的代价。

130. 保险赔款 指保险事故发生后，经查证确属保险责任范围以内的保险标的损失，保险人根据保险合同的规定履行赔偿义务，给予被保险人的款项。

131. 景气指数 亦称景气度，是对企业景气调查中的定性指标通过定量方法加工汇总，综合反映某一特定调查群体或某一社会经济现象所处的状态或发展趋势的一种指标，景气指数的数值介于0和200之间，100为景气指数的临界值。当景气指数大于100时，表明经济状况趋于上升或改善，处于景气状态，越接近200状态越好;当景气指数小于100时，表明经济状况趋于下降或恶化，处于不景气状态，越接近0状态越差。

132. 企业景气指数 亦称企业综合生产经营景气指数，是根据企业家对本企业综合生产经营情况的判断与预期（通常为对“好”、“一般”、“不佳”的选择）而编制的景气指数，用以综合反映企业的生产经营状况。

133. 企业家信心指数 亦称宏观经济景气指数，是根据企业家对企业对外部市场经济环境与宏观政策的认识、看法、判断与预期（通常为对“乐观”、“一般”、“不乐观”的选择）而编制的指数，用以综合反映企业家对宏观经济环境的感受与信心。

134. 年底实有铺装道路长度 指除土路外，路面经过铺装宽度在3.5米以上的道路，包括高级、次高级道路和普通道路。

135. 城市桥梁 指城市范围内，修建在河道上的桥梁和道路与道路立交、道路跨越铁路的立交桥，以及人行天桥。包括永久性桥和半永久性桥，不包括临时性桥、铁路桥、涵洞。

136. **城市下水道总长度** 指所有排水总管、干管、支管及暗渠、检查井、连接井进出水口等长度之和。

137. **城市污水日处理能力** 指污水处理厂每昼夜处理污水量的设计能力。

138. **城市园林绿地面积** 指城市公共绿地、专用绿地、生产绿地、防护绿地、郊区风景名胜区的全部面积。

139. **公园绿地** 指城市中向公众开放的、以游憩为主要功能，有一定的游憩设施和服务设施，同时兼有健全生态、美化景观、防灾减灾等综合作用的绿化用地。

140. **年底自来水生产能力** 指年底城建部门管理的自来水厂和自备水源的社会单位取水、净化、送水、出厂输水干管等环节的实际生产能力。

141. **年底实有公共汽车** 指年底可参加营运的全部车辆数，包括年底营运车辆和库存查封未参加营运的车辆，不包括非营运车辆，如架线车、油罐车、工程车、货车及其他专用车辆和借入的客运车辆。

142. **营运线路长度** 指设置的固定营运的线路长度，包括郊区营运线路长度。不包括临时行驶的线路长度。

143. **年底供水管道长度** 指从送水泵到用户水表之间所有管道的长度。

144. **全年供水总量** 指公用自来水厂和自备水源的社会单位全年的供水总量，包括有效供水量及损失水量。

145. **生活用水量** 指居民日常生活与公共福利设施的用水量。包括居民、饮食店、旅馆、医院、理发店、浴池、洗衣店、游泳池、商店、学校、机关、部队等单位的用水量。

146. **城市人口用水普及率** 指城市用水的非农业人口数（不包括临时人口和流动人口）与城市非农业人口总数之比，计算公式：

用水普及率＝城市用水的非农业人口数/城市非农业人口数×100%

147. **输气管道长度** 指由压缩机、鼓风机、储气罐的出口到用户立管之间的全部管道长度。

148. **全年供气总量** 指全年售给各类用户的全部煤气量。包括工业用量、家庭用量和其他用量。

149. **城市用气普及率** 指使用煤气（包括人工煤气、液化石油气、天然气）的城市非农业人口数（不包括临时人口和流动人口）与城市非农业人口总数之比。计算公式：

城市用气普及率＝城市用气的非农业人口数/城市非农业人口数×100%

150. **废水排放总量** 指生产废水和生活污水的排放总量。生产废水指企、事业单位在生产、科研过程中向外排放的所有排放口的废水量总和。生活污水指城镇居民区和企、事业单位职工集中居住区排放的污水量。

151. **工业废水排放总量** 指经过工业企业厂区所有排放口排到企业外部的工业废水量。包括外排的直接冷却水、超标排放的矿井地下水和与工业废水混排的厂区生活污水，不包括外排的间接冷却水（清污不分流的间接冷却水应计算在内）。

152. **工业废水排放达标量** 指全面达到国家、地方排放标准的外排工业废水量。包括经过处理后达标外排的和未经处理达标外排的两部分工业废水。国家排放标准见国标（GB8978—88）。

153. **废气排放总量** 指燃料燃烧和生产工艺过程中排放的各种废气总量，以标准状态下每年万标立方米表示。

154. **工业固体废物综合利用量** 指已用作农业肥料、造田、生产建筑材料、筑路以及其他方式综合利用的固体废物量（包括当年利用往年的工业固体废物堆存量）。综合利用量由原产固体废物的单位统计。

155. **工业固体废物处置量** 指以符合环境保护要求的方式将固体废物放置在不再回取的场所的固体废物量，如填埋、焚烧、经封场处理的专业贮存场（库）、深层灌注、回填矿井等（包括当年处置往年的堆存量）。

156. **工业粉尘排放量** 指工业企业在生产工艺过程中排放的固体微粒总重量。如钢铁企业的耐火材料粉尘、焦化企业的筛焦系统粉尘、烧结机的粉尘、石灰窑的粉尘、建材企业的水泥粉尘等。不包括电厂排入大气的烟尘。

157. **R & D** 是“研究与发展”（Research and Development）的英文缩写。其含义是指在科学技术领域（包括自然科学、农业科学、医药科学、工程与技术科学、人文与社会科学领域），为了增加知识的总量，以及运用这些知识而进行的系统的、创造性的活动。R&D包括基础研究、应用研究、试验发展三类活动。

158. **独立研究与开发机构** 指有明确的任务和研究方向，有一定学术水平的业务骨干和一定数量的研究人员，具有研究、开发、开展学术工作的基本条件，主要进行科学研究与技术开发活动，并且在行政上有独立的组织形式，财务上独立核算盈亏，有权与其他单位签订合同，在银行有单独户头的单位。

159. **科学家和工程师** 指具有大学本科以上学历的人员和不具备上述学历但已评定为高、中级职称的人员。

160. **独立研究与开发机构职工** 指在科学研究与技术开发机构工作，并由其支付工资的各种人员。包括长期职工和临时职工，不包括编制以外的离休、退休人员和停薪留职人员，但包括招聘人员。

161. **研究与发展经费支出** 指报告期内用于研究与实验发展课题活动（基础研究、应用研究、实验发展）的全部实际支出。包括用于研究与发展课题活动的直接支出，还包括间接用于研究与发展活动的一切支出。

162. **发 明** 专利法及其实施细则所称的发明是指对有关产品、方法或其改进所提出的新的技术方案。

163. **实用新型** 专利法及其实施细则所称的实用新型是指对产品的形状、构造或者其结合所提出的适于实用的新的技术方案。

164. **外观设计** 专利法及其实施细则所称的外观设计是指对产品形状、图案、色彩或者其结合所作出的富有美感并适于工业上应用的新设计。

165. 网上登记技术合同数　指本地区在全国技术合同网上登记系统中登记的技术合同数。

166. 网上登记技术合同成交金额　指本地区在全国技术合同网上登记系统中登记的技术合同成交金额。

167. 科技企业孵化器　是指以促进科技成果转化、培养高新技术企业和企业家为宗旨的科技创业服务机构。包括科技创业服务中心、大学科技园、归国留学人员创业园、软件园等综合型、专业技术型科技企业孵化器。

168. 在孵企业总收入　指在统计年度内由孵化器孵化的企业所实现的技、工、贸等各种收入之和。

169. 在孵企业从业人员　指本报告期末在孵化器孵化的企业的人员总数。

170. 毕业企业　指经孵化器扶持，发展到一定规模后脱离孵化器实现独立发展的企业。（毕业企业的数据仅按毕业时的数据累计，不进行跟踪）。

171. 普通高等学校　是指按国家规定的设置标准和审批程序批准举办的，通过全国普通高等教育统一招生考试，招收高中毕业生为主要培养对象，实施高等学历教育的全日制大学、独立设置的学院和高等专科学校、高等职业学校及其他机构（独立学院和分校、大专班）。

172. 成人高等学校　是指按国家规定的设置标准和审批程序批准举办的，通过全国成人高等教育统一招生考试,招收具有高中毕业或同等学历的人员为主要培养对象，利用函授、业余、脱产的多种形式对其实施高等学历教育的学校。包括：职工高等学校、农民高等学校、管理干部学院、教育学院、独立函授学院、广播电视大学、其他机构。

173. 专任教师数　教师是指专职从事教学工作的人员，包括临时调去帮助做其他工作的人员，不包括调离教学岗位担负行政领导工作的原教学人员。

174. 文化事业机构　指从事专业文化工作和为专业文化工作服务的独立建制的单独核算的单位。不包括这些单位另外举办独立核算的其他机构和各部门的业余文化组织。

175. 艺术表演团体　指从事戏曲、音乐、舞蹈、杂技等专业艺术表演，有独立账户，实行单独核算的团体。不包括半工半艺、半农半艺的业余剧团。

176. 艺术表演观众人数（人次）　指售票、包场演出或民族地区免费演出的艺术表演观众人次数。不包括彩排审查和内部观摩演出的观看人次数。

177. 医　院　指名称为医院，设有固定床位能收容病人住院并能为病人提供医疗、护理服务的医疗机构。包括县及以上医院、其他医院两部分。按所属性质分为卫生部门、工业及其他部门、集体所有制单位3类。其中县及以上医院按业务性质分为综合医院和专科医院。

178. 卫生技术人员　指卫生事业机构支付工资的全部固定职工和合同制职工中现任职务为卫生技术工作的专业人员。包括中医师、西医师、中西医结合高级医师、护师、中药师、西药师、检验师、其他技师、中医士、西医士、护士、助产士、中药剂士、西药剂士、检验士、其他技士、其他中医、护理员、中药剂员、西药剂员、检验员、其他初级卫生技术人员。

179. 医　生　指经卫生部门审查合格，从事医疗工作的专业人员。分为中医医生和西医医生。包括卫生技术人员中的中医师、西医师、中西结合高级医师、中医士、西医士和其他中医。

180. 等级运动员人数　指经考核正式批准授予等级运动员称号的人数。运动员等级分为国际级运动健将、运动健将、一级运动员、二级运动员。

181. 等级裁判员人数　指经考核正式批准授予等级裁判员称号的人数。裁判员等级分为国际裁判、国家级裁判、一级裁判、二级裁判、三级裁判。

182. 社会福利事业单位　指集中收养社会孤老、残、幼的机构。包括由民政部门管理的社会福利院、儿童福利院、精神病人福利院和城镇集体办的福利院，以及农村集体办的敬老院。

183. 社会福利事业单位收养人数　指由民政部门管理的和城镇及农村集体举办的社会福利事业单位中收养的老人、少年儿童、缺乏生活自理能力的残疾人员和精神病人。

184. 社会福利企业单位　指以安置城镇有一定劳动能力的盲、聋、哑和肢体残疾人员就业为目的，享受国家减免税待遇的国有或集体经济性质的企业。包括福利工厂、福利商品服务业、假肢厂和安置农场等单位。

185. 律　师　指受聘参加法律顾问处工作，担任法律顾问、刑（民）事代理人、刑事辩护人，办理非诉讼事件、解答法律询问，代写法律事务文书等主要从事律师业务的专职法律工作者和兼职律师。

186. 公证人员　指在国家公证机关依法办理公证事务的司法人员。包括公证员、助理公证员和在公证处工作的其他人员，

187. 办理公证文书　指公证处在一定时期内办结的公证文书件数。公证文书应按司法部规定或批准的格式制作。包括国内公证和涉外公证两部分。其中国内公证分为经济合同公证和民事法律关系公证两大类。

188. 调解人员　指在人民调解委员会担负调解民间一般民事纠纷和轻微违法行为所引起的纠纷的工作人员。包括调解委员会的委员和调解小组的调解员。

189. 调解民间纠纷　指调解委员会依照法律规定，根据自愿原则，用说服教育的方法调解民间发生的有关民事权利和义务的争执，促成当事双方达到协议和谅解，解决纠纷. 包括婚姻家庭纠纷，财产权益纠纷等。不包括法院受理的纠纷案。

APPENDIX7 EXPLANATORY NOTES ON MAIN STATISTICAL INDICATORS

1 Gross Domestic Product (GDP) refers to the final products of all resident units in a country (or a region) during a certain period of time. Gross domestic product is expressed in three different forms, i.e. value, income, and products respectively. The form of value refers to the total value of all products and services produced by all resident units during a certain period of time minus total value of intimidate input of materials and services of the nature of non-fixed assets or the summation of the value-added of all resident units; the form of income includes all the income created by all resident units and distributed primarily to all resident and non-resident units; the form of products refers to the value of all final goods and services for final use by all resident units plus the value of net exports of goods and services during a given period of time. In the practice of national accounting, gross domestic product is calculated with three approaches, i.e. production approach, income approach, and expenditure approach, which reflect gross domestic product and its composition from different aspects.

2 Comparable Prices refers to prices that removed the factors of price change so as to exactly reflect the change of aggregate when comparing the value of different periods. Two methods are used for calculating comparable prices: 1. Multiplying the output of products by their fixed prices of certain year; 2. Converting prices by relevant price index.

3 Constant Price refers to the average price of a given product in certain year, which is used for comparison of output value over time. As the output value at constant prices removes the factor of price changes, it reflects the trend of production development over time. Since 1949, with the changes in general price level, National Bureau of Statistics has issued nationally unified constant prices five times: the 1952 constant prices for 1949-1957; the 1957 constant prices for 1957-1971; the 1970 constant prices for 1971-1981; the 1980 constant prices for 1981-1990; and the 1990 constant prices have been used since 1991.

4 Various Planning periods The conventional division of time period in this statistical yearbook is as follows: Economic Rehabilitation Period, 1950-1952; the First Five-Year Plan period, 1953-1957; The Second Five-Year Plan period, 1958-1962; The Third Five-Year Plan period, 1966-1970; The Fourth Five-Year Plan period, 1971-1975; The Fifth Five-Year Plan period, 1976-1980;The Sixth Five-Year Plan period, 1981-1985; The Seventh Five-Year Plan period, 1986-1990;The Eighth Five-Year Plan period, 1991-1995;The Ninth Five-Year Plan period, 1996-2000;The TenthFive-Year Plan period,2001-2005;The Eleventh Five-Year Plan period,2006-2010;The Twelfth Five-year Plan period ,2011-2015.

5 Average Annual Growth Rate refers to the average growth rate year after year in a long period of time. There are two methods for calculating: one is "level approach", or the method of geometric level calculation, is the annual average growth (decrease) rate, which derived by comparing the level of the last year of the interval with that of the beginning year; the other is called "accumulative approach", or algebraic average or equation method, is the annual average growth (decrease) rate, which is derived by summation of the actual figure of each year in the interval divided by the figure in the base year. Usually, the results calculated by the two methods are fairly close, but they differed sharply when uneven economic development occurred with striking fluctuations in growth.

The average annual growth rates listed in this statistical yearbook are all calculated by "level approach". The base years are not listed when the years are listed for average annual growth rates. For example, the average annual growth rate of the 33 years since reform & opening-up implemented is listed as 1979-2011 without listing the base year 1978, the rest of the years are analogized as the same.

6 Registration Status of Enterprises Enterprises are classified into 3 categories, namely domestic-funded enterprises, enterprises with investment from Hong Kong, Macao and Taiwan, and enterprises with foreign investment, in the light of the registration status of an enterprise in industrial and commercial administration agencies. Domestic-funded enterprises include state-owned enterprises, collective-owned enterprises, cooperative enterprises, joint ownership enterprises, limited liability corporations, share-holding corporations Ltd., private enterprises and other enterprises. Included in the enterprises with investment from Hong Kong, Macao and Taiwan and enterprises with foreign investment are joint-venture enterprises, cooperative enterprises, sole investment enterprises and share-holding corporations Ltd. For government agencies, institutions and social organizations, which are not requested to be registered in industrial and commercial administration agencies, they are classified mainly by their sources of funds and way of management.

7 State-owned Enterprises refer to non-corporation economic units where the entire assets are owned by the state and which have registered in accordance with the Regulation of the People's Republic of China on the Management of Registration of Corporate Enterprises. Excluded from this category are sole state-funded corporations in the limited liability corporations.

8 Collective-owned Enterprises refer to economic units where the assets are owned collectively and which have registered in accordance with the Regulation of the People's Republic of China on the Management of Registration of Corporate Enterprises.

9 Cooperative Enterprises refer to a form of collective economic units (enterprises) where capitals come mainly from employees as their shares, with certain proportion of capital from the outside, where production is organized on the basis of independent operation, independent accounting for profits and losses, joint work, democratic management, and a distribution system that integrates remuneration according to work with dividend according to capital share.

10 Joint Ownership Enterprises refer to economic units established by two or more corporate enterprises or corporate institutions of the same or different ownership, through joint investment on the basis of equality, voluntary participation and mutual benefits. They include state joint ownership enterprises, collective joint ownership enterprises, joint state-collective enterprises, and other joint ownership enterprises.

11 Limited Liability Corporations refer to economic units established with investment from 2-50 investors and registered in accordance with the Regulation of the People's Republic of China on the Management of Registration of Corporations, each investor bearing limited liability to the corporation depending on its share of investment, and the corporation bearing liability to its debt to the maximum of its total assets. Limited liability corporations include exclusive state-funded limited liability corporations and other limited liability corporations.

12 Share-holding Corporations Ltd. refer to economic units registered in accordance with the Regulation of the People's Republic of China on the Management of Registration of Corporations, with total registered capitals divided into equal shares and raised through issuing stocks. Each investor bears limited liability to the corporation depending on the holding of shares, and the corporation bears liability to its debt to the maximum of its total assets.

13 Private Enterprises refer to profit-making economic units invested and established by natural persons, or controlled by natural persons using employed labour. Included in this category are private limited liability corporations, private share-holding corporations Ltd., private partnership enterprises and private-funded enterprises registered in accordance with the Corporation Law, Partnership Enterprises Law and Interim Regulations on Private Enterprises .

14 Other Domestic-funded Enterprises refer to domestic-funded economic units other than those mentioned above.

15 Enterprises with Investment from HongKong, Macao and Taiwan refers to enterprises set up in mainland China in the forms of joint investment,cooperation or solely-owned investment by investors from HongKong, Macao and Taiwan in accordance with foreign-related economic laws & regulations of China. They include joint-venture enterprises, cooperative enterprises & solely-owned enterprises.

16 Enterprises with Foreign Investment refers to enterprises set up in mainland China in the forms of joint investment, cooperation or solely-owned investment by foreign investors in accordance with foreign-related economic laws & regulations of China. They include joint-venture enterprises with foreign investment, cooperation enterprises with foreign investment and enterprises with sole (exclusive) foreign investment.

17 Three Industries Industry structure has been classified according to the historical sequence of development. Primary industry refers to extraction of natural resources; secondary industry involves processing of primary products;and tertiary industry provides services of various kinds for production and consumption. The above classification is universal although it varies to some extent form country to country. Industry in China comprises:

Primary industry: Farming, Forestry, Animal Husbandry and Fishery (including farming, forestry, animal husbandry ,fishery and Services).

Secondary industry: industry (including mining and quarrying, manufacturing, production and supply of electricity, water and gas) and construction.

Tertiary industry: all other industries not included in primary or secondary industry.

18 Total Population refers to the total number of people alive at a certain point of time within a given area.The annual statistics on total population is taken at midnight, the 3lst of December, excluding migrant population without household register in Changzhou city.

19 Birth Rate (or Crude Birth Rate) refers to the ratio of the number of births to the average population (or mid-period population) during a certain period of time (usually a year) which is often expressed in ‰. Birth rate in the chapter refers to annual birth rate. The following formula is used:

Birth Rate = Number of Births/Average Number of Population×1000‰

Number of births refers to live births i.e. the births when babies had showed any vital phenomena regardless of the length of pregnancy.

The current calculation of birth rate is based on data residency by the public security data of permanent residency by the family planning commission at city levels, and can also be based on annual population sampling at country and provincial levels, including the late registration for births of previous year.

Annual average number of population is the average of the number of population at the beginning of the year and that at the end of the year, and can be substituted with the mid-year population.

20 Death Rate (or Crude Death Rate) refers to the ratio of the number of deaths to the average population (or mid-period population) during a certain period of time (usually a year) which is often expressed in ‰. Death rate in the chapter refers to annual death rate. The following formula is used:

Death Rate= Number of Deaths/Annual Average Number of Population×1000‰

21 Natural Growth Rate of Population refers to the ratio of natural increase in population (number of births minus number of deaths) in a certain period of time (usually a year) to the average population (or mid-period population) of the same period which is often expressed in ‰. The following formulas are applied:

Natural Growth Rate of Population = (Number of Births-Number of Deaths)/Average Number of Population×1000‰

Natural Growth Rate of Population = Birth Rate-Death Rate

22 Life Expectancy refers to the average number of years a person of a certain age will live (or the average life-span of an age group if the pattern of morality for this age group remains as it is.)

23 Employed Persons refers to the persons engaged in social labor and receive remuneration payment or earn business income, including:(1)fully employed staff & workers in state-owned, collective-owned or other kinds of economic sectors and otherwise employed persons; (2)private and individual economic laborors in towns; (3)rural social laborers.

Persons employed in various units refers to all the persons working in government agencies of various levels, political and party organizations, social organizations, enterprises and institutions, and receiving wages or other forms of payment. They include fully-employed staff and workers, re-employed retirees, foreigners and Chinese compatriots from Hong Kong, Macao, and Taiwan working in various units, part-time employees, employees of other units working temporarily at current posts, and employees holding the second job, but exclude staff and workers who have left their working units while keeping their labour contract(employment relation)unchanged. This indicator reflects the total number of laborers actually engaged in production or other operations in various units.

24 Staff and Workers refer to the persons who work in (and receive payment therefrom) enterprises and institutions of state ownership, collective ownership, joint ownership, share holding, foreign ownership, and ownership by entrepreneurs from Hong Kong, Macao, and Taiwan, and other types of ownership and their affiliated units and get paid also include the staff and workers who have left their working units while keeping their labour contract/employment relation unchanged.

25 Fully Employed Staff and Workers refer to persons who work in, and receive wages from their working units, as well as persons who have their work posts, but are temporarily absent from work for reasons of study or on sick, injury or maternal leave and still receive wages from their working units.

26 Staff and Workers Who Have Left Working Units but Still Remaining the Relationship with the Units refer to those who have left the production or working posts due to various reasons and are not taking other positions in the same units, but whose labor relationship still remained in the units.

27 Total Wages of Persons Employed refer to the total remuneration payment to the whole staff and workers in various units during a certain period of time, including the total wages of fully employed staff and workers, the total salaries of assigned personnel and the total earnings of other employed persons.

28 Total Wages of Fully Employed Staff and Workers refers to the total remuneration payment to fully employed staff and workers in various units during a certain period of time. The calculation of total wages is based on the total remuneration payment to the staff and workers. Therefore, all the wages and salaries and other payments to staff and workers are included in the total wages regardless of their sources, category, and forms(in kind or cash).

29 Average Wage of Fully Employed Staff and Workers refers to the average wage in monetary terms per person during a certain period of time for fully employed staff and workers in various units, which is one of the main indicators reflecting the general level of wage and is calculated as follows:

Average Wage of Fully Employed Staff and Workers = Total Wages of Fully Employed Staff and Workers in Given Period / Average Number of Fully Employed Staff and Workers in Given Period.

30 Registered urban unemployed people refer to unemployed people at working age (from 16 years old to retirement age) in urban areas that have the ability to work and the need for jobs and have registered at public employment service agencies.

31 Consumer Price Index Consumer price, refers to the price that consumer goods and services purchased by urban and rural residents, is the final price of social products and services, which influences the people's livehood and lay a prominent role in the whole national economic price system. Consumer price index reflects the trend and degree of changes in prices of consumer goods purchased by residents.

32 Retail Price Index The retail price refers to the price that the residents afford for the living consumer and service. It is the final price of social products and service has a direct bearing on the people's lives and has a fairly important states in the whole national economy system.

33 Service Price Index refer to the comparative number of the expenditure of non-commercial and service consumption. The items involve: telecommunication expense, postal expense, transportation expense, hairdressing & beautification expense, culture and entertainment expense, school and baby-sitting expense, mending and other expense, medical insurance service expense, total classifications.

34 Employment Population in Urban Households refer to urban residents engaged in certain work and receiving payment for the labor or income from their business operation, including those who work in state-owned or collective units, joint ventures, foreign-owned units and private with permanent or temporary jobs. The self-employed individuals and re-employed retirees are also included. This indictor reflects the situation of urban employment and is the basic data for calculating employment rate and dependency ratio.

35 Total income of urban families refers to the total income of sample families living in urban areas, which is comprising of salary income, net income from business operation, earnings from properties and income of transfer, not including the income of rent and sale of their properties. The income is calculated on what is actually occurred. The figure, whether redeemed or paid in advance, will not be further divided when calculated.

The income from properties refers to the income from the family owned chattel (saving deposits in banks, securities), real estate (such as housing, automobiles, land and personal collections). This includes the remising of one's own properties, such as interests, rents, earning from patents, dividends from one's property circulation, added profits of properties.

The income of transfer refers to the income of sample families, made up of the country's payment transfer and inter-family payment, including retirement pension, unemployment welfare, compensation etc. The unit's transfer of payment, including job compensation, insurance premium, public reserve of housing and inter family donations.

36 Disposable income of Urban Households refers to the total amount of sample urban residents' income, which is comprised of income direct available for consumption, non-compulsory expenditure plus savings deposits, i.e. the income which could be disposed of freely. The formula of calculation is: disposable income=total income of the family – personal income tax – expenditure on social insurance – received subsidiary.

37 Total expenditure of Households refers to total actual expenditure of a household excluding that from rending, which includes all daily expenditure, housing expenditure, transfer expenditure, property expenditure and expenditure on social insurance. The statistical calculation is based on actual value of commodities or service bought, regardless of the means of payment, whether on installment or not, so long as the commodity and service has been consumed. If the commodity or service was bought on tally or installment, the difference of actual payment and payment due is put into the categories under the title of income from debit and credit.

38 Consumer Expenditure of Urban Households refers to total daily expenditure of residents, including the expenditure on foods, clothing, household appliance and service, health, education, cultural and entertainment service, housing, occasional costs and service. including goods or services used for donation.

39 Net Income of Rural Households refers to the total income of the permanent residents of the rural households during a year after the deduction of the expenses for productive and non-productive business operation, the payment for taxes and the payment for collective units for their contracted tasks, which can then be spent for investments in productive and non-productive construction, for consumption in daily life and for savings deposit. It is a comprehensive indicator to show the actual level of the income of the peasants' household. The net income of the rural households includes not only the income from the productive and non-productive business operation, but also the income from the non-business operation, such as the money remitted or brought back by the members of the household who are in other places, the government relief payment and various subsidies. It includes not only the money income, but also the income in kind. But the income from borrowing from banks, friends and relatives is excluded.

40 Able-bodied and Semi-able Bodied Laborers of Rural Households refers to permanent residents of rural households who are able to work and actually engaged in social labor, which is one factor of production and sources of rural households income. According to the relevant regulations, male aged 18-50, female aged 18-45 are considered as able bodied laborers; male aged 16-17 and 51-60, female aged 16-17 and 46-55 are considered as semi-able bodied laborers. Those who are not in above age but able to work and actually engaged in social labor are also considered as able-bodied or semi-able bodied laborers, while those who are within the above age range but unable to work are not counted as able-bodied or semi able bodied laborers.

41 Expenditure of Rural Households for Consumption refers to total expenses of rural households on daily life, including expenses on food, clothing, housing, fuel, articles for daily use, and expenses on cultural life and services. This indicator is used to show the actual consumption level of peasants, including expense on food, clothing, housing, fuel, articles for daily use, and expenditure on daily life and services.

42 Total Investment in Fixed Assets in the Whole Municipality Investment in fixed assets is the essential means for social reproduction of fixed assets. Amount of investment in fixed assets refers to the volume of activities in construction and purchases of fixed assets in monetary terms. It is a comprehensive indicator which shows the size, pace, proportional relations and use orientation of the investment in fixed assets. Total investment in fixed assets in the whole society is classified into the following parts investment as categorized by ownerships. Total value of investment: city &town collective units, real estate development, investment in rural area.

43 Investment in Real Estate Development refers to the investment by the real estate development companies, commercial buildings construction companies and other real estate development units of various types of ownership in the construction of house buildings, such as residential buildings, factory buildings, warehouses, hotels, guesthouses, holiday villages, office buildings, and the complementary service facilities and land development projects, such as roads, water supply, water drainage, power supply, heating, telecommunications, land leveling and other projects of infrastructure. It excludes the activities in simple land transactions.

44 Sources of Funds for Investment in Fixed Assets refer to various funds received during the year by fixed assets investment for construction and purchase of fixed assets. They include balance of funds bought forward from the previous year, subtotal of sources of funds in this year, and various payable funds. The subtotal of the sources of funds in this year is further divided into six categories: state budgetary investment, domestic loans, bonds, foreign investments, self-raised funds, and other sources of funds.

45 Investment in Fixed Assets by Structure refers to the three major parts of investment activities, i.e. construction and installation, purchase of equipment and instrument, and other expenses.

46 Newly Increased Fixed Assets refer to the newly increased value of fixed assets through investment, including the value of projects completed and put into production, the value of equipment, tools, and vessels considered as fixed assets, as well as the relevant expenses as investment in fixed assets. This is a comprehensive indicator of investment in fixed assets, reflecting the achievements of investment in fixed assets in different periods, different sectors, and different regions.

47 Rate of Projects of Fixed Assets Completed and Put into Operation refers to the ratio of the newly increased fixed assets to the total investment made in the same period. This is a comprehensive indicator, reflecting the speed of the employment of fixed assets and the investment efficiency.

48 Projects under Construction refer to projects having construction and installation activities undertaken in the reference period, including projects started in the reference period, or continued from the previous period, or completed and put into production or suspended in the reference period.

49 Projects Completed and Put into Use Industrial projects refer to the major projects and accessory facilities completed which result in forming production capacity and have been checked and accepted while the living and welfare facilities have been completed and can ensure normal production and formally put into production. Non-industrial projects refer to the major projects and accessory facilities completed which possess the designed capacity and have been checked, accepted and formally put into production.

50 Floor Space of Buildings under Construction and Completed refers to total floor space in each story of buildings calculated from the outside line of building walls, including both usable space and the space occupied by constructions like pillars or walls. The floor space of multi-story buildings includes the total floor space of each story (including basement).

51 Floor space under construction refers to the floor space of all buildings (including basement, semibasement and supporting buildings) is being constructed within the period of the report. It consists of the floor space newly constructed in current phase and the floor space constructed from last year to current phase, and the floor space which stopped constructing in the previous phase but restarted to construct in current phase. The floor space completed in the current phase and the floor space stopped constructing or delayed construction of the current phase shall be included in the floor space under construction. As to multi storey building, floor space completed shall be filled in the total floor space of each storey.

52 Floor space completed refers to the total of building area of all buildings which are completed as per design requirement, meet the requirements for residence and use, and are inspected and accepted as qualified or meeting the completion acceptance criteria and can be transferred to normal use.

53 Floor Space of Residential Buildings refers to the floor space of the residential buildings under construction and completed among the total space of buildings under construction and completed.

54 Gross Output Value of Farming,Forestry,Animal Husbandry and Fishery refers to the total volume of products of farming, forestry, animal husbandry and fishery in value terms and the value of all kinds of supporting serving activities to farming, forestry, animal husbandry and fishery producing activities, which reflects the total scale and total result of agricultural production during a given period of time.The statistical scopes for Farming, Forestry,Animal Husbandry and Fishery are:

(1)Farming include crop cultivation and other farming crop cultivation, include planting of grain, beans, tubers, cotton, oil bearing crops,sugar crops,fiber crops,tobacco,vegetables,medicinal materials, melons and others, as well as tea,mulberry and fruit plantation.

Other farming include gathering of wild plant fruits, fiber,gum, oil, firewood, wild medicinal materials, fungi and commodity industry run by rural household.

(2)Forestry include planting of trees (not including planting,management & harvest of tea, mulberry and fruit plantation), collection of forest products,cutting and felling of bamboo and trees by villages and other cooperative organizations under villages.

(3)Animal Husbandry include raising and grazing of any kind of animal and hunting and raising of wild animal, excluding fish breeding.

(4)Fishery include cultivation and catches of acquatic animals and seaweed.

(5) The trade of farming, forestry, animal husbandry and fishery, including irrigation service, elementary processing service of farming products, other agricultural service, forestry service, veterinarian service, other animal husbandry service, fishery service, and so on.

55 Grain Yield refers to the yield in the whole country including grains produced by state farms, collective units, industrial enterprises and mines.(Grain includes rice, wheat, corn, sorghum, millet and other miscellaneous grains as well as tubers and beans). Data on grain production before 1989 were obtained through the Comprehensive Statistical Reporting System.Since 1989,data from sample sunveys are used.

56 Yield of Oil-bearing Crops refers to the total yield of oil bearing crops of various kinds, including peanuts, (dry, in shell) rapeseeds, sesame, sunflower seeds, flax seeds, and other oil bearing crops. Soybeans, oil-bearing woody plants, and wild oil-bearing crops are not included.

57 Output of Aquatic Products refers to catches of both artificially cultured and naturally grown aquatic products, including fish, shrimps, crabs and shellfish in sea and inland water as well as seaweed. Freshwater plants are not included.

58 Output of Pork, Beef, and Mutton refers to the meat of slaughtered hogs, cattle, sheep and goats with head, feet, and offal taken away.

59 Cultivated Area (Area under cultivation) refers to farmland which is plowed constantly for growing crops, including cultivated land, newly cultivated land in the current year, farmland left without cultivation for less than three years and fallow land in the current year, rotation land, rotation land of grass and crops, farmland with some fruit trees, mulberry trees and other trees and cultivated seashore land, lake land, and etc. The land of mulberry fields, tea plantations, orchards, nurseries of young plants, forestland, reed land, natural and man-made grassland and other land are not included in cultivated land.

60 Sown Area of Crops refers to area of land sown or transplanted with crops regardless of being in cultivated area or non cultivated area. Area of land re-sown due to natural disasters is also included.At present ,the sown area of crops:grain,oil-bearing crops, cotton, hamp, sugar crops,tobacco,medicinal materials,vegetables,melons and other farm crops.

61 Irrigated Area refers to areas that are effectively irrigated, i.e. level land which has water source and complete sets of irrigation facilities to lift and move adequate water for irrigation purpose under normal conditions. Under normal conditions, irrigated area is the sum of watered fields and irrigated fields where irrigation systems or equipment have been installed for regular irrigation purpose.

62 Consumption of Chemical Fertilizers in Agriculture refers to the quantity of chemical fertilizers applied in agriculture in the year, including nitrogenous fertilizer, phosphate fertilizer, potash fertilizer, and compound fertilizer. The consumption of chemical fertilizers is required in calculation to convert the gross weight into weight containing 100% effective component (e.g. 100% nitrogen content in nitrogenous fertilizer, 100% phosphorous pentoxide contents in phosphate fertilizer, 100% potassium oxide contents in potash fertilizer). Compound fertilizer is converted with its major component.

63 Total Power of Farm Machinery refers to total mechanical power of machinery used in farming, forestry, animal husbandry, and fishery, including ploughing, irrigation and drainage, harvesting, transport, plant protection, stock breeding, forestry and fishery. The power of internal combustion engines is required to convert horsepower into watts and the power of electric motors is required to be converted into watts. Machinery employed for non-agricultural purposes, such as the machines used in township run and village-run industry, construction, non-agricultural transport, scientific experiments and teaching, is excluded.But mechanical power that engage in agriculture and sideline products for primary processing of villiage industrial mechanical power are included.

64 Number of Livestock or Poultry in Stock at Beginning (or End) refers to the total number of large animals, pigs, sheep, fowls, etc. raised by rural cooperative organizations, state farms, rural individuals, government agencies, schools, industrial and mining enterprises, army, and urban residents at the beginning (or end) of the reference period. The investigated method of the pigs and poultry has changed from overall investigation to sampling investigation since 1997.

65 Industry refers to the material production sector which is engaged in extraction of natural resources and processing and reprocessing of minerals and agricultural products, including (1) extraction of natural resources, such as mining, salt production, logging (but not including hunting and fishing); (2) processing and reprocessing of farm and sideline produces, such as rice husking, flour milling, wine making, oil pressing, cotton ginning, silk reeling, spinning and weaving, and leather making; (3) manufacture of industrial products, such as steel making, iron smelting, chemicals manufacturing, petroleum processing, machine building, timber processing; water and gas production and electricity generation and supply; (4)repairing of industrial products such as the repairing of machinery and means of transport (including cars).

66. Light Industry refers to the industry that produces consumer goods and hand tools. It also refers to the industry that produces consumer goods. The light industry consists of the following two branches: (1) the industrial sectors using agricultural products as raw materials, such as textile and sewing of cotton, wool, hemp and silk, leather and relative products, pulp and paper production, food production, etc.; (2) the industrial sectors using non-agricultural products as raw materials, such as metal, chemicals, glass, porcelain and ceramics, chemical fiber and relative fabric, matches, wood products and so on for daily use. Most of the light industrial products are production consumer goods, while some of them are used in the production of raw materials and semi-finished products, such as chemical fibers, industrial fabrics, paper products, salt, etc.

67 Heavy Industry refers to the industry, which produces capital goods, and provides various sectors of the national economy with necessary material and technical basis. It consists of the following three branches according to the purpose of production or the use of products:(1) Mining, quarrying and logging industry refers to the industry that extracts natural resources, including extraction of petroleum, coal, metal and non-metal ores and logging.(2) Raw materials industry refers to the industry that provides various sectors of the national economy with raw materials, fuels and power. It includes smelting and processing of metals, coking and coke chemistry, chemical materials and building materials such as cement, plywood, and power, petroleum refining and coal dressing. (3) Manufacturing industry refers to the industry that processes raw materials. It includes machine-building industry, which equips sectors of the national economy, industries of metal structure and cement products, industries producing means of agricultural production, such as chemical fertilizers and pesticides.

According to the above principle of classification, the repairing trades, which are engaged primarily in repairing products of heavy industry, are classified into heavy industry while these engaged in repairing products of light industry are classified into light industry.

68 Gross Industrial Output Value refers to the total volume of final industrial products produced and industrial services provided during a given period in monetary terms, including the value of finished products, the income of processing rendered to other units and the changes in the value of home-made semi-finished products between the beginning and closing of the period.

69 Industrial Sales Output Value refers to the total volume of industrial products sold by an industrial enterprise during a given period and in the form of currency. It includes the value of finished products, semi-finished products, and industrial operations rendered to other units, products, industrial operations and self-made equipment provided to the basic construction department, welfare department, etc. of the enterprise. As to those finished products and semi-finished products, no matter whether products are manufactured in this calculation period or the previous one, so long as they are sold out in this calculation period, they should be included. The industrial operations are industrial services rendered to other units according to contracts. The products, industrial operations and self-made equipment provided to basic construction department, welfare department, and etc. of the enterprise should be regarded as act of sale, and included in sales statistics.

The scope, price and method of calculation of industrial sales output value are the same as those for gross industrial output value. However, the calculation base are different: the base for sales output value is the total volume of products sold; the base for gross industrial output value is total volume of production of industrial products.

70 Accounts Receivable refer to money owed to a business on the sale of products, services and other business activities by its customers that have purchased goods or received services, mainly including money owed by concerning debtor(s) to a business on the sale of products or services, as well as the packaging costs, transport charges and so on paid in advance by a purchasing agent.

71 Paid-in Capital refers to the total capital (or equity) actually contributed to a corporation by investors in monetary terms, in kind, with intangible assets, etc. The investment entities can be divided into state capital, collective capital, corporate capital, personal capital, Hong Kong, Macao and Taiwan capital, and foreign capital.

72 Total Assets refer to all resources collected via past transactions or events of a business, owned or controlled by the business and expected to bring economic benefits to the business.

73 Total Circulating Assets refer to assets that meet one of the following conditions: (1) assets expected to be liquidated, sold or consumed within a normal business cycle, including inventory, accounts receivable, etc.; (2) assets held for trading purposes; (3) assets expected to be liquidated within one year (including one year) after the balance sheet date; and (4) cash or cash equivalents that have unrestricted ability for exchange of other assets or to pay off the liabilities within one year after the balance sheet date.

74 Total Fixed Assets refer to tangible assets, with service life over one fiscal year, held by a business for production, services, rental or operation and management.

75 Original Value of Fixed Assets refers to the cost of fixed assets, including the total amount of all expenses incurred at the time of purchase, construction, installation, reconstruction, expansion and technical improvement of a particular fixed assets.

76 Accumulated Depreciation refers to the accumulated amount of depreciation on fixed assets of a business during the past years drawn in the end of given period.

77 Depreciation Drawn in Current Year refers to the total amount of depreciation on fixed assets of a business drawn within given period, the data of which is collected according to the "Depreciation of Fixed Assets" of "Statement of Changes in Financial Position" in accounting.

78 Total Liabilities refer to the current obligations that are expected to result in outflow of economic benefits of a business incurred from past transactions or events of the said business. Liabilities are generally divided into liquid liabilities and non-liquid liabilities based on the length of the repayment period.

79 Total Liquid Liabilities refer to liabilities that meet one of the following conditions: (1) liabilities expected to be settled within a normal business cycle; (2) liabilities held for trading purposes; (3) liabilities that shall be settled within one year after the balance sheet date; and (4) liabilities that a business has no right to defer the settlement to more than one year after the balance sheet date by their own. Such liabilities include short-term borrowings, bills payable, accounts payable, remuneration payable to employees, taxes payable and other items.

80 Non-liquid Liabilities refer to liabilities other than in current liabilities, including long-term loans, bonds payable and so on, the data of which is collected according to the ending balance of "Total Non-liquid Liabilities" of "Balance Sheet" in accounting.

81 Total Creditors' Equity refers to residual interest owned by creditors in corporate assets after deducting liabilities. Company creditors' equity is also known as shareholders' equity, including paid-up capital, capital surplus, earned surplus, undistributed profits, etc.

82 Main Business Income refers to income of sales of goods and services and other main business recognized by a business.

83 Main Business Tax and Surcharges refer to the business tax, consumption tax, urban maintenance and construction tax, education surtax, etc. that should be borne by a company from main business.

84 Total Value of Profit and Tax (pre-tax Profits) refers to the total sum of profits, products sales tax and surcharges and the value added tax payable of industrial enterprises. It is also called pre-tax profits.

85 Ratio of Profits to Total Industrial Costs refers to the ratio of profits realized in a given period to the total costs in the same period, which reflects the economic efficiency of input cost and is calculated as follows:

Ratio of Profits to Total Industrial Cost(%)=(Total Profits/ Total Costs)×100%

86 Sales Ratio of Industrial Products refers to the sales of industrial products to the gross industrial output value in given period, which is important in reflecting the linkage between production and sales and the extent of the needs of the society that has been met by the supply of industrial products. It is calculated as follows:

Sales Ratio of Industrial Products = [Industrial Sales / Gross Industrial Output Value (at current prices)]×100%

87 Gross Output Value of Construction refers to total output value as expressed in monetary terms of the production and service of construction enterprises within certain period of time. The total value consists of three parts:

(1) Output value of construction projects, that is the value of projects covered by the project budgets;

(2) Output value of installation projects, that is the value of the installation of equipment, (excluding the value of the equipment to be installed);

(3) Other output value: refers to the value of production including repairing of auxiliary parts of housing, non-standard equipment manufacturing, administration cost of contractor on sub-contractor and other construction output which cannot be clearly categorized.

88 Output Value of Completed Projects usually refers to output value of single construction project concerned within reference period, calculated when the projected is completed as required by the plan of the project, meeting the requirements of turning over to the user and pass the examination of authorized department. The scope of output includes: the value created from start to completion of the projects. If the construction of the projects took more than one year, the output value should include the value completed in previous year. The output can be calculated on section by section bases on large projects if they can be divided by sections, levels of construction. Large plants, deluxe hotels, pipe work, highway, railway etc are examples of these large projects.

89 Floor Space of Buildings Under Construction refers to all the floor space of buildings in construction reported in reference period, including those starting construction, construction relayed from previous period, construction resumed after the delay of the previous period, completed construction and construction started in present period and stopped at present.

90 Floor Space of Buildings Completed refers to floor space of construction project concerned within reference period, calculated when the projected is completed as required by the plan of the project, meeting the requirements of turning over to the user and pass the examination of authorized department. The calculation of the floor space should strictly adhere to the standard requirements for check up the completion of the construction projects. For civil construction projects, generally speaking, the floor space should be calculated when the building itself and its water, sewage, gas, heating, ventilation, elevator etc have been completed according to the construction plan, passed the examination for completion and turned over to the user. For the industrial construction as well as the construction of R&D buildings, the floor space should be calculated, generally speaking, when the building was completed with water, heating, sewage and ventilation as well as auxiliary parts in living quarter and operational quarter, even without the installation of manufacturing equipment as well as pipelines.

91 Total Number of Machinery and Equipment Owned by the End of Year refers to the number of machines and equipment owned by the enterprises, and listed as the fixed assets of the enterprises by the end of the year, including machinery and equipment for construction, production and transportation.

92 Total Power of Machinery and Equipment Owned by the End of Year refers to the total power of machinery and equipment owned by the enterprises, and listed as the fixed assets of the enterprises by the end of the year, including machinery and equipment for construction, production and transportation. The power of the machinery is calculated on basis of the designed or verified capacity, covering the power of the machinery/equipment and the separate power equipment serving the machinery/equipment (such as electric motors), but excluding welders, transformers and boilers. The unit used for the calculation of power is kilowatt, with horsepower converted to kilowatt by 1 horsepower=0.735 kilowatt.

93 Income from Settlement of Projects refers to the income received by the construction enterprise from the contracted project through settlement procedures, and other charges to the contractoree as operational costs in addition to the value of the project, such as temporary facility fee, labour insurance premium , moving cost of construction equipment, as well as various types of claims to the contractee.

94 Profit from Settlement of Projects refers to profit realized through settled projects."-"expresses loss-incrring.It is calculated with the following formula:

Profit from Settlement of Projects=Income from Settlement of Projects-Settled Cost-Settled Taxes and Extra Charges

95 Length of Highways refers to the length of highways which are builted in conformity with the grades specified by the Highway Engineering Standard JTJ01-88 formulated by the Ministry of Communications,and have been formally checked and accepted by the departments of highways and put into use. The length of highways includes that of the suburb highways at large and medium-sized cities, highways passing through streets at small cities and towns, and also the length of bridges and ferries. It does not include the length of streets in big and medium-sized cities and highways built for the production purpose at factories, mines, forest areas and agricultural areas. If two or more highways go the same section of the way, the length of the section is only calculated for once and no duplication is allowed. The length of highways is an important indicator to show the development of the highway construction and to provide essential information to calculate the transport network density.

96 Length of Navigable Inland Waterways an indicator reflecting the size and development of inland water network, it refers to the length of the natural rivers, lakes, reservoirs, canals, and ditches open to navigation during a given period, which enables the transport by ships and rafts. It includes the channels open to navigation for over an accumulative 3 months in a year, yet this does not include the river courses which are only used to float odd logs and bamboo rafts.

97 Freight (Passenger) Traffic refers to the volume of freight (passenger) transported with various means. Freight transport is calculated in tons and passenger traffic is calculated in the number of persons. Despite the type of freight and travelling distance, the freight transport is calculated in the actual weight of the goods: and despite the travelling distance and ticket price, the passenger traffic is calculated by the principle that one person can be counted only once in one travel. The passenger who travels with a half price ticket or a child ticket is also calculated as one person. The freight (passenger) traffic provides a quantitative measure to show how the transport industry serves the national economy and people, and is also an important indicator for planning the transport industry and for studying the development scale and speed of the transport industry.

98 Freight Ton-kilometers (Passenger-kilometers) refer to the sum of the products of the volume of transported cargo (passengers) multiplying by the transport distance, usually using ton-kilometer and passenger-kilometer as units for measurement. Normally, the shortest distance between the departure station and the destination station (i.e., the payable distance) is the basis to calculate the freight ton-kilometers. This is an important indicator to show the total results of the transport industry, to prepare and examine the transport plan and to measure the efficiency, the labor productivity and the unit cost of transport.

99 Business Volume of Post and Telecommunications Services refer to the total amount of services provided to society by post and telecommunications enterprises with the form of value. Post and telecommunications services can be divided by category as letter, parcel, bill of draft, newspaper and magazine distribution, EMS, philately, fixed telephone, lending circuit, mobile phone, packet switched data traffic and lending telephone switchboard maintenance. The calculation method shall be the sum of various kinds of product time average unit price (fixed price) then plus the service incomes from lending circuit, telephone switchboard and circuit maintenance on behalf of customers.

100 Mobile Telephone Subscribers refer to subscribers of the telephone using mobile telephone network, and occupying mobile telephone number. The number of subscribers shall be calculated as per the number dealt with the formalities of mobile telephone network at cell-phone business office as of the report date, each cell-phone shall be recorded as one subscriber.

101 Number of Internet Subscribers refers to the number of subscribers who have registered and accessed into the international network, including local network area, metropolitan area network, wide area network, and dial-up network subscribers and private wire network subscribers.

102 Total Retail Sales of Consumer Goods refers to the sum of retail sales of consumer goods sold by all sectors of the national economy to urban and rural residents and social groups. This indicator is used to show the supply of consumers goods through various channels to households and institutions, and is very important for the study on people's livelihood, on the purchasing power of consumer goods and on the circulation of money.

103 Wholesale and Retail Sales Trade refers to units not directly involved in the manufacturing of commodities, rather purchasing the commodity from manufacturers or circulating units without processing, or with simple processing (cleaning, tidying, categorizing, packaging, etc) and achieving benefits by reselling the commodities.

104 Accommodation refers to service provided to clients with payment.

105 Catering trade refer to the units offer various food and drinks consumed at once in certain places and this kind of service is more important than other services (entertainment, e.g.) offered.

106 Wholesale enterprises above designated size refer to wholesale companies with the main business income of more than RMB 20 million yuan.

107 Retail enterprises above designated size refer to retail companies with the main business income of more than RMB 5 million yuan.

108 Catering enterprises above designated size refer to catering companies with the main business income of more than RMB 2 million yuan.

109 Total Sales of Commodities refer to value of commodities sold by the establishments to other establishments and individuals (including direct export). This indicator reflects the total value of sales of commodities at domestic markets and export, including: (1) commodities sold to urban and rural residents and social groups for their consumption;(2) commodities sold to establishment in all industries for their production and opration;(3) commodities sold to wholesale and retail establishments for re-selling with or without further processing;(4) commodities for direct exprt to abroad.

110 Value of Business Transaction in Trading Markets refers to the total volume between the buyers of consumption market and sellers of production goods market, which includes farmers, non-agricultural people, government offices, organizations, industrial and commercial enterprises and individual sellers, and which serves as the comprehensive index of the dimensions of trading markets.

111 Registered Capital of Private Enterprises refer to the checked registered capital when the private enterprises do the start or change registered, exclude the bank loans.

112 The Units of the Private owned industrial and Commercial Enterprises refers to the amount of the private owned industrial and commercial enterprises, which have got the business licence or the temporary business licences.

113 Staff and Workers in the Private Owned Industrial and Commercial Enterprises refer to the whole people take part in the business and get paid, which are checked by the industrial and commercial department, involved the manager of the private industrial and commercial enterprises, helper and the apprentices.

114 Registered Capital of the Private owned Industrial and commercial enterprises refer to the checked registered capital when apply for or change the registration.

115 Utilization of Foreign Capital refers to remittance, equipment and technology financed from abroad, by loans, foreign direct investment and other forms undertaken by the Chinese governments at all levels, by various departments, enterprises and other economic units.

116 Direct Investment by Foreign Entrepreneurs refers to the investments inside China by foreign enterprises and economic organizations or individuals (including overseas Chinese, compatriots from Hong Kong and Macao, and Chinese enterprises registered abroad), following the relevant policies and laws of China, for the establishment of ventures exclusively with foreign own investment, Sino-foreign joint ventures and cooperative enterprises or for cooperative exploration of resources with enterprises or economic organizations in China. It includes the re-investment of the foreign entrepreneurs with the profits gained from the investment and the funds that enterprises borrow from abroad in the total investment of projects which are approved by the relevant department of the government.

117 Contracted Projects with Foreign Countries refers to projects undertaken by Chinese contractors (project contracting companies) through bidding process. They include: (1) overseas civil engineering construction projects financed by foreign investors. (2) overseas projects financed by the Chinese government through its foreign aid programs. (3) construction projects of Chinese diplomatic missions, trade offices and other institutions stationed abroad. (4) construction, projects in China Financed by foreign investment.(5) sub-contracted projects to be taken by Chinese contractors through a joint umbrella project with foreign contractor(Including bear terrain mapping; geological resource exploration and census ;construction regional planning; provide the design documents, drawings, production technology and engineering technical economic advice; feasibility investigation, research and evaluation of project;carry out technical guidance and training personnel);(6) housing development projects. The business income from international contracted projects is the work volume of contracted projects completed during the reference period, expressed in monetary terms, including completed work on projects singed in previous years.

118 Service Cooperation with Foreign Countries refers to the activities of providing technology and labor services to employers or contractors in the forms of receiving salaries and wages. Labor services providing by contractual joint ventures of Chinese international contracting corporations should be included in the statistics of service cooperation with foreign countries. The business income of labor service cooperation is the income in the form of wages and salaries, overtime pay, bonuses and other remuneration received from the employers during the reference period.

119 International Tourists refers to foreigners, overseas Chinese, Chinese compatriots from Hong Kong, Macao and Taiwan coming to China for sightseeing, visits, tours, family reunions, vacations, study tours, conferences and other activities of a business, scientific and technological, cultural, educational and religious nature. It does not include representatives and employees of resident institutions of foreign countries in China such as embassies, consulates, news agencies and offices of foreign companies and organizations, nor does it include long term foreign experts or students residing in China, or persons in transition without spending a night in China.

120 Total Electricity Consumption refer to the total amount of electricity consumed, it can be divided into "countryside used electricity","industry used electricity","transportation used electricity","urban and rural residents used electricity"and so on, all kinds of the electricity consumption all involved the electricity sold to the city's consumer by power stations, the electricity produced for self use (involved the electricity made by the waste heat).

121 Energy Consumption of Industry Enterprises refer to the energy, artificial used energy and energy used in other fields as fuel, material and supplementary material.

122 Total Fiscal Revenue refers to the revenue obtained of the government finance by means of participating in distribution of social products, including normal budgetary revenue and fund budgetary revenue. The normal budgetary revenue mainly includes as follows:

(1) Taxes, including VAT, consumption tax, business tax, business income tax, individual income tax, resources tax, tax of adjustment for the orientation of fixed investment, urban maintenance and construction tax, housing property tax, stamp duty, land value increment tax, city and town land use tax, tariff duty, contract tax and tax on occupancy of cultivated land, etc.

(2) Administrative charges revenues refer to administrative charges revenues included in budgetary management in accordance with related stipulations.

(3) Special revenues, including revenue collected from imposing fee on sewage treatment, revenue collected from imposing fee on urban water resources, and extra-charges for education, etc.

(4)Other revenues, including revenue from the repayment of capital construction loan, revenue from capital construction projects, and donations and grants.

Fund budgetary revenue mainly consists of fund revenue from industrial and communication authorities, social insurance fund revenue, income from compensated use of land and government housing fund revenue, etc.

123 Government Expenditure refers to the distribution and use of the funds the government finance has raised, so as to meet the needs of economic construction and various causes. It includes the following main items:

(1)General public services indicating the expenditure on general public services provided by the government.

(2)National defense indicating the government expenditure on active military, reserve forces of national defense and national defense mobilization, etc.

(3)Public Security indicating the government expenditure on maintaining public security.

(4)Education indicating the government expenditure on education.

(5)Science and technology indicating the expenditure on science and technology.

(6)Culture, sports and media indicating the government expenditure on culture, sports, radio and film and news publishing, etc.

(7)Social security and employment indicating the government expenditure on social security and employment.

(8)Medical treatment and health indicating the government expenditure on medical treatment and health.

(9)Environmental protection indicating the government expenditure on environmental protection.

(10)Urban and rural community affairs indicating the government expenditure on urban and rural community affairs.

(11)Agriculture, forestry and water affairs indicating the government expenditure on agriculture, forestry and water.

(12)raffic and transportation indicating the government expenditure on traffic and transportation.

(13)Industrial, commercial and financial affairs indicating the government expenditure on industry, commerce and finance.

(14)Other expenditures indicating other government expenditures that cannot be categorized in the above function subjects.

124 State revenue and local government revenue refer to the revenue owned by the central government and the revenue belongs to local government in accordance with the financial system.

Since the reform of tax system and financial system in 1994, the revenue belonged to the central government includes tariff, consumption tax, value added tax of imported goods levied by the customs, income tax of railway transportation enterprises, state-owned banks, state-owned post enterprises, sales tax of railway and banking and insurance (central government), offshore petroleum resources tax and vehicle purchasing tax (charges), etc. The taxes belong to the general budgetary revenue of local governments include regular sales tax, vehicle and vessel usage tax, animal slaughter tax, tax on occupation of cultivated land and deed tax, etc. The revenue shared by the central government and local governments includes value added tax, business income tax, urban maintenance and construction tax, individual income tax and stamp tax, etc. One point demands explanation is that the data over the years can't be compared fully due to the changing revenue-sharing pattern and sharing proportions between the central government and local governments in recent years.

125 Deposit is a form of credit by which enterprises, institutions, organizations or households can put money into banks and other credit institutions for safekeeping and interest earning under the principle of free withdrawal. According to different depositors, deposits are divided into enterprise deposits, treasury deposits, deposits of government agencies and organizations, capital construction deposits, urban savings deposits, rural deposits and other deposits. Deposits are major sources of the credit funds of banks.

126 Saving Deposits Balance of Urban and Rural residents Saving deposits include the bank savings deposits of organizations such as industrial and mining enterprises, army units, institutions, ect. The outstanding amount of savings deposits refers to the money put into banks and rural credit unions at certain time points (balance between deposit and withdrawal), such as the end of the month, quarter or year.

127 Loan is a form of credit by which banks and other credit institutions provide funds at certain interest rate to enterprises and individuals in the light of the principle of unconditional repayment. Loans from Chinese banks include circulating capital loans, fixed assets loans, loans to urban and rural individuals engaged in industrial and commercial business and agricultural loans.

128 Amount Insured refers to the maximum that the insurant will get for the claim of the case insured.

129 Premium is the fee paid by the insurant to the insurer to obtain the obligation of compensation from the insurance within the agreed terms.

130 Insurance Indemnity refers to the compensation paid by the insurer to the insurant in accordance with the stipulations of the insurance contract after confirmed the insured event within the scope of insurance coverage by means of verification.

131 Prosperity Index refers to status and trend of development of sample groups or certain economic and social phenomenon, derived from quantitative processing of qualitative indicators regarding enterprise's degree of prosperity. The prosperity index varies from 0 and 200 with 100 as its critical point. When the prosperity exceeds 100, it is indicated that the economy is turning for better, while the index is below 100, vise versa.

132 Prosperity Index of Enterprises refers the index reflecting soundness of general operation, derived form management's judgment and estimation on performance of the company,(variables being sound,common and bad),which is used to reflect the general operation status of the enterprises.

133 Business climate index also known as comprehensive production and management climate index of enterprises, is the prosperity index constituted based on entrepreneurs' judgments and expectations of overall production and operation conditions of their enterprises (usually evaluated as "good," "fair" or "poor"), which is used to reflect a company's comprehensive production and management status.

134 Length of Paved Roads at the Year-end refers to the length of roads with a paved surface, and with a width of more than 3.5 meters, including high quality, medium quality and ordinary roads.

135 Urban Bridges refer to bridges over river courses, great separated junctions and overpasses in urban areas. Permanent bridges and semi-permanent bridges are included. Temporary bridges, railway bridges and culverts are excluded.

136 Length of Urban Sewage Pipes refers to the total length of general drainage, trunks, branch and blind drainage, inspection wells, connection wells, inlets and outlets, etc.

137 Daily Disposal Capacity of Urban Sewage refers to the designed 24-hour capacity of sewage disposal at the sewage treatment works.

138 Floor Space of the Park, Gardens and Green Area Of Urban refers to the total area of urban public green land, special green land, production green land, protection green land and suburban scenic spots.

139 Green Space in Park refers to the green area with main function of opening for the public, and recreation, which possesses certain recreation facilities and service facilities, integrated the effects of ecology perfection, scenery beautification, prevention and mitigation of the effects of disasters.

140 Production Capacity of Tap Water at the Year-end refers to the actual comprehensive production capacity of the waterworks administered by the urban construction department and those owned by enterprises or institutions, taking the capacity of the main links, such as water inflow, purification, conveyance and outflow of the trunk pipelines into account.

141 Number of Public Vehicles (Buses and Trolley buses) at the Year-end refers to the total number of operational buses available at the year-end, including the year-end operational vehicles and vehicles in stock. Non-operational vehicles such as stringing cars, tank cars, machine shop cars, trucks and other special vehicles and the borrowed passenger vehicles are excluded.

142 Length of Roads in Operation refers to the length of designated regular routes in operation, including the length of suburban routes in operation. The length of temporary operational lines is not included.

143 Length of Water Supply Pipelines at the Year-end refers to the total length of all the pipelines between the water pumps and the users water meters.

144 Annual Volume of Water Supply refers to the total volume of water supplied by the public water-works and those owned by individual enterprises and institutions during the whole year, including both the effective water supply and loss during the water supply.

145 Consumption of Water for Residential Use refers to the water consumption of households for daily life and the water consumption of public welfare facilities, including the consumption of restaurants, hotels, hospitals, barber shops, public bathhouses, laundries, swimming pools, shops, schools, institutions, army units and other units.

146 Percentage of Urban Population with Access to Tap Water refers to the ratio of the urban non-agricultural population (excluding temporary and mobile population) with access to tap water to the total urban non-agricultural population. The formula is:

Percentage of Population with Access to Tap Water=(Urban Non-agricultural Population with Access to Tap Water) / (Urban Non-agricultural Population) ×100%

147 Length of Gas Pipelines refers to the total length of pipelines between the outlet of the compressor, blower or gas tank and the gas meters of users.

148 Volume of Gas Supply refers to the total volume of gas sold to users in a year, including the volume for industrial use, residential use and other uses.

149 Percentage of Urban Population with Access to Gas refers to the ratio of the urban non-agricultural population with access to gas (including gas, liquefied petroleum gas and natural gas) to the urban non-agricultural population (excluding temporary and mobile population). The formula is:

Percentage of Population with Access to Gas =(Urban Non-agricultural Population with Access to Gas) / (Urban Non-agricultural Population) ×100%

150 Total Amount of Waste Water refers to the total amount of industrial waste water and resident waste water. The industrial refers to the total of the waste water produced in the producing, studying period of the enterprises and institutions. The resident waste water refers to the waste water produced in the residences.

151 Volume of Industrial Waste Water Discharged refers to the volume of industrial waste water discharged, through all outlets, to the outside of industrial enterprises, including waste water produced, direct-cooling water, underground water from mines that does not meet the standard of discharge, and the domestic sewage mixed up with industrial waste water when discharged, but excluding discharged indirect-cooling water.

152 Volume of Waste Water up to the Standard for Discharge refers to the volume of discharged industrial waste water that, with or without treatment, has come up to the national or local standards for discharge.

153 Total Amount of Waste Gas Discharged refers to the volume of various kings of waste gas discharged to the air in the process of fuel burning or in the production process, and is measured by 10,000 standard cubic meters each year under normal condition.

154 Volume of Industrial Solid Wastes Utilized in a Comprehensive Way refers to the volume of solid wastes from which useful materials can be extracted or which can be changed to be utilizable resources, energy or other materials, including the volume of industrial solid wastes stored up in the previous years and utilized in the current year, such as the solid wastes utilized as fertilizers, building materials, for making roads or for other purpose. Statistical data on utilization of industrial solid wastes are collected by solid wastes producing units.

155 Volume of Industrial Solid Wastes Treated refers to solid wastes disposed of in a non-recoverable place that meet the requirement of environmental protection, such as burying (The dangerous wastes should be buried safely), burning, piling in designated sites, pouring water into the deep strata, filling of old mines, etc. (including treatment of solid wastes piled up in the previous years).

156 Industrial Dust Discharged refers to the total weight of solid dust discharged by industrial enterprises in the production process, such as dust of refractory materials from iron plants, dust from coke-screening system or from sintering machines of coking plants, dust from lime kilns, cement dust from building material enterprises, etc., but excluding smoke and dust discharged by power plants.

157 R & D is the abbreviation of research and development, and refers to the systemic and creative activities for the purpose of increasing knowledge and applying the knowledge within the field of science and technology (including the fields of natural science, agricultural science, medical science, engineering and technological science and humanities and social science). R & D consists of three kinds of activities, including fundamental research, application research and experimental development.

158 Independent Research and Development Institutions refer to the state- owned institutions which have direct mission and research purpose, a certain number of core members with higher research level and certain number of research personal, favourable conditions for R&D and engaging in scientific research and technological development. The institutions also have their own independent organization and finance, authority to sign contracts with other units, their bank accounts. Independent research and development institutions include the institutions attached to central government agencies, Chinese Academy of Sciences, Chinese Academy of Social Sciences and the institutions attached to the local government.

159 Scientists and Engineers refer to persons who have completed university or higher education or obtained titles of senior and middle level professional positions.

160 Personnel of Independent Research and Development Institutions refers to the persons working in and receiving payment from research and development institutions. It includes regular full-time and temporary staff and workers and employees working on contracts, but excludes retirees and persons leaving their work without payment but still retaining their posts, who are not on the employee list.

161 Total Expenditure on Research and Development refers to all actual expenditure made for R&D (basic research, applied research and experimental development)in reference period. It includes direct expenditure on R&D and indirect expenditure on R&D (including management and necessary administrative expenses of research institutes, investment in capital construction relating to R&D).

162 Inventions refer to the inventions as specified by the patent law and its detailed rules and regulations for implementation. They refer to the new technical proposals to the products or methods or their modifications.

163 Utility Models The utility models specified by the patent law and its detailed rules for implementation refer to the new technical proposals on the shape, structure or combination of shape and structure of product, which is suitable for practical use.

164 Designs refer to the designs as specified by the patent law and its detailed rules and regulation for implementation. They refer to the aesthetics and industry applicable new designs for the shape, pattern and color of the product, or their combinations.

165 Number of online registered technology contracts refers to the number of local technology contracts registered via the national technology contracts on-line registration system (http://www.ctmht.net.cn/).

166 Business volume of online registered technology contracts refers to the business volume of local technology contracts registered via the national technology contracts on-line registration system (http://www.ctmht.net.cn/).

167 Science and Technology Enterprises Incubator refers to the scientific and technological innovation service organization aiming to promote the transfer of scientific and technological achievements, and to nurture high-tech enterprises and entrepreneurs. It includes technological innovation service center, university technology parks, innovation (venture) park for returned overseas students, software parks and professional technological enterprises incubators.

168 Total income of enterprises under incubation refers to the sum of various incomes achieved from technology, industry and trade by the enterprises under incubation within the statistical year.

169 Persons employed by enterprises under incubation refer to the total number of persons employed by the enterprises under incubation at the end date of this report.

170 Incubated Enterprises refer to the enterprises realize independent development after developed to a certain scale so that divorce from the incubator. (The data of incubated enterprises is only accumulated based on the data of graduation time, without tracking).

171 Regular Institutions of Higher Learning refer to educational establishments set up according to the government evaluation and approval procedures, enrolling graduates from senior secondary schools via national entrance examination and providing higher diploma education. They include full time universities, independent colleges and senior professional schools, senior vocational universities and other institutions (such as independent institutes, branch schools and junior colleges).

172 Institutions of Higher Learning for Adults refer to educational establishments set up according to the government evaluation and approval procedures, enrolling personnel with senior secondary school or equivalent education via national entrance examination and providing higher diploma education by means of correspondence, part time or full time. They include workers' colleges, peasants' colleges, institutes for administration, educational colleges, independent correspondence colleges and etc.

173 The number of Full-time Teachers refers to the number of personnel engaged in education as full-time teachers, including those who are temporarily designated (within one year) to assist in other fields. The former teachers transferred from teaching to undertake administrative management are excluded.

174 Cultural Institutions refer to units which have their own organizational system and independent accounting system and specialize in or serve cultural development. They exclude other establishments run by these cultural institutions and amateur cultural groups established by various departments.

175 Art Troupe refers to the troupe which is engaged in drama, opera, music, dance, acrobatics or other art performance, opens independent accounts with banks and has self-supporting accounting system; excluding the troupes which are engaged partly in industrial or agricultural activities, partly in art performance and the professional troupes organized by the people.

176 Number of Spectators at Art Performance refers to the number of attendants at commercial shows, completely booked shows or free shows given in minority national areas, and does not include the number of spectators at rehearsals for examination and internal shows for study.

177 Hospitals refer to medical institutions with permanent hospital beds, which are able to take in patients and provide them with medical and nursing services. Hospitals are classified into three categories: hospitals at or above the county level, hospitals of rural townships, and other hospitals. According to their ownership, hospitals can be classified into three categories: hospitals under the public health departments, hospitals under industrial and other departments and collective-owned hospitals. Hospitals at or above county level are divided into comprehensive and specialized hospitals.

178 Medical Technical Personnel refers to all medical staff and workers employed by medical institutions, including doctors of Chinese and Western medicine, senior doctors who integrate traditional Chinese therapeutics with Western therapeutics in practice, senior nurses, pharmacists of Chinese and Western medicine, laboratory specialists, other specialists, paramedics of Chinese and Western medicine, nurses, midwives, druggists in Chinese and Western medicine, laboratory technicians, other technicians, other practitioners of Chinese medicine, nursing attendants, pharmacological workers of Chinese and Western medicine, laboratory workers, and other primary medical personnel.

179 Doctors refer to qualified professional medical workers approved to practice by public health departments. They are classified into doctors of Chinese medicine, doctors of Western medicine, senior doctors who integrate traditional Chinese therapeutics with Western therapeutics in practice, paramedics of Chinese medicine and Western medicine, and other specialists of Chinese medicine.

180 Number of Athletes in Grades refers to the number of athletes who have been given titles through examination. The titles of athletes include international masters of sports, masters of sports, first-grade and second-grade.

181 Number of Referees in Grades refers to the number of referees who have been given titles after examination. They are classified as international referees, national referees and referees of the first, second and third grades.

182 Social Welfare Institutions refer to institutions taking care of old people without children,handicapped people and orphans. They include social welfare institutions run by civil affairs departments, children welfare institutions, social welfare institutions for mental patients, and collective-owned old peoples homes in rural areas.

183 Number of People Taken in by Social Welfare Institutions refers to the number of old people, children, totally dependent handicapped people and mental patients taken in by social welfare institutions run by civil affairs departments and those run by collective units in urban and rural areas.

184 Social Welfare Enterprises are collective owned enterprises which employ the blind, deafmute, and other handicapped people who are able to work in cities and towns and enjoy exemption from state taxes, including welfare plants, welfare commercial services, artificial limb plants and farms, etc.

185 Lawyers are legal workers who are employed full time by legal counseling firms to act as legal advisers, agents in criminal or civil lawsuits, or defenders in criminal lawsuits, or to handle non-litigious legal affairs, to advise on matters of law or to write legal papers for others. Both full-time and part time lawyers are included.

186 Notary Personnel refers to judicial workers of the state notary offices handling notarization work according to law. They include notaries, assistant notaries, and other people working for notary offices.

187 Notarized Documents refer to the documents settled by notary offices in a year. The notary documents are drawn up in accordance with the regulations of the Ministry of Justice, including domestic documents and foreign-related documents. Domestic documents are divided into two major categories, documents on economic contracts and documents on civil legal relations.

188 Mediators refer to workers on peoples mediation committees responsible for mediating in civil disputes and cases of slight infraction of the law. They include members of the mediation committees and mediators of mediation groups.

189 Mediation of Civil Disputes refers to mediation committees work in mediating in civil disputes concerning civil rights and duties through persuasion and education in accordance with the provisions of law on a voluntary basis, so as to solve disputes by helping the parties involved come to an agreement and understanding. These disputes include divorce cases and disputes over property ownership, but exclude the civil cases to be handled by the court.

中国统计出版社最新图书简目

（仅供参考，以最后出书为准）

统计资料

中国统计年鉴-2012　中国统计摘要-2012　国际统计年鉴-2012
2012中国发展报告　中国第三产业统计年鉴-2012　中国区域经济统计年鉴-2012
中国劳动统计年鉴-2012　中国社会统计年鉴-2012　中国城市统计年鉴-2009
中国建筑业统计年鉴-2012　中国人口和就业统计年鉴-2012　中国工业经济统计年鉴-2012
中国商品交易市场统计年鉴-2012　中国房地产统计年鉴-2012　中国能源统计年鉴-2012
中国民政统计年鉴-2012　中国贸易外经统计年鉴-2012　2012中国地区经济监测报告
中国科技统计年鉴-2012　中国农村统计年鉴-2012　中国农产品价格调查年鉴-2012
中国高技术产业统计年鉴-2012　中国教育经费统计年鉴-2010　中国农村贫困监测报告-2012
全国农产品成本收益资料汇编-2012　中国科学技术协会统计年鉴-2012　工业企业科技活动资料-2012
大中型批发零售和住宿餐饮企业统计年鉴-2012　中国城市（镇）生活与价格年鉴-2012　中国县（市）社会经济统计年鉴-2012
中国农村住户调查年鉴-2012（中、英文）　中国农村全面建设小康监测报告-2012　第二次全国R&D资源清查资料汇编—综合卷
第二次全国R&D资源清查资料汇编—工业企业卷　中国零售和餐饮连锁企业统计年鉴-2012　中国民族统计年鉴2011、2012
2010年中国第六次人口普查公报

2012年省级综合统计年鉴系列

北京　天津　河北　山西　内蒙古　辽宁　吉林　黑龙江　上海　江苏　浙江　安徽　福建　江西　山东
河南　湖北　湖南　广东　广西　海南　重庆　四川　贵州　云南　西藏　陕西　甘肃　青海　宁夏
新疆　新疆生产建设兵团

2012年市（县）级综合统计年鉴系列

天津滨海新区　石家庄　唐山　邯郸　太原　大同　长治　阳泉　晋城　朔州　晋中
运城　忻州　临汾　呼和浩特　包头　沈阳　大连　长春　吉林市　四平　哈尔滨　黑龙江垦区
上海浦东新区　苏州　无锡　常州　徐州　南通　盐城　镇江　江阴　丹阳
杭州　宁波　绍兴　台州　温州　金华　嘉兴　衢州　福州　福州经济技术开发区
厦门经济特区　南昌　上饶　济南　青岛　潍坊　郑州　洛阳　三门峡　南阳　武汉　宜昌
十堰　荆州　咸宁　长沙　广州　东莞　惠州　深圳　桂林　南宁　柳州　来宾　河池　海口　成都　绵阳
贵阳　昆明　庆阳　西安　兰州　银川　乌鲁木齐

2010年人口普查资料系列

中国2010年人口普查资料　北京　天津　河北　山西　内蒙古　辽宁　吉林　黑龙江　上海　江苏
浙江　安徽　福建　江西　山东　河南　湖北　湖南　广东　广西　海南　重庆　四川　贵州　云南
西藏　陕西　甘肃　青海　宁夏　新疆　新疆生产建设兵团　河南省各市2010年人口普查资料丛书
中国分县2010年人口普查资料　中国分乡镇、街道2010年人口普查资料　中国分民族2010年人口普查资料

“十一五”规划教材

非参数统计　医学统计学　概率论与数理统计　统计学　现代金融投资统计分析
多元统计分析　经济计量学教程　应用时间序列分析　统计指数理论及应用
统计数据处理概论　质量管理统计方法　社会统计学　多元统计分析实验
企业经营管理统计　市场调查与预测　统计学原理（非统计专业使用）
统计学：从数据到结论　国民经济核算教程（国民经济统计学）　概率论与数理统计（经济、管理类专业使用）

重点图书

挑大学选专业2012—高考志愿填报指南　挑大学选专业2012—考研择校指南